MW01256193

I Have Avenged America

Ulrick Jean-Pierre, *General Jean-Jacques Dessalines, 1803*, 2013.
Oil on canvas, 52 × 96 in. (132 × 244 cm). Courtesy of the artist.

I Have Avenged America

JEAN-JACQUES DESSALINES AND HAITI'S FIGHT FOR FREEDOM

Julia Gaffield

Yale UNIVERSITY PRESS

New Haven & London

Published with assistance from the Annie Burr Lewis Fund
and from the Louis Stern Memorial Fund.

Copyright © 2025 by Julia Gaffield. All rights reserved. This book
may not be reproduced, in whole or in part, including illustrations, in any form
(beyond that copying permitted by Sections 107 and 108 of the U.S. Copyright Law
and except by reviewers for the public press), without written permission from
the publishers.

Yale University Press books may be purchased in quantity for educational, business,
or promotional use. For information, please email sales.press@yale.edu (U.S. office)
or sales@yaleup.co.uk (U.K. office).

Set in Adobe Garamond type by Integrated Publishing Solutions.
Printed in the United States of America.

Library of Congress Control Number: 2024949780
ISBN 978-0-300-25547-8 (hardcover : alk. paper)

A catalogue record for this book is available from the British Library.

Authorized Representative in the EU: Easy Access System Europe,
Mustamäe tee 50, 10621 Tallinn, Estonia, gpsr.requests@easproject.com

10 9 8 7 6 5 4 3 2 1

For Mark, Stevenson Thomas, and Pierce James; I love you with all my heart

Contents

I Have Avenged America

My Name Has Become a Horror to All Those Who Want Slavery

"We must destroy all of the black people in the mountains—men and women—and spare only children under twelve years of age," wrote French general Charles Leclerc from Saint-Domingue, now called Haiti, in 1802. Once the world's largest sugar-producer, Haiti had been the most profitable colony of any European power anywhere on earth. Leclerc was on a mission from Napoléon Bonaparte to reinstate slavery after France had abolished it during the violent revolution that had engulfed the colony over the previous decade. The French had only outlawed slavery to win the loyalty of many of the revolutionary generals and their troops. They had particularly sought to secure the allegiance of Black officers and soldiers, who eventually joined the side of the French Republic because they believed that they would have equal rights as French citizens. General Leclerc understood that violence would be required to reinstate slavery. The only way to save the colony, he believed, was to try to undo the revolution. "We must destroy half of those in the plains," he continued, "and must not leave a single person of color in the colony who has worn an epaulette."[1]

Ordered by Leclerc to kill all the Black people in his district, General Jean-Jacques Dessalines sought out peers and former political and military rivals and made a proposal. "The era of disunion has passed . . . and it is against the white people only that we should feel resentment; as for me, my decision is already made to die as their most cruel enemy; follow me or you are doomed."[2] Enslaved for thirty years, Jean-Jacques Dessalines had served the French Republic loyally since 1794. Yet he finally broke with France at the news that universal abolition had ended: "I raised the banner of revolt, because it is time to teach the French that they are monsters that this earth is devouring too slowly for the good of humanity."[3] Within two years, Dessalines was crowned emperor of an independent and free Haiti.

Haiti under Dessalines was the first country to permanently outlaw claims to people as chattel, three decades before the British committed to gradual abolition, and some six decades before US president Abraham Lincoln's Emancipation Proclamation. On the very shores where Christopher Columbus first brought European rapacity into the Americas, Haiti, forged in slavery, was born in abolition.

"Yes, we have rendered to these true cannibals war for war, crime for crime, outrage for outrage," reflected Dessalines after he and his generals had proclaimed Haiti's independence. "Yes, I have saved my country—I have avenged America."[4]

Jean-Jacques Dessalines has been a hero to Haitians for centuries, but as Haitian-Canadian writer Dany Laferrière put it, "he is the strongest Haitian figure but the least known abroad."[5] The founding father of the most radical nation-state of the age, Dessalines, unlike his contemporaries in France and the Americas, didn't just claim to fight for freedom; he was fully committed to destroying slavery, racism, and colonialism.[6] Dessalines's commitment to abolition was shaped by the fact that he had personally experienced slavery. In less than five decades, Dessalines journeyed from "slave" to revolutionary to French republican general to founding father and, finally, to his death at the hands of political rivals. All along, he boldly insisted on his own and his people's right to liberty and equality. His life—and Haiti's very existence—exposed the lie in Enlightenment values that celebrated universal rights while excluding Black people and expanding slavery.

This standard bearer of the modern ideals of freedom and equality is not only *not* remembered for his role in the Age of Revolution, in the history of anti-colonialism, and the history of the abolition of slavery; he is maligned. In 2018 Fox News anchor Tucker Carlson, incensed that a street in the Little Haiti neighborhood of Brooklyn, New York, was renamed Jean-Jacques Dessalines Boulevard, called him a "genocidal nutcase."[7] Dessalines represented a bold and unapologetic demand for full Black liberation, and he terrified those who supported the racist colonial system. "*War to the death against tyrants!* that is my motto," Dessalines declared a few months after independence, *"freedom, independence; that is our rallying cry."*[8]

As the Haitian Revolution was unfolding (1791–1804), and especially after Dessalines became its primary leader, onlookers—mostly, but not solely, white people—tried desperately to undermine his success by claiming that he was barbaric, "uncivilized," a "tiger" dripping with the blood of his victims.[9] They did so to explain why French and British colonists had lost battles against Dessalines's army, why the abolition of slavery was a bad idea, and why Black people were not fit for self-rule. Dessalines's success in establishing and sustaining Haitian independence was a problem for racist people in colonies and countries that supported slavery. Thus, for over two hundred years, slanderous or incomplete accounts have shaped popular opinion and scholarly interpretations of the revolution and especially of Dessalines, pushing the man who declared Haitian independence into the background of histories of the making of the modern world.[10]

In a way, Dessalines seemed to know that he, and the revolution he embodied, would be marginalized. When he addressed his citizens in the Haitian Declaration of Independence on January 1, 1804, he already anticipated how his memory would be exploited and ignored two centuries later: "Remember that I have sacrificed everything to fly to your defense," Dessalines pleaded, "parents, children, fortune, and now I am rich only with your freedom; [remember] that my name has become a horror to all those who want slavery, and that despots and tyrants never utter it unless to curse the day that I was born."[11]

Born Jean-Jacques Duclos on a small coffee plantation in Grande Rivière du Nord in French Saint-Domingue around 1758, the future emperor was enslaved for more than three decades on two different coffee plantations. In 1791 Jean-Jacques Dessalines became a revolutionary; for the rest of his life, he fought against slavery, racism, and colonialism. In his most spectacular victory, in 1803, he defeated Napoléon Bonaparte's expeditionary forces, who were no match for Dessalines's revolutionary Armée indigène (Indigenous Army). Faced with the gruesome plan that Leclerc proposed in 1802, Dessalines and his troops fought for their freedom and their lives.

Because of his successful leadership in the Haitian Revolution, Dessalines was officially shunned by the international community. When he wrote to US president Thomas Jefferson—popularly remembered as a proponent of individual rights, democracy, and equality—he never even received a response. In fact, Jefferson refused to recognize Dessalines as a state leader and Haiti as a nation.

Louis Rigaud, *Portrait of Jean-Jacques Dessalines,* 1878. YPM ANTAR.028683,
Courtesy of the Yale Peabody Museum, New Haven, Connecticut.

The scorn of Jefferson and Bonaparte, however, failed to stop Dessalines or,
for that matter, Haiti. Consider how the first issue of the Haitian *Gazette* in
November 1804 celebrated the empire, claiming that "on the ruins of the French
government in Saint-Domingue, the Empire of Haiti rises before the eyes of the
astonished Universe."[12]

Dessalines valued courage and bravery on the battlefield and loyalty to the
shared cause of freedom. He was unwilling to submit to or collaborate with
those who did not deserve his respect. He relied on his community, assembling

an inner circle of officers, administrators, friends, and family who supported him during his enslavement and during his revolutionary fight. These men and women were equally dedicated to ensuring freedom, and he loved them dearly. Dessalines was fiercely devoted to his community—up to a point. If he suspected one of his friends or allies of betraying the cause, he was ruthless. He interpreted a betrayal of the revolution as a personal attack. Still, with these companions, he famously loved to dance and took time to celebrate victories, holidays, and important life events. And Dessalines maintained a wry sense of humor, delighting in outwitting a foe and confidently laughing in the face of unwarranted audacity, even when he was the target.

To remember Dessalines only as warrior, either in celebration or condemnation, is not enough. Such an account would overlook his complexity and other aspects of his life that truly reveal his humanity. While Dessalines was unquestionably successful in leading the revolutionary forces to victory, he failed to secure widespread support for his rule. Unsurprisingly, he had many enemies abroad, and, despite his diplomacy, he was unable to secure international recognition of Haitian independence. He also failed to sustain the coalition of revolutionary leaders who had rallied together during the war for independence or to creatively reimagine what freedom would look like for those who had previously been enslaved. These failures would ultimately lead to his demise.

There is no doubt, however, that Dessalines was indeed a warrior. He fought on the front lines with his troops and achieved renown on the battlefields. After all, the two phrases popularly associated with him are "*liberté ou la mort*" (freedom or death) and "*koupe tet boule kay*" (cut off their heads, burn down their houses). Both signaled his willingness to die and to kill for freedom from enslavement and independence from colonial rule. "Swear to the whole universe, to posterity, to ourselves," Dessalines encouraged his citizens in the Declaration of Independence, "to renounce France forever, and to die rather than live under its dominion. To fight until our last breath for the independence of our country."[13]

His stubborn commitment to abolition made him into a survivor, and throughout the revolution he strategically evaluated when to bend and when to break.

His fight for freedom would provide plenty of opportunities for both.

PART ONE

Jean-Jacques

ca. 1758–1791

CHAPTER I

You Have Your Own Language

"In the middle of the colonial system under which we groaned, Dessalines was born," an article in a Haitian newspaper recounted after the revolution had overturned that system.[1] The experience of coming into the world under this collective agony shaped every aspect of Jean-Jacques Dessalines's life. At first he fought against the conditions of his own individual enslavement, but eventually he fought to destroy the entire legal system. The personal and the collective were connected, Justin Lhérisson recounted in Haiti's national anthem, "Our traditions demand, Be ready, heart and hand."[2]

Dessalines grew up in a brutal slavery society, which the French had systematically constructed for more than six decades. And it was all the more terrible that this system of slavery was built on the first island that Spanish explorers encountered in the Americas.

Before the Europeans invaded, the Indigenous people of the island called it *Ayti* (which meant "mountainous"), a name that would be recalled over three hundred years later to signal the end of the colonial period. The island is the second largest island in the Caribbean; it sits slightly southeast of Cuba, and only 850 miles off the coast of Florida. In 1492 Christopher Columbus claimed it as a Spanish colony and christened the island as "Hispaniola." Despite it being the land first claimed as a Spanish colony, Hispaniola remained a backwater of the empire for centuries.[3] The Spanish capital of the colony, Santo Domingo,

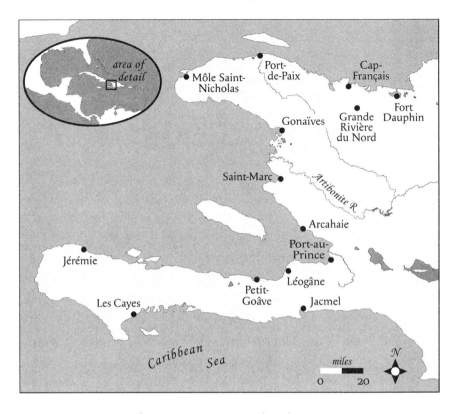

Map of Saint-Domingue. Drawn by Rebecca Wrenn.

was on the southeastern side of the island. But the rest of the island was un-claimed—according to the European empires that ignored the sovereignty and land claims of Indigenous peoples—and therefore up for grabs.

This made the western side of Hispaniola an ideal haven for pirates and a new kind of outlaw, "buccaneers" (land-based pirates, named for the wooden frames they used to smoke meat, *boucans*). Far away from the Spanish capital in the east, French buccaneers claimed territory in the island's west. In the seven-teenth century, interimperial competition in the Atlantic increased; now the French government took advantage of the presence of these French buccaneers to establish an official colony. They gained control of the western third of His-paniola from the Spanish in the late seventeenth century (a fact that the Spanish only conceded almost a century later), though the mountainous interior of the colony remained contested territory.[4] As a French colony, Haiti was called Saint-Domingue (the French version of Santo Domingo).

The French colonists soon learned that the elevated plains that surrounded the port cities on the island proved ideal for growing the world's newest obsession: sugar. With brutal speed, the crop became central to all facets of colonial life in Saint-Domingue.[5] But sugar production was punishing and dangerous work. So the French, like people from other imperial powers, maximized their profits by importing captive Africans.

In the eighteenth century, French slaving ships would visit multiple ports on the West African coast to purchase men, women, and children, before embarking on the months-long journey across the Atlantic to the Caribbean.[6] Enslaved Africans who endured the transatlantic slave trade were susceptible to disease, malnourishment, mental and emotional trauma, and physical and sexual violence. Many did not survive the voyage.[7] On the island, the colonists divided the plains into large plots of less than one square mile, each of which used the labor of one hundred and fifty to two hundred enslaved people.[8] Where sugar would not grow because of the topography, landowners established coffee, cotton, and indigo plantations. On these large plots the French forced enslaved men, women, and children to cultivate, plant, harvest, and process their crops—overwhelmingly, sugar cane—from sunrise to sunset under strict and violent supervision.

Over the course of the eighteenth century, enslaved people in Saint-Domingue produced more wealth than in any other colony in the world, making French enslavers and merchants rich.[9] During the same period, the French forced almost one million African captives into slavery in Saint-Domingue.[10]

For enslaved Africans, especially for those who toiled on sugar plantations, forced migration to the colony would usually become a death sentence.[11] From the plantation owners' perspective, it was cost-effective to work a man or woman to death and then replenish the workforce with incoming men and women dragged off large slaving ships in chains. In the early eighteenth century, the French imported between 10,000 and 20,000 African captives annually; by the end of the century that number had climbed as high as 48,000 each year.[12] By this point the sheer numbers of people dying and being imported meant that of the enslaved population in Saint-Domingue, more than half had been born in Africa and thus were newly enslaved.[13]

These newly enslaved people were called *bossales* (born in Africa), while those born in the colony—like Jean-Jacques Dessalines—were known as "creoles." Although the distinction between the two groups was not rigidly defined, the divide was important.[14] Enslaved creoles had grown up within the plantation system and, consequently, the worldviews of their enslavers. Meanwhile, the *bossales*—who were the majority of the enslaved—had been uprooted from their kinship groups, cultures, and political associations; as such, the plantation system in Saint-Domingue was completely foreign and at odds with their worldviews.[15] This broad division—between those who were enslaved at birth and those who were enslaved later in life—resulted in conflict-ridden relationships during the independence period, based on the two groups' different definitions of freedom.[16] Born on the island, creoles inherited a version of freedom from the colonizers that prioritized the idea of productive citizenship; drawing on their own past lives, *bossales,* in contrast, prioritized family relations, collective property, and relations of reciprocity.[17]

But the line between these two cultural groups was blurry. Some people at the time described Dessalines as being of "Congo" origin.[18] "He had less of the habits of a Black creole than those of an African," one writer remarked; "the food, the way of life of the Europeans disgusted him."[19] "Congo" was a catchall term, which colonists used to describe a culturally and linguistically diverse group of captives from West Central Africa.[20] People from that region composed a significant part of the enslaved population of northern Saint-Domingue in the late eighteenth century; in the region where Dessalines lived, this percentage was even higher. There, "Congo" men, women, and children made up more than a third of the enslaved population.[21] These people were often captives from the frequent African civil wars of the eighteenth century, and they brought with them military experience, revolutionary ideologies about diffusing power under monarchies, and spiritual beliefs and practices, all of which shaped the parishes of northern Saint-Domingue.[22]

Moreover, the diverse groups that made up the general colonial category of "Congo" people maintained community networks across plantations, despite efforts by the enslavers to prevent interplantation communication and socialization.[23] These societies sustained precaptivity rituals and beliefs.[24] Living in this milieu, Dessalines may have adopted some of the cultural, social, and political practices of the "Congo" peoples in his community.[25]

Similarly, Dessalines spoke Creole, a language with many roots that developed over generations by speakers of African languages and French dialects.[26] Later in his life, a French naturalist overheard him scolding a creole colonist for speaking to him in French: "*Tiembé langue à vous* [you have your own language]."[27] Dessalines rejected French culture and prioritized his "creole-Congo" identity. His ability to move effortlessly between these cultures would serve him well.

Jean-Jacques's home parish lay on the margins of Saint-Domingue's colonial life, with a distinct geographic, social, and demographic history that shaped his future. The sloped terrain of the mountains in Grande Rivière did not support sugar cultivation, but the climate and geography were ideal for coffee production.[28] The coffee plantations of Grande Rivière included small plots that were set aside for subsistence gardens. The parish was well-known for the quality and price of its food crops; regular rainfall made growing foodstuffs a worthwhile investment, and some sugar planters therefore purchased plots in the region for food production.[29] The food surplus allowed for an internal trade, which tightened this region's connections to the northern sugar plains and port cities. A network of roads facilitated this exchange, winding through the mountains, often alongside the riverbeds, between the borderland region of Grande Rivière and the port city of Cap-Français.[30] But beyond the built environment of the roads and plantations, the uncultivated and uncolonized mountains provided a place of refuge for those who dared to escape slavery.[31]

In Saint-Domingue in the late eighteenth century, enslaved people far outnumbered free people; in the colony there were about sixty thousand free people, compared with half a million enslaved people. Being outnumbered by their captives, the French routinely used violence and torture on the plantations. This included whipping, beating, amputation, burning, and, in some instances, slow and painful executions.[32]

To try to maintain their authority, the tiny minority of the population who were enslaving the majority also instituted restrictive laws for all residents. In 1685, even before they had acquired Saint-Domingue, the French published an edict that applied to their other Caribbean colonies, aiming to protect white colonists and their property and limit crime among the enslaved population.[33] This *Code Noir* regulated the behavior of the enslaved, the formerly enslaved, and the enslavers. Without much oversight, however, the limits on the unrestrained dominance of the enslavers were largely ignored.[34] Officials in the colony periodically updated or reiterated the laws of the colony to suit their changing needs in a growing plantation economy. The code remained in place until the Haitian Revolution, but it was only selectively and strategically used by the free population, and usually only when it served their own interests.[35]

Whatever the *Code Noir* may have stipulated, enslaved people resisted the authority of their enslavers. They did so by refusing to work, destroying equipment, and stealing. They also escaped captivity by running away (*marronage*):

enslaved people might sometimes disappear for days or weeks (*petit marronage*) or might try to permanently escape enslavement (*grand marronage*). Escape was dangerous, yet common enough across the island that the colonial government early on established a specialized police force, the *maréchaussée,* to capture and return fugitives to their plantations.[36] In response to *petit marronnage,* enslavers could use their discretion in punishing enslaved men and women: they often whipped, chained, or isolated captive fugitives in the stocks, a restraining device for corporal punishment and public humiliation.[37] But for those enslaved people who escaped for longer than a month, the *Code Noir* mandated they be brandished with the fleur-de-lys and disfigured or disabled to make it harder for them to abscond in the future.[38] The state brutally executed those who tried to escape repeatedly.

There is no question that Saint-Domingue was a profoundly hostile and dangerous place for enslaved men, women, and children.

When Dessalines was born around 1758, France was at war with Great Britain. The Seven Years' War (1756–1763) was a truly global conflict, fought primarily among European nations, but which sprawled throughout their empires. It marked a turning point for Atlantic empires in the eighteenth century. Even distant battles dramatically changed official policy and daily life, especially for those in the colonies.

In the war, France lost considerable territory in North America, which only made its Caribbean colonies more important. Now overseas administrative and financial policy fixated on the Caribbean, because the French government in Europe believed it was losing control of the colonies.[39] It issued deep and sweeping reforms, reasserting metropolitan authority with the goal of maximizing profits. To strengthen the connections between the colonies and the metropole, the French empire formally and informally prioritized solidarity among the empire's white people, rather than among its free people.[40]

These reforms disrupted the existing socioeconomic hierarchy of Saint-Domingue. Until then the social order had enabled the development of a large and wealthy class of free people with African ancestry, some of whom were themselves plantation owners and enslavers. The new reforms, however, implemented a race-based hierarchy among free people, setting the stage—not immediately— for an eventual collaboration between free people of color and enslaved men and women.[41] This new colonial hierarchy, however, remained fluid and depended on individual and interpersonal relationships.[42]

By the 1780s there were about twenty-seven thousand "free people of color" (*gens de couleur libres*) in Saint-Domingue, about the same number as the free white population.[43] "Free people of color" was a legal category that included all free people who had any Black ancestors, but it was a stratified and diverse group. People of this legal and social status may have been recognized as free from their birth or they may have secured this status though manumission (the act of being freed from slavery). Most free people of color were creole people of "mixed race" and tended to be wealthier, benefiting from the economic and social capital of their white parents or ancestors. Many of them used this wealth to buy land and enslaved people, receive training and education in France, and lobby the colonial state for access to political and social rights. These free men, women, and children were often referred to as *mulâtres* (mulattoes), a derogatory term used for people who had one white parent and one Black parent.[44] Yet a significant part of the population of free people of color had no white ancestors and were called *noir* (black) or *nègre* (negro).[45]

In the decades after the Seven Years' War, France tried to regain financial and political control of its colonies by targeting free people of color. The metropole implemented new and increasingly discriminatory restrictions on jobs, marriages, titles, social and cultural behavior, and even surnames.[46] Priests and notaries were now mandated by the colonial administration to describe free people of color using racial categories in official documents.[47] From that time on, priests and notaries listed free people of color using the labels *nègre libre, mulâtre, quarteron,* and *griffe,* allegedly referring to their degree of racial mixing.[48] Consider how the only use of *libre* (free) was next to the word *nègre,* the label for people who did not have any white ancestors; this reflected the real and perceived association between Blackness and slavery. For all free people of color, their names always now appeared alongside these racial descriptors, asterisks marking them as "lesser" colonial subjects. Furthermore, beginning in the 1770s, white people in the colony started calling all free people of color—even those who had never been enslaved—by a new term: *affranchis* (freed persons). This labeling implied that the natural state of people of color was enslavement.[49]

Colonial administrators coupled this newfound insistence on marking people as nonwhite with new policies that forced free people of color to document and prove their free status. This necessarily made their freedom precarious.[50] Under the new system, the so-called *blancs* (white people) were "free"; meanwhile, the so-called *gens de couleur libres* were legally free, but were socially and economically unequal in their freedom. These new regulations pushed them closer to those who were enslaved and required them to constantly prove their free status.[51]

Still, while many free people of color chafed against these restrictions and bemoaned their treatment as "slaves," their social and legal status remained different from that of people in bondage. It was only the stringent racism of the white colonists that would eventually push free people of color to find common cause with enslaved people.

CHAPTER 2

Un Mauvais Esclave

Neighborhood children called out to a young Jean-Jacques Dessalines as he passed on the dirt roads of his home parish of Grande Rivière du Nord, south of the large port city Cap-Français on the northern coast of Saint-Domingue. "*Papa Jacques, ba nous oranges* [Father Jacques, give us oranges]," the children shouted.[1] And he did, handing out the fruit for free.

Long before he was a general, let alone a freedom fighter or emperor, Dessalines was enslaved on a coffee plantation. Some claim that he had always been destined for greatness. "He descended from a man and a woman to become a demigod," Timoléon C. Brutus argued in a twentieth-century biography.[2] Refusing to work in the fields, he was assigned the menial task of selling fruit in the parish. In this job he became well-known and well-liked across the parish. Dessalines formed such strong bonds of friendship that they lasted a lifetime. Years later, when he had become a military leader, many of the officers in the unit under his command were the same childhood companions he'd befriended as "Papa Jacques." These officers affectionately called their general after his childhood name, Duclos.[3]

By that time Dessalines was far from his enslaved youth, and had long since abandoned the surname Duclos. But as he grew up, Dessalines would have primarily been known by his first name, or even just Jacques, as the parish's children called him.[4] As was customary for enslaved people, he was also known by the last names of his enslavers, and the first man to enslave him was a white man named Duclos.[5] (After abolition, many formerly enslaved people used only one name because they rejected their former enslavers' surnames.) Although owning a small coffee plantation in Grande Rivière, Duclos, by most accounts, was a poor white man (*petit blanc*), a socioeconomic category that by the 1780s comprised a full third of the thirty thousand white people in the colony.[6] Many of the *petits blancs* were frustrated with their failure to find the fortunes they had expected in Saint-Domingue.[7] Their economic status did not match the racial hierarchy of the colony, but their race nevertheless conferred political and social power. For Duclos, this discrepancy between wealth and power must have made Jean-Jacques's defiant attitude all the more aggravating.

Jean-Jacques stole moments of personal freedom by escaping from Duclos for short periods of time, in what the French called *petit marronage*.[8] Instead of working, he was allegedly frequently drunk. In fact, the only reason he was distributing fruit to children was that Duclos was apparently at his wits' end trying to find jobs from which Jean-Jacques would not run. Not even the "cruelest punishments" could force Jean-Jacques to obey his enslaver. Ineffectively, Duclos tied Jean-Jacques to a ladder and whipped him so frequently that his backside was covered in scars.[9] While this brutality did nothing to make him more obedient, Jean-Jacques carried the physical scars of these violent attempts to control him for the rest of his life.

No wonder he was described by others at the time as a *"mauvais esclave"* (bad slave).[10] Perhaps it was his early noncompliance that later made him so effective as a freedom fighter. After all, the first three decades of his life were shaped by slavery. Under the harsh labor system, Dessalines fought for time, autonomy, and community. He suffered, but he resisted by forming a network of family and friends. These relationships lasted a lifetime and were the foundation for his success in the revolution.

There is near consensus regarding the year Jean-Jacques was born, 1758, but the day of his birth is uncertain.[11] Haitian historian Jules Rosemond argued in 1903 in preparation for the centenary of Haitian independence that Dessalines was born on September 20, 1758, and that date is popularly celebrated as his birthday. July 25, the patronal holiday of his namesake, Saint James (Saint Jacques), was celebrated as his *fête* during his rule and has sometimes been interpreted as his "birthday."[12]

The reason for the confusion is that enslaved people were almost entirely excluded from the parish records, the documents that historians typically use to learn more about a person's life and lineage. Enslavers were legally required to have enslaved people baptized, but they often did not comply with the law. Even when they did, the parish priests kept separate records of the baptisms of enslaved people—if they kept them at all—and those documents largely no longer exist.[13]

The exact details surrounding Dessalines's birth itself are also difficult to pinpoint. His parents were almost certainly enslaved, and because slavery was a hereditary sentence, by law he would have been the "property" of his mother's enslaver when he was born.[14] According to the *Code Noir,* enslaved people were allowed to marry if they were enslaved on the same plantation, and their marriage would have legally prevented them from being sold separately.[15] For this reason, it is unlikely that this law was actually enforced.[16] Similarly, the law discouraged enslavers from separating children from their parents, yet the plantation system provided little support for family structure and prioritized plantation work.[17] Infant mortality on Caribbean plantations was high, but if enslaved children survived their first few years of life, they started working on the plantations when they were about five or six years old.[18]

Even before that age, Jean-Jacques was probably separated from his mother. She may have been sold to another plantation or perhaps she died. In her absence, the young Jean-Jacques developed a close friendship with a woman named Victoria—or Toya—Montou, whom he later called his "aunt."

Together, Jean-Jacques and Toya suffered the brutality of slavery on the Duclos coffee plantation. Years later—in a rare moment in which Dessalines reflected on his life under slavery—he described the bond that he formed with Toya. "Like me," he recalled, "she had to endure all the pain, all the emotions during the time that we were condemned to work side-by-side in the fields."[19] A white doctor who knew them both later claimed that Toya and Jean-Jacques's relationship became a problem for Duclos. "She chatted with him so often, and they were so intimate," he wrote, that Duclos separated them by sale.[20]

Toya was displaced to the large Déluger plantation in Montrouis, south of Saint-Marc on the Gulf of Gonâve. There she worked as the leader of a fifty-person plantation unit (*atelier*).[21] In that position, claimed the white doctor, Toya looked, acted, and sounded much like a military general.[22]

When Jean-Jacques was still in his youth, Duclos sold him to a free Black man named Philippe Jasmin, sometimes called Désir.[23] He was identified in the parish and notarial records as a creole—that is, born on the island—and as a *nègre libre.*[24] His parents, Pierre and Rose, were also free; it is likely that he was born free and inherited the plantation from his father.[25] Someone born free, like

Philippe Jasmin, would have had more evidence of their freedom and therefore protection against the new colonial laws that discriminated against people of African descent; someone enslaved at birth, like Jean-Jacques, would instead have had only evidence of their status as a "slave."[26]

Jean-Jacques's new enslaver was part of a growing community of free people of color in the northern province who grew coffee in the mountains south of Cap-Français, including the parishes of Grande Rivière and neighboring Dondon.[27] The landowners of the coffee-growing region of Grande Rivière were primarily (though not exclusively) free Black men and women, and Jasmin owned a small coffee plantation in the Cormier Valley.[28] One reason for this demographic majority was that coffee required smaller plots of less fertile land, far lower start-up costs, fewer laborers, and no irrigation, unlike sugar.[29] The free Black population of the north province was larger than elsewhere in the colony, and free people of color outnumbered the white population by almost half.[30]

Jean-Jacques's new home was along the river for which the valley was named and less than two miles from the town of Grande Rivière.[31] The steep hillside of the Jasmin plantation rose from the base of the Cormier Valley, covered in trees and fields.[32] The climate was temperate, ideal for coffee and food production, and it kept enslaved people relatively healthy.[33]

The sale of enslaved people often separated families and sent them into communities of strangers. But by chance, when Duclos sold Jean-Jacques to Philippe Jasmin, the future general was reunited with twelve extended family members, including aunts, cousins, and an uncle.[34] Jean-Jacques and his family worked side by side with Jasmin, a standard practice where free people of color owned and lived on smaller plantations.[35] Together they cultivated and harvested the coffee plants and the food crops. Given that all the enslaved people on the plantation were a creole family, social relations would have been less hierarchical, especially in terms of gender relations.[36] In fact, after Duclos sold him, Jean-Jacques's quality of life and life expectancy would have increased.[37]

Unlike sugar, coffee cultivation required a similar pace of labor throughout the year.[38] Field work on a coffee plantation included cutting down trees and clearing uncultivated land, planting new coffee trees, fertilizing new plantings, pruning, weeding, and picking the coffee cherries. Overall, enslaved people shared the work on a coffee plantation, but managers designated certain tasks to specific groups. For example, Jean-Jacques and his uncle Etienne likely would have been responsible for clearing new land, because it required strength. Etienne and his sisters, as the more experienced workers, would have used their specialized knowledge to prune the trees. Jean-Jacques's aunts and younger cousins

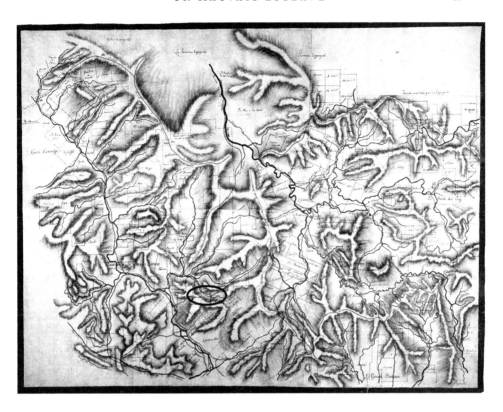

Quartier du Dondon, et de la Grande Rivière. 1802. This map shows the Jasmin plantation in the Cormier Valley (circled). Courtesy of the Maps and Imagery Library, Special and Area Studies Collections, George A. Smathers Libraries, University of Florida, Gainesville, Florida.

would have weeded, fertilized, and protected the trees.[39] The harvesting season, in which everyone on the plantation participated, began in September and lasted about four months. A secondary harvest season followed in March. Shelling, drying, and sorting the coffee beans was difficult work but did not usually require the entire labor force on the plantation; a group of workers completed the task after a full day in the fields.[40]

According to the *Code Noir*, enslavers had to provide a minimum amount of food for their enslaved people. Most, like Jasmin, instead chose to set aside plots of land where enslaved men and women would grow their own food.[41] In addition to cultivating coffee, therefore, Jean-Jacques and his extended family raised their own crops, such as cassava, sweet potato, taro root, yam, squash, plantains, beans, corn, cabbage, leafy greens, coconut, and peppers.[42] Although growing their own food added to their workloads, enslaved people appreciated these gar-

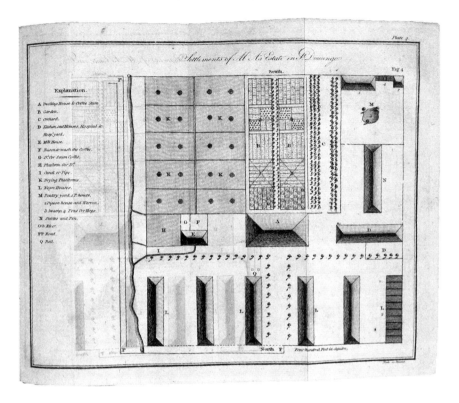

This is a diagram of a slightly larger coffee plantation that included twice
as many *"cases à nègres,"* but was also along a river. From Pierre-Joseph Laborie,
The Coffee Planter of Saint Domingo (London: T. Cadell and W. Davies, 1798),
inserted after page 198. Courtesy of the John Carter Brown Library, Providence.

den plots for the autonomy they provided. They could choose what and how
to plant in their gardens, and they owned the food and medicine that they
produced.[43]

This food supply was not just meant for subsistence; it was central to the
colonial economy. On Sundays enslaved people—taking in hand the written
permits that their enslavers issued to them—traveled to regional markets to
exchange provisions and medicines.[44] The region's largest market was in Cap-
Français, where some fifteen thousand people attended every week. And each
week these thousands were policed and surveilled by agents of the state. Nevertheless, in the hustle and bustle of the market, enslaved people also found freedom, kinship, and community, using these occasions to socialize and worship.[45]

The Jasmin coffee plantation was home to seven buildings. There was a "big house," where Jasmin and his wife lived; a kitchen; a coffee store; a managerial house, where a plantation manager or overseer may have lived and done business; and three *cases à nègres,* houses for Jean-Jacques and his extended family. All the buildings were made of wood and thatch; posts hammered into the ground were bound together with wattling that formed the seven- or eight-foot-high walls. Builders wove palm, sugar cane, or plantain leaves together to form the roofs.[46] Each house would have been less than fifty feet long, typically divided into two rooms, one of which was reserved for sleeping. These three small houses were shared by the thirteen enslaved people living on Jasmin's plantation.[47]

Remarkably, Jean-Jacques (possibly now going by the surname Jasmin or Désir) was not just reunited with his family on the Jasmin plantation. He also met the daughter of a man with whom his fate would be entwined for decades: the famous revolutionary later known as Toussaint Louverture. These two heroes of the Haitian Revolution met more than a decade before the first flame was lit, on a plantation in the mountains near the Spanish border, one enslaved and the other renting his labor. This hierarchical beginning would define them for years in a fraught relationship in which the two men became friends, then revolutionaries, then colleagues—but one giving orders and the other quick to follow them.

Philippe Jasmin was married to a free Black woman named Marie-Marthe, sometimes called Martine. A creole like her husband, Marie-Marthe was the daughter of a free Black woman, Cécile, and an enslaved Black man, Toussaint de Bréda (who would later change his name).[48] Marie-Marthe's father had secured his freedom by about 1776, and he now worked as a coachman on the Bréda plantation in the nearby town of Haut-du-Cap.

It is unclear when Jean-Jacques first met Toussaint de Bréda. But their close relationship likely began in 1779, when Jean-Jacques was a young man of about twenty-one. In August that year, Philippe Jasmin officially leased his coffee plantation to his father-in-law.

When they signed the lease, Toussaint de Bréda had already been renting the plantation for six months.[49] The lease, at a rate of 1,000 colonial *livres* per year, included the labor of the thirteen men, women, and children whom Jasmin enslaved. When writing up the lease document, the notary described the plantation and listed and valued all of Jasmin's property.[50] "Jean-Jacques nephew," he wrote about twenty-one-year-old Dessalines, "fifteen hundred *livres,* here. . . . 1500." His uncle Etienne was valued at 2,400 *livres,* well above the average price of 1,300 *livres* for an enslaved man, suggesting that he was a skilled laborer.[51]

Three of Jean-Jacques's aunts—Marie Rose, Marie Françoise, and Marie Marthe—
were valued at 1,800 *livres* and one, Marinette, at 1,500. His cousins Moise,
François, and Marie Louise were valued at 1,200 *livres,* while his cousins Anne,
Modeste, Joachim, and Joseph, likely being much younger, were valued at 300
and 900 *livres.*[52] It is unclear whether Toussaint de Bréda lived on the plantation
during his lease or whether he managed it from his residence in Haut-du-Cap,
but according to the contract Jasmin expected Bréda to "enjoy and use" the coffee plantation "as a good father."[53] This meant that he had to maintain the buildings and the crops and provide for the enslaved people. If he shirked these duties,
he was accountable for the losses that resulted. For example, during the lease,
one of Jean-Jacques's aunts and her son died; as such, Toussaint de Bréda had to
reimburse his son-in-law for the loss of their labor.[54]

Still, it is likely that Bréda did live on the plantation during the lease. As
Marie-Marthe's father, he may have previously met the enslaved people on the
Jasmin plantation, but during the lease he was able to give orders. Therefore, for
two and a half years, Jean-Jacques labored on the Cormier Valley coffee plantation under and alongside Toussaint de Bréda.

Though they later fought together as colleagues, the relationship from the
start was always hierarchical. Dessalines respected Bréda and yearned for his
approval. This was an interesting turn for Dessalines, who for years had acquired
a reputation as a *mauvais esclave.* Perhaps Dessalines respected Bréda's leadership, or perhaps Bréda respected Dessalines's rebellious spirit. For whatever reason, though, throughout the rest of their relationship, Bréda continued to give
orders and Dessalines obeyed.

When Toussaint de Bréda canceled his lease on July 31, 1781, the plantation
returned to Philippe Jasmin, who, three years later, died at the age of forty-five.[55]
Jean-Jacques was then about twenty-six; according to customary practice, after
Jasmin's death his property would have been split between his wife, Marie-
Marthe, and any children they may have had.[56] It is likely, therefore, that Jean-
Jacques legally became Marie-Marthe's property.[57] For the next three years,
Jean-Jacques remained enslaved on the Jasmin coffee plantation, with ten of his
extended family members.

On October 4, 1787, when Jean-Jacques was about twenty-nine, Marie-
Marthe married a free Black man from the parish of Cap-Français named Jeanvier Desaline.[58] By the time he married Marie-Marthe, Desaline had been a free
man for at least twenty years and was a militia leader and a skilled tradesman,

which would have given him freedom of movement and social status in the parish of Cap-Français.[59] He probably managed the day-to-day operations of his wife's property with her permission, as the law required.[60] Between 1787 and 1791 Jean-Jacques worked alongside Jeanvier Desaline as his apprentice in carpentry or roofing.[61]

It was during Jean-Jacques's enslavement under Jeanvier Desaline that he adopted the name that he used for the rest of his life, Jean-Jacques Dessalines.[62] Out of all his enslavers, including Toussaint de Bréda (later Louverture), why did Dessalines choose to keep Jeanvier Desaline's name? Perhaps he wanted to maintain a connection to his family and to sustain his network of connections in Grande Rivière.[63] But he may have particularly valued Jeanvier Desaline's status as a militia leader among free people of color.[64]

In 1767 a new colonial law had required every free man over fifteen years old to serve in the militia, which was when Jeanvier Desaline began his service as a soldier in the colonial militia.[65] White colonists resented this law and regularly shirked their militia duties, which meant that free men of color made up most of the militia.[66] (Even so, as part of the reforms following France's losses during the Seven Years' War, the colonial state prevented free men of color from serving as commanders, and white men led all militia companies in the colony.)[67] In Saint-Domingue, as in France, the militia system was central to local governance, helping to maintain "order" by assisting in infrastructure maintenance, bureaucratic administration, policing, and capturing people who had escaped from slavery.[68] Jeanvier Desaline clearly excelled at this form of service and was quickly promoted from soldier to corporal and then sergeant, even though he was prevented from entering the ranks of the commanding officers.[69]

By 1779 France had joined the American colonists fighting the British during the War for Independence. To aid their new allies, Jeanvier Desaline joined several hundred free men of color in the Chasseurs Volontaires unit, which sailed north from Cap-Français to the North American mainland to help reclaim the city of Savannah from the British.[70] The siege was a disaster for the Chasseurs, but many of the men who survived the battle later became leaders in the fight against slavery and racism in Saint-Domingue. When he returned from Savannah, Jeanvier Desaline rejoined the colonial militia as a sergeant major. Seven years later he married Marie-Marthe. Thus, by the time Jeanvier Desaline enslaved Jean-Jacques he had served in the colonial militias for eighteen years. Free people of color used militia service for social and economic mobility and built extensive kin-like networks based on their service. The social status that

Jeanvier Desaline gained through leadership positions in the militia was likely his appeal as a second husband for Marie-Marthe and perhaps also as a model for Jean-Jacques.

Dessalines may have followed Jeanvier Desaline into the militia, where he would have gained some military experience.[71] Enslavers could authorize their enslaved men to undertake militia service as a path to eventual freedom (indeed, by the 1790s, this was one of the only tax-free ways to secure legal freedom from slavery).[72] Enslaved servicemen occupied the lowest rank of the *maréchaussée* and served in policing units of unpaid volunteer adjutants. They worked alongside poor free people of color as the "muscle of the colonial state," locating and capturing maroons in the remote mountains.[73] Perhaps Dessalines's later military success stemmed from this training. If it did, it was another of the many contradictions of his life: serving in the colonial militia meant that his own personal freedom would have come at the expense of other people's.

Meanwhile, Dessalines became a father. On October 2, 1789, his daughter Marie-Françoise Célimène was born in Saint-Marc, the parish where his friend Toya now lived. Célimène's birth mother remains unknown, but she may have been Dessalines's first wife.[74] Seventeen years later Dessalines registered his daughter with the state, recognizing her as a legitimate child with his new wife. It is possible he met Célimène's mother at a regional market, traveling for or with Jeanvier Desaline doing carpentry work, or while visiting Toya. Four years later he fathered another daughter, Célestine, who was also born in Saint-Marc.[75]

Over the course of his life, Dessalines would father more than a dozen children, but details about their lives are hard to come by. He was rumored to have had multiple mistresses who may have been the mothers of some of these children. Yet his second wife, Marie-Claire Heureuse Bonheur, is believed to have never given birth to any of their children.[76]

While Dessalines was building a family, the French nation was in turmoil. Earlier that year in Paris, members of the Third Estate had formed a National Assembly, claiming to be the legitimate representatives of the nation. In response, white colonists in the Caribbean demanded representation in the National Assembly and tried to wrest power from the overseas government by strengthening local control over legal, political, and economic policies.[77] By the end of 1789, white colonists in Saint-Domingue had formed assemblies in each of the island's provinces and parishes, aiming to elect men who would represent the colony in France.[78] They saw an opportunity for themselves in the French

Revolution; they wanted to limit the distant state's control over colonial economic policy, and sought to achieve this goal by seizing political power.[79]

But this power was limited to white men. By limiting voting rights and membership in the new assemblies to white people, the new democratic institutions excluded fully half of the colony's free men.[80] Immediately, Black and mixed-race men saw this exclusion for what it was and objected.[81] Over the next year and a half, Dessalines's home parish became a critical site for the struggle among the free population for rights and representation. Free men of color met on multiple occasions in the town of Grande Rivière, where they petitioned the colonial state, demanding equal rights as French citizens. Nearby, Dessalines would certainly have been aware that free people of color were advocating for equal rights, and that a deep-seated conflict was brewing between the enslavers of different "races" in Saint-Domingue.[82]

On October 30, 1789, a group of free men of color from Grande Rivière wrote to the Colonial Committee, in session in Cap-Français, demanding the right to submit their grievances. Since they were free residents of Saint-Domingue, the group argued, that meant they were citizens of France. It was in the best interests of the colony to include them, they continued, because they were essential for "public security": an explicit reference to their critical role in the colonial militia. Moreover, they insisted, they had sacrificed their health and personal interests to "maintain order and the safety of their fellow citizens."[83] Consequently, the group argued, they should have the right to speak to the assembly.

This request from the free men of color in Grande Rivière was ignored by the Colonial Committee in Cap-Français. But the militiamen submitted their grievances anyway. In eight articles, forty-two men reiterated their loyalty to the colony and to the French king; they also reminded the committee of their value as keepers of public order, both by fending off "enemies of the state" and returning enslaved fugitives to their plantations.[84] In return for their service, the free men of color from Grande Rivière asked for the same "rights, privileges, immunities, and exemptions that all honest citizens have the right to claim." They wanted to be able to choose free men of color as officers in the militias and to be "known only by our names and surnames, and place of residence"—that is, without the asterisks that parish priests and notaries always added to denote their racial status and mark them as lesser citizens.[85]

Alongside their demands, the men of Grande Rivière issued a gentle yet pointed warning to the white assembly: it would be unjust and impolitic to refuse them their rights, since they managed the precarious balance of the plantation system.[86] Even so, the Colonial Assembly once again ignored the petitioners.

They were not dissuaded.

The group of militiamen had elected as one of their two commissioners Jean-Baptiste Chavanne, a mixed-race plantation owner from Grande Rivière, who was part of the military elite of the region, though not particularly wealthy.[87] Like Jeanvier Desaline, Chavanne and many of the men who supported him in Grande Rivière had fought in the Battle of Savannah.[88] Now Chavanne and his supporters made their case again to the assembly by strategically using one of the key texts of the French Revolution. In October 1789 King Louis XVI had ratified the National Constituent Assembly's Declaration of the Rights of Man and of the Citizen, which declared that "men are born and remain free and equal in rights."[89] Now, in March 1790, Chavanne's group asked for authorization to participate in the parish and provincial assemblies since "we are duly and legally called to the presentation and discussion of our rights," insisting that the colonial assembly could not disobey what had been "decreed by the nation and promulgated by the King."[90]

That same day, on the other side of the Atlantic, deputies in the French National Constituent Assembly approved voting instructions for the colonies. But rather than resolving the conflicts in the colonies about whether free men of color were eligible to vote, the assembly sidestepped the issue, leaving it up to the colonial administrations to decide.[91]

Less than a month later, a free man of color was executed in Cap-Français; the reason was that he had demanded that the French Declaration of the Rights of Man and of the Citizen be applied to free people of color.[92] The colonists' decision was clear: the assemblies would remain open only to white people. By continuing to insist on equal rights, the men from Grande Rivière were explicitly risking their lives.[93]

Consequently, Chavanne fled across the island's Spanish border to escape the wrath of the French colonial government. He remained there until October 1790, when he returned to Dessalines's home parish of Grande Rivière.[94] There Chavanne was joined by Vincent Ogé, a free man of mixed race from neighboring Dondon. Ogé had recently returned from Paris, where he advocated for the rights of free men of color in the colonies in front of the National Constituent Assembly. Now he and Chavanne (as well as Ogé's brothers Jacques and Joseph, the latter of whom would later serve in Dessalines's administration) agreed to turn a paper protest into an armed revolt.[95]

Together Chavanne and Ogé assumed leadership of the Grande Rivière uprising. They wrote to the provincial assembly again, demanding that all free men
be allowed to vote. What was different from earlier in the year, however, was
that now Chavanne and Ogé warned that if their demands were denied, they
would "resist force with force."[96] Predictably, the assembly again refused their
demands, so Chavanne and Ogé organized and armed their supporters.[97]

In Grande Rivière about three hundred men of color prepared for battle.
Similar actions were taken elsewhere in Saint-Domingue by other free men of
color.[98] This was how a political and ideological fight among the free population
gradually turned violent: the white population committed to defending the status quo, while the free men of color risked their lives to demand social and political equality.

Over the next two weeks, Chavanne and Ogé led groups of Black and mixed-
race rebels throughout the parish, seizing arms from plantations owned by white
men.[99] They did not use violence, and even issued receipts to those they disarmed, explaining that they would eventually return the munitions.[100] After a
small skirmish in Grande Rivière on November 1, Chavanne and Ogé retreated
beyond the border and fled to the Spanish city of Santo Domingo on the eastern side of the island.[101] The Spanish government arrested and questioned the
fugitives and then, at the insistence of the French colonial governor, extradited
them and about two dozen of their followers to Cap-Français. There the French
colonial administration subjected them to a days-long secret trial.

The Superior Council of Cap-Français found Chavanne and Ogé guilty of
the crime of rebellion and condemned them to death.[102] The council made examples of Chavanne and Ogé, warning free people of color of what would happen if anyone challenged the exclusive authority of the white colonists. An executioner smashed their bones and then removed their heads to display on pikes.[103]
Soon after, twenty-one more men were executed for having participated in the
rebellion; their decapitated heads joined those of Chavanne and Ogé.[104]

Local newspapers were keen to emphasize that it was *"mulâtres"* men who
were responsible for the revolt.[105] But the unfair treatment and violent execution of the group's leaders, and the council's flagrant disrespect for them, affected the entire population of the region, both free and enslaved. Thus the
gruesome deaths of Chavanne and Ogé served not only as a warning for future
insurgents but also as an inspiration.

Jean-Jacques Dessalines grew up in this complex world of localized terrorism
and global warfare. From his enslavers' perspective, his sole value was his labor

productivity. In contrast, Dessalines saw himself as more than a "slave." As he grew into a man, he resisted his enslavers' framework and found ways to protect himself from the violent and dehumanizing impulses of colonialism and slavery. He rose from obscurity by refusing to submit to the authority of the colonizers and enslavers. And he inspired others who would join him in establishing and defending—against all odds—Haitian independence. For the first time anywhere in the Americas, Haitian revolutionaries would abolish slavery for good. His life and legacy are at the heart of the centuries-old and ongoing fight for Haitian freedom and sovereignty, and indeed for global racial equality.

Dessalines's childhood and early adulthood were trapped in this tense, precarious, and violent world of the plantation. This life, along with the anti-revolutionary violence he would have witnessed or learned about in his own home parish, showed him just how hard it would be for people of African descent to secure true freedom and equality in the colony. Yet he, and thousands of others, soon decided that it was worth the risk.

PART TWO

Dessalines

1791–1804

CHAPTER 3

He Felt Like He Was Born for War

Nearly six months to the day after Jean-Baptiste Chavanne and Vincent Ogé were executed, a survivor from their short-lived rebellion spoke before a secret nighttime gathering deep in the woods. "The moment of vengeance is coming," claimed this free man from Grande Rivière; "tomorrow, during the night, all the white people must be exterminated."[1] Knowing the ghastly fate of his fellows from the revolt, he had personally experienced the state's violent resistance to demands for equality.

It was mid-August 1791, and enslaved men and women—mostly people in positions of authority, influence, and mobility on the plantations—in the northern province of Saint-Domingue met to plan a war.[2] They were joined by some free people of color, like the survivor of Chavanne and Ogé's revolt. Claiming they were going to a Sunday dinner, they secured permission from their enslavers and gathered at night in the woods of the Lenormand de Mézy plantation, southeast of Cap-Français.[3]

They met again a week later, this time in Bois Caïman, a wooded area on the Choiseul sugar plantation of Petite-Anse, a parish directly south of Cap-Français. Men and women danced and worshipped and prepared to fight for their lives. They sacrificed a black pig and called on the spirits for assistance, collecting the blood and hair of the pig to use as protective talismans in the upcoming fight.[4] "Powerful Liberty!" a religious leader named Dutty Boukman shouted as he addressed the crowd in the forest, "come . . . speak to every heart."[5]

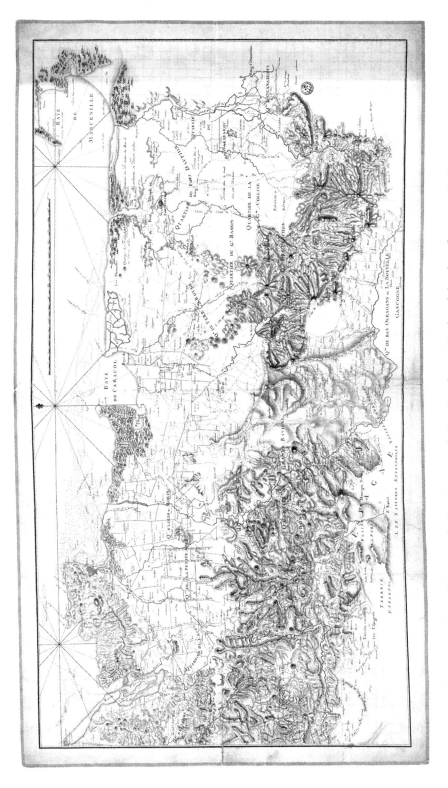

Carte topographique de la région du Cap-Français et du Fort-Dauphin, au Nord-est de la colonie française ou St. Domingue, 1760. Bibliothèque nationale de France, Département des cartes et plans, GE SH 18 PF 150 DIV 2 P 8.

Soon after, on the night of August 22, 1791, the revolutionaries rose up.[6] In large groups they spread east and west from Acul, recruiting insurgents along the way. To the west they reached neighboring Limbé. To the east they burned cane fields, houses, and sugar mills; killed enslavers and managers; and stole livestock for food and transportation in Plaine du Nord, Petite-Anse, Quartier Morin, and as far east as Limonade.[7] It was an "insurrection of an infinity of plantations units," one colonist lamented.[8]

Within a week, the revolutionaries attacked seven parishes and destroyed 184 sugar plantations. One group of colonists estimated that it would take two decades to recover from the damage.[9] Dark clouds billowed up from the fires that engulfed the sugar crops, creating a macabre landscape for those viewing the scene from ships in the Cap-Français harbor.[10]

But it was not senseless destruction; in fact, the enslaved rebels were careful in their attacks.[11] They scoured the plantations for valuables and weapons before destroying the equipment and setting fire to the mills, buildings, and crops.[12] They aimed to destroy the material objects associated with their enslavement, while salvaging resources for their freedom.

The colonial authorities rallied some defenses, punishing and executing suspected insurgents and crucially protecting the city of Cap-Français.[13] Stymied, the revolutionaries retreated to the mountain range of the Massifs du Nord, where they formed three armies under the leadership of Jean-François Papillon (Petecou), Georges Biassou, and Jeannot Bullet.[14] All three of the revolutionary leaders had previously been enslaved in the region around Cap-Français; Papillon had escaped as a fugitive, and Biassou had secured his freedom and was working as a driver in 1791.

As the revolutionary armies moved south into the mountains, they destroyed nearly 1,200 coffee plantations, even while marshaling shelter, food, trade partners, and recruits. In the early days of the war in late August, the revolutionaries had accumulated about two thousand supporters; but quickly they increased their ranks to about ten thousand fighters and by the end of September they were at least twenty thousand strong.[15] Now they solidified their positions farther east in Fort-Dauphin and Ouanaminthe, establishing strongholds in Grande Rivière and Dondon—the parishes that surrounded the Cormier Valley where Dessalines lived.[16] Dessalines likely joined the revolution then. "The movement of 1791 marked the hour impatiently awaited by the centuries-old forces that seethed within Dessalines," Haitian historian Gérard M. Laurent wrote.[17]

From the mountains, the revolutionary leaders looked across the border and appealed to Spanish royalism and Catholicism to secure material support. While the revolutionaries in Saint-Domingue were fighting for freedom and equality, many of their political and religious beliefs and affiliations would have been considered counterrevolutionary from the perspective of France. Republicanism had not yet evolved into a political ideology that supported abolition, and in fact would only do so at the insistence of the enslaved revolutionaries in Saint-Domingue.

It was in the mountains, only a few weeks after the initial uprising in Acul, that Jean-Jacques Dessalines was likely recruited into the revolutionary armies. It is also possible that he participated in the initial August uprising.[18] Regardless, given that the revolutionaries took control of Grande Rivière in the first weeks of September, Dessalines must have joined their ranks by then.[19] "Without ambition, modest and blindly obedient to the orders of his leader," Dessalines's secretary would recount much later, "he felt like he was born for war, making it as a happy soldier and finishing it as a hero."[20]

From the beginning, Dessalines fought in a unit led by Toussaint de Bréda, the father-in-law of his previous enslaver, with whom he'd struck up a relationship more than a decade earlier. Before the uprising, Bréda had known Biassou, one of the three leaders of the mountain-based armies; as such, he joined the revolutionaries as Biassou's aide-de-camp in Grande Rivière and Dondon.[21] Later, when Bréda established his own unit, Dessalines followed him. Most likely, Bréda had recruited him.

"Since the beginning of the Revolution," Bréda later wrote about a group of his top generals, including Dessalines, "[they] never ceased to assist me in my operations."[22] This assistance came in many forms, including advice and protection. Indeed, Dessalines was "the heart of [Toussaint's] armies," argued Dessalines's secretary, Boisrond-Tonnerre, "his constant support, his counsel, his right-hand man; from the earliest days of the Revolution he saved him several times in the northern plains when [Toussaint] was still only considered one of the black leaders of the revolt."[23]

As Dessalines rose in the ranks of the revolutionary army, his extended family from the Cormier plantation likely supported the revolution from the outset. Some may have fought themselves, possibly including his uncle Etienne and some of his cousins, who may have served with Dessalines under Jean-François, Biassou, and Jeannot. Others, like his aunts and younger cousins—with whom he maintained contact even as he spent the next years away fighting—could contribute by sustaining their subsistence plots on the plantation, allowing the revolutionaries the time to regroup and rest. Meanwhile, in another parish Dessalines's aunt Toya quickly set out to reunite with him in battle. Gun in hand, she led a unit of several men who were armed with wooden pikes. Colonists captured her unit and interrogated them. "Where are you going?" they asked Toya. She was going to find her leader, she replied. "Who is he and where is he?" they asked. "Jean-Jacques," she answered, noting that she did not know where he was.[24]

Unbeknownst to Toya, Dessalines was not far from home. Since he and Bréda were both familiar with Grande Rivière, they had chosen the parish as their base. In the first months of the revolution, Dessalines's topographical knowledge of the mountainous region would have made him an effective soldier. Many of the revolutionaries, both those who had been enslaved and those who were recognized as free, were former members of the *maréchaussée* and the colonial militia, and they likely had deep knowledge of the landscape, especially the most effective places to hide. The revolutionaries who were born in Africa may have fought in civil wars at home and would have known how to use firearms.[25] They had experience fighting in small units—or what one historian calls "platoons"—that harassed their enemies into confusion by attacking, retreating, and regrouping for repeated quick assaults.[26]

For the next decade, the revolutionaries perfected their fighting style, an approach that could be described as swarming, to best suit the terrain and capitalize on the geography.[27] During this period they occupied the plantations of the mountainous region and set up camps in the fields. There they honed their skills and coordinated their attacks. The violence of the uprising was initially irregular, and insurgents used whatever tools they could find as weapons. Through plantation raids and trade with the Spanish, they soon expanded their cache of weapons by securing guns, swords, and cannons and developed a strategy of attack and retreat.[28] Combatants would descend covertly from the mountains and target French-controlled plantations, killing enslavers and stealing supplies, and then disappear into the heavily forested terrain for protection before retreating to their camps.

As the revolution intensified in the final months of 1791, colonists and government officials blamed everyone but themselves for their losses. They claimed that some white people were spreading rumors that the French king had abolished slavery, and they accused free people of color of agitating for equal political rights. They also blamed the French National Constituent Assembly for expanding political participation.[29] Few of the colonists understood that their own acts of violence had motivated enslaved people to rebel, and that enslaved men and women had their own ideologies and aspirations for freedom and autonomy.

In fact this revolution had been brewing for years. There were countless enslaved people like Dessalines, who had defended themselves against the violence of the plantation, engaged in multiple forms of defiance, and denounced the system of slavery itself.[30] Now they were simply working together.

By November 1791 the white colonial armies realized that they were in trouble. They may have successfully pushed the insurgents back from Cap-Français, but nevertheless they were too weak to completely defeat the revolution. But if free people of color would ally with the white planters, urged Anne Louis Tousard—the lieutenant colonel of the regiment of Cap-Français and a veteran of the American War for Independence—then those in his district would be rewarded for their loyalty. "Do you believe," Tousard asked them in a public speech, "that after you helped us save our properties that there will be any among those whom you have fought alongside, who will not be your most ardent defender and who will not help you secure your just and reasonable demands in exchange for the essential services that you rendered?"[31] Tousard knew that he could use their desire for equal rights to secure their assistance in the war. Many free people of color did join the white French colonial troops, a sign that their loyalty was primarily to the free population or that they assumed the colonial state would defeat the revolution.[32]

One of the free men of color who answered Tousard's call was Jeanvier Desaline, the person who was, at least nominally, still the enslaver of Dessalines. Building on his previous experiences as a sergeant major in the militia and a sergeant in the Chasseurs Volontaires in Savannah, in November 1791 Jeanvier Desaline led a national guard unit of free people of color, itself a revolutionary reconfiguration of the militia.[33] In this capacity he fought against at least one of the people whom he had formerly enslaved and against his own father-in-law.[34]

The choices that Jean-Jacques Dessalines, Jeanvier Desaline, and Toussaint de Bréda made at the outbreak of the revolution reflected the different opportunities then available to Black men in the northern province. Each of them had a lot to lose and a lot to gain, and they made difficult decisions based on their own personal histories. Dessalines had been enslaved his entire life, while Toussaint de Bréda had once been enslaved but now had been a free man for more than fifteen years. Meanwhile, Jeanvier Desaline managed a coffee plantation and an extended family of enslaved men, women, and children; moreover, he had built a career in the militia by supporting the plantation economy even though it limited his political and social rights. Remarkably, the three men knew each other as workers, plantation owners, and family members.

Joining the revolution was dangerous. Rebels could lose their lives in battle, but even if they survived they could face backlash if the movement itself failed. Assuming a leadership position and attaching one's name to the written record of the revolution was even riskier. Even so, both Dessalines and Bréda decided that the collective fight for freedom was worth the risk.

Military service had previously been an avenue for social and economic advancement for free men of color. Men like Jeanvier Desaline therefore chose the more certain path and joined the combined colonial forces opposed to the uprising. As a plantation owner and an enslaver, he was also likely trying to protect or recover his assets.

Additionally, he and many other free people of color believed that the revolt was losing strength. They anticipated an imminent return to the previous colonial system, meaning renewed control over their plantations and the people whom they enslaved. And they weren't wrong. By the end of 1791 the insurgents had killed about four hundred enslavers; moreover, they were no longer working on the plantations and had freed themselves from slavery.[35] But securing long-term freedom was far from guaranteed. Insurgent leaders worried that France had sent troops to help the colonists. And now, with veterans such as Jeanvier Desaline joining, the insurgents faced a combined colonial force of all free men: white colonists and free people of color.[36]

Because the revolutionaries wanted to secure permanent outcomes, they elected to open negotiations with colonial officials.[37] The conditions that Jean-François and Biassou proposed for peace reflected their deep concerns for their safety and freedom. Worried about possible retribution, they asked for a general amnesty for all revolutionaries and documented freedom for the leaders. They also insisted that it was essential for them to keep their weapons. Throughout the revolution enslaved men and women interpreted any attempts to disarm them as signaling the return of slavery or further restrictions on their safety and freedom. In exchange for these demands, Jean-François and Biassou promised that they would make the rest of the insurgents return to their plantations—as slaves again.

The two generals thus did not ask for general abolition.[38] They likely recognized that they had to limit their demands, and at this point complete abolition seemed unattainable.

Before Jean-François and Biassou received a response, three civil commissioners arrived in Cap-Français from France, unaware that a significant revolution was underway.[39] They carried two proclamations that had momentous consequences for the colony. On September 24, 1791—almost two months before they landed in Saint-Domingue—the French National Constituent Assembly had awarded the colonial assembly authority over the laws that regulated slavery and the political rights of free people. This was a victory for the white colonists, since it overturned a previous law from Paris that had recognized the political equality of a limited number of free men of color in the colonies.[40] But just four days later, the National Constituent Assembly also extended a general amnesty for "acts of revolution" if the person was willing to submit to the new order.[41] For some Black insurgents in the colony, this second proclamation seemed like it might let them claim amnesty, too. Still, they knew that the chances that their fight would be recognized as a full-scale "revolution" were slim, because that would have entailed recognizing that the insurgents' actions were political.[42]

Ultimately, the colonial state instead considered their actions as crimes. Still, asked Jean-François, Biassou, and the "*citoyens de couleur*" (citizens of color)—as they tried to negotiate a settlement—"what crime would it be to reclaim the legitimate authority of the rights that have become sacred?"[43] The colonial assembly simply ignored their question. One person who did respond, days later, was Anne Louis Tousard, the lieutenant colonel of the regiment of Cap-Français, who seized the opportunity to belittle the insurgents. "Do not believe," Tousard scoffed, "that the white people and especially an assembly of representatives of the colony will ever debase themselves by receiving conditions dictated and demanded by their revolted slaves." Tousard issued his own set of demands, including the return of all enslaved insurgents to their plantations, the complete disarmament of the Black population, and the return of white prisoners.[44]

Now it was the insurgent leaders' turn to ignore their enemy's demands. Instead they wrote to the new civil commissioners, hoping that the conflicts among the various branches of colonial governance would offer room for consideration of their proposals.[45] In these negotiations, Toussaint de Bréda and other insurgent leaders joined Jean-François and Biassou.[46] "By ordering each of us to return to our homes," the insurgents explained to the French commissioners, "you have ordered an impossible and simultaneously perilous thing."[47] The leaders claimed they were beholden to the will of the masses.[48] "And what will but that of a multitude of *Negres de la Cote* [born in Africa]," they argued, "most of whom barely know how to say two words in French but who in their country were accustomed to warfare and in that way still?"[49]

A week later, Jean-François and Biassou sent another letter to the commissioners, explaining that their soldiers wanted slavery reforms and noting that they had good reason to make these demands: the colonizers had committed "a thousand cruelties against the slaves."[50] Like Dessalines, enslaved people carried the evidence of this violence, and the physical and emotional scars of the punishments remained vivid. It was the enslavers' own actions, the insurgent leaders decried, that "forced their slaves to become executioners by all kinds of torments."[51]

As leaders of the uprising, Jean-François and Biassou were also worried that, even if a truce was agreed, they might not even have the chance to reach the plantations and instead would be executed like Chavanne and Ogé. Just six months earlier, those two leaders, "after voluntarily surrendering on the word of the superiors of Cap and believing themselves in complete safety, were sacrificed in pieces!"[52] The memory of Chavanne's and Ogé's executions loomed large in the north—and continued to do so for years to come. The enslaved insurgents in 1791 saw themselves as the heirs to that earlier insurrection, and anticipated— reasonably—that the colonial state would respond similarly to their actions. They did not want to be punished for protesting the injustices of slavery and demanding better treatment, which was, they argued, well within their rights.

But even if the commissioners from France had found these arguments persuasive, they could not overrule the colonial assembly, which held firm.[53] The diplomatic route had failed. The insurgents therefore turned their focus southward, across the poorly defined border with the Spanish colony where they had already secured illicit trade partners.[54] There they found willing allies who, though cautious, formed a precarious alliance with the Black soldiers by acknowledging their freedom and providing financial incentives.

Within weeks of the failed negotiations with the French commissioners, the rebellion resumed. Now Jean-François's unit attacked Ouanaminthe, a border parish east of Grande Rivière. There they would fight against Jeanvier Desaline's national guard unit, composed of free people of color.[55]

Already the revolutionaries were changing the world of the colony, even for their adversaries. One of the demands that Chavanne and Ogé had made before the Grande Rivière revolt was for the militias to allow for Black and mixed-race officers. Jeanvier Desaline and other men of color who fought with the colonial troops likely expected to lead their own national guard units. Tousard was annoyed by this demand but found it expedient and acquiesced. "I am angry that the citizens of color are not convinced of the necessity of having white officers," he wrote on January 13, 1792. But "because I see that those of Barbo and Dessalines [sic] are well served," he concluded, "the company of Ouanaminthe can keep their officers of color, let them know."[56]

Tousard's concession wasn't enough to bring victory to the colonists. Jean-François defeated Jeanvier Desaline and Barbo, claiming Ouanaminthe for the insurgents.

In April 1792, with the war still raging, the French government in Europe finally forced the colony of Saint-Domingue to apply the Declaration of the Rights of Man and of the Citizen to all free people equally.[57] To implement this new policy, which was sure to be contentious, Paris sent another group of commissioners to the colony, but news of the change preceded them.[58] Knowing that the metropole could be played against the colony, the leaders of the insurgency tried to use the change to advocate for the rights of enslaved people. In July 1792 Jean-François and Biassou along with Gabriel Aimé Belair, one of Biassou's aides-de-camp, wrote a letter addressed to a broad cross section of colonial society, including government and military personnel and the free citizens of the colony.[59] They strategically used the vocabulary of the French Revolution to make their case, noting that they were following in the footsteps of the "brave French" in the "Mother Country."[60]

"Yes, Messieurs," they noted, "we are born free like you, and it is only by your avarice and our ignorance that we have been held in slavery up to this day." They argued that the French had treated them like livestock, but that it was time for enslaved people to "demand the rights that all men can claim." "Have you forgotten," they asked their enslavers, "that you have formally sworn to the declaration of the rights of man that says that men are born free and equal in rights." After noting this hypocrisy, the revolutionaries issued another set of demands. This time they called for *la liberté générale* (general emancipation), amnesty for all, and freedom for all enslaved people to leave the colony.[61] In exchange they would ensure that plantation work resumed, but under a system that paid workers for their labor.[62] The letter was intercepted, however, and it never reached its intended public audience.[63]

Paris had a different plan for Saint-Domingue. It was a compromise position that would make neither the colonists nor the insurgents happy, but would—perhaps—preserve the lucrative economic system that sent such riches back to France. When the new commissioners (Léger-Félicité Sonthonax, Étienne Polverel, and Jean-Antoine Ailhaud) arrived in September 1792, they brought six thousand French troops with them, in addition to orders giving them the power to suspend any administrators who opposed them.[64] The commissioners dissolved the colonial assemblies and formed new ones that included free men of color.[65]

This was a desperate attempt on the part of the French government to stop the revolution and secure the place of slavery in colonial society. To reassure the free residents of Cap-Français that political representation for free men of color would not lead to abolition, the commissioners immediately affirmed their commitment to slavery and promised to end the insurgency.[66] "We declare," Sonthonax announced as soon as he arrived in the city, "that only the colonial assemblies, once they are constitutionally formed, have the right to pronounce on the condition of the slaves. We declare that slavery is necessary for the agriculture and the prosperity of the colonies."[67]

Not long afterward, however, news arrived that the French Legislative Assembly had deposed Louis XVI, established a National Convention, and declared the French Republic.[68] This change called into question the authority of the civil commissioners, who had traveled to the colony on the king's behalf.[69] Were the reconstituted colonial assemblies legitimate?

In the mountains, far from the compromises of the commissioners below, the insurgents continued their revolution. The new year came and went. For Dessalines, Bréda, and other Black leaders who had been fighting for almost two years, the life of fugitivity and warfare was difficult. But surrender to the French was not an option, because they would most certainly be executed. Even the commissioner Sonthonax realized this, remarking that "there seems to be a considerable mass who are resolved to die rather than surrender."[70] Dessalines supported Bréda when he served as Biassou's second in command, but the hardships of war generated rivalry among the insurgent leaders, and Bréda started acting autonomously.[71]

In late February 1793 news reached Saint-Domingue that Spain and Britain had declared war on France.[72] Hoping to undermine the new French Republic, France's enemies also saw an opportunity to seize what had been the world's most lucrative colony.[73] The revolution in Saint-Domingue swiftly expanded, and the insurgents suddenly secured bargaining power. The British encroached on French territory from Jamaica, occupying parts of the south and west of Saint-Domingue. The Spanish attacked from the island's eastern side, using their ongoing trade relationship with the revolutionaries to gain ground in the north. Remarkably, even in the face of these attacks, the French republican administration, although mired in chaos, stood steadfast in its support for slavery and unified in the goal of quelling the insurgency.[74] It would not bend in its commitment to slavery, even with its possession of the colony at stake.

The British and Spanish attacks on Saint-Domingue created new battlefronts and also new opportunities for the insurgents.[75] The changes within the French government, and the ongoing refusal of the administrators to accept the insurgents' demands, pushed the revolutionaries into an official alliance with the Spanish. The alliance secured legal freedom for the revolutionaries under Spanish law. In June 1793 they were incorporated into the Santo Domingo military forces as a separate unit of about fourteen thousand troops called the Black Auxiliaries of King Carlos IV.[76] As part of the auxiliaries, the four thousand men in Toussaint de Bréda's unit—including Jean-Jacques Dessalines—secured full rights as free Spanish subjects.[77]

Now under Spanish authority, the insurgents expanded their territory in the northern part of the French colony. Dessalines and his colleagues attacked westward, and by December they had occupied the coastal town of Gonaïves.[78] But conflict among the generals of the Black Auxiliaries about strategy and control continued to undermine their collective unity.[79] Although Bréda and Jean-François vied for leadership, Biassou maintained official control for the time being.[80]

By this point, the revolutionaries had made enough gains to force the French republican commissioners to make concessions. Not only did Sonthonax now face British and Spanish adversaries, but he also had to work with a new French governor, François-Thomas Galbaud, whose mother owned plantations in the colony and who was committed to defeating the revolution.[81] Sonthonax and Galbaud clashed in a power struggle because both had been appointed by the metropole to help govern the colonies, but Galbaud had the support of the local planter elite.[82] In late June, Sonthonax offered freedom and full French citizenship rights to any Black men who were willing to join the republican military forces, including those whom they still considered to be "slaves."[83] An insurgent leader named Pierrot joined forces with Sonthonax along with a few thousand troops and together they forced Galbaud out.[84] Sonthonax's strategy was working.

News of the decree inspired Bréda to negotiate a temporary truce with the colonial army in Dondon.[85] Included on his list of thirty ranked officers who followed his lead and were committed to the truce was "Jacques, Major"—very likely Jean-Jacques Dessalines.[86] The name "Janvier, prêt à faire cap'n" (Janvier, ready to become captain) also appeared on the list.[87] It is possible that this was Jeanvier Desaline, and that sometime between November 1791 and June 1793 he had switched sides to join his father-in-law on the battlefield.[88] Regardless, for the men who agreed to the truce, this may have been an opportunity to solidify their gains, secure their safety, and even find a future within the new colonial structure.

It was around this time that Toussaint de Bréda became Toussaint Louverture. The new surname, which means "the opening," could have referred to his potential for an alliance with the French; or it may have been a statement about his gift for strategic military operations.[89] Either way, the new name signaled that further changes were afoot.

There was still terrific disagreement about the future of Saint-Domingue. It is true that Louverture and his troops—including Dessalines—may have agreed to the temporary truce. But other insurgent leaders and newly freed Black citizens pressured the French commissioners to abolish slavery in its entirety, arguing that full abolition—not amnesty and selective freedom for officers—was the only way to end the war.[90] After all, Sonthonax's previous efforts to recruit insurgents had largely failed; most of them had simply joined France's enemy on the eastern side of the island. But now his victory over Galbaud showed the strategy's potential. During a "festival of liberty" in Cap-Français, a contingent of Black soldiers petitioned the French commissioner for general liberty—and now Sonthonax was ready to listen.[91]

On August 29, 1793—facing ongoing internal strife and a likely attack from the British in Jamaica—Sonthonax finally conceded. Despite his original opposition, the commissioner abolished slavery within his administrative region in the northern province of Saint-Domingue.[92]

Almost exactly two years after the first uprising, enslaved people in Saint-Domingue had successfully forced the government of the world's most profitable colony to abolish slavery. They had developed battle tactics and strategies that supported their cause; they had used interimperial warfare to their advantage; and they had played colonial officials against each other to secure the best outcome. In doing so, enslaved people in the north of Saint-Domingue secured, at lightning speed, the first universal abolition of slavery in the Americas.

Sonthonax's proclamation, however, was not as transformative as it first appeared. The French administration's primary goal was to revitalize and sustain the colony's export economy. Therefore the newly declared freedom for formerly enslaved men, women, and children was limited. While canceling the *Code Noir*, the proclamation replaced it with thirty-eight articles that aimed to regulate the colony's new labor system.

This document was the first in a long lineage of work codes through which the French and later Haitian governments tried to sustain the plantation economy without slavery.[93] It also marked the beginning of a lasting conflict about the definition of freedom between formerly enslaved men and women and the colonial and national administrations. Under the new French republican colonial labor system, formerly enslaved men, women, and children would be paid as contract laborers, or *cultivateurs* (cultivators), working on the colony's plantations under the control of their former enslavers.[94] The state set their wages as profit shares and allowed them two hours per day to cultivate their own subsistence food crops.[95] But while French colonists remained focused on maximizing the production of crops for export, Saint-Domingue's formerly enslaved men and women aspired instead to small-scale subsistence farming, ownership of the land, and control over their time.[96]

Sonthonax framed abolition as an achievement of the new French Republic; and, despite his earlier emphatic protection of slavery, he even claimed that his own mission had always included preparation for its gradual abolition. Instead, he blamed the tyrannical Bourbon monarchs for the perpetuation of slavery. Even with this rhetorical turn, however, Sonthonax clarified that freedom was tied to work. "Do not believe however that the freedom that you will enjoy is a state of laziness of idleness," he announced. "In France, everyone is free, and everyone works; in Saint-Domingue, subject to the same laws, you will follow the same example."[97] But since the colony's labor system and economy were drastically different from those in Europe, formerly enslaved men and women were limited to plantation citizenship, where, paradoxically, they had to work to be free.[98]

Although the proclamation promised a new beginning, the precarity of Sonthonax's authority in the new French Republic did not inspire confidence among the insurgent leaders. Instead Louverture called the French "deceivers, who only want to bring you down." He recalled how the French had treated Chavanne and Ogé when they submitted to French authority and warned his troops that the proclamation might be a trick.[99] The commissioners seemed to confirm Louverture's warning, threatening that the insurgents would "meet an end similar to that of Ogé" unless they defected from the Spanish.[100]

Toussaint Louverture and Jean-Jacques Dessalines, still allied with the Spanish, learned about this end of slavery in the French colony, but were skeptical that the proclamation would stick. Within two months of the abolition proclamation, however, the commissioner in the south, Polverel, established policies to match Sonthonax's in the north. Now slavery was illegal in the entire French colony—at least according to the top-ranking officials there at the time.[101] Yet both of the commissioners established restrictive labor systems and forced formerly enslaved people back to the plantations.[102] Military commanders paired up with commercial agents; together they visited various plantations in the south to read the new labor codes to formerly enslaved people, as well as to secure commitments from them to work six days per week from sunrise to sunset.[103]

In late January 1794 a delegation from Saint-Domingue arrived in Paris, bringing with them copies of Sonthonax's proclamation of abolition. They were not immediately welcomed by the republican government.[104] After all, within the current National Convention in France, even the most ardent so-called abolitionists only argued for its gradual implementation. But who ultimately persuaded the French lawmakers was Louis Dufay, one of the white delegates from Saint-Domingue; he gave a speech in the National Convention that convinced the members to vote to ratify Sonthonax's decree.[105] Dufay argued that Sonthonax had acted out of desperation and that immediate abolition was the only way to save the colony and the lives of their fellow citizens.[106] He also placed primary blame for the change on the Spanish and the British, whose military support of the insurgents and direct attacks of their own had put the commissioners in Saint-Domingue in an impossible position. Now, he argued, abolition would help preserve the plantation economy, and the commissioners' restrictive labor codes essentially created the conditions for gradual abolition.[107] Thus, both in the colony and in the metropole, French abolition was not a principled decision, but a last-ditch effort to send the insurgents back to the plantations.

For years, in fact, the revolutionaries in France had supported slavery in the colonies, whether overtly or by sidestepping the issue (knowing that the colonial assemblies would never abolish it). Only after the enslaved insurgents forced the issue did the National Convention ratify the decision and immediately reframe the abolition of slavery in the language of republican rights, claiming it as one of the triumphs of the French Revolution. Once they abolished slavery, the republicans claimed to have always been abolitionists.[108]

The republicans also tied slavery to royalism, both in their effort to defeat the British and Spanish and to secure the allegiance of Black soldiers in Saint-Domingue. After rumors of the Convention's ratification arrived in the colony, the news divided the revolutionaries.[109] Now there was competition between the insurgents who had allied with monarchical Spain and those who allied with republican France. These were sophisticated political operatives who were seeking to secure the best terms for themselves and for their troops by playing the great powers off one another.

Secretly, in May 1794 Toussaint Louverture established a covert alliance with the French republican forces in Saint-Domingue, thereby breaking with the other leaders who remained steadfastly loyal to Spain. It was only when the official French abolition decree reached the colony in July 1794 that Louverture made the alliance public.[110] Louverture's troops, including Jean-Jacques

Dessalines, were now no longer considered insurgents. In the space of three years, Dessalines had been an enslaved man, a revolutionary, a free Spanish subject and military officer, and now a free citizen-soldier of the revolutionary French Republic.

For the next two years France turned its attention elsewhere, leaving the colony to its own devices.[111] During this time Louverture expanded his military authority, sometimes in partnership and sometimes in competition with a new colonial governor-general, Étienne Laveaux. Together Louverture and Laveaux defended the colony and attacked invading English and Spanish forces.[112] They also coordinated the reconstruction of the smoldering plantation economy.

Jean-Jacques Dessalines, now a French citizen, became a lieutenant colonel in Louverture's army. In the months after they struck their alliance with France, he prepared for a multipronged campaign against the people whom the colonial administration called "rebels" in the east.[113] On December 30, 1794, Lieutenant Colonel Dessalines and four other columns attacked Jean-François and the Black Auxiliaries in Grande Rivière.[114] The initial attacks were successful, and Dessalines's forces pushed the Black Auxiliaries back to Camp Flamin, where they launched an additional strike to take the camp. From their new headquarters, Dessalines and others pressed for more action and reaffirmed their allegiance to Louverture. They routed the Spanish forces and even occupied Grande Rivière. In the southeast region of Dessalines's home parish, the lieutenant colonel assumed control over Camp Denis.[115]

In July 1795 Laveaux authorized Louverture to reorganize the military, and Dessalines assumed command of the 4th demi-brigade in the Artibonite region.[116] Dessalines was among a cohort of officers, including Louverture's nephew, Moyse, as well as Henry Christophe (who would later become king of independent Haiti), Desrouleaux, Duménil, Clervaux, Maurepas (or Morpas), and Bonaventure, who supported Louverture in the years to come.[117]

Over the next several years, Dessalines led four thousand troops with a tightly knit group of officers, including some childhood friends from Grande Rivière, to whom he was forever known as "Duclos."[118] Some of his inner circle of loyal officers included Biret, Dominique, Michaud, and Ferbos. One of his senior officers was Jean-Baptiste Rousselot; he was nicknamed "Dommage" (sometimes spelled "Domage") because when he suffered an injury Louverture had cried out, "*C'est dommage!*" (that's a shame!).[119] Dessalines loved Dommage like a cousin and trusted him deeply.[120] Louis Gabart, another senior officer, was a mixed-race young man who had grown up in Dondon, the parish to the west of Grande Rivière and close to Dessalines's home in the Cormier Valley. Gabart was only about nineteen years old in the early days of the revolution, but he earned the nickname "Vaillant" (Valiant) for his courage and ruthlessness in battle.[121] At some point Dessalines was joined by his younger cousin Joseph Dessalines, who became an officer in the 4th demi-brigade.[122] These officers and the troops they commanded received the nickname of the "sans-culottes"; that is, the name of the radical, militant lower class of the French Revolution. Dessalines's troops earned this powerful name both because most of them had previously been enslaved and because they engaged in no-holds-barred fighting.[123]

In a few short years, the insurgents—through a combination of violence and diplomacy—had successfully abolished slavery in the colony. Yet their fight was far from over. The officers and soldiers were now officially part of the French republican army, and France was at war. In the battles to come, Dessalines and the officers and soldiers of the 4th demi-brigade would commit themselves to defending the French Republic. But whether they would be successful was unclear, as was whether the republic would defend them in turn.

CHAPTER 4

To Spill Our Blood . . .
for the Freedom of the Nation

"We deposit here in your hands the oath that we have sworn to spill our blood, to the last drop, for the freedom of the nation," wrote 150 soldiers and officers in Toussaint Louverture's army in a 1795 collective letter to the National Convention in Paris.[1] Committed to fighting with France as republicans, Louverture's men were responding with gratitude to a decree issued by the National Convention on July 23, 1795, which declared the soldiers of the colonial army "were deserving of the nation."

In the middle of the second page of signatures appears the name "Jean-Jacques Dessalines," alongside his officers of the 4th demi-brigade. Although it was a secretary who signed Dessalines's name (he would later drop his first name, after he learned to compose his own signature), this is the first known and confirmed instance of Dessalines as a signatory to a document. It was around this time that "by his energy and his bravery, by his aversion against the system of exploitation, [Dessalines] caught the attention of his superiors." Haitian historian St. Victor Jean-Baptiste argued that "his ascension began" that year.[2]

The same 1795 decree from Paris appointed Toussaint Louverture to the position of brigadier general alongside three mixed-race officers: Jean-Louis Villatte, Louis-Jacques Beauvais, and André Rigaud. Each of these four officers were to defend the French Republic in the colony, but they acted nearly independently of each other within their respective regions. Moreover, the decree (under regulations dictated by the governor and the *ordonnateur,* the public

spending director for the colony) also ordered all cultivators—previously enslaved people now forced to work the land again—who were not in the military
to return to their plantations.

In response to the decree, Dessalines and the rest of Louverture's men expressed their gratitude and promised to continue defending the republic. "You
have decreed that we are deserving of the nation," they wrote. "It is for republican hearts a sweet comfort, a prize worthy of envy! Receive our thanks, fathers
of the nation."[3]

In the years to come, however, as he fought courageously for the republic,
Dessalines repeatedly had to convince the French administrators that his heart
was in fact truly republican. Even while the French reluctantly admitted Black
officers into their ranks, the local administrators clashed over the governance
of Saint-Domingue. White French officials may have accepted free Black men
as soldiers, but they nevertheless tried to regain administrative control from the
clearly more powerful generals. Dessalines balked, quarreling with a new set of
colonial agents. It was starting to become clear that the abolition of slavery did
not signal equality among free men. The fight continued, even if—for now—
they were on the same side.

"We only have left, Citizen Representatives," the letter concluded, "to give
you our assurance that under Laveaux and Toussaint Louverture whom you have
retained for us, we begin our march with a firm & steady stride in the battlefields of victory, & will rip from the English the part of this unfortunate colony,
that the traitors, the royalists basely delivered to them."[4]

The letter thus addressed the key issues that would define Black resistance in
Saint-Domingue for a decade to come. Louverture and Governor Laveaux, even
when not formally allies, had maintained an affable relationship based on respect and a commitment to the same values.[5] But within a year Laveaux was no
longer governor. Moreover, the four generals promoted in the July 23 decree
soon turned on each other as they vied for power. For the rest of the Haitian
Revolution, conflict over legitimacy and authority within the French colony
pitted geographical, political, and racial factions against each other.[6]

It took more than a piece of paper to heal the deep wounds of generations
of slavery. Divisions multiplied, as a person's legal status prior to the abolition of
slavery—either as "slave" or "free"—continued to affect their social status and
political and military allegiances. People who had previously been enslaved were
now referred to as *nouveaux libres* (newly freed people), and those who had
previously been free were called *anciens libres* (formerly free people). These new
labels accompanied another shift in terminology; after the abolition of slavery,

de couleur (of color) increasingly referred only to people of mixed race, used as a synonym for *mulâtre* and especially for mixed-race people who were free before abolition in 1793, or *anciens libres*. Therefore, after 1793, an *homme de couleur* was typically someone with lighter skin who had been free before the Haitian Revolution. In contrast, someone who was called *noir* (black) typically had darker skin but may have been either enslaved *or* free before 1793. The ambiguity of the latter term implicitly and explicitly associated people with darker skin to an enslaved past.

As brigadier general, Louverture faced a delicate task in supporting the French Republic. On one hand, Paris had stated a mission to sustain and expand legal freedom; on the other hand, France wanted to maintain "order" within the new labor system, which was designed to keep formerly enslaved men and women working on the plantations and to keep the colony profitable for France. To accomplish both at once was extremely difficult, let alone for someone who themself had previously been enslaved.

The first actions of the newly enfranchised Black officers—including Dessalines—were immediately split between the necessity of both fighting foreign enemies and securing domestic "order." Despite the government's urging to secure the borders in the south, Louverture's attention was quickly drawn back to the north. There discontented plantation workers engaged in a series of uprisings, furious that their new role too closely resembled their old enslavement.[7] These northern men and women, called *cultivateurs* (cultivators), often refused to work and, even more disruptively, destroyed their crops or withheld them from the government. To rally support, they spread rumors that Louverture was collaborating with the British and that he planned to reenslave them.[8] Indeed, for decades to come, the specter of slavery's return remained a powerful tool to garner support among factions and fuel revolution.

To support Louverture's negotiations with these rebels, Dessalines and five hundred soldiers headed north.[9] The diplomatic route in Port-de-Paix initially failed, but eventually Louverture conceded to the *cultivateurs*' demands to be paid in cash and to choose their overseers.[10] But elsewhere in the region he used intimidation. "I asked them," Louverture recounted, "while threatening them, if they wanted to return to order by working on their respective plantations or if they wanted to go to war."[11] After almost a year of intermittent uprisings, Louverture successfully regained control of the Port-de-Paix region.[12]

The rebellions in Port-de-Paix were punctuated by an attempted coup d'état against Governor Laveaux in Cap-Français: an insurrection by Villatte and his supporters, who claimed to be the legitimate heirs of colonial power.[13] Louverture defended the governor, saving him from imprisonment.[14] But Louverture found another way to sideline his sometime ally; he encouraged Laveaux to leave for Paris, and seek election in the lower house of the French parliament (the Council of Five Hundred). The general suggested this to the governor because conservatives had regained power in France, and Louverture wanted someone he trusted advocating for Saint-Domingue.[15] Laveaux agreed and departed for Europe, where he defended abolition.[16]

In early 1796 a new set of French commissioners arrived in the colony, including the returning Léger-Félicité Sonthonax, who had been recalled to France in 1794 but who was celebrated among the population for having abolished slavery. At first, Sonthonax and Louverture collaborated, with Sonthonax promoting Louverture to the position of division general.[17] Louverture advocated for Sonthonax to represent the colony in Paris—as he had for Laveaux—but this was largely because of emerging political disagreements and power struggles between the two men.[18]

With domestic order somewhat restored in the north, Louverture turned his attention back to the war with the British in the south and west. In March 1797 he departed from his stronghold in Gonaïves and headed toward Mirebalais with twelve thousand troops.[19]

Before the uprising of the *cultivateurs,* the French commissioners had urged Louverture to focus on the British-occupied region around Mirebalais, a commune northeast of Port-au-Prince. This territory was valuable because it was centrally located, and it contained hundreds of small plantations that were still in operation.[20] Moreover, Mirebalais bordered the important Artibonite River that wove through the mountains near the Spanish border, then snaked northwest to meet the ocean above Saint-Marc.[21] Two roads ran along either side of the river, with smaller routes branching off and zigzagging up the adjoining mountains from the riverbed valley below.[22] The artery was essential to the colonial economy, and it facilitated the transport of export crops to the coast. To preserve its borders and ensure unfettered transport of goods out of the colony, France needed to secure the region.

The campaign against the British was therefore central to the revolutionary fight for freedom. The British forces had wasted no time in fortifying their positions while Louverture was busy putting down domestic strife. Dessalines proved to be an effective leader in these battles. During the operation in Mirebalais, he took command of the center column, while Augustin Clervaux and Christophe Mornet led the left and right columns.[23] On March 25, 1797, Dessalines led his troops along the main road to La Selle, west of Mirebalais, since Louverture anticipated that the success of the attack would depend on the capture of that town.

The vanguard of Dessalines's forces carried a four-caliber cannon and a six-inch howitzer along the arduous mountain terrain, sometimes using stretchers to hoist the heavy weapons on their shoulders. They reached the peak of the mountain and began bombarding the British fort. But the British defended themselves by shutting the blockhouse, which was strong enough to protect them from the four-caliber cannon. Reveling in this achievement, the British returned Dessalines's fire with insults and chants of "*vive le Roi*" (long live the King).[24] Their taunts were silenced by the arrival of the much more powerful howitzer. As Dessalines's troops fired the artillery weapon, the British fled the fort.

Throughout the attack, Dessalines maintained communication with Louverture. And after learning about the victory at La Selle, the general prepared for a joint attack on Mirebalais. The combined troops succeeded in taking Mirebalais, but then faced the wreckage that they had inflicted. "Dessalines and the other officers tried uselessly to stop the terrible fire," Louverture recounted in his report to the commission about the campaign. "The violent wind rendered all the efforts ineffective; everything was devoured by the flames; the explosion of a mine dug in the fort for that purpose destroyed all of the interior buildings."[25] Before the fort was gone, Dessalines saved about a hundred prisoners whom the British had arrested on suspicion of being traitors and who would have been burned alive.

Next Dessalines turned his attention south to the Grand Bois region. The area was heavily forested but also contained almost one hundred coffee plantations. The plantations were newer and the infrastructure of the region was underdeveloped, which limited its agriculture as well as any military campaigns, because the army's food and supplies would have to be transported on the backs of mules.[26] At this point Louverture—having recovered from an injury—rejoined the fray by taking command of Clervaux's column. The columns divided to retake the smaller forts surrounding Grand Bois and met at the captured forts to reorganize. The soldiers were "indefatigable in their marches," Louverture crowed, "courageous in their combat, their conduct merited the highest praise."[27]

He singled out Dessalines for his leadership during the attack. "I can only applaud the firmness, the valor, and the caution of brigade commander Dessalines," Louverture reported to the French commissioners. "I recommend the army, and above all this commander, to the attention of the commission."[28]

Because of his successful campaign, Dessalines was promoted on April 18, 1797, to the rank of brigadier general.[29] He had risen to military prominence through skillful leadership and bravery on the battlefield. Dessalines and the 4th demi-brigade were building a reputation for their effective warfare. "These officers," Louverture reported, "as experienced as brave, did not disappoint my expectation."[30] They were using European-style military organization, troop movements, and weaponry, and using them to great effect.[31] In the coming years they would continue using swarming strategies that worked best for irregular forces in the mountains; but in these first engagements of 1797, Louverture's troops showed that they could adapt to win on traditional European battlefields.[32]

Commissioner Sonthonax celebrated the victory at Grand Bois by naming Louverture commander in chief of Saint-Domingue. This promotion elevated him to a position that outranked Beauvais and Rigaud, the remaining men with whom he had been promoted by France's National Convention in 1795. These victories, however, did not mark the end of the fight over the Mirebalais region. Within months the British crept back into the territory they once occupied.[33] In August Dessalines led five demi-brigades composed of about eight thousand men back to Mirebalais, but he was forced to retreat to the Artibonite region.[34]

The ongoing warfare exacerbated conflicts among the colonial leadership. Civil representatives were vying for political power among themselves, as well as with the much more powerful local military leadership. The 1795 French constitution had declared that there was no legal distinction between France and the colonies; but the document had also set the colonies apart from the legal and political infrastructure of the French Republic by reinforcing that the colonies were ruled by commissioners appointed from Paris.[35] Thus, even though the generals in Saint-Domingue were powerful, French-appointed officials used the constitution to limit the military's authority. The ambiguous applicability of the constitution and the inconsistencies of civil and military government heightened the existing tensions over political legitimacy, all of which fueled further local conflict.

Skillfully maneuvering to secure local and metropolitan support, Louverture framed all opposition to his authority as anti-French and anti-republican. He also threatened his adversaries with violence.[36] Using persuasion and intimidation, Louverture forced Sonthonax out of the colony, supposedly to join Laveaux on the Council of Five Hundred to represent the colony's interests.[37] In a letter, Louverture and his chiefs of staff explained to Sonthonax that they no longer needed him in the colony since peace had been reestablished, despite the fact that they were still at war with the British occupying forces. Dessalines's sig-nature was notably absent from this document, even though he was a brigadier general like some of the others who signed. It is likely that he could not sign the document, however, because he was on the battlefield in Mirebalais.[38]

With Sonthonax gone, Louverture focused his attention on the south, try-ing to secure French control—administered through him—over the entire col-ony.[39] At the end of 1797 and into 1798, Louverture worked with André Rigaud to sustain a coordinated campaign against the British.[40] Rigaud, the mixed-race commander of the south, operated semiautonomously from Louverture, but in collaboration with Beauvais he was willing to temporarily team up against the British.[41]

As part of this uneasy collaboration, Dessalines led twelve thousand troops to retake Arcahaye, the coastal region directly west of Mirebalais. Christophe Mornet joined him again, leading the other column, but the two generals ap-pear to have experienced personal conflicts.[42] When Dessalines failed to capture the plains of Arcahaye, Mornet seized the opportunity; he reported to Louver-ture that Dessalines had retreated instead of attacking the *ancien libre* (free be-fore abolition) and British collaborator, Jean-Baptiste Lapointe, as Louverture had ordered. Louverture was furious to have missed the opportunity to defeat Lapointe and revoked Dessalines's command of the campaign for not following his instructions. He even detained Dessalines at the Morne Blanc fort in Go-naïves, temporarily assigning Mornet command of the army.[43] Even under a strict military hierarchy, it seems, Dessalines sometimes let his own instincts or inter-ests dictate his movements.

But Dessalines was too valuable to languish in detention for long; soon he was back in the field leading another attack on Grand Bois. "The General Des-salines commanding the right wing of the army," Louverture wrote in his in-structions, apparently still unhappy with Dessalines's previous insubordination, "remains personally responsible for the execution of my orders and for our suc-cess in the undertaking if he does not take all of the measures to which the present instructions subject him."[44] In a series of detailed letters, Louverture told him to coordinate with General Moyse, who would, after Dessalines suc-ceeded in taking Grand Bois, begin another attack on Mirebalais.[45] Having learned a lesson from the previous assault on Mirebalais, Louverture ordered them to take Grand Bois first, thereby preventing a British retreat to the moun-tains. Dessalines quickly captured the town as ordered and took command of the right wing in the upcoming attack on Mirebalais.[46]

On February 6, 1798, the assault began. Louverture sent the 6th battalion of the 4th demi-brigade to attack Camp Trianon in the Plain du Mirebalais, blocking all routes from which the British could have received reinforcements. The 6th battalion quickly captured the fort and secured a two-piece cannon. Dessalines and his troops then pressed forward to attack the fort at Mirebalais. On February 10 Moyse joined Dessalines, and together they surrounded the fort. Their cannons, however, were no match for the impenetrable citadel—Louverture called it a "Gibraltar in St. Domingue"—so they settled in for a siege. Every time British troops left the fort to take water, the colonial forces attacked.[47]

While each skirmish hurt the British, Dessalines's and Moyse's troops suffered serious casualties: dozens of men were injured, three were taken prisoner, and seven died. "Among the latter," Louverture wrote, "is the brave Captain Jacques Robin who fought as a hero and died a Republican, yelling *long live the French republic* at the foot of the wall of this fort where he died."[48]

Frustrated by the failure to capture the fort at Mirebalais, Louverture dispatched Dessalines and his troops on February 15 to Boucasin, leaving Moyse to blockade the fort. Dessalines secured positions in the elevations around Boucasin and sent the courageous brigadier chief Biret to attack Camp Cabaret. This was an aggressive move, and Dessalines soon regretted it. The British sent troops to Boucasin, with two columns launching a surprise attack on Dessalines's rear. It was a disaster for the 4th demi-brigade, and at least twenty men died. Fighting on the front lines, Biret was captured by the British, who bayoneted him to death rather than holding him prisoner. "A hero's death," Louverture mourned, "for a man who had lived as one."[49] Dessalines's troops carried Biret's memory with them as they continued the fight.

Dessalines eventually rallied his troops and on February 19 headed to the mountains of Mirebalais, aiming to cut off communication routes from Arcahaye. Then three men defected from the fort at Mirebalais, claiming that the British intended to evacuate, enabling Louverture to hatch a new plan of attack; he sent Dessalines to rejoin Moyse. The British, however, managed to evade Moyse and Dessalines's troops by taking unknown routes in the middle of the night. Dessalines pursued them, found their trail not far from Mirebalais, and trapped the British between his and Brigadier General Morin's forces. Both units inflicted heavy casualties on the British, killing, wounding, or taking prisoner 150 of them.[50]

On February 25 Moyse finally took possession of the fort at Mirebalais, finding only a small group of women, elderly, wounded, and prisoners left behind by the British. He secured the weapons that the British had abandoned, including eleven cannons. To prevent the British from ever recapturing the area, Louverture ordered Moyse to demolish the fort.[51]

Dessalines, now at the head of the left column, leading the 4th and 7th demi-brigades and a detachment from Gros Morne, took over access roads and attacked Camp Sabourin.[52] The poorly garrisoned forts fell to Dessalines's troops, forcing the British to abandon the mountain chain of Arcahaye.[53] Now the republican forces continued their march toward Verrettes, seeking vengeance for the death of Biret. Louverture claimed that Dessalines was unable to "stop this moment of fury," when the troops of the 4th killed any British nationals who remained. They also razed the forts and moved on to capture Camp Martine.[54]

Because they were achieving so many victories in the region, Louverture ordered the troops to rest until they received further instructions. On March 23, while his troops recuperated, forty Black and mixed-race armed British allies surrendered to Dessalines.[55] They said that the residents of Arcahaye were waiting for the French colonial army to arrive, so that they could join the republic. Based on this information, Louverture readied his generals to attack. Dessalines (left), Moyse (center), and Christophe Mornet (right) led the three columns that marched to Arcahaye.

The defectors who surrendered, however, had been lying. Rather than joining the French republican forces, the enemy fought hard, attacking Moyse's center column on an open plain. Dessalines sent two battalions, under the orders of Battalion Chief Michaud, to assist Moyse. The British caught Michaud and his troops in an ambush, taking the battalion chief and several others prisoner, killing seventy soldiers, and wounding another thirty. The center column retreated from the plain to the surrounding hillsides.

One of the soldiers who had been captured with Michaud escaped to report that the British had stripped and executed Michaud, even though he had claimed the rights of war and told them that British prisoners had been treated humanely. "These atrocious acts of cold barbarity," Louverture reported, "revolted me and amplified the bitterness that I felt in my soul because of the loss of such a brave officer that will leave a void in the army that I command."[56] He proclaimed that French republican values made their forces superior to the barbaric British troops. "This is the end that menaces the generals defending France and its constitution and the rights of humanity in Saint-Domingue," Louverture recounted. "This is the enemy that we are combatting."[57] He wrote directly to the local British general to voice his indignation.

Louverture next learned that British forces were assembling off the coast of

Môle Saint-Nicolas, on the western point of the colony's northern peninsula. He therefore diverted his troops to the region.

Meanwhile, in April 1798 two European representatives arrived in Saint-Domingue and changed the trajectory of the revolution. Because the Directory of the French Republic declared the colony to be in a "state of siege," they sent Marie-Théodore Joseph Hédouville to the island as the French government's agent. His goal was to seize political control from Louverture.[58] When Hédouville landed in Cap-Français, Louverture wrote to him, regretting that he could not immediately come meet him because he was preoccupied with the British in Arcahaye, the region on the coast to the west of Mirebalais.[59] Not long after, as Louverture launched a full-scale attack on the British in Mirebalais and Arcahaye, Gen. Thomas Maitland arrived in Saint-Domingue to assume command of the collapsing British military occupation.[60] Immediately, however, he realized that defeat was inevitable. To avoid further embarrassment, he tried to withdraw under the best terms possible.[61] On April 23 he proposed a complete British withdrawal from the west in exchange for the safety of the colonists in the region. Louverture agreed.[62]

While in Saint-Domingue, Maitland gathered intelligence that might be useful for the British, including the colony's shifting political hierarchy. According to his observations, Dessalines and Moyse were in line for the top military positions. Dessalines "is next to Toussaint in point of standing and nominal ranks," Maitland wrote, while "[Moyse] is Toussaint's nephew, and it is presumed is intended by Toussaint in the event of any accident to succeed him." Moyse's succession was not a given, and Maitland noted that "the claims of the first [Dessalines], I apprehend, are strongest both from his character and conduct."[63] Within his demi-brigade, Dessalines was fiercely loyal to his officers and vice versa. Among the military leadership, however, Dessalines appears to have had personal and professional differences with several officers. He had clashed earlier with Christophe Mornet over his alleged insubordination, and he maintained an uneasy working relationship with Moyse. Perhaps he was jealous of Moyse's relationship with Louverture; it is also possible that he did not respect the general and saw his rank as unearned.

The British were waiting for Louverture to sign a treaty that would guarantee their safety in an evacuation. But while Louverture claimed that he was waiting for confirmation from the colonial government for permission, Major Gillespie (the British agent whom Maitland had sent to negotiate) insisted that he only had permission to talk with Louverture and pressed him to decide. Louverture later recounted that since the British offer was to evacuate and leave the occupied forts intact, and since time was of the essence, he was convinced "to open negotiations before a Response from the agent, sure that he would have approved of my conduct."[64]

Acting on his own initiative and strategic understanding, Louverture received and amended the British proposal. Next he ordered a halt on the French attacks in Arcahaye and Croix des Bouquets. The British wanted to keep Jérémie and Môle Saint-Nicolas because the two port cities were valuable military assets. Located on the southern and northern peninsulas, respectively, they strategically bordered the windward passage between Saint-Domingue and Cuba and were key sites for naval operations. Given how much territory he would gain, even with the concession of the two ports, Louverture unilaterally decided to approve the agreement. In addition, Louverture offered amnesty to the French militiamen who had served under the British, noting that "they were rather forced to follow the general impulse than their own particular will."[65]

In early May the British evacuated the west of the island. However, they retained control of Môle Saint-Nicolas and Jérémie, where Maitland stationed his remaining troops.[66]

Maitland's negotiations with Louverture exposed a new and potentially explosive conflict among the colony's French republican leadership. As the top civilian authority, Hédouville should have been the one to negotiate with British emissaries. Maitland, however, understood that Louverture was the leader with the most power in the colony.[67] He was well aware of the tension between Louverture and Hédouville, and used it to get better terms for the evacuation, including amnesty for former allies.[68]

Hédouville represented the pro-planter faction in the metropolitan government that had appointed him. His goal was to reassert French control over the colony and reduce the size and strength of Louverture's colonial military.[69] He arrived with hundreds of civil servants but no troops, so he was limited in how he could challenge Louverture's authority.[70]

Louverture initially maintained a collegial relationship with Hédouville, in part because he needed the new agent to approve his nominations for various military positions.[71] In late May Louverture traveled to Cap-Français to meet Hédouville, leaving command of the places his armies had just seized with his "trusted men."[72] Louverture's forces needed to establish French republican rule in Saint-Marc and Arcahaye, and to defend these cities against further attacks. "In consequence," he told Hédouville, he sent Dessalines to Saint-Marc, "where his lengthy experience will guarantee that place from all enterprises, internal and external."[73]

It was in Saint-Marc that Dessalines's two daughters had been born. Though small, during the occupation it had been an important British post. The city had single-story stone houses, a large church, a hospital, and a government building.[74] Military forts in the hills that rose above the town protected the city. Hédouville approved Dessalines's appointment to Saint-Marc, and on June 3, 1798, Dessalines became brigadier general and commander of the arrondissement of Saint-Marc.[75]

This was an important moment in Dessalines's career. Hédouville told Louverture that the Directory was pleased with the colonial military's successes, and he promised that he would update French leaders on the colony's agricultural and military progress. In Paris the Directory was already well aware, Hédouville told Louverture, of "the wisdom of your [Louverture's] disposition, crowned with brilliant success, the zeal and activity of the Generals & the officers who seconded you, the bravery of the soldiers & their constancy to bear, at the same time, the greatest fatigue & the harshest deprivations." In recognition of Louverture's victories, the Directory had even sent gifts with Hédouville to distribute to the military leadership in Saint-Domingue.[76] Louverture himself received a rifle manufactured at Versailles, a sash or scarf, and a saddle. Dessalines, Moyse, Laplume, and Christophe Mornet, "who had particularly distinguished themselves in your last campaign," received similar gifts.[77]

In the places that they had recently recaptured from the British, agent Hédouville tried to erase any traces of their previous occupation. On June 23, 1798, he wrote to Citizen Boener, the civil commander of the city of Saint-Marc, enclosing copies of an *arrêté* (decree) outlining the process for renaming the streets and military forts. In their current form, Hédouville argued, the names "recall the royalism, feudalism, slavery and the English domination."[78] For example, two of the city's military forts were named after British generals.[79] This seemingly innocuous directive, however, became the center of a power struggle between Hédouville and the local military leadership.

Hédouville's high praise of Dessalines was short-lived, because the general refused to obey the new agent after receiving a directive to change the place names in his district. Dessalines, who had not personally received official copies of the document from Hédouville, prevented Boener from publishing and executing the instructions—not because he objected to the renaming but because he disapproved of the process.

In a fury, Hédouville wrote two letters to Louverture condemning Dessalines's behavior. "You would please, Citizen General," Hédouville instructed, "order the arrest for four days, of general Dessalines for allowing himself to suspend the execution of the decree." Since the *arrêté* did not have to do with troop movements, it had been unnecessary to send Dessalines a personal copy, Hédouville claimed.[80] He told Louverture that he was including a copy of Dessalines's refusal and his subsequent orders. If Dessalines did not comply, Hédouville threatened, he would discharge him. "However painful it would be for me to deprive the republic of the service of such a good officer," he told Louverture, "I would have no other choice, if he repeated a similar act of disobedience, to dismiss him, because no one has the right to oppose the orders of the Government whose power lies in the subordination and obedience of the authorities who are subordinate to it."[81] In this particular conflict, Hédouville won; Dessalines was detained for four days in Saint-Marc for insubordination.

Clearly, however, Dessalines's perceived disobedience continued to rankle Hédouville. He revisited the issue in another letter to Louverture. "I am coming back to the disobedience of general Dessalines," he wrote, "who forgot that all of my orders must be executed as promptly as those of the Directory itself."[82] He was "sure that bad advice convinced him [Dessalines] to take a step that could not have been in his heart."[83] This may have been a subtle dig at Louverture. Hédouville walked back his earlier threat of removing Dessalines but did express "sincere regret that he is forcing me to use such severity; but either authority is recognized, [or] there can be no order."[84]

Dessalines's detention did not lead to an increased respect for Hédouville's authority. Instead the general continued to struggle with Boener over local control in Saint-Marc. Dessalines was clearly irked that Hédouville had circumvented his authority by communicating directly with the civil commander.[85] And he was not afraid to alienate Hédouville with a minor squabble, just to prove that he was not subservient to an authority he did not respect. Dessalines refused to blindly take orders. He may have even intentionally derailed the street renaming, simply to get a rise out of the French agent.

On letterhead that officially announced him as brigadier general and commander in chief of the district of Saint-Marc, Dessalines replied to Hédouville, defending his actions. "Being the commander-in-chief of the district," he explained, "I thought I should only publish and execute the decrees and orders that reached me officially."[86] Dessalines did not personally sign his July 5, 1798, response to Hédouville; his secretary, Birot Sr., signed on Dessalines's behalf.[87] Although he eventually learned to sign his name, Dessalines did not transcribe his own letters, and he likely composed letters in collaboration with a secretary who then read the correspondence back to him before signing.[88] This was not unusual; most military and political leaders in Saint-Domingue used secretaries for their public and sometimes private writing, but people at the time, especially as he gained more power, tried to use Dessalines's alleged illiteracy to undermine his political achievements.[89]

In his July 1798 letter to Hédouville, Dessalines feigned niceness, assuring the agent that he had remedied the situation after Louverture gave him the go-ahead to execute Hédouville's orders.[90] It was a simple error, he explained, and he hoped that his future conduct would prove his loyalty. Dessalines closed the letter by asking for forgiveness. He had delayed the street renaming to make a point but was not willing to cause too much trouble; he was likely also responding to orders from Louverture.

After Hédouville received Dessalines's letter, he wrote a note on the back of it, describing how he responded to Dessalines (in a letter not yet found). "[I] responded that I am convinced," he recorded, "that he did not have bad intentions by suspending the execution of my decree."[91] He nevertheless took the opportunity to reprimand Dessalines one more time, reminding him that "the form of government would become null if the military was not essentially obedient."[92]

This was not the end of the dispute. Four days after Dessalines reported to Hédouville that he had executed the orders, Louverture himself addressed the issue with Hédouville. He noted that he had instructed Dessalines to obey orders "because you are our senior leader."[93] Louverture claimed that he had sent an officer to Saint-Marc to sentence Dessalines to detention for fifteen days, but upon learning that Hédouville had only set it for four days which had already been served, he mandated Dessalines's release.[94]

Louverture wanted Hédouville to know that he intended to reprimand Boener too, because of the "misinformation that reigns between him and the general Dessaline [sic]."[95] Boener, Louverture claimed, was making decisions—including personnel matters—without telling Dessalines, or only telling him after the fact. He had previously explained to Boener that "it was important for the good of the project that there be good intelligence between the authorities."[96]

The incident suggests that while Dessalines was engaged in a local quarrel with Boener, both of their superiors seized the opportunity to flex their own administrative muscles. While each expressed the need for collaboration, Hédouville emphasized military obedience and subordination within the republic, while Louverture stressed communication and harmony. Of course, Dessalines's

actions further fanned the flames of the existing power struggle between Hédouville and Louverture. The minor issue of renaming buildings and roads in Saint-
Marc was a small part of the larger and continuing clash between imperial control of the colony and local colonial autonomy.

Thus, even as he fought in the name of the French Republic, Dessalines
showed contempt for French metropolitan authority. His behavior reflected a
keen awareness of the changing political tides in France, as well as a wariness
about the future of the colony and the freedom of the men and women who
lived and worked there.

During this power struggle, Boener wrote to Dessalines to denounce the
soldiers of the 4th demi-brigade. They were, Boener alleged, threatening plantation owners in large groups, and sometimes stealing from them. In one case, he
claimed, they had destroyed an entire cane field, although it is unclear what the
point of that act of vandalism would have been.[97] Boener told Dessalines that it
was his job to stop this "insubordination," and made five recommendations on
how to accomplish the task, including punishing the officers and reporting them
to Louverture and Hédouville.

Dessalines was not happy with the letter from Boener and denied culpability in a subsequent letter to Hédouville. Dessalines had collected statements
from the plantations that Boener claimed had been raided, which he forwarded
to Hédouville, condemning the accusations against his troops. With all this
evidence, Dessalines told Hédouville, surely the agent would understand how
painful it was to see his troops belittled in this way. "It has always been a glory
to command [them]," he insisted, highlighting their support for the French
Republic.[98]

Hédouville appears to have agreed with Dessalines, replying on July 23 that
he had reprimanded Boener for blaming an entire corps for the actions of a few
individuals. He told Dessalines that he was sure that Boener's complaints were
simply caused by "a love of order."[99]

Those whom Boener had accused were not convinced. On July 28 Hédouville received a petition from the officers of the 4th and 7th demi-brigades com-
plaining about Boener.[100] This petition was contrary to article 364 of the republic's constitution, Hédouville believed, which stated that only individuals could
petition the government and not groups.[101] Furthermore, he hoped to clarify
their alleged misinterpretation of Boener's actions, saying "there was nothing
but a love of order that could have misled that officer & made him confuse the
innocent with the real culprits."[102] "Love of order" clearly meant different things
to different people. The officers and soldiers of Dessalines's demi-brigades were

unimpressed with the colony's French civil administration. Like Dessalines, they pushed back and demanded fair treatment. Dessalines loyally defended them, pointing out that they never once complained about their suffering for the republic and that they did not deserve to be treated with suspicion.[103]

While these petty conflicts among French republican administrators and generals flared, the fight against the British finally came to an end. By July, General Maitland had finally secured permission from his government to evacuate Saint-Domingue completely, including the important ports of Jérémie and Môle Saint-Nicolas.[104] Later news would break that Louverture had independently negotiated a "secret" trade treaty with Maitland to secure access to manufactured goods and war matériel.[105] Building on the previous ceasefire and truce, the treaty stipulated that neither side would attack the other or the United States; in addition, the ports of Cap-Français and the newly renamed Port-Républicain (formerly Port-au-Prince) would be open to British trade.[106] In contradiction to French policy, Louverture offered amnesty to those who had fought against the republic.[107] An addendum to the treaty limited Dominguan maritime movements, a clause inspired by British fears that contact and communication among the Caribbean islands might inspire slave revolts in other colonies.[108]

Louverture signed the treaty without prior approval from Hédouville or from the government in France. According to some at the time, this was essentially a declaration of independence.[109] The "secret" treaty was not much of a secret at all, however, and the agreement was made public before the document had even been officially signed. The *London Gazette,* for example, reported that "no event has happened in the history of the present war, of most interest to the cause of humanity, or to the permanent interests of Great Britain, than the treaty which General Maitland has made with the Black general Toussaint upon the evacuation of the St. Domingo." Treaties carried diplomatic weight far beyond the contents of the document.[110] As such, the "secret" treaty had major implications; even though it was not a formal declaration of independence, the document implied that Louverture was acting autonomously from France. "By this treaty," the newspaper reported, "the independence of that most valuable island is, in fact, recognised, and will be secured against all the efforts which the French can now make to recover it."[111] To some, it seemed, Louverture had made his first move.

In Paris the French minister of war evaluated the treaty alongside a handwritten copy of the London newspaper article and other correspondence relating to the agreement between Louverture and Maitland. Taken together, the minister considered the "secret" treaty to be a direct attack on French dominion.

The changing political context in France also shaped the reaction from Europe. Napoléon Bonaparte, who came to power as First Consul in 1799, clashed with Louverture about the treaty. Bonaparte even considered sending an expedition to Saint-Domingue in early 1800. The minister of war opposed such action because of lack of support and resources.[112] Nevertheless, it was clear that tensions were rising between France and the Caribbean colony.

By this point Hédouville was deeply unpopular among the military leadership of Saint-Domingue. He also antagonized the cultivators with a new set of labor codes.[113] Hédouville anticipated that the codes might elicit resistance, and he instructed local administrators to explain "with a lot of patience, to the cultivators, the motivations of each of the dispositions that it contains."[114] He wanted the administrators to read the codes to the *cultivateurs* in Creole, so that they understood them completely. But although Hédouville claimed that he was acting to preserve liberty, in fact his primary motive was to increase plantation productivity.

Hédouville's new codes limited plantation laborers' mobility, increased control over their time, and outlined punishments for not working or not working hard enough. To leave the plantations for any reason, for example, a cultivator would be required to secure a signed passport from the managers of their contracted plantations, as had been the case under slavery. A key point of contention was an article that tied cultivators to the same plantation for three years, as opposed to the previous one-year contracts. Hédouville argued that through these longer contracts the workers could reap increased rewards from their productivity.[115] The previous labor codes had restricted freedom, but the new codes would restrict cultivators in ways that further paralleled the previous system of enslavement. Distrust of this French official and unrest over worsening working conditions were growing throughout Saint-Domingue.

About two months after he published the labor codes, on September 17, 1798, Hédouville tried once again to have Dessalines removed from his post. Hédouville heard that Dessalines had executed a soldier who was suspected of stealing. According to Boener's report about the incident, Dessalines did so "without any formality."[116] If what he had been told was true, Hédouville wrote to Louverture, "I would discharge General Dessaline [sic]."[117] "Whatever motivations of discipline that could have inspired an act even more atrocious than arbitrary," Hédouville threatened, "he cannot be excused, &, if he was brought before a tribunal, he himself would face the death penalty."[118]

Clearly Dessalines could not win with Hédouville. The agent wanted to reprimand the general for executing a soldier without trial, even while also alleging that his troops were rampaging throughout his district. Somehow Dessalines was always either too harsh or not harsh enough. Hédouville's letter did not provide any details about the soldier whom Dessalines had executed. It is possible that the soldier was not local, and therefore the incident might have been another example of Dessalines's resistance to metropolitan authority in the colony.

The festering conflict was wearing on Louverture. He wrote to his associate Charles Vincent, the director of fortifications of Saint-Domingue, who was in Paris, to complain about Hédouville's behavior.[119] He thought Hédouville's larger goal was to have Louverture removed from power.[120] "Since I am well convinced," Louverture explained, "that it is impossible for a lower grade officer to do good if he does not have the confidence of his government, I would rather end my public career than to allow myself to become a victim of the traps that are laid for me and that it will be impossible to evade."[121] Louverture noted that he had welcomed Hédouville to the colony, but the relationship had quickly soured and he was not confident in the agent's leadership. "He sowed the seeds of division," Louverture wrote. "He is suspicious of all men who have served the republic the best, he dreams of nothing but conspiracies, rallies, of uprisings."[122]

Dessalines was not the only one of Louverture's generals with whom Hédouville clashed. The agent's insistence on oversight of the military leadership also led to open conflict with Moyse, Louverture's nephew. At that time, Moyse was the commander of Fort Liberté near Cap-Français. Hédouville accused Moyse of conspiring with *cultivateurs* on a plantation.[123] The agent ordered the disarmament of Moyse's district in October 1798, sending a unit of white troops to seize their weapons.[124] After a violent clash, Hédouville discharged Moyse from his post for insubordination, as he had repeatedly tried to do to Dessalines. Louverture quickly responded in support of Moyse, rallying the *cultivateurs* to launch an insurgency against Hédouville.[125]

Together Louverture and Moyse marched against Hédouville, and Dessalines arrested the agent.[126] The colonial military leadership claimed victory over what they perceived as metropolitan overreach. Details of Hédouville's arrest are scarce, but it was likely a moment of celebration for Dessalines. The agent and his men had undermined, antagonized, and threatened Dessalines, and now, about a month after Hédouville had tried to have him discharged, the general had succeeded in removing the hated agent from his post.

The administrators of Cap-Français partnered with Louverture to defuse the conflict between the *cultivateurs* and Hédouville. As part of the accord, Dessalines and the 4th demi-brigade went to the city to ensure the safety of the residents and their property.[127] At the end of October 1798 Hédouville boarded a ship bound for France.[128] The municipal administration reported that Louverture had saved the colony by removing Hédouville. All was calm, they argued, and it was thanks to Louverture's vigilance and "his love for France, for his country and for humanity."[129]

Months later, Louverture defended his actions to the French government, describing himself as someone who loved liberty, order, and work, reassuring the minister of the colonies that Saint-Domingue would remain productive.[130] Similarly, on December 9, 1798, thirty-eight generals and brigadier chiefs from the north, east, and west of Saint-Domingue—including Dessalines—wrote to the municipal administrators to pressure them to report to the Directory on recent events in the colony, knowing how their arrest of Hédouville would be spun. "Hold in your hands the scales of justice," the letter urged the administrators, "& you will see that our actions had no other goal but the maintenance of freedom & the desire to secure for France its possessions. That of these agents, in contrast, were bent on annihilating freedom, & depriving France of its colonies."[131]

Dessalines's name appears first on the printed list of signatories.

With their appeal to justice out of the way, Dessalines and the other officers turned in the letter to issuing a thinly veiled threat to the Directory. "Sound the trumpet of truth without bias," they advised, "& reveal without fear, in the eyes of the Directory, the perfidy of its Agents. If you take in this circumstance, a pusillanimous approach, you will lose the confidence of the People, without whom you will not be able to return Saint-Domingue to its tranquility."[132]

Dessalines and the other letter writers were right, but in a way it was Hédouville who got the last word. As he departed the colony, the former agent dropped one last bomb: he wrote to André Rigaud (the general who had been promoted with Louverture in 1795) and named him commander in chief of the south.[133] From that point forward, Rigaud refused to take orders from Louverture. So began a new conflict, which soon plunged the colony into outright civil war.

CHAPTER 5

The French People Will Never Forget Your Republican Virtues

"When they speak about black people they always use the terms *Révoltés, insurgés* [Rebels, insurgents]," complained Toussaint Louverture in an April 1799 letter to an ally in Paris.[1] "But if black people are treated as such for having demanded their rights," he argued, "what Epithets should we give to the French people who Overthrew the Bastille and decapitated Louis 16, then King of France?"[2]

This wasn't an idle complaint. Louverture was concerned that the French *papiers publics* were systematically misrepresenting the revolution in Saint-Domingue, which would have long-term consequences in terms of diplomacy, military aid, and the metropole's approach to its colony's experience with abolition. Moreover, Louverture was already concerned that if a conflict broke out between him and André Rigaud—the commander of the south, recently elevated by Hédouville as a parting shot—France might not support him.

"What term should we use," he wondered, "to describe the arming of the men of color or *mulâtres*? They were reclaiming, we'll say, their political rights too, they obtained them."[3] The rhetoric of rebellion and insurgency were creating consequences for him personally, as well as for the class of formerly enslaved men and women who formed most of the population in Saint-Domingue. "The black people, in contrast," he continued, "making the same reclamations, were Rebuffed, injured, vexed, and mutilated. What a shocking contrast; eh! Can we blame the black people, because they aspired to a Freedom, that they never

69

should have lost."[4] Moreover, he condemned the *"hommes de couleur"* and *"nègres Libres"* for not supporting formerly enslaved men and women. "Newly having secured their political rights," he argued, "these same men of color joined up with the White people whom they had just fought, to turn their unified weapons, against the black people, always, according to them, revolted and insurgent. Eh! I ask them: who set this example?"[5]

By insisting that Saint-Domingue's revolution should be considered both rhetorically and practically on the same level as the French Revolution, Louverture legitimized his own leadership within the context of the French Republic and framed generals such as Dessalines as true defenders of France.

This letter was not the beginning of Louverture's rhetorical campaign to equate the two revolutions. Two months before, on February 4, 1799, Philippe-Rose Roume de Saint-Laurent, the new special agent of the French Directory in Saint-Domingue, hosted a celebration of the five-year anniversary of the abolition of slavery. As the party gathered around a "tree of liberty" in Port-Républicain, Roume claimed that the now defunct French National Convention, "by one of those spontaneous acts that had produced the miracles of the revolution, had risen *en masse;* it avenged Africa of European greed; it avenged republican France of the Machiavellianism of monarchical France."[6] In doing so, Roume rewrote the history of the French Revolution, which until 1794 had been pro-slavery.

During his speech Roume praised Louverture for his role in defeating the British and ending their occupation, thereby ensuring that freedom was protected by the rule of law throughout the colony. At the same time, however, Roume did not credit the revolutionaries in the colony for initiating the abolition of slavery; rather, he insisted that they were inspired by events in France. He admitted, however, that the revolutionaries were "tireless republicans"; "it is you," he conceded, "who freed Saint-Domingue from the despotism of England, who broke the chains of slavery in this precious island."[7]

Louverture then took the stage to reply. "Citizen agent," Louverture addressed Roume directly, "the same unity that you see existing among the generals Toussaint Louverture, Rigaud, Beauvais, Laplume, and the other military chiefs; the same will to work with you for the establishment of constitutional order; the same spirit of republicanism and attachment to France that they are showing you on this day of celebration that brought them here, you will find in the generals Desaline [*sic*], Moyse, Clervaux, Agé, and in all of the other commanders in the *arrondissements* that you still have to visit."[8] It was a victory for Louverture that a Parisian newspaper published both his and Roume's speeches in June 1799. Louverture's declaration of his and his generals' commitment to republicanism was meant to demonstrate their collective pledge to the same values and laws as metropolitan France, affirming the legitimacy of their leadership in the colony.

What "republicanism" meant, however, was ambiguous at this moment. Colonial generals and administrators stated their loyalty to France and linked republicanism with freedom; in so doing, they highlighted the degree to which the French had succeeded in co-opting the narrative of abolition in Saint-Domingue. They also connected their republicanism to the fight against the British. Louverture and especially Dessalines drew on their military victories against the British as evidence of their republicanism. Finally, republicans in Saint-Domingue supported France by sustaining plantation agriculture—by framing productivity as nationalism—so that France could continue to profit from the overseas colonies and the labor of Black men and women. Louverture, Dessalines, and other colonial generals thus curated colonial republicanism for a European audience; this was a necessary measure, since pro-slavery factions were gaining power in the French government and the return of slavery in the colony seemed like a possibility. "By identifying with his brothers in misfortune," Haitian historian Emmanuel C. Paul argued, "[Dessalines] proved to be a collective genius."[9]

The republican messaging proved quite effective. Shortly after the anniversary celebration in Port-Républicain, Roume approved Louverture's request to install Dessalines as commander of the west and then approved Dessalines's own appointment and promotions of his officers. "You have, citizen General, made me very happy," Roume congratulated Dessalines on February 27, 1799, "by providing me with your letter, the commissions given by the virtuous General in chief, to the brave soldiers who rendered so many noteworthy services to the republic fighting under your command, and chasing the English and the counterrevolutionaries from French territory."[10] Roume assured Dessalines that "the French people and their government will never forget neither your work nor your military success, or your republican virtues."[11]

Roume's claims may have been genuine. But the French government would in fact soon forget and carefully excise any memory of Dessalines's republicanism or his military victories for the French nation. For now, however, Roume's praise still stood, as Dessalines threw himself into the civil war that had erupted in the colony. Now that the British were no longer a common enemy, the uneasy alliance between Louverture in the north and Rigaud in the south became untenable. The two generals went to war, competing over territorial control and political power.[12] Each tried to prove that they were "true" republicans, accusing the other of being a traitor to the French Republic, whether because of aspirations to monarchy, independence, or the reestablishment of slavery.[13]

Despite the rhetoric of revolution, the civil war was at its heart a battle over political power: Louverture wanted to bring the entire colony under his authority.[14] M. Longchamp, a sergeant major in the southern army who would eventually become a senator in the Haitian government, later referred to the civil war as a "quarrel between Toussaint and Rigaud [*querelle entre Toussaint et Rigaud*]."[15] On June 2, 1799, Rigaud publicly denounced Louverture for allegedly collaborating with the British and accused him of instigating civil war. He then sent his soldiers to violently occupy several towns in the south that were loyal to Louverture. Louverture responded with a full-scale military invasion.

In this civil war, where the fight over true republican virtues turned violent, Dessalines fought for Louverture, taking ten thousand troops south toward Port-Républicain. He rode on horseback dressed in his general's uniform and wearing a lace-trimmed hat over his headwrap.[16] To claim the capital city, Dessalines called the national guard to the parade and then disarmed the unit. They did not resist, with one exception. Instead of laying down his weapons as ordered, a young *homme de couleur* named Moreau broke his sword.[17] Rather than punishing him, however, Dessalines respected his courage and protected him. "He told Moreau's mother," historian Thomas Madiou wrote later, "that God had blessed her womb, because she gave birth to such a determined boy."[18]

This was not an unusual act for Dessalines; he repeatedly pardoned enemies who earned his respect. Perhaps he saw a reflection of himself in acts of defiance. He did not suffer cowards but triumphantly recruited men who fought with conviction.

Dessalines led one of three divisions in the attack on the south; generals Moyse and Laplume led the other two.[19] Another ten thousand troops from the north joined Dessalines's forces as he pushed farther west along the southern peninsula.[20] Together they attacked Léogâne and then retreated to the mountains around the city.[21]

In late June Dessalines moved on to the coastal city of Grand Goâve, on the north side of the southern peninsula. It was a coastal town, surrounded by sugar cane and fruit trees. Rigaud had recently captured the Tauzin plantation from the northern troops, and Dessalines wanted to retake it.[22] Dessalines's troops attacked from the cane fields of the plantation and pushed Rigaud's troops back, but during a break in the firing Rigaud's troops began to yell so that Dessalines's

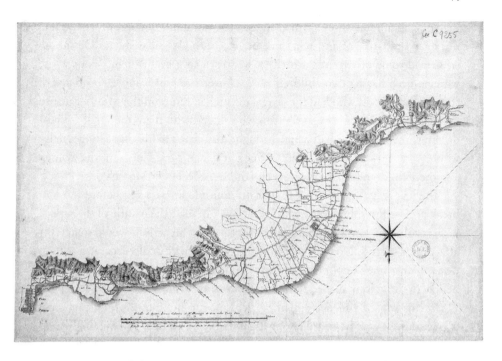

Carte de l'Ouest depuis Port-au-Prince jusqu'au Grand Goave, 1780.
Bibliothèque nationale de France, Département des cartes et plans, GE C-9255.

soldiers could hear: "[You] will not succeed . . . Môle [Saint-Nicolas] has been secured by Rigaud, and he claimed it."[23] This was not the only time the combatants shouted at one another to bolster their chances and emphasize their cause. Dessalines's troops would later face off against southern troops who were singing the "Marseillaise."[24] The fight on the Tauzin plantation was bloody, and both armies suffered casualties. Dessalines retreated to Grand Goâve.

Dessalines hoped to reassure the plantation laborers that Louverture was fighting this new war to defend their freedom. But Louverture's rival had gotten to them first, and so Dessalines's troops arrived to cries of *"Vive Rigaud!"* "He [Rigaud] told them that we are fighting for the English," Louverture protested, "that we want slavery, and that it is necessary to assassinate all of the white people to have freedom."[25] Rigaud's accusations were designed to elicit sympathy from both formerly enslaved people and colonists alike.

Yet there was evidence, discovered by Dessalines's troops, that it was in fact Rigaud who was attacking white colonists. Dessalines uncovered the body of a white plantation owner, Louverture reported, "stretched out naked in the main

road having suffered three bayonet stabs in the side and still warm because it had
not been a quarter of an hour since he had been assassinated." As Dessalines
witnessed some of Rigaud's atrocities, he strove to prevent them. "Four white
women, each having two children . . . ," Louverture told Roume, "residents of
that neighborhood who had for several days taken refuge in the woods, came to
throw themselves in Dessalines's arms who shared with them the small amount
of refreshments that he had which brought them back to life that a longer delay
would have caused them to lose."[26] After a brief rest, Dessalines sent the women
and their children back to the port city of Léogâne, under Moyse's protection.

The war was already being fought on multiple levels. Even before the outbreak of hostilities, Louverture had been eager to seize the mantle of the republican revolution, knowing that how Europeans saw his actions would materially
affect their success. Now the alleged protection of white colonists (and accusations against one's opponents of harming them) became a critical part of how
people in the colony shaped their narratives of events for a European audience.

In this war of violence and rhetoric, Louverture's months-long campaign
was working. After he heard about Rigaud's initial attacks, Roume finally officially authorized Louverture to initiate a campaign against the southern insurgency. On July 3, 1799, he declared Rigaud to be an outlaw and made French
ships available to Louverture.[27] Despite this, Louverture still felt the need to
make his case against Rigaud for support. "Rigaud, after the crimes that he committed," Louverture reported to Roume, "he would never believe that he would
obtain a pardon and he would never believe the sincerity and the guarantee
of your promises and of mine."[28] Louverture was shocked by Rigaud's tactics.
"So, Citizen Agent," he told Roume, "the great deeds of the General Rigaud,
the women, the slaughtered children, the assassinated authorities; the burned
plantations. His trophies are the dismembered bodies of his fellow citizens
after having provoked a revolt among the *cultivateurs,* fired on the national flag,
despised the constituted authorities, would he believe he could obtain a pardon,
no doubt, no."[29]

Each side's narrative about the civil war was just as important as the victories
on the battlefields, and Rigaud's supporters offered a different interpretation of
events. In an anonymous letter to Étienne Mentor, a representative from Saint-
Domingue in Paris's Conseil des Anciens, a man from Jacmel argued that "the
civil war is at its height, the General *Toussaint-Louverture* has finally taken off
his mask."[30] Louverture was a counterrevolutionary, the writer argued, who was
collaborating with the British. Referring to the recent trade treaty with Jamaica,

the author argued that "it must be in this counter-revolutionary meeting that they ensured the loss of St. Domingue, the massacre of the republicans truly loyal to France, because since leaving this confabulation, *Toussaint-Louverture* permitted the entry of neutral and enemy ships into the ports of St. Domingue. Already an English frigate has anchored for thirty-six hours in the harbor of Gonaïves."[31] Louverture was the true traitor, the author claimed, and he was the one who had instigated the war against Rigaud. Mentor shared the letter with a Parisian newspaper, illustrating how the battles in Saint-Domingue were replaying across the Atlantic in the pages and on the streets of Paris.

In July 1799 Louverture headed north with Moyse and ten thousand men, intending to quell the rebellion that had broken out in Môle Saint-Nicolas. He assigned command of the southern expeditionary army to Dessalines, who continued fighting against Rigaud's forces.[32] Rigaud's troops pushed Dessalines back east to Léogâne.[33] From there on August 17, Dessalines forwarded a document to Louverture that he had discovered hidden in the hat of a prisoner. "At this letter," Dessalines told Louverture, "you will no doubt shudder, and in the end, it will make known the extent of the project of your Enemies."[34] The contents of the confiscated letter are unknown, but given that the soldier tried to keep it hidden, it likely had to do with military strategy or movements. Even though they were up against a ruthless adversary, Dessalines assured Louverture that he and his troops would succeed, "because I do not sleep night or day when it comes to securing the place of my country and the places assigned to my command."[35]

Dessalines himself was also unsparing in the campaign against Rigaud's forces. He executed several of his own soldiers for refusing to fight.[36] On the front lines he compelled his soldiers into battle by hitting them with a cane.[37] His tactics were effective, and Dessalines saved the army from defeat.[38] His bravery and effectiveness earned him another promotion. "I charged the general Dessalines, with the command of the army of the West," Louverture reported to Roume on August 23, 1799, "given the need to establish a solid Chief who can preserve this department from its misfortune." There was much he admired about Dessalines and his command of his troops: "the exactitude of this General, his bravery and his prudence combined with his Republican principles made me look to him."[39]

Dessalines assumed command of the western forces even before Roume could confirm Louverture's decision. With Louverture's assistance, he was developing a reputation for both military success and political legitimacy within the French

Republic. This was doubly confirmed a few weeks later in early October, when Louverture asked Roume to confirm Dessalines's and Moyse's appointments in an official document so that he could publicize their new roles.

Roume was delighted.[40] Dessalines had used the new title in his correspondence before the official approval and even before Louverture initially reported his promotion to Roume, so the request was more a matter of making it official.[41] First Roume had to secure formal approval from the Agence du Directoire Exécutif à Saint-Domingue in Cap-Français, which he stated he would do quickly.[42]

That same day the Agence claimed that it had previously approved Dessalines's appointment in the west and that it likewise approved Moyse's appointment in the north. "Considering that one and the other choice are equally worthy of the approbation of the Agency," the Agence's registry noted, "because these two brigadier generals have constantly rendered the most remarkable services and have always conducted themselves according to the most pure principles of republicanism."[43] Louverture's campaign for republican legitimacy was working.

Dessalines would do more than simply take praise from above. He also created his own publicity and framed his own narratives. For example, on September 8, he warned another officer, Henry Christophe, of a deceitful trap that had been laid by Rigaud. This letter not only demonstrates how Dessalines maintained lines of communication with his fellow officers; since he ended up publishing it, it also shows how the rising general could engage in propaganda warfare on his own.

The trap had been laid for Charles Bélair, an officer and, like Moyse, another nephew of Louverture's.[44] A plantation manager approached Bélair, claiming that the cultivators on his plantation, mostly women and children, repented for having followed Rigaud; now they wanted to ask for a pardon. The manager convinced Bélair to come speak with them, leaving his troops behind and bringing only fourteen of his officers. Just as they arrived at the plantation, however, Bélair's company realized the trap. "These officers then found, instead of cultivators, armed men of color who plunged their murderous daggers into their hearts," Dessalines recounted. "The brigadier chief Charles, who was not mounted, abandoned his horse, and only escaped the death awaiting him by killing with a gunshot a *mulâtre* who raised his murderous weapon to him."[45]

Although Bélair himself escaped, all fourteen of the officers who had accompanied him were killed. "Too cowardly to fight Belair head on," Rigaud had resorted to trickery, explained Dessalines: "The traitor Rigaud employs perfidious weapons, that he wields so well; to trap in his net this officer whose valor he knew and whose fearlessness he dreaded."[46]

One could hardly discount Dessalines's words of concern here for Bélair. Yet since he ultimately printed this letter for broader circulation, Dessalines may have hoped to kill two birds at once: to expose Rigaud's tactics and also undermine Bélair's leadership and embarrass him personally, painting him as a dupe. Even Louverture knew this debacle was bad news for his nephew. "I will not hide it from you," he wrote to Roume, "that if the past services of the Brigadier chief Charles Belair did not remind me of his bravery that was so often fatal to the enemies of France, I would put him under the results of the judgment of a war tribunal which, per the Penal Code, would inevitably make him pay with his life for this deadly imprudence."[47] (Louverture noted, however, that he had instead ordered Bélair's imprisonment until Roume decided what to do with him. Bélair survived his misjudgment and later resumed a leadership position in the French army.) Publicizing Bélair's blunder made sense, since Dessalines was jockeying for position among Louverture's officers and perhaps hoped to keep another of Louverture's nephews from rising in rank.

Still, the primary purpose of Dessalines's public letter was to smear Rigaud. It reported that according to deserters from Rigaud's forces, the southern general had killed almost the entire white population in the south.[48] This was an exaggeration, but the northern forces seized every opportunity to highlight the southern army's attacks on white colonists.

"Let this perfidious fact," Dessalines emphasized, "make known to you the enemy that we have to combat, the wickedness of the men of color from the South, and what we can expect from them."[49] The war between Louverture and Rigaud has often been characterized as a "color" war—the Black troops of the north versus the mixed-race troops of the south—but in his letter about Rigaud's duplicity Dessalines made sure to note that he did not condemn *all* men of color. "It is very unfortunate," Dessalines regretted, "that the men of color from the South do not behave like the ones who make up the army whose command is entrusted to me, principally the brave officers of the sans-culottes, who knew, by their obedience and good conduct and their courage, that they would earn the esteem and the confidence of the General in chief, mine and that of all good citizens."[50] Dessalines was likely referring to his officers Gabart (Vaillant), Ferbos, and Rousselot (Dommage), who were all *hommes de couleur* and well respected for their bravery.

Again and again, Dessalines and Louverture insisted that they were not fighting a race war. Instead, as they had claimed before and after hostilities broke out, they were only defending true republicanism and the freedom of the citizens in the colony.

While Dessalines was embroiled in the fights in the south, Louverture was busy keeping order in the north. He offered the "traitors" in Môle Saint-Nicolas amnesty in exchange for their surrender—but to no avail.[51] He then enlisted Augustin Clervaux to help him attack the city, ordering the blockade of the port by two French ships. This tactic worked, and they claimed the city. "The death of the traitors, the imprisonment of their accomplices," Louverture reported, "rendered the city calm, and it enjoys today a complete tranquility, under the laws of the Republic."[52]

In the meantime Rigaud retreated to Les Cayes, but then outmaneuvered Dessalines to push him back.[53] Louverture left the north, leaving it under Moyse's command. "The unfortunate war that afflicts the colony," he wrote on October 4, "demands the greatest surveillance, and it being impossible to see everywhere myself, it is necessary that I am seconded in my operations by men who are capable of bearing part of the burden of this war ignited by Rigaud's ambition."[54]

With Louverture's return from the north, Dessalines now had his assistance in the attacks against Rigaud in the south, as well as that of over two thousand white men from the national guard whom Louverture had recruited in the north and west.[55] From his camp in the wooded region between Port-Républicain and Grand Goâve, Dessalines launched a new attack. "They arrived, Bayonets forward," he reported of the attack led by Rousselot (Dommage), "they overtook the retrenchments, fell into the camp and put to the sword anyone they found, they took about 200 guns, five crates, all of their luggage, before they even had the chance to save the value of a pin."[56]

On the lower coast of the southern peninsula sat the city of Jacmel, which had remained neutral during the beginning of the war between Louverture and Rigaud. Now, however, an unauthorized attack by an overzealous southern colonel, Birot (not the man who served as Dessalines's secretary), briefly propelled General Beauvais, the local officer, into the civil war in support of Rigaud.[57] Soon, however, Beauvais boarded a ship in an effort to stay out of the civil war, and died in a shipwreck on his way to France.[58]

Now stationed south of Léogâne, Dessalines did not rush. Instead he familiarized himself with the layout. Small forts on the outskirts of the city formed the first line of defense.[59] Dessalines learned that he had the support of the *cultivateurs* of the region and the benefit of the white population's neutrality. "It is possible," Longchamp, a soldier who fought for Rigaud's forces, later speculated, "that he also hoped for a defection in his favor as a result of the maneuvers that he was trying to implement with the help of the white people in the area."[60] After this reconnaissance, Dessalines decided to avoid outright battle, electing instead to lay siege to the city.

To begin he distributed copies of one of Louverture's proclamations, documents that, "rather than spilling blood," aimed to peacefully "disabuse the unfortunate French people."[61] The proclamation countered the accusations that Rigaud had made against Louverture, including the intentions behind the Maitland treaty with Great Britain, as well as Rigaud's attempt to frame the civil war as one between Black people and *hommes de couleur*. (Louverture himself had previously accused Rigaud of anti-Black prejudice, which Rigaud had denied.)[62] Louverture claimed that it was Rigaud who was the traitor, that the Maitland treaty was in the best interests of the colony, and that "there are many men of color who have been chiefs, and are now commanding in the northern and western departments, therefore this is not the class of men of color which we wish to chastise; we punish none but traitors."[63] This persuasion method did not work. Since those in Jacmel refused to surrender, Dessalines ordered the attack.

The siege continued for a month and a half, and Louverture's forces cut off provision routes to Jacmel by land and sea.[64] The night of January 5, 1800, Dessalines's troops attacked from all points. The defenders of Jacmel fought so valiantly, Longchamp claimed, that Dessalines himself wished that they were in his command. "Dessalines admired from afar the order of Auger [Ogé] and of his companions," the veteran wrote. "Stomping his foot, he expressed his regrets that he could not count these brave men among the ranks of his army."[65]

Eventually Dessalines pushed Benjamin Ogé into retreat. The day was a victory for Dessalines's forces, who secured the post of Talavigne, on the outskirts of Léogâne.[66] From there they "rained bombs and cannonballs on us."[67]

In the battle for Jacmel, some observers contended, Dessalines took no prisoners. "Desalines [*sic*]," a British captain named Hugh Cathcart told Maitland, "lately surprized [*sic*] a camp with two hundred Mulattoes in it. They were all put to the sword."[68] Cathcart had heard this, he claimed, from Henry Christophe. "They have gone too far ever to be reconciled," Cathcart concluded. "The Mulattoes never will forgive him [Louverture], for the cruelties he has exercised upon their colour, and he is determined to exterminate them."[69] This was an exaggeration, but it is possible that the northern officers disagreed about how to treat the southern leadership.

The capture of Talavigne convinced Birot, the officer who had instigated the

conflict in the first place, to convene a war council with the officers of the southern army to plan their evacuation from Jacmel. On January 10 they began their
retreat west toward Baynet. The southern troops abandoning Jacmel were starv-
ing, reduced to eating four ounces of bread and whatever meat they could find,
including scavenged rats.[70]

One of the southern generals, Alexandre Pétion, decided to let some of the
southern women seek aid from the northern army. Those who approached the
ranks commanded by Henry Christophe, according to Longchamp, were fired
upon and pushed back, for "that monster did not know how to sympathize with
the misfortune of his peers."[71] (Longchamp's anti-Christophean sentiments likely
stemmed from his experiences during the postindependence civil war, during
which Christophe was the president and then king of Haiti and controlled the
north.)

"Dessalines," on the other hand, "welcomed with benevolence the unfortu-
nates who came over to his side."[72] His enemies in the southern armies, however, assumed he was lying: they saw this strategy as "perfidious and seditious"
and thus continued to frame Dessalines and the northern army as vengeful and
cruel.[73] Dessalines did offer "full and complete amnesty to all who submitted
without delay to the legitimate authority."[74] At this point in his career as a commander, Dessalines clearly saw the value of winning over the civilian population; he welcomed defectors and explicitly encouraged southerners to join forces
with him.

In early March Pétion called another war council. The southern generals decided to retreat farther west, hoping to join their troops in Jérémie.[75] The retreat
was arduous; dozens of women and children joined the soldiers in their march,
creating chaos along the road. They left Jacmel with 1,500 men and 50 to 60
military wives and an unknown number of children, recalled Longchamp; by
the end of their journey, only six or seven hundred men and eight women remained. Not all of them had died; it was likely that many left to seek safety with
Dessalines. "Those who fell into Dessalines's power," Longchamp wrote, "were
the least unfortunate; the men were incorporated into the 4th demi-brigade
and the women received aid."[76] Dessalines appears to have gotten his wish to
have some of the brave soldiers who had defended Jacmel among his own troops.
Again, he knew the value not only of winning battles but also of winning public
approval.

When Dessalines recounted his efforts to Louverture, his commanding officer was pleased. "The General Dessalines," Louverture reported, "having pre-

sented to me such a great number of prisoners, I made them swear an oath of fidelity to the republic & to the constituent authorities; I sent those who were soldiers back to their respective plantations."[77] Some weren't worth pardoning, but these were few: "Only one, named CHARLES, former officer of the gendarmerie of Port-Républicain," Louverture wrote, "who, at the beginning of Rigaud's revolt, abandoned his post, and brought his company to the rebels, & who since then, came back to assassinate several people in the plains of the Cul-de-Sac, that man only, I say, was shot."[78] Dessalines and Louverture were not only abiding by European rules of warfare—which attempted to limit the wholesale killing of adversaries after the cessation of hostilities—they were also highlighting these actions, as they tried to situate themselves and their armies within the French Republic.

Dessalines's benevolence to his prisoners, Longchamp wrote, was emblematic of his character. "If Dessalines had not received the benefits of an education," the author claimed, "at least, in his raw nature, he knew how to appreciate courage and especially courage among the unfortunate; left to his own impulses, his heart was not closed off from good sentiments."[79] Unlike his colleague Henry Christophe, Longchamp claimed, Dessalines resisted unnecessary violence and even incorporated mixed-race troops into his own unit upon their defection or defeat.[80] For example, Dessalines recruited one of the southern officers who had defended Jacmel, Louis Bazelais.[81] Bazelais soon became his chief of staff and remained loyal to Dessalines for the rest of his life.

Throughout the civil war, Louverture and Dessalines intentionally framed their conduct for a public audience, knowing that the war would not just be won on the battlefields but also in the minds of the civilian population and the distant onlookers in Europe. Even knowing these conscious efforts, it can't be denied that Dessalines developed a reputation as a courageous general guided by republican virtues, who abided by "civilized" standards of warfare.

Amid the chaos of the civil war, Dessalines met his second wife, Marie-Claire Heureuse Bonheur. A Black woman from the southern city of Léogâne, she sought refuge with the northern army during the siege of Jacmel.[82] Marie-Claire was likely born in the 1760s and had never been subjected to slavery.[83] Like Dessalines, she was previously married, but by 1795 she was widowed. Reportedly a beautiful woman with a kind and generous heart, Heureuse was beloved in her community and later throughout the country.[84] On April 2, 1800, Dessalines and Heureuse were married in Léogâne.[85]

In the coming years, Dessalines's new wife traveled with him during campaigns and sometimes served as a nurse to the 4th demi-brigade.[86] Moreover, she oversaw ceremonial events and supported Dessalines's leadership. She would even later adopt his children as her own.[87]

People at the time claimed that Heureuse changed Dessalines and inspired him to be more merciful.[88] Historians and chroniclers have repeated these claims, arguing that she was the "good genius to her ferocious husband."[89] Prior to their marriage, however, Dessalines had repeatedly shown compassion and clemency to his enemies, especially those who had earned his respect with their courage. By framing Marie-Claire Heureuse as purely good, later writers strategically defined Dessalines by violence, thus undermining his authority and legitimacy.

Dessalines's wedding in Léogâne must have been quick and intimate, because he was soon back on the battlefield. Louverture promised Dessalines that they would properly celebrate the union later.[90] But for now, both men had to focus on the civil war.

To completely defeat Rigaud and unite the colony under Louverture's leadership, the northern forces now had to push west. As he marched, Dessalines achieved several quick victories, receiving compliments for the "military precision" with which he secured Grand and Petit Goâve.[91] Moving westward, Dessalines observed the deserted and scorched plantations that Rigaud's forces left in their wake.[92]

Meanwhile, Louverture was emboldened by the arrival of emissaries from France, which had been experiencing turmoil of its own. In the past six months Napoléon Bonaparte had gone from victorious general to the ruler of France as First Consul. Now he sent proclamations to Saint-Domingue, one of which confirmed Louverture as "general-in-chief" of the colony's military.[93] Louverture seized the opportunity to try to persuade his opponents to join his side. "I have received orders from the French Government," he wrote in a proclamation addressed to the citizens of the south, "which enjoins me to re-establish peace and tranquility in this unhappy colony, to put an end to the civil war, by the ravages of which you are all desolated, and to employ to that effect all the powers with which I am invested."[94] He offered a full pardon and amnesty to anyone willing to surrender, but he followed this offer with a threat: "Reflect, Citizens, your fate depends on yourselves: should you still continue deaf to the voice of your friend, you must perish, and I shall have nothing to reproach myself with."[95]

While Bonaparte had confirmed Louverture's military rank, the new 1799 French constitution called for "special laws" for the colonies, setting them juridically apart from France. Over the next year, this clause would set the stage for a power struggle between Louverture and Bonaparte's government in Paris.

Louverture's proclamation inspired some opponents to defect. Just over a week after the amnesty proclamation, several refugees arrived at Dessalines's camp. Their defection was useful to Louverture, confirming the soundness of his "hearts and minds" strategy. It also brought other benefits. "I learnt from the refugees," Dessalines reported to Louverture, ". . . that Rigaud had advanced with a number of troops into the plain [of] Fond des Nègres; and that their infantry was encamped upon a neighboring plantation to that in which I had fixed the headquarters of the army, with two pieces of brass cannon 4 lbs. caliber; and that the cavalry was upon another, a little farther off with Rigaud, who came yesterday to where his infantry was, and administered an oath to everyone to die upon their entrenchments, rather than make one retrograde step, or abandon the two pieces of cannon."[96]

This was valuable information, and Dessalines wanted to put it to good use. He was determined to retrieve those two cannons. He was unable to lead the charge himself, however, because he was sick with a fever. Dessalines instructed Rousselot (Dommage) to attack Rigaud, and "not to return to me without the two pieces of cannon, which Rigaud's troops had sworn not to abandon."[97]

The artillery was not easily won. "The combat was bloody," Dessalines reported. Nevertheless, Rousselot and the 4th and 10th demi-brigades secured the two cannons, along with prisoners, rations, flints, and cannon cartridges. Dessalines sent the two cannons to Petit Goâve, because "my soldiers are too much weakened by hunger to take them with us."[98] Having pushed Rigaud's troops southwest to Aquin during the struggle, Dessalines and his troops—although exhausted, poorly supplied, and sick—continued their pursuit of the last of the southern army.

On the plains outside Aquin, Rigaud's forces were camped on the Dufrete plantation. It was here that Dessalines made his attack, dividing his right column in three for the assault. "The first division had scarcely arrived at its destination (the two others being still on their march)," Dessalines reported, "when the enemy seeing this manœuver, made a sally from the plantation and took to flight."[99] Leaving the battlefield and retreating to Aquin, Rigaud and his forces then "rallied & gave battle." The 4th and 8th demi-brigades were in the vanguard and fought for two hours before the other divisions joined the fight. At this point Rigaud was "beaten and put to rout."

Dessalines ordered the cavalry to advance, and they "made a great slaughter, and the enemy were pursued to the sea shore, where a number of them, who attempted to embark, were destroyed in the water or among the reeds."[100] Although a column from Anse-à-Veau made one last desperate attempt to take the field, it was Dessalines and the armies of the north who claimed Aquin.

Dessalines captured more prisoners and war matériel in the victory, all of which he sent to Louverture. "Many of the white and colored inhabitants of the parish of Acquin [*sic*] have flocked to us," he told Louverture, "and I have treated them with all the compassion and humanity which you have prescribed in your instructions."[101] He also noted that while Rigaud himself had managed a narrow escape, Dessalines had been able to secure the outlaw's personal archive. Rigaud fled to Les Cayes, which Dessalines immediately put under siege. Finally, a few weeks later in late July, Rigaud escaped the colony.[102] The civil war was over.

"After general Rigaud's departure, some black people seeing the country without government, began plundering," a French newspaper reported, "but the general Dessaline [*sic*] entered aux Cayes with an army of 10,000 men, and put an end to the brigandage, by announcing that whoever committed the smallest theft would be shot."[103] This latest praise in the Parisian press is worth pausing on. Throughout the civil war, Dessalines's conduct was praised by many local observers, including one of Rigaud's soldiers. These all emphasized Dessalines's humane treatment of defectors and prisoners. French newspapers published similar accounts, celebrating his military leadership and his honorable victory as evidence of republican triumphs. Here at the end of the civil war, even in France itself, it seemed that Roume was right: Dessalines would continue to be praised for his labors, his victories, and his embodiment of the French Revolution itself.

Within weeks of Rigaud's flight—in August 1800—Louverture assumed control of the south and indeed the entire colony. "[Rigaud] departed, citizens," he announced to the residents, "and this day was that of your deliverance; the army of the republic arrived, and its conduct in this takeover must have proven to you, that if it was able to defeat you when you took up arms against justice and reason, it also knew, that as soon as you recanted your error, could only see in you a people of friends and brothers."[104] Dessalines and Louverture incorporated many of the prisoners into the 3rd and 4th demi-brigades and continued to treat nonmilitary personnel with benevolence.[105] When she was with Dessalines in camp, Marie-Claire Heureuse welcomed asylum seekers, sometimes under her own roof.[106]

Not all his enemies sought asylum, however. One southern officer, who had earned an offer to join the 4th demi-brigade from Dessalines, refused; instead he proclaimed that if he secured a gun, he would use it to assassinate Dessalines. Believing him, Dessalines ordered the officer's execution.[107] Dessalines admired courage, but he was not reckless. He needed to cultivate an image of fairness and firmness, but he would not tolerate the presence of conspirators against the republic within his ranks.

In recognition of his critical role in defeating Rigaud, Dessalines was promoted to division general, one of only four men with such a position in the colony. At a ceremony in Léogâne, Dessalines received his rank and then delivered a speech in Creole.[108] After congratulating his troops on their victory, Dessalines readied them for further battles. "The war that you recently ended," Dessalines told them, "was a small war; but there remain two more important wars to wage, the one against the Spanish who do not want to cede their territory and who insulted your brave General in Chief." The Treaty of Basel between France and Spain on July 22, 1795, had concluded peace in Europe and had ceded control of the colony of Santo Domingo to the French, while disbanding the Black Auxiliaries of King Carlos IV. For more than five years, France had legally owned Santo Domingo. But control on paper was not power in fact.[109] The other war, Dessalines argued, was "against the French who unfettered by their enemies will try to put you back under slavery." He tried to instill confidence in his troops. "These two wars," he claimed, "we are in a good position to win." Dessalines knew that pro-slavery factions in France were gaining ground. The free people of Saint-Domingue had to be ready.

In fact, war was already upon them. While Louverture and Dessalines were embroiled in their civil war against Rigaud, Louverture had learned that the Spanish in Santo Domingo were kidnapping people from the French colony and enslaving them. To secure control of the eastern side of the island, he had sent General Âgé to the region, but Spanish residents denied that Louverture had the authority to assert control without instructions from the French government.[110] Following the victory over Rigaud, Louverture renewed efforts to subdue the east. Finally, by the end of 1800, he effectively controlled the entire island of Hispaniola.[111]

There were some exceptions. Along the former border between the east and west, several communities refused to recognize Louverture's authority and so lived independently. The rebel leader Lamour Dérance occupied Henriquille (Henriquillo) while Lafortune was stationed in Maniel.[112] Still, Louverture's victory seemed effectively complete.

As he turned to asserting political power, Louverture ordered an administrative reorganization of some of the island's cities, renaming streets and batteries. In Aquin, among the proposals for new names for the east–west streets were rue

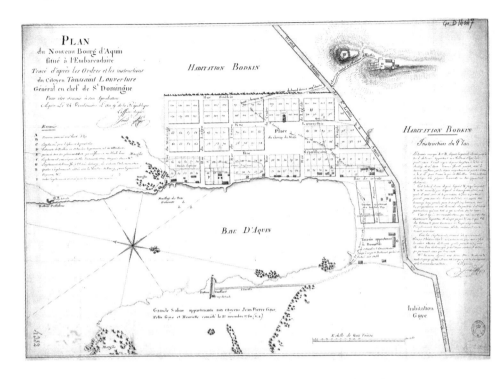

L. Sonis, *Plan du nouveau bourg d'Aquin, situé à l'embarcadaire,*
Tracé d'après les ordres et les instructions du citoyen Toussaint Louverture,
Général en chef de St. Domingue pour être soumis à son approbation, October 16, 1800.
(The catalogue entry dates it to 1799, but the map includes the later date.) Bibliothèque
nationale de France, Département des cartes et plans, Registre C, 04332.

Louverture and rue Républicain. They intersected with streets such as rue de
l'Union, rue de l'Égalité, and rue du Peuple. On the coast, west of the city center, the proposal suggested renaming the fort "Batterie Dessalines."[113] A note by
the engineer indicated that these names for the roads, squares, and batteries
were simply projections, but that "they were recommended by the municipal-
ity and the military commander." Dessalines had become so deeply integrated
within the colonial republican project that his name alone now represented
French values.

In October 1800 Louverture issued another new labor code. This was intended to replace Hédouville's unpopular code from 1798 and also, crucially, to
ramp up agricultural production.[114] These new regulations moved oversight of
the colony's agricultural economy to the military, with Louverture as the top

authority. Consequently, the army would adjudicate conflicts between workers and employers and punish recalcitrant parties on both sides.[115] "All managers, drivers, and cultivators," article 1 of the code declared, "will be required to complete with exactitude, submission, and obedience, their duties,—*like the military.*"[116] So-called "vagrancy" was also cracked down on by the 1800 code, which sought to limit the *cultivateurs'* movements and the use of their time. Now laborers were confined to the plantations, as well as subject to harsh discipline. Anyone caught breaking the laws or assisting a lawbreaker would be arrested.[117]

Louverture's code aligned closely with the previous labor codes imposed by the French Republic since the end of slavery—that is, those issued by Sonthonax, Polverel, and Hédouville. What really separated the 1800 code from theirs was that Louverture expanded the boundaries of the codes by applying his to the former Spanish side of the island.[118]

It was at this time that Louverture and his officers also acquired the rights to plantations left vacant by colonists who had died or fled.[119] The state took possession of these plots as *domaines nationaux* (government-owned property), leasing many of them on five-year contracts. For his part, Dessalines leased plantations in Jérémie, Louverture, Petit Goâve, Arcahaye, Saint-Marc, Artibonite (here his wife Marie-Claire also leased one), Ennery, Jacmel, Cap-Rouge, and Port-Républicain, including the Déluger plantation in Saint-Marc where his aunt Toya had been enslaved. Dessalines may have done this to protect Toya or her associates as they worked as *cultivateurs*.[120] In total, Dessalines acquired leases for between twenty and thirty sugar and coffee plantations in the south and west.[121]

Dessalines's cousin Joseph Dessalines, who fought with him in the 4th demi-brigade, also leased a plantation in Jérémie.[122] Dessalines's former enslaver, Jean-vier Desaline, secured the rights to his old coffee plantation in the Cormier Valley. As the concierge of the government house in Cap-Français, Jeanvier Desaline also managed the land in Grande Rivière.[123] It is possible that Dessalines's uncle, aunts, and other cousins were still *cultivateurs* in the Cormier Valley.

Attempting to increase productivity, Louverture held his officers personally accountable for strictly enforcing the new code among the populace.[124] He appointed Dessalines as the inspector of agriculture for the west. As compassionate as he was in war, Dessalines proved equally severe in his new job. He carried out his duties with a thoroughness that earned him a reputation for stringent discipline. He harshly reprimanded laborers and managers both for shirking plantation duties and for not meeting expected production rates.[125] He also sought to disband covert religious organizations that would challenge the authority of Louverture's administration and might thus also slow down production.[126]

Using these tough methods, Dessalines helped revive the colony's plantation economy.[127] Like the other military generals now in command of agricultural laborers, he had a vested interested in ensuring the success of the plantation system. Many officers now managing plantations worried that a decrease in productivity would invite their reenslavement.[128]

While Louverture and his generals had successfully eliminated local rivals and had begun to revive the smoldering plantation economy, their biggest adversary was already plotting their overthrow. Across the Atlantic, First Consul Napoléon Bonaparte's eye was turning back toward what had been the world's most profitable colony. He had, in fact, already interpreted Louverture's treaty with Maitland and Jamaica as a move toward independence. In 1801 it was Louverture's efforts to better regulate the colony that was the final straw.

The revolutionaries' fears, especially concerning the return of slavery, had been right all along. Now, Louverture and Dessalines's next battle would be against France.

CHAPTER 6

He Will Betray Them a Hundred Times

In December 1801, a year after Louverture and Dessalines's victory in the civil war, a French expedition of more than twenty thousand troops sailed from Brest, headed for Saint-Domingue. Leading the expedition was Bonaparte's brother-in-law, Charles Leclerc, whose second-in-command was Donatien Rochambeau (son of the French general who fought at the Battle of Yorktown). Although Leclerc had never set foot in the colony, Rochambeau had briefly served as governor in Saint-Domingue in the 1790s. Memories of his governance and his pro-slavery advocacy in France meant he was already despised by the current colonial leadership.

With them, Leclerc and Rochambeau carried a government document that compiled public information and private perceptions about the colony's military leaders. Preparing for any military and political attacks on them, the expedition's leaders would have studied the briefing carefully. It described anyone "who it would be dangerous to keep in the colony, or who needed to be monitored."[1]

One such person was "Dessalines, division general," who the document noted was both deeply loyal to Louverture and yet also competed with him. While Louverture later insisted that Dessalines "knows military subordination," the French hoped that such perceived divisions might be exploited by the expedition.[2] More important, however, the briefing suggested that despite the acclaim he had received from France, Dessalines was not as loyal as he might have once appeared. Referring to Dessalines's speech in Léogâne after the civil war less than a year ago, the document warned the French commanders that Dessalines was already prepared for a fight against them. "He told a large corps of troops and a lot of assembled cultivators," the author recounted, "that there were still two wars to sustain, the one from the Spanish part that would not be a big deal, and the one against France, *si la France velé gater Bagage cila-là* (if France wanted to bring back slavery), that for that war *everyone would have to rise together, the women, like the men,* they replied with cheers."[3]

Dessalines had been right to worry: Bonaparte was sending Leclerc and Rochambeau to Saint-Domingue to reconquer the island for France, and the colony's revolutionary leaders feared that they also planned to violently reimpose slavery.[4]

The expedition was to proceed in three stages, according to the plans of Bonaparte and the French minister of the navy, Denis Decrès. During the first phase, Leclerc would occupy the cities, organize the national guard, and assure the colonists of France's good intention. "All of the black people who are there," Bonaparte told his brother-in-law, "have to be flattered during the first phase, well treated, but in general we have to deprive them of their popularity and their power. Toussaint, Moyse and Dessalines must be well-treated during the first phase."[5]

Meanwhile, Leclerc should get the European soldiers of the expedition accustomed to the island's terrain, while taking control of the plains. He would also begin disarming the "black people who are rebels," meaning the independent revolutionary leaders who had resisted joining Louverture's forces and who lived in remote inland regions.[6]

During the second phase, the "two armies" would pursue the "rebels by any means necessary," first in the French part, then in the (formerly) Spanish part. Bonaparte hoped to use a similar strategy that the French had used in the Alps: "eight or ten columns [of 300 to 400 men total] at the same time combining their movements against a single position."[7] If at this point Dessalines and the others supported the expedition's efforts, then Leclerc would allow them to keep their ranks.

But all that would change in the third phase, when Leclerc—regardless of the officers' loyalty—would deport Louverture, Moyse, and Dessalines and all of Louverture's allies as "traitors to the nation and enemies of the French people."[8] The only remaining opposition, they assumed, would be three to four thousand independent revolutionaries whom they would eventually destroy. During this final phase, the French troops would disarm all the Black people. Bonaparte even assured Leclerc that they would receive help from the United States because "[Thomas] Jefferson promised that from the moment the French army arrived, all measures would be taken to starve Toussaint and to help the army."[9]

Finally, when the third phase was complete, Leclerc was authorized to proclaim that Saint-Domingue was finally "restored to the Republic," and all French colonists who had remained loyal to France could reclaim their properties.[10] For his part, the minister of the navy told Leclerc directly that the goal was to "reconquer without violence, the former St. Domingue for the metropole, and to add a new scale of agriculture, two times as big. It is necessary to base this vast empire on the foundations of liberty and work, sagely in coordination."[11]

How such a balance was to be coordinated may not have been included in Bonaparte and Decrès's official instructions. But it is clear that Leclerc's ultimate goal was to reinstitute slavery in the colony. Soon, it seemed, Dessalines would need to fulfill his promise that "everyone would have to rise together."

So much had changed in Saint-Domingue since the end of the civil war. Just one year earlier, Jean-Jacques Dessalines had led the northern army to victory, delivering a united colony to his general in chief. Louverture was grateful for Dessalines's efforts and for the rest of the senior officers, and he wanted their valor to be known beyond the borders of the colony. So, in a letter to First Consul Napoléon Bonaparte on February 12, 1801, Louverture argued that the French nation should celebrate his officers. "The zeal & all of the dedication of the officers committed to their duty, loyal to their country," he wrote, "they are all meritorious officers and equally worthy of your trust and of national recognition."[12] He highlighted the accomplishments of Brigadier General Moyse, his nephew, during his capture of Môle Saint-Nicolas, whom he had rewarded with the rank of division general. He also wanted Bonaparte to recognize the same promotion for Dessalines, "after the pacification of the South, at which he was one of the ones who contributed the most by his reliability and bravery."[13] Both division generals had already assumed their new roles, but Louverture stressed that the French should know of their valiant defense of the colony during the civil war. Moreover, he wanted the government to validate and compensate them accordingly.

The government in Paris, however, heard conflicting reports about Dessalines. In April 1801, Jacques Péries, the public spending director, wrote to the minister of the navy and colonies, contradicting Louverture's claims of fidelity to France among his officers. Péries was distraught following news from the western coastal town of Gonaïves. "Two hundred men of color among whom were three white people were recently slaughtered," he claimed, "by order, by a detachment sent by the Gen'al Dessalines; these men of color were *anciens libres* and owned big plantations in part of the South, and during the war against Rigaud asked for refuge from the Gen'al who assigned them to Saint-Marc and to Gonaïves."[14]

This alleged massacre—which Dessalines had supposedly ordered of the refugees from the south—Péries presented as evidence that France had lost control of the colony; the Black generals were acting on their own accord. "It will, they say," he warned the minister, "soon be a question . . . of the independence of the colony." Péries described his understanding of the colony's current military leadership, noting that "Dessalines is division general without having more ability than Moyse but is perhaps more cruel, which is saying something, and was recently named inspector gen'al of agriculture of the island, and this was to pit him against the insubordinate Moyse, because this role put him in position to dispose of the cultivators."[15]

Péries suspected discord and conflict among the military leadership and noted that Moyse in particular was advocating for independence. He pitted Dessalines and Moyse against each other but reported that "Toussaint recognized the need to maintain division among these officers; there is also talk that Dessalines will be named gen'al in chief, if that is the case what will Toussaint be?"[16] For years tension had simmered between Dessalines and Moyse; perhaps Louverture even sustained the conflict to prevent any challenges to his leadership.

In July 1801 Louverture issued a colonial constitution on his own initiative. Suddenly accusations and rumors of a Saint-Domingue independence movement increased exponentially. The general was frustrated with waiting for the "special laws" that the 1799 French constitution had decreed for the colonies, and he simply published his own.[17] His intent was to ensure that the "special laws" preserved abolition and ensured full citizenship for people in the colony.[18]

Later Louverture explained that the colonial constitution was a last resort for the sake of the "tranquility" of the colony. Because France had not declared any laws or instructions specifically for Saint-Domingue, Louverture assembled elected representatives from each commune and asked them to create a colonial constitution.[19] The committee was composed entirely of people who had been free before the Haitian Revolution, many of whom had been enslavers.[20] Reflecting the interests of France and of the plantation owners, Louverture believed that the new constitution would increase agricultural production. Given this strategy, the export economy was critical to the abolition of slavery, since

Louverture hoped that sustaining the plantation system would inspire France to leave the colony alone.[21]

The colonial constitution therefore reaffirmed the abolition of slavery, while simultaneously insisting on the centrality of the plantation economy.[22] *Liberté* in Saint-Domingue, then, meant the legal abolition of slavery but not the ability of individuals to freely decide how to use their time or have equal access to resources like land. Work, especially plantation work, was conceived as a civic virtue; people who did not work were therefore undermining the moral basis of the colony.[23] The document thus constitutionalized the labor code of October 1800, while strengthening the military oversight of agriculture.

The constitution included a total of seventy-seven articles. Some of these (such as the articles that named Roman Catholicism as the official religion and outlawed divorce) contradicted the existing laws in France, taking advantage of the "special laws" clause.[24] Still, Louverture maintained that the constitution was not a declaration of independence and that in fact he was simply filling a void left by the neglect of the French republican government. The constitution named Louverture governor-for-life and committed him to maintain direct communication with the metropole.

Bonaparte and his administration, however, interpreted it as a de facto declaration of independence. In the United States as well, onlookers similarly understood the constitution as a break from France.[25] It was this 1801 constitution, following the previous "secret" treaty between Louverture and Maitland, that pushed Bonaparte to attack the colony.

As the French military in Europe readied for battle, Dessalines and Marie-Claire Heureuse—along with several other military couples—finally got to celebrate their hasty nuptials that had taken place during the civil war. They had no idea what was coming their way. The celebration in early October lasted for days in Saint-Marc. Dessalines and other officers had been anxious for the party because Louverture "had promised [it], for a long time, in the name of the Government."[26] One former colonist claimed that the group ceremony was to ensure that all the generals were properly married in the church, per Louverture's wishes. This created an embarrassing situation for Dessalines, because he did not have a record of his baptism. The matter was resolved when Dessalines visited Jeanvier Desaline in Cap-Français to buy his baptismal certificate from his former enslaver. There is no remaining record of such evidence existing, but the colonist insisted that he had heard this account from Jeanvier Desaline himself.[27]

Louverture oversaw the beginning of the festivities but left early to tend to administrative duties. He notified Dessalines that his wife Suzanne would rep-

resent him at the event.[28] Dessalines was known for his love of dancing, and it
is likely that the lengthy celebration involved a feast after which guests danced
to music late into the night. "Like all of the Congos from whom he originated,"
a French consul later described, "he [Dessalines] was gay, loved pleasure, and
above all else dancing; relentlessly, he sought to perfect himself at it."[29] After
she oversaw the celebrations, Suzanne traveled with Marie-Claire, while their
spouses set out to defend the colony against the French invasion. Their respite
from battle did not last long.

Only weeks after the wedding party, Dessalines was leading the first battalion of the 4th demi-brigade in a march against Plaisance to quell a revolt in the
north.[30] "The first of Brumaire, reports were arriving from all sides," Louverture later recounted, "telling of the sudden uprising of the districts of Acul, of
Limbé, of Port-Margot, of Marmelade, of Plaisance and of Dondon, and the
unfortunate who escaped the massacres, announced that the cry of the Revolted
was: *Death to all the Whites*."[31] The cultivators in those regions had revolted in
opposition to Louverture's labor policies. They were led by none other than Louverture's nephew, Moyse.[32]

Dessalines may have welcomed the opportunity to engage his longtime rival.
He successfully dispersed the insurgents, forcing them to return to their plantations. French newspapers published unsourced accounts of the revolt, claiming
that "in all of the insurgent regions that Dessalines visited, he shot the driver
and the *nègres domestiques* of the plantation, and he decimated the *nègres* cultivators."[33] Another report from a resident of Cap-Français was less explicit, alleging that he "brought terror among all these brigands, during his tour always
making an example of the chiefs of the revolted."[34] Increasingly, public and private descriptions of Dessalines's tactics would emphasize the use of violence to
quell dissenters.

"The unanimous reports of the Generals, the military Commanders, the cries
of the Revolted, the interrogations of those who were arrested," Louverture wrote
in his official report about the revolt, "are in agreement in indicating the division
general *Moyse,* as the author of the Conspiracy."[35] Louverture believed that the
revolt had been stoked by false claims that he had sold Black people into slavery.

In an emotional proclamation on December 14, 1801, published in the *Bulletin officiel du Port-Républicain,* Louverture professed his disappointment at
his nephew's recent rebellion. Men in power were responsible to their people, he
argued, but they also had to honor the chain of command. "This is the standard
to which I have held Moyse, for ten years, in all of our private conversations," he
wrote, "that I repeated to him a thousand times in front of his peers, in the pres-

ence of the generals; that I repeated in my correspondence; these are the princi-ples and sentiments detailed in thousands of my letters."[36] Indeed, Louverture was devastated by Moyse's treason. "Instead of listening to the advice of a father, of obeying the orders of a leader devoted to the well-being of the colony," he regretted, "he wanted to let himself be guided by his passion, only to follow his fatal penchants; he died miserably." Moyse was executed on Louverture's orders. Louverture used this bitter episode as an opportunity for a warning: "That is the fate reserved for all who want to imitate him."[37]

In the same proclamation Louverture praised Dessalines. He was an exam-ple of the path Moyse could have taken, and Louverture declared that Dessalines would retain his position as division general. By defeating Moyse, Dessalines eliminated a major obstacle in the way of his own advancement, and he secured his place as a loyal leader in Louverture's army.

Despite being put down swiftly, Moyse's defection and rebellion could not have come at a worse time. In fact it was at this moment that Leclerc and Ro-chambeau's expedition left France. Saint-Domingue needed all the help it could get. And while the ships sailed for weeks across the Atlantic, Leclerc and Ro-chambeau would have read more of their briefing on the island's military leaders and planned how to divide and defeat them.

"It is probable that [Dessalines] will be the one chosen by g'al Toussaint to succeed him" the report concluded. "But for him to be, as much as it is possible, in a position to replace him it would have to be delayed for several years."[38] There were portraits of other officers including Martial-Besse, Charles Bélair, Le Franc, Joseph Benoit, Mameselle, Jean Pinau, Noel Guedon, Lamour Derance, Laplume, Agé, Clervaux, Pageot, and Christophe. And, of course, there was much more about Dessalines.

Dessalines had previously been "ferocious," the briefing reported, but Lou-verture and Marie-Claire Heureuse had influenced him; now he was "much softened." "His wife, who is gifted with an excellent heart," read the report, "has improved his character. This woman is sweet, humane, likes white people a lot; he has become kinder, more humane and has more deference for the white peo-ple."[39] After his marriage, onlookers consistently attributed any of Dessalines's actions that were rooted in empathy and compassion to his wife. Indeed, an-other report warned that he was "naturally volatile, his temper is abrupt and he is difficult, he has, despite his civilization, retained a savage air which repulses at first; but, rest assured that while he is cruel in his outbursts, his heart, when he calms down, is no stranger to pity, and good feelings."[40] To secure Dessalines's allegiance, this report recommended, the French expedition should use his wife to help convince him of their good intentions.

Charles Vincent, a director of fortifications who had significant experience in the colony, also wrote with advice for Leclerc. After assuring Leclerc that Henry Christophe would be a willing collaborator because he "loved white people," Vincent recommended that Leclerc exploit any existing conflicts among Louverture's generals. Although not knowing about Moyse's rebellion and subsequent execution, he argued that publicizing Louverture's favoritism toward Moyse would anger Dessalines. "The goal would be to cause conflict if necessary between the G'l dessalines and the G'l in chief," he advised, "and I believe there exists that possibility; we read in all of the newspapers a letter from the G'l in chief to the first consul by which he requested that Moyse be recognized as division general before Dessalines."[41] Vincent recommended reprinting that letter in local newspapers to publicly embarrass Dessalines. "If the top black leaders can be divided," he concluded, "they will submit faster, this is evident."[42]

This advice echoed letters from Bonaparte and Minister Decrès, which emphasized, above all, not alarming the Black leaders at the outset, only dividing them slowly. But Leclerc ignored this strategic advice. Instead "they came with a large army to bring desolation to this island, alarming the inhabitants and chasing them into the woods & the mountains," as Louverture later recalled. "The innocent victims fled in all directions abandoning their lands and their valuables."[43] Even if it hadn't inspired fear on arrival, however, the expedition did itself no favors by assigning Donatien Rochambeau as Leclerc's second-in-command. "Who is the person who will engage G'al Rochambeau with confidence," Louverture would later ask Leclerc, "well-known enemy of freedom in Saint-Domingue & of black people? This same Rochambeau, who after having vomited horrors in this very country was in France publishing *mémoires* against the freedom of black people."[44]

More important than the mistakes of the French expedition, however, were the planning and strategy of Louverture and his officers. They had worried that such a fleet might come for some time. Secretly Louverture had instructed his generals, remembered Dessalines's secretary-general, Louis Félix Boisrond-Tonnerre, to "be on their guard, to prepare for a vigorous defense, to oppose any disembarkation by the French, and to burn the cities in the event that it was not possible to resist them."[45] Burning the cities and retreating to the mountains was a defensive strategy that enabled the revolutionaries to take advantage of their inland forts and food sources, while weakening the defensive positions of the occupying forces.

This was the plan followed by the defenders of Saint-Domingue. In February 1802 the French expedition arrived in the Cap-Français harbor; there were additional French ships near Saint-Marc, as Dessalines reported.[46] But in Cap-Français Henry Christophe refused to let the French troops disembark without orders from Louverture. Instead he promised to burn the city to the ground if Leclerc and his troops proceeded, just as Louverture had instructed.[47] Leclerc ignored the warning, and as the French troops disembarked, Christophe evacuated and set fire to the town.

After the French landed in the scorched remains of Cap-Français, Leclerc distributed a proclamation from Bonaparte, dated November 8 of the previous year: "Inhabitants of Saint-Domingue, whatever your origin and your color, you are all French, you are all equal before God and before the republic."[48] To help his expedition's military efforts, Bonaparte thus attempted to divide the colonial population's allegiance by denying that the expedition was there to reinstitute slavery. "If someone tells you: *these forces are here to wrest your freedom,*" Bonaparte counseled, "reply: *the republic would not suffer that it be taken from us.*"[49] He concluded with a threat: anyone opposing Leclerc was a traitor to the nation, and "the wrath of the republic will devour them like fire devours dried cane."[50]

Louverture was quick to see the difference between Bonaparte's words and Leclerc's actions. "I thought that the conduct of the general Leclerc was very much contrary to the intentions of the government," Louverture wrote in his *Mémoires,* "because in his letter the first consul promised peace meanwhile he waged war."[51]

When the Leclerc expedition arrived, Dessalines was in Saint Raphaël, near the border between the Artibonite River and the north. He quickly headed south toward Port-Républicain to help defend the southern and western regions.[52] In Léogâne he allegedly instructed the local commander Pierre Louis Diane to execute some of the white population, perhaps to eliminate potential accomplices of the invading French.[53]

According to an anonymous account by a white colonist, on February 10, 1802, Dessalines publicized news of the burning of Cap-Français and other regions and "declared himself to be the enemy of the white people."[54] He claimed the French were ungrateful for his services to the nation and vowed that his forces would destroy the expeditionary army.

Beginning with the French reinvasion of 1802, Dessalines's actions suggest a change in his ideological commitments; he was convinced that the abolition of slavery was not guaranteed under colonial rule. The roots of an independence movement started taking shape.

Dessalines ordered civilians and troops to evacuate and camp at the base of the mountains, preparing for a French assault. Many white French people wrote publicly and privately about Dessalines's actions at this point in the conflict. Their accounts were hyperbolic, intending to elicit support for the French and to damage Dessalines's reputation.

From Léogâne, Dessalines instructed the regional leaders of the south to prepare themselves. He told the commander of Petit Trou to recruit two hundred men and increase the size of his gendarme company to sixty. "Courage, stand guard," he counseled, "and do not let yourselves be surprised."[55] He also wrote to his longtime colleague Brigadier Chief Rousselot (Dommage) in Jérémie to warn him of a potential attack by the French ships. But rather than ordering Rousselot to kill all the white people, as the anonymous author claimed he had done in Léogâne, Dessalines simply cautioned him against trusting them. "Be wary of all the White people," he warned, "because they can play everyone like they did at [Port-Républicain]."[56]

Dessalines did, however, conclude the letter with a postscript noting that there were some French people in Jérémie who "deserve that we bring them within an inch of death" (*mérite qu'on leur fasse voir le Bon Dieu par le petit trou*), instructing Rousselot to act accordingly.[57] It is unclear exactly what Dessalines meant by this phrase and whether he wanted Rousselot to threaten the French or to torture them. But rather than a wholesale massacre of the French, he insisted only that his generals intimidate some of the French colonizers.

Dessalines warned Rousselot that the French might try to distribute proclamations on shore to help their invasion. He therefore instructed his officer to confiscate such documents. His own strategy in Port-Républicain and Léogâne, he told Rousselot, was to burn the towns and the plains and retreat to the mountains. "Do not lose courage," he implored his longtime friend, "the circumstance requires it."[58] "I am leaving tomorrow for Jacmel," he signed off, "because my presence is necessary everywhere so that I can make it known to the people of St. Domingue that they want to take away their freedom."[59]

Rousselot did not receive Dessalines's letter in time, and only escaped the French after putting up a weak defense against a seventy-four-cannon French warship in the harbor.[60] Dessalines saw this as a betrayal. "I left with you," he told the population of Jérémie years later, "as your chief, my cousin Domage. Domage! I loved him more than myself!"[61] Years later, he was still pained by Rousselot's "treason." Dessalines believed that instead of defending Jérémie against the French invasion, Rousselot had been bribed by local colonists, who flattered him into becoming "a traitor to his superior's orders and to his own color."[62] That said, Boisrond-Tonnerre's account of the event blamed Rousselot's troops rather than the officer himself.[63] Others attributed Rousselot's weak defense to the appearance of a large French fleet and believed that he had remained loyal to Louverture and Dessalines.[64]

Dessalines left Léogâne and headed south to Jacmel, where he similarly spread the word that the French were invading. He reprimanded the commander Pierre Dieudonné for asking permission to let French women, children, and the elderly board the ships in the harbor. Instead, Dessalines allegedly told Dieudonné that "he should have let them embark," an anonymous white colonist claimed, "and then sink all of the ships with cannon fire, and destroy all the white people (those were his exact words)."[65] This same witness claimed that Dessalines threatened the lives of all white people in the town. "He announced to the White people that he was declaring War on them," the author wrote, "and that he was going to set the black people on them, that he already saw death painted on their faces, and that in his eyes they were no more than cadavers."[66] The witness focused on what he perceived to be the violent threat that Dessalines posed. But the account also hints at Dessalines's belief that the white colonists could not be trusted.

Another white French author, the naturalist Michel-Étienne Descourtilz, also claimed to have escaped Dessalines's wrath because of outside intervention. After Dessalines returned to Petite Rivière, according to Descourtilz, "the time was therefore fixed! streams of blood will flow! the executioners are ready and roar with impatience."[67] Descourtilz was a prisoner at the time but a local surgeon, falsely claiming that Dessalines had sent for the prisoner, secured his release. Descourtilz might have eventually been killed, he claimed, had Dessalines's wife not intervened on his behalf. Marie-Claire Heureuse hid Descourtilz under a bed, and when he was discovered by Dessalines she pleaded for his life. "Mercy! Mercy! *Messieurs,* demand mercy with me," she implored Dessalines and his officers. "This is a doctor, do not kill him; he could be useful to us."[68] Dessalines conceded, and Descourtilz lived.

At this point, Dessalines left Jacmel to head back north. His goal was to continue evacuating towns, burning them and the surrounding plains, and then absconding to the mountains.[69] Upon Dessalines's departure, Dieudonné declared his allegiance to the French, read the French proclamations, and allowed the white colonists to board the ships in the harbor—this may have been the only reason why the anonymous chronicler lived to tell his (tall) tale.[70]

By mid-February 1802, Leclerc had secured surrenders from Maurepas (or Morpas), Paul Louverture (Toussaint's younger brother), and Clervaux.[71] On

February 17 Leclerc issued a general proclamation to the inhabitants of Saint-Domingue, claiming that he wanted to work with them and that he had even promised to make Louverture his lieutenant general. "I promised the inhabitants of Saint-Domingue their freedom," he claimed, "I will make sure that they enjoy it. I will ensure that people and property are respected."[72] But because the revolutionary generals resisted the French expeditionary army, Leclerc was obliged to denounce Louverture and Christophe as *hors la loi* (outlaws) and to declare that they were rebels against the French Republic.[73]

Several days later, Dessalines updated Louverture about troop movements and threats from the French army, emphasizing that he was ready to fight. "I have no news from St. Marc, at the moment," Dessalines told his commander in chief. "All that I can tell you is that the garrison and I are always well prepared to defend ourselves in case of an attack from our enemies, and I can assure you that they will not remove me from this place except after a strong defense."[74]

On March 1 Leclerc had to admit that his campaign was not moving as quickly as had been anticipated. "Dessalines, the most ferocious of all," Leclerc wrote to the minister of the navy, "massacred a few white people. It is good that we still have the entire month of *ventose* and *germinal* before the strong heat and rains of winter begin. We are pursuing Toussaint from mountain to mountain without rest. As long as he has 2000 men with him we are sure to reach him. All the coast and all the ports are ours."[75] The strategy that Dessalines had outlined—burning the towns and retreating to the mountains—was working. The French forces were in disarray and already exhausted.

Still, some in the colony remained optimistic about Leclerc's chances. A white priest, Père Guillaume Lecun, argued that the French expeditionary army would, by starting a war, "bring back peace, true liberty and goodwill, of which they have only been kept in the most absurd and perfidious name."[76] Peace for white people in the colony depended, Lecun believed, on the subjugation of the Black population.

On March 1 Dessalines received a letter from Louverture. He replied immediately, asking forgiveness for not updating him on his whereabouts and explaining that it was only because he did not know where Louverture was. He had been determined, he told his commanding officer, to secure the important fort at Crête-à-Pierrot, which sat along the Artibonite River and directly east of Saint-Marc. He therefore installed troops at the fort and two battalions from the 4th demi-brigade on a nearby hillside. He fortified the garrison with six cannons and prepared for battle. "This post," Boisrond-Tonnerre later explained, "was essential to Dessalines and offered him the means of defense. He ordered his troops to surround the site with stakes where the fort used to exist and within forty-eight hours put the fort in a state to resist the attack that they antici- pated."[77]

This fort became the site of the fiercest battle that Dessalines would fight against the French expeditionary army when they first invaded. It would also consume his energy and attention for weeks and ultimately bring him both per- sonal tragedy and military setbacks.

Later that month, Dessalines defended the fort at Crête-à-Pierrot with seven hundred men, who reinforced and repaired the building, bringing can- nons and munitions from nearby regions.[78] As the French approached the base, Dessalines lowered the gates. "'Soldiers,' he said, with the energy that he always put into his speeches," Boisrond-Tonnerre recounted, "'these gates are lowering for those who are not resolved to die; while there is still time, let the friends of the French leave, they have only to hope for death here.'"[79] He filled a barrel with gunpowder, promising his troops that he would blow the fort up if they did not fight hard.

An envoy from the French army approached the fort with a letter held high, requesting permission to deliver it to Dessalines. The general refused, ordering the soldier's execution. "A swarm of Frenchmen led by more than twenty offi- cers," Boisrond-Tonnerre recounted, "surrounded the fort and rained down a hailstorm of cannonballs, bombs, bullets and shells on a group of seven hundred men, resolved to die."[80]

Yet Dessalines's forces withstood the assault and returned fire. After the first day, the fort still stood. The French were humiliated, Boisrond-Tonnerre de- scribed with glee. Dessalines's mere seven hundred men had sent fifteen thou- sand troops *of the most powerful nation in the world* (the expression from the letter from Leclerc to Toussaint-Louverture)" running for cover.[81] In contrast, a French report simply noted that the French general, recognizing that "the enemy was superior in number, and had several pieces of artillery," ordered the retreat.[82]

With a respite from the attack, Dessalines left the fort and ventured toward Plassac (southeast, toward Grand Cahos) to retrieve munitions that he had stored in the woods.[83] Yet on his march he was engaged by the French and nearly lost an entire battalion.[84] Marie-Claire Heureuse, Suzanne Louverture, and other military wives and children were hiding nearby. Dessalines reassured Louver- ture in a March 9 letter that "your spouse and mine escaped to the woods"—but, he admitted, "with nothing."[85] Later Dessalines would send some of his forces (a battalion from the 4th, some troops from the 8th, and the national guard) to protect his wife and the other families, who by then were hiding in Grand Fond in the Grand Cahos Mountains.[86]

Before Dessalines could make it back to the fort, the French returned.[87] On March 11, at 8 a.m., the French launched an attack on the fort that continued nonstop until March 24.[88] Dessalines could not break the attack from the outside, nor could he get back in. In the middle of the fighting, Dessalines's artillery lieutenant, Pierre Charles Marion, defected—perhaps acting as a plant—and allegedly gave the French a full report on the status of Dessalines's troops.[89] He offered a detailed description of the fort, including a summary of the quantity and grade of Dessalines's weapons, as well as the location of their munitions stores.[90] He claimed that Dessalines was in the fort—a lie—and that he was commanding about two thousand troops—another lie. Based on this information, the French expedition drew up a map of the firing range from each point of the fort's defense. The map also showed a series of French camps surrounding Crête-à-Pierrot.[91]

On March 22 Pierre Thouvenot, a French chief of staff, reported to the commander of Le Borgne that he had Dessalines surrounded. He told his commanding officer that he expected to take the fort.[92]

At some point during the battle at Crête-à-Pierrot—where his wife had been endangered nearby—Dessalines may have sustained an injury to the chest.[93] Descourtilz, the white doctor who was Dessalines's prisoner at the time, claimed to have tended to the wound. But Dessalines refused to drink an herbal remedy from the doctor, because he was worried that Descourtilz might poison him. As the battle at the fort dragged on, Dessalines could see that the stakes were dire. They still had not been able to lift the siege nor reenter the fort. He tried to reassure his troops. "Take courage . . . take courage, I tell you," Dessalines told his men, "the white Frenchmen are not capable of standing up to the good men of Saint-Domingue; they will go, go, go, but then they will stop; they will get sick, they will die like flies. Listen well: if Dessalines surrenders a hundred times, he will betray them a hundred times."[94] "So, I repeat to you," Dessalines continued, "take courage and you will see that when they get smaller and smaller, we will chicane them, we will fight them, we will burn their harvests; and we will hide in our mountains."[95]

For six days the Saint-Dominguan army held off the French, as Dessalines tried to get closer to the fort. He did manage to get an emissary inside to communicate with his trusted battalion chief Lamartinière, who reported that the fort's troops were out of water. When Dessalines's troops attempted to obtain water from the nearby river, the French attacked with fury.[96] Dessalines then sent

Lamartinière a ring that he always wore on his finger; this, the battalion chief knew, was the signal to evacuate.[97] The French captured and occupied the fort as Dessalines's troops fled under chase toward Grand Cahos.[98]

Seeing that the retreat was putting the munitions stores—and their wives and children—in jeopardy, Dessalines changed course. He ordered his aide-de-camp Jean-Philippe Daut (or Daux) and the commander Lafortune to go to Grand Fond to protect Marie-Claire Heureuse, Suzanne Louverture, and the other women and children. Instead, however, Lafortune went to find his own wife; as a result, the French claimed the weapons stores.

Dessalines's wife had been secured by Daut, but only because she had escaped to the same plantation where his own wife and children were hiding. When she saw Daut, Marie-Claire demanded to know whether her husband had died in the fight. "It would have been a good thing," the aide replied, "because he would not have had so much misery & sadness & suffered less harm."[99] Daut then left the group for unknown reasons and was followed by the enemy.

When he returned to the hideout where Marie-Claire and the others were concealed, the French followed him, and captured Dessalines's wife as a prisoner. They took several other military wives and children, including the wife of Dessalines's loyal officer Gabart, a few officers, and another one of Dessalines's aides, Maurice.[100] Dessalines did not comment on his wife's imprisonment in writing, although he must have considered her safety in the coming weeks.

The next month a newspaper in Philadelphia confirmed that "Madame Dessalines, wife to the black general, had been made prisoner." Marie-Claire's reputation was growing, and the US newspaper repeated the narrative about her alleged resistance to Dessalines's violence. "She is a black woman, and represented by those who have been in that country, as amiable and humane. The jewels and other ornaments found on her person were extremely valuable. It is stated, that during the convulsions in the colony, many lives and much property were preserved by her interposition."[101]

After a hard battle at Crête-à-Pierrot, the defeated Saint-Domingue troops met at Marchand in the Artibonite region, as Louverture had instructed. Dessalines remained there for several weeks, setting up camp on one of the properties.[102] He explored the possibility of building a new fort in the nearby mountains and sent envoys to secure salt and food, seizing livestock from local residents.[103] But his spirits and health faltered, as he and others succumbed to illness. "For eight days," Boisrond-Tonnerre recounted, "Dessalines was at Marchand in a state of languor and sickness that made him despair for his life."[104] "My dear Governor," Dessalines described his illness to Louverture, "in this moment, I am sick to the point of not being able to stand up with a terrible colic and a tenesmus in which I only produce blood."[105] He was too weak to even sign the letter, as was his secretary Benoit, and so his chief of staff Bazelais signed on his behalf.[106] His wife not being there to help nurse him must have made his illness even more of a hardship.

As his condition worsened, his soldiers started to lose hope. "We saw several soldiers come to his bedside, and question him," Boisrond-Tonnerre wrote, "and when weakness prevented him from encouraging them, they retreated with their hands on their heads, a sign of the greatest pain among black people; we are lost, they cried, the general Toussaint abandons us and our Father will die."[107] Some of his troops and regional leaders chose this moment to defect to the French; others were still scattered in the mountains of Grand Cahos, separated since the defeat at Crête-a-Pierrot.[108]

When Dessalines finally recovered, he learned that of the several hundred troops he'd had before the rout and sickness, only about sixty now remained. As punishment, Dessalines executed two captains, and he threatened to kill any other officers who failed to bring back his troops. Within four days, Boisrond-Tonnerre claimed, he was "at the head of five thousand men armed and burning with the desire for revenge."[109] Even though they had lost their last battle, they now knew what they were up against and were convinced victory was still within reach. "Crête-à-Pierrot had destroyed the great French bogeyman," Boisrond-Tonnerre recounted, "and the black soldiers, proud of their general's resistance, gradually rallied around him."[110]

But while Dessalines and his troops were animated and prepared to fight, other Saint-Dominguan units were being defeated. For three months Louverture and his forces had held out against the invading French, but now their resistance was collapsing. "I have reason to be surprised," Louverture wrote to Leclerc on April 23, 1802, "when you told me that the general Christophe has submitted to the Republic, with the troops that he commands, because none of the Generals, Soldiers and other citizens who are with me, have ever ceased to be submitted and devoted to it."[111] Louverture denied that he and his army were traitors and maintained that Leclerc could have avoided conflict if he had simply followed traditional protocol by sending an envoy when his ships arrived in Cap-Français.

The situation was dire. Henry Christophe was now fighting for the enemy, and even Louverture himself had opened negotiations with Leclerc. But Dessalines—without knowing about this turn of events—continued waging war. He plotted an alternative defense strategy with Charles Bélair.[112] On April 26 he advised Louverture on the best military formation for their current situation and geography. He wanted to deploy a tactic that they had previously used in which Dessalines fought on foot. "When it was an attack, & when we were camped in one place," Dessalines reminded Louverture, "you made us put our horses on the various plantations in Marmelade & you only kept close to you as many guides as were necessary, so that we were all employed in fighting the enemy."[113] A similar strategy was essential at this moment, Dessalines argued. Without their horses, they could take advantage of the familiar terrain to surprise and exhaust the French expeditionary army. Recognizing that everyone in the Saint-Domingue army needed to fight, he wanted to join his men on the battlefield. "If you find my advice & my memory of it timely, you will adopt it," Dessalines ended on a deferential note to Louverture. "In the opposite case, please excuse me, having only in mind to be of Good service, & to earn your esteem."[114]

But Dessalines's defense proposal was moot, since Henry Christophe had reassured Louverture that "he believed in the frankness and the righteousness of [Leclerc's] intentions."[115] After Christophe had surrendered to the French, Leclerc publicly announced that he was no longer an outlaw.[116] Not too long before, Christophe had burned the city of Cap-Français to the ground, all to defend Saint-Domingue from the French invasion, but now he assisted Leclerc in securing Louverture's capitulation. Perhaps Christophe had analyzed the current situation, and concluded that the Saint-Domingue forces could not win.

Louverture himself soon concluded that he was out of options. He knew he was defeated. He asked to meet Leclerc in person, demanding that he "ensure forever general liberty, and the equality of all of my fellow citizens on a solid and unwavering foundation; and because nothing is more dear to the military than honor, repair ours."[117] Not knowing about Louverture's communications with Leclerc, Dessalines sent his commander two sacks of salt, and even requested a large quantity of tafia (a drink distilled from molasses) in preparation for the next battle against the French. Dessalines reported that his officers sent words of respect and loyalty, especially Dessalines's longtime colleague Louis Gabart.[118]

But Louverture's mind was made up. He went to meet Leclerc in Cap-Français and surrendered.[119] Leclerc guaranteed that Louverture could retire to one of his plantations in safety. But Louverture also had some advice. He assured Leclerc that Dessalines would also surrender, but recommended that he be allowed to resume his command in Saint-Marc (and likewise that Charles

Bélair take his command in Arcahaye).[120] In these positions, he believed, they would assist the expedition in defeating any remaining insurgents.

So, on May 1, 1802, Louverture and Leclerc officially declared a ceasefire. And Bonaparte's brother-in-law reversed the decree that had condemned Louverture as an outlaw. He also ordered Louverture to invite Dessalines to see him, because "I want to know him."[121] Louverture agreed to pass on the message but cautioned, "I am afraid that he will not want to if you do not give him your word of honor."[122] He knew Dessalines would be wary of Leclerc's intentions and hoped to reassure him before their meeting.

On May 3 Leclerc publicly announced his ceasefire agreement.[123] The next day he asked Louverture to come to Cap-Français, adding, "bring the G'al Dessalines with you."[124] Leclerc clearly sensed how important it was for his mission to secure Dessalines's surrender, and he hoped that Louverture would facilitate an easy transition.

Dessalines, still stationed at Marchand, had not yet received news of the surrender. Still addressing Louverture as *mon cher gouverneur* (my dear governor), on May 3 Dessalines notified him that he was sending more salt.[125] The next day, however, Dessalines sensed that something was amiss. Bélair notified Dessalines that he had received instructions from Louverture to bring his troops to a meeting, without further explanation. Dessalines wrote to his commander, insisting that the plan was misguided. "I beg you to remember," Dessalines wrote to Louverture, "what we resolved on the Lory plantation, even though I am a Soldier and ready to obey all of your Orders, please allow me to say; that it is impossible for two companies to remain camped in that place."[126] He did not reveal what they had sworn to do, but their Lory plantation pact may have involved a commitment to an independence movement.

"My Dear Governor," Dessalines wrote the next day, "I recently received your letter dated the 12th of the current [May 2, 1802], in which you explained your embarrassing position, because of the treason of general Christophe, who joined the enemy."[127] "What do you expect, My Dear Governor," Dessalines told Louverture in response to Christophe's defection. "This is what we have to expect from cowards, you have known *Christophe* for a long time, and he was incapable of resisting with us to continue waging war."[128] Dessalines sent reinforcements to Louverture and awaited further instructions, regretting that he could not come meet Louverture himself, since his presence was necessary in Marchand.

Eventually Dessalines learned about Louverture's surrender. He was furious, remaining in denial even as he received more information. The commander Jean-Pierre Nicolas had forwarded to Dessalines a packet of papers from the

French general stationed in Santo Domingo, François Kerverseau, who attempted to win him over with tales of French victories in Egypt, in the Pyrenees, and in the Alps. The packet also contained several letters from Paul Louverture that Dessalines was convinced were forged, because they described how happy Paul was to have joined the French forces in the east. "As I read this treachery to myself," Dessalines told Louverture, "I was so angry that I tore them up."[129]

Dessalines was a whirlwind, trying to keep his armies moving. After destroying the damaging evidence, Dessalines sent a letter to the commander Jean-Pierre Nicolas, forbidding him from receiving mail or communicating with the enemies. Dessalines told Nicolas about Christophe's "treason" and asked Louverture to help secure the commander's commitment to fight. Finally, Dessalines reported that another colleague, a citizen Pierre, had asked for reinforcements to secure some white prisoners; Dessalines reminded him of the men in the national guard who were already under his orders. If these men were not up to the job, Dessalines told Pierre, he could send the prisoners to him. "I will put them in a place of safety," Dessalines assured Louverture, "because the moment that the war reignites again, I will dispose of anything that will deter me."[130]

The next day, however, the full picture became clear when Dessalines and Louverture met face to face on the road that connected their respective plantation camps. Louverture revealed his alliance with Leclerc, arguing that it was in the "public interest" to surrender, and assuring Dessalines that he would keep his military command. Bélair was also at the meeting, and he and Dessalines both protested their commander's decision. Louverture eventually managed to convince Dessalines and Bélair to surrender, "despite all their repugnance and their regret and their tears, and they threatened to leave and break away from me."[131]

A furious Dessalines told Louverture "that he would be responsible for the disasters that he would unleash on his compatriots, because of his weakness." Dessalines only yielded to Louverture's pressure, Boisrond-Tonnerre argued, because of his troops' loyalty to the now former governor.[132] Moreover, Dessalines's wife was being held as a prisoner by the French, which may have factored into his decision to surrender. Marie-Claire Heureuse was released as Dessalines resumed his command in Saint-Marc.

Dessalines never forgave Louverture for this decision. Ultimately, it was this action that broke his trust in his longtime friend and mentor.

Boisrond-Tonnerre later argued that Dessalines's submission to Leclerc was a ruse. "Dessalines swallowing his wrath," Boisrond-Tonnerre wrote, "recognized the virtue of necessity, and went to lead them in Saint-Marc. It was therefore for his troops or rather by the desire to prevent them from the horrors that he anticipated, that Dessalines appeared to have surrendered; but the plan to raise the banner of insurrection as soon as the French gave him the pretext remained strong in his heart."[133] In May, Dessalines and Leclerc reached an uneasy détente. Neither one trusted the other entirely, but both were willing to pretend out of necessity, at least for the moment.[134]

It is likely that Dessalines allied with the French for practical reasons in 1802. He could not continue to defend the colony against the French expeditionary force without Louverture's support or that of the other top generals in the colony. Yet he probably was not convinced by Leclerc that the French would not ultimately reinstitute slavery, and he likely imagined a future in which he would once again fight against the French. He may have also used this alliance to target his own military and political rivals, knowing that he also would have had to contend with the independent revolutionary units who had rejected Louverture's authority. He probably tried to eliminate rival leaders and potential future enemies, in the event that he would later defect from the French to fight for independence. As he had said at Crête-a-Pierrot, no matter how many times he surrendered, he would always resume the fight.[135]

As Leclerc had promised Louverture, Dessalines resumed command of Saint-Marc.[136] Now Dessalines's demi-brigade, along with the rest of Louverture's forces, were integrated into the French expeditionary army as "colonial demi-brigades," and the officers kept their ranks. He would never leave the men of the 4th demi-brigade, Boisrond-Tonnerre believed, for "in all the campaigns that he undertook, [they] always served as the avant-garde and the aegis of his division." "[The French] tried to corrupt them," he wrote, "but this corps was steadfast in the face of seductions."[137] Because the troops were loyal to Dessalines and trusted him deeply, they supported him even during his alliance with Leclerc.

At this crucial moment Leclerc made a major mistake in his dealings with Dessalines. Despite Louverture's warnings, he placed Dessalines under Rochambeau's command. "If you had instructed him to report directly to you, or to any other General under your orders," Louverture told Leclerc, "it would have been better."[138] Hoping that Leclerc would change his mind, Louverture waited for a response before contacting Dessalines.

But Leclerc did not heed Louverture's warning, and Dessalines reported to Jean-Baptiste Brunet, an experienced French officer who had fought with Rochambeau in Italy and who now served under Rochambeau's command in the Artibonite.[139] Brunet was "commonly called Leclerc's gendarme."[140] Dessalines was aggravated by the appointment but decided to work with Brunet, voicing false professions of friendship and loyalty that masked deep tension and distrust. For the time being, they both needed the other to accomplish their military assignments within the French expeditionary army.

In this moment of crisis, transition, and general distrust, Dessalines also began concealing his true intentions from Louverture.[141] "You can count on, citizen general, the fact that I know nothing other than obedience," Dessalines wrote, "since I have had the honor of serving in the republican army, I have always made it my duty to obey both verbal and written orders from my leaders."[142] This was an outright lie; Dessalines had been detained several times for disobeying commands. Moreover, he had a long history of disregarding instructions and orders from people he did not respect; it was likely that after his surrender to the French, Louverture was now in this category of those Dessalines felt free to disobey.

The new arrangement did not start off smoothly. Leclerc summoned Dessalines to Cap-Français, but he was again too ill to travel. Afflicted with a "*grand fluë de sang*" that prevented him from mounting his horse, he sent the battalion chief Lamartinière in his place: an officer who—like Dessalines himself—was uneasy with the new French alliance.[143]

Moreover, Dessalines's communications with Leclerc were deceitful. While he would have preferred to answer to a French officer who had never previously served in the colony, he said, he was nonetheless keen to show his "obedience." Thus, Dessalines lied, he would happily serve under Rochambeau. He hoped that they could discuss the matter when they met face to face.[144] And Leclerc was deceived; he did not seem to understand the depths of Dessalines's loathing. "The general Dessalines is a bit scared of you," Leclerc told Rochambeau. "He would have liked to have not been under your orders, but I told him that these were my intentions and he obeyed immediately."[145]

Dessalines turned to more pressing matters in Saint-Marc.[146] His first task as an officer in the French expeditionary army was to ensure that the *cultivateurs* returned to plantation work. He spoke to the officers and workers, assuring them that Leclerc's "intention was pure concerning liberty."[147] Dessalines reported to Rochambeau that several letter carriers had been assassinated by insurgent plantation workers in Arcahaye, but he stressed that he had given orders for the *cultivateurs'* immediate return to the plantations. "If after this report," he told Rochambeau, "you judge that my presence is necessary next to the *cultivateurs,* all you have to do is give me your orders, you will see the zeal and the activity that I will put into quickly quelling the disorder."[148] In Saint-Marc, as division general, he oversaw almost 1,800 troops, most of whom were armed.[149]

Madame Dessalines was now with him in Saint-Marc. "As we were told," Brunet wrote, "she is a beautiful *négresse,* who seems to me to be a good wife and who does not belie the reputation that she has made for the gentleness that she exhibits." Brunet invited her to dinner and promised Rochambeau he would show her respect.[150] He never followed up about the dinner, but his closeness with Dessalines in the coming months—even if it was all a lie—suggests that Brunet and Marie-Claire Heureuse would have had plenty of opportunities for conversation. The French army occupied old sugar plantations for campgrounds and food, and the generals used the large plantation houses, hosting meetings and dinners and conducting business. In addition to letter writing, Dessalines and Brunet—maybe sometimes with Marie-Claire—would have met to discuss troop movements and military strategy.

From Saint-Marc Dessalines launched campaigns against units in Saint-Domingue that had not yet submitted to the French expeditionary army. He soon put Verrettes, Mirebalais, and Plassac under Bélair's command, as Rochambeau had ordered.[151] Rochambeau did not trust Dessalines, however, and so assigned battalion chief Margeret to spy on him in Saint-Marc.[152]

Soon all the contradictions of this unstable alliance came to the surface. After years of warfare and the chaos of the French assault, "order" could not simply resume. Agricultural production—the key to France's extraction of wealth from the colony—had not resumed nearly as uniformly as planned. That was in spite of Dessalines's repressive efforts on the ground and Leclerc's harsh orders announcing a return to agricultural production. Many officers, soldiers, and laborers simply refused to follow Leclerc's directives.[153]

This was trouble for the officers who had surrendered to the French, and they knew it. For his part, Louverture claimed to be helping the French effort by advising Dessalines on how to discipline the workers and soldiers. But Leclerc did not trust the former governor and still believed that he was a threat.[154] To undermine his authority, French soldiers, while at Ennery, pillaged Louverture's properties, threatening his safety and livelihood.[155] Just weeks after Leclerc issued a public truce with Louverture, the French began plotting his arrest and deportation.

The French knew that they would have to manage Dessalines in their plot to arrest Louverture. But Brunet, Dessalines's supervising officer, was confident that he would not be a problem. In mid-May, Brunet dined with Dessalines and Bélair and "buttered them up to make them talk."[156] "They said that they do not like TOUSSAINT very much," Brunet told Rochambeau, "that he is the cause of the losses that they suffered, that they were mistaken because they had no knowledge of the orders from the consul concerning Toussaint, that surely if they had they would not have fired a single bullet. They showed me enough confidence."[157] "The general Dessalines finally opened up to me," Brunet recounted, "and told me that Toussaint only used him as a drudge [*bête de somme*], that during all of the meetings that took place he was never invited, and that he thought that Toussaint feared him more than he loved him; he wants to have a meeting with the general-in-chief; and I believe that would be a good idea."[158]

Most likely, Dessalines and Bélair saw through Brunet's plan and told the French officer what he wanted to hear.[159] After all, Dessalines's prior actions and letters when the French expeditionary army arrived contradicted what he said to Brunet. He and the other Saint-Domingue generals knew that their positions and lives were at risk, which is why they fought so hard against Leclerc's forces. At this point, however, Dessalines and Bélair protected their own safety and refused to defend Louverture. They were still reeling from when Louverture had cornered them into surrendering, something that Dessalines had denounced as his former leader's "weakness."[160] So Dessalines distanced himself from Louverture and denied past or continued loyalty to the former governor, insisting that his only loyalty was to France.

In truth, whatever loyalty Dessalines may have felt either to Louverture or to France was superseded by his commitment to freedom. And in this moment, that commitment required him to pretend to be loyal to the Leclerc expedition.

"[I] consider you," Dessalines told Brunet, "a special friend after the marks of rank and favorable reception that you were pleased to honor me with when I arrived here."[161] Dessalines secured his position within the reconfigured expeditionary army by flattering Brunet and obsequiously professing his loyalty. And his deception worked. After their meeting, Brunet supported Dessalines in his alliance with Leclerc and defended Dessalines's allegiance to France.

Brunet's support came in handy soon after Dessalines assumed his position in Saint-Marc. Sylla (or Cila), one of Louverture's former officers, had visited Dessalines in Saint-Marc "to learn from me the measures that they should take, that is to say if they should still remain in rebellion."[162] Dessalines told Brunet and Leclerc about this visit, and he claimed to be shocked at the question. He was worried that the appearance of these two emissaries would give Leclerc the impression that he was secretly collaborating with Sylla, who had not yet surrendered, and so he expressed surprise and confusion at their appearance. "My status as a man of honor and of character," he assured Leclerc, "leads me to notify you so that I do not lessen the confidence that you have been pleased to give me."[163] Dessalines enclosed a letter to Sylla that he asked Leclerc to forward after reading it, if he found it appropriate. It was a short letter in which Dessalines said he was shocked that Sylla had not followed the orders of "l'ex G'al Toussaint," and exhorted him to send his followers back to their plantations.[164] Sylla obeyed.

Over the next week Dessalines reported a new problem to Rochambeau: the French troops were often drunk or hungover. "The garrison at this place is completely out of wine," he regretted, "which means that they are given rum as a substitute. The European troops suffer singularly."[165] Other European troops were getting sick from drinking from local water sources. While Dessalines was asking for more supplies for the European troops, it is also possible that he was amused by the French troops' inability to hold their liquor or was noting weaknesses as he covertly planned his next moves.

Eventually Dessalines became worried that his letters were being intercepted because Rochambeau did not respond. Nevertheless, he carried on with his duties. "I will leave tomorrow," Dessalines told Rochambeau on May 23, 1802, "to go do my tour throughout the area that the general in chief put under my command so that I can see the *cultivateurs* and to revive agriculture."[166] He requested oxen or mules for the colonial troops, because they had no way of transporting food stuffs.[167] This was essential since the rains had started, and the roads were impossible to navigate due to the mud.

By May 26 Dessalines's concern about his correspondence not getting through had turned to frustration. The lack of communication delayed the execution of his duties, and he told Rochambeau that he would have to act without his approval. "I am worried enough to believe that you are sick and that is what is creating this delay," he wrote. "As I am awaiting your orders about different areas of service, I am unable to act as a result."[168] The next day he wrote again to follow up on a previous letter about "young people of color" who had defected from the 4th demi-brigade. He wanted Rochambeau's permission to send an officer to round them up in Port-Républicain and bring them back.[169] The day after that, he wrote to ask for permission to allow the war commissioner to give rations to newly arrived European troops.[170] At the very end of May, Dessalines finally received instructions from Rochambeau, and he sent troops to Verrettes, Mirebalais, and Plassac accordingly.

On June 1, 1802, Dessalines and the sans-culottes were officially integrated into the French expeditionary army as the 3rd battalion of the 5th demi-brigade. Colloquially, however, they continued to be referred to as "the 4th."[171] On June 3 Dessalines left Saint-Marc for Cap-Français, accompanied by his chief of staff Bazelais and several of his officers, to meet with Leclerc.[172] While in Cap-

Français, he wrote to Rochambeau to update him on his movements and to highlight that he had Leclerc's approval. "I reserve the right to prove to you in person," he told Rochambeau, "my sincere attachment to the French government as well as to all the chiefs, since I had the privilege of reuniting with your values."[173] This was something that was hard to do while Rochambeau was ignoring his letters. Leclerc's "favorable reception" to his visit offered Dessalines protection to counterbalance Rochambeau's distrust, since Dessalines knew that the support from the top-ranking officer mattered more.

Whatever Dessalines told Leclerc during their meeting in Cap-Français convinced the French general of the former rebel's loyalty. This was probably why Leclerc proceeded with his plans to arrest and deport Louverture, even though Dessalines remained in the colony. (He thus contradicted the official orders he'd been provided with in France, which was to have all the officers deported together.) "Toussaint is acting in bad faith," Leclerc reported to Bonaparte on June 6, "as I had expected. But I got what I wanted from his surrender, which was to separate Dessalines and Christophe and their troops from him."[174] "I will order his arrest," he continued, "and I believe I can count enough on Dessalines, the mind of whom I have made myself master, to charge him with going to arrest Toussaint."[175]

But Dessalines had proven over the course of his life that no one was the master of his mind. Now, despite his efforts to ingratiate himself with the French, Dessalines refused to arrest Louverture although, in accordance with his agreement with Leclerc, he did nothing to stop it. Dessalines later blamed Louverture for his own capture, arguing that the former governor "had the fatal weakness to believe in the sincerity of the promises of Bonaparte's envoy."[176] While he was not willing to actively participate in the arrest, Dessalines understood the event as one of Louverture's own making.

Leclerc assigned the task to Brunet and battalion chief d'Esquidoux.[177] According to Louverture's memoir, Brunet tried to trick him and his wife into a meeting. "This I will repeat to you, general," Louverture recalled Brunet's letter stating, "you will never find a friend more sincere than I, in the confidence of the captain general, in love for all who are subordinate to him and you will enjoy tranquility."[178] Brunet had planned to wait for Dessalines to return to the Georges plantation from Cap-Français, and claimed that Louverture "is not suspicious of me."[179]

He was wrong. Louverture suspected that Brunet was conspiring against him, and he showed up unexpectedly at the Georges plantation on June 7. "Pushed to his limit by their insolence," Boisrond-Tonnerre recounted, "this general mounted his horse with the goal of going to complain."[180] Brunet seized the opportunity. While Louverture was in the main house of the plantation, Brunet exited and ordered a squadron leader to seize Louverture and his guards.[181]

"O! The infamy! What treason!" Louverture exclaimed.[182] Louverture was furious to have been treated like a criminal, especially because Brunet had promised that he was safe.[183] "It was in this state," Boisrond-Tonnerre lamented, "that they embarked and conducted to Cap this unfortunate and too gullible leader whom they did not even deign to tell the reasons for his arrest."[184] Two days later Leclerc announced Louverture's arrest, claiming, "The general TOUSSAINT did not want to enjoy the Amnesty that was granted to him; he continued to Conspire; he was going to reignite the civil War; and I had to arrest him."[185] Leclerc also noted that he had proof of Louverture's conspiracy and that there was nothing else to worry about for those who had put down their weapons.[186]

Leclerc claimed that Dessalines had provided him with the evidence on his recent trip to Cap-Français. "He [Louverture] had sent one of his accomplices to general Dessalines," Leclerc wrote in a proclamation published in the colonial newspaper, "to urge him not to surrender in good faith; the general Dessalines declared this to me."[187]

From prison in France, Louverture contradicted these assertions, demanding to see the alleged proof that Leclerc claimed to have. "We will see if the lie and the slander that he vomited against me," Louverture argued in his *Mémoires,* "we will see that the general dessaline [*sic*] surrendered following my orders while the general leclere [*sic*] said that I only surrendered after the surrender of general dessaline; why did general leclere not follow the order that had been established for a long time?"[188]

Remarkably, noted one French general, Pamphile de Lacroix, the Saint-Domingue population reacted to the news of Louverture's arrest and deportation with surprising indifference. "They did not appear to miss the man who had been for so long their idol," Lacroix wrote, "they even showed themselves to be apathetic to his fate." But perhaps this apathy was a performance. "This indifference, which was too great not be an affect," Lacroix concluded, "contributed in no small part to the confidence that the General Leclerc had in the good intentions of most of the Black officers."[189] On his way back from Cap-Français, Dessalines spoke with Sylla, who had rebelled at the news of Louverture's arrest, and implored him to return to order.[190] Sylla refused. Dessalines also visited Brunet at the Georges plantation, and his officers harassed Brunet into giving them some of the money that had been confiscated from Louverture's plantation.[191] He later requested that Louverture's horses, staff, and guides be incorporated into his own division.[192]

At this point Dessalines was in a dangerous position. If he wavered in his professed commitment to the French expeditionary army, his position and life were at risk.[193] Dessalines continued to blame Louverture for his deportation, believing that the former governor-general had let himself be duped by the French. Before Louverture's arrest and deportation, Dessalines had remained steadfast in his public commitment to Leclerc's expeditionary army. According to Boisrond-Tonnerre's account, however, the moment of Louverture's arrest was the "flash of light [*coup de lumière*] for Dessalines," when his rebellion against the French now seemed inevitable.[194] He only had to bide his time.

CHAPTER 7

I Will Remedy It by Force

By August 1, 1802, an insurrection was brewing in the region—at least, so claimed Citizen Cabal, the "capitaine du port de St. Marc"—and Dessalines was at the center of it. "Dessaline [*sic*] is the worst person on earth," Cabal told General Rochambeau. "He at least knows everything that is going on, if he is not secretly directing it." Rather than making an example of Black insurgents, Cabal argued, Dessalines let them off the hook, including one of the men recently arrested in Saint-Marc. Even more worrisome for the French was that Dessalines was hosting nighttime meetings with "various scoundrel officers," including his longtime companion Louis Gabart. "The judgement that I pass on this *nègre* general," Cabal concluded, "who I see from time to time and who I never cease to observe, is that he is unhinged, deceitful to excess and that he has an ulterior motive, far from being surrendered to the government."[1]

In fact, it may have been Dessalines's hatred for Rochambeau that was pushing him toward defection. As Louverture had predicted in May 1802, the two were not a good fit. Rochambeau antagonized Dessalines, distrusted him, and continued to spy on him. Cabal recommended to Rochambeau that he consult with Hautière, a French captain who had been placed as Dessalines's aide-de-camp to spy on him, to confirm his claims.[2]

The simmering conflict surfaced when Rochambeau ordered the execution of several officers and soldiers from the national guard in Saint-Marc, who were under Dessalines's command.[3] On August 1 Dessalines's chief of staff notified

Rochambeau that the executions had taken place, but evidently the letter did not reach him promptly.[4] "I cannot hide from you," Rochambeau told Dessalines on August 4—perhaps thinking of Cabal's letter—"that your conduct lacks strength, lacks energy, and does not correspond in any manner to what we should expect."[5] He warned Dessalines that he would have to report to Leclerc about his purported bad behavior. "It is with facts and not promises," he advised Dessalines, "that we make ourselves worthy of his benefaction."[6]

At the end of the letter was an appended postscript, which acknowledged that Dessalines had in fact punished the prisoners according to Rochambeau's orders. Yet he sent the letter anyway as a gratuitous jab to undermine Dessalines's place in the French military.[7] Rochambeau then forwarded Cabal's letter to Leclerc and noted that this evidence "confirms for me even more what I already knew about Dessalines and those around him."[8] Rochambeau concluded that it was high time to arrest him. He called Dessalines a deceitful man (*homme faux*) and a hypocrite, arguing that "there is no hope for tranquility with men like this, since it is obvious that they have not for an instant been in good faith."[9]

In the months after Louverture's arrest and deportation, the French rightfully distrusted Dessalines and were never fully convinced of his loyalty. Rochambeau in particular doubted him, and perhaps that was why Dessalines was assigned to his jurisdiction. When Dessalines returned to Saint-Marc after his meeting with Leclerc in Cap-Français in early June 1802, he boasted about his good relationship with the general in chief, emphasizing Leclerc's welcome reception.[10] Others supported Dessalines in his efforts to assuage Rochambeau's skepticism. "He [Dessalines]," General Martial-Besse told Rochambeau, "appears to be infinitely flattered by the reception that the General in chief gave him in Cap."[11] Brunet joined the chorus of reassurance with his own letter to Rochambeau: "Dessalines is happy with Toussaint's arrest, from whom he never received anything but expressions of ingratitude. He reiterated a hundred times the assurance of his entire devotion to the orders of the French government."[12] Even Leclerc tried to convince Rochambeau of Dessalines's loyalty, or at least of his utility. "You know about Toussaint's arrest," Leclerc wrote to Rochambeau from Cap-Français. "Dessalines was here when we were told about it, I am happy enough with him, he will serve you well for the disarmament."[13] "Dessalines exalting the ardor of his companions," Haitian historian Jules Rosemond claimed, "won the respect of the Napoleonic army."[14] But whether it was respect or practicality, Dessalines successfully convinced the French that he was necessary.

Nevertheless, Rochambeau remained sure that Dessalines's ultimate plan was to rebel, which was likely true. But Leclerc assumed he could use Dessalines to expedite his mission to return the colony to French control. In fact Dessalines was simply biding his time and carefully ensuring his own safety within the French expeditionary army. In mid-1802 he was in no position to launch a war for independence.

In the months following Louverture's deportation, Dessalines spent most of his time traveling throughout the region that bordered the divisions of the north and the Artibonite with a mostly Black unit. They were scouring the woods (*fouiller les bois*) for "rebels" or *brigands,* confiscating their guns and sending at least some of them to his superiors in Plaisance.[15] He and his troops focused on the regions around Gros Morne, Pilate, Plaisance, and Limbé; they knew the mountains well and were in shape to traverse them. European troops would not have been able to survive.

In these campaigns Dessalines fought against both some of his former colleagues who refused to join the French expedition (like Sylla), and against independent revolutionary leaders who had previously resisted Louverture's authority (men such as Mathieu, Macaya, Comus, Zéphirin, Léveillé, and Paul Ballerat).[16] During his time in the French expeditionary army, it is likely that Dessalines targeted specific rebels whom he viewed as threats to his own leadership, particularly those whom the French called "Congos"—a term that in the context of the Leclerc expedition had taken on a new meaning and referred to autonomous revolutionary leaders, many of whom were African-born.[17] The term, however, was not exclusively used to describe people who were considered *brigands* and the context mattered. While attacking potential rivals, Dessalines likely also planned for his own eventual defection by supplying allies with weapons and hiding munitions depots in the mountains, out of reach and undetectable by the French army.[18] Despite his professions of loyalty, Dessalines was calculating a dramatic and decisive blow against his enemies.

In undertaking these jobs, Dessalines developed a reputation among many of the French leaders as exceptionally effective. "Confidence appears to have been renewed in this canton," battalion chief d'Esquidoux argued in June. "The appearance of General Dessaline [*sic*] will contribute a lot to the return to order and tranquility."[19] The next week Brunet told Leclerc that he needed Dessalines deployed to a particularly disruptive region called Champagne that lay inland and west of Cap-Français: "I believe that General Dessalines's presence will be necessary in that damned district."[20] Dessalines used his violent reputation to secure obedience from soldiers and workers and alliances with other military leaders, aiming to convince the French that he was necessary for their multistage

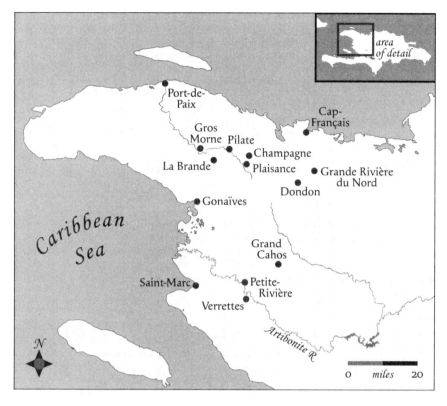

Map of the Artibonite and the north of Saint-Domingue. Drawn by Rebecca Wrenn.

plan for subduing the colony. In his reports he emphasized the effectiveness of these methods, claims which his French commanding officers then repeated. A brigadier chief even reported that in terms of subduing the rebels, Dessalines alone was more effective than a column of two hundred soldiers.[21]

But the French understood that Dessalines's effectiveness could be turned against them. So they sometimes sent captured insurgents to him for execution, in an attempt to alienate Dessalines from the insurgent population.[22] The implication was that he used force or violence to defuse the threat of rebellion, but few of the people reporting on Dessalines's alleged achievements would have witnessed his actions. Rumor and reputation contributed to the narrative of Dessalines's success, a story that he himself crafted for the most part and that his French allies repeated. Regardless of its origin, Dessalines's allegedly unparalleled ability to subdue and punish rebels was the reason that he was still in the colony and not imprisoned on a ship bound for France like Louverture.

The French expeditionary army also tasked Dessalines with demilitarizing the *cultivateurs* and forcing them to be productive plantation laborers.[23] Reports of resistance were coming in from Verrettes, the region inland from Saint-Marc under Charles Bélair's command.[24] Bélair secured the allegiance of the commander Jean-Louis François and gave "the necessary orders for agriculture." He and François disarmed the *cultivateurs*.[25] Dessalines ordered his own troops to carry out similar tasks, assuring Rochambeau that if he encountered any obstacles, "I will remedy it by force."[26]

To assist Dessalines and the other generals with their efforts to force cultivators back to work on their assigned plantations, Leclerc introduced another new labor code. On June 30, 1802, he reaffirmed the military oversight of agricultural production that Louverture had included in his constitution. In addition, he threatened cultivators with punishment if they did not follow orders or if they submitted unjustified complaints.[27] The document also restricted the size of agricultural land to be fifty *carreaux* (about 160 acres) minimum, thereby limiting small-scale agriculture and reinforcing the sugar-centered plantation economy.

By early July Martial-Besse reported that the disarmament campaign in the division of Saint-Marc was well underway, and the regions under Dessalines's control were "perfectly tranquil."[28] "Everything is in order, General," Dessalines told Rochambeau on July 6, "and I pray that you believe that if in the districts under my orders, there formed even the smallest gathering [*rassemblement*], I would have the honor to inform you that they were dispersed, and the leaders were punished for their crimes."[29]

This same month, illness wrecked the French expeditionary army. "I have just learned from the chief general's aide-de-camp," Dessalines wrote Rochambeau, "that you are bedridden & sick, which distresses me greatly. I sincerely wish you a speedy recovery."[30] Dessalines conveyed his and Marie-Claire's well wishes as a form of diplomacy. Not long after, Brunet also fell ill. "I am convinced that if he [Dessalines] knew I was bedridden," Brunet told Leclerc, "he would have already come to offer me his services. I dare say, I have his complete confidence, and that I can make him do whatever I judge appropriate."[31]

Thus Dessalines had effectively convinced Brunet that he was committed to the French expeditionary army. At that moment, however, Dessalines himself was ill, so ill that he could not compose or sign his own letters, and his chief of staff Bazelais notified Rochambeau instead.[32]

Leclerc claimed to be pleased with Dessalines's efforts, but he was wary of the professed allegiance of many of the "colonial" (Black and *mulâtre*) generals.[33]

He commissioned a secret report to assess their loyalties. The anonymous report concluded that both Dessalines and Bélair were "two deceitful men, and cunning, scheming new crimes in the shadows, seeking to deceive us by appearances, and I conclude that it would be very urgent to confirm it."[34] Rochambeau repeated these claims almost verbatim in a letter to Leclerc four days later and assured the general in chief that he would arrest suspected insurgents.[35]

Leclerc was also finding that establishing French "order" in Saint-Domingue was harder than he had presumed. On July 24 he wrote a letter to the minister of the navy, partly in numerical code because of the topic. "Do not think of establishing slavery here before some time," he warned. "After the countless proclamations that I made here to reassure the black people of their liberty, I do not want to contradict myself; but assure the first Consul that my successor will find everything ready."[36]

As Dessalines had suspected when the French expedition first arrived, the French fully intended to reestablish slavery in the colony. It was only a matter of waiting for the right time to do so. Leclerc lied to Dessalines, to other military leaders, and to the cultivators to secure their allegiance. But the implementation of this plan proved to be too much for him. In August 1802 Leclerc began planning for his exit from Saint-Domingue.[37]

Around this time, Dessalines forwarded Rochambeau's patronizing letter to Brunet and detailed his alleged feelings of offense upon reading it. There was no evidence of an insurrection in Saint-Marc, Dessalines argued, and yet Rochambeau had ordered the execution of six former officers of the national guard under suspicion of revolt. Rochambeau had done so without Dessalines's knowledge or consent, while he was bedridden with a fever. Dessalines knew these officers personally and admitted to Brunet that he would have shot them himself if he had discovered any evidence of rebellion.[38] "I did not want, given that you were sick," Dessalines explained to Brunet, "to let you know as my best friend [*meilleur ami*], all of these things and painful sentiments that agitated me, it would have increased your suffering, without alleviating mine."[39] While Dessalines had developed a reputation for excessive violence, his response to Brunet highlights that violent retribution was reserved for circumstances in which Dessalines was convinced that the person or people were deserving of the punishment.

Leclerc might have been planning his own escape, but the French army at large was there to stay. And although Dessalines knew that Rochambeau hated and distrusted him, it is unclear whether he knew about the more widespread opposition to his continued presence in the colony. The officers of the expeditionary army were at odds about how to treat or use Dessalines; Brunet served as an intermediary between Dessalines and other high-ranking officers, placating both parties in an uneasy alliance. Some French officers worried that Brunet had been duped and criticized him for putting blind faith in Dessalines.[40] Dessalines used Brunet for self-preservation and to help secure a reassignment out of Rochambeau's jurisdiction.

Dessalines was deeply frustrated with Rochambeau. He had carried out the general's orders, but still he complained. "The affair should have been finished," Dessalines protested to Brunet, "and his reproaches, not being warranted, should have been suppressed; he did not do it; I am therefore authorized to believe that he only wrote to me to give me trouble." "It is to my best friend only," Dessalines told Brunet, "that I address the narrative of my complaints, it is in his eyes only that I want to justify the accusations that men of passion dare to make; the letter from G'al Rochambeau is the third one of this kind that I have received from him." Dessalines let Brunet know that he wanted to talk with Leclerc about being reassigned, since "I do not want, nor can I remain under the command of a general who does not want to know me, nor respect me."[41]

While waiting for a potential reassignment, Dessalines continued his disarmament duties. On August 11 Brunet's chief of staff, Pierre Thouvenot, ordered Dessalines to focus on the region between Gros Morne and Plaisance and to "annihilate every last one of the bad subjects and to not leave a single trace whatsoever."[42] "It would be desirable to only employ the Colonial troops in the campaigns against the Brigands," Thouvenot advised. "Ours go to the hospital by the dozen and the corps are reduced to nothing."[43] The European (white) troops who had been dispatched for the campaign near Gros Morne were recalled by the French military leadership to their respective quarters, so Dessalines only kept the Black troops with him.[44]

But instead of annihilating the rebels of Gros Morne as ordered, Dessalines—according to Boisrond-Tonnerre—spent this time preparing for his own defection. "Dessalines reorganized the insurrection in Gros Morne and in Plaisance," Boisrond-Tonnerre reported. "In the most dangerous posts in two neighborhoods, he put strong ambushes composed of soldiers and cultivators whom he had armed, and arranged to make French battalions pass through, company by company."[45] Boisrond-Tonnerre's account is plausible, especially since the French expeditionary army removed the European soldiers from Dessalines's unit, enabling him to act covertly.

Furthermore, French assessments of Dessalines's success in "dispersing" the rebels were based on his own accounts of events, so it would have been possible for him to conceal any contradictory movements. For example, Dessalines wrote to Brunet that he had been chasing the *brigands* in the woods in La Brande, south of Gros Morne, since sunrise, reporting that they were completely dispersed. The rebel leader Mathieu, he claimed, feared Dessalines's attack and had fled with his followers (including a group of women) to the region farther north. "It will be difficult for you to see," Dessalines told Brunet, "an idea of the desolation, and the terror that I brought to all these insurgents. Their leaders have lost their minds, and are the first to pressure the *cultivateurs* to return to their plantations. They do not want them, they said, to share the fate that menaces them." To help find the remaining insurgents, Dessalines sent a spy to whom he promised a reward if he found them. Dessalines signed off with words of affection. "Goodbye, my dear general," he told Brunet, "I hope to embrace you soon."[46]

Based on reports like these, Brunet's chief of staff remained convinced that Dessalines was still working for the French. "Dessalines has been hunting the Brigands for 7 days in la Brande," Thouvenot wrote on August 13, "like one chases wild animals. Shooting, the baton, the gallows, are all employed by him every day because of the quality of subjects who fall into his hands. La Brande will remember for a long time the punishments that he administers."[47] Now Brunet ordered Dessalines to find the locations of the remaining insurgents and their munitions, using whatever means necessary, "either by force or with money."[48]

Since Dessalines and his troops were allegedly working relentlessly to support the expedition's mission, on August 14 Brunet requested that they be given a few days' rest before his next attack. "He has done us great services in the arduous march that he recently made," Brunet told Leclerc about Dessalines's recent achievements. "His troops also are in need of a few days rest; he is asking for a little for himself before the disarmament that he is proposing to do in all of the regions which he has traveled."[49] Despite his achievements, Dessalines did not get the rest he requested.[50] Instead he remained camped on a plantation, where he continued to "search all the woods," sometimes claiming to fire on the rebels.[51]

Even though he declared that he had dispersed the insurgents of La Brande, Dessalines said he was frustrated with his progress. "Like you, my dear General," he wrote to Brunet on August 15, "I knew how important it would be to discover the arms depots and the munitions that we thought the insurgents had in the mountains. I used everything to get some information on it. Threats, rewards, neither gave me the slightest indication."[52] He even claimed that he was starting to doubt that these munition stores existed. He sent Brunet sixteen guns, although it is possible that this was a cover to prove that he was disarming the insurgents, when in fact he may have been confiscating munitions for his own purposes.

Even as he planned for his own rebellion, Dessalines still worked to extricate himself from Rochambeau's authority. Dessalines recounted the alleged injustices from his commanding officer to Brunet, who then forwarded the complaints to Leclerc. But he added a warning that if Rochambeau's behavior continued, it might affect their ability to recruit and retain insurgents.[53] "I guarantee Dessalines's fidelity, his zeal and his activity for the service," Brunet concluded, "but I think to get the most out of him, it is necessary to take him out of the Division of G'al Rochambeau, with whom he will never agree."[54] In a second letter on the same day, he told Leclerc that Dessalines had completely "dispersed" the brigands, but that he had not managed to capture any of the leaders. "I remain convinced," he concluded, "that he will get them dead or alive."[55]

Brunet tried to calm and reassure Dessalines, writing that he was certain Dessalines would be reassigned. "Do not worry about these nuisances, my dear General," Brunet told Dessalines, "complete your operation and let me do the rest."[56] The next week Dessalines claimed to have completely disarmed the Champagne valley, but regretted that he only had collected forty or fifty guns. The small number of guns, he told Brunet, reflected the small number of *cultivateurs* currently in the region.[57] He planned to travel south toward Gonaïves, where he intended to capture four insurgents who fought for Sylla, and from whom he hoped he could extract information about the rebel leader's whereabouts. He proposed capturing Figaro, Simon Chatard, Latulipe Saint Amand, and Laurent Saint Amand in a surprise attack at night.[58] The next day Dessalines sent Brunet sixty-six more guns and reported that he had arrested six men who had assassinated a French officer.[59] He alleged that he had them executed in front of an assembly of *cultivateurs,* and expected that "this example will prove to them that the government will never leave crimes unpunished."[60]

Brunet's chief of staff replied with his congratulations for Dessalines's success. "Your remedies are violent," Thouvenot wrote, "but they are indispensable to purge the colony of atrocious scoundrels."[61] Thouvenot enthused to the French general Bertrand Clauzel about Dessalines's efforts: "The General Dessalines works like a god. In three days, Plaisance and its dependencies will be disarmed, the rebels punished, their leaders hanged or shot, or so defeated that they will not be able to do any harm or escape for much longer from the patrols of the gendarmerie."[62] Thouvenot updated the other officers under Brunet's command about Dessalines's movements; yet the chief of staff remained camped in Plaisance and therefore based his analysis and praise entirely on Dessalines's own reports.

Dessalines, however, never captured any of the main rebel leaders in his jurisdiction. Perhaps he was working like a god: but was he cleaning up a mess for the French or laying the groundwork for his defection?

In a summary of Dessalines's recent campaign in the northwest, Brunet reported to Leclerc on August 24 that "the General Dessalines is still doing well: he already sent me 500 guns, and he rid the country of more than a hundred incorrigible scoundrels." Some insurgents had broken their weapons as they fled. Brunet suspected that the leaders had moved farther west, but he assured Leclerc that "more than 300 men or women were beaten by Dessalines for information: none of them could give him any."[63] Once again, French officers repeated up the chain of command Dessalines's carefully crafted stories.

For the next several days, Dessalines passed back through the regions he had searched, intending to return to Plaisance in late August for a few days' rest before heading south to Verrettes. He reported during his final tour of the region that he had found abandoned *ajoupas* (temporary huts built out of branches and leaves) in the mountains, and that one of his captains had collected another sixty-eight guns. He called all of the *cultivateurs* to assembly, shot four "bad subjects," and searched the others.[64] He secured only eight more guns and noted that many of the *cultivateurs* and administrators from the several plantations were missing. "I'm leaving this region today," he reported to Brunet on August 24, "in part to give time to the cultivators to return, they will not do that as long as I am here, and in part because there are no plantain trees, and my troops are suffering infinitely from the deprivation."[65] His plans for resting his troops were interrupted, however, by news of an uprising in Verrettes, part of the region under his command.

On August 20, 1802, twenty-eight men from the national guard of Verrettes testified that Charles Bélair—Dessalines's counterpart in a region neighboring Saint-Marc—had recently defected from the French army and ordered them to rebel.[66] Bélair may have assumed that he would meet a fate similar to Louverture's.[67] Bélair instructed them, they recounted, to unite with the insurgents under Joseph Dessource, Destrade, and Noël Bucquet, at which point Bélair would acquire munitions in Saint-Marc under the guise of marching against them. The goal, the men from the national guard said, was to kill all the white people and their allies. "If they let this moment pass," the men claimed that Bélair had told them, "the white people were going to put them back under Slavery or Kill all those who had served under the orders of Toussaint."[68]

The following day the leader of the national guard unit, Faustin Repussard, wrote to Rochambeau to tell him of Bélair's insurgency. "For four days, I have been chasing the revolted," Repussard reported. "Numerous families and brave people have succumbed to the daggers of the assassins. I captured some of them, all of them agreed in their reports that Charles Belair was the promoter and se-cret instigator of these movements."[69] On August 23, from Saint-Marc, Bazelais wrote to Dessalines with the alarming news. While Bazelais anxiously awaited Dessalines's return, he wrote to Rochambeau to say that he was working with the local commanders to suppress the insurgency.[70] The news spread quickly, and Brunet told Leclerc the following day that Bélair was leading two hundred insurgents.[71]

The French could not afford to lose many troops in battle with Bélair's reb-els. So Leclerc tried diplomacy first, ordering Bélair in a letter to return peace-fully to Cap-Français. He also warned the rebel general that the prompt return of his followers to their stations or plantations was the only way to obtain leni-ency. It was up to Brunet to actually pass the letter on to Bélair, and he used the opportunity to implore his former ally to surrender.[72]

While Brunet wondered how he'd subdue Bélair, he was also obliged to worry about Dessalines, but for a different reason. Given this latest insurgency, Brunet needed to redeploy his forces and so intended to send Dessalines to the Artibonite. He suspected, however, that Rochambeau's petty antagonizing of Dessalines would interfere with the new mission. According to Brunet, Rocham-beau had appointed Auguste Duquesne as commander of the Artibonite, "only placed there to annoy the general Dessalines, and to disrupt what had been done."[73] Similarly, Leclerc's first communication to Rochambeau about the mat-ter also put Duquesne at the center of the conflict. "I have learned citizen gen-eral that Charles Belair is in revolt," Leclerc told Rochambeau. "He was nearly forced to do so by the conduct and the inconsiderate words by the named Duquesne. Dessalines was no more spared than him."[74] Another French general argued that Rochambeau had executed several of the wives of the officers in Bélair's unit, and Bélair responded by deserting the French expeditionary army.[75] For his part, Brunet's chief of staff Thouvenot also named Duquesne as the source of Bélair's rebellion, but included Rochambeau in his analysis. "Rocham-beau behaves clumsily," he told Clauzel. "He irritated Dessalines, Belair, & &. He exercises a despotism that displeases everyone. He appointed the C'n Duquesne who is the terror of this district because of the horrors that he committed with the English during the occupation. How many idiots we have in the Army."[76]

Bélair did not coordinate with Dessalines in his rebellion. Weeks earlier, the secret nighttime meetings that Cabal had observed in Saint-Marc may have been about a possible defection and insurgency against the French; even if so, however, Dessalines and Bélair did not agree on the method or timing. Some have attributed Dessalines and Bélair's contentious relationship to Dessalines's jealousy over Louverture's favoritism to his nephew. Outsiders assumed that one of the two would have succeeded Louverture, and it is likely that both thought that they were the right man for the job.[77] Yet it is also possible that the two disagreed not just about hierarchy but strategy too. After all, although both would ultimately rebel, they failed to work together.

Because it was accepted that Rochambeau's antagonism had led to Bélair's revolt, Leclerc finally pulled Dessalines out from under his command. Now Dessalines was officially in charge of Brunet's former region, Gonaïves, and one of Brunet's chiefs of staff, Haque, was placed under Dessalines's command to serve alongside Dessalines's chief of staff Bazelais, likely as a spy.[78] Dessalines saw through the scheme and isolated Haque.[79]

During the first days of the Bélair insurrection, Dessalines remained unaware of the new battlefront in Verrettes.[80] He regularly updated Brunet on his progress but also cautioned him not to believe unfounded rumors that questioned Dessalines's loyalty to the French government. It is unclear whether these accusations were in connection with the Bélair rebellion (he may have been responding to unrelated rumors that he had been arrested).[81] Dessalines continued collecting weapons, but the number that he forwarded to Brunet was disappointing to the general. Brunet was quick to explain the discrepancy: "If the G'al Dessalines has only sent me 565 guns," he told Leclerc, "it is because he has broken a lot of them, and a lot were thrown in the woods and in the rocks by the brigands as they fled for fear of being caught with their guns, because they knew they would have been shot on the spot."[82]

On August 26 Dessalines finally received a report of Bélair's break with the French. "I am in despair at this news," he told Brunet, "but I ardently desire to contribute to stopping this insurrection. Also my dear General, use me. I am writing to the General-in-chief, to offer him my services again."[83] Dessalines thus exploited the moment of Bélair's defection to affirm his loyalty to France, swearing his "perfect devotion to the French Government."[84] After disarming the region inland of Gonaïves, he promised to return to Plaisance to meet Brunet, and he sent his prisoners to his commanding officer for sentencing.[85] Dessalines clearly believed it was not enough to express his dismay only to Brunet, so he sent a letter directly to Leclerc. "It is with as much pain as astonishment," Dessalines told the French general, "that I learn the news of the recent shameful defection and the cowardly betrayal of the miserable Charles Belair."[86]

On August 27 Brunet prepared to send Dessalines with a detachment from the 13th colonial demi-brigade to arrest Duquesne, the commander whom Rochambeau had appointed to antagonize Dessalines and Bélair. Duquesne had tried to instigate conflict between the Black officers and officers *de couleur* in Saint-Marc—as Bonaparte himself had suggested to Leclerc and Rochambeau—a tactic that perhaps he thought would enable the French to better control the leadership of the colony. Leclerc and Brunet now blamed Duquesne for Bélair's insurrection and regretted that Rochambeau's petty taunts had created a new enemy for the expedition.[87] Conflict between the Black and mixed-race generals, Brunet argued, would not help the French expedition's efforts to regain control over the colony. "They are idiots, imbeciles," Brunet told Leclerc about Duquesne, "those who remember that there were factions, who ruin all our affairs. Our position requires politicking, caution, and all measures that are not, set us back."[88]

Indeed, Bélair's revolution was spreading, and Leclerc grew increasingly desperate. He wrote to Rochambeau on August 27, regretting that he could not send more troops. Another rebellion had broken out in Dondon and Grande Rivière, and he did not have enough men to control that area. Writing in code, he told Rochambeau that "we are not strong enough to crush our enemies. We must limit ourselves at this moment to destroying all those who revolt, if their deaths could have a negative effect, capture them and send them aboard a ship." A vessel was in Rochambeau's department for that express purpose.

Leclerc also warned Rochambeau about the potency of Dessalines's name. Dessalines claimed that the population was terrified of him, so terrified that they would return to "order," working on the plantations. Rochambeau believed that the population was also loyal to the general and would be ready to fight with him as soon as he gave the orders. "Never speak against Dessalines in public," Leclerc advised.[89]

Leclerc's use of code was not unusual. Revolutionaries throughout the Americas were known to have used them in letters to protect their contents should they be intercepted.[90] It is, however, relatively rare to find documents in code from the Haitian Revolution.[91] Leclerc's use of code suggests that he did not know whom he could trust and that he suspected more of his alleged allies would soon defect.

Dessalines inspected his new headquarters at the Georges plantation near Gonaïves and then continued to Petite Rivière.[92] He met with General Pierre Quantin to discuss a plan of action in the likely case that Leclerc's letter to Bélair did not inspire him to surrender.[93] Rumors that Dessalines had been arrested and that Bélair would be next were the principal causes of the uprising, Dessalines told Leclerc in a letter on the same day. "I only need to know my responsibilities," he reassured the general in chief, "by fighting the rebels without pity & returning to this division order and tranquility."[94]

Bélair was currently beyond his jurisdiction, but Dessalines nonetheless requested permission to track the rebel down. "The region that they occupy," he argued to Leclerc, "their numbers, the circumstances, everything necessitates a deployment of force & examples such that the insurrection is annihilated in its entirety."[95] One French general assumed that Dessalines wanted to march against Bélair to evaluate whether his forces were large enough to succeed, in which case Dessalines would join the rebellion.[96] Another French observer claimed outright that Dessalines "had raised up all the *nègres* of the Artibonite to join with Charles."[97] There is little evidence to support the idea that Dessalines would have joined Bélair. But the first claim that Dessalines wanted to assess the rebellion himself makes good sense.

This interpretation is supported by how Dessalines went out looking for Bélair. Rather than bringing his full forces, he led a battalion of only 180 troops from his sans-culottes, a negligible number of white troops, and forty gendarmes; he also requested an additional four to six hundred infantrymen from Leclerc, which was an unrealistic demand.

Before he signed off, Dessalines warned Leclerc about another possible source of opposition in Saint-Marc: several *hommes de couleur* in Saint-Marc were allegedly denouncing Dessalines to avenge Rigaud, arresting people "left and right," and antagonizing Dessalines by seizing his livestock and horses. This was likely the fallout of Duquesne's interference. Dessalines recommended arresting them to stop the "partisan hatreds" (*haines de partis*).[98]

Writing from Petite Rivière, on his alleged mission to find Bélair, Dessalines said that he was continuing his disarmament and return-to-the-plantations efforts. He declared that he had easily convinced 180 *cultivateurs* to return to work. "On the response that I gave them," he reported to Brunet, "on the assurance that I made of the intentions of the government with respect to them, all of them made me listen to their protest of devotion and their promise to return peacefully to their plantations; and all were reminded that when you were in Gonaïves, they were calm and happy."[99] All was quiet on the right bank of the Artibonite, Dessalines assured Brunet.

Because he had not received any response from Bélair, Dessalines on September 3 gathered only about 350 men from his sans-culottes and various other units. He sent a contingent under the direction of Gabart to chase Bélair in the north, while he went to the east of Verrettes to track down Bélair's accomplice, Larose, commander of the 8th colonial demi-brigade and a man who had previously served under Dessalines. Dessalines's spies had informed him that Larose had broken off from Bélair. Dessalines then received word that Bélair was back in the region, and he headed even farther east toward Grand Cahos. He requested munitions and reinforcements from Saint-Marc and Gonaïves.[100] He planned to march against Bélair to ensure "his and his party's destruction."[101]

Dessalines signed off a lengthy report to Brunet with a promise of fidelity. "Believe, my General," he asked Brunet, "that I will always find myself happy when I can serve the government and prove to it that I will never be a perjurer."[102] While making his rounds in the plains, he secured the allegiance of 180 men by assuring them of Leclerc's good intentions.[103] Quantin supported Dessalines in his mission by publishing news of Dessalines's recent disarmament efforts and even proactively notifying the units in Saint-Marc that Dessalines was currently marching against Bélair, Larose, and several other insurgents and their followers. "If those and their partisans persist in their rebellion," Quantin announced, "the General Dessalines proposes & permits their extermination. I take it upon myself to publicize this operation of the Division General Dessalines as testimony of the high esteem & consideration that the entire army and the good citizens of St. Domingue owe him."[104]

But a different account of events emerges from the correspondence of Brig. Gen. Wladyslaw Jablonowski, a Polish officer in the French expeditionary army, who contradicted Quantin's assertion of Dessalines's loyalty.[105] While Dessalines claimed to have convinced 180 insurgents to put down their weapons, Jablonowski contended that "none of these brigands have laid them down." Dessalines's troops, Jablonowski wrote, had burned down the gallows in Petite Rivière. "I would certainly not have confronted Dessalines head on, I would have used him," Jablonowski concluded. "I would have spared him; but I never would have put unlimited trust in him. He overtly protects scoundrels and seeks to render honest people suspect."[106]

On September 5, after attacking Plassac, Dessalines received an envoy from

Larose asking him for a private meeting. Instead Dessalines showed up with his aide-de-camp, his chief of staff, a battalion chief, and a few dragoons, with his infantry not far behind. Larose shouted orders and threats at Dessalines, which angered him. "He approached, trembling, within firing range," Dessalines recounted to Brunet, "and perceiving that I had anticipated the trap that he had set, he answered my reproaches and questions by stammering."[107] The officers of the 8th demi-brigade immediately abandoned Larose and defected to Dessalines's side, telling Dessalines that they did not support the rebel.

Larose spurred his horse to action and escaped at full speed. Dessalines chased him until it was too dark to continue. The next day he discovered that Larose had fled all the way south to Mirebalais to unite with the rebel leader Lamour Dérence. After a day and a half of intense chase, Dessalines returned north to help fight Bélair, because Larose was now out of his jurisdiction. He brought with him the soldiers and officers from the 8th who had defected from Larose's rebellion. "Peace and tranquility reign now in the plain of the Artibonite," Dessalines reported, "and the insurrectionary fire that the brigand la Rose fomented, who ordered those who did not follow him in his criminal revolt to be shot, was extinguished as quickly as it had started in the Grand and Petit Cahos."[108]

Bélair may have been coordinating with Larose, but he was also collaborating with his wife, Sanite. One of the French reports for the expedition had described Sanite Bélair as "an extremely wicked [*mauvais*] woman, constantly animated against them [white people] and provoking her husband to the most glaring injustices."[109] About a month and a half earlier, Bélair had requested permission to go to Cap-Français to tend to family affairs, and Dessalines supported his request.[110] His trip may have been to retrieve Sanite. Many of the generals' wives traveled with their spouses during battles, but Sanite Bélair sometimes fought alongside her husband, and the pair were ideologically opposed to white rule in the colony.[111] Few details are known about her participation in the rebellion, but Dessalines viewed her as a threat. "I am very keen on capturing his tiger of a wife," Dessalines told Leclerc, "who is always thirsty for blood!"[112]

Despite Dessalines's efforts to quell the rebellion, Jablonowski continued to blame him for Bélair's actions. "I beg you to believe," he told Rochambeau, "that Belair would no longer exist if his demise was up to me."[113] He claimed that Bélair had passed through the right bank of the Artibonite River precisely because that was Dessalines's jurisdiction. But Dessalines remained protected; Brunet and Quantin both made assurances of his loyalty, and Leclerc himself thought that he was still necessary for their mission.

Meanwhile Dessalines prepared to march against Bélair in the Cahos mountains. He divided his troops into two columns of sans-culottes, which would coordinate with the European and colonial infantries. Before Dessalines arrived, Repussard, leading the first column cavalry, discovered Sanite Bélair hiding in some tall grass and took her into his custody.[114] Upon learning of his wife's capture, Charles Bélair surrendered to Repussard. Dessalines learned of their capture on September 6.[115] He confronted his former colleague where he was being held and then took the Bélairs to Petite Rivière.

While the Bélairs were in his custody, Dessalines demanded that Charles recognize him as the *chef* of a possible united insurgent army; this was alleged by the French general Pamphile de Lacroix. But when Bélair was unwilling to submit, Dessalines sent him to Cap-Français, "so that the captain General can decide their fate."[116] Lacroix's account may have been shaped by the knowledge of later events, but he suggested that had Bélair conceded to Dessalines's orders, the two might have collaborated in rebellion.

Dessalines publicly claimed he was pleased with Bélair's arrest and took credit for quelling the rebellion. "In five days," he wrote to Brunet, "I stopped, by my marches and the deployment of my various forces, an insurrection that was taking on a hallucinating character and that was going to envelop one of the most beautiful parts of the colony." He did, however, offer a mild defense of his former colleague, suggesting that the rebellion may not have been Bélair's idea. "There are different versions of *Charles's* story," he told Brunet, "and it is said that *Larose* was the leader. Since Charles surrendered willingly and that he did not show any resistance I thought that it was important to send him to the Captain General so that we can get clarification on a revolt that did not seem to have been spur of the moment."[117] From Petite Rivière Dessalines brought the Bélairs to Gonaïves and put them on a boat sailing for Cap-Français for questioning and sentencing by Leclerc.[118]

News of Bélair's arrest became public on September 8, 1802, when Quantin announced that Bélair and his troops were in Dessalines's custody. He also praised Dessalines, who he claimed was "unwavering in his fidelity to the R[e-publi]c & the mother country despite the treacherous insinuations at one time spread against this very excellent General officer and no less a very devoted French citizen."[119]

Soon after, Leclerc published his own account that included a letter from Dessalines dated September 10, the same day that he wrote his lengthy report to Brunet about his campaign against Larose and Bélair. In his letter to Brunet, Dessalines had highlighted the uncertainty surrounding Bélair's involvement in the insurrection. However, his letter that Leclerc published expressed confidence of the rebel's ultimate culpability. "I have certain proof that Charles Belair was the leader of the recent insurrection," Dessalines's letter to Leclerc claimed. "This proof was made evident by the officers of the 8th, who appeared to me to be more unhappy than guilty in these events."[120] "God forbid, however, we excuse any of those who dared to revolt against the Government," Dessalines wrote to Leclerc. "I have for all those who followed the scoundrel Charles in his criminal revolt the most profound indignation. It is Charles who ordered the assassination of his secretary in his home and his ferocious wife contributed in no small part to the acts of barbarism that were committed against our unhappy brothers, the friends and defenders of the French Government. Let Charles and his wife be punished accordingly."[121]

How can one explain the different approaches in the letters? Because of his closer relationship with Brunet, Dessalines may have tried to ensure some leniency for Bélair, despite their contentious history. Brunet forwarded his letter to Leclerc, and Dessalines likely would have anticipated this.[122] Did Dessalines feel guilty for betraying his longtime colleague? Or was he just playing both sides?

Dessalines was unlikely to show any sympathy for the rebels in a letter to Leclerc, because the Frenchman would interpret it as wavering in his commitment to France. Dessalines likely prioritized self-preservation at the expense of a political rival. It is also possible that Dessalines wrote to Brunet before his alleged conversation with Bélair, during which the rebel refused to recognize Dessalines's leadership, and that he wrote the letter to Leclerc after the conversation.

Finally, Leclerc may have edited the letter before publishing it, thus linking Dessalines more solidly with the French expedition and against any insurrections. The most emphatic claims regarding Bélair's involvement had come from Repussard, both at the beginning of the insurrection and in his capture. Instead of any of Repussard's letters, however, Leclerc chose to publish the letter from Dessalines.

Perhaps this choice was an attempt to isolate Dessalines from any opposition to the French expeditionary forces, and to undermine the widespread loyalty to the general.[123] Leclerc had taken a similar approach when he publicly folded Dessalines into his scheme to arrest and deport Louverture. He may have fabricated evidence so that he could do the same with Charles Bélair. It is more likely, however, that Dessalines knew his audience and was willing to sacrifice Bélair and his wife as he waited for a more opportune moment for defection.

"Charles Belair was shot with his wife," Boisrond-Tonnerre wrote. "The resolve of this couple astonished the executioners who sentenced them."[124]

Almost immediately after Bélair and Larose's rebellion, Dessalines returned to his assigned disarmament campaign.[125] Leclerc claimed he was pleased with the general's recent operations, which he publicized in an *ordre du jour,* but it was essential, Brunet told him, to disarm the cultivators without delay.[126] The French campaigns for complete control, however, remained largely unsuccessful. Other Black leaders deserted the French expeditionary army, including Jean-Baptiste Sans Souci in Grande Rivière and Dondon, and Macaya and Capoix in Port-de-Paix.[127] Sans Souci's troops, Lacroix reported, "continually harassed our posts, they keep them in an anxiety that is so exhausting that it contributes in no small way to increasing the ravages wrought by sickness."[128] Moreover, men, women, and children took over the mountains of the north, and many *cultivateurs* joined the insurgents. Thouvenot encouraged the French officers to "work the brigands *à la Dessalines,*" likely a reference to Dessalines's alleged use of violence to quell dissent.[129]

Leclerc repeated his praise for Dessalines in a letter to Bonaparte himself on September 16, claiming that "Dessalines is at this moment the butcher of the black people," but also reporting that he had assigned two aides to spy on Dessalines. Leclerc reminded Bonaparte that he was sick and wanted to leave Saint-Domingue. He again asked him to send a successor, because he did not recommend any of the existing generals, including Rochambeau, to take over the leadership of the colony.[130] Although Leclerc told Bonaparte that he used Dessalines "to execute all the odious measures," he noted that he would only "keep him as long as I need him."[131]

Leclerc had always been wary of Dessalines's loyalty. But now even Brunet was starting to waver. Brunet wanted to make clear to Leclerc that he was not being reckless in his evaluation of Dessalines's position. "Do not think, my general," he told Leclerc, "that I have in dessalines a blind confidence."[132] He wrote the second half of that claim in a simple alphabetic code. "I know that you need him," he continued, switching out of coded writing, "& that if you do not have a man of his temper and character we would need to find one or create one in order to finish what needs to be done in the colony." Brunet probably believed that the rebels who might intercept the letter were illiterate or semiliterate (as many people suspected or claimed about Dessalines), and therefore he thought that even a simple code would have prevented or delayed their reading of the document.

Dessalines's reputation among the French as a ruthless enforcer protected him for the time being. "Here is my opinion of him. He has put all his confidence in me, & his support in you," Brunet concluded. "I will make him do everything," he promised. "He has a lot of self-confidence; he loves his country; he wants freedom, or what he believes to be the freedom of his color: the mention of slavery will undoubtedly make him revolt. I approve of everything that he has proposed to me, but I know how to make him do what I want, especially when he is with me."[133]

Brunet was wrong about his ability to make Dessalines do whatever he wanted. But he was correct that the return of slavery would push Dessalines to revolt.

CHAPTER 8

It Is Time to Teach the French That They Are Monsters

Only one month after Dessalines helped defeat Bélair's uprising, General Pierre Quantin in Saint-Marc received a remarkable letter from him. The letter itself has yet to be uncovered, but Quantin's response implied that Dessalines had asked him as a friend and fellow soldier to join him in rebellion. Dessalines apparently argued that he was rebelling because of rumors circulating that France would soon reimpose slavery in Saint-Domingue. Over the previous months, Quantin and Dessalines had worked well together, and Dessalines respected the French general because Quantin opposed slavery. Because of their friendship, Dessalines was not willing to attack him without giving him fair warning and a chance to escape.

"Someone must have made you sign the letter, general, without reading you the contents!" Quantin wrote to Dessalines, "at least that's what I want to believe, my friend."[1] Quantin's suspicion that Dessalines did not write his letters reflected the common beliefs that he was illiterate and that his secretaries wrote his correspondence. Quantin closed his brief response with a long postscript. "I would be the first to lay down my weapons if it is true that I am a tool of the return of slavery," he wrote, and he guaranteed that Dessalines was mistaken.[2]

The next day Dessalines responded to Quantin. He claimed that the "people of Saint Domingue" had truly believed that the French were "animated by the principle of Liberty" when they arrived on their shores earlier in 1802. But they had sadly been mistaken. "By what fatality do we now clearly see," Dessalines wrote, "that its intentions are different."³ "I am French, friend of my country and of liberty," he went on. "I cannot see with a dispassionate eye such atrocities."

Dessalines tied the ideal of liberty to France and claimed legitimacy based on his true defense of the European nation. He argued that he was defecting from Leclerc's army, but not from France. The struggle in Saint-Domingue, he believed, was a battle over legitimacy within the French Republic. Dessalines was not yet aiming for political independence. He encouraged Quantin to board a ship bound for France, because he intended to take the city of Saint-Marc "either willingly or by force." "I will defend myself as a true soldier," Dessalines concluded, "a friend of freedom and of his country."⁴ He sent off the letter to Quantin and prepared to march against Saint-Marc and against his former ally.

So much had changed in just a few weeks. As the dust had settled after the Bélair rebellion, Leclerc became increasingly suspicious of Dessalines. On September 26, 1802, he wrote to Napoléon Bonaparte again, now noting a change in Dessalines's behavior.⁵ "One month ago, in the expeditions that I ordered him to undertake," Leclerc observed, "he destroyed the rebels' weapons. Today, he does not destroy them anymore and he no longer mistreats the black people, like he did before."⁶

Leclerc even hinted at a revelation he must have been loath to admit, even to himself: that throughout his campaign against Bélair, Dessalines might have been stockpiling weapons for himself. One French officer worried that previously Louverture had hidden up to 150,000 stores of gunpowder, and that now Dessalines had done the same. "The General Leclerc was well aware," the officer wrote, "that Toussaint never ceased for ten years to preach to the Black people that their freedom depended on the preservation of their weapons; he similarly knew that he [Toussaint] had advised the Black people to use them the day their white officers demanded them; because such a demand could only ever signal the return of slavery."⁷

The day after Leclerc wrote the letter to Bonaparte, Brunet's chief of staff Thouvenot contradicted these claims in a lengthy summary for another general of Dessalines's recent actions against the rebels. Dessalines and eight hundred troops from the sans-culottes and 8th colonial demi-brigades (the latter was Larose's former unit), Thouvenot insisted, were working hard day and night to defeat the rebels in the woods and mountains near Marmelade. Thouvenot also noted that Dessalines had told Brunet that "these two units were very tired and that a lot of them were sick. He asked for remuneration for the 4th who were nearly naked."[8] Dessalines's troops did not receive permission to rest, however, and they continued their attacks with reinforcements from Gonaïves.[9]

Already, then, some of Dessalines's powerful allies were beginning to suspect him of treachery. This concern only accelerated in early October 1802, when several men from another French Caribbean colony, Guadeloupe, escaped imprisonment as their ship anchored in Cap-Français.[10] The escapees brought the Black residents of Saint-Domingue a warning: slavery was returning to the French empire.[11] The men from Guadeloupe carried a copy of a French law from May 20, 1802, which affirmed the legality of slavery in the parts of the empire that had previously been under British occupation, and where French abolition had therefore never gone into effect. Leclerc had tried to hide the law by preventing its publication in Saint-Domingue, knowing how it would be interpreted.[12]

While the May law did not apply to Guadeloupe and Saint-Domingue, which had remained in French hands, the law made clear that slavery and the slave trade were once again legal in parts of the French empire. In fact, unbeknownst to the escapees from the ship, a July 1802 consular decree had re-legalized slavery in Guadeloupe and other French territories.[13]

Uncertainty quickly gave way to fear and dread as the voices supporting slavery multiplied and grew louder in France and echoed in Saint-Domingue. "I want slaves in our colonies," the French colonial minister, Denis Decrès, wrote in a report. "Liberty is a food for which the stomachs of the negroes are not yet prepared. We must seize any occasion to give them back their natural food, except for the seasonings required by justice and humanity."[14] With such voices in France, and the May proclamation now in hand, people in Saint-Domingue understood that their freedom was precarious, and the door was now open to the possibility of the expansion of slavery everywhere.

Abolition—the cause for which they had fought, and for which their family, friends, and colleagues had died—could be undone. Pro-slavery factions had taken over the French government, and they no longer embraced and took credit for the ideal of universal freedom.

The slavery rumors exacerbated an increasingly tense situation in the colony. Leclerc had continued his mission to disarm the "brigands," and it was a violent process. Resistance to the French army was growing as more and more troops defected and escaped to the mountains to join the insurgents, where they encamped in small groups, using the woods as cover for ambushes. They were mostly men, but some women participated too.[15] To sustain themselves, the rebels stole food from the plantations that they attacked and then burned the fields, houses, and mills to the ground before returning to the hills.[16]

Leclerc had come to believe that all Black soldiers and officers—including Dessalines—were traitors or potential traitors. On several occasions, Leclerc rounded up hundreds of Black troops and had them executed under suspicion of conspiracy.[17] He assumed that these public displays of force would make his soldiers and officers reluctant to challenge the French army. It had the opposite effect.

The signs pointing to a general rebellion were everywhere. Some French officers—paranoid that rebels might attack through the woods surrounding them—ordered plantation laborers and Black prisoners to cut down trees to clear their field of vision. Consequently, some regions were completely deforested.[18]

In addition to the French fears of uprisings, there was now a growing chorus of French complaints focused on soldiers' illness and inadequate supplies. The rainy season was brutal for the unseasoned French soldiers, and illness spread rapidly through the ranks. Leclerc was losing 130 soldiers per day to yellow fever alone—he estimated this in early October, when the news from Guadeloupe broke—and he had fewer than four thousand white troops who were fit for combat.[19]

Leclerc explained to Bonaparte that his hopes for the future of the colony were dwindling. His troops were dying in battle and in the temporary camps and hospitals that dotted the colony. The rebels knew this, and exhausted the French further by leading them on chases through the harsh terrain of the mountainous interior.

Leclerc realized that the insurgency was growing rapidly; everywhere he looked, he saw signs of open rebellion. He told Bonaparte that they needed to kill all the revolutionaries, even those who were now their allies.[20] The French were making an all-out, last-gasp effort to assert their political and racial control of Saint-Domingue. Their tactics were increasingly repugnant, and their desperation was obvious. Now was the time for the Black soldiers to turn against them and take back control of the island.

Slowly the weakened French realized that the reinforcements they had been promised were not coming.[21] As a solution, desperate local leaders recruited white colonists, reversing an earlier policy of disarming the local elite.[22] Leclerc ordered all male merchants and planters between the ages of sixteen and fifty, regardless of race or nationality, to join the war effort under the national guard, with the specific goal of defending the port cities.[23]

Even faced with an uphill battle, Brunet faithfully voiced his certainty of success. He was increasingly worried, however, about Dessalines's loyalty and continued to write about the general in alphabetical code, in case his letters fell into any of the Black officers' hands. The code itself was simple, much easier to crack than Leclerc's numerical code. Brunet used the alphabetical letter following the intended letter (for example, "*révolte*" was "sfwpmuf"), and he often shortened Dessalines's name to "eftt . . . . . ." or merely "D . . ."[24] Writing to Leclerc, Brunet claimed that Dessalines was loyal to the general, but that his hatred of Rochambeau could provoke Dessalines into leaving the army. "If you were no longer in the colony," Brunet warned Leclerc, "he would no longer want to serve."

Dessalines's recent victories in a series of skirmishes had, Brunet reported to Leclerc, further elevated his reputation and fueled his ego.[25] The French needed him, and he knew it. But Dessalines was also worried, Brunet sensed, because a massive uprising was underway, and he believed that the French were losing ground.

In a conversation the night before Brunet wrote the letter, Dessalines had told him that the French needed to take *grandes mesures* (extreme measures) to effectively subdue the rebellion. "He is certainly not a friend of the blacks [*ami des noirs*]," Brunet concluded. The Amis des Noirs had been France's main abolitionist organization. Brunet's choice of words, therefore, implied that Dessalines was neither a rebel ally nor a supporter of universal freedom. In the context of the reestablishment of legal slavery elsewhere in the Caribbean, the word choice mattered. Brunet argued that just as the French had relied on Toussaint Louverture, they could count on Dessalines to "bring back the peace": to once again subdue the rebellion and return the laborers to their assigned plantations.

The next day Brunet wrote to Leclerc again, still using code interspersed with normal alphabetical handwriting. He reported that the rebels had crossed to the northern bank of the Artibonite River to attack the plantations, and Dessalines had gone to the region to reestablish order with the regiment from Saint-Marc.[26] "I made two columns of the small army that I had," Dessalines told Brunet, "because of my good guides, who I brought, I found them. I completely defeated them."[27] He collected thirteen guns and chased after the insurgents, all recent defectors from the French expeditionary army, who dispersed in the woods.

Like Brunet, the French general Pamphile de Lacroix also believed that Dessalines still supported the French army. He recapped Dessalines's actions in the

IT IS TIME TO TEACH THE FRENCH

Artibonite and his subsequent meeting with Leclerc, to whom he "renew[ed] his protests of fidelity and devotion."[28] Yet it was this precise meeting between Dessalines and Leclerc in early October, ironically, that set Dessalines's defection in motion. According to Brunet, Dessalines had asked for the meeting to give Leclerc "a plan (these were his words) to save the colony."[29] In actuality, he needed Leclerc to believe his allegiance was real because he was requesting money and ammunition that he would need for his defection. He also needed time to coordinate with other leaders. "I'm thirsty for the blood of the rebels," Dessalines allegedly told Leclerc.[30] "That day he seemed to give rise to all his indignation," Lacroix claimed, "and that the agitation of his limbs showed his rage even more than his words. The General in chief told him with certainty that the troops that he was expecting from France would put him in a position to strike a terrible blow. *It must,* cried Dessalines furiously, *be a complete earthquake.*"[31]

Dessalines must have been convincing, because Leclerc approved the transfer of military supplies despite his earlier wariness of Dessalines's allegiance, and he gave Dessalines new marching orders. He was to lead six thousand Black troops to kill the dissidents. Meanwhile, the white troops would take control of the coastal towns.[32] In other words, the Black soldiers would take on the most dangerous and difficult tasks, while the white soldiers camped in the fortified cities. As a second phase of the plan, Leclerc intended to disband all the Black regiments and disperse the soldiers among the white regiments—at which point it would be easier to kill them.[33]

Having secured further support and credulity from Leclerc, Dessalines now needed to rally allies. Perhaps most difficult, he had to unite the historically antagonistic colonial factions of the military leadership, mainly those who had been free before the abolition of slavery (*anciens libres*) and those who had been freed by the 1793 decree (*nouveaux libres*).

After his meeting with Leclerc—giving him no sign of his true intentions—Dessalines departed Cap-Français with the sans-culottes and headed directly east to Petite-Anse, a small town on the coast just past the outskirts of Cap-Français.[34] His wife Marie-Claire Heureuse, who had previously been camped on the Georges plantation, was with him, traveling with her luggage on a *cabrouet*, a small two-wheeled cart pulled by an ox or a mule.[35] She was likely traveling with Dessalines for safety, since the French imprisoned, killed, and deported rebels' families during the war. Marie-Claire had already been captured and imprisoned once, so she stayed close to her husband and his troops.

In Petite-Anse, Dessalines met with Alexandre Pétion, a general from the south whom he had fought against during the civil war, and who had returned to the colony from France with the Leclerc expedition. Their relationship was strained, but Dessalines knew he needed Pétion's support to ensure the allegiance of the *hommes de couleur*. This was a necessary collaboration if they hoped to defeat the French.[36] Although the French had successfully exploited the conflict between them, Dessalines made clear to Pétion that their interests were aligned and they had to work together to succeed. Dessalines showed Pétion his orders from Leclerc to secure the coastal towns and disband the colonial units, and, after reading them, Pétion agreed to fight for freedom.[37]

Soon after Dessalines left Cap-Français, however, Leclerc had second thoughts about giving him the military supplies. After a massive desertion from the colonial units, Leclerc issued an order for Dessalines's arrest. But, although he didn't know it yet, it was too late. Dessalines's plan was already underway.[38]

Desperate to assuage the fears that slavery was returning to the colony, Leclerc organized a fancy ball at the government palace in Cap-Français for the officers of his army. This was a common tactic that Leclerc used to secure the allegiance of Black and mixed-race leaders. On October 12 army officials gathered in the halls of the palace. They ate, listened to music, and danced, even while a rebellion brewed in the hills nearby.[39]

At the soirée, the officers of color appeared nervous. Concerned, Leclerc's wife, Pauline (who was Bonaparte's sister), asked what the matter was. It was Clervaux who replied, saying that although he had personally been free long before the Haitian Revolution, he was nevertheless against slavery. "If I believed that there was ever a question of slavery here," he insisted to the sister of the most powerful man in France, then "in an instant I would become a brigand."[40]

The officers' demeanor at the party heightened Leclerc's suspicions that a rebellion was imminent. He decided to focus on defending the city of Cap-Français itself, assembling the remaining Black units, the national guard, and foreign merchants in the region. But their numbers were small, however: fewer than two thousand soldiers.[41]

Two days after the ball in Cap-Français, the rebellion broke into view. The troops of the 10th and 13th colonial demi-brigades descended from the hills of Haut-du-Cap under the cover of night and attacked.[42] They were led by none other than Pétion, the former commander of the south during the civil war, who had just allied with Dessalines, and Clervaux, the officer who had confronted Pauline Leclerc at the ball. The two had allied with the influential rebel leader

Macaya and increased their ranks with *cultivateurs* from the surrounding plantations. These new rebels were able to overtake several forts on the outskirts of the city.[43] Facing this formidable force, the French could only retreat deeper into the city.

Sixty miles west of Cap-Français, another city was attacked. This was Port-de-Paix, which was quickly occupied by Henry Christophe, who had also allied with the other rebel officers. Meanwhile, Pétion and other defectors and independent revolutionary leaders, including Petit-Noël, continued their attack on Cap-Français. They vastly outnumbered the French, but the French had the defensive advantage of a well-fortressed city, and they staved off the rebels' attacks for the time being.

As his collaborators attacked Cap-Français, Dessalines remained in the west. He was biding his time, even continuing to play the part of a loyal French officer. When he stopped in Plaisance, for example, news had not arrived of his arrest warrant, so he was able to assure the local military administration that he would diligently disband any rebels he encountered. He continued along the route to Gonaïves, and when he was close to Plaisance he distributed guns and cartridges to the plantation laborers—supplies he had recently secured from Leclerc— readying them for revolution.[44]

As Dessalines continued west, he was attacked by independent revolutionary units that still believed he was loyal to France—he was, after all, still pretending that was the case. "Look at my face! Am I white?" Dessalines is alleged to have said to Jacques Tellier. "Do you not recognize the soldier from Crête-à-Pierrot? Was I white at Petite-Rivière de l'Artibonite, on the arrival of the expedition? Interrogate these mountains covered with French skeletons. They will name Dessalines as the hero of these trophies."[45] Tellier let him pass but did not join him.

At this point Tellier was one of the very few to know of the general's defection. Dessalines had only told his inner circle about his plans, for fear that the news would leak. Most of his troops, especially the few white ones, still thought he was loyal to France. As he traveled west, therefore, the Black troops formed Dessalines's front line, while the white troops brought up the rear. The front of the march passed through the mountains relatively unscathed, communicating with the rebels hidden in the woods and conveying their plans. As the white troops came through, Dessalines's new allies ambushed and decimated them.

Continuing to maintain the secrecy of this strategy, Dessalines publicly used these attacks on his white soldiers as evidence that he needed more troops and supplies from Leclerc. He railed against the rebels and promised that he would kill them. All the while, however, Dessalines was secretly collaborating with them.[46]

Back in Cap-Français, Leclerc scrambled. He no longer trusted the loyalty of any Black soldiers and ordered the arrest of all the remaining colonial troops in the city. He forced about a thousand of them onboard ships in the harbor. The French weighted them down and then threw them overboard to drown. The aftermath of this slaughter multiplied its horror, as the bodies washed to shore and lay exposed in the blistering sun.[47]

When Dessalines reached Gros Morne, he encountered an insurrection in progress led by Paul Prompt and Magny, officers who had fought alongside Dessalines at Crête-à-Pierrot.[48] But since he continued to claim allegiance to France, he told his garrison—following his orders from Leclerc—to descend on Gonaïves, a city directly south of Gros Morne along the coast. At the same time, Dessalines tipped off the rebels, coordinating with another Black general, Julien Labarrière, to ambush the French soldiers on their way.[49] The French units from the surrounding areas recognized the coordinated attacks and retreated to Gonaïves. But they had believed Dessalines; his past loyalty to France, even as he was engaged in open revolt, was strong enough to leave him unquestioned.

Dessalines was setting the stage for his first large-scale battle as a rebel leader during the last phase of the revolution. A mixed-race general, André Vernet, rallied his troops outside of Gonaïves and camped on the Pougaudin plantation where he awaited orders from Dessalines, who arrived nearby at the Georges plantation. From outside Gonaïves, Dessalines wrote to Brunet on October 9 to report on his efforts. He had two hundred men, he told Brunet, and he was worried about the insurgent attacks on Ennery and Gonaïves. "My General," Dessalines wrote, "I am very confused as to how I can save this district with so few people."[50]

In addition to his tried-and-true tactics of professing loyalty to secure more troops, Dessalines needed one last favor from Brunet. He asked him to write to Leclerc to order the release of his cousin Joseph Dessalines, whom Rochambeau had imprisoned on a ship in Port-au-Prince along with the rest of the regiments from Jérémie and Saint-Marc.

After sending the letter, Dessalines cautiously approached the big house of the Georges plantation, which was full of white officers.[51] He had secretly prepared to attack Gonaïves, but the French there were now on to him. An officer warned Dessalines, but rather than retreating or giving up his cover, Dessalines leapt on his horse and raced to see the French commanding officer in Gonaïves, leaving his wife and her coterie at the Georges plantation.

When he arrived in Gonaïves, he met the commander and demanded to know where the rumors of his defection had started. The commander backed down, pleading that the French government would never doubt his allegiance.[52] In response Dessalines promised to push the rebels back into the mountains. But the visit was another ruse. Before he left, Dessalines secretly secured the alliance of the colonial officers; they would stay in the city and switch sides when Dessalines attacked with the troops who were waiting on the outskirts.[53]

Dessalines then rode southeast to Petite Rivière, where he rallied the support of three thousand *cultivateurs*. He placed a man named Cottereau in charge, with orders to attack the French when he gave the signal. He ordered the gallows, a physical symbol of French oppression, to be brought to the center of town, where Dessalines cut it down. The town responded with exuberant celebrations. He knew he had their support.[54]

Despite his efforts to quell the rumors, suspicion of Dessalines's defection was spreading among the French officers. When Dessalines confronted the local squadron leader in Petite Rivière, Gen. Marie Martin Antoine Andrieux, he learned that news of his arrest warrant had spread. Although Dessalines remained steadfast in his assertion of loyalty to France, Andrieux was not convinced. He set a trap for Dessalines. The local priest invited Dessalines to lunch at the rectory, and the general accepted the invitation, even though he had been warned not to trust the priest. During the meal, when a woman of color signaled to Dessalines that he was about to be ambushed, he abruptly stood up and went to the window, claiming that he saw smoke in the mountains. The rebels were coming to attack, he argued, and he needed to go meet them. He raced out to the parade ground and shot his gun twice in the air, the signal for the three thousand *cultivateurs* to rise.[55] Hearing the general uprising, Andrieux and the other local French commanders fled to nearby towns.

Dessalines followed Andrieux to Crête-à-Pierrot, captured him, and ordered him to go to Saint-Marc. But Andrieux had fired three cannon shots to alert the French in Saint-Marc. As the French prisoners marched to the coastal town, the rebels ambushed and harassed them during their entire eighteen-mile route. By the time he reached Saint-Marc, Andrieux only had ninety soldiers left. Andrieux's departure was a victory for Dessalines; it also left the munitions stores from the interior region in the rebels' possession. Dessalines gathered the supplies and sent word to Vernet, who was still stationed outside Gonaïves, before he headed west to meet him.

During this initial phase of the war, Dessalines once again fell ill. Despite this being a crucial moment, the severity of his fever forced him to dismount and stop several times in transit.[56]

In Gonaïves, the French, with only a few hundred soldiers to defend their position, knew they were in trouble. They abandoned the perimeter and built a ditch around their encampment, securing the doors with cannons. They filled old barrels with dirt and piled them high to form a rampart.

As he prepared to attack Gonaïves, Dessalines continued writing to Brunet, updating him on his supposed actions against the rebels in the north. The continued deceit, even in the midst of active campaigns, was impressive. "I could not start my march to meet you in Port de Paix," he wrote from Petite Rivière on October 15, "given the presence of big number of enemies in this district. I thought it better to oversee the revival of the old fort here." Dessalines emphasized that Brunet needed to tell Leclerc that not just the north but the entire colony was in revolt. "I am told that the rebels said loudly that they would rather die altogether than be assassinated one by one," Dessalines argued, "& that we cruelly tricked them because we assassinate them instead of protecting them."[57] He was worried, he wrote, because he had heard that all the officers who had been called to Port-Républicain, like his cousin Joseph, had been imprisoned on a ship.[58] He claimed that his eighteen-year-old nephew had also been captured and hanged. "See how much I have suffered! . . ," he wrote in desperation, "but they will not make me revolt. Despite everything, I will stay loyal to my promises & to the government!"[59] It was another deliberate obfuscation; his letters to Brunet had become part of his revolutionary strategy.

In Saint-Marc, Quantin sensed something was amiss, perhaps because of the warning shots fired by Andrieux. On October 17 he complained to Dessalines that he had not received any communication from him while he was in Petite Rivière. He learned, however, that Dessalines was not at Petite Rivière, but at the Georges plantation; Quantin assured him that a ship was sailing from Port-au-Prince to Gonaïves filled with war munitions to support his defense.[60]

From the Georges plantation, Haque, the French chief of staff who had been assigned to spy on Dessalines, claimed that he had observed suspicious behavior among the Black troops. "For a few days an agitation reigns among the black people," he warned a French colleague, "a worry difficult to describe; their faces are no longer the same; they whisper, they appear to confide and all of this makes the observant eye think: meanwhile nothing is happening." He noted that Dessalines had seemed happy when he left for Gros Morne, still claiming unwavering allegiance to Leclerc. Haque also reported that Madame Dessalines was at the Georges plantation and that she and her ladies had been so ill for twelve days that he referred to them as "half dead."[61] He concluded by reporting that he had not heard from Dessalines, but he was supposed to be at Plaisance. The next day Dessalines wrote a letter to Brunet, claiming instead to be at Petite Rivière. He reported difficulty in suppressing the rebellion that he himself was coordinating.[62]

Finally, on October 23—ten days after the initial attack on Cap-Français—Dessalines ambushed the city of Gonaïves with two thousand men. The battle began at 11 a.m. and continued until 2 a.m. that night. As Dessalines's troops descended on the city, some residents and the national guard took up arms to join the defense; others packed their valuables and fled to ships waiting in the harbor. Initially the revolutionaries sustained some losses after two leaders were impatient and did not wait for the signal before attacking. The French pushed back. Vernet convinced the rebels to regroup and wait for Gabart, who descended from the Pougaudin plantation, leading about a thousand men. He halted outside the ramparts and presented himself to the French, still claiming loyalty to the republic. The French tested him on which regiment he was leading, because the 4th (sans-culottes) was divided into the 3rd battalion and the 5th light infantry unit. Gabart answered correctly, but he was betrayed by an overzealous soldier. "Death to the French! Fire to the ramparts!" the soldier cried. Chaos ensued.[63]

Dessalines, still outside the city, ordered Gabart to form two columns. The soldiers on the right, commanded by Gabart, attacked from the salt flats. On the left, soldiers commanded by an officer named Victor attacked on the side of the tannery. The revolutionaries burned the church and the houses, they broke down the doors to the barricaded areas where the French had retreated, and they infiltrated the roads.

At this point the ambush turned to hand-to-hand combat. Dessalines continued along the road to Gonaïves, despite his illness, and he arrived to find the city in flames. He hurried to join the fray. "At his presence," Boisrond-Tonnerre recounted, "the troops let out their usual cry, the general Dessalines is with us, the general Dessalines has arrived."[64]

The revolutionaries pushed the French soldiers to the shore at Fort Mouneau, where French colonists had boarded ships to flee. The rest stayed to continue firing on the rebels. They held out until 2 a.m., when they started destroying as much as they could within the fort, especially the artillery, lest it fall into the hands of the rebels. They threw away any provisions that they could not carry into the bay. By 4 a.m. the French troops embarked on ships in the harbor and sailed for Saint-Marc, firing their cannons at the city as they fled.[65]

After the siege on Gonaïves, Dessalines retreated to Petite Rivière to re-group. From there he sent the letter to Quantin advising him that he planned to attack Saint-Marc. It was only now that he finally ended the charade of loyalty to Leclerc. "The contents of [the letter] surprised me! They cannot express your intentions!" Quantin replied to Dessalines.[66] Dessalines told him that it was true, "I have taken Petite-Rivière and Gonaïves tomorrow I march against Saint-Marc."[67] Dessalines pointed to Leclerc's order calling for his arrest, and closed the letter detailing the atrocities the French were committing against the Black and mixed-race soldiers under Leclerc's orders.[68] The two generals exchanged several letters, each trying to convince the other of their case, and each invok-ing the ideals of the revolution. Ultimately Dessalines found himself marching against his friend.

Following his attack on Gonaïves, news of Dessalines's defection spread quickly.[69] The *Gazette officielle de Saint-Domingue,* the colonial newspaper, pub-lished a proclamation issued three days before, on October 20, by General Le-clerc. "An incredible betrayal has been committed," Leclerc announced. "Cow-ards plush with the benefits of the government, have abandoned their posts to join the rebels."[70] He claimed, however, that Dessalines's treasonous actions had not been successful. Leclerc made sure to highlight that the rebel attack on Cap-Français had also failed because of the loyalty of the colonists and the colonial army.

In response to the coordinated defection, Leclerc redistributed his army and ordered them to consolidate in the large coastal cities to maximize their resources and manpower. Loyal colonists were allowed to enter the cities, and they were recruited into the war effort via the national guard. He ordered the sick to evac-uate to a small island off the north coast, Tortuga. Arms stores and provisions were loaded onto ships to prevent rebel forces from taking them.[71]

Leclerc's movements had sparked rumors of a French evacuation. The pur-pose of his October 20 proclamation, therefore, was to reassure the French col-onists that they were not withdrawing. After they reconquered the colony with the help of reinforcements from France, Leclerc announced, they would "pun-ish the traitors and the rebels." He did not specify what that punishment would be, but given the expedition's history in the colony, Leclerc was likely planning to execute Dessalines and his allies. "Citizens, stay calm," he urged. "Confidence and support for the government; this must be your motto. The army has prom-ised that it will not abandon you, it will keep its word."[72]

Rochambeau, who had never supported Dessalines, was not surprised by the news. "Everything that you can tell me on account of g'al Dessalines," he told Quantin, "will not surprise me, and for a long time you know what I have never ceased to tell you."[73] Rochambeau reported that the insurgents had captured the Arcahaye and warned Quantin that he should prepare to be attacked.[74]

The mountains had always provided refuge for revolutionaries in Saint-Domingue, and the war was now clearly geographically divided. The French army occupied the ports while the insurgents retreated inland, ready to attack the coasts and then escape to the center. The only exits for the French were the ships in the harbor. Still, Leclerc hoped that inbound vessels would soon be bringing reinforcements from France.

On October 25 Dessalines's forces attacked Saint-Marc in a fierce battle. Quantin had amassed several battalions and infantry units to defend the city. A Polish unit was among them; their lackadaisical efforts—they allegedly did not believe in slavery and therefore were not willing to fight or kill to support it— apparently helped Dessalines's forces. The revolutionaries would not forget this assistance.[75]

During a break in the fighting, Quantin discovered that the soldiers of the 12th demi-brigade were loyal to the uprising. He rounded up the entire unit on the parade; then the French attacked from all sides, killing about four hundred troops.[76] The next day the city's residents were said to be unable to open their doors because of how high the bodies were piled in the streets.[77]

In Saint-Marc, Quantin's defenses withstood Dessalines's attack. Dessalines established his headquarters outside the town on the Lacombe plantation, a small plot of land on the north side of the Rivière des Guêpes that ran north of Saint-Marc. He rallied support from other revolutionary leaders in the area, some of whom were hesitant given his involvement in Bélair's arrest and execution. Dessalines's duplicitous alliance with the French came at the cost of trust among some local leaders—clearly, he had fooled both friends and foes alike.

At 8 p.m. on October 25, Dessalines and his new allies attacked Saint-Marc again; the siege lasted for eight days.[78] This was a well-coordinated attack, and all points fired at the same time. They were expecting inside help from the 12th demi-brigade, not knowing that these soldiers had been killed. When Dessalines realized this, he backed off, which enabled Quantin to counter. Quantin was lucky to have successfully defended the city against Dessalines's attack, because he was low on supplies and war matériel and did not receive any support from Rochambeau in Port-Républicain. Instead, on October 31 Rochambeau ordered him to evacuate the city.[79]

Dessalines and his allies retreated to the plains of the Artibonite and set up camp at Petite Rivière.[80] He was seething from the failed attack on Saint-Marc and blamed his soldiers for their half-hearted efforts, scolding them for not fighting like their lives depended on it. He accused them of longing for the comforts of the French army, even when their freedom was in jeopardy. If they hoped to win, he railed, they would have to be ruthless.

To emphasize his own fierceness, he selected three soldiers at random and killed them.[81] He then ordered his officers to scour the plains and the mountains to find every last plantation laborer and rebel and recruit them into his army. They needed a mass uprising for their revolution to succeed. Dessalines ordered his officers to kill anyone who refused to join.[82]

Within days Dessalines rallied over four thousand troops in the region of Petite Rivière. He reorganized the 4th, 7th, and 14th demi-brigades and formed a new unit that he called the "Polonais." This was not a nod to their Polish allies—many of whom had defected to join Dessalines—but because the soldiers were mostly African, and their languages were so poorly understood by the creole troops that it may as well have been Polish.[83] Even under the most dire circumstances, the revolutionaries gave in to humor and levity.

The French officers in the region of Saint-Marc reported to Rochambeau about Dessalines's whereabouts and anticipated his movements. In these reports they imposed a new identity on Dessalines. He was now the *brigand Dessalines*—no longer their ally or their friend.[84]

Philibert Fressinet, a French brigadier general in Saint-Marc, told Rochambeau that Dessalines may have been badly injured in the attack on Gonaïves. "All of my information leads me to believe that the day after my encounter with Dessaline [*sic*]," Fressinet noted, "he was wounded by the troops from Gonaïves before their evacuation & that his wound is fatal."[85] Fressinet was wrong about the severity of the injuries, but it is possible that during the October revolution Dessalines suffered high fevers and a serious battle wound. Fressinet did not elaborate on his sources, and no other records suggest that Dessalines was actually near death at the end of October.

It is possible that Dessalines's allies spread this misinformation about his health to make the French overconfident in their ability to quell the rebellion.[86] The rumor that Dessalines had died in the attack on Saint-Marc even made it to the United States by December.[87] Just as Dessalines had deceived his enemies and allies for months, so too did the revolutionaries use rhetoric and deception to support their efforts on the battlefield.

After Dessalines's retreat to Petite Rivière, the revolutionaries spread out along the north side of the Artibonite River in small bands. Fressinet set out on a reconnaissance mission to the east, but he only reached the south bank of the Artibonite. He claimed to have seen a small number of rebels on the other side of the river who fired their guns several times to warn the other camps. The sequence of shots was repeated by different groups along the river, as each group let the more distant groups know that French troops were near.[88] To Fressinet's dismay, the rebels were clearly many in number and well-coordinated.

From the cover of the hillsides near Petite Rivière, Dessalines plotted his next moves. By occupying the bank of the Artibonite River, Dessalines and the revolutionaries took advantage of the mountainous landscape, while also remaining connected to the main artery of the region.

While Dessalines was on the attack, Leclerc fell ill with yellow fever. He remained in Cap-Français, where he received news of Dessalines's actions in Gonaïves and Saint-Marc.[89] The illness was quick and vicious, and Leclerc died on November 2, 1802. For months he had requested permission to leave the colony; now it was too late for Bonaparte's brother-in-law.

Dessalines had professed his allegiance to Leclerc but then defected, even while Leclerc was still leading the French army. His death seemed to free Dessalines from any hope he may still have had in the French. Dessalines soon turned his revolt into a full-scale war for independence. The week before Leclerc died, Dessalines had written to Quantin. "I will defend myself as a true soldier, friend of liberty and of my country," he declared.[90] This was his last profession of loyalty to France. The French were now his sworn enemy. "Jean-Jacques, like some spirit from God," the Haitian poet Ignace Nau recounted, "dictated independence by firelight!"[91]

CHAPTER 9

The Eve of Making Our Executioners Disappear

On June 23, 1803—eight months after Quantin evacuated Saint-Marc—Dessalines composed a remarkable letter to the governor-general of Jamaica, George Nugent.[1] The handwritten letterhead announced Dessalines as the "General in Chief of the Army of Saint-Domingue." Writing from the Frère plantation on the plains of the Cul-de-Sac region east of Port-au-Prince, Dessalines presented his vision for the transition of Saint-Domingue from a slavery-based colony to a free country.

Dessalines's letter referenced the recent peace between France and Britain but nonetheless emphasized that Jamaica and Saint-Domingue shared interests due to their geographic proximity. The British had little incentive to support a slave rebellion, let alone an independence movement; but they had more pressing concerns, and Dessalines knew this. He argued that the Saint-Domingue independence movement was necessary because of French atrocities during the war, a fact for which he knew the British would show sympathy. Because the peace between France and Britain was fragile and war would likely resume, Dessalines made the case for British support for his army by depicting France as their common enemy. Dessalines reminded Nugent of the recent Leclerc expedition, made possible because of the peace with Britain. But, he argued, even the impressive French forces were "too weak to return under the most humiliating and harshest yoke the men whom it had held in the time of its calamities."[2]

This was also a warning. The British in the Caribbean were still reeling from their defeat in Saint-Domingue in 1798, and Dessalines was indirectly cautioning Nugent that any future British invasion would meet the same fate.

Dessalines also reminded Nugent of the peace treaty that the French had signed with Toussaint Louverture, which they had broken when they arrested and deported him. In doing so, Dessalines wrote, they "trampled on the laws of honor and humanity and broke the seal of reconciliation."[3] Breaking a treaty might seem like a small or tangential critique, but the ability and willingness of a nation to honor its existing treaties was a critical part of statehood in the early nineteenth century. By targeting French trustworthiness, Dessalines set the stage for his own negotiations with the British. He, unlike the French, would not break a treaty.

Dessalines went on to attack French morals by defending his decision to rebel as a matter of life and death. Recalling the outbreak of revolution in the fall of 1802, Dessalines argued, "It was at the moment when the entire population of Saint-Domingue would have disappeared, because of the tortures invented by the assassin government, that the people took back the weapons that they never should have abandoned." Dessalines framed himself as the legitimate leader of the movement because the people had called him to lead the battle. Their goal was clear: "the expulsion of the tyrants." Dessalines was honored to inform Nugent that "in the name of this people, weary with humiliation . . . all the ties that attached Saint-Domingue to France are broken, and that they would suffer death, the death of cowards, rather than return to its fatal protection."[4]

All this was masterful diplomacy. But it was also assuredly true. Beginning in October 1802, there is no doubt that Dessalines viewed his people's struggle as one of life or death, and that the ultimate goal was independence, no matter the cost.

As strongly as Dessalines must have felt at the outset, now he must have been even more certain in the rightness of his actions. In the months separating his defection from the French army and this carefully considered letter to Nugent, the French had shown their inhumanity in full. "I must stop here . . . ," Boisrond-Tonnerre wrote as a preamble to his description of Rochambeau, Dessalines's enemy in the war. "I am going to produce a monster of such an extraordinary nature that I need to collect myself so as not to be accused of crossing the boundaries of the strictest impartiality, by showing its true colors."[5]

Boisrond-Tonnerre and Dessalines were right. Because what Rochambeau and the French expeditionary army did in Saint-Domingue in 1802 and 1803 was almost too horrific to recount.

Following the mass defection of soldiers, including Dessalines, from the French army in October 1802, the already brutal and deadly war magnified in its intensity. Rochambeau, who took over command of the French army after Leclerc died, was "inconceivable in his cruelty," Boisrond-Tonnerre wrote. "The blood of the black and mixed-race [*jaunes*] people appeared to cascade on the dependencies of the French government."[6]

Under Rochambeau's leadership, the French expeditionary army ramped up the scale and the violence of their battle tactics, treating the revolutionaries outside the customary practices of European "civilized" warfare. Rochambeau concluded that it would be impossible to return the colony to its former productivity without drastic measures and decided to continue Leclerc's "war of extermination." The general imported hundreds of dogs from Cuba to attack the insurgent army; he burned people alive; and he drowned, asphyxiated, and shot prisoners.[7]

He was not alone in this violent depravity. The French general commanding in Saint-Marc, Charles d'Henin, recommended to the French government that it was necessary to kill *all* the Black people in the colony. "We will be forced to the cruel necessity of destroying the entire existing caste of *nègres* in Saint-Domingue," he wrote in a *mémoire* while he was still in the colony, "because it seems demonstrably impossible, to return to slavery men who have enjoyed their independence and have learned to fight for their freedom."[8]

When Rochambeau assumed command of the French army in Saint-Domingue, he had the support of the troops and of the remaining white colonists, who had been frustrated with Leclerc's perceived incompetence. One resident of Cap-Français reported to a plantation owner in Paris that he anticipated that Rochambeau would easily restore the colony.[9]

But who was leading the new revolution of Saint-Domingue was not clear. By some accounts, Dessalines was already recognized as the leader within a month of his defection from the French army.[10] The French general Pamphile de Lacroix, on the other hand, claimed that it was only some six months later, in March 1803, that Dessalines became the "*Général en chef des révoltés.*"[11] Another French report from the same month emphasized the decentralized structure of the revolution, with different military generals commanding regions alongside units of insurgent *cultivateurs*. In this version of events, Dessalines controlled about six thousand troops in the region between Gonaïves and Arcahaye, but not the entire army. The regions south of Dessalines's command were led by Cangé, Pétion, and Michel Sell, while the independent rebel leader Lamour Dérance controlled significant territory. In the north Henry Christophe and Clervaux controlled the regions in the mountains of Marmelade and Dondon.[12]

Most likely a combination of these accounts was true. As the leader of the revolutionary army, Dessalines promoted the generals who first joined the October rebellion. In addition, he maintained his leadership among the regional commanders, including assigning the post of Marmelade to his brother-in-law, L'Encens. [13] This novel approach made it harder to defeat Dessalines's army, according to Lacroix, because the French could not focus on any one target; instead they had to fight on many fronts.[14]

Dessalines was chosen to lead, recounted Boisrond-Tonnerre, because of his extraordinary skill set. He knew how to discipline the troops and was skilled in mountain-based warfare.[15] This made him an effective leader. "The seniority of his rank, the quality of the services rendered, the prestige of his personal valor, the ascendancy acquired over the armed masses," Haitian ethnographer Jean Price-Mars argued, "designated Jean Jacques Dessalines to supreme power."[16]

Dessalines and the revolutionary army, however, still had to contend with independent rebel leaders who refused to join forces, fighting a "war within the war" even while they battled the French.[17] One such leader, Jean-Baptiste Sans Souci, was a formerly enslaved man who in the early days of the revolution had been under Louverture's command.[18] Later he was integrated into the French army under Leclerc, but had defected long before Dessalines and the other generals. Therefore Sans Souci claimed the title of general in chief. As early as July 1802 he had attacked the French with a large force of soldiers and cultivators in the regions of Grande Rivière, Dondon, and Plaisance.[19] Now the revolutionary army invited Sans Souci to join them, but he remained independent even after the October rebellion, refusing to recognize his former allies as his superiors.[20]

Nevertheless, during the year following the October uprising and after assuming leadership of the revolution, Dessalines defeated French-controlled zones one by one. By December 1802 Dessalines and his troops were making incursions toward the south. Then the revolutionary army captured the Mirebalais region and planned to attack the southern peninsula.[21] Dessalines drew on his lengthy experience fighting in the woods to harass, evade, and assail the French army. In this kind of warfare, "those designated to attack [chariner] a post," Lacroix explained, "advanced in silence, entirely naked from their feet to their heads, and with the help of a brush that the incredible vegetation produces, they track you down without you suspecting where they are coming from, you cannot attack them without them hearing you, meanwhile, carefully marching completely naked, they advance or retreat without making the slightest noise."[22]

Dessalines was fighting the French army by keeping them constantly on the move, Lacroix believed, and thus exhausting them. Yet he did not argue that the French should adapt to the local terrain to combat these tactics. Instead, curiously, Lacroix maintained that the French must continue to wage regular warfare.[23]

While the focus of the revolutionary military strategy was centered in the mountains and the forests, Dessalines's army also used small boats and barges to assist their attacks on the port cities. Sometimes these small craft grouped together to attack France's larger ships, sinking at least one in 1803.[24] They cut off communications between French-controlled ports and forced the French to defend the cities from both land and sea.[25] The revolutionary army also used fire to combat and intimidate the French.[26] Very quickly, most of the northern part of Saint-Domingue was scorched.[27] In addition, although people at the time and subsequent historians have credited yellow fever for France's loss in Saint-Domingue, it is clear that the revolutionary army strategically magnified the impact of the disease. Taken together, Dessalines was pursuing independence by every means, and assaulting the former enslavers and colonizers on all fronts.

In early 1803, as Dessalines and the other generals gained ground in their campaign against the French, Sans Souci was willing to negotiate. General Christophe, however, imperiled the alliance. After capturing Sans Souci in an ambush, Christophe ordered his execution. The northern general's troops also killed the independent revolutionary leader Macaya. In retaliation, Noël Prieur assumed leadership of these rebel units.[28] Prieur was joined in Dondon by Dessalines's former officer Rousselot (Dommage), who likely refused to join Dessalines or who had lost his rank in Dessalines's army because of his actions when the French arrived in Jérémie in early 1802.[29] The French soon captured and condemned Rousselot for conspiring against them and executed him by hanging in November 1802.[30] Thus, one of Dessalines's earliest officers died, accused of being a traitor by both sides. Dessalines remained devastated by this loss more than a year later.

Because Christophe had been unwilling to negotiate with the rebel leaders, Lacroix claimed that the leadership of the insurgent army passed to Dessalines. Even amid personal tragedy, then, Dessalines was consolidating his forces.

Dessalines's military strategy was indeed effective. "I am not dead yet, my dear general," the French general Thouvenot wrote morosely to a colleague in March 1803, "and I continue to enjoy perfect health. . . . Our troops are getting tired chasing these rascals of *nègres* in the woods and in the mountains; and at the moment when we are about to catch them they hide in some hollows or in some *fourès de bois;* they lie on their stomachs on the ground; and we pass next to them, without seeing them, and they reappear behind us, when we descend."[31] The revolutionary forces knew that the terrain and climate were hard on the French soldiers, and they strategically forced them to fight under conditions that further depleted their energy and resources.

The revolutionary army fought with the memories of the tortures of slavery guiding them. This explains the ferocity of their violence. In this last struggle, both sides killed and burned without mercy. Yet it is Dessalines who has been singled out as ruthlessly violent. His critics have condemned what they consider his excessive use of violence. But his supporters have celebrated his willingness to secure freedom and independence by any means necessary. "Cut off their heads, burn down their houses [*Coupé têtes, boulé cases*], iron and fire," the Haitian historian Philippe-Armand Thoby recounted a century later, "in one hand, the sword dripping with blood, in the other, the burning torch,—here are our fathers in their terrible glory."[32]

In May 1803 the officers of the revolutionary army met in Arcahaye. They had assembled to devise a coordinated final military strategy to defeat the French and exile them from the island.[33] It was at this point that Dessalines was solemnly recognized as the leader of the independence movement.[34]

As a visual representation of their battle for independence, on May 18 Dessalines ripped the white stripe from the French tricolor flag. This left only the red and blue stripes, which now symbolized the alliance of the Black people and *gens de couleur* in Saint-Domingue.[35] Some accounts suggest that the revolutionary army used the blue and red flag before May 1803 alongside other flags, including a black and red flag. In that case, Dessalines's performance on May 18 may simply have been a tactic to reenergize his troops or to concretize the red and blue flag as *the* flag of the revolution.[36] The popular version of this history recounts that a woman named Marie Catherine Flon diligently sewed the red and blue stripes back together.[37] Dessalines knew that the alliance between the various factions of the revolutionary army was fragile, and he sought to reinforce it with symbols that emphasized unity.

Under their new banner, Dessalines and the revolutionary army adopted the slogan *Liberté ou la Mort* (Liberty or Death).[38] For the island's formerly enslaved people, the word *liberté* meant not just political sovereignty but also personal freedom. This slogan was quickly broadcast by Dessalines to the other revolutionary generals across the island. General François Capoix (also known as Capoix-la-Mort) hosted a ceremony in which four to five thousand troops and cultivators on the Fouché plantation swore to fight to the death.[39] Per Dessalines's instructions, Capoix also announced that France's local Black allies would not be spared in the war for independence.

The desperation of the French army was now palpable, and efforts were made to damage Dessalines's reputation and undermine his credibility. On June 11, 1803, the *Gazette officielle de Saint-Domingue,* the official mouthpiece of the French government in the colony, published a *feuilleton extraordinaire:* an additional page with printing only on one side.[40] The page reprinted two letters from the previous year on September 12. The first letter, from Dessalines, was addressed to Leclerc and had led to Charles Bélair's execution. It had originally circulated widely as propaganda for the French army. The second letter was a cover letter by Leclerc, outlining the process by which Charles and Sanite Bélair would be judged and punished for their revolt. The French wanted to remind Dessalines's troops of his alleged responsibility for the Bélairs' capture, condemnation, and execution, calling into question Dessalines's trustworthiness and his loyalty to the rebellion. Why had Dessalines been so steadfast in his support for France just eight months prior, the circular implicitly asked? When would he turn on his current allies and supporters?

Dessalines shrugged off this propaganda and what it suggested about his loyalties. He had the upper hand, and victory was imminent. Before moving to officially declare independence, however, he knew that he needed to establish new regional connections that would safeguard that victory and protect freedom.

Later that month Dessalines wrote his impassioned but calculated letter to Nugent, the governor of the British colony of Jamaica. He made a strong and reasoned case for why the two colonies might help each other, and why he and Saint-Domingue were far more trustworthy than the French.[41] At the end of the letter Dessalines turned to more practical concerns. He wanted a good relationship with Jamaicans because he wanted to trade with them. "Our ports will henceforth be open to all of His Britannic Majesty's ships," he told Nugent, "that will find trade security and good faith in treaties." He was tentatively hoping for a commercial alliance and promised that British merchants would benefit from this new relationship. He was similarly willing to commit to "military relations and those of a different nature."[42]

Dessalines left the door open for Nugent to shape the alliance. But by condemning the French and tapping into their on-again, off-again war with the British, Dessalines positioned his independence movement as compatible and even beneficial to Jamaica. At first, however, Nugent did not respond to Dessalines's letter.

On the same day and on the same letterhead proclaiming himself "General in Chief of the Army of Saint Domingue," Dessalines wrote another letter to a foreign leader: Thomas Jefferson, the third president of the United States, itself not even three decades old.[43] Dessalines's letter to Jefferson was shorter, and the tone reflected the greater geographic distance between Saint-Domingue and the United States. Dessalines reported that Haitian patrol boats had forced the US ship *Federal* into the port of Petit-Goâve and that he was taking the opportunity to send the US president a letter. This opening was a shot across the bow; any US ships sailing in Saint-Domingue's coastal waters, Dessalines suggested, would be subject to search.

Dessalines did not assume that Jefferson would know the details of the ongoing war on the island, so he highlighted "the events that have occurred in our unfortunate island since the arrival of the French and the revolution that was brought about by the tyranny of their oppressive government."[44] The France of Napoléon Bonaparte, he implied, was no longer an ally of the United States, and Saint-Domingue and the United States had more in common than it might appear. "Tired of paying with our blood the price of our blind allegiance to a mother country that cuts her children's throats," Dessalines wrote, "and following the example of the wisest nations, [we] have thrown off the yoke of tyranny and sworn to expel the torturers."[45]

Rather than framing his revolution as a "slave rebellion," he depicted it as an independence movement like that of the United States. Dessalines assumed that the "tyranny" of the European metropole was something to which Jefferson could relate. Indeed, after his first reference to the French reinvasion, Dessalines never mentioned France or the French by name. Instead, to Jefferson, Dessalines attacked them with broader statements about tyrannical and rapacious governments.

In communicating with Nugent, Dessalines aimed to bring Saint-Domingue and Jamaica together as allies against the French. Yet in communicating with Jefferson, he envisioned uniting Saint-Domingue and the US as allies in the broader fight against colonialism. The small but significant differences between the two June 23 letters highlight Dessalines's expanding diplomatic savvy. After months—and possibly years—of deceit and subterfuge, he was now in a position to negotiate more openly, and for more dramatic ends.

Dessalines closed the letter to Jefferson by emphasizing the commercial opportunities in Saint-Domingue that would be available to US merchants if the island's independence movement should succeed. He told Jefferson that he would do everything in his power to ensure that US merchants would profit from Saint-Domingue's sugar and coffee crops, and even tempted him by highlighting the big harvest that was expected the next year.

He did not say it in his letter, but what Dessalines most needed from Jefferson and the US merchants were weapons. And even though Jefferson never responded to Dessalines's overture, US merchants soon took advantage of the trade opportunities now available to them in Saint-Domingue. Dessalines maintained relationships and correspondence with several merchants, using the former French plantation manager and diplomat under Louverture, Joseph Bunel.[46] He had his wife's assistance, and Marie-Claire later exchanged letters with Joseph's wife, Marie Bunel.[47] These relationships paid off, and in August the US ship *Connecticut* delivered 300,000 pounds of gunpowder hidden in flour barrels to Dessalines, on behalf of a group of merchants from Philadelphia.[48] The ship itself was sold to Dessalines, with the promise of two additional ships that were en route.[49]

As he managed the regional and Atlantic context of the independence war, Dessalines also sustained and extended his alliances within Saint-Domingue. With the help of the mixed-race general Nicolas Geffrard, a former ally of Rigaud's during the civil war, Dessalines secured the support of several important generals in the south, and he recruited thousands of cultivators in the Cul-de-Sac region following his alliance with Lamour Dérance.[50] But even though Dessalines assumed his expanded army could win, the French still controlled key areas of the south; the war was not yet over.[51]

In July 1803 Dessalines learned that the French and British had once again declared war on each other.[52] Convinced that this renewed global conflict fully guaranteed his success, Dessalines decided to go on the offensive.[53] He met up with Geffrard in Les Cayes and delivered a speech to the troops. "My brothers," Dessalines announced in Creole, "after the capture of Petite Rivière in the Artibonite from the French, I was proclaimed general in chief of the independent army by the people of the Artibonite. The generals of the North and West, moved by their love of freedom, forgetting the political conflict that pitted them one against the other, came successively to recognize my authority."

Dessalines then tried to explain his earlier role in the civil war against the south. "I have always fought for freedom," he continued, "and if I was during the civil war blindly obedient to Toussaint Louverture, it was because I believed that his cause was that of freedom."[54] He reminded his audience that he had done everything possible to save their brave compatriots after Rigaud's defeat. He urged his audience to move on from this previous conflict. "My brothers, let us forget the past," he implored. "Forget these horrible times, when we were misled by the white people, we armed ourselves one against the other. Today we are fighting for the Independence of our country, and our red and blue flag is the symbol of the union of *noir* and *jaune*." The crowd roared in response: "War to the death against the *blancs*."[55]

Dessalines promised to defeat the factions of the "Congos," including Lamour Dérance, and this commitment enabled him to secure the allegiance of Larose, Bélair's former accomplice and the man whom Dessalines chased out of his jurisdiction in 1802.[56] He also promoted Geffrard and several other generals in a reorganization of the southern troops, while Louis Félix Boisrond-Tonnerre became Dessalines's secretary.[57] Dessalines was well aware that the memory of the civil war was still fresh, but he hoped that the factional divisions within the revolutionary army would fade as they united in the goal for independence and fought against their common enemy.

The French still held key enclaves in the south, which they needed to defend. The French general now in Jérémie, Philibert Fressinet, tried to fragment Dessalines's forces. Fressinet wrote to the newly promoted revolutionary commander Laurent Férou, who had only recently joined Dessalines's army and had fought against Dessalines during the civil war between Louverture and Rigaud. Fressinet tried to instigate "racial" tension between Dessalines and Férou, since Férou was an *homme de couleur*. The French general warned Férou that if the French departed, old racial animosities would resurface. "The era of fighting between Toussaint & Rigaud will happen again," Fressinet argued in his July 9, 1803, letter. "Dessalines without restraint and without obstacles," he warned, "who embraces you now with the mask of cordiality, hides the heart of a tiger, he burns to bathe once again in your blood and to tear you to shreds."[58]

The white French army, Fressinet claimed, was Férou's only hope. "Dessalines was previously your executioner, is he then preferable," Fressinet asked Férou, "to a wise and beneficent power, to a power that carried the glory of its name, the news of its exploits, all the way to the most distant regions—What does he promise you? Assure you? Guarantee you? A life of worry, proscribed, incessant alarms, and in peril and overwhelmed with privations of all kinds."[59] Fressinet anticipated the violent murder of the wives and children of the mixed-race officers under Dessalines, and predicted a "land stained with every crime."[60]

Instead of joining the French, Férou sent Fressinet's letter to Dessalines. The general in chief responded personally to the insults and accusations, sending his response to the French general. "Your letter to Brigadier General Férou," Dessalines wrote to Fressinet on July 13, "was given to me yesterday evening, by this officer full of honor to whom you deny the most common sense and whom you insult so gratuitously."[61] Dessalines argued that Fressinet was sorely mistaken in his analysis of the allegiance of the mixed-race generals, since they too had been the "victims of the cruelty" of the white French armies. "The past, the present, the future even, warns them that all of their misfortunes come from and will come from those whom you call their fathers," Dessalines countered, "and that more natural ties connect them to their mothers."[62] He noted that Fressinet's claims regarding the morality of the French government were hollow, since gibbets "will never be the attribute of beneficence."[63] What relevance were Fressinet's claims to the global glory of the French empire, Dessalines asked, "if it reserved for Saint Domingue cruelties with which no power had yet been tainted?"[64] In conclusion, Dessalines declared, white French colonists were the source of racial tensions. Without the French on the island, he predicted, conflicts among the Black people and the *gens de couleur* would fade.

Less than a month later, Férou and Fressinet negotiated the terms of Fressinet's evacuation from Jérémie. During these negotiations, Férou identified himself as the "Brigadier General commanding the army of the incas, united against Jérémie, acting under the powers entrusted to them by the chiefs; who themselves took it from the English Government."[65] The copy of the peace preliminaries included a note at the end, which recorded that on August 3 General Férou assumed control over Jérémie after the French and their allies departed, but that "the remaining [French people] were respected upon entry of the army of the incas."[66]

By using the name "army of the incas," the document signaled a transition among the revolutionary army, which in the coming months would begin to adopt Indigenous references.[67] Until this point, Dessalines's title was "General in Chief of the Army of Saint Domingue," but in the second half of 1803 the army's name changed. Dessalines's first reference to *Indigène* (Indigenous) was on August 2, 1803, in a letter to the British admiral John Thomas Duckworth. In the letterhead, the revolutionary army was called the "armée des Indigenes," and Dessalines was identified as the "Général en Chef de l'armé indigene."[68] Less than two weeks later, however, Dessalines returned to using "Armée de Saint Domingue" and continued to do so for another month and a half.[69]

Perhaps Dessalines was testing out the new name and assessing the best way to unite the military and the population under his leadership. This was not an assertion of membership among the Indigenous nations of the Americas; rather, it was an ideological claim to territorial legitimacy and rightful ownership of the land.

Locally and internationally, Dessalines emphasized France as the common enemy. And his strategy of aligning the revolutionary army with the British appears to have been effective. For example, he tried to coordinate with the British admiral Duckworth during his land-based attacks. Then, crucially, the news of war between France and Britain had opened the door for a possible treaty with the governor of Jamaica.[70]

On August 18, 1803, Nugent finally responded to Dessalines's June letter. "I have taken the earliest opportunity," Nugent wrote, "of sending two persons to Gonaïves to treat with your Excellency relative to a commercial intercourse etc, between Jamaica and St. Domingo, and we hope that the result will prove advantageous to both parties."[71] The two emissaries met with Dessalines and his generals several times, reporting to Nugent that "the following he said was his present view: to throw off all allegiance to France, and declare the colony independent, under the government of himself and his officers."[72]

The emissaries, James Walker and Hugh Cathcart, asked Dessalines to let the white inhabitants of Saint-Domingue retain or regain possession of their plantations. They also asked him to let the British reoccupy two key ports at Tiburon in the south and Môle Saint-Nicolas in the west. Dessalines declined both these proposals from British-controlled Jamaica. "The soil should be exclusively possessed by the natives (Blacks and Mulattos)," they said Dessalines replied. "They would never agree to the whites holding property in the soil."[73]

The British clearly wanted a return to the terms of their treaty with Toussaint Louverture, while Dessalines emphasized absolute territorial sovereignty. As Walker and Cathcart cruised off the coast of Saint-Marc, they received an envoy from the French general d'Henin, who capitulated to them and evacuated the city, providing further evidence for Dessalines's claims to his imminent victory.[74]

Buoyed by the overture from Jamaica, Dessalines continued to recruit allies. General Geffrard wrote to the governor of Cuba to try to establish diplomatic and trade relations. He even asked him to convey to the king of Spain, on Dessalines's behalf, the homage of the "nascent state." "I have the honor to inform [Your Excellency]," Geffrard wrote to Governor Sebastián de Kindelán y Oregón, "that by expelling from this territory the monsters who have tainted it for too long by their presence and by their crimes, shaking off the abominable yoke of the Government that paid for our services with such ingratitude and barbarity, we intend never to disturb the tranquility of our neighbors, to promote the opposite between us, by all sorts of good measures, trade connections that our Government will do itself a sacred duty to favor and protect."[75]

Geffrard anticipated an official declaration of independence and noted that "as long as a solemn act has proclaimed our independence of the French government and that our political existence is consolidated by treaties of friendship and trade with powerful nations, we open the ports that are in our control to all foreign ships that, due to the need for assistance or commercial speculation, may enter them." Like Jefferson, Kindelán never replied to Geffrard's invitation, likely because Spain was not currently at war with France.[76]

While Dessalines was increasingly confident in his success, he knew that it was not a time to be reckless. When he learned that Geffrard and Férou had allowed the French to evacuate with their weapons, he sent a reprimanding letter to General Gérin, commander of the southern division. "What! On the eve of making our executioners disappear [*disparaître nos bourreaux*] from our unhappy country," Dessalines wrote on September 11, "we would consider ourselves happy to negotiate, and to let our enemies keep their arms? What a shame!"[77] The war was not yet won, and Dessalines knew the next few months would be decisive. He returned to Petite Rivière to let his troops rest.[78]

Having taken possession of Saint-Marc, Dessalines turned his attention to Port-Républicain, where Pétion connected with residents to support the Indigenous Army.[79] Using the artillery that they had acquired from Saint-Marc, Dessalines and Pétion coordinated their efforts, attacking together on September 18, 1803. "From the moment that I put myself at the head of those of my compatriots who had pledged to prefer death over servitude," Dessalines announced in an official report about the attack, "I swore to relentlessly pursue the French, our executioners: but also, I promised to humanity to avoid, as long as it was in my power, the shedding of blood of the innocent and of the unfortunate, instruments of an atrocious government."[80]

It was in the printed account of this campaign, on October 17, that the first public use of "Armée indigène" appeared. The document rejected the French revolutionary name for the city and returned to its previous colonial name, Port-au-Prince, something Dessalines had already been doing in private correspondence.[81] The document also used the heading "Liberty or Death" (*Liberté ou la Mort*).[82]

This sequence of names and slogans highlights Dessalines's layered strategy as he entered the final phase of the independence war. He laid claim to territory by insisting on his and his army's nativity to the island; he foreshadowed his rejection of French republicanism; and he announced to the world that his people would die before returning to slavery.

Dessalines knew that the French would defend the city using multiple tactics. In the face of defections to Dessalines's side, he noted, the French would "try to scare them by representing me as a monster who sacrifices in a blind fury all of the white people whom French tyranny drove under my flags."[83] The evacuation of Jérémie, he claimed, had revealed the compassion of the Indigenous Army. Dessalines was mindful of the customary practices of European warfare—practices that the French had refused to follow in Saint-Domingue because they viewed the population as "savage" and therefore beyond the rules that governed "civilized" society. Dessalines also wanted recognition from the European "family of nations." He tried to demonstrate his and his nation's worthiness by publicizing evidence of their own "civilization," at the same time as he highlighted French "barbarism" in Saint-Domingue.

At first, Dessalines's forces cut off communication to Port-au-Prince from the surrounding regions. In this initial phase, Dessalines and Pétion worked with their former adversary Larose as well as Cangé, Gabart, and Marion. Despite wanting to spare the inhabitants, Dessalines deemed it necessary to cannonade the city. Quickly, however, an envoy from Jean Lavalette, the commanding general in Port-au-Prince, arrived with a proposal to save the city from a general attack.

The envoy was Joseph Balthazar Inginac, a man who would go on to serve as a high-level diplomat in several Haitian administrations. "I remember the reason that made you leave your country during the reign of General Toussaint," Dessalines greeted Inginac. "It was because of the colonists, General Pétion gave me your letters, and told me what you have done for our cause, I am happy with you. So, tell me what is new in town."[84] Inginac replied that he had been sent to negotiate an evacuation. Dessalines burst out laughing (*"se prit à rire aux éclats"*) and proceeded to dictate the terms upon which he would agree to a ceasefire.[85]

Dessalines sent the envoy back with an address to the inhabitants of Port-au-Prince. "Citizens of all classes," Dessalines told them on September 19, "there is still time to rally yourselves to our flags, under which you will find safety, protection and loyalty; Remember, Citizens, the humanity that always guides me dictates this final measure in your favor, and if you do not profit from it, you will have no one to blame but yourselves for the misfortunes that threaten you."[86] Dessalines framed himself as a benevolent leader and promised that those who joined his fight would be fully welcomed in the Indigenous Army. During and after the civil war, after all, Dessalines had previously welcomed units from the south. Now he continued this policy to bolster his forces during the war for independence. Several garrisons from the city and surrounding regions surrendered to him, swelling his ranks.

In response, Lavalette replied to the proposal with several modifications.[87] Dessalines granted him four days to complete the evacuation, ensuring time to load water and supplies, on the condition that he send a hostage to Dessalines to guarantee the agreement. Dessalines similarly sent Lavalette a hostage.[88] On October 8 the French embarked, and Dessalines returned the prisoner Andrieux, the general who had tried to ambush him in Petite Rivière a year earlier.

The next morning, less than a month after the beginning of the siege, "the ships set sail," Dessalines recounted, "and I entered Port-au-Prince, at the head of the army, with the consolation of having spared it as much as my heart desired."[89] He rode into the city flanked by Gabart and Pétion and wearing a red military uniform trimmed with gold.[90]

At this moment of triumph, the Indigenous Army was on the precipice of victory. But it came at great cost. The colony was a dystopian scene. Cities and countryside alike had been burned, and tens of thousands of people had died.[91] The forts were charred and surrounded by the bones of fallen soldiers.[92]

Dessalines and his troops rested in Port-au-Prince for eleven days, preparing for what they assumed would be the final confrontation of their war for independence. The French troops who evacuated Port-au-Prince went to reinforce the deteriorating French army in "Cap." This was Dessalines's new official name for the city (and its nickname); the general in chief removed "Français" from the name, and now he hoped to remove the French people from the city.[93]

He and his troops headed north on October 21, 1803. The attack was delayed by incessant rain, but Dessalines coordinated with generals Christophe, Cangé, Clervaux, Vernet, Gabart, Jean-Philippe Daut, and Capoix. The key battle occurred at Vertières, a fortified plantation near Cap, during which Capoix led the attack.[94] Dessalines coordinated the various movements from the headquarters of the Lenormand plantation—the same plantation on which the revolutionaries had planned the first uprising in 1791.

The Indigenous Army was poorly clothed. But they were well-armed because of the munitions stores that they claimed in Port-au-Prince. They fought for their freedom with pride.[95] On November 18, 1803, they attacked the fort at Vertières. The French responded with a cannonade against the fort at Bréda, killing troops and taking out the battery. Inspired by this success, the French general in chief Rochambeau marched toward Vertières from Cap. The independent revolutionary leaders Jacques Tellier and Cagnet had recently struck a deal with the French in response to rumors surrounding Dessalines's negotiations with the British; Rochambeau had claimed that Dessalines, in his treaty negotiations, was selling the colony to the British.[96] The two independent leaders and their two to three thousand soldiers therefore supported the French, preventing the Indigenous Army from securing food during the battle.[97]

The Indigenous generals who were posted along the main road from Cap were exposed. To protect them, Dessalines coordinated an offensive from all points. He ordered Capoix to seize an overlook on the Charrier plantation, two hundred feet from the fort at Vertières. This was a dangerous mission, which put Capoix and the soldiers of the 9th, 7th, and 14th demi-brigades in the French army's direct line of fire. Dessalines ordered the 3rd, 11th, and 20th demi-brigades to support the attack. As the French rained artillery shells on his troops assailing Charrier, Capoix encouraged his men. "You must, my brave men, make yourselves master of this overlook," he shouted from the front line, "the success of the army depends on it; onward!"[98]

The battle was bloody, and French fire from the fort overwhelmed the Indigenous Army. Leading his troops on horseback, Capoix launched another attack, once again heading directly into the line of fire. Capoix's horse was shot in the attack, but the general scrambled to his feet, shouting "Onward! Onward!"[99] The army had not yet captured the overlook on the Charrier plantation, and Dessalines coordinated with Gabart to secure the post. "I want the Indigenous flag to fly within a half hour on the summit of Charrier," Dessalines exclaimed, "even if I see the army corps disappear, unit by unit."[100]

Finally, the Indigenous Army secured the overlook at Charrier. This assault, in turn, supported the troops at the foot of Vertières. Observing the battle at a distance, Dessalines noticed that Rochambeau was changing position, so he ordered Clervaux to reinforce their position at Charrier. Then the Indigenous Army exploded a caisson in the heart of the fort at Vertières, which forced the French out. Dessalines pressed his generals forward; it was now or never. "Dominique," Dessalines encouraged an officer who had fought with him in the 4th demi-brigade, "I took away your battalion because of your weakness in various battles; well! this is your opportunity to prove yourself and to regain my respect; charge with bravery, and I will give you back your battalion."[101] Dominique fought courageously and died in the battle.

Dessalines and his chief of staff Bazelais went up to Charrier. Here on the high point overlooking the besieged French fort, the troops celebrated their general, knowing victory was within reach. At dawn the next day, recognizing that they could not withstand another assault by the Indigenous Army, the French set

Ulrick Jean-Pierre, *The Battle of Vertières, 2, 1803*, 1995 (with Dessalines in the foreground).
Oil on canvas, 48 × 60 in. (122 × 152 cm). Courtesy of the artist.

fire to the fort and fled to Cap. "The white people are fleeing," the Indigenous
troops cried. "Forward!"[102]

As Dessalines and the Indigenous Army claimed Vertières, the French troops
from other surrounding forts also retreated to Cap under the cover of night.
The Indigenous Army captured several other key posts outside the port city, and
Dessalines established his headquarters in Haut-du-Cap. "I have to say that the
success of this affair," Dessalines recounted, "was due to the constancy of the
generals, to make a fearless assault with their soldiers; each demi-brigade maintained its reputation there."[103]

"On 8 brumaire [October 31], he passed the revue of his troops in the Artibonite," Boisrond-Tonnerre later boasted, "and on the 26th of the same month
[November 18] he found himself at Haut-du-Cap with his entire army. This one
day was enough to make Rochambeau capitulate."[104]

On November 19, 1803, Dessalines, general in chief of the Indigenous Army,
and Duveyrier, adjutant commander of the French army, signed a treaty for the
surrender (*reddition*) of Cap. In the treaty the two generals agreed that in ten
days Dessalines would take control of the city and its surrounding forts. While

the French concurred that the arsenals would remain untouched, Dessalines agreed that French war and merchant ships carrying troops and colonists were free to clear out on November 28.[105] The treaty also stipulated that the sick and injured French soldiers who were unable to travel would be cared for in the hospitals until they were cured or healed. These individuals were "especially under the protection of the humanity of General Dessalines, who will embark them for France in neutral ships."[106] Similarly, in exchange for the release of *des hommes du pays* (men of the country) by Rochambeau, Dessalines assured protection for the French colonists who chose to stay in Saint-Domingue after the evacuation.

One year later, Boisrond-Tonnerre claimed that the evacuation treaty was an implicit recognition of independence. "Conquerors of Egypt which is no longer yours," he addressed the French people in his *Mémoires*, "detractors of the English who defeat you and block your ports, you fled, you capitulated, you surrendered to a brigand. Did you forget that the French republic does not treat with her enemies if they are in her own territory, if they are rebellious subjects, or are you persuaded that Saint Domingue does not by right belong to France, and that we are not rebels, because we only want to be free like you."[107]

It would quickly become clear, however, that in fact the French did not view the evacuation agreement as either an official peace treaty or a recognition of independence.

To support the commitments of the treaty, Dessalines issued a public proclamation on the same day to the "citizen inhabitants" of Cap. In it Dessalines explained the treaty that he signed with Rochambeau for the "evacuation of the city of Cap" by the French troops.[108] "The war that we have waged up to this day," Dessalines stated, "is completely foreign to the *habitans* [*sic*] of this miserable colony. I have always offered safety and protection to the inhabitants of all colors, you will find the same in me on this occasion."[109] Here *habitans* referred to the planters and landowners who lived in Saint-Domingue, and who had in fact often supported the French in the national guard.[110] Dessalines pointed to his treatment of the inhabitants "of all colors" in other cities; this, he argued, proved his promise that those who chose to stay would find "safety and protection," both in person and property, under his government.

The government printing press in Cap printed the proclamation, with a note from the president of the Council of Notables of Cap, who declared that the following demonstrated the "peaceful disposition of the new Government, and the protection and safety accorded to all individuals who will continue to live in this colony."[111] A French officer claimed to have overheard Dessalines committing to these promises in private. "Ten days before the departure of the army, being at his [Dessalines's] house," Armand Levasseur de Villeblanche recounted, "I heard him say in Creole, with the insinuation of truth that this language gives: 'during the war I ravaged everything, but now that the French army retreats from our coasts, that we are now at peace, I will reestablish agriculture. I make no distinctions between colors, I will forget what happened between the white colonists and myself, I assure them my protection; their persons and their fortunes will be respected.'"[112] If Dessalines did in fact say these words, his understanding of the evacuation treaty establishing "peace" was the basis upon which he made subsequent claims and decisions.

The inconsistencies among the evacuation documents highlight the ambiguity of this event. The joint French and Indigenous document called it a surrender (*reddition*), but Dessalines's proclamation noted that it was an "evacuation of the city." The introductory note by the president of the Council of Notables, dated the day after the treaty, admitted that Dessalines was establishing a "new government," yet Dessalines also claimed that Saint-Domingue remained a "colony." Finally, the treaty itself specifically applied only to the city; but there were clearly broader implications, since Cap was the last major holdout of French troops in Saint-Domingue.

Perhaps because of these ambiguities, three Indigenous generals—Dessalines, Henry Christophe, and Augustin Clervaux—magnified the significance of the evacuation treaty by issuing a declaration of independence.[113] "In the name of the black people and the men of color of St. Domingue," the three generals announced on November 29, 1803, "the independence of St. Domingue is proclaimed. Restored to our primitive dignity, we have reclaimed our rights: we swear that no power on earth will ever make us lose them." These rights were based on the Dessalinean concept of *liberté,* which prioritized anti-colonialism and the legal abolition of slavery.[114]

Dessalines, Christophe, and Clervaux foreshadowed the subsequent name change for the island by framing "the independence of St. Domingue" as a return—they had "restored" the island by protecting it against any other "power on earth." Colonialism, from their perspective, necessarily enforced "prejudice," but by expelling the French they secured their dignity and would protect it "forever."

Like the treaty with Duveyrier and Dessalines's proclamation to the inhabitants of Cap, the November 29 proclamation offered protection for the "landholders [*propriétaires*] of St. Domingo." "We are not ignorant," the generals continued, "that there are some among you that have renounced their old errors, abjured the injustice of their exorbitant pretensions, and acknowledged the lawfulness of the cause for which we have been spilling our blood these twelve years. Toward these men who do us justice, we will act as brothers."[115]

Then, however, Dessalines, Christophe, and Clervaux issued a warning: "But as for those who, drunk with foolish pride and selfish slaves to a guilty pretentiousness, are blinded so much as to think that they are the essence of human nature, and they affect to believe that they are destined by heaven to be our masters and our tyrants, let them never come near the land of St. Domingue; if they come here, they will only see chains and deportation."[116]

The generals claimed that any line of defense was justifiable if it was in the name of freedom: "Nothing is too dear, and every means are lawful, to men from whom it is wished to tear the first of all blessings. Were they to cause rivers and torrents of blood to run; were they, to maintain their liberty, to conflagrate seven-eighths of the globe, they are innocent before the tribunal of providence, that has not created men to see them groaning under harsh and shameful servitude." Dessalines, Christophe, and Clervaux situated their anti-colonial struggle within a divine system of justice. The worldly courts of the nations and empires and the customary practices of the law of nations had, for centuries, supported the expansion of European empires throughout the globe. These same courts could not be trusted to accurately judge anti-colonial movements. But the generals were confident in the righteousness of their movement, since slavery was contrary to God's will. The anti-slavery revolution, therefore, had to be fought by every means necessary.

The generals closed with a prediction that this declaration of independence signaled the end of the war. "But nowadays the Aurora of peace lets us have the glimmer [*rayon*] of a less stormy time," they argued. "Now that the calm of victory has succeeded to the troubles of a dreadful war, everything in St. Domingo ought to assume a new face, and its government henceforward to be that of justice."[117]

On the night of December 3, the last of the French troops evacuated the western side of the island from the city of Môle Saint-Nicolas.[118] News of the French evacuation traveled across the countryside. As Saint-Domingue's men and women embraced, they cursed the French.[119] The Indigenous Army hoisted their flag in the forts and on their ships, announcing their independence to all visitors.[120]

The aurora of peace, however, was a phantasm. The French were already plotting their return.

CHAPTER 10

Liberté ou la Mort

On January 1, 1804, in the city of Gonaïves, Dessalines and his generals announced to their citizens and to the world the independence not of Saint-Domingue, but of a new country called "Haiti."[1] The country's new name was, in fact, its old name: what the Indigenous people had called the island before Christopher Columbus arrived in the Caribbean. Dessalines initially spelled it "Hayti," but over the course of the first decades of independence, the spelling gradually and inconsistently changed to "Haïti."[2] This new name paid homage to those who had earlier fought to the death for their freedom.[3] Recovering the name "Hayti" erased French colonialism and emphasized sovereignty at every mention of the nation and its citizens.

"Let us swear to fight to our last breath," Dessalines cried to his fellow citizens in Creole on January 1, "for the independence of our country."[4] He recounted their suffering under French colonialism and slavery and reminded them of the atrocities committed by the recent French expeditionary army.[5] Dessalines's secretary, Boisrond-Tonnerre, then read the oath of independence, which the generals in attendance repeated together: "to renounce France forever, and to die rather than live under its dominion."[6] He also read the text that he had composed the night before and that Dessalines signed and approved. It was a speech in French in Dessalines's voice and addressed to the citizens of Haiti.[7] Finally, the generals nominated Dessalines to the position of governor-general for life.

These three elements (the oath, the speech, and the nomination) together make up the official Haitian Declaration of Independence, or the *Acte de l'In-dépendance*. It was the world's second successful declaration of independence.[8]

At the same time, Jean-Jacques Dessalines became the first abolitionist head of state in the Americas.[9] In his speech he warned the assembled citizens, "Know that you have accomplished nothing, unless you give to the nations a terrible, but just, example of the vengeance that must be wrought by a nation proud of having recovered its liberty, and jealous of maintaining it; let us frighten all those who would dare to try to take it from us again: let us begin with the french." The French had dared to try to reenslave them, Dessalines argued, and Haitians would never be safe with French colonizers in their midst. "Let them shudder when they approach our coasts," he warned, "if not from the memory of the cruelties they perpetrated there, then by the terrible resolution that we shall enter into of putting to death, anyone who is born French, and who would soil the territory of liberty with their sacrilegious foot."[10] From then on, Dessalines vowed, the war with France would be "eternal." He counseled his citizens to "swear at last, to pursue forever the traitors and the enemies of your independence."[11]

Dessalines's tone toward the French had changed dramatically between Rochambeau's evacuation in late November 1803 and January 1, 1804. In those few weeks, it became clear that the "stormy time" spoken of after the evacuation treaty at Cap was not over; instead, the war with France would continue.

General Rochambeau had been careful to sign a treaty that allowed his evacuation but did not concede defeat. This did not mean that he or his troops would be able to keep fighting, however. When the French cleared out from the port at Cap, they were immediately apprehended by the British navy and transported to Jamaica. From there they sailed as prisoners of war to Europe; Rochambeau himself remained interned in England for the next decade.

But remnants of the French expeditionary army stayed on the island. General Jean-Louis Ferrand escaped with his soldiers and made his way to the eastern side of the island by mid-December 1803; there they joined a contingent of about five hundred French troops based in the city of Santo Domingo.[12] Evacuating troops from Jacmel and Croix-des-Bouquets joined them. Still, the combined forces in Santo Domingo remained under a thousand.

And indeed—as Dessalines would decry in the formal proceedings of independence the next month—Ferrand's *raison d'être* was to destroy Dessalines's armies and the nascent state so that he could reestablish French rule and slavery.[13] Claiming to be the legitimate governor of "Saint-Domingue," Ferrand waged war using proclamations, piratical attacks on foreign shipping to the island, and a blockade of Cap.[14] He declared that more French troops would soon arrive from Europe to help reconquer the colony. On nearby Jamaica, George Nugent, the British governor with whom Dessalines had exchanged letters, was not convinced that Ferrand and the remaining troops from the French expeditionary army could defeat Dessalines's forces. As he told his superiors in London in December, "the incapacity and atrocious conduct of their [France's] chiefs in St. Domingo are proverbial, and that colony is most decidedly lost to France at least as long as the present Rulers there bear sway."[15]

From Dessalines's vantage, however, it was too early to know that Ferrand was dreaming or bluffing.[16] So he prepared for a reinvasion. His men destroyed the coastal forts and readied the port cities for easy destruction, while fortifying the mountainous interior with military barracks, provisions grounds, and munitions depots.[17] His goal for the next several years was to establish and protect Haitian sovereignty.

It was in preparing for invasion that Dessalines conceived of the January 1 Declaration of Independence. This would replace the previous declaration from November 29, demonstrating a dramatic shift in Dessalines's vision for an independent country and what was needed to protect it.[18]

At first Dessalines instructed one of his secretaries, Jean-Jacques Charéron, to write the new declaration. Charéron composed a text (yet to be recovered) that closely mirrored the 1776 US Declaration of Independence, but Dessalines and his other secretaries complained that it lacked emotion and did not reflect their nation's needs.[19] At this point Boisrond-Tonnerre stepped up and famously declared, "to draft the act of independence, we need the skin of a white person for parchment, his skull for an inkstand, his blood for ink, and a bayonet for a pen!"[20] This statement allegedly convinced Dessalines, and he told Boisrond-Tonnerre to create a document that would match his own fury toward the French.

On December 31, 1803, Boisrond-Tonnerre wrote through the night, guided by the memory of the hundreds of thousands of Black people who had died under French colonialism.[21] He wanted to ensure that these ancestors would welcome the founders of the new nation in the afterlife. Dessalines approved his text for the next day's ceremony. It is possible that Dessalines edited the document as Boisrond-Tonnerre was writing it, or after he saw the finished version; but there is little evidence about the process through which the Declaration of Independence was authored or coauthored. Dessalines signed the document in his name and claimed the words as his own.

In the new declaration Dessalines referred to "Hayti" as "the country that saw our birth," even though most of the population had been born in Africa. Moreover, he even called Hayti's people *citoyens indigènes* (indigenous citizens). It may be that Dessalines meant that Haitians, regardless of where they were born, had earned Haitian citizenship during the revolution.[22] Alternatively, Dessalines may have been referring to the fact that most of the revolutionary leaders were born in the colony, and their rights to territorial legitimacy extended to the population more generally.[23] Either way, Dessalines's act of renaming validated the revolutionaries' claims to the island, positioning the French as foreigners. It was not they who belonged in Hayti.

The concept of indigeneity also provided a new homeland for those who had been rendered stateless by colonialism and slavery throughout the Americas. This was especially salient for those like Dessalines who were of African descent but had been born in the Americas, and who from birth had been dispossessed of all claims to a homeland.[24]

Dessalines's Hayti explicitly challenged the colonialist notion of rights and nationality to offer a place of freedom and belonging, a physical and moral place of refuge. Hayti was now a homeland for the dispossessed and downtrodden of the Americas, and Dessalines enacted policies to put this idea into practice. He advocated for the "return" of "indigenous people" (*indigènes*), whom he defined as *noirs* and *hommes de couleur,* to Hayti.[25] In January 1804 he even offered to pay for their safe return from the United States. He issued similar offers to "*noirs et gens de couleur*" in Martinique and Guadeloupe.[26]

The name "Hayti" was also symbolically important, since it meant "mountainous" in the language of the Indigenous peoples who previously had inhabited the island.[27] The mountains had, for more than a century, been a refuge from enslavement and imperialism.[28] More recently they had been home to the military camps of Dessalines's Indigenous Army. Haitians owed their lives to the protection afforded by the mountains, and Dessalines continued to rely on the topography for national defense in the years to come.

Dessalines understood that the intention of the remaining French soldiers and colonists was to reenslave the Black citizens of his new country. His January 1 speech to the "indigenous of Hayti," therefore, was a warning and a call to arms. Dessalines was worried because "the French name still haunts our country."[29] In the previous November 29 declaration, Dessalines, Henry Christophe, and Augustin Clervaux had promised that those who respected their freedom would be treated "as brothers." A month later, however, Dessalines emphasized that his citizens had nothing in common with the French, that it was clear that "they are not our brothers, that they will never be."[30] He now reversed the claim that the French would find safety under his government and argued, "If they find asylum among us, they will again be the instigators of our troubles and our divisions."[31]

Clearly the fear of another French attack shaped the content of the Declaration of Independence and Dessalines's actions afterward in a way that had been absent from the November 29 document.[32] It is impossible to know whether Dessalines intended all along to recant his November 19 and 29 commitments to protect the French colonists who remained in the country, or whether he reconsidered the promise after the French continued waging war. Toussaint Louverture had similarly promised the safety of the white inhabitants who remained in Saint-Domingue, as well as those who had fled the colony but were keen to return to their plantations. Many of these people had supported the French army under Leclerc and Rochambeau; Dessalines likely assumed that they would do the same if Bonaparte sent more troops from France.

Alternatively, Dessalines may have given the French a second chance but then changed course when he learned that another French invasion was likely, after Ferrand established his base in Santo Domingo in December. Dessalines claimed that the new country encompassed the entire island—which had legally been the territory of the French colony—and therefore the continued French presence in the east was a direct challenge to Haitian sovereignty.

Finally, it is plausible that Dessalines intentionally deceived the French to enact revenge. After the French expeditionary army evacuated, Dessalines allegedly announced that he would never take pity on the French as long as he bore the scars of his enslavement.[33] In his address, Dessalines asked the "Indigenous citizens" to look around the island and to remember what had been done to their families. They had become "the prey of these vultures."[34]

The problem now, Dessalines argued, was that their "assassins," these "tigers still covered with their blood," remained in the country, and their "atrocious presence reproaches your insensitivity and your culpable slowness in avenging them. What are you waiting for before appeasing their spirits; remember that you want your remains to rest near those of your fathers, when you have driven tyranny out; will you descend into their tombs without having avenged them? No, their bones would repulse yours."[35] Dessalines understood the urgency of defending the new nation from attack; the French had made it clear that the war was not over.[36] He hoped to fend off another attack by boosting his troops' morale and by warning the French that any attempts to recolonize the island and reenslave its citizens would fail.[37]

Dessalines ordered the government press to print and publish the Acte de

l'Indépendance. Between the second and third week of January, Pierre Roux—
the longtime printer of the colonial government, who assumed the same duties
for the independent government—printed both broadside copies to be posted
in public spaces and pamphlets to be distributed by mail.[38] Only two official
printed copies of this text are known to have survived; one is an eight-page pamphlet, and the other is a one-page broadside.[39]

In addition to an explicit act of renaming and an assertion that "Saint-
Domingue" no longer existed, the published versions of the Declaration of Independence also rejected the French republican calendar and adopted the Haitian dating system as an addendum to the Gregorian calendar.[40] The Declaration
of Independence was dated "the first of January, eighteen hundred and four, the
first year of independence."[41] Beginning with this declaration, every document
that the Haitian government produced, including proclamations, letters, and
newspapers, reminded readers that Haiti had existed as an independent country
for a specific number of years.

The day after he declared independence, Dessalines published two decrees.
One canceled all existing leases on plantations, targeting military officers or
other people who had secured land leases from the French government.[42] These
may have been leases like the ones that Dessalines himself had secured when
Toussaint Louverture was in power, or they may have been leases between personal contacts or family members. The decree was likely laying the groundwork
for the state to nationalize plantation land as *domaines nationaux,* as the French
republican state had done in the colony during the revolution.[43] This way they
could ensure consistent revenue to support the Haitian state and protect against
invasion.

The second decree regulated the uniforms of the military officers. They were
to wear blue uniforms with red lining, with either red or blue sashes and red,
blue, or black plumes, depending on their ranks.[44] These two short decrees highlighted Dessalines's focus as he set out to protect his new country and ensure
that it remained independent. A well-organized agricultural export economy
and military hierarchy were key elements that would support a centralized, independent Haiti.

The new nation needed a new plan of defense. Rather than fight to hold
onto the ports—which might be impossible, given France's navy—Haiti would
defend itself in the mountains that had always sheltered its revolutionaries. Dessalines ordered new forts to be constructed inland from all the major cities
throughout the country. At one of these forts in Marchand, he established his

headquarters, which he renamed "Dessalines."[45] The Haitian army later started manufacturing their own gunpowder at the forts in Marchand-Dessalines.[46] Soldiers and cultivators built the forts during mandatory, limited-term work assignments, after which they returned to their designated plantations or stations. The state also pulled tradespeople such as masons and carpenters from their own work or from plantations to assist the efforts.[47] The whole island supported the defense efforts. Just one month after the Declaration of Independence, on January 31, 1804, Henry Christophe ordered the entire city of Cap to help move the arms and ammunition out to the plantations of Grand Pré and Ferrière, where they would construct new forts.[48]

Dessalines's goal was to maintain a standing army of over twenty thousand men ready for battle and a militia that could be called to arms in times of need.[49] In the event of a French attack, alarm cannons would fire on all points and the generals would order their troops inland, while the *cultivateurs* joined their ranks. The elderly, women, and children would cultivate subsistence gardens near the forts, which would then feed both soldiers and civilians in the event of an attack.

Even this was not the end of the plan. In fact, some of the forts were not meant to be permanent structures. Instead they were part of a larger defensive strategy on the ground. "Their main objective, when ambushed," a French doctor who spent two years under Haitian authority argued, "is to wait for their enemies on the narrow routes that lead to the forts, to attack them, they also took care to leave them all covered with woods to better achieve their goal."[50] By withdrawing inland, Dessalines would force the French to fight in the mountains, where the Haitian army had a tactical advantage. Furthermore, when evacuating the towns, the Haitians planned to leave poisoned foodstuffs. Newly free Haiti thus initiated a stratified defense system.

As he built his country's morale and its defenses, Dessalines also looked beyond his new country's borders for help. Only the governor of Jamaica had replied to his circular, but the precise elements of a potential alliance were not simple or straightforward.[51] By the new year, Governor Nugent was prepared to propose a formal trade treaty, which could have had much broader implications for Haitian sovereignty.[52]

To that end, he sent Edward Corbet to "St. Domingo." Having previously served as an emissary to the colony when Louverture was governor, Corbet arrived in mid-January 1804, in the wake of Dessalines's declaration of an independent Haiti.[53] Once there, he exchanged letters with Dessalines and held lengthy in-person meetings that included other Haitian generals. Corbet did not mention the presence of a translator, so it is likely that the two men spoke French and Creole to one another. After witnessing the interactions among Haiti's leaders, Corbet concluded that Dessalines "pays or appears to pay a considerable degree of deference to the opinion of his Officers *of Colour.*" But Corbet also understood that the relationship was strained by their prerevolutionary and revolutionary history, and he assumed that "altho' they contributed to elevate him to his present situation of 'Governor-General of Hayti for Life,' I entertain great doubts of there being much sincerity on either side." Corbet noted that even though Dessalines consulted with his generals, "the Government of the Island, which they now call Hayti (its primitive appellation) is perfectly despotic under the chief Dessalines."[54] Framing the Haitian government as unenlightened and tyrannical became common among foreigners such as Corbet. In effect, a multilayered strategy emerged to undermine Haitian sovereignty and equality on the international stage.

The treaty Nugent proposed to Dessalines included fourteen articles designed to renew the previous peace agreement between Jamaica and Haiti, while also creating an alliance against enemy nations and privateers. Nugent wanted to regulate and limit Haiti's marine navigation and set guidelines for the ships of other independent nations that traded with them. The goal was to confine Haitians within their territory, so as to prevent communication between the "brigands" and the enslaved people of the British West Indies. They worried that otherwise the Haitians might intentionally or inadvertently inspire a rebellion in Jamaica.

In return the British would protect Haiti's coastal trade. To secure maximum economic advantage, Nugent wanted exclusive trading rights. According to the treaty, when trading with Haiti, British ships would sail under a flag of truce and carry a trade license from the British government. Since flags of truce implied that the two nations were at war, this article assumed some degree of continued French authority over the island. At the same time, the treaty aimed to secure more British influence in Haiti. The Jamaican governor's proposal was an attempt to control Haitian trade and to monitor other international trade, bringing Haiti into the British sphere of influence.

In addition to discussing Nugent's formal treaty proposals, Corbet emphasized the British desire to acquire a military post on the island for the duration of the current Franco-British war; he requested temporary possession of Môle Saint-Nicolas, a port they had held during the British occupation of Saint-Domingue. Dessalines rejected this request as an unacceptable infringement of

the island's territorial sovereignty. Furthermore, since he had ordered the destruction of the military fort at Môle Saint-Nicolas, he argued that it would not
be any use to the British army, and the issue was therefore moot.[55] Dessalines did
not let this request derail the negotiations, however, stating that "the demand
by the British Government did not inspire any distrust of its loyalty and good
faith" and that he was ready to continue the treaty talks.[56]

After meeting with Dessalines on January 15 and 17, 1804, in Port-au-Prince,
Corbet returned to Jamaica. Upon arrival, he gave Nugent a French-language
copy of a revised trade agreement, which included Dessalines's reactions, his
proposed amendments to each article, and two additional articles. The revised
treaty proposal did not reflect any special relationship with Great Britain. Dessalines had explained that he wanted to give preferential treatment to the British, but that he would not do so at the expense of trade relationships with other
nations. "It is my responsibility," Dessalines told Corbet on January 16, "to offer
protection to all (the French rigorously and rightfully excepted) who want to
establish amicable relations and trade relationships with the indigenous people." Dessalines did not elaborate on the potential content of any official trade
treaties or a political and military alliance; instead he promised that "all diplomatic and commercial measures on the part of the British that would not prove
detrimental to the sacred independence in these lands, nor to the exclusive privilege of rights, will be taken into consideration by me."[57]

Dessalines likely did not want to offer the British preferential treatment,
because it might jeopardize Haitian trade with the United States. One account
by a US merchant noted that there were ten American ships in the harbor at
Port-au-Prince in mid-January 1804. The merchant said that his fellow citizens
were treated well and, almost as an afterthought, reported that "the new government in this island was instituted on the 1st of this month and the island is
called aïty [sic]."[58] In another letter, this American wrote that he hoped the new
government would soon put its affairs "on a permanent footing" and reported
that Dessalines was currently touring the country to that effect.[59] Another US
merchant in Port-au-Prince highlighted that there was plenty of coffee for sale,
that the British did not interfere with US shipping, and that their cargos were
protected by armed Haitian vessels.[60] A third US merchant hoped that a Haitian treaty with the British would benefit the US by providing protection for
American merchants clearing out from Haitian ports, who were otherwise at risk
of being captured by French privateers.[61] If Dessalines offered the British preferential trade terms, he might disrupt this balance.

The first of the two articles that Dessalines added to Nugent's proposed treaty requested that British agents arrange for the sale of arms and ammunition for the defense of the country. It also—shockingly—requested that these same agents "deal with the sale of black people brought to the island for the restoration of its agriculture."[62] His second additional article required the governor of Jamaica to repatriate any Haitians onboard British ships or in British prisons.

The people whom Dessalines purchased through the slave trade would be free upon their arrival in Haiti, since the 1804 Declaration of Independence had reaffirmed the abolition of slavery. Dessalines's proposal followed the example set by Louverture, who had also requested that Jamaican traders sell enslaved people in Saint-Domingue, where they would then become *cultivateurs*.[63] These articles reflected the fact that Dessalines wanted to revive the island's plantation economy, which required a large labor force. Corbet estimated that the population in Haiti after the revolution was between 150,000 and 160,000 men, women, and children. Dessalines's conviction that the new nation required the support of a plantation economy pitted him against most of the population, who saw plantation labor as a feature of slavery. He thus continued the policies set by the French republican administration and by Louverture, requiring formerly enslaved men and women to work on plantations. The *cultivateurs'* refusal to work on sugar plantations, however, resulted in the near collapse of the sugar industry; coffee and cotton quickly became the nation's primary export crops.[64]

While in Port-au-Prince, Corbet gathered as much information as he could about circumstances in the new country. He noted that the white population in Haiti was "insignificant" and concluded that their situation was "extremely deplorable."[65] He explained to the governor of Jamaica that Dessalines had encouraged French civilians to stay, but that the promises of safety and security in persons and property had been empty, since the white inhabitants were "called upon for heavy contributions and beyond the possibility of many to produce."[66] A US merchant in Port-au-Prince also described violence in Port-au-Prince in the wake of the declaration, reporting that "they kill white people daily and I am of the opinion that they will kill all the French white people in this island."[67] Corbet recounted that the executions continued during his stay in Port-au-Prince, "for which I could hear no reason assigned, except that they were not sufficiently revenged for the cruelties exercised towards them by the French and in retaliation for which those unfortunate individuals to whom the General in Chief Dessalines has assured protection, are now to become the victims."[68]

After he returned to Jamaica, Corbet claimed that "upon very slight pretences & in some cases without any pretext whatever, [French] lives have been put in requisition. At the dead hour of night they are taken from their houses

and are heard of no more and their property, as far as it can be found, is generally disposed of before the morning." While he had not personally witnessed
these alleged occurrences, he asserted that "this happened about 10 days before
our arrival at Port-au-Prince to about a dozen persons, and the only reason I
ever hear pretended for this severity was, that some of them in their correspondence, which had been intercepted, had been writing rather too freely respecting the existing government."[69]

According to Corbet, then, the Haitian state was monitoring the correspondence of local French colonists; when they found evidence of anti-government
support, they sentenced the authors to death. Such letters would have indicated
to Dessalines that the French colonists were potential collaborators in the event
of a French attack. He had issued a warning in the Declaration of Independence,
and the alleged executions appear to have been the manifestation of that promise. "What do we have in common with these executioners?" Dessalines had
asked his citizens. He had warned that if they found "asylum" in Haiti, they
would conspire against the new state.[70] Within a week of the Declaration of Independence, according to Corbet, Haitians targeted white French people who
threatened the new government.[71] The intercepted letters among white French
residents showed that Dessalines was right about the potential French threat,
and that French colonists could be just as dangerous as French soldiers.

In February 1804 Dessalines began a nationwide tour of the major port cities. He began in Les Cayes in the south, looped around the southern peninsula
before heading back to Port-au-Prince, and then traveled up the coast through
Saint-Marc and Gonaïves, ending in Cap in mid-April. Even before he set out
on his tour, reports had begun circulating about a "massacre" in Les Cayes.

One US captain claimed that on January 22, seventy white inhabitants were
"massacred by the brigands, and thrown into the river."[72] The term "massacre"
had been used throughout the revolution, and did not necessarily signal the killing of unarmed adversaries or "civilians." But it was also a term that white colonists used to describe Haitian revolutionary warfare, putting them outside the
rules of "civilized" warfare.[73] It is also difficult to parse who could be considered
a "civilian" in the context of a war for independence and a war against slavery,
since colonialism and slavery necessarily entailed a constant war between the
enslavers and the enslaved and the colonizers and the colonized.[74] The Haitian
state treated all white French people as the enemy, both as colonizers and enslavers. To Dessalines, French people posed a serious threat, both while living in the
country and beyond its borders.

Part of Dessalines's preparation for another French attack was the network of inland, mountain-based forts and a standing army. But since a French attacked seemed imminent, Dessalines took the extraordinary step of eliminating the would-be collaborators of the French army. Everywhere he stopped on his tour, his generals and soldiers publicly executed white French citizens who threatened the new nation or who had participated in the campaigns of the recent French expedition. Estimates of the dead range from hundreds to thousands.[75] The French propagandist Louis Dubroca immediately seized the opportunity of the hyperbolic accounts of "massacres," printed in newspapers throughout the Atlantic world, to condemn Dessalines as a leader and Haiti as a country. How, he argued, could the world recognize a nation of "Africans [who] slaughter without pity"?[76] Dessalines's decisions during these four months have almost universally been condemned—then and now—and contributed to European and US decisions not to recognize Haiti's independence.[77]

But what actually happened during the first five months of 1804, and why did it happen? This has been difficult to assess, because most of the archival record is composed of writings by panic-stricken white onlookers, who were either terrified for their own lives or fearful that legal slavery was coming to an end. They reproduced tropes about violent Black men murdering white women and children and targeting "civilians" after the war with France was over. It is true that Dessalines did order the executions of white French people whom he viewed as a threat to the new nation or who had supported the French expeditionary army. But the extent of these killings has been misconstrued and exaggerated both at the time and by later historians.

Dessalines later assumed responsibility for these executions, but some observers believed that he had been influenced by his officers and citizens. The Jamaican diplomat claimed that the "people of colour"—by which he meant Haitians of mixed race, the *hommes de couleur*—"are urging Dessalines to the total destruction of the white people now in his power, so that whatever may happen hereafter there may be no claimants to many of those properties of which they now get possession."[78] Several nineteenth-century accounts suggest that Juste Chanlatte, a former free man of color who was one of Dessalines's principal secretaries, seized the opportunity to target white people whom he knew personally.[79] The French priest Father Guillaume Lecun also argued that the *mulâtres* generals were more vindictive against the white people because of their own ambition.[80]

There were likely two central reasons why Dessalines began his first national tour in the south. First, the remaining French troops on the island were in the city of Santo Domingo, on the southern coast and only a short sail to Jacmel. General Ferrand had previously been stationed in the south and likely still had contacts or potential collaborators in the region. Ferrand could have also drawn on pre-independence divisions to find support among southern republicans.[81] These political divisions remained even after the tenuous alliance, despite Dessalines's efforts to symbolically unite the country during the war for independence. The south was the region over which Dessalines had the least amount of power, and he likely wanted to assert his authority.

Second, while Dessalines was in Les Cayes, he issued another ordinance.[82] On February 7, 1804, he determined that "all sales or donations either of movable or immovable items made by people who emigrated to those who remained in the country, are and remain annulled; of course only those since the Indigenous Army took up arms to expulse the French from the Island of Haiti."[83] The article targeted people who had refused to join Dessalines's fight for independence but who passed on their land to people still on the island.

The ordinance contained a total of twenty articles, in which Dessalines tried to assert his authority over a region that had long been outside his sphere of political and military power. Dessalines ordered plantation owners to first pay cultivators their quarter share of revenue, followed by the territorial tax owed to the state. It abolished the councils of notables throughout the country, centralizing power under his authority. It restricted the sale of the harvest from year eleven of the French republican calendar to those who had been allied with the Indigenous Army on July 9, 1803; those who had been allied with the French at that point would be forced to give up their crops to the state, although they were allowed to return to their properties. Dessalines revoked the leases of sugar plantations that had been awarded to military officers and placed those properties under the authority of the Haitian government. In addition, the ordinance regulated the communication networks within the military and government, and prioritized status reports on the construction of the inland forts. The document was an explicit attempt on Dessalines's part to govern more effectively.

While in Les Cayes, Dessalines received word from Corbet and from John Thomas Duckworth, the commander in chief of the Jamaican fleet, that Ferrand in Santo Domingo "professes to be in expectation of succours from France."[84] "I sincerely thank your Excellency," Dessalines responded to Duckworth on February 12, "for the notice that you gave me concerning the armament being prepared in France against the Island of Hayti. I have been on my guard for a long time and I am ready to receive the French, who would want to see the country that they could not defend."[85]

France apparently was preparing for a reinvasion. Likely reacting to this claim, Dessalines (sometime between his letter to Duckworth on February 12 and his arrival in Jérémie on the 25th) ordered the commanding general at Les Cayes, Nicolas Geffrard, to execute the white French people in the city and confiscate their possessions for the state.[86] The white Polish soldiers who had arrived with the French army—and who had defected to the Indigenous Army or who had been left behind when the French evacuated—were, however, safe.[87] Dessalines welcomed these units into the Indigenous Army and into the new nation as full citizens.

"The most horrid massacres were going on at Aux Cayes," reported a US ship captain who claimed to have witnessed the events, "a few nights before he sailed, most of the whites of that place were put to death."[88] The US *Mercantile Advertiser* and the French *Journal de Paris* both published lists of names of the people who were executed in Les Cayes and the surrounding area.[89] The two lists contained the names of 151 people, including planters, doctors and surgeons, merchants, a carpenter, a priest, a baker, a notary, and two women.[90] Three of the men recorded on these lists had committed suicide. Not long after, another newspaper reported that "no massacres had taken place since the sailing of the *Ann;* and there was a reasonable prospect from the interference of General Dessalines, of a restoration of 'order and good government.' Proclamations were distributed that the whites should be protected in their lives and property."[91] Perhaps the Haitian government had made its point, or perhaps it had executed all the people whom it viewed as a threat.

While Dessalines focused on protecting the nation, his wife, Marie-Claire Heureuse, celebrated independence in the north. On February 12 she threw a dinner and ball for 250 people, including US, British, and French guests. "It was elegantly ornamented inside with flowers, branches of trees, *three hundred* small lamps of colored glass hung round the room," one attendee noted, "four large chandeliers over the table, twelve great looking glasses, and a marble statue at each end of the room in a recess." The guests feasted on "beef, mutton, turkies, ducks, fowls, oranges, pine-apples, alligator pears, apples, pies, puddings, jellies, sweet-meats, cakes, and claret, Madeira, and Champaign [*sic*] wines."[92] Madame Dessalines hosted the event with Henry Christophe and his wife, Marie-Louise.

After dinner the room was cleared, and the partygoers danced through the night. Days later, Christophe hosted another dinner in Madame Dessalines's honor, which featured a hot air balloon and fireworks. Tensions were high in Haiti in early 1804, but independence was still a moment to celebrate.

On February 10, back in the south, Corbet arrived again from Jamaica to continue the treaty negotiations, this time equipped with "presents to Dessalines and his principal officers, to the value of several hundred pounds, chiefly composed of hats, gold lace, epaulettes and sabers."[93] Dessalines met him in Jérémie on February 25. While discussing the new version of the proposed treaty, Dessalines and Corbet quickly came to terms regarding the articles that did not concern British regulation of other foreign merchants and of Haiti's maritime movement. It remained clear, however, that they had conflicting goals in establishing a trade treaty.

Most notably, Nugent had agreed to omit the article requiring British ships to trade under a flag of truce. Therefore Jamaica—on behalf of Great Britain itself—had implicitly conceded that Haiti was no longer a French colony. Still, Governor Nugent was not yet ready to recognize national independence. Corbet and Nugent continued to call the island "St. Domingo," and instead of calling Dessalines "Governor-General," they addressed him as "General in Chief of the Army Indigene." Dessalines responded to these diplomatic insults by reiterating that he would not accept articles that limited his country's sovereignty.[94] Corbet told Dessalines that he had not been instructed to address him as anything more than "General in Chief," and his refusal to call Dessalines by his new title on his second visit made it clear that at the heart of the negotiations for a trade treaty was really the question of sovereignty.

In response, Dessalines insisted that he wanted to be recognized as the leader of an independent nation. He wanted more than implicit acceptance that Haiti was no longer a French colony.

Nugent had readily accepted Dessalines's request regarding expatriated Haitians, and so the British returned 154 prisoners "belonging to this island." Nugent modified Dessalines's demands for military supplies because, as he explained, it was not the duty of the British agent to promote the arms trade in Haiti; "everything of that sort must be left to private merchants, who will, with permission of the Governor of Jamaica, be allowed to import to this Island a reasonable quantity of ammunition and as the public service of that Island may admit of."[95] With this concession, Dessalines achieved one of his main objectives, since the British would not only allow but also encourage a limited arms trade to Haiti for the purpose of internal security.

In contrast, Corbet explained to Dessalines that the second half of the article, "respecting the importation of negroes for sale," was "inadmissible and of a tenor which was not within His Excellency's [Nugent's] comprehension."[96] Nugent was likely reluctant to expand the reach of the British slave trade given that the Parliament in London was debating its abolition, even if those people would have secured their freedom on arrival in Haiti. Furthermore, increasing the population in Haiti would also have been risky for Nugent, who wanted to ensure that Jamaica was protected from the Haitian Revolution. Despite this last disagreement, Dessalines asked Nugent to submit the proposed article for review in London.

Corbet was also concerned about the lives of the white inhabitants of the Grande-Anse region, "of which there is no inconsiderable number." He had previously emphasized how few white people there were in the country, and so he either corrected himself after he visited a different region (he had previously been in Port-au-Prince) or he exaggerated the number to elicit more concern. On February 29, after returning to Jamaica from Haiti, he reported to Nugent that "the white people in the Grand Ance [*sic*] . . . now hold their lives by the most precarious tenure; indeed I much fear the greatest part if not the whole are doomed to destruction. Many of them intimated to me, that the only hope they had of escaping it (for all permission to leave the island is refused) was the idea of a British Commercial intercourse taking place and the residence of a British person among them in a public character."[97]

At this point, Corbet was convinced that his negotiations with Dessalines had reached an impasse, but he believed that he had to keep the possibility of a treaty open, since the white residents argued that their lives depended on it. Corbet and other foreign merchants emphasized that Dessalines had specifically targeted the French during the executions and that all other white people were completely safe.[98] Corbet was among several witnesses to claim that the French inhabitants were prevented from leaving; it is likely that Dessalines and his government suspected that if they left, they would assist a reinvasion effort.[99] The policy of preventing white French people from leaving the country—even those who became permanent residents—continued throughout Dessalines's time in office.

In his meetings and letters with Corbet and his correspondence with Nugent, Dessalines did not address the issue of the executions or the French colonists who remained in Haiti. His public proclamations highlighted the ongoing war with France, but his private and diplomatic correspondence avoided any mention of his radical anti-colonialism.[100] Dessalines simultaneously asserted Haitian anti-colonialism through physical and rhetorical violence, even while attempting to peacefully establish trade and diplomatic relations with a neighboring colony. Both were required if the Haitian state had any hope of survival in the early nineteenth-century Atlantic.

Two puzzling and perhaps related events occurred in Jérémie that seem to
have affected Dessalines's attitude toward the remaining French colonists. The
first happened before Dessalines's arrival at the southern city, likely at the end of
January.[101] John Perkins, a British free man of color and captain of the ship *Tartar,* while sailing off the coast of Jérémie, helped smuggle several white French
colonists onto his ship, one of whom had previously joined the Haitian army.[102]
Given that white people were prohibited from leaving Haiti, Laurent Férou, the
local commander, asked Perkins to return the men. Perkins resisted initially but
eventually conceded, in exchange for the return of some British prisoners who
had been apprehended for illegally landing outside the port city.[103] Some interpreted the incident as an attempted conspiracy, and Férou court-martialed the
French men and ordered their executions.[104] The British subjects, who had come
ashore to get water in Abricots and whom Férou had arrested, also sparked rumors of a possible conspiracy against the Haitian government. Tensions were
high, and the slightest possibility of an invasion or rebellion put the new government at risk.

The second event that occurred in Jérémie was that Dessalines was informed
about a letter in which white colonists and merchants had advocated for the
return of slavery and voiced their support for Rochambeau.[105] He did not yet
have a copy of the letter, but someone told him what it said. In response, before
leaving the southern city, he ordered his generals to execute the white French
colonists in the region.[106] Perkins, the captain of the British *Tartar,* wrote to
Duckworth about the executions at Jérémie. "The evening we came to an anchor," he related on March 17, "several bodys [*sic*] got entangled in it, in fact such
scenes of cruelty and devastation have been committed as is impossible to imagine or my pen to describe."[107] The "massacre" that Perkins described had allegedly
taken place the day after he set sail from Jérémie. In another letter Perkins claimed
that 308 French people had been executed, but he only provided the names of 35
of them. His list included one priest and one woman; the rest were not identified beyond their surnames.

When he arrived in Port-au-Prince on February 28, Dessalines secured a
copy of the colonists' letter of support that had been transcribed in the records
of a local notary.[108] Neither the original version of this letter nor the two extant
copies include a date or a location, and it is not clear whether Dessalines knew
when or where the colonists wrote the letter. When he publicized its contents,
he left the timeline ambiguous, but he noted that the letter and its authors were
likely responsible for the "evil that had rained down on our heads but called for
our independence."[109]

The contents of the letter appear to have been shocking for Dessalines and for the Haitian people. The original document had been attached to a cover letter written on December 21, 1802, more than a year earlier, and the letterhead announced that it was from "the merchants and inhabitants of Port-au-Prince." It was signed by over one hundred merchants and colonists, some of whom may have still been in the country, and some of whom Dessalines believed were *hommes de couleur* but, because of their light skin, they claimed to be white.[110] The letter was addressed to the residents of the main commercial centers in France.

The colonists' letter recounted Rochambeau's allegedly heroic efforts during the revolution and the confidence they had in his ability to bring back "stability" to Saint-Domingue—through the reestablishment of slavery.[111] "Rochambeau is the leader who is needed in Saint-Domingue . . . ," they argued, "this is, gentlemen and dear fellow citizens, our most ardent desire."[112] In the aftermath of Leclerc's death, the letter claimed that France could send all the troops it wanted, but any campaign would fail without a "leader removed by these principles and the morality of the vain abstractions from a false philosophy that is inapplicable in a country where the soil cannot be fertilized but by Africans, whom a strict discipline must control."[113] Only Rochambeau could rise to this task, the colonists claimed.

The original document included a clause of a sentence that is curiously missing from the two 1804 copies: "the man [Rochambeau] who was deported by Sonthonax and his adherents, because of his favorable views on the system indispensable to St. Domingue . . ."[114] It is unclear whether it was the notary, Dessalines's secretary, or a British secretary who introduced this omission, and whether it was an error or an intentional deletion. The discrepancy is noteworthy, however, because it is the clearest reference to the reestablishment of slavery in the original letter. The letter outlined a plan to ask Bonaparte to confirm Rochambeau as governor, at which point, they promised, "Saint-Domingue will rise again from the ashes and will send once again, to the heart of the metropole, products that will increase its commerce, and will be for it, a new source of abundance and prosperity."[115]

News of the letter spread, and Haitians demanded that Dessalines publish the names of those who signed it.[116] They wanted to know who had advocated for the return of slavery. Dessalines conceded and published the letter in Port-au-Prince.[117] Later he circulated copies of the document throughout the country.[118]

The next day, from the city of Gonaïves, Dessalines published a decree calling for the arrest and execution of those who had collaborated with Leclerc and Rochambeau; not just those who had signed the 1802 letter of support for Rochambeau, but anyone who was known to have supported the expedition, materially or rhetorically.

"There remains on this island people who contributed," Dessalines declared on February 29, "either by their writing, or by their accusations, to the drowning and suffocation, assassination and hanging or shooting of over 60,000 of our brothers under the inhumane government of Leclerc and Rochambeau. Considering that all these men, who have dishonored human nature by the zeal with which they fulfilled their office as denunciators and executioners, must be classified among the assassins, and left without remorse to the sword of justice."[119] He instructed his generals to arrest these individuals, collect the appropriate evidence to prove their treachery, and keep a list of their names so that Dessalines could publish them. "What terrible lessons," Boisrond-Tonnerre recounted not long after, "for the only inhabitants who dared write to ask that Rochambeau's nomination be confirmed by the first consul."[120]

When he published the letter, Dessalines also ordered the arrest of the French people who had secured naturalization documents in neighboring islands. He suspected that they would return and foment a rebellion of their own. "Considering that French people who were outlawed and banished from this island, solicit naturalization papers in foreign countries with which they want to return to the country to sow discord," Dessalines wrote, they should be arrested and their papers confiscated.[121]

By this point, news of the executions was circulating throughout the Atlantic world. Foreign newspapers immediately connected Dessalines's Declaration of Independence speech to rumors of so-called massacres of French people in Haiti. For example, the first news concerning a "massacre" in Haiti in the *Journal de Paris* that appeared on March 4, 1804, was pure speculation. "There are rumors here that this chief [Dessalines] plans to destroy from top to bottom all of the cities of the colony," the newspaper reported, "and to drive out all the whites."[122] The article's author clearly expected nothing more from a person of Dessalines's "character," described as a "rebel" and a "leader of black people" (*chef de noirs*). The *Journal de Paris* followed up in May with a story reprinted from a New York newspaper, including five paragraphs from the Declaration of Independence ending with *commençons par les Français* (let us begin with the French). "The recent massacre of the whites in Saint-Domingue," the newspaper commented, "was preceded by a proclamation that we believe is curious enough to transcribe it here in its entirety."[123]

The executions gripped the attention of white foreign onlookers, who feared a future without slavery and colonialism. The French vice consul in Virginia, Martin Oster, connected Dessalines's Declaration of Independence with the deaths of the white French colonists in Haiti. In a letter to the French foreign minister, he noted that sick and injured French troops in Cap had been killed, along with "almost all of the inhabitants of the southern part of Saint-Domingue, [who] were bayoneted or shot, or drowned." Oster, however, emphasized that the tour of the port cities in the south was also important for Dessalines's military strategy: "We are informed that Dessalines emptied all of the arsenals in the cities and he had all of the artillery transported, all of the war matériel, to the interior of the country, to take refuge."[124]

Dessalines divested the cities of the tools that the French might use if they returned to try to reconquer Haiti. Both French people and war matériel could be weaponized against the citizens of Haiti. They had to be moved, or removed, it seems.

Perhaps in response to news of the executions, Ferrand, from his base in Santo Domingo, persisted in advocating for French colonialism. He issued a proclamation promising that former plantation owners would be able to return to their land once the French had reconquered "Saint-Domingue." "You should anticipate that France," Ferrand announced on March 17, "after having reestablished tranquility in this island, will put you in possession of your plantations. You will live under a paternalistic government, in a country where the provisions are in abundance, and where trade and confidence make new progress each day."[125]

Dessalines's executions continued to generate attention. Corbet recounted news from a British merchant, Mr. Dunbar, who had recently been in Port-au-Prince and who claimed to have learned from Captain Perkins of the events in the south. When the French protested to Dessalines that they had been promised safety under his government, Dunbar related, "he is said to have replied that those assurances were only given them to induce them to remain, that he might get them into his power!!!"[126]

Such descriptions framed Dessalines as someone who sought out violence rather than someone who was protecting the new nation. Instead of recognizing France as the aggressor, stories like this depicted Dessalines as a wanton killer.

But not all the accounts aligned in their reporting on events in Haiti. One report in the *Columbian Centinel* in Boston cautioned that "no credit ought to be given to the accounts circulated in the United States, of the massacres in cold blood of the whites in the devoted colony of St. Domingo." Their source conceded that perhaps "in the moments of assault and engagement some excesses have been committed; but since the evacuation of the island by the French, the blacks have treated the whites who have not been in arms against them with hospitality and good faith."[127] Even though not everyone believed the alarmist accounts coming out of Haiti, however, Dessalines's international reputation was increasingly negative and hyperbolically violent.

After the February 29 proclamation, Dessalines returned to Port-au-Prince, where he instructed his generals to follow his orders and execute the white colonists. Descriptions of these executions used racist language that framed them as unjustified and extreme. "Dessalines arrived here on Friday afternoon last," Perkins wrote, now sailing off the coast of Port-au-Prince, "and turned loose 400 to 500 blood thirsty villains on the poor defenseless Inhabitants, he gave an order for a general massacre (strangers accepted) [sic]." "The poor victims were slaughtered in the streets, in the squares and on the seaside," he continued, "stripped naked and carried out of the gates of Léogâne and St. Joseph and thrown in heaps. A few days I fear will breed a pestilence. Had you seen with what avidity these wretches flew at a white man you would have been astonished."[128] Perkins, who claimed to have been on land and witnessed these events, framed the colonizers as victims and tried to garner maximum sympathy for the former enslavers in Haiti.

Perkins also contended that Dessalines was killing for profit: "The plunder Dessalines is supposed to have collected by the sacrifice of so many lives is calculated at no less a sum than one million of dollars."[129] After the executions at Jérémie, Dessalines had allegedly traveled to Port-au-Prince followed by seventy mules loaded with goods and treasures confiscated from the dead white French.[130] As was typical at the time, Perkins detached the killing from the ongoing war and depicted the dead as "poor victims." The rationale for the executions, according to Perkins, was only the Haitians' "thirst" for blood, an accusation that some historians continue to repeat.[131]

By characterizing those who were executed as "poor victims" and "civilians," Perkins and other observers placed the executions outside the customs of regular warfare. In doing so, they framed Dessalines (and by extension Haiti) as not "civilized." Therefore, it was not worthy of recognition as a sovereign state. Furthermore, because the French considered the Haitian revolutionaries to be outside the bounds of "civilized" society, they themselves had not and did not need to follow the rules of regular warfare. They claimed to be shocked that the Haitian state did not treat them with the respect that they had never shown the revolutionaries on the battlefields or in peacetime.

From Port-au-Prince Dessalines traveled north to Arcahaye, Saint-Marc, and Marchand-Dessalines, ordering executions at each city.[132] From Marchand-Dessalines, on April 1, 1804, Dessalines distributed copies of the colonists' letter of support for Rochambeau to his generals. "If the resolution that we have taken to exterminate our oppressors, needed any apologists in the heart of Hayti," he reassured his generals, "I would address to each of my fellow citizens a copy of the piece that you will find here included."[133] Dessalines reiterated his vow from the Declaration of Independence that the war with France would be eternal.

"Generals," he commanded, "in reading this piece, cry: *To arms!* and remind yourselves that your country cannot exist but by shouting *to arms* every six months."[134] In a footnote in his *Mémoires,* Boisrond-Tonnerre similarly implored his readers to look to the address before jumping to any conclusions about the executions. "Read this address," he advised, "and then pity these inhabitants if you find them to be pitied. *Ranae regem petentes* [the frogs who desired a king]."[135]

On the same day (April 1) that Dessalines published the pro-Rochambeau letter and the order, Dessalines's secretary, B. Aimé—who may have been his son, Jacques Bien-Aimé—wrote to the editor of the *Philadelphia Gazette,* asking him to publish Dessalines's February 29 decree, in which he ordered the arrest of those who had contributed to the "drowning, suffocating, hanging and shooting of more than sixty thousand of our Brethren under the inhuman Government of Le Clerc and of Rochambeau."[136] The publication of this proclamation in the United States was necessary, since an "evil disposed person (of whom unfortunately there are too many) will not fail to charge us with causing an indiscriminate destruction of the whites, whether good or bad, who have remained in the Island, it is right that the world should be undeceived by exposing the true motives which induced the Government to a measure which has never affected and never will effect [*sic*] any but the guilty."[137] Dessalines emphasized the culpability of those whom he targeted, but the executions were not limited to those who had signed the pro-Rochambeau letter.

On April 21, 1804—less than four months after the Declaration of Independence—Dessalines ordered the final executions in Cap.[138] Around that time, a British admiral claimed, "a general massacre of the White French took place; full three thousand, men women and children, were victims of it, and I believe very few remain; I understand some are concealed, but how they will get off the island is uncertain."[139] The French priest Guillaume Mauviel later described a "massacre" of "all the white people, without distinction of age or sex" on Dessalines's orders.[140] A French doctor in Cap claimed he was among only fifteen of 2,700 white people to survive the "massacres."[141] Six months later, however, a

British captain stated that he expected another massacre of about 200 white women in Cap, a claim that contradicts the admiral's report that few remained after the alleged April executions.[142]

While many of the foreign accounts, as well as those of both Haitian and foreign historians, describe a "general massacre" that had taken place in various cities, other evidence reveals that in fact hundreds of white people remained in Haiti in 1804 and beyond, many of whom were or had been French. A rare and partial census report from Gros Morne in the northern part of the Artibonite counted over six hundred white people in October 1804.[143] One US merchant who spent time in Cap in 1804 and 1806 estimated that in 1806 about three hundred "French" men, women, and children lived in Cap, and between six and eight hundred elsewhere in the country.[144]

Rather than a "general massacre," then, Dessalines had targeted select colonists for execution, while allowing others to remain and become citizens. Some of these white Haitians found jobs as local administrators.[145] For those who remained, the government facilitated their naturalization through an official process. A copy of a naturalization certificate—the cover letter of which noted specifically that the document was intended for white people—described the person in question as eligible for citizenship because the government was "convinced of the religion, the mores and the civic virtues of the citizen." If they signed the document, the naturalized white citizen renounced France forever and swore to live and die according to Haitian laws, to never challenge the Haitian government's legitimate authority, and to contribute to the prosperity of the country. Once the white person was accepted as a "child of Haiti," the naturalization document declared, they would "enjoy, regardless of their color, the same rights and prerogatives as the natural born citizens."[146] Some of the white French people who remained in Haiti, however, eventually escaped and wrote extensive reports about their time in Haiti, including details about the Haitian defense system, just as Dessalines had feared.[147]

One week after the final executions, Dessalines delivered another proclamation from Cap, this one destined to become one of his most famous.[148] On April 28, 1804, he addressed the *habitans d'Haïti,* arguing that the executions were justified and necessary. He presented the executions as retribution for past wrongdoings and stated that "finally, the hour of vengeance has rung, and the implacable enemies of the rights of man have suffered the punishment due for their crimes."[149]

He held the French accountable for their fate and claimed that Haitians had done what was necessary to secure their own country. "Yes, we have retaliated against these true cannibals," he claimed, "war for war, crime for crime, outrage for outrage; yes, I saved my country, I have avenged America."[150] In doing so, Dessalines established a bond between his citizens and the new nation.[151]

Dessalines highlighted the crimes that the French were guilty of: first, the centuries of slavery to which they had subjected the Haitians and their ancestors; and second, the atrocities committed by the French expeditionary army, including the "massacre of the entire population of this island," which, he noted, the French army had instructed him—when he was still a seemingly loyal French general—to carry out.[152]

These crimes also included the "plot very recently contrived in Jérémie": this was likely an amalgamation of the white Frenchmen who tried to escape with Perkins's help, the British citizens who illegally came ashore in Abricots, and the pro-Rochambeau letter that was revealed to Dessalines while he was in Jérémie. Dessalines connected these acts to "the terrible explosion that would have ensued, despite the general pardon granted to these incorrigibles upon the expulsion of the French Army; their emissaries answered them quickly in all the cities to spark a new internecine war."[153]

The executions, according to Dessalines, prefigured the fate that enemy invaders would encounter if they dared challenge Haitian freedom and sovereignty. "Tremble tyrants, usurpers, scourges of the new world!" he warned. "Our daggers are sharpened; your punishment is ready! sixty thousand men, equipped, inured to war, obedient to my orders, burn to offer a new sacrifice to the manes of their assassinated brothers."[154]

The French might come as far as the port cities. But if they ever approached the mountains, Dessalines promised, they would be "devoured by the anger of the children of Haiti."[155] He made sure to note that some white people, "commendable by the religion they have always professed," and innocent of the crimes committed by the French, were accepted into the new nation.[156] Furthermore, all neutral nations—so long as they respected Haitian sovereignty—would be welcome in Haiti for commercial relations. Dessalines was emphatic, however, that neither of these concessions should jeopardize Haitian sovereignty.

"*No colonist or European will ever set foot on this territory,*" he clarified, "*as master or proprietor,* this resolution will forever be the fundamental basis of our constitution."[157] And for the most part, this rule remained in place for over a century, until the US occupation of Haiti that began in 1915.[158] The exceptions to this rule in 1804, however, were the "handful of white people" who were "innocent of the mistakes of their counterparts." "It is repugnant to my charac-

ter and my dignity," Dessalines professed, to punish people who had "sworn to
live with us in the woods." He offered them clemency and ordered the nation
to treat them with respect.

Dessalines explicitly outlined the political project of the executions in the
April 28 proclamation, and he systematically supported his anti-colonial violence with rhetorical violence.[159] "Nature shuddered at hitherto unheard-of
crimes," Dessalines announced to the citizens of Haiti, "their actions were at
their worst." Haitians had had no choice but to respond.[160]

Dessalines's act of constitutive justice was, he argued, a necessary act of nation building, because the former colonizers had worked for so long to divide
the population.[161] "*Noirs et jaunes*," he argued, "which the refined duplicity of
Europeans has so long sought to divide; you who today make a single whole, one
single family, do not doubt it, your perfect reconciliation needed to be sealed
with the blood of your executioners."[162]

Four days later, Dessalines turned his attention outward. Now, rather than
to Haitians themselves, Dessalines addressed another proclamation to the "inhabitants of the Universe."[163] "Do not, unheard, accuse us of cruelty," Dessalines
pleaded with the international community. "Remember our past sufferings, and
you will judge less severely our present acts of necessity—of despair." Dessalines
accused white French revolutionaries, Bonaparte, and Leclerc of having committed horrific crimes in Saint-Domingue, which stemmed from their "desir[e]
to tyrannize over the Blacks." As in the Declaration of Independence, he called
the French "slaves," and tied Haiti's experiences to those of the nations of Europe
whose inhabitants had recently been "butchered, plundered, or enchained" by
Bonaparte.

"The Republic of Hayti," Dessalines declared, "wishes to live in peace with
all mankind, except with the White slaves of a BUONAPARTE; to them they
swear an eternal hatred, destruction and death, should they ever dare to set their
feet on this island of liberty, which their baseness, wickedness, and ferocity, have
so often and so terribly inundated with the blood of our unfortunate country-
men." Few white foreigners, however, would remember the Haitians' past sufferings as they read the inflammatory reports about the executions.

This proclamation was the only instance in which Dessalines called Haiti
a republic during his tenure as head of state. It is possible that the label was
an error inserted by the British printer, since the only known available version
of this proclamation is one that was printed in the *London Times*. But it is also
possible that Dessalines tailored it to his audience. Perhaps he wanted to em-

phasize that the Haitian Revolution was the true manifestation of liberty and equality. The proclamation also referenced "English invaders" from the British occupations of the south and west; indeed, the timing of this proclamation suggests that Dessalines no longer believed that he had to accommodate a British audience, since the treaty negotiations with Nugent were falling apart.

In his final response to Nugent—eleven days after this proclamation—Dessalines made clear that he was not willing to submit to a restrictive British treaty, since it did not reflect Haiti's new political reality. "First off, Your Excellency will Allow me to Recount," Dessalines explained to Nugent, "that the general Toussaint treated with the British government as a Subject or official of the French government, [but] that under these circumstances, I cannot nor do I have to, treat but as ruler of the people that I Command." By emphasizing how he differed from Louverture, Dessalines challenged the British officials in Jamaica and London to come to grips with a new sovereign nation in the Caribbean. In return, he offered promises of nonintervention abroad, assuring the British that the revolution would remain within the island. From Dessalines's point of view, Jamaica and Haiti could coexist peacefully. "The intention of my government," Dessalines explained in his response to Nugent's final letter, "is solely to defend itself from the French government and their allies, to fight against oppression and to attempt nothing against the powers who are charitable enough to see the French government as treacherous, regicidal, and tyrannous."[164] Nonintervention abroad, Dessalines hoped, would ensure that other nations would not invade Haiti, thereby protecting the legacy of the revolution at home.

Ultimately, however, Dessalines's letter marked both an end and a turning point, as the governor-general insisted that he did not need other nations for his to be free. "I, leader of a country, treat for my Citizens," Dessalines stated plainly. "I do not Owe anything to any power nor am I seeking to be attached to any government or to comply with any accommodations or treaties."

Before the might and opportunity offered to him if he simply conceded to the British—he would gain a powerful ally against France—Dessalines remained absolutely defiant. If he could not secure help on terms that acknowledged Haiti as an equal, then Haiti would go it alone.

The stakes were no less dire than when the revolution had begun over a decade earlier. French warships continued blockading Haitian ports and attacking and capturing foreign ships in Haitian waters. The troops in Santo Domingo remained, menacing the Haitian state. And on July 17, 1804, Ferrand—still encamped in force on the island's east side—wrote to the French minister of the navy about "the need in St. Domingo, to annihilate each and every last Black person, they who pollute this earth so precious for France."[165]

Facing such an existential threat, Dessalines had no choice but to lead his newly freed nation on the attack.

PART THREE

Jacques I

1804–1806

CHAPTER 11

The Empire of Hayti Rises before
the Eyes of the Astonished Universe

"The title of Governor general, heretofore referring to the citizen Jean-Jacques Dessalines, does not fulfill, in a satisfying manner, the general will," the nomination document declared, "because it supposes an outside power, dependence on a foreign authority, whose yoke we have forever thrown off."[1] In two short pages, Dessalines's advisors, on behalf of the nation, argued that the most effective method of governing was to have but one ruler. "Let us give to the citizen Jean-Jacques Dessalines," they concluded, "the title of EMPEROR OF HAYTI and the right to choose and name his successor." In a brief reply, Dessalines accepted the nomination.

"If any considerations can justify in my eyes," Dessalines announced, "the august title that your confidence awards me, it is no doubt my zeal to see the salvation of the empire and my hearty desire to consolidate our enterprise, an enterprise which will allow us to give, to the nations least friendly to freedom, not the impression of a bunch of slaves, but one of men who preferred their independence."

Dessalines recognized that this was not an easy task, since Haitians were "the artisans of their own freedom," and they had not "had to beg for foreign help to break the idol to which we are sacrificing." He understood that there might be skeptics within Haiti and abroad, but he explained that "if sober passions make common men, halfway measures halt the rapid progress of revolu-

tions." He emphasized that Haiti was still at war and that the country needed a
soldier to lead it, but that in becoming emperor he was also becoming the "father of my fellow citizens, of whom I was the defender, but the father of a family
of warriors never puts down his sword."[2]

On coronation day, October 8, 1804, military and civilian leaders paraded
onto the Champ-de-Mars in Cap. On the square the state had constructed an
amphitheater with a throne. Father Corneille Brelle, the white priest of Cap and
a naturalized citizen, crowned Dessalines emperor as his generals crowded
around. After the ceremony, the procession went to the cathedral to sing the *Te
Deum* while the military fired their muskets.[3] Jean-Jacques Dessalines, enslaved
at birth and raised on the plantations and on the battlefields of the French colony of Saint-Domingue, was now Emperor Jacques I of a free and independent
Haiti.

The procession returned to the government palace for an evening celebration.[4] At the coronation celebration, C. Cezar Télémaque, the inspector of the
north, sang a song dedicated to Jacques I (set to the popular tune of the vaude-
ville in *Le devin du village,* a famous play by Jean-Jacques Rousseau):

> He is the one who punishes the arrogance
> Of the French, our true enemies
> His name, his valor, his courage,
> Make all the conspirators tremble;
> Enemy of vile slavery;
> He only sees us as his children.[5]

The tune highlighted Dessalines's core values and reminded the nation of his
accomplishments. Their freedom was guaranteed by his victory over the French
and would continue to be secure, all because of his vigilance.

Although he established an empire and took the title of emperor, Dessalines
did not establish a corresponding nobility. He refused to confer titles of nobility
to his generals. When counseled to do so to secure the allegiance of some of his
detractors, he famously responded, "I alone am noble."[6] The military generals,
however, served as an upper sociopolitical class. Their positions, appointed by
Dessalines, were earned based on past and continued service to the nation. The
only exception was his wife, Marie-Claire Heureuse, who became Madame Dessalines, Empress of Hayti. Yet Dessalines did not make his new position hereditary. "I renounce," he told his generals, "yes I formally renounce the unjust custom of perpetuating power in my family."[7]

Abroad, this news traveled quickly. Within four days the governor of Jamaica reported that Dessalines was emperor in a letter to his superiors in London.[8] By the next month, the word had spread throughout the Caribbean.[9]

The decision to make Dessalines emperor was not made lightly. Indeed, it was part of a broader strategic plan to deal with domestic unrest and foreign pressure. In mid-1804 the prognosis was dire. Negotiations with George Nugent had deadlocked, meaning the Haitians could not count on Great Britain for aid. Meanwhile, French soldiers remained encamped in Santo Domingo under the direction of General Ferrand, who continued to threaten Haitian independence.[10] Other foreign governments simply refused to recognize Haitian independence.

Haiti's uncertain status on the international stage magnified its internal divisions, as people inside and outside the country questioned whether Dessalines was the right person to lead the country. Dessalines thus found himself in an increasingly precarious position.

On May 8, 1804—six months to the day before he was crowned emperor—Dessalines responded to Ferrand's attempts to undermine Haitian sovereignty by directly addressing the people of the eastern regions. In a proclamation that was printed in French and Spanish, Dessalines claimed that people in the east had previously supported the Haitians, but that they had been "seduced by treacherous innuendos" into seeking the protection of the French. "Spaniards, think about it," Dessalines warned them. "On the edge of the precipice dug beneath your feet, will this fanatic Minister save you when, iron and flame in hand, I pursue you to your last entrenchments? Ah! No doubt his prayers, his grimaces, his relics will not be able to stop me in my course."[11] Rumors had been spreading that Dessalines was planning an attack on Santo Domingo, and in this proclamation he threatened as much.[12]

Before initiating a military campaign against the French in the east, however, Dessalines had to attend to his own administration and defuse escalating internal challenges to his leadership.[13] On the western side of the island, he faced opposition from about two thousand independent revolutionaries who lived in the mountains outside the reach of the new state of Haiti. Some of these rebels he had fought against during the revolution.[14] The rebels had allied with different sides, sometimes even with the French, depending on what suited their immediate and longer-term needs and goals.[15] Some of the French leaders who dreamed of reconquering Haiti after 1804 even assumed that these independent revolutionary groups would support their reinvasion.[16]

As the Haitian government faced internal and external attacks that undermined independence and sovereignty, the French propaganda machine had gone into full effect.[17] Dessalines knew that his government had to publicize its own version of events. Haitians therefore put pen to paper to defend their freedom and independence. So that the Haitian account could be "entered into the historical record that we are transmitting to our posterity," Dessalines's secretary, Louis-Félix Boisrond-Tonnerre published his *Mémoires* of the war for independence.[18] The book's title page announced that it had been published with Dessalines's permission and by the government printing press.

"Haytiens, whom the courage of a hero has raised from the anathema of prejudice," Boisrond-Tonnerre addressed the nation as Haiti's first secretary of state in 1804, "by reading these memoirs, you will gauge the eye of the abyss from which he has taken you!" Boisrond-Tonnerre then turned his attention to those still suffering around the world: "And you slaves of all countries, you will learn from this great man, that people naturally carry freedom in their hearts, and that they hold the keys to it in their hands."[19]

Despite the trauma he faced by recounting the crimes committed by the French during their recent expedition, Boisrond-Tonnerre declared that it was a necessary task.[20] "How can we persuade the nations that the French contagion has not yet won," he asked, "that a tyrant usurping the throne of his master [Bonaparte], who bases his power on nothing other than liberty and equality, who claims the title of restorer of morals and religion, has decreed in cold blood the massacre of a million men, who wanted nothing other than liberty and equality."

He finished with a warning to the outside world. Now that liberty had been secured, he counseled, Haytiens "will defend it against the entire universe."[21]

At almost the exact moment that Boisrond-Tonnerre's *Mémoires* was released in Haiti, a propagandistic "biography" of Dessalines was published in France. Very quickly, the more powerful voice of Louis Dubroca—mouthpiece for the Napoleonic government—drowned out the Haitian accounts of events, including Boisrond-Tonnerre's remarkable *Mémoires* that yearned to combat the "French contagion."[22]

Two years earlier, Dubroca had written a similarly false portrait of Louverture with *La vie de Toussaint Louverture*.[23] Now he repurposed his earlier work to attack a new Haitian leader. In fact he adapted entire passages from his 1802 Louverture book, editing them to vilify Dessalines and the Haitian state and to simultaneously defame the British Empire. Dubroca's so-called biography was not a biography at all, but rather a propagandistic articulation of white French fears of Black revolution and independence. The Caribbean leaders were to some degree interchangeable, depending on the political needs of the author.

Key to Dubroca's approach in his Dessalines "biography" was to implicate the British in the success of the Haitian Revolution. "Is there any political consideration," Dubroca asked his readers, "that can justify this shameful association that the British government have with the leader of a population of assassins, whose crimes have terrified the whole world?"[24] Dessalines's army, Dubroca claimed, could not have defeated the French without outside assistance. The book began with a castigation of the British for allegedly allying with Haiti, and concluded by returning to British culpability.

While the book was explicitly written to malign the British, Dubroca's fictional account of Dessalines's life has had remarkable staying power. His purported biography shaped public opinion of Dessalines on two important topics: the first was his claim that Dessalines was born in Africa, and the second was his description of the so-called massacres of 1804.

"This ferocious African," as Dubroca described Dessalines, "transported very recently to Saint Domingue from the coast of Guinea, was a domestic to a free *nègre* property owner, named Dessalines, when the insurrection broke out."[25] The detail was important for Dubroca, because it substantiated his contention that Dessalines was "entirely a stranger to European custom, to the influence of their habits, of their civilization, and of their language, he had conserved all the ferocity, all the ignorance of the climate that saw his birth."[26] Dubroca used racist descriptions of Dessalines's physical appearance to support his claim about Dessalines's "savagery."[27]

Dubroca was not the first person to assert that Dessalines had not been born in the colony. Indeed, many white people at the time claimed that Dessalines was "African"; while some specified that they thought he was born in Africa, others left the claim ambiguous, since the term was sometimes simply a synonym for "Black" or "slave" and was also used as a derogatory term to emphasize a person's alleged lack of "civilization."[28] These characterizations occurred in private correspondence, official reports, and published accounts.

In most cases, the authors attached the birthplace claim to related allegations of "barbarism." For example, in an 1800 report on the state of the colony, a French author described Dessalines as "of the congo nation, a ferocious and barbarous man, says that he will drink the blood of white people."[29] Similarly, Edward Corbet recounted in 1803 that "Dessalines is an African, brutal and sanguinary in his disposition and altogether illiterate."[30] Levasseur, an officer in the

French army, published a short book in 1804 on the evacuation of the French army in which he called Dessalines a "former Bossale slave," defining "Bossale" as "from the coast of Africa."[31]

While these descriptions have the trappings of legitimate reporting, they in fact perpetuated the "monstrous hybrid" trope, with which white writers dehumanized Black men to justify and excuse their own racism, cruelty, and warfare. Indeed, Levasseur even went so far as to refer to Dessalines as an *"homme-tigre"* (tiger-man).[32] The implication was that he was so violent, he could not be considered human.[33] Foreigners described Dessalines as being African-born to bolster their claims about his supposedly "natural" ferocity and violence.

But these accounts did not stop at their character descriptions. Dubroca's 1804 "biography" imagined a narrative of Dessalines's revolutionary life as one whose sole purpose was violence for violence's sake. He filled one break in a passage—derived from his Louverture "biography"—with a pages-long lurid description of Dessalines's alleged violence in the early 1790s, including claims that he and his followers had raped and disemboweled women and drowned babies in boiling water.[34] Dubroca cranked up the gore, reproduced stereotypes, and played fast and loose with the evidence—if he had any at all.

Dubroca peppered *La vie de J.-J. Dessalines* with such graphic descriptions of violence, building to the most urgent event that he needed to spin, the so-called massacres of 1804. "While the spirits were reassured by the intentions of the black people," Dubroca purported, "their treacherous leader accelerated, by any means possible, the fatal moment; he traveled throughout the various sections of the colony, gathering the military officers, rousing them to carnage, and assuring himself of their zeal, by binding them to the execution of his crimes with the most dreadful oath."[35]

Rather than recognizing the crimes committed by the French colonists, Dubroca framed Dessalines as the criminal. Truthfulness was not the point of these early claims—rather, the goal was to discredit the Haitian revolutionaries and to ensure their failure.

The threat of reinvasion loomed large, and Dessalines faced increasingly hostile foreign depictions of him and his country. He understood in 1804 that his top priority had to be consolidating internal power, so that he could focus on defense against a French invasion.

To do this, his advisors counseled that he needed a new title. His current title, governor-general for life, was the same one that Toussaint Louverture had held when they were still under French colonialism. They argued that the title was not appropriate for the leader of an independent nation, since "governor" implied an external superior power or a metropole.[36] Moreover, the state may have wanted to overwrite any evidence that could have supported France's on-going claims to colonial legitimacy. This objective might explain why he tried to eliminate any sign that France still held dominion over the island.

No foreign power had yet officially recognized Haitian independence. Dessalines therefore needed as much evidence as possible that Haiti was indeed a sovereign nation. But what new structure would be most appropriate for the new country? A cohort of generals in the south advocated for a republican government, with a president at its head.[37] Others supported a centralized government under Dessalines's leadership, seeing a need to strengthen his power through an elective monarchy.[38] Dessalines and his advisors left little documentary evidence of this debate, but according to Haitian historian Thomas Madiou, news from Europe tipped the balance in August 1804.

Napoléon Bonaparte was proclaimed Emperor Napoléon I of France in May 1804, and news of this development reached Haiti in August 1804.[39] When Dessalines shared the news with his main political rival in the south, Alexandre Pétion, he explained that he was worried that this shift would elicit an international coalition against Haitian independence.[40] Having officially abandoned republicanism, the French might now find other nations to support their opposition to Haitian independence. And if Haiti did become a republic, the new country might become the target of European anti-republican warfare. It was therefore necessary, Dessalines argued, "to reinvigorate the fortification projects" in preparation for an attack. To support this move, Dessalines instructed Pétion to give workers only Saturdays off and then force them back to work on Sundays. He did not yet broach the possibility of becoming emperor.

But we can assume he spoke with his advisors about the question. Dessalines's primary advisors were secretary of state Louis Félix Boisrond-Tonnerre and secretary-general Juste Chanlatte, two *hommes de couleur* from the south and west, respectively. Both men were wealthy *anciens libres,* who had received their educations in Paris before returning to the colony.[41] Boisrond-Tonnerre and Chanlatte had only recently joined Dessalines's inner circle in mid-1803 and early 1804, respectively. Dessalines likely employed them to help overcome the factionalism that lingered after the civil war, and to help him frame Haitian statehood for a foreign audience with the goal of securing international recognition. Dessalines also relied on advice and friendship from the northern general Henry Christophe, who consistently sent updates to Dessalines and offered guidance on administrative, military, and personal matters. Christophe also maintained a close relationship with his wife, Marie-Claire, whom he called "my dear friend" (*ma chère commère*).[42]

After the news of Bonaparte's imperial title arrived in August, Dessalines and his top advisors and secretaries, including Boisrond-Tonnerre and Chanlatte, devised a plan that would, they hoped, protect his administration from external and internal threats and enable him to govern more effectively.[43] They likely excluded the republican generals of the south and west from this next phase of Haitian statecraft.[44]

To begin the process of converting the "State of Hayti" to the "Empire of Hayti," Boisrond-Tonnerre and Chanlatte composed a petition, a document that has yet to be recovered.[45] Signatures on the petition would provide evidence that support for an elective monarchy was widespread, thus adding legitimacy to Dessalines's rule. Those generals who leaned toward a republican form of government (Pétion, Geffrard, Férou, and Jean-Louis François) were only made aware of the plan to declare a Haitian empire when Dessalines requested their signatures for the document.

Dessalines wrote a personal cover letter to Pétion on August 14, 1804—less than a week after he had notified the general about Napoléon's new title—because he knew that Pétion would oppose such a measure. Dessalines nevertheless went through the motions of requesting his support. He asked Pétion to sign the petition "if you deem it appropriate," and instructed him to "have it signed by the generals and corps commanders of your division."[46] In the cover letter he named the generals François, Geffrard, and Magloire to help get the appropriate signatures. Pétion and the other generals conceded, and the signed petition came back to Dessalines by the end of August.[47]

Ultimately, the official nomination of Dessalines as emperor included six printed pages of signatories' names and positions.[48] The text and signatures may have been the same or like that of the petitions that circulated throughout the country in August. Dessalines likely wanted to give the illusion of universal support for his change of title, even though there were deep and growing divisions within the country.

There are inconsistencies in the official record of the nomination process. The state-issued, printed copy of the official nomination of Dessalines as emperor carries the date—curiously—of January 25, 1804, and the location of Port-au-Prince. It is possible that Dessalines and his administration had been considering a change in title since the first month of independence, but the historian Madiou claims that the documents were backdated, so as not to give the impression that the Haitians were imitating the French. Similarly, the printed version of Dessalines's acceptance of the nomination was dated February 15, 1804, from Marchand-Dessalines. The location may have been symbolic; Dessalines was in Les Cayes on that date.[49]

Wherever and whenever the originals were created, the government press printed both documents in early September 1804. By December the British governor of Jamaica had received copies.[50]

The official coronation ceremony was scheduled for October 8, but in early September Dessalines declared to his officers that he was ready to begin using the new title.[51] His officers responded with cries of *"vive l'Empereur!"*[52] Foreign diplomats in Haiti began using the new title immediately, even though their states did not recognize Haitian independence.[53]

After the coronation, Dessalines may have shared the news himself with his archenemy Napoléon. A copy of a letter dated October 9, 1804—that is, the day after the coronation—is allegedly from Dessalines to Napoléon. This suggests that Dessalines may have initiated contact in an attempt to secure recognition of the new Haitian Empire: "I implore you sire, my brother and cousin, to declare in an authentic manner that you believe that a black man can just like a man of any other color become emperor like you." The authenticity and sincerity of this letter, however, are suspicious.[54]

What *is* known is that when the government distributed the printed version of Dessalines's nomination and acceptance, they appended a short essay by Chanlatte called *"À mes concitoyens."* (In the essay Chanlatte still called Dessalines "governor-general," suggesting that he wrote it before the coronation.)[55] The essay attributed much of Haiti's success to the "grace of the Supreme Being" and argued that "when the Eternal distributed the different races on earth, they did not intend that one particular species would destroy another."

While revolutionary France claimed to be a land of liberty, Chanlatte flipped the script. "Their nation," he wrote, "slaves today under an unjust and ambitious master, are learning from a savage people the secret of being free."[56] While the French had condescended to Haitians for "living in the woods," Chanlatte predicted that "it is there that we will be invincible." The mountains were their refuge and their strength. "It is there that for so long the tutelary genius of Hayti calls its dear infants. At this courageous resolution, the bones of our brothers, these martyrs of liberty, will tremble with joy. Our arsenals, our arms, our munitions, our resources and our families will be under the protection of Nature and the Gods."[57] Dessalines had successfully coordinated the war for independence from the mountains and now focused his national defense in the interior; Chanlatte's essay celebrated his strategy.

Moreover, Chanlatte was optimistic for the future. "And so, the Island of Hayti," he closed the essay, "similar to the Phoenix, after having felt its intestines torn by its own children, after having been consumed by flames, will rise from the ashes, and will emerge from its ruins, more beautiful and more glorious."[58] In 1802 Rochambeau's supporters—those who had recently been executed on Dessalines's orders—had envisioned Saint-Domingue rising from the ashes to revive the slavery-based plantation economy. Now, instead, Chanlatte imagined a glorious future based on liberty.[59]

Soon after Dessalines's coronation in October, the Haitian state celebrated the first anniversary of its Declaration of Independence on January 1, 1805.[60] In just one year, Dessalines and the Haitian state had prevented outside incursions, revived the economy, and established a new form of government. While Haitian independence had not yet been recognized by foreign powers and the French were loudly still claiming dominion, the Haitian state maintained informal trade relations with the British and the US. Most important, they had secured their borders and preserved the abolition of slavery.

This was a moment to celebrate for all Haitians. For Dessalines the festivities began the night of December 31, at a party he hosted in Marchand-Dessalines. Drums and fifes filled the night air as the partygoers danced African dances till dawn.[61] Dessalines's love of dance had a lasting impact on the country, and a French consul later wrote that "we even owe to [his] taste several *bambocha* (*fandangillo*) that he composed for the balls at his court."[62] The carabinier, a dance style that dates back to Dessalines's empire, mimics military marches and was named after cavalry soldiers.[63] The following day, a formal ceremony took place. Thousands of troops gathered to hear a speech by Boisrond-Tonnerre, the secretary who had penned the original Declaration of Independence. His comments focused on the ongoing struggle against the French.[64]

Then Dessalines spoke. To the assembled soldiers, he energetically proclaimed the national oath: to live free and independent, or die.[65] He instructed his generals to repeat the Independence Day festivities in their own districts in the days after January 1.[66] January 6 was the *jour des rois,* when the troops received additional rations of beef and wine for the beginning of a six-day celebration. Soldiers and *cultivateurs* assembled in their town squares to hear readings of the act of independence and Dessalines's independence speech.[67] Those assembled also renewed their oath to live free and independent.

"May divine Providence, that has deigned to give you such clear marks of its protection, and favor the most just of causes," Henry Christophe wrote to Des-

salines, "preserve you for a long time, for the glory and prosperity of your Empire and the happiness of your army and the People, a constant object of your
deepest concerns."[68] On January 12 Christophe reported to Dessalines that the
celebration in his district had included "the Te Deum [which was] celebrated in
the parish to the sound of several artillery salvoes; in the afternoon there was a
meal at the old theater building, and during the following six days of this celebration, we danced continually."[69]

Dessalines continued to support his troops and build his navy, but he only
acted against the French in Santo Domingo after his coronation as emperor.[70]
Throughout 1804 General Ferrand had maintained that reinforcements from
France were expected any day now. He expanded his authority on land by launching expeditions throughout the east, rallying the "Spanish" people and people of
color to his side by spreading anti-Dessalinean propaganda.[71] He acquired land
on behalf of the French colonial state and tried to expand the nascent plantation
economy.[72]

Ferrand repeatedly tried to blur the line between slavery and freedom, pushing more and more Black people into bondage in his territory.[73] In January 1805
Ferrand was still a threat to Haitian independence, and it was clearer than ever
that a French reconquest would mean the repeal of abolition.[74]

Dessalines had claimed the entire island as Haitian territory. And he knew
that if a foreign presence—and specifically a French one—remained on the island, the Haitian state was not safe. "Having decided to recognise as borders
only those traced by nature and the seas," Dessalines later stated as he recounted
his campaign against Santo Domingo, "convinced that as long as a single enemy
still breathes on this territory there remains something for me to do in order to
hold with dignity the post to which you have appointed me. . . . I have resolved
to regain possession of the integral part of my dominions and to destroy even to
the last vestiges the European idol."[75]

As these plans became a reality, the British in Jamaica decided that their best
course of action would be to remain neutral.[76] Their support would have been
decisive, but a battle between the Haitians and the French would, they hoped,
lessen the likelihood of either empire attacking Jamaica.[77]

Other British governors in the Caribbean worried that if Dessalines's empire extended throughout the island, it would increase the likelihood that enslaved people from all the islands would seek refuge there. "All our Negroes, who
wish to elope," the governor of Turks Island wrote in November 1804, "make
directly for that island; formerly if they could be traced and found, they were

restored to their old masters; but such is far from being the case at present, as Dessalines not only protects, but encourages by employing them." This had already happened; several enslaved people from Turks Island had stolen two boats and escaped to Haiti. When Governor Alexander Murray sent emissaries to retrieve the fugitives, Dessalines claimed that he had no knowledge of their presence, which Murray concluded was a lie, since his contacts reported to have seen them on shore.[78]

Around the same time, the governor of Jamaica similarly reported that enslaved people had escaped to Haiti and told his superiors that "the Negroes from those islands [Caicos] desert by every opportunity to the Land of Liberty."[79] It is possible that Dessalines was covertly helping enslaved people secure their freedom as Haitian citizens, while also trying to preserve and expand his provisional relationship with the British.

For months before and after the coronation, Dessalines and his advisors had planned for a campaign against Santo Domingo. A French attack in early January 1805, however, forced their hand.[80] On January 6 General Ferrand authorized and encouraged people living in the departments of Ozama and Cibao, near the contested Haitian border, to capture and enslave Haitian boys under the age of fourteen and girls under the age of twelve. He avoided using the word "slave," but he did note that the prisoners would become the "property" of their captors.[81] Those who were not eligible for enslavement, Ferrand decreed, should be killed.[82]

Ferrand's aggressive tactics put Haitian lives at risk and encroached on the territorial sovereignty of the Haitian Empire. His goal, explicitly outlined in his decree, was to ensure the Haitians' "submission to the emperor of the French, at the hands of the general FERRAND," at which point he would cease the attack.[83]

At the end of the month, Dessalines prepared his troops for battle. This meant they needed new uniforms in accordance with his January 2, 1804, decree.[84] He asked the division generals to procure blue fabric and coordinate with the tailors of their departments.[85] Obtaining enough blue fabric to outfit the twenty thousand soldiers who would march the next month was not an easy task.[86] The troops also received cartridges, flints, provisions, and pay.[87] The soldiers who were physically able to make the arduous journey across the island were organized into demi-brigades, and the generals mustered their troops for review.[88] The generals and their commanders scoured the departments for any citizens who had shirked their military duties.[89]

On February 16, 1805, Dessalines and his generals began their march.[90] "The

Indigene Army take the field next week against St Domingo," one Haiti-based US merchant reported, "headed in person by His Majesty. Dessalines is truly a man of *strong mind and prodigious firmness.* I like him on account of his quick decision."[91] The emperor brought twenty thousand soldiers, but since the overland journey was difficult, they were limited in their weapons, artillery, and cannons.[92] A Haitian ship supported the overland attack by carrying supplies, including biscuits.[93] A contingent from the south, led by Nicolas Geffrard, joined the attack on February 19 with an artillery regiment.[94] The contingent from the north, under the direction of Henry Christophe in Cap, was delayed because of an extended period of *les nords,* periods of heavy wind and rain that occur intermittently between October and April.[95] After Christophe's troops left, the severe rains escalated and a hurricane hit Cap, damaging the city.[96]

The weather would continue to be a problem. Dessalines led a column from Petite Rivière across the central mountains to approach Santo Domingo from the western side, while Christophe's column from Cap headed farther east to the north of the city.[97] Because of high waters caused by the lengthy rains, Christophe used canoes to transfer his troops and supplies from Cap to Monte Christi, after which they began their overland journey south and east as the rain continued.[98]

En route, Dessalines learned that he would not be receiving any support from the Spanish-speaking inhabitants of the eastern side of the island. Consequently, he determined that he would not show them any mercy.[99]

The troops reached the outskirts of Santo Domingo on March 6, two months after Ferrand had announced his policy of restoring slavery.[100] The Spanish colonial city was a well-fortified city surrounded by a fifteen-foot-high stone wall.[101] Ferrand defended it with only about seven hundred troops and two thousand militiamen. The French performed targeted excursions out from the city, but the Haitian army soon established sophisticated ad hoc bastions. As had been the case during the revolution, the army occupied several plantations and set up camps. The columns communicated with each other using cannon shots, and conveyed letters using aides-de-camp who moved quickly overland.[102]

From the Gaillard plantation, three and a half miles northwest of the city, Dessalines wrote to Ferrand to demand that he surrender to his authority. Ferrand responded the next day with cannon fire. Christophe's troops from the north joined Dessalines's attack, resting just briefly on March 7 on a neighboring plantation, before advancing toward the northeast of the city.[103] Christophe and Clervaux settled their troops on the eastern side of the Ozama River, a waterway that runs from the Caribbean Sea through the city of Santo Domingo

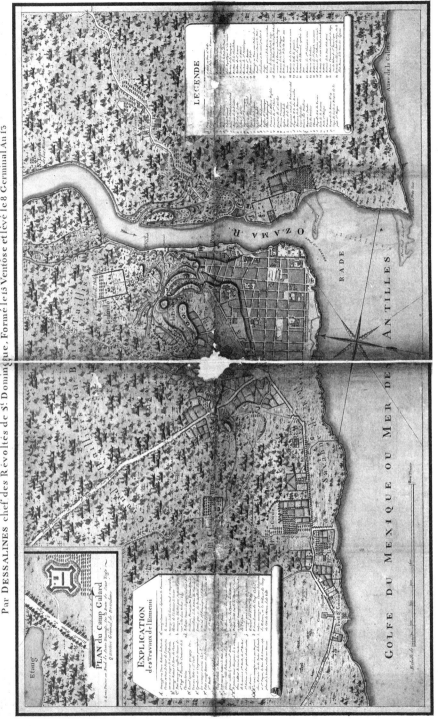

Plan du siège de Santo Domingo par Dessalines, chef des révoltés de St. Domingue, formé le 15 Ventôse et levé le 8 Germinal an 13, 1805. Library of Congress Geography and Map Division, Washington, DC, G4954.

and then forks to create a veinlike network outside the city walls to the northeast.[104] The Haitian army thus surrounded Santo Domingo, attempting to compensate for their limited artillery.[105]

After two days of fighting, Dessalines anticipated that the enemy would retreat, since they were leaving their dead and wounded on the battlefield. On March 11, however, Ferrand sent out three columns to attack the Haitian army. With new reinforcements under Pétion, the Haitian army pushed them back and took prisoners.[106] "I have the honor to inform your majesty," Christophe reported to Dessalines on March 13 from the banks of the Ozama River, "that the gun shots that you no doubt heard last night, were fired by my Division at the Ships that, finding themselves near our lines, wanted to escape." "The enemy had many people killed both on Board the Ships and on land," he continued. "Several of their ships were towed and put under the protection of the fort; despite this, our gunshots will reach their men."[107]

Ferrand continued to cannonade and bombard the Haitians from within the city walls. On March 16 Dessalines ordered his troops to approach within pistol shot of the city walls.[108] While attacking Ferrand's troops, the Haitian army took enslaved Spanish-speaking plantation workers as prisoners; Christophe made sure, however, that they did not take sick or postpartum women.[109] He let one of his battalion chiefs know that Captain Félix "is escorting a convoy of Spanish people, men & women, that you will place on the Grandpré Plantation, and secure for them foodstuffs, until my return." "Do not allow anyone to vex them," Christophe warned the battalion chief, "and you will count them so that no one takes them and places them on other plantations; have some respect for them."[110] The Haitians also stole oxen and other animals to bring back for the state-owned carts (*charrois de l'État*), so that the farmers would not have to give up their livestock.[111]

On March 21, in the middle of relentless gunfire, Christophe learned that Dessalines had welcomed a child. "I congratulate you with all my heart," Christophe wrote to Dessalines, "for the news that you were kind enough to share with me, which gave me great pleasure, because it tends towards the Happiness of our country."[112] This was likely the birth of Dessalines's daughter Serrine, although he does not appear to have publicly celebrated Serrine's birth.

News from the battlefield, in contrast, was not good. "I have the honor to let you know that yesterday at almost noon, an armed brig with a French flag, moored just beyond the other ships," Christophe reported to Dessalines on March 23. "The round of shots that your Majesty no doubt heard were fired at

it, but it was too far away and we could not reach it."[113] Dessalines conferred
with his top generals, who agreed on the need for a coordinated attack.[114]

By the evening of March 26, however, the Haitian army faced a French foe
that had increased significantly in numbers.[115] Ferrand's pleas for reinforcements
from France had finally been answered, as Bonaparte renewed his dreams for a
revival of France's American empire. After a brief stop in Dominica, a fleet arrived in the Santo Domingo harbor.[116] From his position on the Ozama River,
Christophe alerted Dessalines of the arrival of a brig and two schooners, bringing the number of French ships to seven. Unfortunately, the ships were out of
gun range, beyond even the reach of the cannon that Christophe had unearthed
on the plantation where he was stationed.[117]

The arrival of the ships inspired Ferrand to launch an offensive against Pétion's and Geffrard's troops near the coast to the west of the city. After an initial
push, though, the French quickly retreated, leaving their dead and wounded
strewn along the route back to the city walls.

On March 28 the new French troops began disembarking from the ships.[118]
Pétion convinced Dessalines of the possibility that additional French ships
could arrive in the west, and the emperor therefore abandoned the siege to return to the territory over which he already had dominion.[119] "In any other circumstance," Dessalines later explained, "this reinforcement . . . would have been
insufficient to prevent the success of my forces."[120] His troops could not afford
further delays in capturing the city, and he reluctantly conceded that the small
fleet had reversed the likely outcome of his campaign.

Dessalines ordered his generals to evacuate, and the cavalry spread along the
route, destroying and burning everything in their path. As the Haitian troops
retreated, they took prisoners, stole animals and cattle, and burned homes and
villages.[121] This, they hoped, would weaken French power and reduce the likelihood of an attack.[122] Christophe noted that there were about six hundred prisoners, "Spaniards of both colors and the two sexes."[123] "All those who will not
march willingly," Christophe instructed, "we will make them march by force or
leave them on the floor."[124] He made arrangements to feed the prisoners plantains, potatoes, and cassava.[125]

Under Haitian authority, some of the Black Spanish prisoners were sent to
work as *cultivateurs* on plantations in the west, while others were incorporated
into the Haitian army, their freedom guaranteed by Haitian law.[126] "The intention of the Haitian Government is not to mistreat them," Christophe told one
of his generals. "Convince yourselves generals of these truths that I have told
you at different times."[127] Christophe had learned that the Spanish cultivators

were indeed being maltreated in an effort to get them to work, and many of the women had been taken as domestic servants or *femmes de chambres* of members of the army or residents of the east.[128] Any of the Spanish cultivators who tried to escape were executed.[129]

Dessalines himself requested that 130 Black Spanish men and women and their children be sent directly to him.[130] It is unclear why he did so, but it is possible that he intended to have them work on his plantations in Marchand-Dessalines. The white Spanish prisoners, on the other hand, were likely executed.[131] They had supported Ferrand, and Dessalines treated them the same way that he treated his "eternal enemies," the French.[132]

Haitian fears of another French attack heightened after a British ship arrived at Môle Saint-Nicolas. Its sailors reported that they had seen a large fleet of French ships to the east carrying about fifteen thousand troops.[133] When they arrived back in the west, the Haitian generals quickly pivoted to ready the port cities to defend against an attack.[134] Dessalines ordered the generals to redouble their construction efforts on the inland forts, and to remove all war munitions from the port cities.[135] At the same time, the generals shifted more of the Haitian *cultivateurs* to fort-building duties.[136] In early May Christophe tested twelve mortar bombs, most of which were successful.[137] He also reported that he had requested more *vivres* (provisions) for the troops.[138] The French squadron never attacked Haitian territory, but General Ferrand and his troops remained in Santo Domingo until 1809, threatening the new country and assaulting maritime trade.

Upon their return from Santo Domingo, Dessalines asked his generals for detailed reports of their march, so that his administration could compose an official account of the siege.[139] To introduce the official record, Dessalines addressed the nation from Marchand-Dessalines on April 12. He noted that Ferrand had provoked the siege with his January 6 decree, and Dessalines distributed copies of the document as proof of Ferrand's intentions.[140] The address was also a call for vigilance. "At the first sound of the alarm cannon," he instructed, "may the land of Haiti reveal to their greedy eyes nothing but ashes, iron and soldiers; and if we have to die as victims for the most just of causes, let us leave behind the honorable memory of the energy of a people fighting against slavery, injustice and despotism."[141]

When Dessalines returned from the campaign against Santo Domingo, he reinvigorated efforts to fortify the interior, protect the port cities, and bolster agricultural production. He also issued Haiti's first constitution and a series of legal codes designed to regulate the military and various social aspects of Haitian life. The first of these documents was the imperial constitution, which Boisrond-Tonnerre and Chanlatte had drafted during the siege against Santo Domingo. Dessalines signed and accepted it on May 20, 1805.[142] In this constitution Dessalines attempted to define Haiti as a distinctive nation by focusing on citizenship, political organization, and culture.

He made good on his promise to deny white people land ownership rights in article 12: "no white man of whatever nation he may be, shall put his foot on this territory with the title of master or proprietor, neither shall he in future acquire any property therein."[143] The constitution allowed some significant exceptions to this rule, including white women, Germans, and Poles who were naturalized by the Haitian government.[144] These people would, however, have had to renounce all other citizenships.[145] Similarly, Haitians lost their citizenship if they emigrated or naturalized in a foreign territory.[146] Dessalines knew that he could not trust the white colonizers as property owners to protect Black Haitians; the state therefore assumed control of any property that they had previously owned or recently sold.[147] These land confiscations would enable the state to control the economy, while also generating revenue. The "territory" that the constitution considered to be part of the country included the entire island, although of course Dessalines had just failed to recapture the east.[148]

The most well-known article of Dessalines's constitution is number 14: "all exception of color among the children of one and the same family, of whom the chief magistrate is the father, will necessarily cease, the Haytians shall hence forward be known only by the generic appellation of blacks."[149] The constitution, recognizing race as an ideological concept, decreed that Haitians of all skin colors would be recognized as "Black," thereby eliminating the racial hierarchies of the colonial era. Rather than remaining a label that signaled subjugation and inequality, in Dessalines's empire "Black" became the universal and the political basis for citizenship.[150] Instead of being a term associated with subordination, slavery, and savagery, as white colonizers had practiced, Dessalines declared Blackness to be the source of freedom and independence.[151]

This meant, however, that Haitian citizenship was based on exclusion.[152] Not all Haitians welcomed this racialized or colorized version of citizenship, and the *gens de couleur* chafed at being called *noir*.[153] The socioracial hierarchy of the colonial era did not disappear, despite Dessalines's efforts to unite the population.

The constitution reaffirmed the empire and Dessalines's role as both emperor and commander in chief of the army. As in 1801, the leader of the country maintained both political and military power. The highly military structure that developed in Haiti was seen by political leaders as necessary for several reasons. Haiti was a Black, independent nation of formerly enslaved people in a region otherwise characterized by colonialism and slavery. As such, pro-slavery nations viewed the country with apprehension or hostility.[154] Their potential threats to Haitian independence made a strong military necessary during the early years of independence, and so each of the early constitutions asserted state sponsorship of strong military forces.[155] Furthermore, Haiti was still actively at war with France.

By sustaining such a strong military force, however, Dessalines alienated his administration from the nation.[156] *Cultivateurs* were removed from their homes for extended periods to serve in the standing army, draining resources from local communities. The integration of the army into the political development of the state also encouraged military solutions to social and political problems.[157] While the constitution defined citizenship as universal, in practice it emphasized military service, from which women were excluded.[158]

The constitution also valued national unity over internal dissent. It called for allegiance in times of crisis and valued the idea of one national community above local or regional affiliations, a recognition of the continued factionalism within the country.

To foster Haitian nationalism, the constitution designated national holidays and festivals. Article 27 stated that "there shall be national festivals for celebrating independence, the *fête* of the emperor [Saint Jacques's feast day on July 25] and his august spouse [August 12], that of agriculture and of the constitutions."[159] The new flag of Haiti was black and red. Another aspect of Dessalines's constitution, which set his apart from subsequent Haitian constitutions, was that he declared freedom of religion and restricted the state from choosing a religion.[160] The constitution made clear that marriage was "an act purely civil and authorized by the government," and legalized divorce.[161]

Within two weeks Dessalines appointed a public official in each commune who would be responsible for recording births, marriages, and deaths for individuals in their locality.[162] Because Haiti did not have support from the Holy See, Dessalines assumed the leadership of the island's Catholic Church, and he appointed priests, including Corneille Brelle, the priest in Cap who had overseen his coronation.[163] He and his generals also tried to prevent the practice of Vodou. "I am told, general," Christophe wrote to Capoix in late 1805, "that they continually dance *le Vaudoux,* in the region of Bois de l'Anse, if this is true, this region merits your prompt attention, to prevent a dance that is so prejudicial to tranquility, and has always been banned everywhere by the governments."[164]

As with the Haitian Declaration of Independence, the first Haitian constitution had both a domestic and a foreign audience. Dessalines and his government checked the boxes for what would qualify their state as worthy of membership in the European "family of nations." They also hoped to make their state less threatening (thereby securing recognition and treaties) by reiterating their promise not to invade neighboring colonies.[165] It was important to repeat this guarantee in the aftermath of the campaign against Santo Domingo, since some countries may have interpreted the attack as an expansion of the Haitian Empire. Instead, however, Dessalines emphasized that the campaign against the French in Santo Domingo was an anti-colonial battle to reclaim land that was already theirs, not an imperialist offensive.[166]

The constitution was not Dessalines's only attempt to lay the juridical foundation of the nation. Six days after he signed the constitution, he published a military penal code that contained seventy-six articles.[167] "Without honor, fidelity, obedience, and subordination," Dessalines stated in the May 26, 1805, document, "armies are nothing but hordes of brigands."[168] The term "brigand" had been levied against the Haitian armies during the revolution, as the French and the British declared them to be armed enemies of the state and dangerous to public order. The term was also racialized, since it was usually used to describe Black rebels.

To prove that Haiti was a legitimate state, Dessalines had to show that the Haitian army was a legitimate military force. International relations and legitimacy in the European community depended on common understandings of the rules of engagement. By organizing the Haitian military in a way that was legible to Euro-American nations, Dessalines hoped to increase his nation's perceived "civilization," according to foreign metrics. This, in turn, would help protect the new country from foreign invasion.

The code also sought to protect against internal insubordination. It included legislation about desertion to the enemy, espionage, treason, assassination, and revolt, all of which would be punished with death by firing squad. People who deserted "to the interior," even for short periods of time, would receive prison time, shackles, corporal punishment, or solitary confinement.[169] More minor forms of insubordination or negligence would receive similarly strong punishments. Infractions such as looting, stealing, or destroying private or public property and threatening the lives of unarmed Haitian citizens in the process were also punishable by death. The code punished military personnel for raping women and girls: ten years in prison for raping a minor, and five years for raping a woman.[170] If a victim died because of an attack, the guilty party would be sentenced to death.

Dessalines continued building the nation's legal infrastructure by issuing a series of additional laws relating to "illegitimate" children, divorce, and military tribunals.[171] The legal code that permitted and regulated divorce contained forty-nine articles, many of which were copied directly from the 1792 French divorce code (which was no longer in effect), sometimes with minor linguistic changes.[172] The most significant difference, however, was the elimination or reduction of minimum wait times leading up to, during, and after the divorce process. This made divorce and remarriage much quicker and easier than in the French code.

The Haitian code also included several additional articles with no equivalent in the French code. For example, there was an article limiting women's petitions for divorce from men enlisted in the army and away from their commune, and another article facilitating the divorce of spouses who had emigrated from Haiti.[173]

Dessalines was personally invested in a May 28, 1805, law that established the rights of children born out of wedlock and required spouses to recognize their partner's existing children before marriage.[174] The law also allowed married fathers to recognize children born out of wedlock, granting such children the same inheritance rights as those born in wedlock.[175] The following February, Dessalines and Marie-Claire Heureuse had several children recognized by a notary in Marchand-Dessalines. These were children whom Dessalines had fathered before he met Marie-Claire, but she claimed them as her own because she was now allowed to do so by law. Records exist for Célimène, Jacques Bien-Aimé, and Célestine—all born in the 1790s.[176] Dessalines allegedly had several mistresses in different cities who bore other children out of wedlock.[177] Balthazar Inginac claimed that at least one of Dessalines's mistresses, Euphémie Daguih, spent exorbitant amounts of state money in Les Cayes.[178]

The state was also concerned about collective action against the government, and section 8 contained a single article, a response to the escalating political challenges to Dessalines's empire. "All conspiracies or plots," the article declared, "all statements tending to trouble the Empire with a civil war, by propagating disunion, by animating the citizens against one another or against the legitimate exercise of authority, will be punished with death."[179] Dessalines would show no mercy to those who challenged his rule.

On June 16 Dessalines hosted a ceremony in Marchand-Dessalines to publicly present the new constitution and the military penal code. His secretaries read the constitution and the code aloud, explaining the contents to potential critics.[180] Then Dessalines gave a speech.[181] The constitution, he noted, "establishes your rights on invariable bases, and lets you take your place among the ranks of civilized nations."[182] "I swear to respect and uphold the constitution in all its integrity," he promised. "I swear to support freedom and independence, and to force our enemies to recognize them or to bury myself under the rubble of my fortresses."[183]

The evening concluded with a dinner. The emperor and generals toasted the constitution; Haiti's liberty and independence; the emperor, empress, and imperial family; the generals and the army; and the United States and other nations trading with Haiti. Boisrond-Tonnerre drew attention to a specific article of the constitution and toasted "to Union, to Fraternity, to the only denomination under which Haitians will henceforth be known, which is blacks [*noirs*]."[184]

Prior to the June 16 ceremony, Dessalines sent copies of the constitution and military code to his regional generals.[185] The code specified that the minister of war (soon after Étienne-Élie Gérin was appointed to the position) was personally responsible for ensuring that printed copies of the code were sent to the military commanders and war commissioners, and that its articles were followed exactly. Dessalines instructed the generals to distribute the documents to the military leaders throughout each region; they were to read the documents aloud in a public square each Sunday for three weeks, beginning on June 16.[186]

After the constitution and military penal code were read aloud, the crowd in Cap responded with cries of *"Vive sa Majesté l'Empereur!"*[187] The constitution, Henry Christophe enthusiastically claimed in a letter to Dessalines after receiving the printed copies, gave Haitians "a way to repudiate [our enemy's] unjust project to enslave us and to erase us from the list of free peoples!"[188]

Perhaps signaling that Dessalines was not as confident as he would have liked to be about national support for his rule, he reorganized the nation's military leadership at a ceremony at the imperial palace in Cap on July 8, 1805. "By the grace of God and the constitutional Law of the state," Dessalines named Henry Christophe general in chief of the Haitian army (Dessalines maintained the position of emperor and *chef suprême* of the army).[189] The minister of finances and the interior was André Vernet, and the minister of war and the navy was Gérin. Dessalines named Paul Romain, François Capoix, and Jean-Louis François as division generals and Louis Gabart, Alexandre Pétion, and Nicolas Geffrard as commanders in chief of the army's regional divisions. His longtime chief of staff Louis Bazelais retained his position. Dessalines even employed his former enslaver, Jeanvier Desaline, as a concierge in the new imperial palace.[190]

But the military promotions did little to stifle the threats to Dessalines's rule. The republican factions in the south of Haiti, still reeling from the declaration of the Haitian Empire, were further antagonized by the 1805 constitution and legal codes. Internal political opposition to the emperor was growing. Instead of consolidating power within the country, the constitution created an unbridgeable divide between factions.

CHAPTER 12

Tears of Blood

"Surveillance has increased for some time on all points," the governor of Martinique and Guadeloupe wrote to the minister of the French colonies, "after the notice that I received from the agent from our islands in St. Thomas, who told me that *Dessalines* sent emissaries to the neutral colonies charged with organizing a rebellion of the slaves in Martinique & Guadeloupe."[1] This "agent" was the former colonist Roberjot Lartigue, who had owned land in the Artibonite and was one of the signatories to the 1802 letter supporting Rochambeau's nomination as governor.[2] Lartigue wanted the French government to reinvade Haiti so that he could reclaim his plantations, and his fearmongering among Caribbean officials aimed to generate support for such an expedition.

In a series of letters Lartigue managed to convince other governors that Dessalines was planning an imminent Caribbean-wide revolution. Thus, by 1806, claims that Dessalines was fomenting anti-slavery revolts elsewhere in the Caribbean were proliferating, despite the explicit promises in the Declaration of Independence and the 1805 constitution that Haiti would not make such a move.

In February 1806 the US Congress passed a bill—at President Jefferson's insistence—that officially prohibited trade with Haiti. This cut off a key trade relationship for the new nation. News of the prohibition reached Haiti in March.[3] Henry Christophe reported to Dessalines that US merchants in Cap were scrambling to protect their investments. Haiti's political sovereignty and its trade relationships were being jeopardized by Dessalines's reputation for violence and the apparent threat that he might provoke rebellions abroad. "At that time," as Haitian historian Michel Hector noted, "the project of building an anti-colonial, anti-slavery, anti-racist, and anti-plantation society was totally in contradiction with the dominant global hierarchy."[4]

Despite these internal and external challenges, or perhaps because of them, Dessalines determined to celebrate the second anniversary of Haitian independence. In anticipation of the event, the empress began procuring supplies for the feast. She asked Christophe to send her sugar, cheese, and fruits in *eau-de-vie*.[5] Dessalines invited Christophe and Romain to join him in the city of Marchand-Dessalines for the January 1 celebration.[6] Before his departure, Christophe left detailed instructions regarding how his soldiers should celebrate the holiday in Cap in his absence. When the troops, civilian corps, and cultivators from the city had assembled on the Champ-de-Mars, Christophe wanted one of the local generals to read the oath of independence and Dessalines's speech to the citizens of Haiti, and those in attendance would once again renew their vows to live free and independent.[7] The men and women at the ceremony would swear again "to posterity, to the whole universe, to renounce France forever, and to die rather than live under its dominion."[8]

As it had the year before, the sequence of events at the celebration reminded the population of Dessalines's leadership in securing victory over the French expeditionary army, and emphasized the need to remain prepared for another attack. Independence Day provided a moment of unity among the generals. As Dessalines's officers took the oath, "the political hatreds which divided the citizens," Madiou wrote, "were for a moment forgotten . . . for they expressed their horror at all foreign domination by which all hearts were animated."[9]

But the celebrations obscured a rising crisis. Anti-Dessalinean resistance was growing, especially among southern republicans, who believed their political interests would be best served if Dessalines left office.[10] The republicans prioritized their rights as landowners, whereas Dessalines insisted that ensuring freedom and independence trumped individual property ownership.[11] The emperor was unable to unite the country in the face of ongoing foreign challenges to Haitian independence and sovereignty. In response, he tried to further consolidate his authority by nationalizing more land, especially in the south. Instead of securing his position, however, this move pushed the southern military leadership to rebel. Before the third anniversary of independence could be celebrated, Dessalines would lie dead, killed by the leaders of a republican revolution.

"Every country, every people, has had its tyrants," an article in the Haitian *Gazette* claimed on August 1, 1805. "Every people have also had their liberators. The United States had its Washington; Switzerland had its Guillaume Tell; and us, we also have our Dessalines!"[12]

Saint Jacques's feast day, July 25, was the *fête* of His Majesty, Emperor Jacques I, as declared in article 27 of the new constitution. After a mass at the church in Cap, prepared with a "magnificently decorated throne" for the emperor, Dessalines and his retinue returned to the palace for speeches, a feast, and a ball. The emperor toasted the liberty and independence of Haiti, Henry Christophe recognized the emperor and empress, Brig. Gen. Louis Bazelais celebrated Christophe and the generals, and the emperor's aide-de-camp Étienne-Victor Mentor acknowledged the United States and the US merchants in attendance. Finally an American made a toast "to the free Peoples of the universe, and to the conservation of the government and the independence of Haiti, etc."[13]

After the toasts, Secretary-General Juste Chanlatte, whose *À mes concitoyens* had accompanied Dessalines's official acceptance of the imperial crown, performed couplets that he had composed for the occasion: "Around his flags, the same fate brings us together; let us live at his feet, where we will die together; because those who recognize the law of JACQUES the first; Have but one spirit, one Heart, for the state and its king."[14]

Despite this moment of celebration, Dessalines was in the midst of a protracted period of mourning. His aunt Toya had been very ill, and she died not long after he published the state constitution and legal codes.[15] "My aunt is dead," Dessalines said in tears, "my companion for a long time during our days of suffering, is dead." Madame Dessalines knelt in prayer beside her body. Dessalines "placed his hand on Madame Dessalines's shoulder," Toya's doctor, Jean-Baptiste Mirambeau, recalled, "and said while resting his head on that of his good wife, 'Victoria is dead! I now have only you. Only you, near to me, my dear Claire.'"[16]

In late October 1805 Dessalines lost his baby girl Sérrine, the child who had been born while he was on the battlefield in the east. Christophe wrote to him to offer love and support and to give advice to the emperor as a father and a friend. "Call on philosophy Sir to aid [Your Majesty]," Christophe told the emperor. "It will console your afflictions, especially when you reflect on the fact that it is the Inevitable law of Destiny that stole her from you. The Universe that contemplates you, Your People who expect their happiness and felicity from you, impose on you the obligation to Live, to crown the grand Oeuvre that you have so happily begun."[17] Christophe may have been especially pained by the news of Sérrine's death because some of Dessalines's children spent time in Cap with Christophe's wife, Marie-Louise, and a shared governess named Hélène.[18] Dessalines was also godfather to one of Christophe's sons.[19]

To compound Dessalines's grief, one of his most valued and loyal counselors, Gen. Louis Gabart (Vaillant), died on October 30 at the age of twenty-nine.[20] Gabart had been one of Dessalines's loyal officers in the 4th demi-brigade, the sans-culottes; the two men had fought together for more than a decade.[21] Gabart was buried at the church in Saint-Marc, and his heart was interred at Fort Culbuté in Marchand-Dessalines. "As long as he lived," Gabart's gravestone read, "he devoted his time to the freedom of his country, and he deserved the title of friend of his Sovereign."[22] Then, only days after Gabart's death, Dessalines lost his mother-in-law, Marie-Elizabeth, on November 2, 1805, at the age of fifty-six.[23]

Understanding how devastating these losses were for Dessalines, Christophe once again wrote with his condolences. "So many misfortunes in such a short space of time must afflict Your Majesty's heart in a sensible way," Christophe sympathized, "especially when the objects of our affection rightly deserve our regrets." Christophe tried to buoy his spirits by reminding Dessalines that Gabart's "memory is nevertheless dear to the children of haïty [*sic*]. He was one of its courageous defenders, who sacrificed his whole life for the civil and political existence of his fellow citizens; in these distinguished qualities he will inevitably pass to posterity."[24]

Christophe worried that the grief from these losses would affect Dessalines's ability to lead. So he advised the emperor to remain strong. "It is enough, I think, to remind [Your Majesty]," he wrote, "that the salvation of our country, the love of the army & the people of whom you are the Father, & of whom you know the Extent of their attachment must engage you to get a hold of your affliction, so that it does not affect your health, that is so precious to us!"[25]

It was in this time of grief that new political problems emerged for Dessalines. Opposition to his rule was escalating, exacerbated by another push to remove land from the hands of the *anciens libres*. The minister of finances, André Vernet, ordered the verification of all land deeds and instructed the generals to produce registers of the land in their districts.[26] Under this new law, the state would confiscate land from those who could not provide legitimate documentation for their properties.

The new verification regulation angered the *anciens libres,* who wanted to keep the land that they had inherited from former colonists.[27] The *arrêté* elicited an immediate response from landowners who blamed Dessalines for the policy.[28]

Perhaps Dessalines intended to confiscate the land previously owned by

French colonists as the first step of his plan for "agrarian reform."[29] Within a year, his government owned more than two-thirds of Haiti's plantations. But if he did intend to coordinate a large-scale land redistribution program, he never had the chance to implement it.

It was not just internal conflicts that besieged Dessalines. By 1806 geopolitical developments made his leadership increasingly complicated. Foreign recognition of Haitian sovereignty was not forthcoming. Moreover, Dessalines himself was central to racist justifications for withholding that recognition. In 1805 the French propagandist Louis Dubroca's so-called biography of Dessalines had been translated into Spanish and German and published in Madrid and Leipzig.[30] The following year, a Spanish version appeared in Mexico, now featuring several inflammatory images.[31] Christophe was depicted holding a sword and torch in front of a scorched town, with families fleeing burning buildings. The caption claimed that Christophe "toured the island of Saint Domingue burning and killing the unhappy settlers."[32] Dessalines was pictured standing before rows of military tents, sword in hand, holding the decapitated head of a white woman while a severed hand lay on the ground beneath. A final image showed Dessalines in imperial robes and wearing a crown at his coronation ceremony, his throne rising above a crowd of Black faces identified as his "Court and vassals."[33]

Following the celebration of the constitution's anniversary, Dessalines embarked on a tour of the restive southern peninsula. He left on June 17 for Léogâne and then Jacmel. He stayed for several days in Jacmel, noting his approval of how the generals had finished the construction of the fort.[34] During his travels, Dessalines continued sending instructions to Christophe in the north.

But his letters arrived to Christophe with clear evidence of tampering. "I do not know what Strange curiosity & what motives," Christophe replied, "can engage people to violate your Majesty's seal that must be sacred; principally the letters that [Your Majesty] addresses to me."[35] He noted that the typical punishment for opening mail was to have one's hand cut off, but that this instance "well deserves that the head follow the wrist."[36] It is possible that Dessalines's adversaries in the south were spying on the emperor to plot his assassination or to better evaluate whether they would be able to secure Christophe's support.

The emperor continued his tour westward along the southern peninsula, arriving in Jérémie on July 8. Each of his stops was celebrated with feasts as he inspected the various forts. On July 25 the nation again celebrated Dessalines's *fête* on Saint Jacques's feast day at the palace in Jérémie. The solemn celebration was

DESALINES.

Louis Dubroca, *Vida de J. J. Dessalines, gefe de los negros de Santo Domingo* (Mexico: D. Mariano de Zúñiga y Ontiveros, 1806), inserted after page 72. Courtesy of the John Carter Brown Library, Providence.

followed by a splendid meal and a ball.[37] "I feel great satisfaction," Christophe wrote to Dessalines in a letter marking the national holiday, "in seeing my fellow citizens indulge in the sweet outpourings of gratitude, celebrate with gusto Your Majesty's *fête* & bring you, sir, from all parts of the Empire, the tribute of affection and love that is due to the dear father of the great Haitian family!"[38]

The celebrations in the south, however, were deceptive. Dessalines did not in fact have full support from the region's military leaders. Leaving Jérémie, Dessalines headed east toward Les Cayes. He arrived on July 31 and spent more than five weeks there.[39] Far from placating the southern generals, however, in Les Cayes he doubled down on his land policies. Disregarding danger, he directed his administrator of state properties, Joseph Balthazar Inginac, to follow up on the February 1804 decree regarding land inherited from white colonists, and issued severe orders against certain individuals.[40] On September 1 Dessalines, clearly frustrated with southerners' flouting of the law, issued a new decree relating to illegally obtained land from the former colonizers. The new regulations gave the principal administrator of each division full authority over the certification of land inherited from, sold by, or donated by white people.[41] Southerners anticipated that the state would now confiscate most of their properties.[42]

Dessalines left Les Cayes on September 9 to return to the capital and then begin a tour of the north. He left a roiling city in his wake. Those who were in possession of illegal titles and those who had just been dispossessed of their lands were furious. Now they made a pact to revolt against the emperor.[43]

Republican insurgents in the surrounding regions converged on Les Cayes. They called on the cultivators for support, using the clarion of the conch shell to spread the news quickly.[44] In a public declaration on October 12, the rebels claimed that Dessalines intended to wage war against the *anciens libres.* Their primary grievance was land confiscation, but that in and of itself was not sufficient justification for a revolution. The ideology that supported the revolt was Jeffersonian republicanism, according to historian Hénock Trouillot.[45]

The southern republicans outlined their grievances in a document entitled *Résistance à l'oppression* (Resistance to oppression).[46] The authors claimed they were acting on enlightened republican principles and promised to protect individual interests.[47] "A terrible tyranny," the authors began, "exercised for too long on the People and the Army, has finally exasperated all the minds and brought them in a movement worthy of the reasons that caused them to rise en masse to create a worthy levee against the devastating torrent that menaces them."[48] They called out Dessalines for taking away land that they claimed to have owned for decades, and they condemned him as a "stupid man" (*homme stupide*) for hurting international trade by allegedly executing a British merchant. They accused him of cruelty for reorganizing the military so that soldiers were removed from their native regions and therefore lost their means of subsistence. They also attacked him for allegedly spending public money on his mistresses, arguing that "the public Treasury lavishly provided sums of 20,000 gourdes per year to each of his concubines, of whom we can count at least twenty."[49]

The southern republicans railed against the process by which Dessalines had issued the 1805 constitution. They complained that it was "dictated by caprice and ignorance, written by his secretaries, and published in the name of the Generals of the Army who, not only had never approved nor signed this informal and ridiculous act, but also did not know about it except when it was made public and promulgated."[50] They promised to issue a new constitution, one that would protect the rights of soldiers, cultivators, and landowners alike. The authors concluded by declaring Henry Christophe the provisional head of the government—unbeknownst to Christophe himself.

Insurgents in the southern cities took up arms. The rebels from Anse-à-Veau were led by Étienne-Élie Gérin, the minister of war and the navy. On October 13 the leaders of the "Army of the South" wrote to Christophe, advising him that the people had risen and attempting to rally him to their cause, writing that they assumed "your indignation at least equals ours." The southerners knew that the best way to manage the north was through Christophe. To unite the nation after an inevitably divisive move, they swore allegiance to Christophe under whatever title he wanted to assume as the head of a new government: "We are awaiting, General-in-chief, your orders for all our operations; be our protector and that of Haiti; we hope that God will bless our good cause."[51]

Did Christophe ever receive this letter or respond to it? The lack of evidence does not rule out the possibility that he did.

Leading the insurrection into Port-au-Prince were Pétion, Gérin, Yayou, Vaval, and Guy-Joseph Bonnet, who claimed to be fighting for "liberty."[52] When Dessalines learned of the insurrection, he headed south from the capital with a small entourage to quell the uprising. He instructed three demi-brigades from Arcahaye to meet him at Pont-Rouge outside Port-au-Prince, unaware of their allegiance to Pétion.[53]

Christophe initially appeared oblivious to the insurgency.[54] "I have the honor to send your Majesty," Christophe wrote to Dessalines on October 16, as the emperor traveled south to meet the insurgents, "one hundred and fourteen small Mango plants that I had promised you to be planted in the Imperial Palace Gardens of Dessalines."[55] But he wrote again later that day, having just received a letter from Dessalines about the insurrection. "It pained me to learn about the Event," Christophe wrote, "as it will Oblige Your Majesty to deploy the severity of the law, against the authors of this catastrophe, who are no doubt just ambitious."[56] Per Haiti's laws, acts of rebellion were punishable by death, and Christophe anticipated that Dessalines would follow through.

Dessalines's plans to overpower the insurgency, however, were hampered by defections among his ranks. One of the battalion chiefs—whom Dessalines had instructed to rendezvous at Pont-Rouge—instead revealed to the insurrection leaders that Dessalines was on his way to meet the units. The insurgent leaders used the battalion chief's uniform to trap Dessalines, dressing someone else in his clothes. "There is Gédéon waiting for me," Dessalines allegedly told Boisrond-Tonnerre as he approached the meeting spot. "How faithful he is. I will reward his zeal."[57]

The cultivators whom Dessalines passed along his route did not warn him of the ambush that had been laid. Some historians have interpreted their silence as implicit support for his removal from office, as well as fear of the consequences if the uprising failed.[58]

On October 17 Dessalines encountered the group at Pont-Rouge. It quickly became apparent to him that the conspiracies he had long feared had come to fruition.[59] As the insurgents surrounded Dessalines, the emperor fired his pistol, killing a rebel soldier. The republicans fired back, hitting the emperor's horse. Dessalines called for assistance, but the insurgents opened fire and riddled his body with bullets.[60]

At about forty-eight years of age, Haiti's first head of state lay dead at the hands of the generals he had been unable to fully integrate into his administration. Dessalines had survived enslavement and a thirteen-year revolution. But he had antagonized a powerful faction of the military leadership, who saw him as a roadblock to their own and the nation's success. In the moments after the assassination, Yayou, Gérin, and Vaval stripped Dessalines to his undergarments and cut off his fingers to steal his jewel-encrusted rings. Later they sold the fingers as macabre souvenirs to US merchants in Port-au-Prince.[61]

The group dragged Dessalines's body to Port-au-Prince, further mutilating his corpse along the way.[62] When they arrived in the capital, they cast the body aside in the government square. Children then pelted it with stones. A woman named Défilée stopped the assault and collected Dessalines's remains in a sack. Popular accounts claim that she buried the remains of his body with care. While early historians described Défilée as "la folle" (the crazy one), her actions reflected the popular support that Dessalines still had because of his role as Haiti's liberator from slavery and colonialism.[63] Rather than a state funeral, Dessalines's death was marked with conflict, personal connection, and spectacle.

News of the attack on Dessalines spread quickly, but the details were confused. Within two days, Christophe wrote to the minister of finances, André Vernet, not knowing or not convinced that Dessalines was dead. "Get more information on the circumstances of this crime," Christophe instructed, "so that you can clarify for me, because in reality I cannot understand this news nor believe it."[64] Later, crying "tears of blood," he wrote to his generals to let them know that the emperor had been assassinated.[65]

Rather than accepting the leadership of the rebellion, Christophe planned to defend the national capital and the imperial family.[66] He wrote to Pétion, not knowing that he was part of the rebellion, asking for an update and emphasizing the need to defend the empire.[67] He reassured the US merchants that their investments were guaranteed and trade relationships would continue. Christophe readied for war.[68]

In the days after Dessalines's assassination, both Christophe and Pétion wrote to Madame Dessalines. In his October 19 letter, later printed and published, Pétion condemned Dessalines's alleged tyranny but avoided direct culpability for his death—"the memorable day of the seventeenth, had been set by Providence, for the moment of Vengeance." Pétion reassured Madame Dessalines, however, that she was safe: "console yourself, Madame, you are among a People who would dedicate their lives for your happiness: forget that you are Dessalines's wife so that you can become the adoptive wife of the most generous nation, who knows no hate but that against its only oppressor."[69] Pétion knew that Marie-Claire was widely loved and respected, and he likely hoped that with her support he might be able to minimize backlash from the assassination.

Two days later, Christophe, still unclear on the details of the assassination, also wrote to Madame Dessalines. "It would be difficult for my heart, my dear friend," he wrote, "to express to you the sensation that I felt in learning of the news of the disturbances that have taken place & especially the unprecedented attack that was committed on the person of H.M. the Emperor, your spouse, my worry is unequaled about his fate."[70] Christophe was furious that their enemies had chosen to attack on the eve of peace in Europe, when they should have been focused on internal unity and national defense. He regretted that he could not come see Madame Dessalines immediately, but assured her that he had inquired as to whether she and her family were in danger. If they were, "I will send someone to get you with your children to bring you near my Wife, who is alarmed & who weeps like me over this cruel event."[71]

By October 22, however, Christophe learned that Gérin was at the center of the plot and that Dessalines was truly dead. He also learned that the generals of the south wanted him to assume control of the government. "I never showed General Gérin any ambition for the leadership," Christophe wrote to Pierre Toussaint, the commander of Saint-Marc, making sure to distance himself from the assassination. "I desire nothing other than the happiness of my country, and I know how to submit myself to the laws that are established."[72]

It did not take long, however, for Christophe to change his mind. He dried his tears of blood, and he reframed what he had previously referred to as a "crime" as a "cruel necessity." Christophe likely saw opportunity in his nomination, or at least anticipated that this was the best way to ensure his own safety. "Frightened by the burden that the unanimous will of my brothers in arms impose on me, by entrusting me with the reins of the Government," Christophe wrote to Gérin on October 23, "it would pain me to accept, if I were not intimately convinced that your guidance & your counsel will always come to my aid in cases of emergency."[73] He accepted the offer to lead the new government.

Christophe also wrote to Pétion to sympathize with his "dear friend" about the "arbitrary acts to which we were unhappy witnesses & victims & that put us in a state of mediocrity under the reign that has recently passed."[74] Christophe's rally to the republican insurgency led some to conclude that he was in on the plan to remove Dessalines from office. But it is more likely that he quickly reassessed his options and decided that leading a reconfigured Haitian government was in his best interests.[75]

On November 2 Christophe addressed the nation in a document that the *Gazette* published a few weeks later. "Engrave in your souls love of your country, of order," he told the citizens of Haiti. "Print it in indelible characters, that the government wishes to maintain the most perfect union, and the forfeiture of all hatred, of all ambition, of all allegiance to party, and has no other goal than the salvation of the State."[76]

On November 6 the *Gazette* also published an article explaining the events leading up to Dessalines's death. The anonymous article stated that the intention of the insurgents was not to kill Dessalines but instead to depose him according to article 29 of the 1805 constitution, a clause by which they considered the emperor "in a state of war against society" because he had allegedly deviated from the principles of the constitution.[77] Because Dessalines was determined to resist, the *Gazette* claimed, and because of his supposed "violent character," he determined his own fate.

Dessalines's widow, Marie-Claire Heureuse, eventually found residence in the north with Henry Christophe, calling him *mon compère*.[78] Later she resided in Saint-Marc and Gonaïves. Marie-Claire Heureuse Dessalines died more than fifty years after her husband, on August 8, 1858. The Haitian newspaper *La Feuille du commerce* celebrated her reunion in the afterlife with other heroes of the Haitian Revolution, including her friend Suzanne Louverture.[79] The two mothers of the nation would be surrounded by their "adoptive sons," Clervaux,

Lamartinière, Dommage, and Gabart; together, the newspaper promised, they would be "bright stars in the blue sky of freedom."[80]

A US paper memorialized her as the "good genius of her ferocious husband," noting that she had saved several white Frenchmen. Since Dessalines's death, the paper recounted, she occupied her time by "nursing the sick and looking after the welfare of young girls, whom under the title of goddaughters, she was always fond of having about her."[81] During the revolution and throughout her life, Madame Dessalines's reputation at home and abroad were unimpeachable. As the US obituary highlighted, writers usually contrasted her good reputation with Dessalines's. Within Haiti, however, Dessalines's reputation ebbed and flowed as politicians, artists, and historians responded to domestic events and international characterizations.

By the end of 1806 the new Haitian government issued another constitution. This created, for the first time, the Republic of Haiti. The document, declaring itself to be in the name of "the people of Haiti," reaffirmed the abolition of slavery, the nation's promise not to undertake any foreign expeditions, and the prohibition on white landownership. It stated that the rights of citizens included "liberty, equality, safety, and property."[82]

The 1806 constitution built on Dessalines's 1805 anti-colonial and anti-slavery constitution but diverged in several respects. Roman Catholicism, for example, became a protected religion, and government power would reside in a twenty-four-person senate. The first version of the senate would be named by the constituent assembly (the authors of the constitution); thereafter, the parishes would create electoral assemblies to nominate senatorial candidates. The existing senate would then choose the senators from the lists. Executive power was vested in a president whom the constituent assembly would name initially, and thereafter would be appointed by the senate, for a four-year term. Only a senator, a former senator, or the secretary of state could assume the presidency.

Within weeks of the publication of this new constitution, Christophe backtracked on his allegiance to the republicans: "After having massacred the emperor, whom they charged with shedding the blood of the Haytians, did they not cruelly assassinate more than thirty of the superior officers? And, for what reason? One reddens to think of it! Solely because they are blacks, and enlightened." Christophe also blamed the "men of color" in the south and west for the "extermination" of the white population.[83] He returned to Cap and refused to participate in the new republic. Instead he began imagining a new future for the country.

By the end of February 1807, Christophe and the generals of the north issued their own constitution, reviving the "State of Hayti." The government under this 1807 constitution was to consist of a president and commander in chief of the army and navy (Henry Christophe), with a nine-person council of state that would be named by the president. The position of president and commander in chief was for life, and Christophe had the right to choose his successor. Most of Dessalines's generals became officers in Christophe's military.[84]

Because of Christophe's defection, the constituent assembly of the south named Pétion president under their 1806 constitution. Pétion denounced Dessalines as the cause of the civil war and emphasized that the late emperor's rule had been particularly bad for the *gens de couleur.* "The dreadful reign of Dessalines is at an end!" Pétion wrote in an invitation to the "men of colour, who have been forced to leave this Country." "During the life of that Barbarian," he asserted, "you had reason to fear being sacrificed to his blind fury; but now no motives should prevent your return."[85]

Dessalines lived and died among a divided population. In the wake of his assassination, however, both factions distanced themselves from his rule. Christophe continued to celebrate Dessalines as a liberator, but Pétion insisted that he was simply a tyrant.[86] For the next century, the Haitian state remained divided in its memory of Dessalines.

It is clear today, however, that Dessalines was one of the greatest revolutionaries of recent centuries. Jean-Jacques Dessalines issued the world's second successful Declaration of Independence, and in doing so he founded the first abolitionist state in the Americas. His was a revolution fought by enslaved people, but it was also the founding of a modern polity *by* enslaved people. As such, its significance is simply unequaled.

To Haiti and to Dessalines, the world continues to owe an immense debt. Dessalines's Haiti opened the door to abolition around the world.

We Have Dared to Be Free

The memory of any founding father is fraught. For more than two centuries, Jean-Jacques Dessalines's life and legacy have been celebrated, condemned, co-opted, and fictionalized to serve various political, social, and cultural ends both within Haiti and around the world. Haitians call on the memory of Dessalines when the nation's sovereignty is under attack, and the revolutionary leader has come to embody independence and an unwavering opposition to foreign rule.[1] In contrast, for centuries foreigners have used Dessalines to argue the opposite: that Haiti is unfit for self-rule.[2]

The fact that his memory has become an ideological battleground on the international stage in the twenty-first century is no surprise; after all, he was someone who advocated for violent revolution for racial equality and self-determination. He and his troops overturned the racist power structures that still dominate societies across the Americas today, and they terrified colonists and enslavers everywhere in the nineteenth century.

Unwilling to admit to the crimes against humanity that they had committed, colonizers instead made Dessalines out to be a monster.[3] The fictitious accounts of Dessalines's life remain powerful more than two hundred years later, as evidenced by the fact that few people outside of Haiti remember him as a hero of the Age of Revolution. But Dessalines deserves recognition. He founded the first abolitionist state in the Americas, and he did so when none of his contemporaries elsewhere were willing to challenge the institution of slavery, despite loudly professing their commitments to liberty and equality. "It is not only childish, but grotesque," therefore, as Haitian historian Louis-Joseph Janvier argued, "to claim that one can pass definitive judgements on Dessalines."[4]

Much of the foreign conversation about Dessalines in the nineteenth century was tainted by Louis Dubroca's 1804 so-called biography, which was only loosely based on reality. Indeed, Dubroca's vilification of Dessalines in the early nineteenth century helps explain why, centuries later, the former Fox News host Tucker Carlson could refer to Dessalines as a "genocidal nutcase." Dubroca erroneously claimed that Dessalines was born in Africa, for example, to magnify his alleged savagery for his European audience. That falsehood was repeated in various publications, including the popular *Dictionnaire universel d'histoire et de géographie,* the first edition of which was published in 1842 and the thirty-fourth and final edition in 1914.[5] The error was corrected after the publication of Thomas Madiou's multivolume history of Haiti.[6] In the eleventh edition of the *Dictionnaire universel*—published half a century after his assassination—Dessalines was finally listed as "1st emperor of Haiti, born in St-Domingue, in Cormiers, was a *nègre* and was first a slave in St-Domingue."[7]

But Dubroca was not alone. Many foreign observers treated Dessalines less as a person than as an archetype of the "bloodthirsty Negro," publishing accounts of the Haitian Revolution that perpetuated these stereotypes.[8] In 1818 a British writer condemned Dessalines's "extra-judicial military execution[s], and especially the slaughter of unoffending children," claiming that Dessalines committed these alleged acts because he was a "ferocious and illiterate negro," who was merely imitating the examples set by the French generals Leclerc and Rochambeau.[9] A decade later, another British writer condemned the supposed killing of "innocent" French people: "even Nero would have paused; but the infamous and blood thirsty negro Dessalines secretly rejoiced at the success of his inhuman stratagem."[10] Another decade after that, an American writer provided a similar characterization: "While his soldiers were murdering the unfortunate victims of his ferocity, the monster gloated with secret complacency over the scene of carnage like some malignant fiend, glorying in the pangs of misery suffered by those who had fallen a sacrifice to his wickedness."[11] The evidence for these claims was thin, but the descriptions nevertheless passed from generation to generation as foreigners repeated the stories. They did so mostly because they believed the alleged eyewitness accounts left by French colonists, who had a vested interest in Haiti's failure as a country.

In contrast, Haitian authors in the early nineteenth century, many of whom had witnessed the events, treated Dessalines's anti-colonial violence as a minor issue in Haitian history or simply dismissed it altogether, especially when considered within the context of decades of French atrocities under slavery and during the revolution. They tried to ensure that the colonists' writings would not be the sole sources of Haitian history.[12] "The emperor was not the enemy of humanity," Haitian writer and statesman Baron de Vastey declared in 1818, "for having been the enemy of France, and he was not barbarous, for having retaliated against those who wanted to exterminate us."[13] While most foreign witnesses, editors, and writers remained obsessed with Dessalines's "massacres," early Haitian authors focused on his efforts to construct a nation using constitutions, legal codes, and international diplomacy.[14]

Nevertheless, by the mid-nineteenth century, Dessalines's violent defense of the country had become a political liability for Haiti.[15] Beginning in 1825, the European and American "family of nations" excluded Haiti, even after officially recognizing the country and signing treaties with Haitian leaders. Dessalines's violent critique of Enlightenment values was considered "uncivilized."[16] This was why, decades later, Haiti's most prominent intellectuals in the mid-nineteenth century were committed to proving their people's nonviolence, and therefore their ability to be sovereign and "civilized."[17]

Thomas Madiou's and Beaubrun Ardouin's multivolume histories of Haiti, published in the 1840s and 1850s, have had a lasting impact on how the "massacres" have been understood both inside and outside of Haiti—and therefore on how Dessalines is remembered. Both framed the events as aberrations in Haitian history, moments of weakness that were not representative of the new nation. They also contextualized the violence. Madiou pointed out that other nations that had gone through revolutions had initiated similarly horrific acts of violence— Haiti was no different than these other "civilized" nations.[18] Similarly, Ardouin paralleled the executions with French behavior during the Haitian war for independence, even though he admitted that "after a victory, when law triumphs, moderation, generous feelings must prevail over hatred, no matter what. *The vanquished* also have rights in the eyes of humanity, in the eyes of God."[19] In 1804, however, the French had not yet conceded defeat, and Dessalines's "victory" was still illusive.

Haitians were thus being held to a different standard than other European and American nations (those perceived as being white). And Haitian authors were forced to grapple with these injustices, even as they wrote their own versions of the histories of colonialism and the revolution.

It was only in 1904—the centennial of Haiti's independence—that Dessalines secured a permanent place in the national pantheon. "Is it not cowardly and naïve to condemn some of the deeds of Dessalines," historian Louis-Joseph Janvier asked in the lead-up to the celebrations, "which were by the way designed and executed collectively, while accepting the benefits of others, and to try to cover yourselves in his lion's cloak all the while acting diametrically against his plan and ideology?"[20] From this perspective, Dessalines's success could not be separated from his commitment to violent rebellion in the face of France's own violent commitment to slavery and colonialism.

That same year a new national anthem was selected: Justin Lhérisson's poem "La Dessalinienne," which celebrated unity, landownership, loyalty, and the founders. When asked why he named it after Dessalines, the anthem's author replied, "*Dessalines* is the name that made possible and attainable all the great and beautiful things."[21]

In 1906 Haiti commemorated the hundredth anniversary of Dessalines's assassination, and October 17 was inaugurated as a day to honor his memory; it is still observed today.[22] It was an opportunity to declare an end to the factious period that Dessalines's death had begun, and perhaps to move beyond these political divides: legacies of the tensions between *anciens* and *nouveaux libres* during the revolution.[23]

Even before Dessalines was officially commemorated in Haiti, his memory remained powerful among the Haitian people.[24] He is the only leader of the Haitian Revolution to have been incorporated into the popular religion Vodou.

After his assassination, Dessalines became the *lwa* Ogou Desalin.[25] The Ogou family of *lwa* have many forms, but they are related to war and the military. Vodou *lwa* are contradictory characters; the Ogou *lwa* are forces of freedom, but they can also suppress freedom instead of defending it.[26] Just as Dessalines's reputation and memory were inconsistent and fraught, practitioners both celebrate and critique him in song and practice.[27] The Haitian revolutionary is not considered beyond reproach.

Dessalines's inclusion in this family of *lwa* reflects the country's debt to his fight for freedom and independence and predates the official, state-sponsored celebration of Dessalines's life that emerged in the late nineteenth century. A Vodou song recorded in the 1950s emphasizes Dessalines's role as defender of Haiti:

Toussaint died badly . . . ooo
He wasn't afraid to die badly
Dessalines is the Bull of Haiti
Yacanbanda
I've got no mother
No father
They tried to kill my whole race
They didn't kill me[28]

The "they" in this song might be interpreted in a variety of ways, because Dessalines's memory also serves as a warning of the power of the military and political elite who killed him.[29]

Dessalines's example has also offered inspiration for Black men and women outside of Haiti. "Ay, one of those self-freed, much-feared fugitives, who love liberty and hate the master," declared a fictional Dessalines in William Edgar Easton's 1893 play named after the revolutionary leader. "Who, not satisfied with merely breathing words of hatred, wreak vengeance on them for their wrongs upon the race."[30] More recently, the West African country of Benin marked the 220th anniversary of Haitian independence by installing a bust of Dessalines in the city of Cotonou. The sculptor, Borgella Dumond, recounted that the installation "is a tribute to the resilience, the struggle, and the determination embodied by the emperor Jean-Jacques Dessalines."[31]

A decade after the centennial of Haitian independence, the United States invaded Haiti after US banking leaders convinced Woodrow Wilson's administration to take control of the country's political and financial interests. For nearly two decades (1915–1934), these foreign troops occupied the first nation to abolish slavery. During the US occupation, Dessalines's memory became a political tool to rally opposition to foreign intervention and the usurpation of Haitian sovereignty.[32] For example, Haitian soldier and musician Occide Jeanty's commemorative tune "Dessalines ou 1804: Marche guerrière," originally composed for the hundredth anniversary of Haitian independence, gained widespread popularity during the occupation.[33] The Haitian people called on Dessalines's anti-colonialism for inspiration.

After the US Marines finally evacuated, Dessalines's legacy became embroiled in a political battle among Haitian nationalists.[34] The ideology of Haitian Black nationalism, Noirisme, argued that mimicry of French culture among the mixed-race Haitian elite was a tool of oppression. François Duvalier, among this move-

ment's leaders, later adopted Dessalines's red and black flag, positioned himself
in a triumvirate with Dessalines and God (*Dieu, Dessalines, Duvalier*), and claimed
to be his twentieth-century heir.[35] The movement's intellectuals held that Dessalines was representing the will of the people when he had executed white French
people. But they also emphasized Dessalines's willingness to issue the orders: "to
make himself feared, loved and obeyed, and radically rid his country of the specter of slavery."[36]

Dessalines is still a powerful political reference in Haiti. "Fictive kinship with
Papa Desalin," writes Sophie Sapp Moore, "remains the price of entry for the
practice of radical politics in Haiti today."[37]

In the international sphere, however, Dessalines's memory remains intentionally grafted onto a propagandistic version of the 1804 executions. Consequently, abroad it is Toussaint Louverture who has become the most globally
famous hero of the Haitian Revolution, even though he did not live to see Haitian independence. Today he is rightfully celebrated and commemorated as an
icon of Black freedom and anti-slavery resistance.[38]

The most globally popular history of the Haitian Revolution, *The Black
Jacobins*, written by the Trinidadian historian C. L. R. James in 1938, focused
on Louverture and considered Dessalines's anti-colonial violence to be "a tragedy," because they "degrade[d] and brutalise[d]" the Haitian population. "For
these old slave-owners," James argued, "those who burnt a little powder in the
arse of a Negro, who buried him alive for insects to eat, who were well treated
by Toussaint, and who, as soon as they got the chance, began their old cruelties
again; for these there is no need to waste one tear or one drop of ink." The problem for James was that the killing "was not policy but revenge, and revenge has
no place in politics."[39]

More recent accounts mirror James's analysis, but are remarkably less sympa-
thetic to the anti-slavery and anti-colonial war that Dessalines was fighting. In
2005 Philippe Girard—the scholar who has been the most extreme in assessing
these executions in modern historiography—went so far as to describe them as
"genocide." Girard's interpretation, however, hinged on the conclusion that the
war for independence was over, and it ignored the explicit laws and constitutional articles that accounted for the hundreds of white French people who remained in Haiti and who were given a path to citizenship.

Girard has since walked back that assessment and instead uses the term
"massacre" in more recent publications. But the influence of his earlier characterization is unmistakable: white supremacists and other critics of the Haitian

Revolution now deploy the word "genocide" to undermine the achievements of the Haitian revolutionaries.

Central to Girard's claim is that Dessalines ordered his generals to kill French "civilians" after the war was over.[40] By framing the French evacuation as a "surrender"—which the French very explicitly said it was not—and downplaying the significance of the French presence in Santo Domingo as well as the possibility of French reinforcements, Girard's characterization minimizes the reality of the ongoing threats to the new Haitian state.

A second influential historian, Jeremy Popkin, has veered in the direction of calling the "massacres" genocide, but he stops just short.[41] Popkin singles out the executions from the context of the revolution because, he argues, those who died were "completely helpless," suggesting that Dessalines should have instead deported them.[42] He didn't, Popkin concludes, because of his supposed "penchant for violence."[43]

Framing colonizers and former enslavers as "completely helpless" erases the centuries-long history of European domination and violence in the Americas and, more important, their continued threat to the nation. Dessalines knew that white French men and women, once deported, would likely have agitated for a French reinvasion. French people previously evacuated from the colony began plotting reinvasion as soon as they landed elsewhere in the Caribbean, sometimes providing information about the Haitian state.[44] Half a dozen former colonists went on to submit various reconquest plans to the minister of foreign affairs in Paris immediately after the French evacuation.[45] And several French men who had survived the executions but later escaped the country wrote lengthy reports designed to aid the expected French expedition.[46]

Scholarly accounts such as those by Girard and Popkin have influenced more popular accounts of the Haitian Revolution. For example, drawing heavily on Girard's work is popular podcaster Mike Duncan, who, in season 4 of *Revolutions,* offered a sensationalized account of what he called the "genocidal massacres" of 1804 carried out by "Dessalines and his death squad." Duncan alleged that Haitian soldiers raped all the white women, and concluded that Dessalines committed a "heinous crime."[47]

Or consider the Wikipedia page for Dessalines, which—as of the writing of this book—read: "He ordered the 1804 Haitian massacre of the remaining French population in Haiti, resulting in the deaths of between 3,000 and 5,000 people, including women and children, as well as thousands of refugees. Some modern historians classify the massacre as a genocide due to its systemic nature."[48] The entry for the Haitian Revolution includes a subsection called "1804 massacre of the French," which does not use the term genocide.[49] There is, however, a separate Wikipedia entry called "1804 Haitian massacre," which notes that the event is also known as the "1804 Haitian genocide."[50]

At the moment that Haitians first rose up, the pro-slavery and pro-empire powers of Europe and the Americas had a special interest in ensuring that Haiti failed. Both then and now, targeting Dessalines supported their goal. But excluding him from the ideological and political history of the Age of Revolution and the Enlightenment highlights the ongoing effects of nineteenth-century propaganda that championed racist definitions of freedom and equality. "Despite his despotism after the expulsion of our oppressors," urged Madiou, "we must forgive him, honor him deeply, love his memory, set aside his role as sovereign, and think of him only as the glorious warrior and the immortal founder of the independence of Haiti."[51]

Dessalines seemed to foresee the scorn he and his nation would receive in the future. In early 1804 he had addressed a proclamation not to his fellow Haitians, but instead to the "inhabitants of the Universe." "Do not, unheard, accuse us of cruelty," he pleaded with the international community. "Remember our past sufferings, and you will judge less severely our present acts of necessity—of despair."[52] To such a plea, we must surely listen.

But we must also listen to more than pleas. To understand Dessalines truly, listen to his defiance. In another speech, he confessed to "mortals and gods" that he had "avenged America." This defiant act was his "pride and glory."

"What does it matter how present and future races will judge me?" Dessalines demanded. "I have done my duty, I know my worth; that is enough for me."[53]

Notes

ARCHIVES ABBREVIATIONS

ADG	Archives Départmentales de la Gironde, Bordeaux
AGI	Archivo General de Indias, Seville
AN, Paris	Archives Nationales, Paris
AN, Pierrefitte	Archives Nationales, Pierrefitte
ANOM	Archives Nationales d'Outre-Mer, Aix-en-Provence
ASPF	Archivio Storico Propaganda Fide, Rome
BHS	Bibliothèque Haïtienne des Spiritains, Port-au-Prince, Haiti
BPL	Boston Public Library
CKS	Center for Kentish Studies, Maidstone, UK
DNA	Danish National Archives (Statens Arkiver), Copenhagen
MAE	Ministère des Affaires Étrangères, Paris
MSRC	Moorland-Spingarn Research Center, Howard University, Washington, DC
NAM	National Army Museum, London
NARA	National Archives and Records Administration, Washington, DC
NLJ	National Library of Jamaica, Kingston
RWL-AUC	Robert W. Woodruff Library of the Atlanta University Center, Atlanta
SCRBC	Schomburg Center for Research in Black Culture, Kurt Fisher Haitian Collection, New York
SHD	Service Historique de la Défense, Vincennes
TNA	National Archives of the United Kingdom, Kew, London
UF-RP	University of Florida Libraries, Rochambeau Papers, Gainesville
UPR-ANC	University of Puerto Rico, Alfred Nemours Collection, San Juan

INTRODUCTION

1. Charles Leclerc to Napoléon Bonaparte, October 7, 1802, Cap-Français, in Paul Roussier, *Lettres du général Leclerc: Commandant en chef de l'armée de Saint-Domingue en 1802* (Paris: Société de l'histoire des colonies françaises et Librairie Ernest Leroux, 1937), 256.

2. [Louis Félix] Boisrond-Tonnerre, *Mémoires pour servir a l'histoire d'Hayti* (Dessalines: Imprimerie centrale du gouvernement, 1804). Book housed at Harvard University, Houghton Library, FC8 b6366 804m., 48.

3. Boisrond-Tonnerre, *Mémoires*, 58.

4. Dessalines, "Proclamation aux Habitans d'Haïti," Cap, April 28, 1804, *l'an premier de l'indépendance* (Cap: P. Roux, imprimeur du gouvernement), TNA, CO 137/113, f. 138.

5. Dany Laferrière, Louis-Philippe Dalembert, Edwidge Danticat, and Évelyne Trouillot, with J. Michael Dash, moderator, "Roundtable: Writing, History, and Revolution," *Small Axe: A Caribbean Journal of Criticism* 18 (2005): 199.

6. The simultaneous commitment to eliminating slavery, racism, and colonialism is what Marlene L. Daut calls "the 1804 Principle." Daut, *Awakening the Ashes: An Intellectual History of the Haitian Revolution* (Chapel Hill: University of North Carolina Press, 2023), xviii.

7. "NYC Approves Street Name for Advocate of Racial Murder," Fox News, YouTube Channel, August 3, 2018, 3:05, https://youtu.be/x3uubB75tLE?si=JH5JIOG_F1T5ULDy.

8. Dessalines, "Proclamation aux Habitans d'Haïti," Cap, April 28, 1804.

9. On "tiger," see Armand Levasseur, *Événemens qui ont précédé et suivi l'Évacuation de Saint-Domingue, publiés par un Officier de l'État-Major de l'Armée* (Paris: Desprez, 1804), 30–31; Marlene L. Daut, *Tropics of Haiti: Race and the Literary History of the Haitian Revolution in the Atlantic World, 1789–1865* (Liverpool, UK: Liverpool University Press, 2015), 84.

10. This kind of erasure is in line with Michel-Rolph Trouillot's well-known description of the "silencing" of the Haitian Revolution. Trouillot, *Silencing the Past: Power and the Production of History* (Boston: Beacon Press, 1995).

11. Armée indigène, "Liberté ou la Mort," January 1, 1804, *l'an premier de l'indépendance* (Port-au-Prince: Imprimerie du Gouvernement), TNA, CO 137/111/1 and TNA, MFQ 1/184.

12. "Empire d'Haïti, du Cap, le 14 Novembre, Coup-d'Oeil Politique de l'Europe," *Gazette politique et commerciale d'Haïti,* numéro 1, November 15, 1804, *l'an premier de l'indépendance* (Cap: P. Roux, imprimeur de l'Empereur), p. 2.

13. Armée indigène, "Liberté ou la Mort," January 1, 1804.

CHAPTER 1. YOU HAVE YOUR OWN LANGUAGE

1. "Du Cap, le 31 Juillet," *Gazette politique et commerciale d'Haïti,* August 1, 1805, *l'an deuxième de l'indépendance,* no. 34, p. 134.

2. "Notre passé nous crie: Ayez l'âme aguerrie!" Justin Lhérisson, "La Dessalinienne," 1903; English translation by Martin Shaw, available at Haitian Embassy to the United States website, https://www.haiti.org/national-anthem/. See also Justin Lhérisson, "La Des-

salinienne," [1903], in Lélia J. Lhérisson, *La Dessalinienne: Hymne national haïtien* ([Port-au-Prince?]: C. Beaubrun, 1919).

3. For more on Spanish colonialism in the seventeenth century, see Juan José Ponce Vázquez, *Islanders and Empire: Smuggling and Political Defiance in Hispaniola, 1580–1690* (Cambridge, UK: Cambridge University Press, 2020).

4. François Blancpain, "Les droits de la France sur la colonie de Saint Domingue et le traité de Ryswick," *Outre-Mers* 94, nos. 354–355 (2007): 306.

5. Trevor Burnard and John Garrigus, *The Plantation Machine: Atlantic Capitalism in French Saint-Domingue and British Jamaica* (Philadelphia: University of Pennsylvania Press, 2016), 3.

6. Mallory Hope, "Risk and Uncertainty in France's Atlantic Slave Trade," *International Journal of Maritime History* 35, no. 3 (2023): 344–375.

7. Stephanie E. Smallwood, *Saltwater Slavery: A Middle Passage from Africa to American Diaspora* (Cambridge, MA: Harvard University Press, 2008). Once they arrived in the colony, many enslaved Africans had to endure additional trips to other regions of the colony and the traumatic process of being sold. See Nicholas Radburn, "*Au-delà de la traversée:* The Transatlantic Slave Trade within Prerevolutionary Saint Domingue," *William and Mary Quarterly* 81, no. 2 (2024): 319–358.

8. David Geggus, "Slave Society in the Sugar Plantation Zones of Saint Domingue and the Revolution of 1791–93," *Slavery & Abolition* 20, no. 2 (1999): 34; Burnard and Garrigus, *Plantation Machine,* 43.

9. Laurent Dubois, *Avengers of the New World: The Story of the Haitian Revolution* (Cambridge, MA: Belknap Press of Harvard University Press, 2004), 21. The island is often referred to in histories as "the pearl of the Antilles." For a historic use of this phrase, see "la perle d'amerique, isle de St. Domingue," Roulet to Ferrand, Santo Domingo, May 12, 1806, SHD, GR7, B11.

10. Richard Follett, "The Demography of Slavery," in *The Routledge History of Slavery,* edited by Gad Heuman and Trevor Burnard (London: Routledge, 2011), 121. Follett notes between 1680 and 1777 about 800,000 enslaved people were imported. Using data from the Slave Voyages Database, Marlene Daut records that 911,142 captives were transported to Saint-Domingue; see Daut, *Awakening the Ashes,* 53. See also, Dubois, *Avengers,* 39.

11. Gwendolyn Midlo Hall, *Social Control in Slave Plantation Societies: A Comparison of St. Domingue and Cuba* (Baltimore: Johns Hopkins University Press, 1971), 14–17; Follett, "Demography of Slavery," 122–124, 129.

12. Dubois, *Avengers,* 39.

13. John Thornton and Christina Mobley estimate that fully two-thirds had been born in Africa and thus were newly enslaved. John K. Thornton, "'I Am the Subject of the King of Congo': African Political Ideology and the Haitian Revolution," *Journal of World History* 4, no. 2 (1993): 183; Christina Frances Mobley, "The Kongolese Atlantic: Central African Slavery and Culture from Mayombe to Haiti" (PhD diss., Duke University, 2015), 4. David Geggus disputes these claims and argues that about half of the enslaved population was African-born. See David Geggus, "Kongomania and the Haitian Revolution," *The Americas* 81, no. 2 (2024): 222.

14. Carlo A. Célius, "Créolité et bossalité en Haïti selon Gérard Barthélemy," *L'homme: Revue française d'anthropologie* 207/208 (2013): 326.

15. Michel Hector and Laënnec Hurbon, "Introduction: Les fondations," in *Genèse de l'État haïtien (1804–1859)*, edited by Michel Hector and Laënnec Hurbon (Paris: Éditions de la Maison des sciences de l'homme, 2009), 14. See also Jean Casimir, *The Haitians: A Decolonial History*, translated by Laurent Dubois (Chapel Hill: University of North Carolina Press, 2020), 134–138; Johnhenry Gonzalez, *Maroon Nation: A History of Revolutionary Haiti* (New Haven, CT: Yale University Press, 2019).

16. Jean Casimir, "La suppression de la culture africaine dans l'histoire d'Haïti," *Socio-anthropologie* 8 (2000), published online January 15, 2003; Casimir, *Haitians;* Thornton, "I Am the Subject of the King of Congo," 201.

17. Casimir, *Haitians*, 45–46.

18. Gaspard Théodore Mollien, *Haïti ou Saint-Domingue*, tome 2, edited by Francis Arzalier (Paris: L'Harmattan, 2006), 54.

19. Mollien, *Haïti ou Saint-Domingue*, tome 2, 54.

20. Christina Mobley distinguishes between the "Kongo zone," which refers to the geographic area that colonizers called "Congo," and the "political unit of the Kingdom of Kongo." Mobley, "Kongolese Atlantic," 6.

21. Dubois, *Avengers*, 40–42; Mobley, "Kongolese Atlantic," 4–5. David Geggus argues that previous scholars have overestimated the demographic presence and cultural significance of "Congo" people in Saint-Domingue, but he agrees that they were more prevalent in the northern coffee-growing region; see Geggus, "Kongomania," 230.

22. Thornton, "I Am the Subject of the King of Congo," 186, 188–189; Mobley, "Kongolese Atlantic," 283–337.

23. Thornton, "I Am the Subject of the King of Congo," 200.

24. Thornton, "I Am the Subject of the King of Congo," 200.

25. In thinking about Dessalines's birthplace-as-identity, it is instructive to resist the absolute binary of "creole" and *bossale* as distinct social categories, especially for regions of the colony such as Grande Rivière that had a prevalence of "Congos." One historian has proposed a new middle-ground category, "creole-Congo," a label taken from a Haitian Vodou song. See Laurent Dubois, "Thinking Haitian Independence in Haitian Vodou," in *The Haitian Declaration of Independence: Creation, Context, and Legacy*, edited by Julia Gaffield (Charlottesville: University of Virginia Press, 2016), 211; Deborah Jenson, "Jean-Jacques Dessalines and the African Character of the Haitian Revolution," *William and Mary Quarterly* 69, no. 3 (2012): 615; Joan [Colin] Dayan, *Haiti, History, and the Gods* (Berkeley: University of California Press, 1998), 22.

26. Dubois, *Avengers*, 43.

27. M. E. Descourtilz, *Voyages d'un naturaliste et ses observations*, tome troisième (Paris: Dufart, père, Libraire-Éditeur, 1809), 281.

28. Moreau de Saint-Méry refers to the parish as Sainte-Rose, its historic name. Médéric Louis Élie Moreau de Saint-Méry, *Description topographique, physique, civile, politique et historique de la partie française de l'isle Saint-Domingue* (Philadelphia: Chez l'auteur, 1797), 223.

29. Gabriel Debien, "La nourriture des esclaves sur les plantations des Antilles françaises aux

XVIIè et XVIIIè Siècles," *Caribbean Studies* 4, no. 2 (1964): 23–24; Gabriel Debien, *Les esclaves aux Antilles françaises (XVIIe–XVIIIe siècles)* (Basse-Terre: Société d'histoire de la Guadeloupe and Société d'histoire de la Martinique, 1974), 141.

30. Moreau de Saint-Méry, *Description,* 223.

31. "Carte topographique de la région du Cap-Français et du Fort-Dauphin, au Nord-est de la colonie française ou St. Domingue," [n.p., 1760], Bibliothèque nationale de France, Département des cartes et plans, GE SH 18 PF 150 DIV 2 P 8, https://gallica.bnf.fr /ark:/12148/btv1b53103462d; Graham T. Nessler, *An Islandwide Struggle for Freedom: Revolution, Emancipation, and Reenslavement in Hispaniola, 1789–1809* (Chapel Hill: University of North Carolina Press, 2016), 143.

32. Daut, *Awakening the Ashes,* 54–56.

33. Malick W. Ghachem, *The Old Regime and the Haitian Revolution* (Cambridge, UK: Cambridge University Press, 2012), 59–61; "Code Noir ou Edit servant de règlement pour le Gouvernement et l'Administration de la Justice et de la Police des Isles Françoises de l'Amérique, et pour la Discipline et le Commerce des Negres et Esclaves dans ledit Pays," March 1685, in Médéric Louis Élie Moreau de Saint-Méry, *Loix et constitutions des colonies françoises de l'Amérique sous le vent,* vol. 1 (Paris: Chez l'auteur, 1784): 414–424. Original document also available at https://digitalcollections.nyhistory.org/islandora /object/nyhs%253A235290#page/1/mode/2up.

34. Ghachem, *Old Regime,* 62.

35. See, for example, the use of the *Code Noir* by free people of color who sought to secure their freedom through marriage: Robert D. Taber, "The Issue of Their Union: Family, Law, and Politics in Western Saint-Domingue, 1777–1789" (PhD diss., University of Florida, 2015), 106.

36. Stewart R. King, "The Maréchaussée of Saint-Domingue: Balancing the Ancien Régime and Modernity," *Journal of Colonialism and Colonial History* 5, no. 2 (2004): https://dx .doi.org/10.1353/cch.2004.0052.

37. Gabriel Debien, "Le marronage aux Antilles françaises au XVIIIe siècle," *Caribbean Studies* 6, no. 3 (1966): 13–15.

38. Art. XXXVIII, "Code Noir ou Edit," 420; Debien, "Le marronage," 10; on similar laws in Barbados and Jamaica, see Stefanie Hunt-Kennedy, *Between Fitness and Death: Disability and Slavery in the Caribbean* (Urbana: University of Illinois Press, 2020), 108–116.

39. Pernille Røge, *Economistes and the Reinvention of Empire: France in the Americas and Africa, c. 1750–1802* (Cambridge, UK: Cambridge University Press, 2019), 6.

40. Jennifer L. Palmer, *Intimate Bonds: Family and Slavery in the French Atlantic* (Philadelphia: University of Pennsylvania Press, 2016), 206n63.

41. John D. Garrigus, *Before Haiti: Race and Citizenship in French Saint-Domingue* (New York: Palgrave Macmillan, 2006); Burnard and Garrigus, *Plantation Machine,* 164–191.

42. Palmer, *Intimate Bonds,* 16.

43. Stewart R. King, *Blue Coat or Powdered Wig: Free People of Color in Pre-Revolutionary Saint-Domingue* (Athens: University of Georgia Press, 2007), xvi.

44. On these pseudoscientific racial taxonomies, see Daut, *Tropics of Haiti,* 4–7.

45. I am drawing on Laurent Dubois's explanation of his translation of *nègre* that "moved

from the multiplicity of meanings in the French term to words that pointed and flowed well in English." Laurent Dubois, "Translator's Introduction," in *Critique of Black Reason*, by Achille Mbembe, translated by Laurent Dubois (Durham, NC: Duke University Press, 2017), ix–xv. I will keep *nègre* in French and italics when it is in a quotation or context-specific but will otherwise use "Black."

46. Taber, "Issue of Their Union," 88–91.

47. Taber, "Issue of Their Union," 84–85.

48. This was a legal category but also a social category. People who were given the label "free people of color" were either Black or "mixed-race" (at the time they were sometimes called *mulâtre, quarteron,* or *grif,* depending on the ascribed race of their parents). As Marlene Daut thoughtfully outlines, there are limits to "the utility of 'race' or skin color to tell us anything benign about a person," even though these labels had serious legal and social ramifications in the eighteenth and nineteenth centuries. Throughout the text I try to avoid reifying the categories that these labels attempted to create while not issuing anachronistic corrections. See Daut, *Tropics of Haiti,* 45–48. On terminology, see also Grégory Pierrot, *The Black Avenger in Atlantic Culture* (Athens: University of Georgia Press, 2019), 219–220n10.

49. John D. Garrigus, "Vincent Ogé *jeune* (1757–91): Social Class and Free Colored Mobilization on the Eve of the Haitian Revolution," *The Americas* 68, no. 1 (2011): 33; Taber, "Issue of Their Union," 112.

50. Taber, "Issue of Their Union," 111.

51. Jennifer L. Palmer, "'She persisted in her revolt': Between Slavery and Freedom in Saint-Domingue," *Histoire sociale/Social History* 53, no. 107 (2020): 18; King, *Blue Coat or Powdered Wig,* xvii.

CHAPTER 2. *UN MAUVAIS ESCLAVE*

1. Mollien, *Haïti ou Saint-Domingue,* tome 2, 53.

2. Timoléon C. Brutus, *L'homme d'Airain: Étude monographique sur JEAN-JACQUES DES-SALINES, fondateur de la nation haïtienne. Histoire de la vie d'un esclave devenu Empereur jusqu'à sa mort, le 17 Octobre 1806,* vol. 1 (Port-au-Prince: Imprimerie N. A. Théodore, 1946), 28.

3. On his use of the name Duclos, see Edgar La Selve, "La république d'Haïti, ancienne partie française de Saint-Domingue," *Le tour du monde, nouveau journal des voyages,* vol. 38 (1879), 202; and Thomas Madiou, *Histoire d'Haïti,* tome 3 (Port-au-Prince: Imprimerie de Jh. Courtois, 1848), 123n.

4. Jules Rosemond, *Conférence historique sur la vie de Jean-Jacques Dessalines, fondateur de l'indépendance haïtienne, faite le 17 Octobre 1903 à l'Association nationale du centenaire* (Port-au-Prince: Imprimerie de l'Abeille, 1903), 16. On naming practices under slavery, see Debien, *Les esclaves aux Antilles françaises,* 71–73.

5. Jacques de Cauna, *Toussaint Louverture: Le grand précurseur* (Bordeaux: Éditions Sud Ouest, 2012), 111. Some have claimed that he was born in the Cormier Valley, where he was later enslaved; see La Selve, "République d'Haïti," 202; There are two Duclos properties marked on a 1760 map of the region, both south and east of the town of Grande Rivière; see "Carte topographique de la région du Cap-Français et du Fort-Dauphin,"

Bibliothèque nationale de France. A few scholars have proposed that Dessalines was born in the Artibonite region, but little evidence supports this claim. See, for example, Brutus, *L'homme d'Airain*, 34–35n3.

6. For a study on a similar scenario in the southern province, see Garrigus, *Before Haiti*, 22.

7. Garrigus, *Before Haiti*, 118.

8. De Cauna, *Toussaint Louverture*, 110; Brutus, *L'homme d'Airain*, 35; Emmanuel C. Paul, "Le ressentiment Dessalinien," *Revue de la Société haïtienne d'histoire, de géographie et de géologie* 30, no. 104 (1957): 146; [François-Richard de Tussac], *Cri des colons: Contre un ouvrage de M. L'evêque et senateur Grégoire, ayant pour titre "De la littérature des Nègres"* (Paris: Chez Delaunay, 1810), 229; Gérard M. Laurent, "Étude No. 1: L'Ame d'un Libérateur," in *Six études sur J. J. Dessalines* (Port-au-Prince: Imprimerie Les Presses Libres, 1950), 13–14.

9. Mollien, *Haïti ou Saint-Domingue*, tome 2, 53; on the scars, see de Tussac, *Cri des colons*, 229; on Duclos's violence, see Laurent, "Étude No. 1," 12–14.

10. Mollien, *Haïti ou Saint-Domingue*, tome 2, 53.

11. Nineteenth-century historical accounts and archival evidence support this claim. See Edgar La Selve, *Le pays des nègres: Voyage à Haïti, ancienne partie française de Saint-Domingue* (Paris: Hachette, 1881), 36; Madiou, *Histoire d'Haïti*, tome 3, 36; Rosemond, *Conférence historique*, 15; Gaétan Mentor, *Dessalines, l'esclave devenu empereur* (Pétion-Ville, Haiti: Imprimerie Le Natal, 2003), 7; Henry de Poyen-Bellisle, *Histoire militaire de la révolution de Saint-Domingue* (Paris: Imprimerie Nationale, 1899), 475n2. When Thomas Madiou demanded a correction to his biographical entry in a nineteenth-century French dictionary, Dessalines's age did not change in the updated entry. "Partie Non Officielle," *Le moniteur haïtien*, December 5, 1852, pp. 2–4; M. N. Bouillet, *Dictionnaire universel d'histoire et de géographie*, 11th ed. (Paris: Hachette, 1856), 486. Early accounts state that he was born in 1758, and while scholars have hotly debated other aspects of his life, this one fact remains nearly consistent. One notable exception to the consensus is Saint-Rémy, who claimed Dessalines was born in 1749, confusingly citing Dubroca: Joseph Saint-Rémy, *Mémoires du Général Toussaint-L'Ouverture, écrits par lui-même, pouvant servir a l'histoire de sa vie, ornés d'un beau portrait par Choubard* (Paris: Pagnerre, Libraire-Éditeur, 1853), 31n2.

12. Rosemond, *Conférence historique*, 15. Gaétan Mentor claimed that Dessalines was born on July 25, 1758, Saint Jacques's day. Mentor, *Dessalines*, 7. An 1806 newspaper reported on "sa fête," likely referring to the holiday of his namesake: *Gazette politique et commerciale d'Haïti*, no. 41, October 16, 1806, *l'an troisième de l'indépendance*, 162. For a list of other possible birth dates, see Berthony Dupont, *Jean-Jacques Dessalines: Itinéraire d'un révolutionaire* (Paris: L'Harmattan, 2006), 73–74.

13. Dessalines's birth may have been recorded in plantation records, but he was consistently enslaved on smaller coffee plantations with resident property owners, and those kinds of settings produced fewer documents that were rarely preserved in the colonial or state archives. Furthermore, for the most part, the parish records for the colony's northern province only exist for the period after 1777, because priests were required to send duplicates of their registers to France. All originals were destroyed during the Haitian Revolution. Jacques Houdaille, "Quelques données sur la population de Saint-Domingue au

XVIIIe siècle," *Population* 28, no. 4–5 (1973): 861–865; Debien, *Les esclaves aux Antilles françaises,* 106.

14. Rosemond, *Conférence historique,* 15. On the lack of information regarding his parents, see Louis-Joseph Janvier, "Notes sur Dessalines et Toussaint Louverture, Guerre de l'Indépendance, Mort de Dessalines," October 6, 1902, manuscript, courtesy of the Bibliothèque Haïtienne des Spiritains, Haïti, 16–17. Many thanks to Patrick Tardieu.

15. Arlette Gautier, "Les familles esclaves aux Antilles françaises, 1635–1848," *Population* (French ed.) 55, no. 6 (2000): 985; Debien, *Les esclaves aux Antilles françaises,* 262.

16. Gautier, "Les familles esclaves," 987; Debien, *Les esclaves aux Antilles françaises,* 262.

17. Gautier, "Les familles esclaves," 992.

18. Follett notes that infant mortality could be as high as 65 percent. See Follett, "Demography of Slavery," 131; Colleen A. Vasconcellos, *Slavery, Childhood, and Abolition in Jamaica, 1788–1838* (Athens: University of Georgia Press, 2015), 9.

19. Jean-Baptiste Mirambeau, "Victoria, surnommé Toya par ses congénères," in *Le Document: Organe de la Librairie d'histoire d'Haïti et des œuvres de la pensée haïtienne,* vol. 1, no. 2 (1940) [original ms. from 1805]: 107, quoted in Jasmine Claude-Narcisse, "Mémoire de Femmes: Victoria Môntou dite Toya," *Mémoire de Femmes,* https://www.haiticulture.ch/Toya.html.

20. Mirambeau, "Victoria," 107.

21. The term *atelier* is sometimes translated as "work gang" by US scholars. I opt for the term "plantation unit" instead, because of the historical specificity of the term "work gang" in the US South and because the term "plantation unit" captures both the group of people and location. It also implies the regimented and supervised work done by the enslaved people who worked in the fields. I am grateful for lengthy conversations about this term with Chelsea Stieber, Nadève Ménard, and Jean Casimir.

22. Mirambeau argued that Toya was transferred from "les Cahos," which is not in Grande Rivière, to the Déluger plantation. Mirambeau, "Victoria," 107; Brutus, *L'homme d'Airain:* 42n2. The "de Lugé" plantation is listed on a 1790 map, south of Saint-Marc: René Phelipeau, "Plan du quartier de l'Artibonite, Isle St. Domingue," Paris, 1790, University of Florida, Smathers Library, Rare Books, G4943.L3 1790.P5 CARTA.

23. "Bail," August 17, 1779, Saint-Domingue, Nord, Le Cap, Dore 1755/1780, *Doubles minutes,* NOT*SDOM 525, DPPC.

24. Sometimes spelled Dézir. "Sep. Philipe Jasmin nègre, 45 ans," État Civil, Saint-Domingue, Grande-Rivière, 1784, ANOM. Archival evidence confirms that Dessalines was enslaved in the Cormier Valley of Grande Rivière du Nord by 1779 when he was about twenty-one years old. Madison Smartt Bell cited the "Bail" document above in his biography of Toussaint Louverture and noted that a "Jean-Jacques" was among those enslaved by Jasmin, but concluded that "if he had been under Toussaint's authority during slavery time, this circumstance would probably have been noticed later on." Madison Smartt Bell, *Toussaint Louverture: A Biography* (New York: Pantheon Books, 2007), 71. Jacques de Cauna first connected the source to Jean-Jacques Dessalines using the records of Marie-Marthe's second marriage to Jeanvier Desaline. See Jacques de Cauna, "Dessalines esclave de Toussaint?," *Outre-Mers* 99, no. 374–375 (2012): 319–322; de Cauna, *Toussaint Louverture,* 111; Mollien, *Haïti ou Saint-Domingue,* tome 2, 53. La Selve argues

that Duclos sold him when he was still "tout jeune encore." La Selve, "République d'Haïti," 202. Jasmin was less than thirty-nine years old when he purchased Dessalines.

25. It is possible that Philippe and his mother had previously been enslaved, but when she died she was free. His father, Pierre Jasmin, died on February 19, 1785, at about age seventy. He was a widower but had been married to a free Black woman named Rose. In 1760 Philippe Jasmin would have been twenty-one years old, so it is possible he was the owner listed on the map, but it is more likely his father. The Grande-Rivière parish records list a ca. seventy-year-old woman named Rose as having been buried earlier that year on May 16, but the record did not note any family. See "Sep. Rose negresse 70 ans," État Civil, Saint-Domingue, Grande-Rivière, 1784, ANOM, and "Sep. Pierre Jasmin negre, 70 ans," État Civil, Saint-Domingue, Grande-Rivière, 1785, ANOM.

26. Palmer, "She persisted in her revolt," 24.

27. David Geggus shows that after 1763 Saint-Domingue experienced a massive expansion of coffee cultivation. David Geggus, "Sugar and Coffee Cultivation in Saint Domingue," in *Cultivation and Culture: Labor and the Shaping of Slave Life in the Americas,* edited by Ira Berlin and Philip Morgan (Charlottesville: University of Virginia Press, 1993), 73.

28. The notarial records note that the Jasmin plantation was in Petit Cormier, "Bail," August 17, 1779, Saint-Domingue, Nord, Le Cap, Dore 1755/1780, *doubles minutes,* ANOM, Notariat de Saint-Domingue (NOT*SDOM) 525, DPPC.

29. King, *Blue Coat or Powdered Wig,* xviii, 124.

30. David Geggus, "The Slaves and Free People of Color of Cap Français," in *The Black Urban Atlantic in the Age of the Slave Trade,* edited by Jorge Cañizares-Esguerra, Matt D. Childs, and James Sidbury (Philadelphia: University of Pennsylvania Press, 2013), 102. The population of Grande Rivière was 650 white colonists, 950 free people of color, and 9,500 enslaved people. Moreau de Saint-Méry, *Description,* 226; Taber, "Issue of Their Union," 56.

31. A 1760 map shows a plantation in Cormier called "Jasmin": "Carte topographique de la région du Cap-Français et du Fort-Dauphin," Bibliothèque nationale de France. For a list of neighborhoods in the parish, see Moreau de Saint-Méry, *Description,* 223. The *Affiches américaines* make clear that other people lived in the valley, even if they were not marked on the maps. See the digitized versions from 1766–1791: https://llmc.com/title descfull.aspx?type=2&coll=145&div=410&set=31772.

32. The Jasmin plantation was in the smallest quarter of coffee plantations. Geggus, "Sugar and Coffee Cultivation," 76.

33. Laurent, "Étude No. 1," 11; Moreau de Saint-Méry, *Description,* 227.

34. It is possible that he was sold with other members of his family, but it is unlikely that all thirteen men, women, and children were sold together. De Cauna, "Dessalines esclave de Toussaint?," 321.

35. King, *Blue Coat or Powdered Wig,* 92.

36. Geggus, "Slaves and Free People of Color of Cap Français," 108.

37. Follett, "Demography of Slavery," 127.

38. King, *Blue Coat or Powdered Wig,* 90; Geggus, "Sugar and Coffee Cultivation," 84.

39. Debien, *Les esclaves aux Antilles françaises,* 142–143.

40. Debien, *Les esclaves aux Antilles françaises,* 143–144.

41. See Art. XXII and Art. XXIV in "Code Noir ou Edit," 418; Dubois, *Avengers,* 48.

42. De Cauna, *Toussaint Louverture,* 86–87; King, *Blue Coat or Powdered Wig,* 126; Pamphile de Lacroix, "Mémoire secrêt sur l'armée et la colonie de Saint-Domingue," [n.d., likely 1803 or 1804], AN, Pierrefitte, AF/IV/1212; Debien, "La nourriture des esclaves," 10.

43. Laurent Dubois and Richard Turits, *Freedom Roots: Histories from the Caribbean* (Chapel Hill: University of North Carolina Press, 2019), 87–88.

44. Michel-Rolph Trouillot, *Haiti, State against Nation: The Origins and the Legacy of Duvalierism* (New York: Monthly Review Press, 1990), 39; Dubois, *Avengers,* 49–52.

45. Annette Joseph-Gabriel, "Mobility and the Enunciation of Freedom in Urban Saint-Domingue," *Eighteenth-Century Studies* 50, no. 2 (2017): 226.

46. Pierre-Joseph Laborie, *The Coffee Planter of Saint Domingo* (London: T. Cadell and W. Davies, 1798), 97.

47. Laborie, *Coffee Planter,* 96.

48. De Cauna, *Toussaint Louverture,* 81.

49. Jean-Louis Donnadieu and Philippe Girard have argued that Jasmin may have leased his plantation because he was recruited to fight with the Chasseurs Volontaires in the Battle of Savannah in 1779. This would have been unlikely, because Jasmin and Toussaint de Bréda signed the lease the day after the fleet carrying the Chasseurs sailed for Savannah from Cap-Français. Jean-Louis Donnadieu and Philippe Girard, "Nouveaux documents sur la vie de Toussaint Louverture," *Bulletin de la Société d'histoire de la Guadeloupe* 166–167 (2013): 120. On the date of departure, see George P. Clark, "The Role of the Haitian Volunteers at Savannah in 1779: An Attempt at an Objective View," *Phylon* 41, no. 4 (1980): 360; and Roberta Leighton, editor and annotator, "Meyronnet de Saint-Marc's Journal of the Operations of the French Army under d'Estaing at the Siege of Savannah, September 1779," *New-York Historical Society Quarterly* 36, no. 3 (July 1952): 261.

50. De Cauna, *Toussaint Louverture;* Philippe R. Girard, *Toussaint Louverture: A Revolutionary Life* (New York: Basic Books, 2016); Sudhir Hazareesingh, *Black Spartacus: The Epic Life of Toussaint Louverture* (New York: Farrar, Straus and Giroux, 2020).

51. Jean Fouchard, *Les marrons de la liberté* (Paris: Éditions de l'École, 1972), 100; Bryan Edwards, *An Historical Survey of the French Colony in the Island of St. Domingo* (London: John Stockdale, 1797), 208–212.

52. De Cauna, *Toussaint Louverture,* 110. The later cancellation of the lease refers to François as a *"negrillon,"* confirming that he was younger. "Résiliation de bail," July 31, 1781, ANOM, 7DPPC, 5974, cited in Philippe R. Girard and Jean-Louis Donnadieu, "Toussaint before Louverture: New Archival Findings on the Early Life of Toussaint Louverture," *William and Mary Quarterly* 70, no. 1 (2013): 70n76.

53. "Bail," August 17, 1779, Saint-Domingue, Nord, Le Cap, Dore 1755/1780, *doubles minutes,* ANOM, NOT*SDOM 525, DPPC.

54. Jean-Jacques's deceased aunt was Marie Marthe and her son was François; I have not included their names in the text to avoid confusion with Philippe Jasmin's wife Marie-Marthe. On their death, see "Résiliation de bail," July 31, 1781, ANOM, 7DPPC, 5974. The original lease between Jasmin and Bréda was supposed to be for nine years, but ended up lasting only two years.

55. Philippe Jasmin was buried on November 16, 1784 (he died on November 15), État-civil de Grande Rivière, 1DPPC 2384, ANOM.

56. King, *Blue Coat or Powdered Wig*, 186.

57. Gaspard Théodore Mollien mistakenly identified Marie-Marthe as Jasmin's daughter. Mollien, *Haïti ou Saint-Domingue*, tome 2, 53. Another account claimed Dessalines was enslaved by a *maîtresse:* "Mémoire Secret" [marginalia, *présumé de Pascal*], [ca. 1802], SCRBC, Sc Micro R-228, reel 9. No evidence has been found to suggest that Philippe Jasmin and Marie-Marthe had any children together.

58. The priest entered his name as "Janvier dit de Salines" in the marriage record, but he signed his name as "Desaline" and in a later document wrote his name—or had a notary write his name—as "Jeanvier Desaline." ANOM, État Civil, "Le Cap," 1787. His military record is: ANOM, "Dessalines, Janvier, sergent-major dans la milice coloniale, concierge de la maison du Gouvernement, à Saint-Domingue, 1796," ANOM, COL E 129, ark:/61561/up4240mmpny. The priest recorded that he was the eldest son and a *fils naturel* (a son born out of wedlock) of a free Black woman named Marie Jourdain. Given that the priest did not list "Janvier dit de Salines's" father and that he was not identified as *mulâtre*, it is possible that his father was an enslaved man.

59. Joseph-Gabriel, "Mobility and the Enunciation of Freedom," 221.

60. On women's property ownership, see Jennifer L. Palmer, "The Fruits of Their Labours: Race, Gender and Labour in the Eighteenth-Century French Caribbean," *French History* 32, no. 4 (2018): 471–492; King, *Blue Coat or Powdered Wig*, 197–198. Pamphile de Lacroix later recounted that Dessalines "was the slave of a free black person from Cap whose name he uses." However, whether Jeanvier Desaline was legally Dessalines's enslaver is still not conclusive; see Lacroix, "Mémoire secrêt." On Jeanvier Desaline as Dessalines's enslaver, see also Jenson, "Jean-Jacques Dessalines," 628; de Tussac, *Cri des colons*, 229.

61. Brutus, *L'homme d'Airain*, 44, 48; Poyen-Bellisle, *Histoire militaire*, 475; M. Charles-Malo, *Histoire d'Haïti (Île de Saint Domingue), depuis sa découverte jusqu'en 1824* (Paris: Louis Janet, 1825), 306.

62. Rosemond, *Conférence historique*, 16. The initial spelling of his name is inconsistent and was sometimes Desalines or Desaline, but I will only use Dessalines for clarity.

63. I am grateful to my William & Mary undergraduate students in HIST 121 (Spring 2023) for their discussion of Dessalines's name choice.

64. King, *Blue Coat or Powdered Wig*, xiii, 231; Moreau de Saint-Méry noted that the militias were disbanded in 1764 and only reestablished in 1768. Moreau de Saint-Méry, *Description*, 499.

65. Taber, "Issue of Their Union," 89. Jeanvier Desaline was therefore at least six years older than Jean-Jacques Dessalines.

66. King, *Blue Coat or Powdered Wig*, 61.

67. John D. Garrigus, "Catalyst or Catastrophe? Saint-Domingue's Free Men of Color and the Savannah Expedition, 1779–1782," *Review/Revista Interamericana* 22 (1992): 115; King, *Blue Coat or Powdered Wig*, 62.

68. Garrigus, "Catalyst or Catastrophe?," 111; King, *Blue Coat or Powdered Wig*, 59.

69. ANOM, "Dessalines, Janvier, sergent-major."

70. Garrigus, "Vincent Ogé *jeune,*" 39; he fought in the Baur-Bellerive company, ANOM, "Dessalines, Janvier, sergent-major."

71. After the Makandal affair in 1758, enslaved people were not allowed to form separate units but would have to serve under their enslavers. Gwendolyn Midlo Hall, "Saint Domingue," in *Neither Slave nor Free: The Freedman of African Descent in the Slave Societies of the New World,* edited by David W. Cohen and Jack P. Greene (Baltimore: Johns Hopkins University Press, 1974), 174.

72. Frédéric Régent, "Armement des hommes de couleur et liberté aux Antilles: Le cas de la Guadeloupe pendant l'Ancien régime et la Révolution," *Annales historiques de la Révolution française* 2, no. 348 (2007): 44; Ghachem, *Old Regime,* 115; Hall, "Saint Domingue," 177; Boris Lesueur, "Les paradoxes de la liberté par les armes (Antilles, XVIIIe siècle)," in *Sortir de l'esclavage, Europe du Sud et Amériques (XIVe-XIXe siècle),* edited by Dominique Rogers and Boris Lesueur (Paris: Karthala, 2018), 204–206.

73. Garrigus, *Before Haiti,* 100; King, *Blue Coat or Powdered Wig,* 56, 59.

74. Some nineteenth-century accounts claimed that Dessalines was married twice. See Poyen-Bellisle, *Histoire militaire,* 476; "Obituary: Death of the Widow of the First Emperor of Hayti," *Anti-Slavery Bugle,* New Lisbon, OH, October 2, 1858, vol. 14, issue 6 [reprinted from the *Evening Post,* Philadelphia].

75. It is possible that Célimène had a twin brother, Jacques Bien-Aimé, but the baptismal record from 1806 has an error that makes me hesitate. Jacques Bien-Aimé was either Célimène's twin or was twins with a girl born in 1793 named Célestine Dessalines. See Kesner Millien, "L'Empereur Jean-Jacques Dessalines: Père de famille à part entière," *Le Nouvelliste,* October 29, 2012, https://lenouvelliste.com/article/110263/lempereur-jean-jacques-dessalines-pere-de-famille-a-part-entiere; Joseph Eveillard, "Claire Heureuse de son vrai nom Claire Félicité Guillaume Bonheur: Conférence prononcé le dimanche 23 Juillet 1933," *Revue de la Société d'histoire et de géographie d'Haïti* 5, no. 13 (1934): 7; "Acte de Naissance de Célimène Dessalines, fille de Jean-Jacques Dessalines," February 2, 1806, courtesy of the Bibliothèque Haïtienne des Spiritains. Many thanks to Patrick Tardieu for sharing this source; the document is mentioned in Eveillard's 1934 article.

76. Eveillard, "Claire Heureuse," 6–7.

77. Dubois, *Avengers,* 78.

78. Garrigus, "Vincent Ogé *jeune,*" 54. Garrigus footnotes: "Procuration à MM. Grenouillaud et Chavanne," October 30, 1789, ADG, Collection Chatillon, 61 J 15, pièce 21.

79. Dubois, *Avengers,* 78.

80. De Cauna, *Toussaint Louverture,* 51; Dubois, *Avengers,* 78.

81. Dubois, *Avengers,* 80.

82. While there is little evidence about any possible involvement of enslaved rebels in the Grande Rivière revolt, some historians have suggested that Dessalines supported Chavanne and his army in their armed conflict. Rosemond, *Conférence historique,* 20; Mentor, *Dessalines,* 8–9.

83. "Lettre aux Messieurs du Comité Colonial Séant au Cap," October 30, 1789, ADG, Collection Marcel Chatillon, 61 J 15.

84. John D. Garrigus, "'Thy coming fame, Ogé! Is sure': New Evidence on Ogé's 1790 Re-

volt and the Beginnings of the Haitian Revolution," in *Assumed Identities: The Meanings of Race in the Atlantic World,* edited by John D. Garrigus and Christopher Morris (College Station: Texas A&M University Press, 2010), 30.

85. "Messieur le Presidant et membres de l'assemblée général et provinciale de la partie du Nord," November 10, 1789, ADG, Collection Marcel Chatillon, 61 J 15.

86. Garrigus, "Vincent Ogé *jeune*," 55.

87. Garrigus, "Vincent Ogé *jeune*," 54.

88. Garrigus, "Thy coming fame, Ogé!," 30; Garrigus, "Vincent Ogé *jeune*," 39. Jeanvier Desaline may have been among the men supporting Chavanne, but he did not sign any of the documents that they submitted to the white assemblies.

89. "Déclaration des droits de l'homme et du citoyen" (Paris: Chez Jaufret, 1789), Bibliothèque nationale de France, https://gallica.bnf.fr/ark:/12148/btv1b8410817c.

90. Citizens and free people of color of the north province to the colonial assembly, March 28, 1790, ADG, Collection Marcel Chatillon, 61 J 15.

91. Garrigus, "Vincent Ogé *jeune*," 56; Dubois, *Avengers,* 85.

92. Garrigus, "Vincent Ogé *jeune*," 57.

93. Garrigus, "Vincent Ogé *jeune*," 56–57; Garrigus, "'Thy coming fame, Ogé!,'" 31.

94. Garrigus, "'Thy coming fame, Ogé!,'" 31.

95. Joseph Ogé became the principal administrator of the North Department in 1804. Vincent Ogé testimony, "Extrait des minutes du Conseil Supérieur du Cap," 1791, AN, Pierrefitte, DXXV/58, dossier 574. Many thanks to John Garrigus for sharing his images and transcription of this document.

96. Ogé and his brother Jacques later claimed that they were being egged on by some of their colleagues, who were present while they were writing. Garrigus, "Vincent Ogé *jeune*," 58; Garrigus, "'Thy coming fame, Ogé!,'" 21, 31.

97. Garrigus, "Vincent Ogé *jeune*," 58.

98. Garrigus, "'Thy coming fame, Ogé!,'" 35.

99. Garrigus, "'Thy coming fame, Ogé!,'" 31–32; Thomas Madiou, *Histoire d'Haïti,* tome 1 (Port-au-Prince: Imprimerie de Jh. Courtois, 1847), 57.

100. "Extrait des minutes du Conseil Supérieur du Cap."

101. Garrigus, "Vincent Ogé *jeune*," 59.

102. Madiou, *Histoire d'Haïti,* tome 1, 61. The Superior Council of Cap-Français had been disbanded in 1787 because the tribunal's members refused to follow a royal ordinance regulating enslavers' abuse of enslaved people. See Malick Ghachem, "The Colonial Vendée," in *The World of the Haitian Revolution,* edited by David Patrick Geggus and Norman Fiering (Bloomington: Indiana University Press, 2009), 156. The provincial assembly of Cap-Français reestablished the Superior Council in 1790. Dubois, *Avengers,* 78.

103. "Nouvelles Coloniales," *Gazette de Saint-Domingue, politique, civile, économique et littéraire, et Affiches américaines,* March 2, 1791, no. 18, p. 1; Dubois, *Avengers,* 88.

104. Jane Landers, *Atlantic Creoles in the Age of Revolutions* (Cambridge, MA: Harvard University Press, 2010), 59.

105. "Nouvelles Coloniales," *Gazette de Saint-Domingue, politique, civile, économique et littéraire, et Affiches américaines,* March 2, 1791, no. 18, p. 1.

CHAPTER 3. HE FELT LIKE HE WAS BORN FOR WAR

1. Antoine Dalmas, *Histoire de la revolution de Saint-Domingue* (Paris: Mame frères, 1814), 116.

2. Carolyn E. Fick, *The Making of Haiti: The Saint Domingue Revolution from Below* (Knoxville: University of Tennessee Press, 1990), 91, 94; Dubois, *Avengers*, 98–99.

3. David Geggus, "The Bois Caïman Ceremony," *Journal of Caribbean History* 25, no. 1 (1991): 45; on the woods, see Hérard Dumesle, *Voyage dans le Nord d'Hayti, ou Révélations des lieux et des monuments historiques* (Cayes: Imprimerie du Gouvernement, 1824), 85. For a comprehensive analysis of the Bois Caïman ceremony and its historiography, see Daut, "Revolution," chap. 4 in *Awakening the Ashes*.

4. On the date and location of the meeting, see Geggus, "Bois Caïman," 45–46. For a description of the "Savane à Cayman," see Moreau de Saint-Méry, *Description*, vol. 2, 595; Dubois, *Avengers*, 100; Landers, *Atlantic Creoles*, 61; Dalmas, *Histoire de la revolution de Saint-Domingue*, 117–118.

5. Dumesle, *Voyage dans le Nord d'Hayti*, 88; translated and quoted in Daut, *Awakening the Ashes*, 116. These words were later attributed to Dutty Boukman.

6. De Cauna, *Toussaint Louverture*, 151. Before the planned day for the start of the insurrection, enslaved people on several plantations broke out in rebellion. The revolutionaries moved up the date before authorities could uncover the full extent of the conspiracy. For example, a report from Cap-Français on August 20, 1791, noted that twenty-eight people had run away, and others had been arrested in Limbé, concluding, "il n'est rien moins question que du projet de brûler et massacrer." "Extrait d'une lettre du Cap le 20 aoust 1791," copied for M. de Bertrand on October 24, 1791, AN, Paris, microfilm, CC9A 5.

7. On livestock, see Bel__villeneuv, Ladébat [?], Cormiers, and Reynaud to the Minister of the Navy, December 3, 1791, AN, Paris, microfilm, CC9A 5; Fick, *Making of Haiti*, 99–100; Dubois, *Avengers*, 94.

8. Auberts Gueyraud [?] to M. de Gallifet, Cap-Français, August 25, 1791, AN, Pierrefitte, 107AP/128.

9. Bel__villeneuv, Ladébat [?], Cormiers, and Reynaud to the Minister of the Navy, December 3, 1791, AN, Paris, microfilm, CC9A 5.

10. Jean-Baptiste Chapuy and Pierre Jean Boquet, "Vue de l'incendie de la ville du Cap Français, Arrivée le 21 Juin 1793," 1794, Bibliothèque nationale de France, RESERVE QB-201 (171)-FT 5, available on Gallica.

11. Fick, *Making of Haiti*, 105; Dubois, *Avengers*, 113; de Cauna, *Toussaint Louverture*, 151; Auberts Gueyraud [?] to M. de Gallifet, Cap-Français, August 25, 1791, AN, Pierrefitte, 107AP/128.

12. Fick, *Making of Haiti*, 97.

13. Dubois, *Avengers*, 96.

14. Landers, *Atlantic Creoles*, 61–62; Philippe-Albert de Lattre, *Campagnes des Français à Saint-Domingue, et réfutation des reproches faits au Capitaine-Général Rochambeau* (Paris: Chez Locard, Arthus-Bertrand, Amand Koenig, 1805), 48; Fick, *Making of Haiti*, 112; Charlton W. Yingling, *Siblings of Soil: Dominicans and Haitians in the Age of Revo-*

lutions (Austin: University of Texas Press, 2022), 83; Miriam Franchina, "'Only When French Generals Will Give Their Daughters in Marriage to the Nègres': Jean-François Petecou and the Other Path to Haitian Freedom," *Age of Revolutions*, posted May 17, 2021, https://ageofrevolutions.com/2021/05/17/only-when-french-generals-will-give -their-daughters-in-marriage-to-the-negres-jean-francois-petecou-and-the-other-path -to-haitian-freedom/.

15. Some estimates have been as high as 100,000. See Dubois, *Avengers,* 97, 113; Yingling, *Siblings of Soil,* 48; Fick, *Making of Haiti,* 106.

16. Fick, *Making of Haiti,* 111; Miriam Rebekah Martin Erickson, "The Black Auxiliary Troops of King Carlos IV: African Diaspora in the Spanish Atlantic World, 1791–1818" (PhD diss., Vanderbilt University, 2015), 94.

17. Laurent, "Étude No. 1," 14.

18. La Selve, *Pays des nègres,* 167; Rosemond, *Conférence historique,* 20; Adolphe Cabon, *Notes sur l'histoire religieuse d'Haïti, de la révolution au concordat (1789–1860)* (Port-au-Prince: Petit Séminaire Collège Saint-Martial, 1933), 90n1; Mentor, *Dessalines,* 9; Lacroix, "Mémoire secrêt." The consul claimed that Dessalines became an aide-de-camp to Jean-François, though none of Jean-François's letters list him as an aide. See Mollien, *Haïti ou Saint-Domingue,* tome 2, 53; M-N Bouillet, *Dictionnaire universel d'histoire et de géographie,* 11th ed. (Paris: Hachette, 1856), 486. Another aide-de-camp of Jean-François was "Despres" or d'Espres; see Jeremy Popkin, *Facing Racial Revolution: Eyewitness Accounts of the Haitian Insurrection* (Chicago: University of Chicago Press, 2007), 141. Belair and Lefebvre are listed as aides-de-camp to Biassou in Biassou, "Ordre," August 24, 1792, AN, Pierrefitte, D/XXV/12. Lefebvre was also an aide-de-camp to Jean-François; see Jean-François to "Messieurs le Citoyen des Gens de Couleur Campés au haut du Cap," [n.d., ca. 1793], AN, Pierrefitte, D/XXV/12. Watable is listed as an aide-de-camp to Jean-François in Jean-François to "Monsieur et Général," August 25, 1793, AN, Pierrefitte, D/XXV/12; Delile is listed as an aide-de-camp to Biassou in Jean-François to Biassou, July 6, 1793, AN, Pierrefitte, D/XXV/12.

19. "Adresse a l'assemblée Générale de La partie francoise de St. Domingue, par MM Les Citoyens de couleur, de la grande Riviere Ste. Suzanne, et autres quartiers, malheureusement envelopés dans le funeste Evenement du 23 Aoust dernier," [ca. December 1791], AN, Pierrefitte, D/XXV/1.

20. Boisrond-Tonnerre, *Mémoires,* 7.

21. Charles Forsdick and Christian Høgsbjerg, *Toussaint Louverture: A Black Jacobin in the Age of Revolutions* (London: Pluto Press, 2017), 40; Landers, *Atlantic Creoles,* 56, 58, 63–65; Hazareesingh, *Black Spartacus,* 51; Dubois, *Avengers,* 124; Jean-François, Biassou, et al. [including "Toussaint"] to "Messieurs," Grande Rivière, December 12, 1791, AN, Pierrefitte, D/XXV/1.

22. Louverture to Bonaparte, 23 Pluviôse an 9 [February 12, 1801], "Documents précédant l'intervention du general Leclerc à Saint-Domingue, 7 pièces," AN, Pierrefitte, AB/XIX/5002.

23. Boisrond-Tonnerre, *Mémoires,* 7.

24. The doctor footnoted the exchange to clarify that "Jean-Jacques" meant "Jean-Jacques Dessalines." Mirambeau, "Victoria," 108.

25. John K. Thornton, "African Soldiers in the Haitian Revolution," *Journal of Caribbean History* 25, no. 1 (1991): 60; John K. Thornton, "Kongomania and the Numbers Game," *The Americas* 81, no. 2 (2024): 271–272.

26. Dubois, *Avengers,* 109; Thornton, "Kongomania and the Numbers Game," 272.

27. Thornton, "Kongomania and the Numbers Game," 272–273.

28. Dubois, *Avengers,* 116; Thornton, "I Am the Subject of the King of Congo," 202.

29. Léger-Félicité Sonthonax, "Relation des événements qui se sont passés au Cap dans les premiers jours du mois de décembre 1792 adressée à la Municipalité de Paris," AN, Paris, microfilm, CC9A 6; Jeremy D. Popkin, *You Are All Free: The Haitian Revolution and the Abolition of Slavery* (New York: Cambridge University Press, 2010), 43–44, 73.

30. On slavery as warfare, see Vincent Brown, *Tacky's Revolt: The Story of an Atlantic Slave War* (Cambridge, MA: Harvard University Press, 2020). On this history of *marronage* in Saint-Domingue, see Fouchard, *Les marrons de la liberté.*

31. Tousard to "tous les citoyens de couleur de la dependance de l'est," November 18, 1791, Anne Louis Tousard Journal (accession 874), Manuscripts and Archives Department, Hagley Museum and Library, Wilmington, DE, https://digital.hagley.org/874_Tousard _journal_microfilm; Fick, *Making of Haiti,* 105.

32. Popkin, *You Are All Free,* 47.

33. On the national guard, see Popkin, *You Are All Free,* 99.

34. On November 22, 1791, Tousard ordered several units, including those of Barbot, "Dessalines," and d'Arnaud, to prepare to march at 10 a.m. that day. He did not use a first name in the document, but based on Jeanvier Desaline's extensive militia leadership and the documented record of his service, I have concluded that this was Jeanvier Desaline. Tousard, "Order," November 22, 1791, Anne Louis Tousard Journal.

35. Popkin, *You Are All Free,* 41–49.

36. Popkin attributes their limited demands to the influence of their white prisoners, who tried to convince them that troops from France were coming. News of the uprising would have reached France in October, and therefore the metropole could have had time to send a fleet to the rescue (but this would have been extremely fast timing). Popkin, *You Are All Free,* 47, 51.

37. Fick, *Making of Haiti,* 114; Anne-Louis Tousard to Laurent-François de Rouvray, Wilmington, DE, November 27, 1791, Anne Louis Tousard Journal, cited in Erickson, "Black Auxiliary Troops," 77; David Geggus, *The Haitian Revolution: A Documentary History* (Indianapolis: Hackett Publishing, 2014), 86–87.

38. Dubois, *Avengers,* 128.

39. The commissioners were Frédéric Mirbeck, Philippe Roume, and Edmond de Saint-Léger.

40. Only those who had two free and legally married parents would have been free. Dubois, *Avengers,* 125; Popkin, *You Are All Free,* 38.

41. Dubois, *Avengers,* 125.

42. Landers, *Atlantic Creoles,* 65; Fick, *Making of Haiti,* 116.

43. "Adresse a L'assemblée Générale de La partie francoise de St. Domingue, par MM Les Citoyens de couleur, de la grande Riviere Ste. Susanne, et autres quartiers, malheureusement envelopés dans la funeste Evenement du 23 Aoust dernier," [ca. December 1791], AN, Pierrefitte, D/XXV/1; Dubois, *Avengers,* 126.

44. Tousard to Mr. Cator [Deputy of Grande Rivière], December 12, 1791, Anne Louis Tousard Journal.

45. Forsdick and Høgsbjerg, *Toussaint Louverture,* 40.

46. Fick, *Making of Haiti,* 160.

47. Jean-François, Biassou, et al. to the Commissioners, Grande Rivière, December 12, 1791, AN, Pierrefitte, D/XXV/1.

48. Erickson, "Black Auxiliary Troops," 83; Dubois, *Avengers,* 124.

49. Jean-François, Biassou, et al. to the Commissioners, Grande Rivière, December 12, 1791, AN, Pierrefitte, D/XXV/1.

50. Biassou and Jean-François to Messieurs Les Commissaires Nationaux delegué par le Roy, [ca. December 21, 1791], AN, Pierrefitte, D/XXV/1. Dubois, *Avengers,* 127–128; Fick, *Making of Haiti,* 117.

51. Biassou and Jean-François to Messieurs Les Commissaires Nationaux delegué par le Roy, [ca. December 21, 1791], AN, Pierrefitte, D/XXV/1.

52. Biassou and Jean-François to Messieurs Les Commissaires Nationaux delegué par le Roy, [ca. December 21, 1791], AN, Pierrefitte, D/XXV/1.

53. Dubois, *Avengers,* 128.

54. Dubois, *Avengers,* 107–108; Yingling, *Siblings of Soil,* 61–62.

55. Yingling, *Siblings of Soil,* 61.

56. Tousard to M. MacDonald, January 13, 1792, Anne Louis Tousard Journal.

57. Dubois, *Avengers,* 130; see also Léger-Félicité Sonthonax and V. F. Delpech, "Relation officielle des Événemens arrivés au cap les 1ere, 2, 3, 4, 5, 6, 7 et 8 X^{bre} 1792," December 10, 1792, AN, Paris, microfilm, CC9A 6.

58. Jeremy D. Popkin, "A Haitian Revolutionary Manifesto? New Perspectives on the 'Letter of Jean-François, Biassou, and Belair,'" *Slavery & Abolition* 43, no. 1 (2022): 6.

59. The authenticity and authorship of the letter have previously been called into question, and historians have typically assumed that the Belair who signed the letter was Charles Bélair—Toussaint Louverture's nephew, who later joined the revolution but who at this moment was likely too young to have been an aide-de-camp to Biassou. As Erickson shows, the letter was published twice in 1793: in Joseph-Paul-Augustin Cambefort, *Quatrième partie du Mémoire justificatif, de Joseph-Paul-Augustin Cambefort, colonel du régiment du Cap* (Paris: Imprimeries des Frères Chaignieau, 1793), 4–11; and "Lettre originale des chefs des Nègres révoltés, à l'assemblée générale, aux commissaires nationaux et aux citoyens de la partie Française de Saint-Domingue, du mois de Juillet 1792," *Le Créole patriote, journal du soir, bulletin de Milscent-Créole,* no. 282, p. 1147, available on Gallica: https://gallica.bnf.fr/ark:/12148/bpt6k10665183/f1.item. See Erikson, "Black Auxiliary Troops," 98. For examples of claims that this was Charles Bélair, see Landers, *Atlantic Creoles,* 68; and Dubois, *Avengers,* 141. Erickson accurately attributes it to Gabriel Aimé Belair; documents signed in 1792 and 1793 note that he was Biassou's aide-de-camp. On the document's authenticity, see Popkin, *You Are All Free,* 50: Hazareesingh argues that Louverture may have been involved in composing the document, but his claims are highly speculative and it is much likelier that Gabriel Aimé Belair shaped the letter. As Yingling's research shows, Belair was also adept at catering to the ideologies of potential allies. See Hazareesingh, *Black Spartacus,* 55–56; Yingling, *Siblings of Soil,* 83.

Jeremy Popkin concludes that the letter is authentic and was a response to a request from the French commissioner Philipe Roume from June 1792 that they return to the plantations, so that he could arrange a pardon from the colonial assembly; Popkin, "A Haitian Revolutionary Manifesto?," 5–7.

60. Quoted in Nathalie Piquionne, "Lettre de Jean-François, Biassou et Belair, juillet 1792," *Annales historiques de la Révolution française* 311 (1998): 133.

61. Quoted in Piquionne, "Lettre de Jean-François, Biassou et Belair, " 134.

62. Popkin, *You Are All Free,* 51.

63. Popkin, "A Haitian Revolutionary Manifesto?," 6–7.

64. Popkin, *You Are All Free,* 23; Dubois, *Avengers,* 142, 145.

65. The king signed the measure into law on April 4, and therefore it carried that date as a name colloquially. Popkin, *You Are All Free,* 45.

66. Dubois, *Avengers,* 142, 144.

67. Quoted and translated in Popkin, *You Are All Free,* 102.

68. Landers, *Atlantic Creoles,* 68; Dubois, *Avengers,* 145.

69. Popkin, *You Are All Free,* 97.

70. Sonthonax made this declaration on February 18, 1793. Translated and quoted in Popkin, *You Are All Free,* 134–135.

71. Popkin, *You Are All Free,* 131–132, 134; Hazareesingh, *Black Spartacus,* 57; Hazareesingh notes that Dessalines was under Louverture's command, but does not include a citation for that claim. See Dubois, *Avengers,* 148.

72. Popkin, *You Are All Free,* 136.

73. David Geggus, *Slavery, War, and Revolution: The British Occupation of Saint Domingue, 1793–1798* (Oxford, UK: Clarendon Press: 1982), 107; Erickson, "Black Auxiliary Troops," 107; Landers, *Atlantic Creoles,* 69.

74. Dubois calls this "republican racism"; see Laurent Dubois, *A Colony of Citizens: Revolution and Slave Emancipation in the French Caribbean, 1787–1804* (Chapel Hill: Omohundro Institute of Early American History and Culture and the University of North Carolina Press, 2004), 3.

75. Erickson argues that Jean-François and Biassou had "nearly decided to fully embrace the Spanish" in an alliance by February 1793. Erickson, "Black Auxiliary Troops," 106.

76. Yingling, *Siblings of Soil,* 62, 84.

77. Hazareesingh, *Black Spartacus,* 58.

78. Hazareesingh, *Black Spartacus,* 58.

79. Yingling, *Siblings of Soil,* 74.

80. Landers, *Atlantic Creoles,* 73–74.

81. Dubois, *Colony of Citizens,* 155; Popkin, *You Are All Free,* 159–160.

82. Dubois, *Avengers,* 155.

83. Popkin, *You Are All Free,* 208–210, 212; Fick, *Making of Haiti,* 159; Landers, *Atlantic Creoles,* 69.

84. The power struggle between the governor and the commissioners came to a head in Cap-Français as the city erupted in violence and flames on June 20, 1793. Jeremy Popkin argues that this was the beginning of the move toward general abolition. Popkin, *You Are All Free,* 4. In contrast, Sudhir Hazareesingh concludes that it was simply "a bout

of lethal infighting among rival French forces which left thousands dead." Hazareesingh, *Black Spartacus*, 59.

85. Louverture's officers rejected a proposal for a week-long truce and instead agreed to a twenty-four-hour truce. Officers of the Army of Toussaint and Gilles to the Commander of the Cordon de l'Ouest, Quartier g'al du Camp [?], June 27, 1793, AN, Pierrefitte, D/XXV/20/199, cited in Popkin, *You Are All Free*, 3, 251–252.

86. Later instances suggest that Jean-Jacques Dessalines went by just the name "Jacques" rather than the full "Jean-Jacques," and, according to most accounts, Dessalines had joined Louverture's unit by this time and was likely in a ranked position. On his name, see, for example, [Juste Chanlatte], "Hymne Haytien," [January 21, 1804], TNA, CO 137/111, f. 81; "Empereur Jacques Dessalines," in *Constitution d'Haïti*, May 20, 1805, *l'an deuxième de l'indépendance d'Haïti, et de notre règne le premier*, Aux Cayes, de l'Imprimerie Impériale, American Philosophical Society, Philadelphia, Pamphlets, vol. 26, no. 13; Madiou, *Histoire d'Haïti*, tome 1, 208.

87. While the spelling on the list is not how Jeanvier Desaline spelled his own name, other documents such as his marriage record and his record of military service include this same misspelling, and it is not unusual to see names spelled differently among documents.

88. Several sources have mentioned a "man of color" or a "mixed-race" man named Dessalines who was a colonel of the cavalry; it is possible though unlikely that this instance is that other Dessalines, rather than Jeanvier Desaline. See Hazareesingh, *Black Spartacus*, 86; Charles W. Mossell and Thomas Prosper Gragnon-Lacoste, *Toussaint L'Ouverture, the Hero of Saint Domingo, Soldier, Statesman, Martyr* (Lockport, NY: Ward & Cobb, 1896), 144; Isaac Louverture, "Notes diverses d'Isaac, sur la vie de Toussaint-Louverture," in *Histoire de l'expédition des Français, à Saint-Domingue, sous le consulat de Napoléon Bonaparte*, edited by Antoine Métral (Paris: Fanjat ainé, 1825), 337–338.

89. Yingling, *Siblings of Soil*, 74.

90. Fick, *Making of Haiti*, 161; Dubois, *Avengers*, 141.

91. Popkin, *You Are All Free*, 269.

92. Fick, *Making of Haiti*, 163.

93. Carolyn E. Fick, "The Haitian Revolution and the Limits of Freedom: Defining Citizenship in the Revolutionary Era," *Social History* 32, no. 4 (2007): 401.

94. Popkin, *You Are All Free*, 271–272; Léger-Félicité Sonthonax, *Au nom de la République: Proclamation*, August 29, 1793 (Cap-Français: Imprimerie de P. Gatineau au Carénage, près de la Commission Intermédiaire, 1793), John Carter Brown Library, https://archive .org/details/proclamationaunooosont/page/n1/mode/2up?view=theater.

95. According to the new labor laws, formerly enslaved men, women, and children were required to work either as field laborers (*cultivateurs*) or as domestic servants on the same plantations where they had been enslaved.

96. Fick, *Making of Haiti*, 179–180; Fick, "Haitian Revolution and the Limits of Freedom," 403.

97. Sonthonax, *Au nom de la République*.

98. Vertus Saint-Louis, "Les termes de citoyen et Africain pendant la revolution de Saint-Domingue," in *L'insurrection des esclaves de Saint-Domingue: 22–23 août 1791*, edited by Laënnec Hurbon (Paris: Karthala, 2000), 396, 401.

99. Toussaint Louverture, "Proclamation of Turel," ca. August 29, 1793, cited in Popkin, *You Are All Free,* 274–275. Popkin argues that because Louverture referred to Ogé, the letter was likely only addressed to free people of color. However, the enslaved insurgents repeatedly referred to Ogé in 1791 and continued to do so until general abolition in 1794.

100. Quoted in Yingling, *Siblings of Soil,* 81.

101. Fick, *Making of Haiti,* 167–172; Popkin, *You Are All Free,* 278.

102. Fick notes the publication of laws and codes on February 7 and 28, 1794, and others between April and May 1794; Fick, *Making of Haiti,* 171–172. "Réglement sur les proportions du Travail et de la Récompense, sur le partage des produits de La culture entre Les propriétaires et Les cultivateurs. du 7 février 1794," AN, Pierrefitte, D/XXV/28.

103. See François Baulou, commandant militaire aux Cayes, and Martin Marin, officier municipal, procureur-provisoire de la commune du dit lieu, February 22, 1794, AN, Pierrefitte, D/XXV/28. There are other examples in the same folder.

104. Popkin, *You Are All Free,* 327.

105. Dubois, *Colony of Citizens,* 160.

106. Popkin, *You Are All Free,* 360.

107. Popkin, *You Are All Free,* 351, 360, 362, 363.

108. For example, see a letter by the agent of the Directory, Philippe-Rose Roume, from 16 Pluviôse, 7e [February 4, 1799], on the anniversary of abolition, printed in *Gazette nationale ou le Moniteur universel,* Paris, 25 Prairial an 7 [June 13, 1799], no. 265, p. 1.

109. A ship docked in Jacmel brought the news; see Yingling, *Siblings of Soil,* 86, 89. David Geggus notes that this ship arrived in June. See David P. Geggus, "From His Most Catholic Majesty to the Godless Republic: The 'Volte-Face' of Toussaint Louverture and the Ending of Slavery in Saint Domingue," *Outre-Mers* 241 (1978): 487, 491, 496; Landers, *Atlantic Creoles,* 76. Hazareesingh argues that the ratification of abolition had little impact on Louverture's decision, because he only considers the arrival of the official decree and not the news of the decree, which arrived much earlier; Hazareesingh, *Black Spartacus,* 66. See also Popkin, *You Are All Free,* 256, 286; Dubois, *Avengers,* 179.

110. Dubois, *Avengers,* 179–180; Geggus, "From His Most Catholic Majesty," 496.

111. Dubois, *Avengers,* 180.

112. Yingling, *Siblings of Soil,* 94.

113. Madiou, *Histoire d'Haïti,* tome 1, 208.

114. Dubois, *Avengers,* 182; Madiou, *Histoire d'Haïti,* tome 1, 210–211.

115. Madiou, *Histoire d'Haïti,* tome 1, 211; *Débats entre les accusateurs et les accusés, dans l'affaire des colonies,* tome 1 (Paris: Imprimerie nationale, Pluviôse, an 3 [1795]), 211 (available online at Manioc: https://issuu.com/scduag/docs/sch13020).

116. Laveaux authorized Louverture to reorganize the troops in July 1795. Madiou, *Histoire d'Haïti,* tome 1, 223–224.

117. Madiou, *Histoire d'Haïti,* tome 1, 208.

118. Madiou, *Histoire d'Haïti,* tome 3, 123n.

119. Saint-Rémy, *Mémoires du Général Toussaint-L'Ouverture,* 96–97n1. Madiou also tells this story of how he got his name, in *Histoire d'Haïti,* tome 1, 389. Some sources de-

scribe Rousselot/Dommage as mixed-race, but it is possible that the label reflected his free status rather than his skin color. On Rousselot/Dommage being a Black man, see M. le Comte Mathieu Dumas, *Précis des événemens militaires: Campagne de 1802,* tome 2 (Paris: Treuttel et Würtz, 1819), 229; and Boisrond-Tonnerre, *Mémoires,* 38. On Rousselot/Dommage being *"mulâtre,"* see Vertus Saint-Louis, "L'assassinat de Dessalines et les limites de la société haïtienne face au marché international," in *Rétablissement de l'esclavage dans les colonies françaises, 1802: Ruptures et continuités de la politique coloniale française (1800–1830),* edited by Yves Bénot and Marcel Dorigny (Paris: Maisonneuve & Larose, 2003), 165; and "Nottes," [n.d., ca. September 1802], UF-RP, box 23, ff. 2268.

120. Peter S. Chazotte, "A Survivor of Dessalines's Massacres," in Popkin, *Facing Racial Revolution,* 239.

121. Saint-Rémy, *Mémoires du Général Toussaint-L'Ouverture,* 32; "Nécrologie," *Gazette politique et commerciale d'Haïti,* Cap, August 8, 1805, *l'an deuxième de l'indépendance,* no. 47, p. 188.

122. Dessalines to Brunet, Habitation Georges, 17 Vendémiaire an 11 [October 9, 1802], SHD, GR7, B8.

123. On the use of "sans-culottes," see Madiou, *Histoire d'Haïti,* tome 3, 339; "Copie de la lettre écrite par le Citoyen Dessalines, général de Brigade, commandant en chef le Département de l'Ouest, datée de Léogane le 21 Vendémiaire, an 8ᵐᵉ [October 13, 1799] au Citoyen Toussaint Louverture, général en chef de l'armée de St. Domingue" [Louverture forwarded the letter to Roume on 24 Vendémiaire an 8, cover letter in same folder], AN, Paris, microfilm, CC9A 26; Jean-Jacques Dessalines to Henry Christophe, 22 Fructidor an 7 [September 8, 1799], AN, Paris, F3/201; Pierre Quantin to Donatien Rochambeau, 7 Vendémiaire an 11 [September 29, 1802], UF-RP, box 12, ff. 1122 or microfilm, BN0864, lot 109.

CHAPTER 4. TO SPILL OUR BLOOD . . .
FOR THE FREEDOM OF THE NATION

1. "Les officiers & soldats de l'armée sous les orders de Toussaint Louverture" to the National Convention, 14 Frimaire an 4 [December 5, 1795], AN, Paris, microfilm, CC9A 11 (2/2) and 12 (1/2).

2. St. Victor Jean-Baptiste, *Le fondateur devant l'histoire* (Port-au-Prince: Imprimerie Eben-Ezer, 1954), xxiv.

3. "Les officiers & soldats . . ." to the National Convention, 14 Frimaire an 4 [December 5, 1795].

4. "Les officiers & soldats . . ." to the National Convention, 14 Frimaire an 4 [December 5, 1795].

5. Hazareesingh, *Black Spartacus,* 71.

6. Hazareesingh, *Black Spartacus,* 117–118.

7. Dubois, *Avengers,* 185.

8. Dubois, *Avengers,* 191.

9. Dubois, *Avengers,* 191; Hazareesingh, *Black Spartacus,* 104.

10. Dubois, *Avengers,* 191.

11. Toussaint Louverture, *copie conforme* by Pascal, October 28, 1796, AN, Paris, microfilm, CC9A 13 (2/2).

12. Geggus, *Slavery, War, and Revolution,* 204.

13. Geggus, *Slavery, War, and Revolution,* 180.

14. Dubois, *Avengers,* 201–202; Hazareesingh, *Black Spartacus,* 99.

15. Hazareesingh, *Black Spartacus,* 109; Dubois, *Avengers,* 205.

16. Miranda Frances Spieler, "The Legal Structure of Colonial Rule during the French Revolution," *William and Mary Quarterly* 66, no. 2 (2009): 405; Dubois, *Avengers,* 205.

17. Hazareesingh, *Black Spartacus,* 110.

18. Dubois, *Avengers,* 205–206.

19. Hazareesingh, *Black Spartacus,* 81.

20. Geggus, *Slavery, War, and Revolution,* 165.

21. Geggus, *Slavery, War, and Revolution,* 204.

22. Mailliart, "Plan Figuratif de la Dépendance de Saint Marc," 20 Frimaire an [7 or 9] [December 11, 1798 or 1800], UF-RP, https://original-ufdc.uflib.ufl.edu/UF00003725 /00001/ix.

23. Toussaint Louverture, "Procès-verbal de l'expédition du général divisionnaire Toussaint Louverture sur le Mirebalais et sa dépendance," 20 Germinal an V [April 9, 1797], ADG, Collection Marcel Chatillon, 61 J 18; Hazareesingh briefly discusses the siege: Hazareesingh, *Black Spartacus,* 81.

24. Louverture, "Procès-verbal de l'expédition . . ."

25. Louverture, "Procès-verbal de l'expédition . . ."

26. Geggus, *Slavery, War, and Revolution,* 237–238.

27. Louverture, "Procès-verbal de l'expédition . . ."

28. Louverture, "Procès-verbal de l'expédition . . ."

29. "Dessaline est promu au grade de General de Brigade," 29 Germinal an 5 [April 18, 1797], "St. Domingue Agents du Directoire Répertoire des Arrêtés, 1796–1799," AN, Paris, microfilm, CC9B 5 to 7; Geggus, *Slavery, War, and Revolution,* 223; Hazareesingh, *Black Spartacus,* 114.

30. Louverture, "Procès-verbal de l'expédition . . ."

31. Hazareesingh, *Black Spartacus,* 70.

32. Thornton, "Kongomania and the Numbers Game," 273.

33. Hazareesingh, *Black Spartacus,* 80, 82.

34. Dubois, *Avengers,* 204; Madiou, *Histoire d'Haïti,* tome 1, 287.

35. Spieler, "Legal Structure," 402; see also Dubois, *Avengers,* 196.

36. Dubois, *Avengers,* 203.

37. Hazareesingh, *Black Spartacus,* 114; Dubois, *Avengers,* 206–207.

38. Le Général en chef et les officiers composants l'état major de l'armée de Saint Domingue to Sonthonax, 3 Fructidor an 5 [August 29, 1797], SHD, GR7, B1.

39. Geggus, *Slavery, War, and Revolution,* 227.

40. Geggus, *Slavery, War, and Revolution,* 374–375.

41. Jeremy D. Popkin, *A Concise History of the Haitian Revolution* (Malden, MA: Wiley-Blackwell, 2012), 74.

42. Madiou, *Histoire d'Haïti,* tome 1, 298.

43. Madiou, *Histoire d'Haïti,* tome 1, 297–299.

44. Toussaint Louverture, "Copie de l'ordre de marche donné au Général de brigade Dessaline, et instructions pour la marche sur le mirbalais," 15 Pluviôse an 6 [February 3, 1798], AN, Paris, microfilm, Colonies, CC9A 18 & 19 (1/2) (reel 19); Hazareesingh, *Black Spartacus,* 87. Louverture's report confirms this is what happened: Toussaint Louverture, "Procès Verbal de la campagne ouvert le 13 pluviôse l'an 6ème contre les Ennemis de la République française par l'armée de St. Domingue," [May 21, 1798], AN, Paris, microfilm, CC9A 19 (2/2).

45. Toussaint Louverture, "Plan d'attaque donné aux Généraux de brigade Moyse et Dessaline," 9 Pluviôse an 6 [January 28, 1798], AN, Paris, microfilm, CC9A 18 & 19 (1/2) (reel 19); Hazareesingh, *Black Spartacus,* 87.

46. Louverture, "Copie de l'ordre de marche . . ."

47. Louverture, "Procès Verbal de la campagne . . ."

48. Louverture, "Procès Verbal de la campagne . . ."

49. Louverture, "Procès Verbal de la campagne . . ."

50. Louverture, "Procès Verbal de la campagne . . ."

51. Louverture, "Procès Verbal de la campagne . . ."

52. Toussaint Louverture, "Plan d'attaque sur les postes du cordon de l'arcahaye et instructions aux divers chefs, qui sont chargés de la faire," 17 Ventôse an 6 [March 7, 1798], AN, Paris, microfilm, CC9A 18 & 19 (1/2) (reel 19).

53. Geggus, *Slavery, War, and Revolution,* 375–376: Madiou, *Histoire d'Haïti,* tome 1, 306.

54. Louverture, "Procès Verbal de la campagne . . ."

55. They were called the York Dragoons, see Madiou, *Histoire d'Haïti,* tome 1, 306n.

56. Louverture, "Procès Verbal de la campagne . . ."

57. Louverture, "Procès Verbal de la campagne . . ."

58. Fick, "Haitian Revolution and the Limits of Freedom," 407.

59. Louverture, "Procès Verbal de la campagne . . ."

60. Hazareesingh, *Black Spartacus,* 135.

61. Dubois, *Avengers,* 216–217.

62. Geggus, *Slavery, War, and Revolution,* 376.

63. General Thomas Maitland to the Earl of Balcarres, onboard HMS *Camilla* off l'Arcahaye, June 19, 1799, NAM, 6807-183-1, p. 43.

64. Louverture, "Procès Verbal de la campagne . . ."

65. Louverture, "Procès Verbal de la campagne . . ."

66. Geggus, *Slavery, War, and Revolution,* 377.

67. Geggus, *Slavery, War, and Revolution,* 379.

68. Hazareesingh, *Black Spartacus,* 135–136.

69. Dubois, *Avengers,* 217; Hazareesingh, *Black Spartacus,* 128, 140.

70. Hazareesingh, *Black Spartacus,* 128–129.

71. Hazareesingh, *Black Spartacus,* 132.

72. Louverture to Hédouville, Port-Républicain, 3 Prairial an 6 [May 22, 1798], "Correspondance entre les généraux Hédouville et Toussaint Louverture," AN, Paris, microfilm, CC9B 5 to 7.

73. Louverture to Hédouville, Port-Républicain, 3 Prairial an 6 [May 22, 1798], "Corre-

spondance entre les généraux Hédouville et Toussaint Louverture," AN, Paris, micro-film, CC9B 5 to 7.

74. Geggus, *Slavery, War, and Revolution,* 231–232.

75. "Dessalines, général de brigade, commandera l'arrondissement de Saint Marc," 15 Prairial an 6 [June 3, 1798], "St. Domingue Agents du Directoire Répertoire des Arrêtés, 1796–1799," AN, Paris, microfilm, CC9B 5 to 7; Boisrond-Tonnerre, *Mémoires,* 7.

76. Louverture to Hédouville, "Réponse, au discours ci-contre," [n.d., but with documents from Prairial an 6, about June 1798], "Correspondance entre les généraux Hédouville et Toussaint Louverture," AN, Paris, microfilm, CC9B 5 to 7.

77. Louverture to Hédouville, "Réponse, au discours ci-contre."

78. [Hédouville] to Citoyen Boerner, Cap-Français, 5 [Messidor] [an 6] [June 23, 1798], "Premier régistre de la Correspondance du citoyen Hédouville, agent-particulier du Directoire Exécutif à St. Domingue," AN, Paris, microfilm, CC9B 7.

79. "Fort Churchill" is mentioned in Geggus, *Slavery, War, and Revolution,* 224; on the initial street renaming see Geggus, *Slavery, War, and Revolution,* 143. The forts are marked on the following map: Major Pechon, "Carte générale de la partie françoise de l'Isle de St. Domingue assujettie aux observations astronomiques de Messieurs de Puységur, de Borda et de Verdun, et dédiée à l'Honorable Thomas Maitland" (London: Robt. Wilkinson, 1799), available on Gallica. This was not the only instance when street renaming—or lack thereof—had political implications. See, for example, Popkin, *You Are All Free,* 165.

80. Hédouville to Louverture, Cap-Français, 13 Messidor an 6 [July 1, 1798], "Correspondance entre les généraux Hédouville et Toussaint Louverture," AN, Paris, microfilm, CC9B 5 to 7.

81. Hédouville to Louverture, Cap-Français, 13 Messidor an 6.

82. Hédouville to Louverture, Cap-Français, 13 Messidor an 6.

83. Hédouville to Louverture, Cap-Français, 13 Messidor an 6.

84. Hédouville to Louverture, Cap-Français, 13 Messidor an 6.

85. Dessalines to Hédouville, 17 Messidor an 6 [July 5, 1798], Archives nationales d'Haïti, A-68, available online: https://ufdc.ufl.edu/CA00510254/0001.

86. Dessalines to Hédouville, 17 Messidor an 6.

87. This is the earliest known extant document for which he claimed sole authorship with a signature.

88. The French general Pierre Quantin later assumed that a secretary had not read Dessalines a letter before signing, because Quantin could not believe what he was reading—an allegation that suggests it was the norm for a secretary to read a letter aloud for Dessalines's approval before he signed it. It is reasonable to think that Dessalines would have witnessed this kind of practice while he had been a general in Louverture's army, and he may have adopted it as his own military status rose. To compose his letters and proclamations, for example, Louverture had several secretaries compose drafts that they then read aloud while he offered edits until the document was exactly to his liking. See Deborah Jenson, *Beyond the Slave Narrative: Politics, Sex, and Manuscripts in the Haitian Revolution* (Liverpool, UK: Liverpool University Press, 2011), 64.

89. Pierrot, *Black Avenger,* 119.

90. Dessalines to Hédouville, 17 Messidor an 6.

91. Dessalines to Hédouville, 17 Messidor an 6.

92. Dessalines to Hédouville, 17 Messidor an 6.

93. Louverture to Hédouville, Quartier Général du Port-Républicain, 21 Messidor an 6 [July 9, 1798], "Correspondance entre les généraux Hédouville et Toussaint Louverture," AN, Paris, microfilm, CC9B 5 to 7.

94. Louverture to Hédouville, 21 Messidor an 6.

95. Louverture to Hédouville, 21 Messidor an 6.

96. Louverture to Hédouville, 21 Messidor an 6.

97. Boener to Dessalines [signed on his behalf by Birot], 25 Messidor an 6 [July 13, 1798], BPL, MS Haiti 71-18.

98. Dessalines [signed on his behalf by Birot] to Hédouville, 28 Messidor an 6 [July 16, 1798], BPL, MS Haiti 70-2 (1–2), item 1.

99. Hédouville to Dessalines, Cap-Français, 4 Thermidor an 6 [July 23, 1798], BPL, MS Haiti 70-2 (1–2), item 2.

100. Hédouville to Louverture, Cap-Français, 10 Thermidor an 6 [July 28, 1798], "Correspondance entre les généraux Hédouville et Toussaint Louverture," AN, Paris, microfilm, CC9B 5 to 7.

101. Constitution, 1795, printed in J. B. Duvergier, *Lois, Décrets, Ordonnances, Réglemens, et Avis du Conseil-d'État,* tome huitième (Paris: Imprimerie de A. Guyot, 1825), 298, available on Gallica.

102. Hédouville to Louverture, Cap-Français, 10 Thermidor an 6 [July 28, 1798], "Correspondance entre les généraux Hédouville et Toussaint Louverture," AN, Paris, microfilm, CC9B 5 to 7.

103. Dessalines [signed on his behalf by Birot] to Hédouville, 28 Messidor an 6 [July 16, 1798], BPL, MS Haiti 70-2 (1–2), item 1.

104. Geggus, *Slavery, War, and Revolution,* 380.

105. Geggus, *Slavery, War, and Revolution,* 381. The United States was unofficially part of the secret treaty; see Ronald Angelo Johnson, *Diplomacy in Black and White: John Adams, Toussaint Louverture, and Their Atlantic World Alliance* (Athens: University of Georgia Press, 2014), 89; Gordon S. Brown, *Toussaint's Clause: The Founding Fathers and the Haitian Revolution* (Jackson: University Press of Mississippi, 2005), 88.

106. Maitland to Louverture, "Conventions Secrètes," June 13, 1799 [signed version], SHD, GR7, B1. See also "Copy of Articles agreed upon between Edward Corbet acting by the direction of Major General Nugent and Joseph Bunel acting in behalf of General Toussaint Louverture . . . ," NAM, 6807-183-1.

107. Hazareesingh, *Black Spartacus,* 137–138; Popkin, *Concise History,* 93–94.

108. "Suitte de l'article cinquième de la convention secrette" and "suitte de l'article huitième," SHD, GR7, B1.

109. Dubois, *Avengers,* 218.

110. Eliga H. Gould, *Among the Powers of the Earth: The American Revolution and the Making of a New World Empire* (Cambridge, MA: Harvard University Press, 2012), 2.

111. "Extrait de la Gazette de Londres du Douze Décembre 1798," SHD, GR7, B1; also quoted in C. L. R. James, *The Black Jacobins: Toussaint L'Ouverture and the San Domingo Revolution*, 2nd ed. rev. (New York: Vintage Books, 1989), 226.

112. "Rapport fait au premier Consul, par le Ministre de la guerre, le 6 Prairial an 8 de la République [May 26, 1800]," SHD, GR7, B1.

113. These were documents that he discussed with Louverture and which Louverture claimed to support, but that were only published in Hédouville's name. Dubois, *Avengers*, 220; Hazareesingh, *Black Spartacus*, 144.

114. Hédouville to "Administrations Municipales; aux Tribunaux Correctionnels et de Paix, aux Commissaires du Directoire Exécutif; aux Officiers Généraux; aux Commandans d'Arrondissement; et aux Officiers superieurs de Gendarmerie," Cap-Français, 16 Thermidor an 6 [August 3, 1798], printed in *Accounts and Papers of the House of Commons*, vol. 24 (Oxford University, 1829), 94.

115. Hédouville, "Arrete concernant la Police des habitations et les obligations réciproques des Propriétaires, ou Fermiers, et des Cultivateurs," Cap-Français, 6 Thermidor an 6 [July 24, 1798], printed in *Accounts and Papers of the House of Commons, vol. 24* (Oxford University, 1829), 96.

116. Hédouville to Louverture, Cap-Français, 1er jour complémentaire an 6 [September 17, 1798], "Correspondance entre les généraux Hédouville et Toussaint Louverture," AN, Paris, microfilm, CC9B 5 to 7.

117. Hédouville to Louverture, Cap-Français, 1er jour complémentaire an 6.

118. Hédouville to Louverture, Cap-Français, 1er jour complémentaire an 6.

119. Hazareesingh, *Black Spartacus*, 100.

120. Louverture to Charles Vincent, 2ème jour complémentaire [an 6] [September 18, 1798]. Document sold by Swann Auction Galleries (sale 2562—lot 240, on March 25, 2021). I am grateful to Peter Miniaci for sharing images of the document.

121. Louverture to Charles Vincent, 2ème jour complémentaire [an 6].

122. Louverture to Charles Vincent, 2ème jour complémentaire [an 6].

123. Dubois, *Avengers*, 221–222.

124. Hazareesingh, *Black Spartacus*, 145.

125. Hazareesingh, *Black Spartacus*, 145.

126. Dubois, *Avengers*, 222; "L'administration municipale du Cap, aux administrations municipales des communes de la colonie, au Cap, le 7 brumaire an 7," printed in *Chronique universelle (faisant suite au Républicain français)*, 16 Nivôse an 7 [January 5, 1799], numéro 2179, p. 1.

127. "Indes Occidentales, au Cap, le 7 brumaire an 7," *Chronique universelle*, 16 Nivôse an 7 [January 5, 1799]: 1.

128. "L'administration municipale du Cap," *Chronique universelle;* Dubois, *Avengers*, 222.

129. "L'administration municipale du Cap," *Chronique universelle.*

130. Louverture to Minister of the Navy, March 1799, AN, Paris, microfilm, CC9A 18 & 19.

131. "Les Généraux & Chefs de Brigade de divers Régimens Coloniaux des parties du *Nord, Est & Ouest* de Saint-Domingue, tant en leurs noms qu'en ceux des Officiers, Sous-Officiers & Soldats desdits Régimens" to "Administrateurs Municipaux des divers

Départemens de Saint-Domingue," 19 Frimaire an 7 [December 9, 1798], AN, Paris, microfilm, CC9A 19 (2/2).

132. "Les Généraux & Chefs de Brigade de divers Régimens Coloniaux . . . ," 19 Frimaire an 7.

133. Madiou, *Histoire d'Haïti,* tome I, 316, 328; Hazareesingh, *Black Spartacus,* 150.

CHAPTER 5. THE FRENCH PEOPLE WILL
NEVER FORGET YOUR REPUBLICAN VIRTUES

1. Louverture to Louis Antoine Esprit Rallier, 26 Germinal an 7 [April 15, 1799], TNA, CO 245/2. Rallier himself had used these terms in his 1796 defense of Louverture, but Louverture did not call him out for having done so. See, for example, Louis Antoine Esprit Rallier, *Nouvelles observations sur Saint-Domingue* (Paris: Baudoin, imprimeur du Corps législatif, 1796), 14.

2. Louverture to Rallier, 26 Germinal an 7.

3. Louverture to Rallier, 26 Germinal an 7.

4. Louverture to Rallier, 26 Germinal an 7.

5. Louverture to Rallier, 26 Germinal an 7.

6. Philippe-Rose Roume de Saint-Laurent [speech at Port-Républicain], 16 Pluviôse an 7 [February 4, 1799], *Gazette nationale ou le Moniteur universel,* Paris, 25 Prairial an 7 [June 13, 1799], no. 265, p. 1.

7. Roume, [speech at Port-Républicain], 16 Pluviôse an 7.

8. Louverture, "Réponse du général en chef, au discours prononcé au Port-Républicain, par l'agent du gouvernement, le 16 pluviôse de l'an 7," *Gazette nationale ou le Moniteur universel,* Paris, 25 Prairial an 7 [June 13, 1799], p. 1.

9. Paul, "Le ressentiment Dessalinien," 155.

10. Roume to Dessalines, 9 Ventôse an 7 [February 27, 1799], TNA, CO 245/2.

11. Roume to Dessalines, 9 Ventôse an 7.

12. Dubois, *Avengers,* 233.

13. Madiou, *Histoire d'Haïti,* tome I, 340.

14. Dubois, *Avengers,* 233.

15. Longchamp wrote an account of a siege anonymously in four issues of *L'Union* in March 1838: "Siège de Jacmel," *L'Union,* nos. 29–32, March 1–22, 1838. Céligni (or Céligny) Ardouin later reprinted the account of the siege and revealed the author to be Longchamp. Céligni Ardouin, *Essais sur l'histoire d'Haïti,* published by Beaubrun Ardouin (Port-au-Prince: Chez T. Bouchereau, imprimeur, 1865), 60. Longchamp later served in the senate under Jean-Pierre Boyer, and he claimed that his account was based on personal experience and on oral histories with other veterans of the battle.

16. Madiou, *Histoire d'Haïti,* tome I, 338.

17. Madiou, *Histoire d'Haïti,* tome I, 335–336.

18. Madiou, *Histoire d'Haïti,* tome I, 335–336.

19. Madiou, *Histoire d'Haïti,* tome I, 342.

20. Madiou, *Histoire d'Haïti,* tome I, 339.

21. Madiou, *Histoire d'Haïti,* tome I, 341–342, 344.

22. Madiou, *Histoire d'Haïti,* tome 1, 347–348.

23. Dessalines [signed on his behalf by Benoît] to Louverture, Grand Goâve, 4 Thermidor an 7 [June 22, 1799], AN, Paris, microfilm, CC9A 24 & 25 (reel 25).

24. Madiou, *Histoire d'Haïti,* tome 1, 348.

25. Louverture to Roume, 21 Messidor an 7 [July 9, 1799], AN, Paris, microfilm, CC9A 25.

26. Louverture to Roume, 21 Messidor an 7.

27. Madiou, *Histoire d'Haïti,* tome 1, 345.

28. Louverture to Roume, 21 Messidor an 7.

29. Louverture to Roume, 21 Messidor an 7.

30. "Au citoyen Mentor, représentant du peuple français, membre du conseil des cinq cents, Jacmel, 14 messidor an VII [July 2, 1799]," *L'ennemi des oppresseurs de tous les tems* [*sic*], Paris, September 11, 1799, p. 4.

31. "Au citoyen Mentor."

32. Madiou, *Histoire d'Haïti,* tome 1, 345–346.

33. Madiou, *Histoire d'Haïti,* tome 1, 347–349.

34. Dessalines to Louverture, Léogâne, 30 Thermidor an 7 [August 17, 1799], [third of three letters on the same day], AN, Paris, microfilm, CC9A 25.

35. Dessalines to Louverture, Léogâne, 30 Thermidor an 7 [August 17, 1799], [first of three letters on the same day], AN, Paris, microfilm, CC9A 25.

36. Dessalines to Louverture, Léogâne, 30 Thermidor an 7 [August 17, 1799], [second of three letters on the same day], AN, Paris, microfilm, CC9A 25.

37. Madiou, *Histoire d'Haïti,* tome 1, 348.

38. Boisrond-Tonnerre, *Mémoires,* 7.

39. "Copie de la lettre Écrite par le Général en chef Toussaint L'ouverture au Cn Roume agent particulier du Directoire Exécutif en datte au Port de Paix le 6 fructidor an 7e [August 23, 1799]," AN, Paris, microfilm, CC9A 25.

40. Madiou, *Histoire d'Haïti,* tome 1, 359; Roume to Louverture, Cap-Français, 12 Vendémiaire an 8 [October 4, 1799], AN, Paris, microfilm, CC9A 26.

41. See, for example, Dessalines to Henry Christophe, 22 Fructidor an 7 [September 8, 1799], AN, Paris, F3/201; Dessalines to Louverture, Léogâne, 30 Thermidor an 7 [August 17, 1799], [first of three letters on the same day], AN, Paris, microfilm, CC9A 25.

42. Roume to Louverture, Cap-Français, 12 Vendémiaire an 8 [October 4, 1799], AN, Paris, microfilm, CC9A 26.

43. "EXTRAIT du Registre des Délibérations de l'Agence du Directoire exécutif à Saint-Domingue," Cap-Français, 12 Vendémiaire an 8 [October 4, 1799], AN, Paris, microfilm, CC9A 26.

44. Michel-Rolph Touillot, *Stirring the Pot of Haitian History,* translated by Mariana Past and Benjamin Hebblethwaite (Liverpool, UK: Liverpool University Press, 2021), 156.

45. Dessalines to Christophe, 22 Fructidor an 7.

46. Dessalines to Christophe, 22 Fructidor an 7.

47. "Copie de la letter Écrite par le Général en chef Toussaint L'ouverture au Cn Roume agent particulier du Directoire Exécutif à St. Domingue."

48. Dessalines to Christophe, 22 Fructidor an 7.

49. Dessalines to Christophe, 22 Fructidor an 7.

50. Dessalines to Christophe, 22 Fructidor an 7. Madiou made sure to highlight the moments in which Dessalines saved *mulâtre* men, women, and children, and noted that he celebrated the officers "of color" in his own army. Madiou, *Histoire d'Haïti,* tome 1, 359.

51. Louverture to "citoyens composans la Garnison du Môle," 1 Thermidor an 7 [July 19, 1799], AN, Paris, F3/201.

52. Louverture to Dessalines, 22 Fructidor an 7 [September 8, 1799], AN, Paris, F3/201.

53. Madiou, *Histoire d'Haïti,* tome 1, 354.

54. Louverture to Roume, Cap-Français, 12 Vendémiaire an 8 [October 4, 1799], AN, Paris, microfilm, CC9A 26.

55. Madiou, *Histoire d'Haïti,* tome 1, 359.

56. Dessalines to Louverture, 21 Vendémiaire an 8 [October 13, 1799], [Louverture forwarded the letter to Roume on 24 Vendémiaire an 8, cover letter in same folder], AN, Paris, microfilm, CC9A 26.

57. "Siège de Jacmel," *L'Union,* Port-au-Prince, no. 29, March 1, 1838, p. 1.

58. "Beauvais," in Georges Six, *Dictionnaire biographique des généraux et amiraux français de la Révolution et de l'Empire: 1792–1814,* tome 1 (Paris: Librairie historique et nobiliaire, 1934), 70.

59. La Selve, *Le pays des nègres,* 354.

60. "Siège de Jacmel," *L'Union,* no. 29, March 1, 1838, p. 1.

61. Louverture, "Adresse à tous les Citoyens, amis du bon ordre, & à tous ceux qui s'intéressent à la prospérité & à la conservation de cette Colonie Française," 26 Ventôse an 8 [March 17, 1800], MAE, M. D., Amérique, vol. 15.

62. Marlene Daut, "Napoleon's Man in Haiti," *History Today,* March 2024, 71.

63. For a contemporary English translation of the proclamation, see *Independent Chronicle and Universal Advertiser,* Boston, February 3–6, 1800, vol. 32, no. 1970, p. 3. For the French version, see Louverture, "Proclamation," [20 Brumaire an 8, November 11, 1799], printed in *Bulletin officiel de Saint-Domingue,* Cap-Français, 29 Frimaire an 8 [December 20, 1799], no. 12, pp. 49–50, and subsequent issue.

64. Louverture, "Adresse à tous les Citoyens," 26 Ventôse an 8. Louverture convinced the US Navy to blockade the southern ports to help him against Rigaud; see Dubois, *Avengers,* 235.

65. "Siège de Jacmel," *L'Union,* no. 30, March 8, 1838, p. 2.

66. Louverture, "Adresse à tous les Citoyens," 26 Ventôse an 8.

67. "Siège de Jacmel," *L'Union,* no. 30, March 8, 1838, p. 2.

68. Hugh Cathcart to Maitland, November 26, 1799, TNA, CO 245/1, f. 68–75.

69. Cathcart to Maitland, November 26, 1799.

70. "Siège de Jacmel," *L'Union,* no. 31, March 15, 1838, p. 3.

71. "Siège de Jacmel," *L'Union,* no. 30, March 8, 1838, p. 2.

72. "Siège de Jacmel," *L'Union,* no. 30, March 8, 1838, p. 2. Madiou also recounted that Christophe advocated razing the city and killing the remaining inhabitants. Madiou, *Histoire d'Haïti,* tome 2, 26.

73. "Siège de Jacmel," *L'Union,* no. 31, March 15, 1838, p. 2.

74. La Selve, *Le pays des nègres,* 358.

75. "Siège de Jacmel," *L'Union,* no. 31, March 15, 1838, p. 3; Madiou, *Histoire d'Haïti,* tome 2, 23.
76. "Siège de Jacmel," *L'Union,* no. 31, March 15, 1838, p. 3; Historians Thomas Madiou and Jules Rosemond support the claim that Dessalines treated prisoners and "civilians" well; see Rosemond, *Conférence historique,* 27; Madiou, *Histoire d'Haïti,* tome 2, 23.
77. Louverture, "Adresse à tous les Citoyens," 26 Ventôse an 8.
78. Louverture, "Adresse à tous les Citoyens," 26 Ventôse an 8.
79. "Siège de Jacmel," *L'Union,* no. 32, March 22, 1838, p. 2.
80. Some historians have insisted that Dessalines "committed numerous atrocities," during the war against Rigaud. See, for example, Dubois, *Avengers,* 235.
81. On Bazelais's defense of the city, see Rosemond, *Conférence historiques,* 26.
82. Paul, "Le ressentiment Dessalinien," 147–148; Eveillard, "Claire Heureuse," 3.
83. Eveillard, "Claire Heureuse," 3.
84. "Obituary: Death of the Widow of the First Emperor of Hayti," *Anti-Slavery Bugle,* New Lisbon, OH, October 2, 1858, vol. 14, issue 6 [reprinted from the *Evening Post,* Philadelphia].
85. Most accounts place the wedding in Léogâne; the 1806 baptismal records of two of Dessalines's children note that the wedding took place in Saint-Marc, which would have been impossible. Beaubrun Ardouin, *Études sur l'histoire d'Haïti,* tome 4 (Paris: Dezobry et E. Magdeleine, 1853), 242–243. The date April 2, 1800, is taken from the civil register of the births of Célimène and Célestine: Acte de naissance de Célestine Dessalines, fille de Jean-Jacques Dessalines, February 2, 1806, courtesy of the Bibliothèque Haïtienne des Spiritains, Haïti. Eveillard, "Claire Heureuse," 4. Madiou says they were married after the civil war : Madiou, *Histoire d'Haïti,* tome 3, 187n. Some accounts note that they were married by Père Guillaume Lecun, but Lecun was likely in Kingston, Jamaica, at the time; see Lecun to unknown, June 30, 1800, Kingston, Jamaica, ASPF, SC, America Antille, vol. 3, f. 309r–310v.
86. Eveillard, "Claire Heureuse," 4.
87. "Obituary: Death of the Widow of the First Emperor of Hayti"; Eveillard, "Claire Heureuse," 7. Her maternal status was made official in 1806 in accordance with a law issued by Dessalines that allowed parents to retroactively register their children in the civil record: title III, article 13, June 3, 1805.
88. Descourtilz, *Voyages d'un naturaliste,* vol. 3, 304–305.
89. "Obituary: Death of the Widow of the First Emperor of Hayti"; Eveillard, "Claire Heureuse," 7. See also Ardouin, *Études sur l'histoire d'Haïti,* tome 4, 242–243; Poyen-Bellisle, *Histoire militaire,* 476.
90. Louverture, "Récit des événements qui se sont passés dans la partie du nord de Saint-Domingue, depuis le 29 Vendémiaire jusqu'au 13 Brumaire, an dixième de la République française, une et indivisible," AN, Paris, microfilm, CC9B 18.
91. Louverture to Roume, Cap-Français, 18 Floréal an 8 [May 8, 1800], AN, Paris, microfilm, CC9B 2.
92. Louverture to Roume, Cap-Français, 18 Floréal an 8.
93. Dubois, *Avengers,* 236.
94. "Proclamation addressed by Toussaint Louverture, Commander in Chief of the Army of

St. Domingo, to All the Citizens of the Southern Department of St. Domingo [1 Messidor an 8 / June 20, 1800]," *London Times,* no. 4932, October 22, 1800, p. 3.

95. "Proclamation addressed by Toussaint Louverture … [1 Messidor an 8 / June 20, 1800]."

96. Dessalines to Louverture, 10 Messidor an 8 [June 28, 1800], *Federal Gazette & Baltimore Daily Advertiser,* Baltimore, August 11, 1800, vol. 13, no. 2094, p. 3.

97. Dessalines to Louverture, 10 Messidor an 8.

98. Dessalines to Louverture, 10 Messidor an 8.

99. Dessalines to [Louverture], 16 Messidor an 8 [July 4, 1800], *Federal Gazette & Baltimore Daily Advertiser,* Baltimore, August 14, 1800, vol. 13, no. 2097, p. 3.

100. Dessalines to [Louverture], 16 Messidor an 8.

101. Dessalines to [Louverture], 16 Messidor an 8.

102. Dubois, *Avengers,* 236.

103. "Nouvelles Étrangères: Isle de Saint-Domingue: Extrait d'une lettre particulière des Cayes, du 29 nivôse [January 19, 1801]," *Courrier des spectacles: Journal des théâtres et de littérature, Lois et actes du gouvernement, nouvelles, annonces, et cours de la Bourse,* 5 Prairial an 9 [May 25, 1801], p. 1.

104. Louverture, "Proclamation à tous les citoyens du département du Sud," 18 Thermidor an 8 [August 6, 1800], printed in *Gazette nationale ou le Moniteur universel,* Paris, 25 Vendémiaire an 9 [October 17, 1800], no. 25, pp. 3–4.

105. Madiou, *Histoire d'Haïti,* tome 2, 66–67; "Siège de Jacmel," *L'Union,* no. 32, March 22, 1838, p. 2. Some historians have argued that instead of treating the men and women of the south as friends and brothers, the officers of the north violently punished the southerners for their transgressions; see, for example, Dubois, *Avengers,* 236.

106. Madiou, *Histoire d'Haïti,* tome 2, 67.

107. "Siège de Jacmel," *L'Union,* no. 32, March 22, 1838, p. 2.

108. "a-t-il dit dans son jargon," in Anonymous to [a French General], "Détails sur St. Domingue," "copies," Philadelphia, December 15, 1800, AN, Pierrefitte, AF/IV/1212.

109. Landers, *Atlantic Creoles,* 77; Yingling, *Siblings of Soil,* 100; "Traité de paix conclu à Bâle le 4 thermidor an III (22 Juillet 1795) entre la République Française et l'Espagne," in M. Jules de Clerq, *Receuil des traités de la France,* tome 1, *1718–1802* (Paris: A. Durand et Pedone-Lauriel, 1880), 245–247.

110. Yingling, *Siblings of Soil,* 144; Dubois, *Avengers,* 237.

111. Yingling, *Siblings of Soil,* 146; Fick, "Haitian Revolution and the Limits of Freedom," 409.

112. Lacroix, "Mémoire secrêt."

113. L. Sonis, "Plan du nouveau bourg d'Aquin, situé à l'embarcadaire, tracé / d'après les ordres et les instructions du citoyen Toussaint Louverture, Général en chef de St. Domingue pour être soumis à son approbation," 1800, available on Gallica: https:// gallica.bnf.fr/ark:/12148/btv1b84921898.

114. For full text of the labor codes, see Ardouin, *Études sur l'histoire d'Haïti,* tome 4, 247–253. Louverture then issued a proclamation designed to better implement his previous proclamation from November 15, 1798; see Hazareesingh, *Black Spartacus,* 227–228; Ardouin, *Études sur l'histoire d'Haïti,* tome 3, 487.

115. Ardouin, *Études sur l'histoire d'Haïti,* tome 4, 253; Fick, "Haitian Revolution and the

Limits of Freedom," 410. Historians refer to this style of enforcement as *"caporalisme agraire."* The term was first used to describe Louverture's labor policies by Paul Moral in 1961; see Moral, *Le paysan haïtien: Étude sur la vie rurale en Haïti* (1961; repr., Port-au-Prince: Éditions Fardin, 1978), 17.

116. Ardouin, *Études sur l'histoire d'Haïti,* tome 4, 249.

117. Hazareesingh, *Black Spartacus,* 277.

118. Ardouin, *Études sur l'histoire d'Haïti,* tome 4, 247; Nessler, *Islandwide Struggle,* 121.

119. Dubois, *Avengers,* 204–205.

120. "Saint Domingue, État Général des Biens Séquestrés affermés dans l'arrondissement de St. Marc par des Domaines Nationaux Jus__ compris le 30 floréal an 10," May 20, 1802, ANOM, "St. Marc," 10 DPPC 190.

121. Lacroix, "Mémoire secrêt." The archival records at the ANOM support this claim, listing at least twenty-two leased plantations beginning in 1797; the last ones were signed in 1802.

122. For more, see ANOM, 10 DPPC 190 and 191. Many thanks to Marlene Daut for sharing these sources with me. "Bail," August 17, 1779, Saint-Domingue, Nord, Le Cap, Dore 1755/1780, *Doubles minutes,* ANOM, NOT*SDOM 525, DPPC. Dessalines later referenced his cousin Joseph, who had served in Jérémie; see Dessalines to Brunet, Habitation Georges, 17 Vendémiaire an 11 [October 9, 1802], SHD, GR7 B8.

123. In either 1797 or 1798, the plantation burned to the ground, and Jeanvier Desaline asked for a three-year extension on the required subvention payment. The petition does not mention when the fire happened, but it suggests that it had only affected the previous year's harvest. [Jeanvier] Desalines to [Joseph] Verrieu, ordonnateur, ANOM, 10DPPC, 107, 289. I am grateful to Marlene Daut for generously sharing this document with me.

124. On Dessalines's role, see, for example, Dessalines to Citizen Bourgeois [*habitant* at Jacmel], 6 Vendémiaire an 10 [September 28, 1801], ADG, 61 J 18, FRAD033_61J18_0082.

125. Hazareesingh, *Black Spartacus,* 277; Madiou, *Histoire d'Haïti,* tome 2, 91.

126. Madiou, *Histoire d'Haïti,* tome 2, 91.

127. "Mémoire Secret" [marginalia, *présumé de Pascal*], [ca. 1802], SCRBC, Sc Micro R-228, reel 9.

128. Geggus, *Haitian Revolution,* 140.

CHAPTER 6. HE WILL BETRAY THEM A HUNDRED TIMES

1. [Unknown author], n.d. [ca. 1801], "Portraits des chefs de la colonie," AN, Pierrefitte, AB/XIX/5002.

2. "qu'il connait la subordination militaire," "Memoire du General Toussaint Louverture," AN, Pierrefitte, AF/IV/1213.

3. "Portraits des chefs de la colonie."

4. Daut, *Awakening the Ashes,* 169–174.

5. Napoléon Bonaparte, "Notes pour servir aux instructions à donner au capitaine général Leclerc," 9 Brumaire an 10 [October 31, 1801], in Roussier, *Lettres du général Leclerc,* 270.

6. Bonaparte, "Notes pour servir aux instructions," 9 Brumaire an 10.

7. Bonaparte, "Notes pour servir aux instructions," 9 Brumaire an 10.

8. Bonaparte, "Notes pour servir aux instructions," 9 Brumaire an 10.

9. Bonaparte, "Notes pour servir aux instructions," 9 Brumaire an 10. On February 16, 1802, French admiral Louis Thomas Villaret-Joyeuse wrote to Jefferson to notify him of the war between the French and the revolutionaries in Saint-Domingue and "reques[ted] from you and the American government the services that all civilized people must render to one another in such circumstances"; he did not, however, mention any previous promises of support. Villaret-Joyeuse to Jefferson, February 16, 1802, Founders Online, https://founders.archives.gov/documents/Jefferson/01-36-02-0389.

10. Bonaparte, "Notes pour servir aux instructions," 9 Brumaire an 10.

11. Ministre de la Marine et des Colonies, "Instructions pour le Général, ~~Leclerc~~, nommé commandant Général de toute l'île de St Domingue," SHD, GR7, B1.

12. Louverture to Bonaparte, 23 Pluviôse an 9 [February 12, 1801], "Documents précédant l'intervention du général Leclerc à Saint-Domigue, 7 pièces," AN, Pierrefitte, AB/XIX/5002.

13. Louverture to Bonaparte, 23 Pluviôse an 9.

14. Jacques Péries to Ministre de la Marine et des Colonies, Cap-Français, 25 Germinal an 9 [April 15, 1801], AN, Paris, microfilm, CC9B 18.

15. Péries to Ministre de la Marine et des Colonies, Cap-Français, 25 Germinal an 9.

16. Péries to Ministre de la Marine et des Colonies, Cap-Français, 25 Germinal an 9.

17. Spieler, "Legal Structure," 408; Fick, "Haitian Revolution and the Limits of Freedom," 409.

18. Fick, "Haitian Revolution and the Limits of Freedom," 409; Sybille Fischer, "Inhabiting Rights," L'esprit créateur 56, no. 1 (2016): 52–67; Lorelle D. Semley, "To Live and Die, Free and French: Toussaint Louverture's 1801 Constitution and the Original Challenge to Black Citizenship," Radical History Review 2013, no. 115 (2013): 66.

19. Daniel Desormeaux, ed., Mémoires du général Toussaint Louverture (Paris: Classiques Garnier, 2011), 192. For original manuscript, see "Memoire Du General Toussaint Louverture," AN, Pierrefitte, AF/IV/1213.

20. Dubois, Avengers, 242.

21. Fick, "Haitian Revolution and the Limits of Freedom," 409.

22. Fick, "Haitian Revolution and the Limits of Freedom," 411; Philip Kaisary, "Hercules, the Hydra, and the 1801 Constitution of Toussaint Louverture," Atlantic Studies 12, no. 4 (2015): 393–411.

23. Fick, "Haitian Revolution and the Limits of Freedom," 411.

24. Toussaint Louverture, "Constitution de la colonie française de Saint-Domingue," 19 Floréal an 9 [May 9, 1801] (Cap: P. Roux, imprimeur du gouvernement), https://digitalcollections.nypl.org/items/99988061-a1fb-5c37-e040-e00a18066d37.

25. See, for example, letters from James Madison and Thomas Jefferson: "From James Madison to Wilson Cary Nicholas, 10 July 1801," Founders Online, National Archives, https://founders.archives.gov/documents/Madison/02-01-02-0515. (Original source: The Papers of James Madison, Secretary of State Series, vol. 1, 4 March–31 July 1801, edited by Robert J. Brugger, Robert A. Rutland, Robert Rhodes Crout, Jeanne K. Sisson, and Dru Dowdy [Charlottesville: University Press of Virginia, 1986], 393–394.) "From James Madison to Robert R. Livingston, 11 July 1801," Founders Online, National Archives,

https://founders.archives.gov/documents/Madison/02-01-02-0526. (Original source: *The Papers of James Madison*, Secretary of State Series, vol. 1, *4 March–31 July 1801*, edited by Robert J. Brugger, Robert A. Rutland, Robert Rhodes Crout, Jeanne K. Sisson, and Dru Dowdy [Charlottesville: University Press of Virginia, 1986], 402–404.) "From Thomas Jefferson to James Monroe, 24 November 1801," *Founders Online,* National Archives, https://founders.archives.gov/documents/Jefferson/01-35-02-0550. (Original source: *The Papers of Thomas Jefferson*, vol. 35, *1 August–30 November 1801*, edited by Barbara B. Oberg [Princeton, NJ: Princeton University Press, 2008], 718–722.)

26. Louverture, "Récit des événements qui se sont passés dans la partie du nord de Saint-Domingue, depuis le 29 Vendémiaire jusqu'au 13 Brumaire, an dixième de la République française, une et indivisible," AN, Paris, microfilm, CC9B 18.

27. De Tussac, *Cri des colons,* 231; cited in Jenson, "Jean-Jacques Dessalines and the African Character of the Haitian Revolution," 628.

28. Louverture, "Récit des événements . . . 13 Brumaire, an dixième." Several historians have claimed that this was Dessalines's actual wedding, but it was in fact simply a proper *fête* for the earlier ceremony. For example, see Girard, *Toussaint Louverture,* 225; Hazareesingh, *Black Spartacus,* 287; Bell, *Toussaint Louverture,* 207. On having been married for two years already, see "Mémoire Secret" [marginalia, *présumé de Pascal*], [ca. 1802], SCRBC, Sc Micro R-228, reel 9.

29. Mollien, *Haïti ou Saint-Domingue,* tome 2, 54.

30. Louverture, "Récit des événements . . . 13 Brumaire, an dixième."

31. Louverture, "Récit des événements . . . 13 Brumaire, an dixième."

32. Fick, "Haitian Revolution and the Limits of Freedom," 411, fn. 42.

33. "Paris, le 20 pluviôse," *Journal des débats et loix du pouvoir législatif et des actes du gouvernement,* 21 Pluviôse an 10 [February 10, 1802], p. 2.

34. "Extrait d'un lettre écrite du Cap, le 5 xbre 1801, par le Cn Maussac au Cn Stevens," AN, Paris, microfilm, CC9B 2.

35. Louverture, "Récit des événements . . . 13 Brumaire, an dixième." On Moyse's involvement, see also "Extrait d'un lettre écrite du Cap, le 5 xbre 1801."

36. Louverture, "Proclamation," 23 Frimaire an 10 [December 14, 1801], *Bulletin officiel du Port-Républicain,* no. 25 tome II, p. 1. Only the first page is available at UF-RP, box 2, ff. 100.

37. Louverture, "Proclamation," 23 Frimaire an 10 [December 14, 1801].

38. "Portraits des chefs de la colonie," AN, Pierrefitte, AB/XIX/5002.

39. "Portraits des chefs de la colonie," AN, Pierrefitte, AB/XIX/5002.

40. "Mémoire Secret," [marginalia, *présumé de Pascal*], [ca. 1802], SCRBC, Sc Micro R-228, reel 9.

41. Vincent [directeur du génie] to Leclerc, 29 Brumaire an 10 [November 20, 1801], UF-RP, microfilm, BN08270.

42. Vincent [directeur du génie] to Leclerc, 29 Brumaire an 10 [November 20, 1801].

43. Louverture to Leclerc, "L'arrivé du général Leclerc, premiers contacts, 3 pieces," 22 Pluviôse an 10 [February 11, 1802], AN, Pierrefitte, AB/XIX/5002.

44. Louverture to Leclerc, "L'arrivé du général Leclerc, premiers contacts, 3 pieces," 22 Pluviôse an 10 [February 11, 1802].

45. Boisrond-Tonnerre, *Mémoires,* 6.

46. Desormeaux, ed., *Mémoires du général Toussaint Louverture,* 171, 176.

47. Boisrond-Tonnerre, *Mémoires,* 9.

48. Proclamation reproduced in Boisrond-Tonnerre, *Mémoires,* 15–16.

49. Proclamation reproduced in Boisrond-Tonnerre, *Mémoires,* 15–16.

50. Proclamation reproduced in Boisrond-Tonnerre, *Mémoires,* 15–16.

51. Desormeaux, ed., *Mémoires du général Toussaint Louverture,* 176.

52. Boisrond-Tonnerre, *Mémoires,* 12–13.

53. Boudet to Chef de l'état major Général, 26 Pluviôse an 10 [February 15, 1802], SHD, GR7, B15; Boudet to G'al de division Dugua, 3 Ventôse an 10 [February 22, 1802], SHD, GR7, B15.

54. Anonymous, "Récit non signé des Evenemens survenus à Léogâne et Jacmel lors de l'arrivé du G'al Leclerc," an 10 [ca. February 1802], UF-RP, box 3, ff. 114–115.

55. Dessalines to Garcia, Léogâne, 21 Pluviôse an 10 [February 10, 1802], BPL, MS Haiti 66-102 (1).

56. Dessalines to Dommage [Rousselot], Léogâne, 21 Pluviôse an 10 [February 10, 1802], ADG, 61 J 18, FRAD033_61J18_0084.

57. Dessalines to Dommage [Rousselot], Léogâne, 21 Pluviôse an 10.

58. Dessalines to Dommage [Rousselot], Léogâne, 21 Pluviôse an 10.

59. Dessalines to Dommage [Rousselot], Léogâne, 21 Pluviôse an 10.

60. Document cited in Hazareesingh, *Black Spartacus,* 307; Poyen-Bellisle, *Histoire militaire,* 129.

61. Chazotte, "Survivor of Dessalines's Massacres," in Popkin, *Facing Racial Revolution,* 349.

62. Chazotte, "Survivor of Dessalines's Massacres," 349.

63. Boisrond-Tonnerre, *Mémoires,* 30n1.

64. Dumas, *Précis des événemens militaires,* 229.

65. Anonymous, "Récit non signé des Evenemens survenus à Léogâne et Jacmel lors de l'arrivé du G'al Leclerc," an 10.

66. Anonymous, "Récit non signé des Evenemens survenus à Léogâne et Jacmel," an 10.

67. Descourtilz, *Voyages d'un naturaliste,* tome 3, 301.

68. Madiou, *Histoire d'Haïti,* tome 2, 209.

69. Boudet to Dugua, 30 Pluviôse an 10 [February 19, 1802], SHD, GR7, B15.

70. Anonymous, "Récit non signé des Evenemens survenus à Léogâne et Jacmel," an 10.

71. Boisrond-Tonnerre, *Mémoires,* 17; *Courrier des spectacles: journal des théâtres et de littérature,* Paris, 17 Germinal an 10 [April 7, 1802].

72. Leclerc, "Proclamation aux habitans de Saint-Domingue," Cap-Français, 28 Pluviôse an 10 [February 17, 1802], printed in *Gazette nationale ou le Moniteur universel,* 2 Germinal an 10 [March 23, 1802], no. 182, p. 728.

73. Leclerc, "Proclamation aux habitans de Saint-Domingue," Cap-Français, 28 Pluviôse an 10.

74. Dessalines to Louverture, 1 Ventôse an 10 [February 20, 1802], SCRBC, Sc Micro R-228, reel 4.

75. Leclerc to Minister of the Navy, 10 Ventôse an 10 [March 1, 1802], published in *Courrier des spectacles: Journal des théâtres et de littérature,* 17 Germinal an 10 [April 7, 1802].

76. Lecun to Leclerc, March 2, 1802, ASPF, SC, America Antille, vol. 3, f. 339.

77. Boisrond-Tonnerre, *Mémoires*, 19.

78. Boisrond-Tonnerre, *Mémoires*, 21–22.

79. Boisrond-Tonnerre, *Mémoires*, 23.

80. Boisrond-Tonnerre, *Mémoires*, 24.

81. Boisrond-Tonnerre, *Mémoires*, 26.

82. [Dugua] to Ministre de la Guerre, Port-Républicain, 5 Germinal an 10 [March 26, 1802], SHD, GR7, B3.

83. Boisrond-Tonnerre, *Mémoires*, 27; [Dugua] to Ministre de la Guerre, Port-Républicain, 5 Germinal an 10.

84. Dessalines to Louverture, Crête-à-Pierrot, 18 Ventôse an 10 [March 9, 1802], UF-RP, ff. 147.

85. Dessalines to Louverture, Crête-à-Pierrot, 18 Ventôse an 10.

86. Dessalines to Louverture, Crête-à-Pierrot, 21 Ventôse an 10, SCRBC, Sc Micro R-228, reel 4.

87. Boisrond-Tonnerre, *Mémoires*, 27.

88. [Dugua] to Ministre de la Guerre, Port-Républicain, 5 Germinal an 10 [March 26, 1802].

89. L. Valabregne to [Leclerc], 27 Ventôse an 10 [March 18, 1802], "l'avancée de l'armée du general Leclerc," AN, Pierrefitte, AB/XIX/5002.

90. "Renseignemens pris d'après la Declaration du C'en Pierre Charles Marions Lieutenant d'artillerie de l'armée de Dessaline," 27 Ventôse an 10 [March 18, 1802], "l'avancée de l'armée du general Leclerc," AN, Pierrefitte, AB/XIX/5002.

91. Thouvenot to C'en Gingembre, 1 Germinal an 10 [March 22, 1802], "Bulletin analytique," SHD, GR7, B3.

92. "Plan de la Crète à Pierrot et de ses environs," [1802], AN, AB/XIX/5002.

93. Descourtilz, *Voyages*, 356–357.

94. Descourtilz, *Voyages*, 359; quoted in Paul, "Le ressentiment Dessalinien," 150–151.

95. Descourtilz, *Voyages*, 359.

96. [Dugua] to Ministre de la Guerre, Port-Républicain, 5 Germinal an 10 [March 26, 1802].

97. Boisrond-Tonnerre, *Mémoires*, 28. Céligni Ardouin dates the evacuation to March 24, 1804; see C. Ardouin, *Essais sur l'histoire d'Haïti*, 84.

98. Dessalines to Louverture, 9 Germinal an 10 [March 30, 1802], SCRBC, Sc Micro R-228, reel 4.

99. Dessalines to Louverture, Crête-à-Pierrot, 21 Ventôse an 10 [March 12, 1802], SCRBC, Sc Micro R-228, reel 4.

100. Dessalines to Louverture, Crête-à-Pierrot, 21 Ventôse an 10 [March 12, 1802], SCRBC, Sc Micro R-228, reel 4.

101. The newspaper reported, however, that she was captured during an engagement between Paul Louverture and Henry Christophe. "Philadelphia, April 20, from CAPE FRANCOIS," *Connecticut Centinel,* April 27, 1802, pp. 2–3.

102. Rochambeau to Clauzel, Saint-Marc, 27 Germinal an 10 [April 17, 1802], SHD, GR7,

B3; Huin to Thouvenot, Gonaïves, 3 Floréal an 10 [April 23, 1802], SHD, GR7, B3; Desormeaux, ed., *Mémoires du général Toussaint Louverture,* 182.

103. Titus to Rochambeau, L'Artibonite, 19 Germinal an 10 [April 9, 1802], UF-RP, box 4, ff. 215, copy also available at UF-RP, microfilm, BN08265; Bonna la Chicotte to unknown, Saint-Marc, 22 Germinal an 10 [April 12, 1802], UF-RP, box 4, ff. 222.

104. Boisrond-Tonnerre, *Mémoires,* 30.

105. Dessalines to Louverture, Habitation Chasseriau, 14 Germinal an 10 [April 4, 1802], SCRBC, Sc Micro R-228, reel 4.

106. On Benoit's illness, see Dessalines to Louverture, Habitation Marchand, 19 Germinal an 10 [April 9, 1802], SCRBC, Sc Micro R-228, reel 4.

107. Boisrond-Tonnerre, *Mémoires,* 31–32.

108. On the defection of two of Dessalines's guides, see Titus to Rochambeau, 25 Germinal an 10 [April 15, 1802], UF-RP, box 4, ff. 240–242, copy available at UF-RP, microfilm, BN08265; Dessalines to Louverture, Camp Marchand, 27 Germinal an 10 [April 17, 1802], BPL, MS Haiti 66-102 (1–9); Dessalines to Louverture, Habitation Chasseriau, 14 Germinal an 10 [April 4, 1802], SCRBC, Sc Micro R-228, reel 4.

109. Boisrond-Tonnerre, *Mémoires,* 32.

110. Boisrond-Tonnerre, *Mémoires,* 29.

111. Louverture to Leclerc, Marmelade, 9 Floréal an 10 [April 29, 1802], "E—la reddition de T. Louverture," AN, Pierrefitte, AB/XIX/5002.

112. Dessalines to Louverture, Quartier Général à Marchand, 5 Floréal an 10 [April 25, 1802], SCRBC, Sc Micro R-228, reel 4.

113. Dessalines to Louverture, Habitation Marchand, 6 Floréal an 10 [April 26, 1802], SCRBC, Sc Micro R-228, reel 4.

114. Dessalines to Louverture, Habitation Marchand, 6 Floréal an 10.

115. Louverture to Leclerc, Marmelade, 9 Floréal an 10 [April 29, 1802], "E—la reddition de T. Louverture," AN, Pierrefitte, AB/XIX/5002.

116. Leclerc, "Arrêté," 6 Floréal an 10 [April 26, 1802], SHD, GR7, B3.

117. Louverture to Leclerc, Marmelade, 9 Floréal an 10 [April 29, 1802], "E—la reddition de T. Louverture," AN, Pierrefitte, AB/XIX/5002.

118. Dessalines to Louverture, Marchand, 9 Floréal an 10 [April 29, 1802], SCRBC, Sc Micro R-228, reel 4.

119. Desormeaux, ed., *Mémoires du général Toussaint Louverture,* 184.

120. Desormeaux, ed., *Mémoires du général Toussaint Louverture,* 184.

121. Leclerc to Louverture, Cap, 11 Floréal an 10 [May 1, 1802], "E—la reddition de T. Louverture," AN, Pierrefitte, AB/XIX/5002.

122. Louverture to Leclerc, 12 Floréal an 10 [May 2, 1802], "E—la reddition de T. Louverture," AN, Pierrefitte, AB/XIX/5002.

123. "Le Général en Chef au Général Toussaint," 13 Floréal an 10 [May 3, 1802], and Leclerc, "Arrêté," 11 Floréal an 10 [May 1, 1802] (Cap: P. Roux, imprimeur du gouvernement), SHD, GR7, B4.

124. Leclerc to Louverture, Cap-Français, 14 Floréal an 10 [May 4, 1802], "E—la reddition de T. Louverture," AN, Pierrefitte, AB/XIX/5002.

125. Dessalines to Louverture, Marchand, 13 Floréal an 10 [May 3, 1802], BPL, MS Haiti 66-102 (1–9).
126. Dessalines to Louverture, Marchand, 14 Floréal an 10 [May 4, 1802], Manuscript Division, MSRC.
127. Dessalines to Louverture, Marchand, 15 Floréal an 10 [May 5, 1802], Manuscript Division, MSRC.
128. Dessalines to Louverture, Marchand, 15 Floréal an 10.
129. Dessalines to Louverture, Marchand, 16 Floréal an 10 [May 6, 1802], SCRBC, Sc Micro R-228, reel 4.
130. Dessalines to Louverture, Marchand, 16 Floréal an 10.
131. Desormeaux, ed., *Mémoires du général Toussaint Louverture,* 184.
132. Boisrond-Tonnerre, *Mémoires,* 33–34, 36.
133. Boisrond-Tonnerre, *Mémoires,* 37.
134. Boisrond-Tonnerre, *Mémoires,* 45.
135. Descourtilz, *Voyages,* 359; quoted in Paul, "Le ressentiment Dessalinien," 150–151.
136. Boisrond-Tonnerre, *Mémoires,* 38; Leclerc to Louverture, Cap-Français, 17 Floréal an 10 [May 7, 1802], "E—la reddition de T. Louverture," AN, Pierrefitte, AB/XIX/5002.
137. Boisrond-Tonnerre, *Mémoires,* 38.
138. Louverture to Leclerc, Marmelade, 19 Floréal an 10 [May 9, 1802], "E—la reddition de T. Louverture," AN, Pierrefitte, AB/XIX/5002.
139. "Brunet," in Six, *Dictionnaire biographique des généraux et amiraux français,* tome 1, 168–169.
140. Boisrond-Tonnerre, *Mémoires,* 50. Saint-Rémy, *Mémoires du Général Toussaint-L'Ouverture,* 81n3.
141. Dessalines to Rochambeau, Marchand, 21 Floréal an 10 [May 11, 1802], UF-RP, box 5, ff. 350, [22/c-33].
142. Dessalines to Leclerc, Marchand, 22 Floréal an 10 [May 12, 1802], SCRBC, Sc Micro R-228, reel 4.
143. Dessalines to Leclerc, Marchand, 22 Floréal an 10.
144. Dessalines to Leclerc, Marchand, 22 Floréal an 10.
145. Leclerc to Rochambeau, Cap-Français, 22 Floréal an 10 [May 12, 1802], Philippe Rouillac Auction House, Vente Rochambeau, catalog lot 215. Link to catalog communicated by Philippe Girard. (Unless otherwise noted, I have not seen the original documents that are cited from the Vente Rochambeau.) https://www.rouillac.com/fr/lot-16-34463 -q.g._lhabitation_georges_21_prairial.
146. Louverture to Leclerc, Quartier Général de Louverture, 22 Floréal an 10 [May 12, 1802], "E—la reddition de T. Louverture," AN, Pierrefitte, AB/XIX/5002.
147. Dessalines to Leclerc, Marchand, 22 Floréal an 10.
148. Dessalines to Rochambeau, Saint-Marc, [illegible] Floréal an 10 [May 1802], BPL, MS Haiti 66-102 (1–9).
149. For an account of Dessalines's troops, see "État de Situation des Deux Divisions Réunis sous le commandement du Général de Division Rochambeau," 20 Prairial an 10 [June 9, 1802], UF-RP, microfilm, BN08270.

150. Brunet to Rochambeau, Saint-Marc, 30 Floréal an 10 [May 20, 1802], Philippe Rouillac Auction House, Vente Rochambeau, catalog lot 224.

151. Dessalines to Rochambeau, Saint-Marc, 10 Prairial an 10 [May 30, 1803], BPL, MS Haiti 67-8.

152. Philippe Girard, "Jean-Jacques Dessalines et l'arrestation de Toussaint Louverture," *Journal of Haitian Studies* 17, no. 1 (2011): 126.

153. Leclerc, "Ordre du jour," Cap-Français, 25 Floréal an 10 [May 15, 1802], SHD, GR7, B4.

154. Desormeaux, ed., *Mémoires du général Toussaint Louverture,* 186.

155. Desormeaux, ed., *Mémoires du général Toussaint Louverture,* 186.

156. Brunet to Rochambeau, Saint-Marc, 30 Floréal an 10 [May 20, 1802], Philippe Rouillac Auction House, Vente Rochambeau, catalog lot 224.

157. Brunet to Rochambeau, Saint-Marc, 30 Floréal an 10.

158. Brunet to Rochambeau, Saint-Marc, 30 Floréal an 10.

159. Philippe Girard has argued that this is evidence that Dessalines participated in Louverture's arrest. See Girard, "Jean-Jacques Dessalines et l'arrestation de Toussaint Louverture," 127–128.

160. Boisrond-Tonnerre, *Mémoires,* 33–34.

161. Dessalines to Brunet, Saint-Marc, 2 Prairial an 10 [May 22, 1802], "Papiers Rochambeau," AN, Pierrefitte, 135AP/6.

162. Dessalines to Leclerc, Saint-Marc, 2 Prairial an 10 [May 22, 1802], "Papiers Rochambeau," AN, Pierrefitte, 135AP/6; nearly illegible copy available at BPL, MS Haiti 66-102 (1–9).

163. Dessalines to Leclerc, Saint-Marc, 2 Prairial an 10.

164. Dessalines to Cila [Sylla], Saint-Marc, 2 Prairial an 10 [May 22, 1802], "Papiers Rochambeau," AN, Pierrefitte, 135AP/6. Dessalines sent copies of these two letters to Rochambeau to advise him of the situation; see Dessalines to Rochambeau, Saint-Marc, 5 Prairial an 10 [May 25, 1802], UF-RP, ff. 408.

165. Dessalines to Rochambeau, Saint-Marc, 3 Prairial an 10 [May 23, 1802], BPL, MS Haiti 66-102 (1–9).

166. Dessalines to Rochambeau, Saint-Marc, 3 Prairial an 10 [May 23, 1802], BPL, MS Haiti 66-102 (1–9) (second letter on this day).

167. Dessalines to Rochambeau, Saint-Marc, 4 Prairial an 10 [May 24, 1802], BPL, MS Haiti 66-102 (1–9).

168. Dessalines to Rochambeau, Saint-Marc, 6 Prairial an 10 [May 26, 1802], UF-RP, box 6, ff. 410, [22/c-36].

169. Dessalines to Rochambeau, Saint-Marc, 7 Prairial an 10 [May 27, 1802], UF-RP, box 6, ff. 415.

170. Dessalines to Rochambeau, Saint-Marc, 8 Prairial an 10 [May 28, 1802], University of Florida Libraries, Saint-Domingue and Haiti Autograph Collection, MS group 218, box 1.

171. Leclerc, "Au nom du Gouvernement Français," 12 Prairial an 10 [June 1, 1802], printed in *Gazette officielle de Saint Domingue,* Port-Républican, no. 1, 4 Messidor an 10 [June

23, 1802], p. 2, available on Gallica. For a list of the ranks of these troops, see Dessalines, "État Numérique des 4e & 8e coloniales Incorporées dans les 5e & 3e légères, comprenant par grades les militaires conservés, passés dans la gendarmerie & les reformés," Saint-Marc, 17 Messidor an 10 [July 6, 1802], UF-RP, microfilm, BN08270.

172. Margeret to Rochambeau, Saint-Marc, 16 Prairial an 10 [June 5, 1802], UF-RP, box 6, ff. 458.

173. Dessalines to Rochambeau, Cap-Français, 17 Prairial an 10 [June 6, 1802], UF-RP, box 6, ff. 462.

174. Original document is missing, summary in "Bulletin analytique," Leclerc to Bonaparte, 17 Prairial an 10 [June 6, 1802], SHD, GR7, B4; transcription available in Roussier, *Lettres du général Leclerc*, 161.

175. Leclerc to Bonaparte, 17 Prairial an 10 [June 6, 1802].

176. Dessalines to George Nugent, September 2, 1803, TNA, CO 137/110, f. 209.

177. Girard, "Jean-Jacques Dessalines et l'arrestation de Toussaint Louverture," 126.

178. Desormeaux, ed., *Mémoires du général Toussaint Louverture*, 188.

179. Brunet to Leclerc, Habitation Georges, 18 Prairial an 10 [June 7, 1802], "Papiers Rochambeau," AN, Pierrefitte, 135AP/6.

180. Boisrond-Tonnerre, *Mémoires*, 48.

181. Girard, "Jean-Jacques Dessalines et l'arrestation de Toussaint Louverture," 128; Brunet to Rochambeau, Habitation Georges, 19 Prairial an 10, [June 8, 1802], Philippe Rouillac Auction House, Vente Rochambeau, Lot 224. Thanks to Mes Rouillac, Commissaires-priseurs (rouillac.com) for sharing a scan of the original document with me.

182. C. Ardouin, *Essais sur l'histoire d'Haïti*, 99.

183. Desormeaux, ed., *Mémoires du général Toussaint Louverture*, 189.

184. Boisrond-Tonnerre, *Mémoires*, 48; on Suzanne Louverture's kidnapping, see Robin Mitchell, "Notes on Sources: Suzanne Louverture," *Journal of the Western Society for French History* 49 (2023): 88–92.

185. Leclerc to Citoyens de St-Domingue, 20 Pairial an 10 [June 9, 1802], SHD, GR7, B4.

186. Leclerc to Citoyens de St-Domingue, 20 Pairial an 10.

187. Leclerc, "Proclamation," 22 Prairial an 10 [June 11, 1802], printed in the *Gazette officielle de Saint Domingue*, no. 1, 4 Messidor an 10 [June 23, 1802], available on Gallica.

188. Desormeaux, ed., *Mémoires du général Toussaint Louverture*, 197.

189. Lacroix, "Mémoire secrêt."

190. Lacroix, "Mémoire secrêt."

191. Brunet to Leclerc, Habitation Georges, 30 Prairial an 10 [June 19, 1802], "Papiers Rochambeau," AN, Pierrefitte, 135AP/6. Girard argues that this proves Dessalines was involved in Louverture's arrest, but since Brunet claimed he was surprised by the demand for money, it seems unlikely that this would have been payment for services rendered. Girard, "Jean-Jacques Dessalines et l'arrestation de Toussaint Louverture," 130.

192. Brunet to Dessalines, Habitation Georges, 10 Messidor an 10 [June 29, 1802], UPR-ANC, ABR-2. Many thanks to Marlene Daut for sharing this source.

193. Rosemond, *Conférence historique*, 38.

194. Boisrond-Tonnerre, *Mémoires*, 48.

CHAPTER 7. I WILL REMEDY IT BY FORCE

1. Cabal to Rochambeau, Saint-Marc, 13 Thermidor an 10 [August 1, 1802], BPL, MS Haiti 70-24 (1–2). (The BPL catalog lists the date incorrectly.)
2. Cabal to Rochambeau, Saint-Marc, 13 Thermidor an 10 [August 1, 1802].
3. Rochambeau to Dessalines, 10 Thermidor an 10 [July 29, 1802], UPR-ANC, AR-1. Many thanks to Marlene Daut for generously sharing this source.
4. Louis Bazelais to Rochambeau, 13 Thermidor an 10 [August 1, 1802], UF-RP, box 9, ff. 735.
5. Rochambeau to Dessalines, Port-Républicain, 16 Thermidor an 10 [August 4, 1802], "Papiers Rochambeau," AN, Pierrefitte, 135AP/6.
6. Rochambeau to Dessalines, Port-Républicain, 16 Thermidor an 10.
7. On August 9 Bazelais followed up with Rochambeau, to assure him that the man whom Dessalines had freed would in fact be executed as Rochambeau had ordered. Bazelais to Rochambeau, Saint-Marc, 21 Thermidor an 10 [August 9, 1802], UF-RP, box 9, ff. 775.
8. Rochambeau to Leclerc, Port-Républicain, 19 Thermidor an 10 [August 7, 1802] (there is a small chance this could be 15 Thermidor or August 3), BPL, MS Haiti 70-24 (1–2). (Either way, the BPL catalog lists the date incorrectly.)
9. Rochambeau to Leclerc, Port-Républicain, 19 Thermidor an 10 [August 7, 1802].
10. Dessalines to Rochambeau, Saint-Marc, 25 Prairial an 10 [June 14, 1802], ADG, 61 J 18.
11. Martial-Besse to Rochambeau, Saint-Marc, 22 Prairial an 10 [June 11, 1802], UF-RP, box 6, ff. 484.
12. Brunet to Rochambeau or Leclerc, 26 Prairial an 10 [June 15, 1802], Philippe Rouillac Auction House, Vente Rochambeau, catalog lot 224.
13. Leclerc to Rochambeau, Cap-Français, 25 Prairial an 10 [June 14, 1802], Philippe Rouillac Auction House, Vente Rochambeau, catalog lot 215.
14. Rosemond, *Conférence historique,* 34.
15. On Dessalines selecting Black soldiers, see Lachaise to Thouvenot, Camp Bérard, 24 Thermidor an 10 [August 12, 1802], SHD, GR7, B6.
16. Dessalines to Brunet, Habitation La France, 24 Thermidor an 10 [August 12, 1802], "Papiers Rochambeau," AN, Pierrefitte, 135AP/6; Thouvenot to Dessalines, Plaisance, 23 Thermidor an 10 [August 11, 1802], SHD, GR7, B19.
17. On Dessalines's conflict with the "Congos," see Lacroix, "Mémoire secrêt"; on the changing meaning, see Madiou, *Histoire d'Haïti,* tome 2, 322n*.
18. Paul, "Le ressentiment Dessalinien," 152.
19. Desquidoux to Clauzel, D'ennery, 25 Prairial an 10 [June 14, 1802], SHD, GR7, B4.
20. Brunet to Leclerc, Plaisance, 3 Thermidor an 10 [July 22, 1802], "Papiers Rochambeau," AN, Pierrefitte, 135AP/6.
21. Lachaise to Thouvenot, Camp Berard, 24 Thermidor an 10 [August 12, 1802], SHD, GR7, B6.
22. See, for example, Makajoux to Brunet, Pilate, 30 Thermidor an 10 [August 18, 1802], SHD, GR7, B6.
23. On the national guard, see Brunet to Dessalines, Plaisance, 28 Thermidor an 10 [August 16, 1802], "Papiers Rochambeau," AN, Pierrefitte, 135AP/6; Martial-Besse to Rocham-

beau, Saint-Marc, 25 Prairial an 10 [June 14, 1802], UF-RP, box 7, ff. 502; Martial-Besse to Rochambeau, Saint-Marc, 2 Messidor an 10 [June 21, 1802], UF-RP, box 7, ff. 538.

24. Bélair to Dessalines, Verrettes, 19 Messidor an 10 [June 28, 1802], SCRBC, Sc Micro R-228, reel 1.

25. Bélair to Dessalines, Verrettes, 19 Messidor an 10.

26. Dessalines to Rochambeau, Saint-Marc, 2 Messidor an 10 [June 21, 1802], SCRBC, Sc Micro R-228, reel 4.

27. Leclerc, "Arrêté" [draft], June 30, 1802, UF-RP, box 7, ff. 568.

28. Martial-Besse to Rochambeau, Saint-Marc, 17 Messidor an 10 [July 6, 1802], UF-RP, box 8, ff. 587.

29. Dessalines to Rochambeau, Saint-Marc, 17 Messidor an 10 [July 6, 1802], SCRBC, Sc Micro R-228, reel 4.

30. Dessalines to Rochambeau, Saint-Marc, 23 Messidor an 10 [July 12, 1802], BPL, MS Haiti 66-102 (10). (The BPL catalog lists the date as 25 Messidor or July 14.)

31. Brunet to Leclerc, Plaisance, 3 Thermidor an 10 [July 22, 1802], "Papiers Rochambeau," AN, Pierrefitte, 135AP/6.

32. Bazelais to Rochambeau, Saint-Marc, 4 Thermidor an 10 [July 23, 1802], UF-RP, box 8, ff. 689.

33. Dessalines to Rochambeau, Saint-Marc, 23 Messidor an 10 [July 12, 1802], University of Florida Libraries, Saint-Domingue and Haiti Autograph Collection, MS group 218, box 1; Leclerc, Cap-Français, 26 Messidor an 10 [July 15, 1802], UF-RP, box 8, ff. 645. This was later printed as an official "Ordre du jour" on 26 Thermidor an 10 [August 14, 1802], and published in the *Gazette officielle de Saint Domingue,* Port-Républicain, no. 17, 30 Thermidor an 10 [August 18, 1802], available on Gallica.

34. Anonymous to Leclerc, 5 Thermidor an 10 [July 24, 1802], UF-RP, microfilm, BN08270. This last claim is confirmed by Dessalines: Dessalines to Rochambeau, Saint-Marc, le 27 Messidor an 10 [July 16, 1802], UF-RP, box 8, ff. 648a.

35. Rochambeau to Leclerc, Port-Républicain, 9 Thermidor an 10 [July 28, 1802], Philippe Rouillac Auction House, Vente Rochambeau, catalog lot 216.

36. Leclerc to Minister of the Navy, 5 Thermidor an 10 [July 24, 1802], SHD, GR7, B26. A copy of this letter and a translation of the code is available in Roussier, *Lettres du général Leclerc,* 219, but the date is listed incorrectly as August 25, 1802.

37. Thouvenot to Clauzel, Plaisance, 25 Thermidor an 10 [August 13, 1802], SHD, GR7, B19.

38. On Rochambeau's excessive use of executions in Saint-Marc, see also Lacroix, "Mémoire secret."

39. Dessalines to Brunet, Baudin, 22 Thermidor an 10 [August 10, 1802], "Papiers Rochambeau," AN, Pierrefitte, 135AP/6.

40. Jablonowski to [either Leclerc or Rochambeau], 17 Fructidor an 11 [September 4, 1802], Philippe Rouillac Auction House, Vente Rochambeau, catalog lot 220.

41. Dessalines to Brunet, Baudin, 22 Thermidor an 10 [August 10, 1802], "Papiers Rochambeau," AN, Pierrefitte, 135AP/6.

42. Thouvenot to Dessalines, Plaisance, 23 Thermidor an 10 [August 11, 1802], SHD, GR7,

B19; Thouvenot to Dessalines, Plaisance, 23 Thermidor an 10 [August 11, 1802], "Bulletin analytique," SHD, GR7, B6.

43. Thouvenot to Boyer, Plaisance, 26 Thermidor an 10 [August 14, 1802], SHD, GR7, B19.

44. Thouvenot to Lachaise, Plaisance, 23 Thermidor an 10 [August 11, 1802], SHD, GR7, B19.

45. Boisrond-Tonnerre, *Mémoires,* 53.

46. Dessalines to Brunet, Habitation La France, 24 Thermidor an 10 [August 12, 1802], "Papiers Rochambeau," AN, Pierrefitte, 135AP/6. Signed version available at Dessalines to Brunet, Habitation La France, 24 Thermidor an 10 [August 12, 1802], SHD, GR7, B6.

47. Thouvenot to Clauzel, Plaisance, 25 Thermidor an 10 [August 13, 1802], SHD, GR7, B19; for another example, see Thouvenot to Boyer, 4 Fructidor an 10 [August 22, 1802], SHD, GR7, B19.

48. Brunet to Leclerc, Plaisance, 25 Thermidor an 10 [August 13, 1802], "Papiers Rochambeau," AN, Pierrefitte, 135AP/6; Capitaine Le Moucheux, 25 Thermidor an 10 [August 13, 1802], SHD, GR7, B6.

49. Brunet to Leclerc, Plaisance, 26 Thermidor an 10 [August 14, 1802], "Papiers Rochambeau," AN, Pierrefitte, 135AP/6.

50. See, for example, Dugua, "Ordre du jour," 26 Thermidor an 10 [August 14, 1802], (au Cap-Français, Chez P. Roux, imprimeur), SHD, GR7, B6.

51. Lemoucheux, "Rapport," 26 Thermidor an 10 [August 14, 1802], SHD, GR7, B6.

52. Dessalines to Brunet, Habitation Pugeot, 27 Thermidor an 10 [August 15, 1802], SHD, GR7, B6; copy available at "Papiers Rochambeau," AN, Pierrefitte, 135AP/6.

53. Brunet to Leclerc, Plaisance, 28 Thermidor an 10 [August 16, 1802], "Papiers Rochambeau," AN, Pierrefitte, 135AP/6 [second letter on this date]; copy available at SHD, GR7, B19. "Bulletin analytique," available at Brunet to Leclerc, Plaisance, 28 Thermidor an 10, SHD, GR7, B6.

54. Brunet to Leclerc, Plaisance, 28 Thermidor an 10.

55. Brunet to Leclerc, 28 Thermidor an 10 [August 16, 1802], SHD, GR7, B19 [second letter].

56. Brunet to Dessalines, Plaisance, 28 Thermidor an 10 [August 16, 1802], "Papiers Rochambeau," AN, Pierrefitte, 135AP/6.

57. Dessalines to Brunet, Habitation Vali___, 4 Fructidor an 10 [August 22, 1802], SHD, GR7, B6.

58. Dessalines to Brunet, Habitation Dumenil, 4 Fructidor an 10 [August 22, 1802] (third letter on same day), SHD, GR7, B6.

59. Dessalines to Brunet, Habitation Dumenil, 5 Fructidor an 10 [August 23, 1802] (an annotation on the document incorrectly says 24 July 1802), SHD, GR7, B5.

60. Dessalines to Brunet, Habitation Dupé, 6 Fructidor an 10 [August 24, 1802], SHD, GR7, B6.

61. Thouvenot to Dessalines, 5 Fructidor an 10 [August 23, 1802], SHD, GR7, B19.

62. Thouvenot to Clauzel, Plaisance, 5 Fructidor an 10 [August 23, 1802], SHD, GR7, B19.

63. Brunet to Leclerc, Plaisance, 6 Fructidor an 10 [August 24, 1802], "Papiers Rochambeau," AN, Pierrefitte, 135AP/6; copy available at SHD, GR7, B20.

64. Brunet to Leclerc, Plaisance, 6 Fructidor an 10.

65. Dessalines to Brunet, Habitation Dupé, 6 Fructidor an 10 [August 24, 1802], SHD, GR7, B6.

66. Document cited and reproduced in full in Maurice de Young, "Jean-Jacques Dessalines and Charles Belair," *Journal of Inter-American Studies* 2, no. 4 (1960): 454.

67. A letter from Dessalines's chief of staff Bazelais confirmed Bélair's involvement and named Destrade and Jean Charles Corjolles as leaders of about six hundred insurgents camped in the Valadon Mountains. Bazelais to Dupuy, Saint-Marc, 30 Thermidor an 10 [August 18, 1802], UF-RP, box 10, ff. 848. Thouvenot later provided evidence from Bélair that outlined race-based factionalism that had developed in the Artibonite region; Thouvenot to Dugua, 10 Fructidor an 10 [August 28, 1802], SHD, GR7, B20.

68. Repussard et al., 2 Fructidor an 10 [August 20, 1802], UF-RP, microfilm, BN08270. Transcribed in Young, "Jean-Jacques Dessalines and Charles Belair," 452.

69. Repussard to Rochambeau, Verrettes, 3 Fructidor an 10 [August 21, 1802], UF-RP, microfilm, BN08270. Transcribed in Young, "Jean-Jacques Dessalines and Charles Belair," 452.

70. Bazelais to Dessalines, Saint-Marc, 5 Fructidor an 10 [August 23, 1802], SHD, GR7, B6; Bazelais to Rochambeau, Saint-Marc, 5 Fructidor an 10 [August 23, 1802], UF-RP, box 10, ff. 864.

71. Brunet to Leclerc, Plaisance, 6 Fructidor an 10 [August 24, 1802], (second letter on same date), "Papiers Rochambeau," AN, Pierrefitte, 135AP/6.

72. Brunet to Bélair, 8 Fructidor an 10 [August 26, 1802], SHD, GR7, B20.

73. Brunet to Leclerc, Plaisance, 6 Fructidor an 10.

74. Leclerc to Rochambeau, d'Estaign, 7 Fructidor an 10 [August 25, 1802], Philippe Rouillac Auction House, Vente Rochambeau, catalog lot 215.

75. Lacroix, "Mémoire secrèt."

76. Thouvenot to Clauzel, 9 Fructidor an 10 [August 27, 1802], SHD, GR7, B20.

77. See, for example, Lacroix, "Mémoire secrèt."

78. "Bulletin analytique," Thouvenot to Haque, Plaisance, 8 Fructidor an 10 [August 26], SHD, GR7, B6; Thouvenot to Dessalines, 8 Fructidor an 10 [August 26, 1802], SHD, GR7, B20; Thouvenot to Haque, 8 Fructidor an 10 [August 26, 1802], SHD, GR7, B20.

79. [Haque] to Thouvenot, Habitation Georges, 20 Fructidor an 10 [September 7, 1802], SHD, GR7, B7.

80. Dessalines to Brunet, Camp Saint-Amand, 8 Fructidor an 10 [August 26, 1802], SHD, GR7, B6.

81. Dessalines to Brunet, Habitation Dumenil, 4 Fructidor an 10 [August 22, 1802], (second letter on same day), SHD, GR7, B6.

82. Brunet to Leclerc, Plaisance, 6 Fructidor an 10 [August 24, 1802], "Papiers Rochambeau," AN, Pierrefitte, 135AP/6.

83. Dessalines to Brunet, Habitation Pilbareau, 8 Fructidor an 10 [August 26, 1802], SHD, GR7, B6.

84. Dessalines to Brunet, Habitation Pilbareau, 8 Fructidor an 10.

85. Dessalines to Brunet, Camp Saint-Amand, 8 Fructidor an 10.

86. Dessalines to Leclerc, 8 Fructidor an 10 [August 26, 1802], BPL, MS Haiti 71-4.

87. "Bulletin analytique," Thouvenot to Boyer, Plaisance, 9 Fructidor an 10 [August 27, 1802], SHD, GR7, B6; "Bulletin analytique," Brunet to Leclerc, Plaisance, 9 Fructidor an 10 [August 27, 1802], SHD, GR7, B6.

88. Brunet to Leclerc, Plaisance, 9 Fructidor an 10 [August 27, 1802], "Papiers Rochambeau," AN, Pierrefitte, 135AP/6.

89. Leclerc to Rochambeau, 9 Fructidor an 10 [August 27, 1802], Philippe Rouillac Auction House, Vente Rochambeau, catalog lot 215.

90. Rachel B. Doyle, "The Founding Fathers Encrypted Secret Messages, Too: Centuries before Cybersecurity, Statesmen around the World Communicated with Their Own Elaborate Codes and Ciphers," *Atlantic,* March 30, 2017.

91. For another example, see Esquidoux to Brunet, Ennery, 30 Floréal an 10 [May 20, 1802], "Papiers Rochambeau," AN, Pierrefitte, 135AP/6.

92. Thouvenot to Brosselin, 12 Fructidor an 10 [August 30, 1802], SHD, GR7, B20; Thouvenot to Dugua, Plaisance, 13 Fructidor an 10 [August 31, 1802], SHD, GR7, B6.

93. Dessalines to Brunet, Petite Rivière, 14 Fructidor an 10 [September 1, 1802], SHD, GR7, B7.

94. Dessalines to Leclerc, Petite Rivière, 14 Fructidor an 10 [September 1, 1802], SCRBC, Sc Micro R-228, reel 4.

95. Dessalines to Leclerc, Petite Rivière, 14 Fructidor an 10.

96. Lacroix, "Mémoire secrêt."

97. Pierre Joseph Caboteur, Déclaration, Arcahaye, 15 Fructidor an 10 [September 2, 1802], UF-RP, box 10, ff. 944–945; Pageot to Rochambeau, Arcahaye, 15 Fructidor an 10 [September 2, 1802], UF-RP, box 10, ff. 944–945.

98. Dessalines to Leclerc, Petite Rivière, 14 Fructidor an 10.

99. Dessalines to Brunet, Petite Rivière, 16 Fructidor an 10 [September 3, 1802], "Papiers Rochambeau," AN, Pierrefitte, 135AP/6.

100. Dessalines to Quantin, Petite Rivière, 16 Fructidor an 10 [September 3, 1802], UF-RP, box 10, ff. 894 (previously incorrectly filed in ff. 953).

101. Dessalines to Brunet, Petite Rivière, 16 Fructidor an 10.

102. Dessalines to Brunet, Petite Rivière, 16 Fructidor an 10.

103. Dessalines to Leclerc, Petite Rivière, 16 Fructidor an 10 [September 3, 1802], SCRBC, Sc Micro R-228, reel 4.

104. Quantin, "Ordre particulier," Saint-Marc, 17 Fructidor an 10 [September 4, 1802], "Papiers Rochambeau," AN, Pierrefitte, 135AP/6; copy available at UF-RP, box 10, ff. 953 (enclosure from letter in ff. 894).

105. On the Polish troops, see Jan Pachonski and Reuel K. Wilson, *Poland's Caribbean Tragedy: A Study of Polish Legions in the Haitian War of Independence, 1802–1803* (New York: Columbia University Press, 1986).

106. Jablonowski to either Leclerc or Rochambeau, 17 Fructidor an 11 [September 4, 1802], Philippe Rouillac Auction House, Vente Rochambeau, catalog lot 220.

107. Dessalines to Brunet, Petite Rivière, 21 Fructidor an 10 [September 8, 1802], "Papiers Rochambeau," AN, Pierrefitte, 135AP/6; a copy is available at SHD, GR7, B7.

108. Dessalines to Brunet, Petite Rivière, 21 Fructidor an 10.

109. Unknown author, n.d. [ca. 1801], "Portraits des chefs de la colonie," AN, Pierrefitte,

AB/XIX/5002; Dessalines to Rochambeau, Saint-Marc, 21 Messidor an 10 [July 10, 1802], SCRBC, Sc Micro R-228, reel 4.

110. Dessalines to Rochambeau, Saint-Marc, 27 Messidor an 10 [July 16, 1802], UF-RP, box 8, ff. 648a.

111. See, for example, "Portraits des chefs de la colonie."

112. Dessalines to Leclerc, Petite Rivière, 16 Fructidor an 10 [September 3, 1802], SCRBC, Sc Micro R-228, reel 4. First half of the quotation is cited in Girard, "Jean-Jacques Dessalines et l'arrestation de Toussaint Louverture," 132.

113. Jablonowski to Rochambeau, Verrettes, 19 Fructidor an 10 [September 6, 1802], UF-RP, box 11, ff. 964.

114. Repussard to Rochambeau, September 10, 1802, reproduced in Young, "Jean-Jacques Dessalines and Charles Belair," 454–455.

115. Dessalines to Brunet, Petite Rivière, 21 Fructidor an 10.

116. Dessalines to Brunet, Petite Rivière, 21 Fructidor an 10.

117. Dessalines to Brunet, Petite Rivière, 21 Fructidor an 10.

118. Brunet to Leclerc, Plaisance, 23 Fructidor an 10 [September 10, 1802], "Papiers Rochambeau," AN, Pierrefitte, 135AP/6.

119. Quantin, "Ordre particulier, copie," Saint-Marc, 21 Fructidor an 10 [September 8, 1802], "Papiers Rochambeau," AN, Pierrefitte, 135AP/6. Original available at UF-RP, box 11, ff. 986–987; microfilm copy available at UF-RP, microfilm, BNO8264, lot 109.

120. "Ordre du jour," printed as a letter from Dessalines to Leclerc, 23 Fructidor an 10 [September 10, 1802], SHD, GR7, B7; copie conforme by Quantin available at UF-RP, box 11, ff. 1000 and on microfilm at UF-RP, microfilm, BNO8264, lot 109. A translation is available at "Army of St. Domingo," Dessalines to Leclerc, 23 Fructidor [an 10] [September 10, 1802], *Philadelphia Gazette & Daily Advertiser,* October 8, 1802, p. 3.

121. "Ordre du jour" included a printed version of the letter from Dessalines to Leclerc, 23 Fructidor an 10.

122. Brunet to Leclerc, Plaisance, 24 Fructidor an 10 [September 11, 1802], "Papiers Rochambeau," AN, Pierrefitte, 135AP/6.

123. Young, "Jean-Jacques Dessalines and Charles Belair," 456.

124. "Charles Belair a été fusillé avec son épouse; la fermeté de ce couple a étonné les bourreaux qui l'ont condamné." Boisrond-Tonnerre, *Mémoires,* 32–33n1.

125. Brunet to Leclerc, Plaisance, 27 Fructidor an 10 [September 14, 1802], "G—autres documents annexes," AN, Pierrefitte, AB/XIX/5002. A few words and phrases in this letter are in code, but none relating to Dessalines are in code.

126. "Bulletin analytique," Ordre du jour de la division de droit du nord (gros morne), 30 Fructidor an 10 [September 17, 1802], SHD, GR7, B7; "Ordre du jour," Quartier Général du Gros Morne, 30 Fructidor an 10 [September 17, 1802], SHD, GR7, B21.

127. Lacroix, "Mémoire secrèt."

128. Lacroix, "Mémoire secrèt."

129. "travailles les brigands à la Dessalines," in "Bulletin analytique," Thouvenot to Achille, Gros Morne, 5 Jour Complémentaire an 10 [September 22, 1802], SHD, GR7, B7.

130. Leclerc to Bonaparte, Cap-Français, 29 Fructidor an 10 [September 16, 1802], in Roussier, *Lettres du général Leclerc,* 234.

131. Leclerc to Bonaparte, Cap-Français, 29 Fructidor an 10 [September 16, 1802], in Rous-sier, *Lettres du général Leclerc,* 230–231.

132. Brunet to Leclerc, Gros Morne, 2 Jour Complémentaire an 10, [September 20, 1802], Philippe Rouillac Auction House, Vente Rochambeau, lot 224 (parts are originally in code). Thanks to Mes Rouillac for sharing a scan of this document with me.

133. Brunet to Leclerc, Gros Morne, 2 Jour Complémentaire an 10.

CHAPTER 8. IT IS TIME TO TEACH
THE FRENCH THAT THEY ARE MONSTERS

1. Quantin to Dessalines, 1 Brumaire an 11 [October 23, 1802], UF-RP, box 13, ff. 1234–1235.

2. Quantin to Dessalines, 1 Brumaire an 11; initially, Quantin tried to use Dessalines's *beau-père* (father-in-law) to convince him.

3. Dessalines to Quantin, 2 Brumaire an 11 [October 24, 1802], UF-RP, box 13, ff. 1238.

4. Dessalines to Quantin, 2 Brumaire an 11.

5. Maurice de Young incorrectly cites that this evidence was in the September 16, 1802, letter, when it is in fact in the September 26, 1802, letter—it is likely that this was sim-ply a typo. Young, "Jean-Jacques Dessalines and Charles Belair," 456.

6. Leclerc to Bonaparte, September 26, 1802, in Roussier, *Lettres du général Leclerc,* 245–246.

7. Lacroix, "Mémoire secrêt."

8. Thouvenot to Dugua, Gros Morne, 5 Vendémiaire an 11 [September 27, 1802], SHD, GR7, B21.

9. Thouvenot to Dugua, Gros Morne, 7 Vendémiaire an 11 [September 29, 1802], SHD, GR7, B21.

10. Lacroix, "Mémoire secrêt."

11. Madiou, *Histoire d'Haïti,* tome 2, 339; Dubois, *Avengers,* 286.

12. Philippe R. Girard, *The Slaves Who Defeated Napoléon: Toussaint Louverture and the Haitian War of Independence, 1801–1804* (Tuscaloosa: University of Alabama Press, 2011), 190. For the text of the law, see "Corps Legislatif, Séance du 27 floréal," *Journal des débats,* 28 Floréal an 10 [May 18, 1802], pp. 3–4, available on Gallica.

13. Jean-François Niort and Jérémy Richard, "A propos de la découverte de l'arrêté con-sulaire du 16 juillet 1802 et du rétablissement de l'ancien ordre colonial (spécialement de l'esclavage) à la Guadeloupe," *Bulletin de la Société d'histoire de la Guadeloupe* 152 (2009): 31–59.

14. Quoted in Dubois, *Avengers,* 285.

15. For example, see Thouvenot to Dugua, Gros Morne, 5 Vendémiaire an 11 [September 27, 1802], SHD, GR7, B21; Pageot, "Rapport du 28 au 29 Nivôse an 11" [January 19, 1803], UF-RP, box 15, ff. 1531.

16. Pierre Panisse, "Compte que Rend, le Chef de Brigade Panisse, Commandant de la Place et Arrondissement, au Général de Division Rochambeau, de ses opérations mili-taires," 15 Vendémiaire an 11 [October 7, 1802], UF-RP, box 12, ff. 1160.

17. Dubois, *Avengers,* 288.

18. Panisse, "Compte que Rend, le Chef de Brigade Panisse."

19. Leclerc to Bonaparte, October 7, 1802, in Roussier, *Lettres du général Leclerc,* 254; Girard, *Slaves Who Defeated Napoléon,* 207.

20. Leclerc to Bonaparte, October 7, 1802, Cap-Français, in Roussier, *Lettres du général Leclerc,* 256.

21. Lacroix, "Mémoire secrêt."

22. Girard, *Slaves Who Defeated Napoléon,* 208.

23. Leclerc, draft decree, 1 Jour Complémentaire an 10 [September 18, 1802], UF-RP, box 11, ff. 1060; Girard, *Slaves Who Defeated Napoléon,* 208.

24. Brunet to Leclerc, Gros Morne, 8 Vendémiaire an 11 [September 30, 1802], UF-RP, box 12, ff. 1125.

25. Brunet to Leclerc, Gros Morne, 8 Vendémiaire an 11.

26. Brunet to Leclerc, Plaisance, 9 Vendémiaire an 11 [October 1, 1802], UF-RP, box 12, ff. 1129.

27. Dessalines to Brunet, Grand Bois, 12 Vendémiaire an 11 [October 4, 1802], SHD, GR7, B8.

28. Lacroix, "Mémoire secrêt."

29. Brunet to Leclerc, Gros Morne, 5 Jour Complémentaire an 10 [September 21, 1802], Georgetown University Manuscripts, Jean Baptiste Brunct Papers, box 1, folder 7. I am grateful to Scott Taylor for sending me a scan of this document.

30. Madiou, *Histoire d'Haïti,* tome 2, 337; Lacroix, "Mémoire secrêt."

31. Lacroix, "Mémoire secrêt."

32. Madiou, *Histoire d'Haïti,* tome 2, 337.

33. Madiou, *Histoire d'Haïti,* tome 2, 340.

34. Boisrond-Tonnerre places this meeting in Plaisance. Boisrond-Tonnerre, *Mémoires,* 51.

35. On Madame Dessalines being at the Georges plantation, see Vernet to Brunet, Pougadin, 5 Vendémiaire an 11 [September 27, 1802], SHD, GR7, B7; Madiou, *Histoire d'Haïti,* tome 2, 360.

36. Céligni Ardouin, "Comment se concerta la lutte pour l'indépendance," in *Oeuvre des écrivains haïtiens. Auteurs haitiens: Morceaux choisis, précédés de notices biographiques,* edited by Solon Ménos, Dantès Bellegarde, A. Duval, and Georges Sylvain (Port-au-Prince: Imprimerie de Mme. F. Smith, 1904), 29.

37. Madiou, *Histoire d'Haïti,* tome 2, 337, 258. In his *Mémoires,* Boisrond-Tonnere situated this meeting and Dessalines's defection immediately after Louverture's arrest. He skipped the months from June to October, thereby avoiding any need to explain Dessalines's actions against the insurgents who continued to resist the French expeditionary forces. According to Boisrond-Tonnerre's version of events, Dessalines received the letter from Leclerc ordering him to kill all the *anciens libres* at their first meeting in Cap-Français in June 1802 (when Brunet arrested Louverture). Dessalines first spoke with Pétion and convinced him to join the revolution, and then went to Haut-du-Cap to talk with Clervaux and Christophe. The meetings likely played out as Boisrond-Tonnerre described, but occurred in early October rather than June. Given that Boisrond-Tonerre's account was approved by Dessalines, this discrepancy suggests that Dessalines did not think it politically wise to highlight his alliance with Leclerc. Boisrond-Tonnere, *Mémoires,* 48.

38. Dubois, *Avengers of the New World,* 288; Leclerc to Bonaparte, October 7, 1802, Roussier, *Lettres du général Leclerc,* 253-259.

39. Madiou, *Histoire d'Haïti,* tome 2, 337.
40. Madiou, *Histoire d'Haïti,* tome 2, 341.
41. Lattre, *Campagnes des Français à Saint-Domingue,* 63.
42. Dubois, *Avengers,* 288–289.
43. Lacroix, "Mémoire secrêt."
44. Boisrond-Tonnerre, *Mémoires,* 51.
45. Madiou, *Histoire d'Haïti,* tome 2, 359.
46. Madiou, *Histoire d'Haïti,* tome 2, 359.
47. Dubois, *Avengers,* 289.
48. Madiou, *Histoire d'Haïti,* tome 2, 259.
49. Boisrond-Tonnerre, *Mémoires,* 59.
50. Dessalines to Brunet, Habitation Georges, 17 Vendémiaire an 11 [October 9, 1802], SHD, GR7, B8.
51. Boisrond-Tonnerre, *Mémoires,* 54.
52. Boisrond-Tonnerre, *Mémoires,* 54.
53. Boisrond-Tonnerre, *Mémoires,* 56.
54. Madiou, *Histoire d'Haïti,* tome 2, 361.
55. Madiou, *Histoire d'Haïti,* tome 2, 361.
56. Madiou, *Histoire d'Haïti,* tome 2, 362.
57. Dessalines to Brunet, Petite Rivière, 23 Vendémiaire an 11 [October 15, 1802], "Papiers Rochambeau," AN, Pierrefitte, 135AP/6; original signed version at SHD, GR7, B8.
58. In 1818 Henry Christophe made Joseph Dessalines a baron along with Dessalines's son Louis. See "Ordonnance du Roi," *Gazette Royale d'Hayti,* Cap-Henry, December 28, 1818, *quinzième année de l'Indépendance,* p. 1. Available courtesy of lagazetteroyale.com.
59. Dessalines to Brunet, Petite Rivière, 23 Vendémiaire an 11.
60. Quantin to Dessalines, Saint-Marc, 25 Vendémiaire an 11 [October 17, 1802], SHD, GR7, B8.
61. Haque to unknown, Habitation Georges, 26 Vendémiaire an 11 [October 18, 1802], SHD, GR7, B8.
62. Dessalines to Brunet, Petite Rivière, 27 Vendémiaire an 11 [October 19, 1802], "Papiers Rochambeau," AN, Pierrefitte, 135AP/6.
63. Madiou, *Histoire d'Haïti,* tome 2, 362. Boisrond-Tonnerre recounted that the soldier cried, "Nous sommes vos ennemis, tirez, nous allons faire feu." Boisrond-Tonnerre, *Mémoires,* 57.
64. Boisrond-Tonnerre, *Mémoires,* 57.
65. Madiou, *Histoire d'Haïti,* tome 2, 363.
66. Boisrond-Tonnerre, *Mémoires,* 58.
67. Boisrond-Tonnerre, *Mémoires,* 58.
68. Dessalines to Quantin, 2 Brumaire an 11 [October 24, 1802], UF-RP, box 13, ff. 1238.
69. Lacroix, "Mémoire secrêt"; Quantin to Rochambeau, Saint-Marc, 2 Brumaire an 11 [October 24, 1802], UF-RP, microfilm, BN08264, lot 109.
70. Leclerc, "Armée de Saint-Domingue, au nom du gouvernement français," 28 Vendémiaire an 11 [October 20, 1802], published in the *Gazette officielle de Saint-Domingue,* Port-Républicain, October 23, 1802, p. 3, available on Gallica and from SHD, GR7, B8.

71. Levasseur says the remaining cities with French people were Cap-Français, Port-au-Prince (Port-Républicain), Môle Saint-Nicolas, Les Cayes, Fort-Dauphin, and Port-de-Paix. *Événemens,* 7n1.

72. Leclerc, "Armée de Saint-Domingue, au nom du gouvernement français," 28 Vendémiaire an 11.

73. Rochambeau to Quantin, Port-Républicain, 2 Brumaire an 11 [October 24, 1802], SHD, GR7, B8.

74. Rochambeau to Quantin, Port-Républicain, 2 Brumaire an 11.

75. Jonathan North and Marek Tadeusz Lałowski, *War of Lost Hope: Polish Accounts of the Napoleonic Expedition to Saint Domingue, 1801 to 1804* (Seattle: Amazon Digital Services, 2018); Pachonski and Wilson, *Poland's Caribbean Tragedy.*

76. Fressinet to Rochambeau, 5 or 9 Brumaire an 11 [October 27 or 31, 1802], UF-RP, box 13, ff. 1270.

77. Madiou, *Histoire d'Haïti,* tome 2, 365.

78. Boisrond-Tonnerre, *Mémoires,* 58.

79. Rochambeau to Quantin, Port-Républicain, 9 Brumaire an 11 [October 31, 1802], SHD, GR7, B8.

80. Boisrond-Tonnerre, *Mémoires,* 59.

81. Madiou, *Histoire d'Haïti,* tome 2, 366.

82. Boisrond-Tonnerre, *Mémoires,* 59.

83. Madiou, *Histoire d'Haïti,* tome 2, 366.

84. See, for example, Fressinet to Rochambeau, 5 or 9 Brumaire an 11.

85. Fressinet to Rochambeau, 5 or 9 Brumaire an 11.

86. For another possible example of deliberate misinformation, see a letter in which Fressinet reported that one of his spies said that Clervaux was dead (which was incorrect). Fressinet to Thouvenot, Saint-Marc, 5 Ventôse an 11 [February 24, 1803], SHD, GR7, B9.

87. *Gazette of the United States,* Philadelphia, December 15, 1802, p. 4. I am grateful to my W&M HIST 212 student Sydney Ruggieri for bringing this article to my attention.

88. Fressinet to Rochambeau, 10 Brumaire an 11 [November 1, 1802], UF-RP, box 13, ff. 1279.

89. Girard, *Slaves Who Defeated Napoléon,* 221. Girard cites E. Peyre, "Journal de la maladie du général en chef," November 2, 1802, AN, Paris, microfilm, CC9B 20.

90. Dessalines to Quantin, 2 Brumaire an 11 [October 24, 1803], UF-RP, box 13, ff. 1238.

91. Quoted in Deborah Jenson and Doris Kadish, eds., *Poetry of Haitian Independence,* translated by Norman R. Shapiro (New Haven, CT: Yale University Press, 2015), 186.

CHAPTER 9. THE EVE OF MAKING
OUR EXECUTIONERS DISAPPEAR

1. Dessalines to George Nugent, June 23, 1803, NLJ, MS 72; copy available at TNA, CO 137/110.

2. Dessalines to Nugent, June 23, 1803.

3. Dessalines to Nugent, June 23, 1803.

4. Dessalines to Nugent, June 23, 1803.

5. Boisrond-Tonnerre, *Mémoires,* 64.

6. Boisrond-Tonnerre, *Mémoires,* 65.

7. Philippe R. Girard, "Caribbean Genocide: Racial War in Haiti, 1802–4," *Patterns of Prejudice* 39 (2005): 157. On dogs, see Lacroix, "Mémoire secrêt"; Tyler D. Parry and Charlton W. Yingling, "Slave Hounds and Abolition in the Americas," *Past & Present* 246, no. 1 (2020): 86–87; Dubois, *Avengers,* 293.

8. Charles d'Henin, "Mémoire historique et politique sur la Situation actuelle à St. Domingue," Thermidor an 11 [July–August 1803], UF-RP, box 19, ff. 2016.

9. Unknown to Monsieur de Gallifet, Cap-Français, November 3, 1802, AN, Pierrefitte, 107AP/128.

10. Young, "Jean-Jacques Dessalines and Charles Belair," 449; M.-R. Trouillot, *Silencing the Past,* 39.

11. Lacroix, "Mémoire secrêt."

12. P. Boyer to Ministre de Guerre Berthier, Cap-Français, 20 Ventôse an 11 [March 11, 1803], SHD, GR7, B9.

13. "Nottes," [n.d., ca. September 1802], UF-RP, box 23, ff. 2268.

14. Lacroix, "Mémoire secrêt."

15. Boisrond-Tonnerre, *Mémoires,* 60; Lacroix, "Mémoire secrêt."

16. Jean Price-Mars, *La République d'Haïti et la République dominicaine: Les aspects divers d'un problème d'histoire, de géographie et d'ethnologie,* tome 1 (Port-au-Prince, 1953), 65.

17. M.-R. Trouillot, *Silencing the Past,* 42.

18. Sans Souci appeared as a colonel on the list of signatures in 1793: Officers of the Army of Toussaint and Gilles to the Commander of the Cordon de l'Ouest, Quartier du Camp [?], June 27, 1793, AN, Pierrefitte, D/XXV/20/199; M.-R. Trouillot, *Silencing the Past,* 41.

19. M.-R. Trouillot, *Silencing the Past,* 42.

20. M.-R. Trouillot, *Silencing the Past,* 43.

21. Kerversau to Pamphile de Lacroix, Neyba, 23 Frimaire an 11 [December 14, 1802], SHD, GR7, B9.

22. Lacroix, "Mémoire secrêt."

23. Lacroix, "Mémoire secrêt."

24. Pamphile de Lacroix reported that a French ship "été assailli par six barges des revoltés." Lacroix, "Mémoire secrêt."

25. Boisrond-Tonnerre, *Mémoires,* 83; Contre-Amiral Emeriau to Vice Amiral Latouche-Treville, Port-Républicain, 11 Ventôse an 11 [March 2, 1803], AN, Pierrefitte, AB/XIX/5002.

26. Boisrond-Tonnerre, *Mémoires,* 73.

27. Mats Lundahl, "Defense and Distribution: Agricultural Policy in Haiti during the Reign of Jean-Jacques Dessalines, 1804–1806," *Scandinavian Economic History Review* 32, no. 2 (1984): 83. This is likely the table that Lundahl is referring to: "Tableau de la situation de l'Ancienne partie française de St. Domingue à l'époque du 30 Ventôse an 11," March 21, 1803, included in Lacroix, "Mémoire secrêt."

28. Lacroix, "Mémoire secrêt"; "Nottes," [n.d., ca. September 1802], UF-RP, box 23, ff. 2268. This document claims that Sans Souci and Macaya, among others, were killed on Dessalines's orders.

29. "Nottes," [n.d., ca. September 1802].

30. Beaubrun Ardouin, *Études sur l'histoire d'Haïti,* tome 5 (Paris: Dezobry et E. Magdeleine, 1854), 308.

31. Thouvenot to Senneville, Cap-Français, 18 Ventôse an 11 [March 9, 1803], SHD, GR7, B22.

32. Philippe-Armand Thoby, "Les étrangers et le droit de propriété en Haïti: Le fameux article 7, une question d'utilité économique," *La Fraternité: Organe des intérêts d'Haïti et de la race noire, journal hebdomadair* (Paris), no. 14, March 15, 1893, p. 38.

33. Claude B. Auguste and Marcel B. Auguste, *Pour le drapeau: Contribution à la recherche sur les couleurs haïtiennes* (Québec: C. et M. B. Auguste, 1982); Madiou, *Histoire d'Haïti,* tome 3, 31.

34. Mario Rameau and Jean-Jacques-Dessalines Ambroise, *La révolution de Saint-Domingue (1789–1804),* 2ème ed. (Port-au-Prince: Société haïtienne d'histoire et de géographie, 1990 [1st ed. published in 1963]), 379–380.

35. Thomas Madiou, "Dessalines," in *Oeuvre des écrivains haïtiens: Auteurs haitiens: Morceaux choisis, précédés de notices biographiques,* edited by Solon Ménos, Dantès Bellegarde, A. Duval, and Georges Sylvain (Port-au-Prince: Imprimerie de Mme. F. Smith, 1904), 33. In contrast, Philippe Girard disputes these dates and notes that there is no archival evidence for May 18, 1803, as the date of the creation of the flag. He incorrectly states that Madiou made no mention of the flag—that was true for his multivolume history of Haiti, but in a posthumously published article on Dessalines, Madiou did in fact describe Dessalines tearing the white out of the French flag. See Philippe R. Girard, "Birth of a Nation: The Creation of the Haitian Flag and Haiti's French Revolutionary Heritage," *Journal of Haitian Studies* 15, no. 1/2 (2009): 135.

36. C. B. Auguste and M. B. Auguste, *Pour le drapeau.*

37. Nicole Willson, "Unmaking the Tricolore: Catherine Flon, Material Testimony and Occluded Narratives of Female-Led Resistance in Haiti and the Haitian *Dyaspora,*" *Slavery & Abolition* 41 (2020): 131–148.

38. Rameau and Ambroise, *La révolution de Saint-Domingue,* 379–380.

39. D'Henin, "Mémoire historique et politique sur la situation actuelle à St. Domingue," Thermidor an 11 [July–August 1803], UF-RP, box 19, ff. 2016.

40. "Feuilleton Extraordinaire," *Gazette officielle de Saint-Domingue,* 22 Prairial an 11 [June 11, 1803], no. 93.

41. Dessalines to Nugent, June 23, 1803, NLJ, MS 72; copy available at TNA, CO 137/110.

42. Dessalines to Nugent, June 23, 1803.

43. Dessalines to the President of the United States [Jefferson], June 23, 1803, Library of Congress, Manuscript Division, Thomas Jefferson Papers, Series I: General Correspondence, 1651–1827, microfilm, reel 028.

44. Dessalines to [Jefferson], June 23, 1803.

45. Dessalines to [Jefferson], June 23, 1803.

46. Joseph Bunel to Dessalines, on an American ship going to Jérémie, Baltimore, November 9, 1803, SHD, GR7, B10.

47. "Femme Dessalines" to "Madame Bunel," Gonaïves, November 12, 1804, RWL-AUC, Henry P. Slaughter Collection, box 37, folder 63, item 1.

48. Castet to Minister of the Navy and Colonies, [1804], SHD, Marine, BB4 no. 208.

49. Castet to Pichon, August 27, 1804, Philadelphia, SHD, Marine, BB4 no. 208.
50. Madiou, *Histoire d'Haïti,* tome 3, 7–8, 20, 35; Boisrond-Tonnerre, *Mémoires,* 78.
51. Boisrond-Tonnerre, *Mémoires,* 84; Madiou, *Histoire d'Haïti,* tome 3, 17–21.
52. Boisrond-Tonnerre, *Mémoires,* 86; Madiou, *Histoire d'Haïti,* tome 3, 42.
53. Madiou, *Histoire d'Haïti,* tome 3, 43.
54. Madiou, *Histoire d'Haïti,* tome 3, 48.
55. Madiou, *Histoire d'Haïti,* tome 3, 48.
56. Madiou, *Histoire d'Haïti,* tome 3, 67.
57. David Geggus, *Haitian Revolutionary Studies* (Bloomington: Indiana University Press, 2002), 215.
58. "Copie de la lettre que j'écrivis à Ferou, homme de couleur, commandant une partie des insurgés du Sud, à Jérémie le 20 messidor an 11 [July 9, 1803]," in Fressinet's journal of the evacuation de Jérémie, SHD, GR7, B10.
59. "Copie de la lettre que j'écrivis à Ferou."
60. "Copie de la lettre que j'écrivis à Ferou."
61. The copy of the letter is four pages long. "Copie d'une lettre de Jean Jacques Dessalines, Général en Chef de l'armée de St. Domingue; au Général de Brigade fressinet, commandant la ville de Jérémie et sa dependance, du quartier général de Gerard, 24 Messidor an 11, 13 Juillet 1803," SHD, GR7, B10. (A "Bulletin analytique" in the same folder says this document was a response to Fressinet's letter to Férou on July 9.)
62. "Copie d'une lettre de Jean Jacques Dessalines . . . 24 Messidor an 11."
63. "Copie d'une lettre de Jean Jacques Dessalines . . . 24 Messidor an 11."
64. "Copie d'une lettre de Jean Jacques Dessalines . . . 24 Messidor an 11."
65. "Général de brigade Commandant l'armée des incas, combinés contre jérémie, agissant en vertu des pouvoirs qui lui ont été confiés par les chefs; qui eux mêmes les tiennent du Gouvernement Anglais." Peace preliminaries in Jérémie between Fressinet and Férou, SHD, GR7, B10.
66. Peace preliminaries in Jérémie between Fressinet and Férou, SHD, GR7, B10.
67. According to David Geggus, the only other use of "armée des incas" was by Capoix on July 3, 1803. Madiou claimed that Dessalines's troops used it in late 1802, but none of Dessalines's letterheads adopted the name. The name was affiliated with Geffrard's troops in Madiou's version of events, and specifically associated with the south in mid-1803. Geggus, *Haitian Revolutionary Studies,* 215.
68. Dessalines to [John Thomas Duckworth], Gonaïves, 14 Thermidor an 11 [August 2, 1803], "G—autres documents annexes," AN, Pierrefitte, AB/XIX/5002.
69. Eleven days later, he used "armée de Saint Domingue." See, for example, Dessalines to Duckworth, August 13, 1803, TNA, ADM 1/253 (original document with an original signature); he also used the old name in a letter in the same folder from August 17, 1803. On September 17, 1803, a British official called him "General Dessalines commander in chief of the native army of Saint Domingo": [Unknown], Kingston, September 17, 1803, TNA, ADM 1/253.
70. Dessalines to [John Thomas Duckworth], Gonaïves, le 14 Thermidor an 11.
71. Nugent to Dessalines, Jamaica, August 18, 1803, TNA, CO 137/110, f. 176.
72. James Walker and Hugh Cathcart, August [2]7, 1803, TNA, ADM 1/253.

73. Walker and Cathcart, August [2]7, 1803, TNA, ADM 1/253.

74. Madiou, *Histoire d'Haïti*, tome 3, 96.

75. Nicolas Geffrard to Sebastián de Kindelán y Oregón, Jérémie, 27 Fructidor an 11 [September 14, 1803], in *Documentos para la historia de Haití en el Archivo Nacional*, edited by José Luciano Franco (Havana: Archivo Nacional de Cuba, 1954), 152–154, cited in Girard, "Birth of a Nation," 144.

76. Geffrard to Kindelán y Oregón, 27 Fructidor an 11.

77. Dessalines to Gérin, Viet, 24 Thermidor an 11 [September 11, 1803], reproduced in Madiou, *Histoire d'Haïti*, tome 3, 59.

78. Madiou, *Histoire d'Haïti*, tome 3, 61.

79. Madiou, *Histoire d'Haïti*, tome 3, 66–67.

80. Dessalines, "Extrait du Journal tenu pendant l'expédition entreprise contre le Port-au-Prince, par le Général en chef de l'armée Indigène," 24 Vendémiaire an 12 [October 17, 1803], (Port-au-Prince: Imprimerie du Gouvernement), p. 3, SHD, GR7, B10.

81. See, for example, Dessalines to [Duckworth], Habitation Niel, August 13, 1802, TNA, ADM 1/253.

82. By November 6, Dessalines used printed letterhead with "Liberté ou la Mort" and "Le Général en chef de l'armée Indigène." See Dessalines to Nugent, Limbé, November 6, 1803, NLJ, MS 72, box 2, 851N.

83. Dessalines, "Extrait du Journal tenu pendant l'expédition entreprise contre le Port-au-Prince."

84. Joseph Balthazar Inginac, *Mémoires de Joseph Balthazar Inginac, Général de Division, Ex-Secrétaire-Général, près S.E. l'Ex-Président d'Haïti, depuis 1797–jusqu'à 1843* (Kingston, Jamaica: J. R. de Cordova, 1843), 12–13.

85. Inginac, *Mémoires de Joseph Balthazar Inginac*, 12.

86. Dessalines to the inhabitants of Port-au-Prince, 2e jour complémentaire an 11 [September 19, 1803], quoted in *Catalogue of the Unpublished Papers of Generals Leclerc and Rochambeau during the War of Independence in Haiti, 1802–3*, AN, Pierrefitte, 135/AP/1. The dates outlined in the extract conflict with the date of the printed proclamation. It is possible that there were two addresses to the inhabitants of Port-au-Prince, or that the date in either the address or the extract was recorded in error.

87. On the proposal for evacuation, see also Inginac, *Mémoires de Joseph Balthazar Inginac*, 12–13.

88. Inginac, *Mémoires de Joseph Balthazar Inginac*, 12–13.

89. Dessalines, "Extrait du Journal tenu pendant l'expédition entreprise contre le Port-au-Prince."

90. Janvier, "Notes sur Dessalines et Toussaint Louverture," 7–8.

91. Tadeusz Łepkowski, quoted in Lundahl, "Defense and Distribution," 83.

92. Madiou, *Histoire d'Haïti*, tome 3, 82.

93. Dessalines does not appear to have used Cap-Haïtien, as the city was later called under Henry Christophe. Dessalines, "Journal de la Campagne du Nord," TNA, CO 173/111.

94. Jean-Pierre Le Glaunec, *L'armée indigène: La défaite de Napoléon en Haïti,* preface by Lyonel Trouillot (Québec: Lux Éditeur, 2014), 61; Dessalines, "Journal de la Campagne du Nord."

95. Madiou, *Histoire d'Haïti,* tome 3, 84.

96. "Narrative of the proceedings," James Walker and Hugh Cathcart, August 27, 1803, NLJ, MS 72, box 2, 493N.

97. Madiou, *Histoire d'Haïti,* tome 3, 90.

98. Madiou, *Histoire d'Haïti,* tome 3, 86.

99. Madiou, *Histoire d'Haïti,* tome 3, 86.

100. Madiou, *Histoire d'Haïti,* tome 3, 87.

101. Madiou, *Histoire d'Haïti,* tome 3, 89.

102. Madiou, *Histoire d'Haïti,* tome 3, 91.

103. Dessalines, "Journal de la Campagne du Nord."

104. Boisrond-Tonnerre, *Mémoires,* 90.

105. Duveyrier signed on behalf of Rochambeau. Dessalines and Duveyrier, "Armées française et indigène," 27 Brumaire an 12 / 19 November 1803, TNA, CO 137/111, f. 12; copy also available at NLJ, MS 72, box 2, 717N.

106. Dessalines and Duveyrier, "Armées française et indigène."

107. Boisrond-Tonnerre, *Mémoires,* 91.

108. Manuscript copies: Dessalines to the citizens and inhabitants of the city of Cap, 27 Brumaire / 19 November 1803, MS 72, NLJ, MS 72, box 2, 852N and 900N (two copies); and TNA, CO 137/110, f. 278 and CO 137/111, f. 166 (two copies). For the printed copy with the note from the president of the Council of Notables, Reynoard, see AN, Paris, microfilm, F3-284.

109. Dessalines to the citizens and inhabitants of the city of Cap, 27 Brumaire.

110. For more on *habitants* as a socioeconomic status, see Meredith Gaffield, "Trust, Obligation and the Racialized Credit Market in Prerevolutionary Cap-Français," in *Voices in the Legal Archives of the French Colonial World: "The King Is Listening,"* edited by Nancy Christie, Michael Gauvreau, and Matthew Gerber (New York: Routledge, 2020), 197.

111. Dessalines to the citizens and inhabitants of the city of Cap, 27 Brumaire.

112. Levasseur, *Événemens,* 29–30.

113. The only remaining archival traces of the November 29, 1803, document are printed English translations in US newspapers, an English pamphlet printed by the Jamaican *Weekly Entertainer,* and a French manuscript transcription in the French military archives, all of which were created in 1804. "Proclamation de Dessalines, Cristophe & Clervaux, Chefs de St. Domingue," copy dated May 8, 1804, SHD, GR7, B11; Jean-Jacques Dessalines, Henry Christophe, and Augustin Clervaux, "Proclamation, 29 November 1803," *Aurora General Advertiser,* January 5, 1804, Philadelphia, no. 4059, p. 2; *Weekly Entertainer,* 1804, NLJ, Pam972.9403 pro. For more on the historiography of this 1803 declaration of independence, see Patrick Tardieu, "The Debate Surrounding the Printing of the Haitian Declaration of Independence: A Review of the Literature," in Gaffield, *Haitian Declaration of Independence,* 58–71.

114. Chelsea Stieber, *Haiti's Paper War: Post-Independence Writing, Civil War, and the Making of the Republic, 1804–1954* (New York: New York University Press, 2020), 4–5.

115. "Proclamation de Dessalines, Cristophe & Clervaux, Chefs de St. Domingue."

116. "Proclamation de Dessalines, Cristophe & Clervaux, Chefs de St. Domingue."

117. "Proclamation de Dessalines, Cristophe & Clervaux, Chefs de St. Domingue."
118. Madiou, *Histoire d'Haïti,* tome 3, 103.
119. Madiou, *Histoire d'Haïti,* tome 3, 113.
120. Loring to Duckworth, November 30, 1803, in *The Gentleman's Magazine and Historical Chronicle for the Year MDCCCIV, vol. LXXIV, part the first* (London: Nichols and Son, 1804), 169.

CHAPTER 10. *LIBERTÉ OU LA MORT*

1. Armée indigène, "Liberté ou la Mort," January 1, 1804, *l'an premier de l'indépendance,* TNA, CO 137/111/1 and TNA, MFQ 1/184.
2. The spelling was inconsistent from the beginning, but Dessalines primarily used "Hayti."
3. Madiou, *Histoire d'Haïti,* tome 3, 114. Following Keegan and Hofman, I am not using "Taíno" to describe the Indigenous population, since "the name 'Taíno' reflects a misuse of the Spanish chronicles by modern historians." William F. Keegan and Corinne L. Hofman, *The Caribbean before Columbus* (New York: Oxford University Press, 2017), 115.
4. Madiou, *Histoire d'Haïti,* tome 3, 115.
5. Tardieu, "Debate Surrounding the Printing of the Haitian Declaration of Independence," 61.
6. Armée indigène, "Liberté ou la Mort," January 1, 1804.
7. Erin Zavitz, "Revolutionary Commemorations: Jean-Jacques Dessalines and Haitian Independence Day, 1804–1904," in Gaffield, *Haitian Declaration of Independence,* 220.
8. David Armitage and Julia Gaffield, "Introduction: The Haitian Declaration of Independence in an Atlantic Context," in Gaffield, *Haitian Declaration of Independence,* 11–17.
9. Daut, *Awakening the Ashes,* 26.
10. Armée indigène, "Liberté ou la Mort," January 1, 1804.
11. Armée indigène, "Liberté ou la Mort," January 1, 1804. This eternal war continued even after Dessalines's death. See Daut, *Tropics of Haiti,* 577.
12. Nessler, *Islandwide Struggle,* 147–148. Ferrand had been the commander of Fort-Dauphin (today Fort Liberté) a port city to the east of Cap which had fallen to the Indigenous Army on September 12. Ferrand had replaced Dessalines's former colleague Pierre Quantin.
13. Nessler, *Islandwide Struggle,* 138, 148.
14. Jenson, *Beyond the Slave Narrative,* 145; Julia Gaffield, *Haitian Connections in the Atlantic World: Recognition after Revolution* (Chapel Hill: University of North Carolina Press, 2015), 18. For an example of his attacks on foreign shipping, see "Extrait des minutes du sécrétariat de la commission spéciale d'Appel des Prises séante à Santo Domingo," 12 Nivôse an 12 [January 3, 1804], SHD, MAR FF3 22; many thanks to Nathan Perl-Rosenthal for sharing this document.
15. Nugent to Hobart, December 21, 1803, TNA, CO 137/111, f. 303.
16. Ferrand was not the only one aspiring to reconquer the island. Several former French colonists and military officers wrote lengthy reports to the French government with recommendations on the best way to defeat the new Haitian government and reinstate

a French colony based on enslaved labor. For example, see Jacques Gaillard to the Minister of the Navy, "Appercú sur les moÿens que l'on devrat emploÿ pour réconquerire la colonie de St. Domingue ÿ Rétablirent ses habitants et faire respecter le gouvernement français," June 25, 1804, SHD, GR7, B11.

17. Nugent to Camden, December 15, 1804, Kingston, Jamaica, TNA, CO 137-113, f. 28; Lundahl, "Defense and Distribution," 80. Madiou outlines a similar plan: *Histoire d'Haïti*, tome 3, 148–149. See also Roulet to Ferrand, "Apperçu [*sic*] sur l'état actuel de la portion de l'isle de St. Domingue occupée par les noirs revoltés," May 12, 1806, SHD, GR7, B11.

18. David Geggus, "Haiti's Declaration of Independence," in Gaffield, *Haitian Declaration of Independence,* 34–35; Deborah Jenson, "Dessalines's American Proclamations of the Haitian Independence," *Journal of Haitian Studies* 15, no. 1 & 2 (2009): 72–102. Haitian sociologist and manuscript collector Daniel Supplice has in his collection a shorter version of the November 29, 1803, document that includes three additional signatures by Vernet, Pétion, and Capoix. It is unclear whether this document is authentic.

19. Tardieu, "Debate Surrounding the Printing of the Haitian Declaration of Independence," 65.

20. Madiou, *Histoire d'Haïti,* tome 3, 114; for more on Boisrond-Tonnerre, see John Garrigus, "'Victims of Our Own Credulity and Indulgence': The Life of Louis-François Boisrond-Tonnerre (1776–1806)," in Gaffield, *Haitian Declaration of Independence,* 42–57.

21. Madiou, *Histoire d'Haïti,* tome 3, 114.

22. By the nineteenth century, place of birth did not always align with citizenship or political allegiance, but it remained a key marker of nationality. See Nathan Perl-Rosenthal, *Citizen Sailors: Becoming American in the Age of Revolution* (Cambridge, MA: Harvard University Press, 2015).

23. Casimir, *Haitians,* 135.

24. Deborah Jenson, "Before Malcolm X, Dessalines: A 'French' Tradition of Black Atlantic Radicalism," *International Journal of Francophone Studies* 10, no. 3 (2007): 342.

25. "Décret du Gouverneur general qui accorde une recompense aux capitaines des bâtiments américains qui ramèneront des Haïtiens dans leur patrie," January 14, 1804, Ministère de la Culture et de la Communication, Haiti, *Lois et actes sous le règne de Jean-Jacques Dessalines* (Port-au-Prince: Éditions Presses Nationales d'Haïti, Collection Angle Droit, 2006), 13. The English translation that was printed in US newspapers used the phrase "native blacks and men of color"; see "Translation: Liberty or Death, Government of Hayti, Arette, January 14, 1st Year of the Independence of Hayti," *Political Calendar* (Newburyport, MA), April 9, 1804, vol. 1, issue 3, p. 3.

26. Léo Élisabeth, "Les relations entre les Petites Antilles françaises et Haïti, de la politique du refoulement à la résignation, 1804–1825," *Outre-Mers* 340–341 (2003): 179. Twelve years later Alexandre Pétion, as president of the Republic of Haiti, took this policy to its logical conclusion: "all Africans and Indians, and the descendants of their blood, born in the colonies or in foreign countries, who come to reside in the Republic will be recognized as Haitians, but will enjoy the right of citizenship only after one year of residence." For more on this constitutional policy, see Ada Ferrer, "Haiti, Free Soil, and Antislavery in the Revolutionary Atlantic," *American Historical Review* 117, no. 1 (2012): 40–66; *Con-*

stitution of the Republic of Hayti (New York: James Tredwell, 1818), Library of Congress, KGS2914 1816 .C66 1818, https://hdl.loc.gov/loc.law/llscd.201076373969.

27. Daut, *Awakening the Ashes,* 32; Geggus, *Haitian Revolutionary Studies,* 207.

28. Ponce Vázquez, *Islanders and Empire,* 34.

29. Armée indigène, "Liberté ou la Mort," January 1, 1804.

30. Armée indigène, "Liberté ou la Mort," January 1, 1804.

31. Armée indigène, "Liberté ou la Mort," January 1, 1804.

32. Duraciné Vaval, "Le gouvernement de Dessalines," *Revue de la Société haïtienne d'histoire, de géographie et de géologie* 28, no. 99 (1955): 63.

33. Quoted in Paul, "Le ressentiment Dessalinien," 149–150; Madiou, *Histoire d'Haïti,* tome 3, 111–112.

34. Armée indigène, "Liberté ou la Mort," January 1, 1804.

35. Armée indigène, "Liberté ou la Mort," January 1, 1804.

36. Malick W. Ghachem, "Law, Atlantic Revolutionary Exceptionalism, and the Haitian Declaration of Independence," in Gaffield, *Haitian Declaration of Independence,* 109.

37. Stieber, *Haiti's Paper War,* 29.

38. Patrick D. Tardieu, "Pierre Roux et Lemery, Imprimeurs de Saint-Domingue à Haïti." *Revue de la Société haïtienne d'histoire, de géographie et de géologie* 218 (2004): 1–30; Edward Corbet to Nugent, January 25, 1804, TNA, CO 137/111, f. 92; Madiou, *Histoire d'Haïti,* tome 3, 119.

39. I identified both copies at the National Archives of the United Kingdom in 2010 and 2011. For the pamphlet version, see TNA, CO 137/111/1. For the broadside version, see TNA, MFQ 1/184. A special issue of the *Revue de la Société haïtienne d'histoire, de géographie et de géologie,* nos. 233–236 (2014), edited by Lewis Ampidu Clorméus and Gaétan Mentor, included several contributions on the Delaration of Independence. On the distinction between an original signed text and an official printed text, see Leslie F. Manigat, "Considérations historiques brèves: À l'occasion d'une découverte de documents d'archives britanniques d'une 'original' de l'acte d'indépendance d'Haïti," 95–97. For a history of Haitians' efforts to find an original text, see Lewis Ampidu Clorméus, "Où est passé l'original de l'acte de l'indépendance d'Haïti?," 47–85. For a close reading of different available versions of the text, see Gaétan Mentor, "Réflexions autour des documents fondateurs de l'état haïtien," 21–46.

40. The Haitian calendar has been in continual use since 1804 and remains so today. Sometimes leaders have appended additional calendars to the Haitian calendar; for example, during the reign of Haitian Emperor Faustin I (1849–1859) and after the end of the US occupation of Haiti (1915–1934).

41. Armée indigène, "Liberté ou la Mort," January 1, 1804.

42. Dessalines, "Arrêté," January 2, 1804, *l'an premier de l'indépendance,* TNA, MFQ 1/184.

43. Casimir, *Haitians,* 36.

44. Dessalines, "Arrêté relative au costume," January 2, 1804, *l'an premier de l'indépendance,* TNA, MFQ 1/184.

45. Inland from Cap, in Grand-Rivière, south of Dondon, in Limbé, in Mirebalais, inland from Port-de-Paix, inland from Gonaïves, inland from Port-au-Prince, inland from Les Cayes, inland from Jacmel, and a series of forts on the route from Gonaïves to Petite

Rivière. Roulet to Ferrand, Santo Domingo, May 12, 1806, SHD, GR7, B11; Guillaume Mauviel to Bonaparte, July 13, 1805, AN, Pierrefitte, AF/IV/1212, p. 38. Many thanks to Jeremy Popkin for sharing the Mauviel source with me. I call the city Marchand-Dessalines for clarity.

46. Christophe to generals and commanders, July 3, 1805, "Henri Christophe, Copie des lettres 1805 [& 1806]," King's College London, FCO2, FOL.F1924 HEN (hereafter cited as "Christophe, Copie des lettres"), p. 105; Christophe to Dessalines, July 3, 1805, "Christophe, Copie des lettres," p. 105. Many thanks to Cameron Monroe for sharing his images of this source with me.

47. See, for example, Christophe to Capoix, April 11, 1806, "Christophe, Copie des lettres," p. 310; Christophe to Benjamin Janot, April 12, 1806, "Christophe, Copie des lettres," p. 310; Christophe to commandant de place, April 12, 1806, "Christophe, Copie des lettres," p. 310; Christophe to Janot, May 13, 1806, "Christophe, Copie des lettres," pp. 337–338; Christophe to Janot, April 30, 1806, "Christophe, Copie des lettres," p. 326.

48. Madiou notes that the construction of the important Fort Laferrière (about seventeen miles south of Cap-Haïtien) began in January 1804; Madiou, *Histoire d'Haïti,* tome 3, 147. Arnold Antonin's recent documentary about Dessalines includes stunning drone footage of some of these forts. Arnold Antonin, director, *Jean-Jacques Dessalines, le vainqueur de Napoléon Bonaparte,* Fokal, 2022, 1 hr., 34 min. Antoine Frinquier, "Relation des évènements du Cap français depuis l'évacuation de l'armée commandée par le général Rochambeau, jusqu'au 20 mai 1804," SHD, GR1 M 597–598.

49. Edward Corbet to Nugent, [n.d., ca. January 15–20, 1804], TNA, CO 137/111, f. 92; Lundahl, "Defense and Distribution," 80; Madiou estimated that the Haitian army was about fifty-two thousand strong: Madiou, *Histoire d'Haïti,* tome 3, 122.

50. Roulet to Ferrand, Santo Domingo, May 12, 1806, SHD, GR7, B11.

51. Gaffield, *Haitian Connections.*

52. For a full analysis of these negotiations, see Julia Gaffield, "Haiti and Jamaica in the Remaking of the Early Nineteenth-Century Atlantic World," *William and Mary Quarterly* 69, no. 3 (2012): 583–614.

53. Dessalines to [Edward Corbet], "Upon the subject of the commercial proposition, received 17th," January 16, 1804, MS 72, box 3, 902N.

54. Edward Corbet, "No 2 Report," January 25, 1804, NLJ, MS 72, box 3, 349N.

55. Corbet, "No 2 Report," January 25, 1804.

56. Dessalines to [Corbet], "Upon the subject of what was proposed respecting Môle Saint-Nicolas, received 17th," January 16, 1804, NLJ, MS 72, box 3, 812N.

57. Dessalines to [Corbet], "Upon the subject of the commercial proposition."

58. "Extrait d'une letter de W. N . . . à Mr. Robert Ritchie," January 13, 1804, SHD, GR7, B11.

59. "Extrait d'une lettre de Mr. Wm N . . . à Wm & Hug. Wilson à Baltimore," January 13, 1804, SHD, GR7, B11.

60. "Extrait d'une lettre de Mr. Fleury Rose à Mr. Pemock à Norfolck [sic]," January 13, 1804, SHD, GR7, B11.

61. "Extrait de la lettre de Messrs Wilson à Mr. Cunningham," January 18, 1804, SHD, GR7, B11.

62. These additional articles can be found in the revised treaty proposal that Corbet brought to Nugent. "French copy of treaty," NLJ, MS 72, box 3, 741N.

63. "French copy of treaty," NLJ, MS 72, box 3, 741N. On Louverture, see Philippe Girard, "Napoléon Bonaparte and the Emancipation Issue in Saint-Domingue, 1799–1803," *French Historical Studies* 32, no. 4 (2009): 591.

64. Gaffield, "Haiti and Jamaica," 586.

65. Corbet to Nugent, January 25, 1804, TNA, CO 137/111, f. 158. On his next visit in February 1804, Corbet estimated that "except at this place [Jérémie] and here only a few, there is not hardly a single proprietor remaining in the island." Corbet to Nugent, February 16, 1804, TNA, CO 137/111, f. 121.

66. Corbet to Nugent, January 25, 1804, TNA, CO 137/111, f. 158.

67. "Extrait d'une lettre de Mr. Moses Treadwell jr à Mr. moses treadwell à Massachusset [*sic*]," January 1804, SHD, GR7, B11.

68. Corbet to Nugent, January 25, 1804, TNA, CO 137/111, f. 158.

69. Corbet to Nugent, January 25, 1804.

70. Armée indigène, "Liberté ou la Mort," January 1, 1804.

71. Madiou also noted that in the early days of January 1804, some white colonists were discussing their hopes for a French reinvasion. Madiou, *Histoire d'Haïti,* tome 3, 126.

72. "New York, March 5," *The Repertory,* Boston, March 13, 1804, p. 2.

73. Bernard Gainot, "'Sur fond de cruelle inhumanité': Les politiques du massacre dans la Révolution de Haïti," *La Révolution française* 3 (2011), https://doi.org/10.4000/lrf.239, paragraph 30; Ashli White, *Encountering Revolution: Haiti and the Making of the Early Republic* (Baltimore: Johns Hopkins University Press, 2010), 57.

74. Haitians assumed that the French were waging war to reenslave them, and so these white men and women should also be seen within the context of what Vincent Brown calls the "Atlantic slave war," the long and sustained assault of daily violence against enslaved Africans which was interspersed with moments of explosive conflict. Brown, *Tacky's Revolt.*

75. I have found several lists of names of people who were allegedly killed in Les Cayes and Jérémie. The lists for Les Cayes contain about 150 unique names, while the list for Jérémie includes 35 names. The lists from Les Cayes claim that an additional unnamed 150 people were executed on shore, and another 45 people who were aboard a French privateer. For Les Cayes, see "Voilà ce que je viens de copier dans le journal de Paris, Philadelphie, 14 Mars," AN, Paris, microfilm, F3/201; "The following Persons have been put to death at Aux Cayes, by order of General Dessalines," *Mercantile Advertiser,* New York, April 17, 1804, p. 2; "List of Persons," *Times,* Charleston, April 6, 1804, p. 4. For Jérémie, see [Perkins] to Nugent, Off Môle Saint-Nicolas, March 17, 1804, TNA, CO137/111, f. 275. Madiou estimated that three thousand people died; Madiou, *Histoire d'Haïti,* tome 3, 141. Jeremy Popkin and Philippe Girard claim that "a few thousand" died; Popkin, "Jean-Jacques Dessalines, Norbert Thoret, and the Violent Aftermath of the Haitian Declaration of Independence," in Gaffield, *Haitian Declaration of Independence,* 116; Girard, "Caribbean Genocide," 142.

76. Louis Dubroca, *La vie de J.-J. Dessalines, chef des noirs révoltes de Saint-Domingue* (Paris: Dubroca [et] Rondonneau, 1804), 123–124.

77. David Brion Davis, "Impact of the French and Haitian Revolutions," in *The Impact of the Haitian Revolution in the Atlantic World*, edited by David Geggus (Columbia: University of South Carolina Press, 2001), 8.

78. Corbet to Nugent, January 25, 1804, TNA, CO 137/111, f. 158. For an earlier instance in which "people of color" or *"anciens libres"* were accused of initiating a "massacre" of white French people, see Manuel Covo, "Le massacre de Fructidor an IV à Saint-Domingue: Violence et politique de la race sous le directoire," *Annales historiques de la Révolution française* 1, no. 395 (2019): 143–169.

79. Grégory Pierrot, "Juste Chanlatte: A Haitian Life," *Journal of Haitian Studies* 25, no. 1 (2019): 50–51.

80. Lecun to Luc Concanen, May 4, 1804, Kingston, ASPF, SC, America Antille, vol. 3, f. 380–381.

81. Stieber, *Haiti's Paper War*, 33.

82. Dessalines, "Empire d'Haïti, Décret, Relatif aux Testamens et autres Actes portant donation de Bien fonds," September 1, 1806, *l'an trois de l'indépendance, et de notre règne le deuxième*, printed in *Gazette politique et commerciale d'Haïti*, Cap, October 2, 1806, *l'an troisième de l'indépendance*, no. 39, p. 2.

83. Dessalines, Aux Cayes, "Liberté ou la Mort," February 7, 1804, *l'an premier de l'indépendance*, NLJ, MS 72, 879N; copy available at TNA, CO 137/111.

84. Corbet to Dessalines, February 10, 1804, TNA, CO 137/111, f. 125.

85. Dessalines to Duckworth, February 12, 1804, TNA, ADM 1/254.

86. Madiou, *Histoire d'Haïti*, tome 3, 128.

87. Pachonski and Wilson, *Poland's Caribbean Tragedy;* Lavalette to Thouvenot, Port-au-Prince, 27 Thermidor an 11 [August 15, 1803], SHD, GR7, B10; Boisrond-Tonnerre, *Mémoires*, 89.

88. "New York, March 5," *New-York Gazette*, March 5, 1804, p. 3.

89. Transcribed copy from the *Journal de Paris*, "Philadelphia, 14 Mars," AN, Paris, microfilm, F3-201; "Nouvelles Étrangères," *Journal de Paris*, 7 Prairial an 12 [May 27, 1804], p. 1; *Mercantile Advertiser*, New York, April 17, 1804.

90. Many of the names can be found on a 1786 map of the plantations in the region: René Phelipeau, "Plan de la plaine du fond de l'Isle à Vache de l'Isle St. Domingue avec les divers canaux d'arrosage," (1786), https://gallica.bnf.fr/ark:/12148/btv1b7003247x.

91. *Virginia Argus* (Richmond), March 24, 1804, vol. 11, issue 1126, p. 3.

92. [Condy Raguet], "A short account of the present state of affairs in St. Domingo (Continued from our paper of 2d inst.)," *Poulson's American Daily Advertiser*, January 4, 1805, p. 2.

93. "St. Domingo," *Times*, London, June 18, 1804, p. 3.

94. Corbet to Nugent, February 29, 1804, NLJ, MS 72, box 3, 665N.

95. Corbet to Dessalines, February 10, 1804, NLJ, MS 72, box 3, 501N.

96. Corbet to Dessalines, February 10, 1804.

97. Corbet to Nugent, February 29, 1804, TNA, CO 137/111, f. 136.

98. Madiou, *Histoire d'Haïti*, tome 3, 129–130.

99. Many former French colonists and French officers submitted reports on the most effective way to "reconquer" the colony, beginning in 1804 and continuing until French rec-

ognition in 1825. Jean-François Brière, *Haïti et la France, 1804–1848: Le rêve brisé* (Paris: Karthala, 2008), 19–26.

100. On Dessalines's "paper war," see Stieber, *Haiti's Paper War*, 30.

101. On the date, see Madiou, *Histoire d'Haïti,* tome 3, 126, and "Extracts of a letter from Mr. Whitfield, dated Kingston Jamaica 9th March 1804," CKS, U840 0211/4.

102. Madiou recounted that it was four men, one of whom had joined the Haitian army. A British emissary claimed that it was six or seven white Frenchmen. See Madiou, *Histoire d'Haïti,* tome 3, 126, and "Extracts of a letter from Mr. Whitfield."

103. Grégory Pierrot's research concludes that the Haitian officer was a French officer named Raynal. Grégory Pierrot, "Theatre in Early Independent Haiti," in *A History of Haitian Literature,* edited by Marlene L. Daut and Kaiama L. Glover (Cambridge, UK: Cambridge University Press, 2024), 45–62.

104. Juste Chanlatte, *Histoire de la catastrophe de Saint-Domingue* (Paris: Librairie de Peytieux, 1824), 74; Madiou, *Histoire d'Haïti,* tome 3, 127.

105. Dessalines to Generals of the Indigenous Army, Marchand, April 1, 1804, *l'an premier de l'indépendance,* TNA, CO 137/113, f. 133; December 21, 1802, original document with signatures available at UF-RP, box 15, ff. 1450.

106. Madiou, *Histoire d'Haïti,* tome 3, 130.

107. John Perkins to Duckworth, March 17, 1804, TNA, ADM 1/254.

108. Dessalines to Generals of the Indigenous Army, Marchand, April 1, 1804.

109. Dessalines to Generals of the Indigenous Army, Marchand, April 1, 1804.

110. Brutus, *L'homme d'Airain,* 362.

111. Gérard M. Laurent, *Six études sur J. J. Dessalines* (Port-au-Prince: Imprimerie Les Presses libres, 1950), 98.

112. Grand Torbec et al. to "principals places de commerce de France," [December 21, 1802], copied on April 1, 1804, by Dessalines, TNA, CO 137/113, f. 133; also available at TNA, CO 137/111, f. 311.

113. Grand Torbec et al., [December 21, 1802].

114. Grand Torbec et al., [December 21, 1802].

115. Grand Torbec et al., [December 21, 1802].

116. Jean-Baptiste, *Le fondateur,* 62–63.

117. Madiou, *Histoire d'Haïti,* tome 3, 127–128.

118. Dessalines to Generals of the Indigenous Army, Marchand, April 1, 1804.

119. Jean-Jacques Dessalines, "Décret relatif aux individus qui on provoqué ou qui ont pris part aux massacres et aux assassinats ordonnés par LECLERC et ROCHAMBEAU," [date incorrectly listed as February 22], published in Gonaïves, *Lois et Actes,* 21–22. An English translation appeared in the *Relf's Philadelphia Gazette,* April 30, 1804, which dates the proclamation to February 29. It includes a cover letter by one of Dessalines's secretaries, "B. Aimé" [possibly Jacques Bien Aimé]. Beaubrun Ardouin cites the *Recueil des lois et actes du gouvernement d'Haïti,* which dates it February 22, when Dessalines was in Aux Cayes, and claims that Linstant de Pradine got the place of publication wrong. I am convinced that instead Ardouin got the date wrong, and that the decree was published on February 29 in Gonaïves. See "No. 10—Décret relative aux individus qui ont

provoqué ou qui ont pris part aux massacres et aux assassinats ordonnés par LECLERC et ROCHAMBEAU," in A. Linstant de Pradine, *Recueil général des lois & actes du gouvernement d'Haïti depuis la proclamation de son indépendance jusqu'à nos jours, tome 1er 1804–1808*, 2nd ed. (Paris: A. Durand, Pédone-Lauriel, 1886), 15.

120. Boisrond-Tonnerre, *Mémoires*, 74.

121. Dessalines to the Generals of the Indigenous Army, Marchand, April 1, 1804.

122. "Nouvelles Étrangères," *Journal de Paris*, March 4, 1804, p. 1.

123. "Nouvelles Étrangères, New York, 3 Mars," *Journal de Paris,* May 6, 1804, no. 226, p. 1467. Available online at https://books.google.com/books?id=5FtCX9u5LR0C&pg=PA1467#v=onepage&q&f=false.

124. Martin Oster to Charles-Maurice de Talleyrand-Périgord, March 15, 1804, MAE, M.D., Amérique, vol. 15.

125. Ferrand, "Aux Habitans Blancs de l'île de Saint-Domingue, réfugiés dans les colonies voisines," March 17, 1804, DNA, Generalguvernementet, Breve fra fremmede autoriteter, 1774D-1807G.

126. Corbet to Nugent, March 23, 1804, TNA, CO 137/111, f. 228.

127. The article also noted that an excerpt of a proclamation attributed to Dessalines was said to be a forgery, but it is unlikely that the article was referring to the February 29 proclamation because of the timing of the publication; the Haitian government also did not publicly circulate the document until later. "Blacks of St. Domingo," *Columbian Centinel & Massachusetts Federalist,* Boston, March 17, 1804, p. 2.

128. Perkins to [unknown, but catalogued with the papers of the governor of Jamaica, George Nugent], March 24, 1804, NLJ, MS 72, box 3, 721N.

129. Perkins to Duckworth, April 8, 1804, TNA, ADM 1/254.

130. [Perkins] to [Nugent], March 17, 1804, TNA, CO 137/111, f. 275.

131. See, for example, Popkin, "Jean-Jacques Dessalines, Norbert Thoret," 122 and 125.

132. Madiou, *Histoire d'Haïti,* tome 3, 134.

133. Dessalines to the Generals of the Indigenous Army, April 1, 1804.

134. Dessalines to the Generals of the Indigenous Army, April 1, 1804.

135. Boisrond-Tonnerre, *Mémoires,* 74. The Latin phrase is a reference to one of Aesop's fables of that title in which the frogs are scolded: "you scorn'd the good king that you had, and therefore you shall bear the bad." http://www.mythfolklore.net/aesopica/phaedrus/12.htm.

136. On trying to uncover Bien-Aimé's identity, see Jenson, "Dessalines's American Proclamations of the Haitian Independence," 80.

137. B. Aimé [possibly Jacques Bien Aimé] to Mr. Relf, April 1, 1804, published in *Relf's Philadelphia Gazette,* April 30, 1804, p. 3.

138. Madiou, *Histoire d'Haïti,* tome 3, 135.

139. Dacres to Duckworth, May 15, 1804, TNA, ADM 1/254.

140. Guillaume Mauviel to Bonaparte, July 13, 1805, AN, Pierrefitte, AF/IV/1212.

141. Frinquier, "Relation des évènements du Cap français depuis l'évacuation de l'armée commandée par le général Rochambeau, jusqu'au 20 mai 1804."

142. M. Atkinson [?] to unknown, October 30, 1804, TNA, CO 137/113, f. 6.

143. "Recensement," October 12, 1804, Gros Morne, John Carter Brown Library, b6297492, https://archive.org/details/recensement0ohait/page/n1/mode/2up.

144. [Condy Raguet], "Circumstantial account of the MASSACRE in St. Domingo, in May 1806. Its causes &c," *Poulson's American Daily Advertiser,* October 8, 1806, p. 2. For other white French people who remained in Haiti, see Mentor, "Réflexions autour des documents fondateurs de l'état Haïtien," 45.

145. Madiou, *Histoire d'Haïti,* tome 3, 160.

146. Blank naturalization form, "Le Gouverneur General, a tous qu'il appartiendra," [n.d., attached to a document from June 7, 1804], TNA, ADM 1/254.

147. Roulet to Ferrand, Santo Domingo, "Apperçu sur l'état actuel de la portion de l'isle de St. Domingue occupée par les noirs révoltés," May 12, 1806, SHD, GR7, B11; Jean-Claude Nouët, Claude Nicollier, and Yves Nicollier, eds., *La vie aventureuse de Norbert Thoret dit l'Américain* (Paris: Éditions du Port-au-Prince, 2007), 67. Thank you to Jeremy Popkin for sharing a copy of this book.

148. Juste Chanlatte was the secretary. Madiou, *Histoire d'Haïti,* tome 3, 145.

149. Dessalines, "Proclamation aux Habitans d'Haïti," Cap, April 28, 1804, *l'an premier de l'indépendance* (Cap: P. Roux, imprimeur du gouvernement), TNA, CO 137/113, f. 138.

150. Dessalines, "Proclamation aux Habitans d'Haïti," Cap, April 28, 1804.

151. Pierrot, *Black Avenger,* 123.

152. Dessalines, "Proclamation aux Habitans d'Haïti," Cap, April 28, 1804.

153. Dessalines, "Proclamation aux Habitans d'Haïti," Cap, April 28, 1804.

154. This English translation is taken from the *Connecticut Herald:* "Liberty or Death. Proclamation. Jean Jacques Dessalines, Governor-General, to the Inhabitants of Hayti," *Connecticut Herald,* New Haven, June 12, 1804, vol. 1, issue 33, p. 2.

155. Dessalines, "Proclamation aux Habitans d'Haïti," Cap, April 28, 1804.

156. Dessalines, "Proclamation aux Habitans d'Haïti," Cap, April 28, 1804.

157. Emphasis in original. Dessalines, "Proclamation aux Habitans d'Haïti," Cap, April 28, 1804.

158. Two exceptions were Henry Christophe's 1807 and 1811 constitutions.

159. Stieber, *Haiti's Paper War,* 29.

160. Dessalines, "Proclamation aux Habitans d'Haïti," Cap, April 28, 1804.

161. On constitutive justice, see Sophie Wahnich, *In Defence of the Terror: Liberty or Death in the French Revolution* (London: Verso, 2016), 42. See also Pierrot, *Black Avenger,* 123.

162. Dessalines, "Proclamation aux Habitans d'Haïti," Cap, April 28, 1804; see also Boisrond-Tonnerre, *Mémoires,* 92.

163. The article was published in translation in the London *Times,* and I have not located an original copy; see "Proclamation of Dessalines," [May 2, 1804], *Times,* London, September 26, 1804, p. 3.

164. Dessalines to Nugent, May 13, 1804, MS 72, box 2, 628N.

165. Quoted in Jean-Pierre Le Glaunec, *The Cry of Vertières: Liberation, Memory, and the Beginning of Haiti,* translated by Jonathan Kaplansky (Montreal: McGill-Queen's University Press, 2020), 96. Ferrand to Minister of the Navy, 28 Messidor an 12 [July 17, 1804], AN, Pierrefitte, AF/IV/1213.

CHAPTER 11. THE EMPIRE OF HAYTI RISES
BEFORE THE EYES OF THE ASTONISHED UNIVERSE

1. Vernet, Clervaux, Christophe, Pétion, Gabart, Geffrard, et al., "Nomination de l'Empereur d'Hayti," January 25, 1804, *l'an premier de l'indépendance* [date is likely backdated], TNA, CO 137/113, f. 32.

2. "Nomination de l'Empereur d'Hayti."

3. "Ordre des cérémonies du couronnement de Jean-Jacques Dessalines, empereur d'Haïti" at Port-au-Prince on the Champ-de-Mars, Alexandre Pétion, ministère de la culture et de la communication, Haiti, September 6, 1804, *Lois et Actes,* 37–38.

4. Madiou, *Histoire d'Haïti,* tome 3, 174.

5. "Couplets, Chantés et présentés à Sa Majesté JACQUES 1er, Empereur d'Haïti; Par C. Cezar Télémaque, contrôleur du département du Nord," *Gazette politique et commerciale d'Haïti,* Cap, no. 2, November 22, 1804.

6. Madiou, *Histoire d'Haïti,* tome 3, 175. Lundahl argues that by not creating a nobility, "Dessalines put himself in a very dangerous position": Lundahl, "Defense and Distribution," 97. Vaval, in contrast, claims it was a decision "plein de justesse et de raison": Vaval, "Le gouvernement de Dessalines," 67.

7. Dessalines to generals and military personnel, [n.d., late 1804], copy, SHD, GR7, B11.

8. Nugent to Earl Camden, October 12, 1804, CKS, U840 027/6, and TNA, CO 137/112, f. 134. Nugent received a printed copy of the nomination and acceptance and forwarded the documents to London: Nugent to Earl Camden, December 15, 1804, TNA, CO 137/113, f. 28.

9. See, for example, Alexander Murray to Lord Hawkesbury, November 2, 1804, Turks Island, TNA, CO 23/46, f. 166. Cobert referred to Dessalines as "His Majesty the Emperor" in a letter to Dessalines's secretary on December 15, 1804, even though the British had not yet diplomatically recognized Haiti or Dessalines. Corbet to Chanlatte, December 15, 1804, Kingston, TNA, CO 137/114, f. 13.

10. Price-Mars, *La République d'Haïti,* tome 1, 66.

11. Dessalines, "Aux Habitans de la Partie Espagnole," May 8, 1804, *l'an premier de l'indépendance,* TNA, CO 137/113, f. 139.

12. For example, see Corbet to Nugent, June 2, 1804, Jamaica, TNA, CO 137/111, f. 334A, and Corbet to Nugent, June 5, 1804, Jamaica, TNA, CO 137/111, f. 340.

13. Madiou, *Histoire d'Haïti,* tome 3, 160.

14. "No 2 Report," Corbet to Nugent, January 25, 1804, NLJ, MS 72, box 3, 349N; Dessalines to Duckworth, September 16, 1803, TNA, ADM 1/253; Nugent to Earl Camden, October 12, 1804, CKS, U840 027/6, and TNA, CO 137/112, f. 134.

15. See, for example, report by James Walker and Hugh Cathcart, September 27, 1803, TNA, ADM 1/253.

16. Mansuy, "Moyens à employer pour reconquérir St. Domingue," 5 Thermidor an 13 [July 24, 1805], AN, Paris, microfilm, CC9A 38; Gaillard Déjourné, "Projet Présenté à Son Excellence Monseigneur le Ministre de la Marine," 8 Vendémiaire an 14 [September 30, 1805], AN, Paris, microfilm, CC9A 38.

17. These kinds of accounts were already popular, and when Henry Christophe received a

copy of René Périn's 1802 *Incendie du Cap* in December 1805, he sent it to Dessalines "pour vous amuser dans vos moments de repos; le contenu de cette Brochure, ne laisse aucune doute sur les vues de nos Ennemis, puisqu'ils ne nous accordant pas même le titre d'hommes, et jugent que nous ne sommes pas dignes de la liberté que nous jouissons, que nous avons su conquérir par la force de nos armes, & qu'il n'appartient pas à aucune puissance sur la terre de nous Ravir! Mais qu'ils viennent, je leur donnerai de Nouvelles preuves!" Christophe to Dessalines, December 13, 1805, "Christophe, Copie des lettres," p. 230; René Périn, *Incendie du Cap, ou Le règne de Toussaint-Louverture* (Paris: Chez les Marchands de Nouveautés, 1802).

18. Boisrond-Tonnerre, *Mémoires,* 5.

19. Boisrond-Tonnerre, *Mémoires,* 93.

20. Boisrond-Tonnerre, *Mémoires,* 3.

21. Boisrond-Tonnerre, *Mémoires,* 4.

22. On Dubroca and Napoléon, see James Stephen, *Buonaparte in the West Indies; or, The History of Toussaint Louverture, the African Hero* (London: Printed for J. Hatchard, 1803), 5, and Brutus, *L'homme d'Airain,* 28.

23. Louis Dubroca, *La vie de Toussaint-Louverture, chef des noirs insurgés de Saint-Domingue* (Paris: Dubroca, 1802), 6.

24. Dubroca, *La vie de J.-J. Dessalines,* 7–8.

25. Dubroca, *La vie de J.-J. Dessalines,* 16.

26. Dubroca, *La vie de J.-J. Dessalines,* 16.

27. Dubroca, *La vie de J.-J. Dessalines,* 135.

28. Geggus, *Haitian Revolutionary Studies,* 208; Jenson, "Jean-Jacques Dessalines and the African Character of the Haitian Revolution," 620; Vertus Saint-Louis, "Le surgissement du terme 'Africain' pendant la revolution de Saint-Domingue," *Ethnologies* 28, no. 1 (2006): 151.

29. Signed "Gas," "Notes sur l'état politique de St. Domingue, Paris, 9 Nivôse an 9 [December 30, 1800], AN, Pierrefitte, AF/IV/1212.

30. This claim followed a description of Henry Christophe as a "Creole of Grenada." See Edward Corbet, "Submission and afterwards Revolt of the Blacks in St. Domingo," January 28, 1803, TNA, CO 137/110, f. 339.

31. "ancient esclave Bossale," in Levasseur, *Événemens,* 25. For a comprehensive list of white foreigners calling Dessalines an "African" and claiming that he was born in Africa, see Jenson, "Jean-Jacques Dessalines and the African Character of the Haitian Revolution," 615–638. See also Alexander Murray to Lord Hawkesbury, November 2, 1804, Turks Island, TNA, CO 23/46, f. 166; M. A. Matinée, *Anecdotes de la révolution de Saint-Domingue, racontées par Guillaume Mauviel, évêque de la colonie (1799–1804)* (Saint-Lô: Imprimerie d'Élie Fils, 1885), 120.

32. Levasseur, *Événemens,* 30–31.

33. Daut, *Tropics of Haiti,* 84.

34. Dubroca, *La vie de J.-J. Dessalines,* 26.

35. Dubroca, *La vie de J.-J. Dessalines,* 119.

36. Madiou, *Histoire d'Haïti,* tome 3, 168.

37. Stieber, *Haiti's Paper War,* 24.

38. Madiou, *Histoire d'Haïti*, tome 3, 168.
39. Madiou, *Histoire d'Haïti*, tome 3, 169.
40. Dessalines to Pétion, August 8, 1804. Letter reproduced in Madiou, *Histoire d'Haïti*, tome 3, 169.
41. Garrigus, "Victims of Our Own Credulity and Indulgence," 48; Pierrot, "Theatre in Early Independent Haiti."
42. Christophe to Madame Dessalines, October 21, 1806, "Christophe, Copie des lettres," pp. 434–436; letter quoted in Eveillard, "Claire Heureuse," 10.
43. Stieber, *Haiti's Paper War*, 41.
44. Stieber, *Haiti's Paper War*, 41–42.
45. Madiou, *Histoire d'Haïti*, tome 3, 169–170.
46. Dessalines to Pétion, August 14, 1804. Letter reproduced in Madiou, *Histoire d'Haïti*, tome 3, 170.
47. Madiou, *Histoire d'Haïti*, tome 3, 170.
48. "Nomination de l'Empereur d'Hayti, J. J. Dessalines," TNA, CO 137/113, f. 32.
49. Dessalines, "Brevet," February 15, 1804, Les Cayes, BPL, MS Haiti 70-21; on the possible January/February 1804 chronology, see Daut, *Awakening the Ashes*, 213–214.
50. Nugent to Camden, December 15, 1804, TNA, CO 137/113, f. 28.
51. Madiou claimed that Dessalines wrote to Pétion on September 4, 1804, using the title "emperor." See Madiou, *Histoire d'Haïti*, tome 3, 175.
52. Madiou, *Histoire d'Haïti*, tome 3, 171.
53. Jacob Lewis to unknown, October 1, 1804, State Department Consular Despatches, Cap Haitien Series, vol. 4, file microcopies of records in NARA, no. 9, roll 4.
54. Dessalines to Bonaparte, October 9, 1804, *an 1er de l'indépendance et de mon règne le 1er mois*, ADG, Généralités—61 J 25 (1804–1992), https://archives.gironde.fr/ark:/25651/vtae9a5cbc2bf46cb75/daogrp/0/3. Miriam Franchina has identified a second copy of this letter in Trogen, KB AR, Fa Zellweger: 41/b: DessJJ: 1804. 10.09. Several aspects of this letter point to it being a fake: (1) The signature on the letter is "Jacques," and no other letter by Dessalines is signed with anything other than "Dessalines" (with the exception of the 1795 letter signed by a secretary). (2) The letter claims a location of Port-au-Prince, but Dessalines was in Marchand-Dessalines at the time. (3) The letterhead states *"Égalité, Fraternité,"* but Dessalines's letterhead would have said *"Liberté ou la Mort."* (4) The letter claims that Dessalines does not have any children or a wife. Franchina's identification of a second copy of the letter suggests that further evidence might come to light regarding the authenticity of the letter, and I am grateful to her for sharing her research findings with me.
55. Stieber, *Haiti's Paper War*, 43. The printed signature on the document was "CH......" as had been the case with the earlier *Hymne haïtiène*. The signatures are not identical, since the *Hymne haïtiène* only had six periods, but, given that the Haitian press did not consistently spell the name of the country, I do not give that too much weight. [Juste Chanlatte], *À mes concitoyens*, [mid-1804, distributed with the nomination of Dessalines as emperor] (Port-au-Prince: Imprimerie du Gouvernement), TNA, CO 137/113, f. 38.
56. [Chanlatte], *À mes concitoyens*.

57. [Chanlatte], *À mes concitoyens.*

58. [Chanlatte], *À mes concitoyens.*

59. On the letter supporting Rochambeau, see Grand Torbec et al., [December 21, 1802].

60. The new Haitian dating system now included an addendum to mark the establishment of the empire. The first anniversary of Haitian independence, therefore, was "January 1, 1805, year two of the independence of Haiti, and the first of our reign."

61. Zavitz, "Revolutionary Commemorations," 222; Madiou, *Histoire d'Haïti,* tome 3, 234–235.

62. Mollien, *Haïti ou Saint-Domingue,* tome 2, 54; translated and quoted in Jenson, "African Character of the Haitian Revolution," 630.

63. Averill Gage, *A Day for the Hunter, a Day for the Prey: Popular Music and Power in Haiti* (Chicago: University of Chicago Press, 1997), 33.

64. Zavitz, "Revolutionary Commemorations," 222.

65. Madiou, *Histoire d'Haïti,* tome 3, 187.

66. Zavitz, "Revolutionary Commemorations," 222–223; Christophe to Dessalines, January 3, 1805, "Christophe, Copie des lettres," p. 1.

67. Christophe to [Paul] Romain, [Toussaint] Brave, and Military Commanders, January 3, 1805, "Christophe, Copie des lettres," p. 2.

68. Christophe to Dessalines, January 1, 1805, "Christophe, Copie des lettres," p. 1.

69. Christophe to Dessalines, January 12, 1805, "Christophe, Copie des lettres," p. 4. The *Gazette* published an account of the northern Independence Day celebrations on January 10, 1805. "Empire d'Haïti, Du Cap, le 9 Janvier," *Gazette politique et commercial d'Haïti,* Cap, January 10, 1805, *l'an deuxième de l'indépendance,* p. 36.

70. The British counted about thirty-nine ships in addition to barges and feluccas in Haiti's navy in late 1804. Corbet, Kingston, December 14, 1804, TNA, CO 137/113, f. 42.

71. Madiou, *Histoire d'Haïti,* tome 3, 158.

72. Nessler, *Islandwide Struggle,* 150.

73. Graham Nessler frames Ferrand's actions as reactionary (a response to Dessalines's executions), but he was already threatening reinvasion before Dessalines executed some of the remaining white French people. Nessler, *Islandwide Struggle,* 149, 153.

74. Nessler, *Islandwide Struggle,* 138, 141, 155.

75. "Adresse de sa Majesté l'Empereur aux Habitants de l'île d'Haïti, à son retour de la Campagne de Santo-Domingo," *Gazette politique et commerciale d'Haïti,* Cap, May 30, 1805, *l'an deuxième de l'indépendance,* no. 25, p. 1. Quoted and translated in Lundahl, "Defense and Distribution," 81.

76. Christophe to Dessalines, February 14, 1805, "Christophe, Copie des lettres," p. 18; Nugent to Camden, Kingston, December 15, 1804, TNA, CO 137/113, f. 28.

77. Nugent to John Sullivan, July 21, 1804, NAM, 6807-183-3, p. 265.

78. Murray to Lord Hawkesbury, November 2, 1804, Turks Island, TNA, CO 23/46, f. 166.

79. Nugent to Edward Cooke, November 18, 1804, TNA, CO 137/113, f. 4.

80. Vaval, "Le gouvernement de Dessalines," 67–68; Nessler, *Islandwide Struggle,* 161.

81. "Arrêté du general FERRAND, mentionné dans l'adresse du n. 22," January 6, 1805, printed in *Lois et Actes,* 46–48.

82. Nessler, *Islandwide Struggle,* 158.

83. "Arrêté du general FERRAND, mentionné dans l'adresse du n. 22," January 6, 1805.

84. Christophe to Dessalines, January 26, 1805, and Christophe to l'administrateur principal [Roumage, jeune], January 30, 1805, in "Christophe, Copie des lettres," pp. 9–11.

85. Christophe to [Paul] Romain, [Toussaint] Brave, and Raymond, January 26, 1805, and Christophe to administrateur principal [Roumage, jeune], January 26, 1805, in "Christophe, Copie des lettres," pp. 8–9.

86. Christophe to Dessalines, January 26, "Christophe, Copie des lettres," pp. 9–10; on the number of troops, see Archibald Kane to Elias Kane, Saint-Marc, February 20, 1805, TNA, HCA 42/426.

87. Christophe to Romain, February 13, 1805, "Christophe, Copie des lettres," p. 15; Christophe to Brave and Raimond [Raymond], February 8, 1805, "Christophe, Copie des lettres," p. 14; Christophe to Vernet, February 13, 1805, "Christophe, Copie des lettres," p. 15; Christophe to Roumage and l'administeur principal au Cap, January 25, 1805, "Christophe, Copie des lettres," p. 8.

88. Christophe to Noë Joachim, January 21, 1805, "Christophe, Copie des lettres," p. 7.

89. Christophe to Dessalines, January 31, 1805, "Christophe, Copie des lettres," pp. 11–12.

90. Dessalines, "Journal de la campagne de Santo-Domingo (Adresse de l'Empereur au peuple)," April 12, 1805, printed in Lois et Actes, 48–54; Vaval, "Le gouvernement de Dessalines," 68.

91. Archibald Kane to Elias Kane, Saint-Marc, February 11, 1805, TNA, HCA 42/426.

92. Some sources state that Dessalines attacked with thirty thousand troops, but it is unlikely that the entire Haitian army was that numerous at the time. See, for example, Lundahl, "Defense and Distribution," 82. On twenty thousand troops, see "No. 37," extract of a letter from Archibald McElroy Jr. to his wife in Pennsylvania, Saint-Marc, February 22, 1805; "No. 43," extract of a letter from A. J. Lewis to Mrs. Huldah Nandyke, Saint-Marc, February 21, 1805; extract of a letter from M. D. Lewis to Mr. Sam'l McCall, Philadelphia, Saint-Marc, February 19, 1805; "Exhibit No. 17," Archibald Kane to Elias Kane, February 20, 1805; "No. 41," extract of a letter from Nath'l Dillhorn to Mr. C. Collins, Saint-Marc, February 22, 1805; "No. 46," extract of a letter from Wm. Ely to Mr. J. Catling, Saint-Marc, February 20, 1805; all in TNA, HCA 42/426. On munitions, see Christophe to Romain, February 16, 1805, "Christophe, Copie des lettres," p. 19.

93. Christophe to [Roumage, jeune], February 14, 1805, "Christophe, Copie des lettres," p. 16.

94. Dessalines, "Journal de la campagne de Santo-Domingo (Adresse de l'Empereur au peuple)."

95. Christophe to Dessalines, January 17, 1805, "Christophe, Copie des lettres," pp. 5–6; Christophe to Dessalines, January 26, 1805, "Christophe, Copie des lettres," pp. 9–10; on "les nords," see Jean-Jacques-Jules Cornilliac, Recherches chronologiques et historiques sur l'origine et la propagation de la fièvre jaune dans les Antilles (Fort-de-France, Martinique: Imprimerie du Gouvernement, 1867).

96. Christophe to Dessalines, April 11, 1805, "Christophe, Copie des lettres," pp. 38–39.

97. Christophe to Brave, February 3, 1805, "Christophe, Copie des lettres," p. 14; Christophe to Raymond, February 4, 1805, "Christophe, Copie des lettres," p. 14; Christophe to Dessalines, February 14, 1805 (second letter on this date), "Christophe, Copie des lettres," pp. 18–19.

98. Christophe to commandant de la Place du Cap, February 21, 1805, "Christophe, Copie des lettres," p. 22; Christophe to Captain Bernato, February 21, 1805, "Christophe, Copie des lettres," p. 22; Christophe to ministre des finances, February 20, 1805, "Christophe, Copie des lettres," p. 20.

99. Dessalines, "Journal de la campagne de Santo-Domingo (Adresse de l'Empereur au peuple)."

100. Girard, *Slaves Who Defeated Napoléon*, 336.

101. Girard, *Slaves Who Defeated Napoléon*, 336.

102. Dessalines, "Journal de la campagne de Santo-Domingo (Adresse de l'Empereur au peuple)."

103. Dessalines, "Journal de la campagne de Santo-Domingo (Adresse de l'Empereur au peuple)"; Christophe to Dessalines, March 18, 1805 (second letter on this date), "Christophe, Copie des lettres," pp. 27–28.

104. Dessalines, "Journal de la campagne de Santo-Domingo (Adresse de l'Empereur au peuple)."

105. Price-Mars, *La République d'Haïti*, tome 1, 67–68.

106. Dessalines, "Journal de la campagne de Santo-Domingo (Adresse de l'Empereur au peuple)."

107. Christophe to Dessalines, March 13, "Christophe, Copie des lettres," p. 25; Christophe to Dessalines, March 23, 1805, "Christophe, Copie des lettres," p. 30.

108. Dessalines, "Journal de la campagne de Santo-Domingo (Adresse de l'Empereur au peuple)."

109. Christophe to Dessalines, March 18, 1805, "Christophe, Copie des lettres," p. 27. See also Christophe to Colonel Albert, March 25, 1805, "Christophe, Copie des lettres," p. 32.

110. Christophe to Poux, March 22, 1805, "Christophe, Copie des lettres," p. 29.

111. Christophe to Albert, March 24, 1805, "Christophe, Copie des lettres," p. 31.

112. Christophe to Dessalines, March 21, 1805, "Christophe, Copie des lettres," pp. 28–29.

113. Christophe to Dessalines, March 23, 1805, "Christophe, Copie des lettres," p. 30.

114. Dessalines, "Journal de la campagne de Santo-Domingo (Adresse de l'Empereur au peuple)."

115. Nessler, *Islandwide Struggle*, 159.

116. Girard, *Slaves Who Defeated Napoléon*, 337.

117. Christophe to Dessalines, March 27, 1805, "Christophe, Copie des lettres," p. 32; Christophe to Dessalines, March 22, 1805, "Christophe, Copie des lettres," p. 29.

118. Dessalines, "Journal de la campagne de Santo-Domingo (Adresse de l'Empereur au peuple)."

119. Beaubrun Ardouin, *Études sur l'histoire de Haïti*, tome 6 (Paris: Chez l'auteur, 1856), 137.

120. "Adresse de l'Empereur au peuple, à son retour du siège de Santo-Domingo," April 12, 1805, *Lois et Actes*, 43–45.

121. Dessalines, "Journal de la campagne de Santo-Domingo (Adresse de l'Empereur au peuple)"; Christophe to Jean-Jacques Bazile, April 2, 1805, "Christophe, Copie des lettres," pp. 34–35; Christophe to Colonel Antoine, April 2, 1805, "Christophe, Copie des lettres," p. 35.

122. Christophe to Dessalines, April 15, 1805, "Christophe, Copie des lettres," pp. 42–43.

123. Christophe to Etienne Albert and Raymond, April 2, 1805, "Christophe, Copie des lettres," p. 34. He told Achille to obtain *vivres* for about six hundred Spanish people for their arrival in Ouanaminthe: Christophe to Comandant Achille, April 2, 1805, "Christophe, Copie des lettres," p. 35.

124. Christophe to Jean-Jacques Bazile, April 2, 1805, "Christophe, Copie des lettres," pp. 34–35.

125. Christophe to Antoine, April 2, 1805, "Christophe, Copie des lettres," p. 35; Christophe to Achille, April 2, 1805, "Christophe, Copie des lettres," p. 35.

126. Christophe to commander of Fort Liberté, April 26, 1805, "Christophe, Copie des lettres," p. 50.

127. Christophe to Brave, April 17, 1805, "Christophe, Copie des lettres," pp. 44–45.

128. Christophe to Brave, April 17, 1805, "Christophe, Copie des lettres," pp. 44–45.

129. Christophe to Brave, September 2, 1805, "Christophe, Copie des lettres," p. 153.

130. Christophe to Brave, April 23, 1805, "Christophe, Copie des lettres," p. 48; Christophe to Dessalines, April 28, 1805, "Christophe, Copie des lettres," pp. 51–52; Christophe to Romain, May 2, 1805, "Christophe, Copie des lettres," pp. 54–55; Christophe to Dessalines, May 2, 1805, "Christophe, Copie des lettres," p. 55.

131. Christophe to Raimond, April 17, 1805, "Christophe, Copie des lettres," p. 45; Christophe to Romain, April 18, 1805, "Christophe, Copie des lettres," p. 46; Christophe to Brave, April 18, 1805, "Christophe, Copie des lettres," p. 46; Christophe, order to Citoyen Noisy, April 15, 1805, "Christophe, Copie des lettres," pp. 41–42; Christophe to Romain and Brave, April 18, 1805, "Christophe, Copie des lettres," pp. 45–46; Christophe to Brave, April 17, 1805, "Christophe, Copie des lettres," pp. 44–45.

132. Price-Mars, *La République d'Haïti,* tome 1, 69.

133. Christophe to Dessalines, June 6, 1805, "Christophe, Copie des lettres," p. 75.

134. Christophe to Chef de Bataillon Tiphaine, March 27, 1805, "Christophe, Copie des lettres," p. 33.

135. Christophe to Romain and Brave, April 11, 1805, "Christophe, Copie des lettres," pp. 37–38; Christophe to Dessalines, April 15, 1805, "Christophe, Copie des lettres," pp. 42–43; Christophe to Raimond, April 19, 1805, "Christophe, Copie des lettres," pp. 46–47.

136. Christophe to military commanders, April 15, 1805, "Christophe, Copie des lettres," p. 43; Christophe to Raimond, April 19, 1805, "Christophe, Copie des lettres," pp. 46–47; Christophe, circular to all military commanders, April 19, "Christophe, Copie des lettres," p. 47.

137. Christophe to Dessalines, May 8, 1805, "Christophe, Copie des lettres," p. 59.

138. Chistophe to Brave, Romain, and Poux, May 24, 1805, "Christophe, Copie des lettres," p. 71.

139. Christophe to Dessalines, April 15, 1805, "Christophe, Copie des lettres," pp. 42–43; Christophe to General Lamothe, April 11, 1805, "Christophe, Copie des lettres," p. 39.

140. Nessler, *Islandwide Struggle,* 161.

141. "Adresse de l'Empereur au peuple, à son retour du siège de Santo-Domingo," *Lois et Actes,* 43–45. The state printed the official account of the siege and distributed it to each of the departments. On May 22 Christophe gave printed copies of the *Journal* to

his military commanders. He instructed them to publicly read and publish the document and to circulate copies to other military commanders and inspectors to further
publicize it. Soon after, the *Gazette* printed Dessalines's address, Ferrand's proclamation, the full text of Dessalines's *Journal de campagne,* and the full text of Henry Christophe's *Journal de campagne* (across multiple issues). Christophe to military commanders, May 22, 1805, "Christophe, Copie des lettres," p. 69. *Gazette politique et commerciale
d'Haïti,* Cap, May 30, 1805, *l'an deuxième de l'indépendance,* no. 25, contains the address, Ferrand's proclamation, and the beginning of the *Journal de campagne. Gazette
politique et commerciale d'Haïti,* June 6, 1805, *l'an deuxième de l'indépendance,* no. 26,
contains the next portion of the *Journal de campagne. Gazette politique et commerciale
d'Haïti,* June 13, 1805, *l'an deuxième de l'indépendance,* no. 27, contains the end of the
Journal de campagne and the beginning of Henry Christophe's *Journal de campagne
tenu pendant l'expédition de Santo-Domingo, par le général de division H. CHRISTOPHE,
commandant en chef des deux Divisions du Nord. Gazette politique et commerciale d'Haïti,*
June 20, 1805, *l'an deuxième de l'indépendance,* no. 28, contains the end of Henry Christophe's *Journal de campagne.*

142. Stieber, *Haiti's Paper War,* 46; *Constitution d'Haïti,* May 20, 1805, *l'an deuxième de
l'indépendance d'Haïti, et de notre règne le premier,* Aux Cayes, de l'Imprimerie Impériale, American Philosophical Society, Philadelphia, Pamphlets, vol. 26, no. 13; Dessalines, May 20, 1805, *Lois et Actes,* 65; Ardouin, *Études sur l'histoire de Haïti,* tome 6,
145; Madiou, *Histoire d'Haïti,* tome 3, 214.

143. General Dispositions, article 12, *Constitution d'Haïti,* May 20, 1805; Claude Moïse,
*Constitutions et luttes de pouvoir en Haïti: Tome 1, 1804–1915: La faillite des classes di-
rigeantes* (Montreal: Éditions du CIDIHCA, 1988), 32.

144. The inclusion of Germans and Poles as citizens in independent Haiti was a result of
their participation in the war of independence. This topic is discussed in detail in
Pachonski and Wilson's *Poland's Caribbean Tragedy.* The French compiled a list of
Austrian, Hungarian, and Polish deserters in June 1802, available at "Place de Veronne,
État Nominatif des déserteurs Autrichieux pendant le mois de Messidor an 10," SHD,
GR7, B5.

145. For example, see "Déclaration de M. JAMES PHIPPS, April 12, 1805," *Gazette politique et
commerciale d'Haïti,* Cap, no. 24, May 24, 1805, p. 4., and "Déclaration de M. Mullery,
négociant du Cap," *Gazette politique et commerciale d'Haïti,* no. 40, September 12,
1805, p. 4, repr. September 19, 1805, no. 41, p. 4.

146. Article 7, *Constitution d'Haïti,* May 20, 1805.

147. Thoby, "Les étrangers et le droit de propriété en Haïti," 1; General Dispositions, article
12, *Constitution d'Haïti,* May 20, 1805; General Dispositions, article 13, *Constitution
d'Haïti,* May 20, 1805.

148. According to Louis-Joseph Janvier, a July 28, 1805, law clarified this point by creating an administrative division in the east. Janvier, "Notes sur Dessalines et Toussaint
Louverture."

149. Article 14, *Constitution d'Haïti,* May 20, 1805.

150. Sybille Fischer, *Modernity Disavowed: Haiti and the Cultures of Slavery in the Age of
Revolution* (Durham, NC: Duke University Press, 2004), 233; Angela Naimou, *Salvage*

Work: U.S. and Caribbean Literatures amid the Debris of Legal Personhood (New York: Fordham University Press, 2015), 37.

151. Laurent Dubois, *Haiti: The Aftershocks of History* (New York: Metropolitan Books, 2012), 43.

152. Doris Garraway calls this policy "negative universalism." Doris Lorraine Garraway, *Tree of Liberty: Cultural Legacies of the Haitian Revolution in the Atlantic World* (Charlottesville: University of Virginia Press, 2008), 80–82.

153. Dayan, *Haiti, History, and the Gods,* 24–25.

154. Lundahl, "Defense and Distribution," 82.

155. Article 30, *Constitution d'Haïti,* May 20, 1805. Paton and Scully claim that the constitution limited voting to men, but the constitution does not include any specifics about who could vote. See Diana Paton and Pamela Scully, eds., *Gender and Slave Emancipation in the Atlantic World* (Durham, NC: Duke University Press, 2015), 10–11; Vaval, "Le gouvernement de Dessalines," 69.

156. Fick, "Haitian Revolution and the Limits of Freedom," 413–414; see also Price-Mars, *Le République d'Haïti,* tome 1, 65.

157. Trouillot, *Haiti, State against Nation,* 88.

158. Mimi Sheller, "Sword-Bearing Citizens: Militarism and Manhood in Nineteenth-Century Haiti," in *Haitian History: New Perspectives,* edited by Alyssa Goldstein Sepinwall (New York: Routledge, 2013), 162; Paton and Scully, *Gender and Slave Emancipation,* 11.

159. Article 27, *Constitution d'Haïti,* May 20, 1805. The dates of these celebrations have often been celebrated as their birthdays, but they were the dates of the feast days of their namesakes.

160. Articles 50–52, *Constitution d'Haïti,* May 20, 1805.

161. Article 14, *Constitution d'Haïti,* May 20, 1805. (A footnote in *Lois et Actes* refers to a law from June 1, 1805, which I have not yet been able to locate.)

162. Dessalines, "Loi sur le mode de constater l'état civil des citoyens," June 3, 1805, *Lois et Actes,* 98–99.

163. Madiou, *Histoire d'Haïti,* tome 3, 133.

164. Christophe to Capoix, November 14, 1805, "Christophe, Copie des lettres," p. 202.

165. Ada Ferrer, *Freedom's Mirror: Cuba and Haiti in the Age of Revolution* (New York: Cambridge University Press, 2014), 207; Article 36, *Constitution d'Haïti,* May 20, 1805.

166. Jenson, *Beyond the Slave Narrative,* 166.

167. An updated version of the document was published in late November and included two additional articles. Christophe to Roman and Capoix, December 2, 1805, "Christophe, Copie des lettres," p. 224.

168. "CODE PÉNAL MILITAIRE. Pour toutes les troupes de l'empire d'Haïti. À Dessalines, le 26 Mai" [printed in 1828]. Dessalines, "Codes of Hayti, May 26, 1805" (Port-au-Prince: Imprimerie du Gouvernement, 1828), BPL, Reserve 4275.68 no. 1. The document was also printed in the newspaper: [Part 1] "EMPIRE D'HAÏTI, CODE PÉNAL MILITAIRE, Pour toutes les Troupes de l'Empire d'Haïti," *Gazette politique et commerciale d'Haïti,* Cap, July 4, 1805, *l'an deuxième de l'indépendance,* no. 30, pp. 117–199; [Part 2] "Suite du Code pénal militaire," *Gazette politique et commerciale d'Haïti,* July 11, 1805, *l'an*

deuxième de l'indépendance, no. 31, pp. 121–123; and [Part 3] "Fin du Code pénal militaire," *Gazette politique et commerciale d'Haïti,* July 18, 1805, *l'an deuxième de l'indépendance,* no. 32, pp. 125–127.

169. "CODE PÉNAL MILITAIRE . . . le 26 Mai."

170. In late 1805, per Dessalines's orders, a soldier was punished for "violating" a five-year-old girl. See Christophe to Dartiguenave, November 25, 1805, "Christophe, Copie des lettres," p. 218; Christophe to Dartiguenave, November 30, 1805, "Christophe, Copie des lettres," pp. 221–222.

171. Dessalines, "Loi sur l'organisation des conseils spéciaux militaires," May 30, 1805, *Lois et Actes,* 82–90. The state printed each of the new laws to distribute throughout the country. Christophe to Dessalines, July 1, 1805, "Christophe, Copie des lettres," p. 102; Christophe to generals and commanders of the Division of the North, June 30, 1805, "Christophe, Copie des lettres," p. 102; Christophe to Dessalines, July 1, 1805, "Christophe, Copie des lettres," p. 102.

172. Dessalines, "Loi sur le divorce," June 1, 1805, *Lois et Actes,* 91–98. The French divorce code was replaced in 1803 and then again in 1804 with the Napoleonic Civil Code. See Suzanne Desan, *The Family on Trial in Revolutionary France* (Berkeley: University of California Press, 2004), 137.

173. Dessalines, "Loi sur le divorce," June 1, 1805, *Lois et Actes,* 91–98.

174. Lundahl, "Defense and Distribution," 92; Dessalines, "Loi sur les enfants nés hors mariage," May 28, 1805, *Lois et Actes,* 77–81.

175. Title V noted that wives did not have this same privilege. Dessalines, "Loi sur les enfants nés hors mariage," May 28, 1805, *Lois et Actes,* 77–81.

176. These documents reference a June 3, 1805, law—specifically article 13 of title III. I have not been able to find the document, but the articles from the May 28, 1805, law correlate to the recognition of children born out of wedlock. The documents, especially those of Célimène and Jacques Bien-Aimé, are inconsistent and the dates conflict—the page break looks like two different documents were spliced together, or that someone transcribed a document and made errors during the transcription. See "Acte de naissance de Célimène Dessalines, fille de Jean-Jacques Dessalines," February 2, 1806, courtesy of the Bibliothèque Haïtienne des Spiritains, and "Acte de naissance de Célestine Dessalines, fille de Jean-Jacques Dessalines," February 2, 1806, courtesy of the Bibliothèque Haïtienne des Spiritains. Dessalines, "Loi sur le mode de constater l'état civil des citoyens," June 3, 1805, *Lois et Actes,* 98–99.

177. Kesner Millien names the following: Eugénie Fresnel, Euphémie Daguilh (originaire des Cayes), Marie-Thérèse Lauge dit Pourcette, Couloute (originaire de Jérémie), Héleine Mouton, Rosiclaire Chambiou, Marie Magdelein, and Célestine Arène. See Millien, "L'Empereur Jean-Jacques Dessalines: Père de famille à part entière," *Le nouvelliste* (Port-au-Prince), October 29, 2012. Hoffman adds "Madame Poncitto": Léon-François Hoffman, "An American Trader in Revolutionary Haiti: Simeon Johnson's Journal of 1807," *Princeton University Library Chronicle* 49, no. 2 (1988): 196.

178. Inginac, "Mémoires de Joseph Balthazar Inginac," 16; on her residence, see Millien, "L'Empereur Jean-Jacques Dessalines."

179. "CODE PÉNAL MILITAIRE . . . le 26 Mai."

180. Stieber, *Haiti's Paper War,* 46.
181. Madiou claimed that Boisrond-Tonnerre read it on Dessalines's behalf, but the *Gazette* reported that "l'Empereur a adressé au peuple le discours suivant." *Gazette politique et commerciale d'Haïti,* July 25, 1805, *l'an deuxième de l'indépendance,* no. 33, p. 131; Madiou, *Histoire d'Haïti,* tome 3, 217. See also Stieber, *Haiti's Paper War,* 46.
182. Madiou, *Histoire d'Haïti,* tome 3, 217–218.
183. Madiou, *Histoire d'Haïti,* tome 3, 217–218.
184. Madiou, *Histoire d'Haïti,* tome 3, 217–218.
185. Christophe to Joacin, Raymond, and commander of Cap, June 11, 1805, "Christophe, Copie des lettres," pp. 81–82; Christophe to Albert, commander of war of Grande Rivière, Jasmain, Lolotte Poux, and Tiphaine, June 11, 1805, "Christophe, Copie des lettres," p. 82.
186. Christophe to Dessalines, June 11, 1805, "Christophe, Copie des lettres," pp. 80–81; Christophe to Joacin, June 14, 1805, "Christophe, Copie des lettres," p. 84.
187. Christophe to Dessalines, June 16, 1805, "Christophe, Copie des lettres," pp. 85–86.
188. Christophe to Dessalines, June 11, 1805, "Christophe, Copie des lettres," pp. 80–81.
189. Dessalines, "Ordres généraux," July 28, 1805, *l'an deux de l'indépendance d'Haïti, et de notre règne le premier,* printed in *Gazette politique et commerciale d'Haïti,* August 8, 1805, *l'an deuxième de l'indépendance,* no. 35, p. 140.
190. "Dessalines, Janvier, sergent-major dans la milice coloniale, concierge de la maison du Gouvernement, à Saint-Domingue, 1796," ANOM; Brutus, *L'homme d'Airain,* 51. See also Mollien, *Haïti ou Saint-Domingue,* tome 2, 53; [Condy Raguet], *Poulson's American Daily Advertiser,* February 14, 1805.

CHAPTER 12. TEARS OF BLOOD

1. Villaret-Joyeuse to Minister of the Navy and Colonies, January 16, 1806, ANOM, COL C8A 112 F36. See also Villaret-Joyeuse to Minister of the Navy and Colonies, 20 Messidor an 12 [July 9, 1804], ANOM, COL C8A 109 F31, and Villaret-Joyeuse to Minister of the Navy and Colonies, February 10, 1806, ANOM, COL C8A 112 F83.
2. Gaffield, *Haitian Connections,* 44–45; "Les Négociants & Habitants du Port-au-Prince aux Principaux Places du Commerce de France," [n.d., ca. December 1802], UFRP, box 15, ff. 1449.
3. Christophe to Dessalines, March 20, 1806, "Christophe, Copie des lettres," pp. 287–288. Christophe implored Rouanez to withhold the information and not publish the senate debates in the *Gazette du Cap;* see Christophe to Rouanez, March 19, 1806, "Christophe, Copie des lettres," p. 287.
4. Michel Hector, "Jalon pour une périodisation," in Hector and Hurbon, *Genèse de l'État haïtien (1804–1859),* 30.
5. Christophe to administrateur, November 19, 1805, "Christophe, Copie des lettres," pp. 209–210.
6. Christophe to Dessalines, December 3, 1805, "Christophe, Copie des lettres," p. 226.
7. Christophe to Capoix and Romain, December 13, 1805, "Christophe, Copie des lettres," p. 231.
8. Armée indigène, "Liberté ou la Mort," January 1, 1804.

9. Madiou, *Histoire d'Haïti,* tome 3, 261.

10. Stieber, *Haiti's Paper War,* 50.

11. Stieber, *Haiti's Paper War,* 50–51.

12. "Du Cap, le 31 Juillet," *Gazette politique et commerciale d'Haïti,* Cap, August 1, 1805, *l'an deuxième de l'indépendance,* no. 34, p. 133.

13. "Du Cap, le 31 Juillet," August 1, 1805.

14. "Du Cap, le 31 Juillet," August 1, 1805.

15. Brutus, *L'homme d'Airain,* 39–40.

16. Mirambeau, "Victoria," 109.

17. Christophe to Dessalines, October 31, 1805, "Christophe, Copie des lettres," pp. 190–191.

18. Marlene L. Daut, *The First and Last King of Haiti: The Rise and Fall of Henry Christophe* (New York: Alfred A. Knopf, 2025), 299.

19. His godson was likely Christophe's son Victor-Henry; see Daut, *First and Last King of Haiti,* 306, 567n6. Christophe to Dessalines, July 2, 1805, "Christophe, Copie des lettres," p. 104. Christophe to Dessalines, March 6, 1806, "Christophe, Copie des lettres," p. 280. Only some of Dessalines's children were in Cap, because the evidence shows that at least one remained in the Artibonite: Roulet to Ferrand, Santo Domingo, "Apperçu sur l'état actuel de la portion de l'isle de St. Domingue occupée par les noirs revoltés," May 12, 1806, SHD, GR7, B11.

20. On Gabart's diagnosis, see Roulet to Ferrand, May 12, 1806; Ardouin, *Études sur l'histoire de Haïti,* tome 6, 215–216.

21. Boisrond-Tonnerre, *Mémoires,* 27.

22. An article in the state newspaper called on the nation's soldiers to see Gabart as a hero. "Nécrologie," *Gazette politique et commerciale d'Haïti,* Cap, November 14, 1805, *l'an deuxième de l'indépendance,* no. 47, p. 188.

23. "Le 2 de ce mois, madame MARIE-ELIZABETH, mère de son Auguste Majesté l'Impératrice, est décédée à l'Artibonite, âgé de 56 ans," *Gazette politique et commerciale d'Haïti,* Cap, November 14, 1805, *l'an deuxième de l'indépendance,* no. 47, p. 188.

24. Christophe to Dessalines, November 7, 1805, "Christophe, Copie des lettres," pp. 193–195.

25. Christophe to Dessalines, November 7, 1805.

26. "Le Ministre des Finances et de l'Intérieur," *Gazette politique et commerciale d'Haïti,* August 15, 1805, *l'an deuxième de l'indépendance,* Cap, no. 36, p. 144; Lundahl, "Defense and Distribution," 92; Vaval, "Le gouvernement de Dessalines," 71.

27. Hénock Trouillot, *Dessalines, ou La tragédie post-coloniale* (Port-au-Prince: Éditions Panorama, 1966), 71.

28. H. Trouillot quoting Louis-Joseph Janvier quoting Hérard Dumesle: H. Trouillot, *Dessalines, ou La tragédie post-coloniale,* 76.

29. H. Trouillot, *Dessalines, ou La tragédie post-coloniale,* 71. Some have argued, however, that it was simply a land grab on the part of a greedy and tyrannical government; see Lundahl, "Defense and Distribution," 92.

30. The German version included one "portrait" of Dessalines: Louis Dubroca, *Leben des*

J. J. Dessalines, oder Jacob's des Ersten Kaysers von Hayti (Leipzig: Johann Conrad Hinrichs, 1805).

31. Louis Dubroca, *Vida de J. J. Dessalines, gefe de los negros de Santo Domingo* (Mexico: D. Mariano de Zúñiga y Ontiveros, 1806).

32. Dubroca, *Vida de J. J. Dessalines,* image of Christophe inserted after p. 30.

33. Juan Lopez Cancelada, "Al lector," in Dubroca, *Vida de J. J. Dessalines,* [ii]; image of coronation ceremony inserted after p. 82.

34. "Empire d'Haïti, de Jérémie, le 20 Juillet," *Gazette politique et commerciale d'Haïti,* Cap, August 14, 1806, *l'an troisième de l'indépendance,* no. 32, p. 128.

35. Christophe to Dessalines, July 13, 1806, *l'an troisième de l'indépendance,* Connecticut Historical Society, Haiti Collection, correspondence and notebook of Creole proverbs, 1804–1843m Series I: box 1, folder 2.

36. Christophe to Dessalines, September 4, 1806, "Christophe, Copie des lettres," pp. 392–393.

37. "Empire d'Haïti, De Dessalines, le 4 Octobre," *Gazette politique et commerciale d'Haïti,* October 16, 1806, *l'an troisième de l'indépendance,* no. 41, pp. 161–162.

38. Christophe to Dessalines, January 25, 1806, "Christophe, Copie des lettres," pp. 381–382. Weeks later, when Dessalines was in Les Cayes, the nation celebrated the empress's feast day on August 12. Madame Dessalines hosted her own *fête* to mark the occasion in Gonaïves and invited local dignitaries and foreign merchants; see "Empire d'Haïti, De Dessalines, le 4 Octobre." Hoffman erroneously claims this was her "birthday" rather than her feast day: Hoffman, "American Trader in Revolutionary Haiti," 188. See also Julia Sigeneau to Simeon Johnson, "Invitation," August 12, 1806, "Correspondence and Accounts of Simeon Johnson," Simeon Johnson Papers, Princeton University, Firestone Library Manuscript Division: box B-001096. Many thanks to Michael Becker for sharing this source with me.

39. Inginac, *Mémoires,* 17. Dessalines met with local authorities and the family of the recently deceased General Geffrard. He had Geffrard's cabinet searched for evidence of a conspiracy against him.

40. Janvier, "Notes sur Dessalines et Toussaint Louverture," 12; Inginac, *Mémoires,* 15–16.

41. "Décret relatif aux testaments et autres actes portant donation de biens fonds," Aux Cayes, September 1, 1806, *l'an troisième de l'indépendance,* in *Lois et Actes,* 141–143; "Empire d'Haïti, Décret, Relatif aux Testamens et autres Actes portant donation de Biens fonds," [September 1, 1806], *Gazette politique et commerciale d'Haïti,* October 2, 1806, *l'an troisième de l'indépendance,* no. 39, p. 152; Vaval, "Le gouvernement de Dessalines," 73; H. Trouillot, *Dessalines, ou La tragédie post-coloniale,* 67; Janvier, "Notes sur Dessalines et Toussaint Louverture," 13.

42. Lundahl, "Defense and Distribution," 96.

43. Janvier, "Notes sur Dessalines et Toussaint Louverture," 13.

44. Janvier, "Notes sur Dessalines et Toussaint Louverture," 14.

45. H. Trouillot, *Dessalines, ou La tragédie post-coloniale,* 78.

46. Gérin, Pétion, Yayou, Vaval, Bonnet, et al., "Résistance à l'oppression," October 16, 1806, *l'an troisième de l'indépendance, et de la vraie Liberté le premier,* Bibliothèque nationale

de France, département de la Réserve des livres rares, FOL-PU-13, available on Gallica. Janvier, whose grandfather was one of the signatories to the document, claimed, however, that it was composed after Dessalines's assassination and backdated; see Janvier, "Notes sur Dessalines et Toussaint Louverture," 22. The date at the end of the document included the Gregorian calendar, the Haitian independence calendar, and a new insurgent calendar: "October 16, 1806, year three of independence, and of true Liberty the first."

47. Stieber, *Haiti's Paper War,* 52.

48. Gérin, Pétion, Yayou, Vaval, Bonnet, et al., "Résistance à l'oppression."

49. Gérin, Pétion, Yayou, Vaval, Bonnet, et al., "Résistance à l'oppression."

50. Gérin, Pétion, Yayou, Vaval, Bonnet, et al., "Résistance à l'oppression."

51. Voltaire for Warnac, Bt. Beauregard, Papalier, Vancol, Racollier, L. Borniet, J. Rocher, and Lacoude to Christophe, October 13, 1806, *l'an troisième de l'indépendance,* printed in Linstant Pradine, ed., *Receuil général des lois et actes du Gouvernement d'Haïti,* 2nd ed. (Paris: A. Durand, 1886), tome 1, 154–155.

52. Stieber, *Haiti's Paper War,* 48–49.

53. Janvier, "Notes sur Dessalines et Toussaint Louverture," 17–18.

54. Janvier, "Notes sur Dessalines et Toussaint Louverture," 17.

55. Christophe to Dessalines, October 16, 1806, "Christophe, Copie des lettres," p. 419.

56. Christophe to Dessalines, October 16, 1806 (second letter on this day), "Christophe, Copie des lettres," p. 420.

57. Janvier, "Notes sur Dessalines et Toussaint Louverture," 19.

58. Lundahl, "Defense and Distribution," 102.

59. Lewis A. Clormeus, "À propos de l'assassinat de Dessalines (17 Octobre 1806)," *Revue de la Société haïtienne d'histoire, de géographie et de géologie* 263–266 (2017): 233.

60. Janvier, "Notes sur Dessalines et Toussaint Louverture," 20.

61. Janvier, "Notes sur Dessalines et Toussaint Louverture," 21.

62. Janvier, "Notes sur Dessalines et Toussaint Louverture," 21.

63. Eveillard, "Claire Heureuse," 9. Janvier, however, claimed that Défilée was not "crazy." "She was the grandmother of Lorient Bazile," he noted, "a rich fisherman from Morne à Tuf who I remember perfectly and who was still living in 1864." Janvier, "Notes sur Dessalines et Toussaint Louverture," 22.

64. Christophe to Minister of Finances, October 19, 1806, "Christophe, Copie des lettres," p. 423. He wrote again two days later: Christophe to Minister of Finances, October 21, 1806, "Christophe, Copie des lettres," pp. 436–437.

65. Christophe to Romain, Brave, and Dartiguenave, October 19, 1806, "Christophe, Copie des lettres," p. 423.

66. Christophe to Jean Louis Longueval, October 19, 1806, "Christophe, Copie des lettres," p. 425.

67. Christophe to Pétion, October 19, 1806, "Christophe, Copie des lettres," p. 430.

68. Christophe to Groguine, October 21, 1806, "Christophe, Copie des lettres," p. 438; Christophe to John Darcy, October 21, 1806, "Christophe, Copie des lettres," p. 439; Christophe to administrateur principal, October 21, 1806, "Christophe, Copie des lettres," p.

441; Christophe to commandant de la place du Cap, October 21, 1806, "Christophe, Copie des lettres," p. 441.

69. Pétion to Madame Dessalines, Port-au-Prince, October 19, 1806 (Port-au-Prince: Imprimerie de Fourcand), Bibliothèque nationale de France, département de la Réserve des livres rares, 4-PU-14, available on Gallica.

70. Christophe to Madame Dessalines, October 21, 1806, "Christophe, Copie des lettres," pp. 434–436.

71. Christophe to Madame Dessalines, October 21, 1806.

72. Christophe to Pierre Toussaint, October 22, 1806, "Christophe, Copie des lettres," p. 443.

73. Christophe to Gérin, October 23, 1806, "Christophe, Copie des lettres," p. 449.

74. Christophe to Pétion, October 23, 1806, "Christophe, Copie des lettres," p. 448.

75. See, for example, Blanchet to Peltier, TNA, WO 1/79; C. Ardouin, *Essais sur l'histoire d'Haïti*, 122.

76. Christophe to the People and Army of Haiti, November 2, 1806, *l'an troisième de l'indépendance,* quoted in Clorméus, "À propos de l'assassinat de Dessalines," 245.

77. Article 29, *Constitution d'Haïti,* May 20, 1805, *l'an deuxième de l'indépendance d'Haïti, et de notre règne le premier.*

78. Madame Dessalines to Christophe, March [?] 1813, Cap-Henry, courtesy of the Bibliothèque Haïtienne des Spiritains. Many thanks to Patrick Tardieu for sharing this document.

79. "Gonaïves," *Feuille du commerce,* Port-au-Prince, August 14, 1858, no. 33, p. 1.

80. Dorvelas-Dorval, "Nos adieux," Gonaïves, August 9, 1858, in *Feuille de commerce,* Port-au-Prince, August 21, 1858, no. 34, pp. 2–3, British Library, EAP1024/1/1/12/8/3, https://eap.bl.uk/archive-file/EAP1024-1-1-12-8-3; cited in Eveillard, "Claire Heureuse," 18.

81. "From the *Evening Post*—Obituary, Death of the Widow of the First Emperor of Hayti," *Anti-Slavery Bugle,* New Lisbon, OH, October 2, 1858, vol. 14, issue 6.

82. Title I, Article 3, *Constitution et rapport fait à l'Assemblée Constituante par son Comité de Constitution, dans sa séance du 27 Décembre 1806* (Cayes: Imprimerie de la République, 1806).

83. Christophe, "Proclamation to the People and Army of Hayti," January 14, 1807, *4th year of independence,* printed in the *Alexandria Daily Advertiser* (Virginia), February 28, 1807, p. 2.

84. Madiou, *Histoire d'Haïti,* tome 3, 374; Vernet, P. Romain, Toussaint Brave, et al., "Constitution de l'État d'Hayti," February 17, 1807, *l'an quatrième de l'indépendance* (Cap: P. Roux, imprimeur de l'État), TNA, WO 1/79, f. 7.

85. Pétion to "the Men of Colour who have been forced to leave this country and seek an asylum in the United States and other foreign nations," March 10, 1807, *l'an quatrième de l'indépendance,* printed in *The Repertory,* Boston, May 12, 1807, p. 1.

86. Stieber, *Haiti's Paper War,* 49.

EPILOGUE

1. Julia Gaffield, "Haiti Protests Summon Spirit of the Haitian Revolution to Condemn a President Tainted by Scandal," *The Conversation,* November 15, 2019.

2. For examples of fictional accounts of Dessalines, see Anonymous, "Dessalines, Tyrant of the Blacks and Murderer of the Whites in Saint-Domingue: A Canvas from the Gallery of Political Monsters" (1805), and John Wilson Ross, "Dessalines and Toussaint L'Ouverture: An Episode in the History of Haiti" (1848), both translated and printed in *Haitian Revolutionary Fictions: An Anthology,* edited by Marlene L. Daut, Grégory Pierrot, and Marion C. Rohrleitner (Charlottesville: University of Virginia Press, 2022), 12–14.

3. France touts itself as being the first country to officially recognize slavery as a "crime against humanity" because of the 2001 "Taubira Law," but in fact Haitians in the nineteenth century used the phrase to describe their experiences with French slavery. See Daut, *Awakening the Ashes,* 117–118.

4. Janvier, "Notes sur Dessalines et Toussaint Louverture."

5. Bouillet, *Dictionnaire universel,* 1st ed., 1847, 486. Boisrond-Tonnerre's *Mémoires,* a publication that Dessalines officially sanctioned, did not comment on Dessalines's place of birth, but it listed him as the leader of soldiers *"du pays"*—which the secretary contrasted with the "congo" soldiers and the *"noirs de Guinée."* Boisrond-Tonnerre, *Mémoires,* 60.

6. This was likely also because Madiou, as editor of *Le moniteur,* publicly pointed out the error. See "Partie non officielle," *Le moniteur haïtien,* Port-au-Prince, December 5, 1852, pp. 2–4, and Madiou, *Histoire d'Haïti,* tome 3, 36. Other Haitian authors have consistently stated that Dessalines was born in Saint-Domingue; see, for example, Brutus, *L'homme d'Airain,* 29. Emmanuel C. Paul was similarly unconvinced of the claim that Dessalines was born in Africa and noted that the evidence was inconsistent. Paul, "Le ressentiment Dessalinien," 143.

7. Bouillet, *Dictionnaire universel,* 11th ed., 1856, 406.

8. Pierrot, *Black Avenger,* 97.

9. James Barskett, *History of the Island of St. Domingo* (London: A. Constable, 1818), 313–315.

10. James Franklin, *The Present State of Hayti (Saint Domingo), With Remarks on its Agriculture, Commerce, Laws, Religion, Finances, and Population, etc, etc* (London: John Murray, 1828), 179–180.

11. Jonathan Brown, *The History and Present Condition of St. Domingo,* vol. 2 (Philadelphia: W. Marshall, 1837), 152.

12. Marlene Daut, "Un-Silencing the Past: Boisrond-Tonnerre, Vastey, and the Re-Writing of the Haitian Revolution," *South Atlantic Review* 74, no. 1 (2009): 39; Daut, *Awakening the Ashes.*

13. Baron de Vastey, *Réflexions politiques sur quelques ouvrages et journaux français concernant Hayti* (Cap-Henry: P. Roux, 1817), 62.

14. Gaffield, *Haitian Connections.*

15. Julia Gaffield, "The Racialization of International Law in the Aftermath of the Haitian Revolution: The Holy See and National Sovereignty," *American Historical Review* 125, no. 3 (June 2020): 841–868.

16. Stieber, *Haiti's Paper War,* 184.

17. Daut, *Tropics of Haiti,* 597.

18. Madiou, *Histoire d'Haïti,* tome 3, 140.

19. Ardouin, *Études sur l'histoire d'Haïti,* vol. 6, 36–37, 58.

20. Janvier, "Notes sur Dessalines et Toussaint Louverture," 24.

21. L. J. Lhérisson, *Historique de "La Dessalinienne,"* 9.

22. L. J. Lhérisson, *Historique de "La Dessalinienne,"* 5; Saint-Louis, "L'assassinat de Dessalines," 113.

23. Stieber, *Haiti's Paper War,* 208–209.

24. Zavitz, "Revolutionary Commemorations," 226; Dayan, *Haiti, History, and the Gods,* 43.

25. Emmanuel C. Paul, *Panorama du folklore haïtien (présence africaine en Haïti)* (Port-au-Prince: Éditions Fardin, 1978), 57.

26. Karen McCarthy Brown, *Mama Lola: A Vodou Priestess in Brooklyn* (Berkeley: University of California Press, 2001), 98; Dubois, "Thinking Haitian Independence in Haitian Vodou," 206.

27. Dubois, "Thinking Haitian Independence in Haitian Vodou," 207.

28. "Dessalines Toro d'Haïti," originally transcribed by Odette Mennesson-Rigaud, translated and reproduced in Dubois, "Thinking Haitian Independence in Haitian Vodou," 209.

29. Michael Largey, "Recombinant Mythology and the Alchemy of Memory: Occide Jeanty, Ogou, and Jean-Jacques Dessalines in Haiti," *Journal of American Folklore* 118, no. 469 (2005): 328.

30. William Edgar Easton, "Dessalines," in Daut, Pierrot, and Rohrleitner, *Haitian Revolutionary Fictions,* 328.

31. "A Bust of Jean Jacques Dessalines Inaugurated in Benin," *Repeating Islands: News and Commentary on Caribbean Culture, Literature, and the Arts,* January 6, 2024, https://repeatingislands.com/2024/01/06/a-bust-of-jean-jacques-dessalines-inaugurated-in-benin/.

32. Saint-Louis, "L'assassinat de Dessalines," 114.

33. Largey, "Recombinant Mythology," 346–347.

34. Matthew Smith, *Red and Black in Haiti: Radicalism, Conflict, and Political Change, 1934–1957* (Chapel Hill: University of North Carolina Press, 2009), 2.

35. Saint-Louis, "L'assassinat de Dessalines," 118; Laurent Dubois, "Dessalines Toro d'Haïti," *William and Mary Quarterly* 69, no. 3 (2012): 544.

36. Brutus, *L'homme d'Airain,* 372; for other examples, see Laurent, *Six études,* 100; Jean-Baptiste, *Le fondateur,* 73.

37. Sophie Sapp Moore, "Between the State and the Yard: Gender and Political Space in Haiti," *Gender, Place & Culture: A Journal of Feminist Geography* 28, no. 9 (2021): 1313.

38. Constant Méheut and Catherine Porter, "Macron Honors Haitian Revolutionary, but Leaves Much Unsaid," *New York Times,* April 27, 2023, https://www.nytimes.com/2023/04/27/world/europe/macron-toussaint-louverture-speech.html.

39. James, *Black Jacobins,* 373 (p. 308 in the original 1938 printing).

40. Girard, "Caribbean Genocide," 142.

41. His repeated analyses of French "survivor narratives," alongside survivor accounts from the Jewish Holocaust during World War II, imply some truth to the "genocide" claim, even while he resists using the term. Popkin, *Facing Racial Revolution,* 336–362.

42. Popkin, "Jean-Jacques Dessalines, Norbert Thoret," 127. Madiou also argued for deportation as a better alternative: Madiou, *Histoire d'Haïti,* tome 3, 140.

43. Popkin, "Jean-Jacques Dessalines, Norbert Thoret," 122.

44. See, for example, the cases of Louis Ferrand and Roberjot Lartigue in Gaffield, *Haitian Connections,* 17–60.

45. For examples, see Lairoza to the Minister of the Marine and the Colonies, "Mémoire contenant un apperçu succinct des évènements survenus à St. Domingue depuis l'arrivée de l'armée française—les causes qui les ont Déterminés.—quelques réflexions—les moyens qu'il eut fallu prendre dans le principe pour la rétablissement de l'ordre . . ." [1804], AN, Paris, microfilm, CC9A 38; Gaillard Déjourné, "Projet Présenté à son Excellence Monseigneur le Ministre de la Marine," September 30, 1805, AN, Paris, microfilm, CC9A 41; and August Duquesne, "Notice sur le débarquement à opérer, le mode d'attaquer et le genre de Guerre à faire aux noirs," November 8, 1806, AN, Paris, microfilm, CC9B 24.

46. Roulet to Ferrand, May 12, 1806, SHD, GR7, B11; Nouët, C. Nicollier, and Y. Nicollier, *La vie aventureuse de Norbert Thoret.*

47. Mike Duncan, "Death to the French," *Revolutions,* April 2016, season 4, episode 18, https://open.spotify.com/episode/0zKgGkb1GXECyHTSJPvNZR.

48. "Jean-Jacques Dessalines," *Wikipedia,* Wikimedia Foundation, October 2, 2024, https://en.wikipedia.org/wiki/Jean-Jacques_Dessalines.

49. "Haitian Revolution," *Wikipedia,* Wikimedia Foundation, January 18, 2024, https://en.wikipedia.org/wiki/Haitian_Revolution.

50. "1804 Haitian massacre," *Wikipedia,* Wikimedia Foundation, January 18, 2024, https://en.wikipedia.org/wiki/1804_Haitian_massacre.

51. Madiou, "Dessalines," 35.

52. The article was published in translation in the London *Times,* and I have not located an original copy; "Proclamation of Dessalines," May 2, 1804, Gonaïves, *Times,* London, September 26, 1804, p. 3.

53. Dessalines to Habitans d'Haïti, "Proclamation," April 28, 1804.

Acknowledgments

A decade ago, in the acknowledgments for my first book, I thanked my dissertation advisor Laurent Dubois with a quotation by the Haitian revolutionary Henry Christophe, who wrote to the British abolitionist Thomas Clarkson in 1816 to thank him for his "wise and good advice" by "beg[ging] him to continue it." I am deeply grateful that Laurent obliged, and I would like to ask for an extension on that request.

I am likewise still indebted to Melanie Newton, who first introduced me to the Haitian Revolution and Jean-Jacques Dessalines when I was an undergraduate student at the University of Toronto. Her teaching changed the course of my life for the better.

This book has benefited from the generosity and wisdom of many friends and colleagues, but none more than Marlene Daut, Chelsea Stieber, and Grégory Pierrot. They have been mentors, models, and dear friends, and I cannot thank them enough. I reveled and commiserated with Marlene about the joys and complications of writing biographies of famous men, and her meticulousness and lyrical prose has been an inspiration to me since I was a graduate student. Chelsea's compassion and patient ear have been a refuge during this process, and I am grateful for our long walk-and-talks. Her sharp analysis helped me wade through some complicated material. Greg's keen wit and playful skepticism have kept me laughing, and his unmatched sleuthing and generosity have made this book better.

My thinking about the Haitian Revolution and Dessalines also benefited from conversations with Jean Casimir, Anne Eller, Deborah Jenson, Madison Smartt Bell, Barry Gaspar, Vincent Brown, Ada Ferrer, John Garrigus, Michel Hector, Vertus Saint-Louis, Nathan Perl-Rosenthal, David Geggus, Jeremy Popkin, Matthew J. Smith, Laura Wagner, Charlton (Chaz) Yingling, Philip Kaisary, Cristina Soriano, Juan José Ponce Vázquez, Jesús Ruiz, Cameron Monroe, Robin Mitchell, Carolyn Fick, Miriam Franchina, Malick Ghachem, Jane Landers, Gaétan Mentor, Andrew Walker, and Erin Zavitz. And also from the friendship of Mitch Fraas, Liz Shesko, and Erin Parish. My collaborators Chantalle Verna and Nadève Ménard have helped me deal with some of the important theoretical issues around translation, and I am lucky to work with them. Kaiama Glover and Alex Gil have also been sources of scholarly wisdom and levity throughout the writing of this book.

My colleagues at Georgia State University encouraged me at the beginning of this project, especially David Sehat. I am also indebted to Alex Cummings, Jeffrey Trask, J. T. Way, and Jeff Young for their friendship. I have been welcomed into the scholarly community at William & Mary, and I am especially delighted to have the chance to work with Nick Popper, Brianna Nofil, Joshua Piker, Catherine Kelly, Tuska Benes, Fabrício Prado, Paul Mapp, Katherine Levitan, Chitralekha Zutshi, Peyman Jafari, and Simon Middleton.

This project would not have been possible without generous funding from the National Endowment for the Humanities' Public Scholars Fellowship; the University of Florida, Center for Latin American Studies' Library Travel Grant; the College of Arts and Sciences and the Department of History at Georgia State University; the College of Arts and Sciences and the Department of History at William & Mary; and the Omohundro Institute for Early American History and Culture.

I have presented material from this book in lectures, workshops, and conferences at the State University of Haiti, Loyola University Maryland, Delta State University, Princeton University, and the Haitian Studies Association. I benefited from the feedback and good cheer of the Georgia Atlantic Latin American and Caribbean Studies Initiative (GALACSI), funded by the Fox Center for Humanistic Inquiry at Emory, especially Lia Bascomb, Yanna Yannakakis, Jennifer Palmer, Tom Rogers, J. T. Way, Adriana Chira, Pablo Palomino, Cassia Roth, and Alex Wisnoski. I am also grateful for the writing accountability and friendship provided by Sherie Randolph, Erica Williams, and Tiffany Lethabo King. The Library Writing Retreat at William & Mary was essential during the editing stages of the book, and I'm grateful for the structure, camaraderie, and sustenance provided by the library staff. The coaches and members at Orange Theory Fitness, Williamsburg, have helped keep me healthy and sane during the final stages of writing and editing.

Visiting archives is one of the greatest joys of my job, and I thank the library and archives staff at each of the institutions cited in endnotes of this book. I offer special thanks to Patrick Tardieu (Bibliothèque Haïtienne des Spirit-ains), Michele Wilbanks (Smathers Library, University of Florida), Scott Taylor (Georgetown University, Booth Family Center for Special Collections), Jean Wilfrid Bertrand (Archives nationales d'Haïti), Isabelle Dion (Archives nati-onales d'outre-mer), James Cronan (National Archives of the UK), and Poul Erik Mouritzen (Danish National Archives).

I am very grateful to Adina Popescu Berk for her editorial guidance and for believing in this project from the beginning, and to Eva Skewes and the team at Yale University Press. I also benefited from excellent editing from Megan Kate Nelson and Ben Platt, and I am grateful for their patience, encouragement, and expertise. Pierce Monahan was a thorough source checker, Duke Johns was a careful copy editor, and I'm grateful for their attention to detail.

I am eternally grateful for the love and support from my family: Scott Gaf-field, Johanna Spaans, Jillian Gaffield, Aaron Spaans, Grace Spaans, Aidan Spaans, Ryan Spaans, Miles Gaffield, Jameson Gaffield, Griffith Gaffield, Christel Koh-ler, James Kohler, Jacqueling Gang, Scott Gang, Aaron Gang, and Sophia Gang. Scott Gaffield provided crucial advice early in the process. My parents, Pam Gaffield and Chad Gaffield, have listened to me talk unceasingly about this book, and I thank them for their patience and advice. Their love and support have always been unwavering, and I'm so, so lucky. I signed the contract for this book in March 2020, and I would not have finished writing it without the sup-port of Mark Kohler, who has been the best partner and supporter. I am grateful for his love and companionship. I thank my children, Stevenson Thomas and Pierce James, for being the best distractions and for their never-ending aston-ishment that the book was *still* not finished.

Index

PRESS
PLAY

Why Every Company
Needs a Gaming Strategy

PRESS PLAY

BASTIAN BERGMANN

HARVARD BUSINESS REVIEW PRESS • BOSTON, MASSACHUSETTS

HBR Press Quantity Sales Discounts

Harvard Business Review Press titles are available at significant quantity discounts when purchased in bulk for client gifts, sales promotions, and premiums. Special editions, including books with corporate logos, customized covers, and letters from the company or CEO printed in the front matter, as well as excerpts of existing books, can also be created in large quantities for special needs.

For details and discount information for both print and ebook formats, contact booksales@harvardbusiness.org, tel. 800-988-0886, or www.hbr.org/bulksales.

Copyright 2025 Bastian Bergmann

All rights reserved

Printed in the United States of America

10 9 8 7 6 5 4 3 2 1

No part of this publication may be reproduced, stored in or introduced into a retrieval system, or transmitted, in any form, or by any means (electronic, mechanical, photocopying, recording, or otherwise), without the prior permission of the publisher. Requests for permission should be directed to permissions@harvardbusiness.org, or mailed to Permissions, Harvard Business School Publishing, 60 Harvard Way, Boston, Massachusetts 02163.

The web addresses referenced in this book were live and correct at the time of the book's publication but may be subject to change.

Cataloging-in-Publication data is forthcoming.

ISBN: 978-1-64782-615-4
eISBN: 978-1-64782-616-1

The paper used in this publication meets the requirements of the American National Standard for Permanence of Paper for Publications and Documents in Libraries and Archives Z39.48-1992.

To Lynn, Alexis, and Tova—all gas, no breaks.

Contents

Part One

THE BASICS

1

More Than Just
Fun and Games

When Burberry approached Mythical Games, the creator of
the renowned blockchain-based video game Blankos Block
Party, about introducing its new fashion line through
unique in-game characters, the Mythical team, led by cofounder and CEO John Linden, thought it was a joke. But Burberry
was serious: it wanted to tap into a new digital audience with vastly
different expectations and shopping behaviors. The company had
done its homework. Its research into global consumer trends showed
that the target consumers didn't just shop—they interacted with
brands on social media, played video games, and prioritized experiences over physical goods. Personalization was paramount.

Blankos Block Party, with its open-world, blockchain-based format, was the perfect platform. In the game, players can own, create,
buy, sell, and build upon their digital vinyl toys, known as "Blankos." These Blankos are customizable and come with unique designs and abilities, which are influenced by pop culture and various
art styles.

Burberry's goal was to give players an authentic Burberry experience inside the video game. The team created a novel character, called Sharky B, that players could purchase and use as their virtual representation. They could customize this character with virtual Burberry items from the company's 2021 summer collection, merging high fashion with digital play.

With accessories like jetpacks, shoes, and armbands, the limited-edition character—only 750 were available—launched just two months after the partnership had begun. At a price of $299.99 per Blanko, the entire collection sold out in twenty-two seconds. The price tag was high, compared with the average cost of in-game items, but that didn't discourage players. The price signaled exclusivity, a premium experience, and the opportunity to belong to a special club—not unlike the signals sent by real-world Burberry items.

Less than one minute into its video game journey, the fashion company had made $225,000 in revenue. More importantly, it reached a new digital audience while being authentic to its brand. Beyond money, Burberry had created new opportunities as a business, which would bode well for its future endeavors.

Many companies today are similarly trying to meet dramatically changed consumer expectations. People desire experiences more than goods and services, because they continue getting value from them long after consumption.[1] Research shows that 80 percent of customers are more likely to make a purchase when companies offer personalized, deeply immersive experiences, and 64 percent expect the companies offering these experiences to react and respond to their questions and requests in real time.[2] The data is clear that traditional forms of media and consumer engagement—the tried-and-true marketing playbooks—simply cannot meet these desires. While daily TV consumption decreased by 21 percent between 2020 and 2024, for example, consumption of digital media is slated to increase by 28 percent between 2020 and 2026.[3] The key driver of the widening gap? Video games.

Over the past three years, the amount of time that US households spend playing video games every week has increased by 30 percent, from 12.7 hours to 16.5 hours.[4] Today 3.3 billion people play a game almost daily—a number that is projected to jump to 3.8 billion by 2030.[5] These people—a large percentage of the global population—are regular consumers like you and me, not just those who fit into the stereotypic idea of gamers. And as customer expectations regarding immersive experiences that resonate become more prevalent, the boundaries between gaming and other industries blur, driven by the proliferation of games as technological platforms rather than isolated forms of media consumption.

The message to executives and leaders of any business is: to regain the loyalty of your customers, you have to meet them where they are. And where you will find them is playing video games. Fashion designer Tommy Hilfiger nailed it when he told me, "Any industry can leverage video games as a dynamic platform for storytelling, product placement, and consumer engagement in ways traditional media can't match."[6] Major brands, companies, and nonprofits are getting into games and employing different strategies to master tectonic shifts in consumer expectations and engagement. Here are a few examples:

- Mastercard issued League of Legends–themed credit cards that allowed players to redeem cashback offers inside the game and unlock special discounts.

- Louis Vuitton placed its iconic handbag in the same game in the form of a trophy case.

- Mountain Dew created a soda specifically aimed at gamers that was advertised in Call of Duty.

- Balenciaga launched its latest fashion collection virtually in Fortnite before it premiered on runways in Milan, Paris, and New York.

- By selling in-game items in PUBG, SpongeBob, and others, WRTHY and the Eleanor Crook Foundation realized ten thousand days of treatment for malnourished children in under twenty-six hours.

- Peloton let its riders immerse themselves in a bike-racing video game while they're burning calories, paving the way for the company's goal of becoming an immersive, connected fitness platform.

The commitment with which these companies are pushing into video games demonstrates how play is serious business. The benefits they—and potentially you—are able to reap are profound. Games allow your customer engagement efforts to scale quickly and globally, and to reach millions of consumers through a dedicated touchpoint that you can shape to represent your brand and align with your goals. No other channel, not even social media, offers this.

Engagement with your content, brand, and products will be far higher through games than through your website, let alone offline touchpoints. This engagement can be continuous, ensuring that you stay top of mind throughout the modern customer journey. Games can help your company become a part of new communities, interact with customers ongoingly and in real time, and develop far stronger brand identity and loyalty than ever before. You will also gain invaluable data and insights, at scale, from your target audience, allowing you to mitigate risks and lower costs in research and development while increasing revenue. These kinds of benefits are a major reason Microsoft decided to double down on its gaming strategy by acquiring Activision Blizzard for $68.7 billion in 2023, the largest acquisition in the computing giant's history.[7]

Video games are the consumer touchpoint of the twenty-first century, and they're pushing companies to reimagine their approaches to a range of services. Former PayPal president and CEO Dan Schulman put it this way: "People play video games every day. They also make multiple payments every day. But they only use PayPal a few times per week. I wonder if there is anything we can learn from the world of video games and apply it to the world of payments."[8] I'd argue those lessons are relevant to every other industry too.

Games and Gamers Are Everywhere

The 3.3 billion people who played video games almost daily in 2024 represent about 60 percent of the global population that is connected to the internet.[9] The takeaway is this: gaming is a platform and a technological medium unlike any other in how it penetrates our lives.

Even if you don't consider yourself to be a gamer, chances are you are exposed to video games quite frequently anyway. My wife, for example, would never describe herself as a gamer, but she has the puzzle game 2048 on her phone and plays often; she also likes the *New York Times* games bundle, which we'll learn about in detail later on. Your kids probably play some video games and hang out with their friends inside them. Maybe you or your partner like Wordle. Maybe the person sitting next to you on an airplane is frantically matching items to collect colorful gems; roughly 270 million people play Candy Crush Saga at least once a month.[10] My 65-year-old father-in-law pulls out his phone at every dinner party and gets in a few minutes of Royal Match. An executive at a large insurance company, who my colleagues and I recently met at a conference, confidently proclaimed that she isn't a gamer—only for her colleague to ask how often she opens Scrabble Go. The next time you are in the office, at a family reunion, or in a public space, keep your eyes open and you see the following: everybody plays games. The myth of the gamer as a lone person in front of a TV in their basement is not only outdated—it's highly inaccurate.

And that's not just because people play regardless of social, economic, or demographic background. Games are starting to show up in a lot of everyday places. If you watch Netflix or Apple TV+, you've likely been prompted to play games that are an expansion of their traditional content offerings. Instagram doesn't necessarily look like a game, yet at its very core it functions like one, which is a big part of the reason it's been so successful. The same is true of the well-known language learning app Duolingo. If you're currently brushing up on your foreign language skills for your next vacation, you might have noticed that the experience looks and feels a lot like a game.

The more that video games make their way into our lives, the more the potential for applications in the realm of business grow. Today games are being used to diagnose and treat children with ADHD, recruit and hire job candidates, train pilots, educate children, hold concerts enjoyed by tens of millions of people, and revolutionize e-commerce. The list goes on, yet many business leaders, executives, and managers in the areas of product development, customer experience, marketing, innovation, and strategy lack the tools and resources to help them wrap their heads around these shifts, what makes gaming so special, and how they can harness its potential to future-proof their companies.

This lack really struck me a couple of years ago when I was on a video call with the global marketing leaders for two of the biggest beverage brands from a *Fortune* 500 consumer goods company. We were excited to discuss a potential partnership around games, and they started the call by excitedly proclaiming that gaming was one of the three key pillars for their entire digital strategy for the next five years. When I asked what they had in mind, the level of excitement started to subside fairly quickly. "Sponsoring an esports team," replied one leader. That was the strategy: sponsoring a team that plays video games competitively.

On an innovation scale from "mind blowing" to "more of the same," this approach tasted as stale as a pot of cold coffee. We collectively took a deep breath—and spent the next ninety minutes discussing video games, clearing up misconceptions, and painting a picture of what might be possible for their beverage brands. It was all new to them.

But they are not alone.

I have spent my entire career at the intersection of digital strategy, business model innovation, technology (specifically artificial intelligence), and gaming. I was fortunate to begin my journey as a consultant at Boston Consulting Group, advising *Fortune* 1000 companies on how to adapt their business models to stay in tune with the evolving needs of a far more digital consumer. I've built startups that partnered with large industrial organizations, using AI to understand consumer behavior and personalize experiences in physical and digital spaces. And I'm a cofounder and the chief operating officer of Solsten, which leverages psychology and AI to understand global consumers more deeply than ever before, to help companies identify and resonate with them. Our work, rooted in gaming, has included partnering with iconic game developers and publishers like Electronic Arts, Sony, Epic Games, Zynga, and Activision Blizzard. These efforts have opened up pathways to work with companies like DraftKings, Dentsu, and Peloton, which are active in different industries but are all asking the same question:

How do we attract and engage consumers in 2025 and beyond? It's a question that executives raise to me every week. Understanding video games and honing a strategy for them is a big piece of the puzzle.

Looking back, the ninety-minute call with the beverage marketers was the impetus for me to write this book. I wanted to provide a resource to help readers like you feel empowered to set a course for the successful future of your company using the power of video games.

The Journey Ahead

Many of the biggest and most famous video games of all time are so-called open-world titles. Elden Ring, which won Game of the Year at the 2022 Game Awards, is a beautiful example. It boasts what many open-world titles have in common: a vast map that is meant to be explored and a player (or a group of players) who sets out to turn uncharted territory into discovered land by collecting resources, solving challenges, and winning battles.

This is what we are about to do. Think of this book as an open world. You are the player who begins their journey, and your map is the territory we are about to explore. Different parts of the map—our destinations—represent the consumers we are trying to reach and engage. But first we must get to know the terrain, to get a feel for the lay of the land, so we know how best to navigate it.

That's the gist of chapter 2—ever-changing and evolving consumer preferences. Who is your target audience? What are their needs and desires? Where do they spend time? Why? Answering these questions and many more will give us a strong sense of our best mode of transportation to travel across the landscape to reach our audience. The ideal vehicles for our travels are video games.

Chapter 3 explains the power of play, what makes something a video game, and why games are highly effective at engaging consumers.

Before embarking on any long and unfamiliar journey, pausing to plan your trip can pay huge dividends. What are the conditions we should expect? Did we pack everything we need? Do we have the right resources? Do we know the most effective and efficient path to our desired destination? Are there alternative routes we can take? Chapter 4 addresses these questions and shows us how to ensure that our journey will be successful.

There is one more thing we can do to set ourselves up for success. We can look for examples of others who have explored the territory before us to learn from their experiences. Players of video games like Elden Ring, for example, dig into Reddit threads, Discord communities, and YouTube gameplay footage to navigate trickier parts of their journeys and get the execution right. Fortunately, you don't have to start a comprehensive online search to find examples and best practices.

Chapters 5 through 8 take us deep into the strategies and actions of the companies that have successfully blazed new trails in customer engagement, using video games as a vehicle. We will learn from organizations such as Chipotle, NASCAR, the *New York Times*, and Peloton that this vehicle can be leveraged in different ways. From integrating with existing games and creating new ones to leveraging blockchain-based games and ultimately letting the game become the product, we'll explore what these companies did, how they achieved success, and synthesize key learnings for you.

Now, as we prepare to embark on our adventure, we should let our fellow travelers and companions know about our plans and what they can expect. Chapter 9 provides insight into how you can effectively prime your organization ahead of time for the gaming future.

Lastly, the map of any great video game will evolve and expand. So will games' potential use cases for companies, since novel applications will add new parts to our map. The epilogue provides a brief look into what may be around the corner.

There are many companies whose stories would have made for powerful examples in this book. I narrowed my selection down to those that I felt achieve a great balance between providing a broad overview of the opportunity space in gaming and offering rich details of how to set the wheels in motion and find success. Without a doubt, there are many examples that had all the ingredients to be showcased but that we just didn't have room to include. I hope you'll give me the benefit of the doubt for any omissions made, and I hope the following stories deeply resonate with you.

We're now past the instruction screens and the tutorials. Hold on to your game controller (your copy of this book!) and lean forward. It's time to press play.

2

Meeting Consumers Where They Are

A s the boundaries between digital and real-world experiences blur, many companies find that their traditional methods of consumer engagement are increasingly out of sync with the lives of the very people they are striving to reach. How, then, can these companies expect to compete in today's marketplace?

The truth is, they can't. In fact, they won't stay in business much longer if they fail to adapt to these changed (and ever-changing) consumer expectations. So which companies will emerge on top? Those that excel at deeply understanding their customers, recognizing their expectations, and engaging them in meaningful, resonant ways at the right touchpoints. In short, companies that meet consumers where they are.

Traditional forms of engagement, like billboards, radio, or television, are falling short in their abilities to meet expectations regarding personalization and immersion. They are mostly passive and one-directional, and the impact of those limits is profound. Take cable TV consumption as an example: in the United States, cable

TV subscriptions are down nearly 35 percent between 2010 and today. Globally, the share of adults who consume all their news and entertainment content via traditional cable TV channels dropped by an astonishing 42 percent in the last four years alone.[1]

Video games, on the other hand, are on the opposite trajectory. Almost 84 percent of all internet users play them.[2] Total US consumer spending on video games grew from $56 billion to more than $60 billion from 2020 to 2021.[3] And while millennials spend the most, shelling out $86 per month, Gen Zers ($80), Gen Xers ($62), and even boomers ($52) aren't far behind.[4]

Taking a closer look at the behaviors of Gen Z offers a window into the future. Not only have games like Roblox become the place for young people to meet and hang out, but 65 percent of Gen Zers "have spent money on a virtual item that exists only within the confines of a video game."[5] What is even more striking, and hugely important for companies to realize, is that 86 percent of consumers who purchased a virtual item inside of a video game also purchased a corresponding physical item—for example, I bought a pair of Nike sneakers to dress my in-game character as well as for myself in real life—a pattern that is not unique to any one demographic group.[6] Given that 57 percent of gamers have spent money on and inside video games, companies and brands have a massive opportunity to monetize the relationship more effectively (and in some cases unlock entirely new revenue streams and business models as well—some of these we get to later in this book).[7]

But there's more than just monetization at stake. People spend 36 percent of their time in video games doing things other than simply playing the game itself.[8] They create content, socialize, watch live streams, join live events like concerts, or buy content. That means brands can engage consumers deeply across a variety of activities and with different content formats all within the same environment. And since video games can be enjoyed on different devices and platforms, it's important for companies to understand usage patterns to better gauge where all this time is spent.

According to research firm Newzoo, mobile devices are by far the dominant medium for people to play video games. In its 2023 Global Gamer Study, Newzoo found that 79 percent of players use their mobile device for gaming, and 47 percent play on multiple devices. When comparing the preferences of people who stick to one device, the prevalence of mobile is startling: while 35 percent exclusively play on mobile devices, only 9 percent and 8 percent play solely on video game consoles and PCs, respectively.[9] Looking at the big picture, the trend toward cross-platform play is clear. Gamers want interoperability across devices and platforms to enjoy their games whenever, wherever. In other words, people identify more with their games than with their devices.

Everyone Is a Gamer

Gaming today is the most popular active form of entertainment for people between the ages of 10 and 50. And as each new, younger generation emerges, their interactions with video games only become more frequent and deeper. In a recent study, consulting firm Bain & Company found that people between the ages of 13 and 17 spend roughly 40 percent more of their time per week in video game environments—playing, chatting, hanging out with friends, shopping, or learning—than with any other form of entertainment, including social media, music, and TV. Although slightly older consumers (ages 18 to 34) spend the most time on social media, according to the same report, video games come in at a close second.[10] So while the younger generations can be regarded as one of the driving forces behind the continued rise of gaming, the one-time notion that these experiences, and the related possibilities for companies, are predominantly for young people no longer holds true.

The data confirms this: in the United States, 47 percent of the people who regularly play video games are in the age range of 18 to 50 years old. The age group with the biggest increase of gamers in the last two decades? People aged 50 and older, a cohort that grew from 17 percent in 2004 to 29 percent in 2024.[11] And while Gen Zers lead the way on one measure of mobile gaming, with about 48 percent of them having installed at least four games on their phones, millennials (45 percent), Gen Xers (41 percent), the Silent Generation (36 percent), and baby boomers (35 percent) aren't far behind.[12] In fact, the share of people in each demographic group that has installed one to three mobile games is very consistent, at around 30 percent across all groups. To quote the authors of the Bain & Company research: "Though gamers have historically trended younger, our data suggests fewer gamers are aging out. This change will likely be supported as gaming becomes the foundation for other media and nonmedia experiences."[13]

This prevalence of video games as a dominant form of media consumption, and hence a means to engage consumers across demographics and generations, can be attributed to an aging population. People who played video games in the 1970s are now grandparents, a shift that explains why gaming is now a multigenerational force—one that is here to stay. "New gamers are constantly aging in," says Raja Rajamannar, chief marketing and communications officer at Mastercard.[14] It's an evergreen turn.

And gamers are a lot more prevalent than stereotypes suggest. Perceptions have shifted significantly over time. In 2015, of those people who had at least one mobile game installed on their smartphones, only 10 percent identified as gamers. Today 50 percent now refer to themselves by the term.[15] Additionally, two-thirds of gamers influence purchasing decisions in US households.[16] That matters because video games are quickly becoming the place where people discover new things to buy. Half of the consumers who play games state that they discover a new brand while doing so, and 47 percent say they're more likely to buy from a brand that is featured in their favorite games.[17]

I was recently on a flight home from a business trip and was seated next to a gentleman who, by my estimation, was likely in his late fifties. Immediately after takeoff, he took out his iPad and started playing Candy Crush Saga, a popular mobile game by the developer King. After a few sessions of moving the colorful pieces around on his screen, my neighbor proceeded to read a car magazine. Then, having studied the reviews of new models that hit the market, he went back to playing Candy Crush for thirty minutes until our plane touched down. This gentleman is a gamer, whether he is conscious of the fact or not.

So are the 48 percent of all US gamers who are female.[18] One such woman, Erryn Rhoden, a 48-year-old mother of three, saw her story go viral after she accidentally entered a Candy Crush tournament and made it all the way to the semifinals, falling just short of the $250,000 prize money.[19] So much for stereotypes.

The reality, as we can see, is that video games will become, and arguably already are, the dominant form of consumer engagement. They're foundational to entertainment experiences more broadly, across industries and demographic groups.

A Gorilla Hiding in Plain Sight

Despite gaming's cultural presence, a market size north of $200 billion, and a history as a hotbed of innovation and landmark technologies, for the longest time the industry has been a gorilla hiding in plain sight. For years it was treated as a niche or secondary market, failing to receive the recognition it deserved. Only recently has its massive potential and influence begun to be fully acknowledged by industries outside its own sphere.

Samir Agili, chairman of game developer and publisher Tilting Point, has been in the industry for twenty-five years, long enough to have seen this switch firsthand. He recalls that, years ago, his team had a meeting with *Vogue* magazine to talk about how video games and fashion could intersect, but at the time some people found the idea laughable.[20] Today Tilting Point and other developers get proactively invited to boardrooms at the likes of Mars Inc. and Tommy Hilfiger to discuss how they can leverage video games for M&M's candy or the latest Tommy fashion line, respectively, to reach and engage with new audiences. (We'll save the inside scoop on how they did it for later in this book.)

So the real questions are these: Why now? What has changed over the last decade? Looking at the data and the interviews I've conducted with more than a hundred executives across industries, it would be reductive to point toward one single driver for this shift. Instead, I argue there are five factors in how video games went from a nice-to-have to an essential strategic tool for companies to stay relevant and connected to their consumers. Let's take a closer look at each of them.

A spotlight on changed media consumption

Many people view the global pandemic as the key reason for video games' rapid growth. But the gaming market had already more than doubled in the ten years leading up to the crisis. Covid was simply the spotlight needed to help people recognize the growth and size of the video game industry. Jonathan Stringfield, a long-time video game and social media executive, shared this view in his book *Get in the Game*, saying that the pandemic didn't cause the gaming boom but made more people aware of its growing influence on daily life.[21]

Luis Di Como, the former executive vice president of global media at Unilever, who oversaw all of the company's video gaming initiatives as part of the global media strategy, agrees. "The pandemic helped in the sense that the numbers started speaking for themselves. The trends became evident and other non-endemic brands started to move, which further inspired Unilever as well," he told me.[22] In other words, companies finally started to see, and act on, the fact that consumers were spending more and more time and money in games.

These new consumer habits aren't likely to go away. "The pandemic was both a huge accelerator and paradigm shift for digitally savvy companies and brands, and you have to identify and cater to the behaviors that stuck," said Erika Wykes-Sneyd, global vice president and general manager of the virtual goods business unit at Adidas.[23] Doing so is especially important for businesses that want to succeed in a world where video games are becoming increasingly mainstream.

A shift in cultural perception

For Erinrose Sullivan, whose almost thirty-year career spans consumer goods and video games, there's a clear driver that has opened gaming up to everyone: mobile devices. When Sullivan led global analytics and insights for video game giant Electronic Arts from 2008 to 2013, the release of the iPhone in 2007 was a pivotal moment that paved the way for gaming to catch on widely. "About twelve years ago, video games were roughly an $80 billion industry, still on the outside because it was primarily console and PC games," she recalled. "Mobile made it mainstream. Now everyone has access—even your grandma."[24]

What about Esports?

Esports are not the same thing as video games. Many executives who excitedly lead their companies into the gaming world with a new digital strategy believe that esports—the part of the market where digital athletes and teams play video games competitively—*is* the entire gaming industry. This belief couldn't be more wrong. The full industry is about six times larger in terms of audience reach, and roughly one hundred times larger in terms of money being made, than just what's attributed to esports.[a]

This reality is important for you as a leader to take into consideration when strategizing your entry point. Rather than spending hundreds of millions of dollars every year to sponsor esports teams—and reaching a fraction of the consumers you could engage—it will pay off much more to look at video games more holistically. British consumer goods giant Unilever is a prime example of a company that evaluates opportunities across the entire gaming ecosystem, consisting of core gaming, esports, streaming, and cultural events.

So far in this book, we have focused on the area of "core gaming," which we refer to simply as video games—essentially, all those titles that can be played on any one of multiple devices. We will continue to stick with core gaming, not for a lack of merit and potential in the remaining three areas, but for the ability to deeply explore what is arguably the most profound and impactful opportunity for companies looking to stay relevant in consumers' perception.

Note

a. "Esports—Worldwide," Statista, updated August 2024, https://www.statista.com/outlook/amo/esports/worldwide.

As video games became ubiquitous, their potential for various applications grew—transforming industries in unexpected ways. One compelling example is the rise of games as tools for learning. Dan White, the founder and CEO of Filament Games, has been creating award-winning learning games for eighteen years, and they used to be met with resistance. Not anymore. "It feels more common as a pedagogy now, to the extent that there's almost an expectation of schools that video games are an integral part of their curricula," White told me.[25]

The legitimization of video games through use cases, demonstrated efficacy, and financial success has also occurred in a sector quite different from White's field: luxury goods. Traditionally, luxury brands like Gucci or Louis Vuitton have catered to high-networth individuals (translation: not gamers). But things have changed. Ashumi Sanghvi, founder and CEO of MAD Global, a creative agency focused on digital innovation, has worked closely with numerous luxury brands on their ventures into video games. While gamers as a consumer group used to be overlooked, they've now become a core focus. "Fashion and luxury have always been about narrative," Sanghvi said. "The same signaling exists in video games through the novel ways in which we can create and express our identity."[26] She added that a few trailblazing brands have showed what's possible. For example, Burberry and Tommy Hilfiger—whose video game journeys we will explore in later chapters—are at the forefront of this shift, merging the worlds of fashion and gaming in groundbreaking ways.

One last thing it's worth remembering: the people who grew up playing video games in the '70s, '80s, and '90s are now adults, many of whom hold influential roles within the very companies trying to understand and engage with this consumer group. These individuals provide a voice and representation for gaming that challenge the outdated stereotypes we discussed earlier.

Intensified competition, especially for younger audiences

While companies have grown comfortable with the idea of actively engaging with gamers and games, the competition has been dialed up. Once a few first movers demonstrated new approaches and strategies, slower and more risk-averse companies were left with little choice but to follow suit if they want to remain competitive.

For BMW, fully committing itself to venturing into video games ultimately took a nudge from a rival. As Stefan Butz, the company's vice president of engineering information and communication platforms, told me, "Tesla showed the way." The competitive pressure intensified in 2019, when Tesla introduced the ability for customers to play video games on the built-in screen of their cars. This development pushed BMW executives to take video games seriously. They realized they needed to explore how their brand could be represented in an increasingly virtual world and how they could achieve their vision of turning the car into a consumer's "second living room."

BMW's team began by analyzing Tesla's solution in order to focus on what its own entry point could be. "The customer need itself was clear," Butz explained. Customers want entertainment offerings to fill the idle time when charging an electric vehicle or to use the freed-up time when autonomous driving eventually becomes a mass market technology. In 2024 BMW launched its own high-end gaming platform allowing customers to play video games on the in-car display of their BMW using their own smartphone, with plans to roll it out across its various models in the coming years.[27] In addition, BMW conducted its own customer and market research, specifically into China, an important growth market for BMW and the car industry at large. The research resulted in a few clear insights: Chinese consumers, particularly younger ones, play video games. A

of video games has exploded, which in turn has spurred the rise of influencers. (To give you a sense of how powerful these influencers are, one recently signed a two-year contract with a streaming network worth $100 million, putting him neck-and-neck for contract size with NBA icon and future Hall of Famer LeBron James.)[30] Overall, advertising has become far more sophisticated, which is also true of the different partners and service providers in the industry. The list goes on.

This advancement in the gaming ecosystem is precisely why companies like Unilever are now fully integrating video games into their broader strategies. Simply using games for advertising or marketing activation, like Honda did in 2012, is not enough.

A closing skills gap

Related to the matured ecosystem, companies benefit from narrower skill and knowledge gaps with regards to video games because of a workforce with more diverse skills and professional backgrounds. Take Jim Green. Before he became the head of interactive and gaming for Peloton, he spent his career as a video game producer and designer. That means Peloton has access to a true expert internally who can help navigate the unfamiliar territory. The importance of this dynamic cannot be understated, and it's demonstrated well by certain actions Unilever took—and didn't take. We will look at these examples in more detail later.

The consumer goods giant had a deal in place in 2012 to put its shampoo brand Dove in Electric Arts' game The Sims Social. After that, though, Unilever and video games put their relationship on the back burner for almost a decade. "Video games were there ten, fifteen years ago," Luis Di Como told me. "The space was important, but it needed too much ramp-up time for us internally. It has always been on our road map, but we simply didn't have access to the skills and capabilities needed to be successful."[31] This is no longer the case—for Unilever as well as others.

Wrapping Things Up

At this point, I hope two things are very clear. First, video games are serious business. And second, they're a serious business right now. For the longest time, a gaming presence has felt like a nice-to-have for companies. But the moment of truth, or what author Malcolm Gladwell would describe as a tipping point, for virtually any business is here. "Video games and gaming as an entire ecosystem are quickly becoming table stakes," warned Amanpreet Singh, a former professional gamer and Unilever's global media innovation and brand partnerships lead for gaming, metaverse, and sports marketing. "It's no longer about whether companies should be in video games. It's about, What else can you do?"[32] Or in the words of Tommy Hilfiger, "For those aiming to captivate and engage a digitally oriented audience, adopting video gaming strategies is increasingly indispensable."[33]

To identify how your company can effectively leverage video games, we first need to lay the foundation: why games are so engaging to consumers, what makes a video game a game, and how you go about building one. We'll start digging into those topics in the next chapter.

3

The Power of Play

At the core of the gaming industry's continued rise is a fundamental truth: play is innate. It's how primates, and we as human beings, learn most effectively.

Video games are essentially a digital manifestation of play with rules. "The magic of video games is that they are able to grab a person's attention as effective as they are," says Raph Koster, author of the seminal book *A Theory of Fun for Game Design* and design lead for massively multiplayer online games like Ultima Online and EverQuest.[1] In essence, a video game is a portal for grabbing and keeping attention, one that is far superior to, for example, television. The level of immersion that video games can create is next to none. Just ask the actor Henry Cavill, who nearly missed out on an offer to portray Superman in a movie because he was too focused on playing World of Warcraft.[2]

The deep connection between users and games has a direct and tangible business impact. Advertising in these titles is more likely to be watched than ads in other media, and consumers tend to show higher loyalty toward companies they experience in the context of games. Brand recall is also higher, and consumers that play games are more likely to make repeat purchases, too.

In other words, once video games enter the fold, the impact is felt beyond the digital realm. When toy company Spin Master (do your kids watch the popular TV show *PAW Patrol*? Spin Master is behind it) joined the gaming space in late 2021 by presenting a full-length episode of its popular anime series *Bakugan Battle Brawlers* on Roblox, the result was a significant uptick in toy sales. Only three years later, the company attributed roughly one-third of its operating income to video games and expected that soon 20 percent of its entire revenue (which in 2024 totaled $2.2 billion) would come from them.[3]

Tilting Point, which works with big brands such as M&M's as they dip their toes into these waters, sees these kinds of dynamics at work in every game it creates. "There is no other medium that gets a user as immersed as a game does," Samir Agili, chairman, told me. "The relationship with the assets inside of a game creates an amazing emotional connection for the player that causes them to sustain their attention and come back to playing the game, and it's a much stronger connection than just seeing a brand somewhere."[4] As we learned before, the data supports him: 86 percent of consumers who purchased a virtual in-game item also purchased the corresponding physical item.[5]

Putting the "Game" in Video Games

To understand why video games can create such deep levels of immersion and connection with people, we have to for a moment dive into the building blocks of what it means to play a game. What makes games so entertaining?

Researchers Katie Salen and Eric Zimmerman define a game as "a system in which players engage in an artificial context, defined by rules, that results in a quantifiable outcome."[6] Their thinking highlights the structured nature of gameplay: players operate within a world whose design dictates how they can interact with it. Rules create boundaries, goals, and challenges, ensuring that the experience is consistent and measurable. The "quantifiable outcome" refers to the fact that games, by their nature, are designed to produce a specific result—whether it's a high score, a win-or-loss condition, or progression toward an objective.

Think of Nintendo's Mario games, some of the best-selling titles of all time. The hero, Mario, and by proxy the player, moves through an artificial world defined by rules (gravity, enemy behavior, platform physics) with clear goals (rescue Princess Peach, defeat Bowser). Every level has its own quantifiable outcome: you either finish the level or you don't. Your performance is measured by the number of coins collected, the time taken, and how many lives you have left. This system creates a sense of challenge, reward, and progression that defines the experience.

Every video game consists of a loop or multiple loops that sends the player on some kind of journey. When a challenge is completed, the next one awaits. We can say the same even for titles like Wordle and Candy Crush Saga. Both share core design principles—clear rules, structured systems, and measurable outcomes—making them highly engaging in the same way as "traditional" games like Mario's various adventures.

The concept of "flow," which psychologist Mihaly Csikszentmihalyi described as a state of intense and contented focus, is also central to understanding how play functions as both an immersive and an educational experience. In the context of games, flow is when players become so absorbed in the task at hand that they lose track of time and external distractions seem to fade away. This state of deep concentration and engagement, which Csikszentmihalyi defines as "action generating action," is key to both enjoyment and learning.[7] Video games are a digital manifestation of the concept, allowing us to flow from one moment to the next.

Someone could argue that social media is able to rival video games in its ability to engage consumers. Look at TikTok, the platform that has taken an entire industry and generations of people by storm. Its meteoric rise has led the app to amass over one billion active users globally.[8] In 2024 US users on average spent a whopping fifty-eight minutes on it every single day.[9] Geopolitical concerns and national interests aside, there's no denying that TikTok has become and likely will remain a powerful tool that businesses will have to leverage to engage with their customers.

However, social media in its current form has a major disadvantage when compared with video games: the former is a highly passive form of consumption, whereas the latter are much more active. Social media lacks the essence of games: play, rules, and goals. Simply put, social media is a one-way street. Video games are a two-way street—which is why they are the far superior form of effective, and lasting, engagement with consumers. (Fun fact: gaming-related content accumulated more than three trillion views on TikTok in 2022, making it the most watched content on the platform.)[10]

Engaging experiences are good at triggering a human brain pattern, and video games are great at doing that. Our participation is an integral part of the experience. "Video games are active and engaging. You are fully involved in the experience, physically and emotionally," said Erinrose Sullivan, who we met earlier in the book.[11] This doesn't mean that more passive forms of media and entertainment can't capture consumers' attention. TikTok is incredible at doing just that. But the active nature of video games allows people to more effectively form positive associations with brands, which has significant upside for businesses. That's precisely the reason that in 2018 Reed Hastings, at the time the CEO of Netflix, referred to the popular video game Fortnite as the company's main competition, rather than other streaming services or even social media.[12]

And there is another upside to video games, one that may not immediately translate into tangible business metrics but that is important to discuss in light of public conversations around the significant health risks that social media poses, especially to children. Researchers in multiple studies have found that passive forms of media consumption (like using social media) can cause anxiety and even depression, while active forms (like playing video games) significantly lower the risks of mental illness. In fact, multiple studies have shown that games are able to improve attention, memory, hand-eye coordination, task switching, and a variety of additional cognitive functions, especially in children. Other studies suggest that playing video games has a profound effect on people suffering from PTSD and substance abuse,[13] specifically because of the social connections people make with other players, as well as a game's ability to remove the person's focus from their trauma or addiction.

So not only are video games powerful channels for engaging customers, but playing them can actually have real benefits. However, as with many things that can support our well-being, moderation is key.

Different Types of Games

Video games can vary a lot in the visual complexity, richness, depth, and level of immersion they provide. On the simpler end, think of digital versions of analog classics like chess and solitaire. On the more complex end, you have large, open-world titles like EVE Online or Minecraft, which also allow players to create their own content to further enrich the experience. Regardless of the level of complexity, every video game leverages the loops mentioned previously, which center on challenge, reward, and progression.

In terms of generating revenue, at a high level, video games monetize players along three major avenues.

Premium games

People pay an up-front fee to access the content of what I call *premium games*, or what you might think of as traditional video games—anything that, historically, you'd buy as a CD to insert into a PlayStation, Xbox, or other console. Today premium games exist just as often in purely digital form, since demand for hard copies has declined. The price point depends on the platform, with mobile games typically costing around $4.99 or less, whereas PC and console titles often range from $9.99 to $70 or even more. Rumor has it that the new Grand Theft Auto 6 may breach a key price barrier and cost up to $100.[14]

For brands, using premium games to engage with consumers is a double-edged sword. Because of the up-front payment, the financial hurdle for customers is higher than that of other engagement approaches. But if a particular game reaches a highly desired audience, it can offer brands direct access and a focused pathway. Sports video game franchises like Electronic Arts' NHL series is a great example—in it you see hockey brands like Bauer and Sherwood advertise on the boards while a match is in motion.

Subscription-based games

Players pay a monthly fee to enjoy subscription-based video games, as well as to receive updated content. Technically, these games somewhat fall into the same category as premium games because of the up-front payment; however, the subscription fee tends to be far smaller, typically around $4.99 per month, than the cost of a premium game (but depending on how long you keep the subscription, it may cost more than buying a premium game outright).

The benefits of this category are twofold: the initial barrier to adoption for the player is smaller than that of premium games, and if the game is able to retain these consumers, it provides a recurring revenue stream to its developer. These steady cash flows are important to consider because companies with revenue models based on subscriptions or recurring revenue bundles achieve far higher valuations than companies without them.[15] For brands looking to make video games an integral part of their business strategy, this should be an important consideration, along with the fact that subscription-based titles lend themselves nicely to a bundling strategy with other digital services—which increases the potential for cross-promotion and further revenue growth.

The company that arguably provides the playbook for how to implement, execute, and win with this approach is the *New York Times* (*NYT*). Since it decided in 2020 to anchor its gaming strategy with a $5 monthly subscription (or $40 if you feel like committing for a full year) that includes famous titles like Wordle and Spelling Bee, along with the classic *NYT* crossword, the audience that plays its games has grown 10x, surpassing one million subscribers within eighteen months.[16]

Today video games are the driving force behind *NYT*'s overall digital subscription. The company's stock price is up 77 percent over the past five years since making the commitment to video games, and revenues are up more than 30 percent as well.[17] Clearly, video games have been instrumental in *NYT*'s economic success despite the massive headwinds in the broader media landscape. Fortunately for us, the company's head of games, the mastermind behind its playbook, will walk us through its journey and strategy in chapter 6.

Free-to-play games

Players can download and enjoy some video games free of charge. Here, revenues are generated via advertisements placed inside the game or digital items that can be purchased. Free-to-play titles provide almost no financial barrier to entry, making them by far the most adopted type of video game as well as the most lucrative—85 percent of all video game revenue is generated from them.[18]

The revenue possibilities are arguably the number one reason companies in many industries have gravitated toward games. Free-to-plays help them reach more consumers, more quickly, and through a nearly limitless set of options that can fit with the company's strategy. For example, by showing a video ad to players in League of Legends, Louis Vuitton embedded its iconic suitcase as the trophy case for the winning team; fashion house Balenciaga launched its latest collection in the form of digital clothing players could purchase for their characters in Fortnite; and fast-food chains Chick-fil-A and Chipotle flat-out created their own video games. The options are limited only by the imagination and seriousness of companies' strategies. Because of free-to-plays' wide adoption by consumers and the vast potential for organizations, these video games and their business opportunities deserve a closer look. Let's examine them more closely.

As we've discussed, free-to-play games offer perhaps the vastest array of options for user engagement, monetization, and hence touchpoints for companies and brands, with the lowest barrier to entry for customers. One way to monetize the audience is through in-game advertising. The game studio will place ads at different points along the player's journey, such as when they finish a level. The person often receives an incentive for watching an ad, such as an item that allows them to progress faster, and the developer makes money from its advertising partners based on the number of ads watched, the number of eyeballs reached, and so on. (Note: there are a lot of parties involved to make this fairly complex system work in the real world, but for the sake of the discussion here, a simplified explanation will suffice.)

In-game ads can look and feel different depending on the context. The aforementioned example, in which players receive an incentive for watching an ad, is called a *rewarded video. Interstitial ads* tend to occur in between game levels or actions that players are taking. *Display banners*, on the other hand, are static ads that appear continually throughout experience, not unlike banner ads on websites. Lastly, *offer walls* provide players with a series of incentives for activities that can range from watching an ad to registering for a service. Regardless of the format, there is one key commonality between the various approaches: they're incredibly easy for companies and brands to set up and leverage. This relatively low barrier to entry sits atop the list of the reasons ads have historically been the default strategy for companies looking to video games.

Among the first movers in this space was Adidas, which in 1993 put billboards on the sidelines of the field in FIFA International Soccer (made by Electronic Arts), with the ads featuring the brand's iconic three stripes. (You're in for a surprise about how Adidas's stance on advertising in games has evolved. We'll get into the company's strategy later in the book.)

The major challenge that companies are faced with when relying on an ad-driven strategy is that it's much harder to engage players solely through ads. The friction they introduce into the experience diminishes the game's ultimate power—the state of flowing from one action to the next. Ultimately, players can have a negative reaction: *You're keeping me from playing my game. Why should I buy your product?* Fortunately, there are a number of other ways free-to-play games are able to drive engagement and revenue that are also highly effective ways for companies to engage their audiences.

When Jenifer Willig, CEO and cofounder of social impact agency WRTHY, strategized around how to meaningfully bring awareness to child malnutrition, and to quickly have a positive impact, she and her team didn't need to look any further than free-to-plays. "Nobody knows that child malnutrition is the number one cause of child death," Willig told me. "So instead of asking people to donate, we asked them to play a video game. We met them where they were already at."[19]

The idea was to integrate ready-to-use therapeutic food (RUTF) into the game experience. RUTFs are energy-dense and micronutrient-enriched food packets that can help a child who is struggling with malnourishment. Tilting Point was the first developer and publisher to try RUTFs, putting them in the free-to-play SpongeBob: Krusty Cook-Off, which is based on the beloved cartoon character SpongeBob SquarePants. It was a perfect fit. Among the in-game items that players could purchase, some were labeled "LifePack," and buying them (with real money) would help fund the distribution of RUTFs to at-risk children. To date, more than ninety thousand packs have been delivered due to LifePack.

The LifePack example is a powerful showcase for how companies can seamlessly leverage the monetization infrastructure of free-to-play games to create a win-win scenario for themselves and the game developer, and even society. Points of integration with in-game items like this are plentiful and are often connected to the game's economy and monetization system, but author Jonathan Stringfield boils them down to three categories:[20]

- *Soft currencies* are fairly easy to acquire, typically earned or purchased as part of the core gameplay experience, and exchanged for minor or temporary rewards or boosts.

- *Hard currencies* can buy substantial in-game rewards or advantages, and usually are given out in small amounts to encourage players to make in-app purchases.

- *Durables* are permanent rewards that can be earned or purchased, often in the form of cosmetic items that allow for character customization.

The exact currencies that appear inside of a video game vary, but most titles will feature at least one of them, if not a combination. The things they buy vary, too, and include new avatars (virtual representations of players), hidden characters, items, coins, power-ups, and skill boosts. These options have proven to be a proverbial gold mine for video game companies, and they just may be one for other companies as well.

Take industry juggernaut Activision Blizzard, maker of the renowned franchise Call of Duty. Originally the company was in the business of selling physical copies of its games for anywhere from $70 to $100 a pop. In 2021 Activision made more than $5 billion in revenue from in-app purchases in free-to-play games—more than 60 percent of its entire revenue that year.[21]

Electronic Arts, another household name, was also known for selling physical copies of games from well-known series like Madden NFL, NHL, and FIFA. The company increased its market capitalization from $4 billion in 2012 to $30 billion in 2018—partly due to changing its focus to free-to-play games. (EA's market cap today is over $41 billion, meaning the positive impact of this monetization model persists.)[22]

The fundamental driver of these shifts is a concept called games-as-a-service, which enables the monetization of video games after their release. Titles are updated frequently with new experiences and content, which opens up space for long-term in-game purchases. Not only does this strategy allow for content to be added monthly, weekly, or even daily, but games can be streamed to the user's device and accessed from anywhere, anytime. For brands and companies outside of the gaming industry, this represents an opportunity that

Just because an experience doesn't immediately look like a game doesn't mean it isn't one. One of the interview questions that Samir Agili of Tilting Point asks job applicants is the following: *Do you think Instagram is a game?* "You'd be surprised by the different types of answers you get," says Agili.[a]

There is one correct answer, he adds: Of course Instagram is a game. Its experience consists of five core elements that make up a loop the user cycles through: goals and objectives; rules and instructions; interactions; challenges; and outcomes, rewards, and feedback. The goal is to have other users follow you and interact with your content. You can post different types of content. You can interact with content and other users by liking, commenting, resharing, and direct messaging. The more followers you have, the more visible your content will be—and the more likes, comments, messages, and ultimately new followers you receive.

The appropriation and application of game design in more utilitarian systems has been called *gamification*, a concept that has taken off in the last decade. As researchers Jonna Koivisto and Juho Hamari point out, games are known for their ability to engage and excite users, and "it is this nature of playing games that gamification technology attempts to capture, harness, and implement into contexts that commonly have a more instrumental purpose."[b] In other words, gamification aims to infuse the experience of playing video games into information systems to affect user behavior.

In his landmark book on the topic, *Actionable Gamification: Beyond Points, Badges, and Leaderboards*, author and researcher Yu-kai Chou offers a step-by-step guide for how companies can introduce game design into customer touchpoints.[c] Take the B2C email app Superhuman, for example. When its CEO, Rahul Vohra, who worked as a game designer in the past, built the service from the ground up, he applied seven game design principles to how he and his team imagined a modern email tool should work:[d]

- Create concrete, achievable, and rewarding goals.
- Design for nuanced emotion.
- Create rapid and robust controls.
- Make fun toys and combine them into games.
- Make the next action obvious.
- Give clear and immediate feedback with no distraction.
- Balance high perceived skill with high perceived challenge (flow).

Notice how these principles tie into the core tenets of games (e.g., seamlessly moving from action to action) as well as the fundamental gameplay loop (e.g., goals, actions with instructions, challenges, rewards) we introduced earlier in this book. Gamification can sometimes be misunderstood or misinterpreted as simply showering the screen in digital confetti when a user completes a task. Vohra went beyond that superficial approach and actually leveraged a true game design process—which is what gamification represents at its very core. (A talk he once gave was fittingly titled "Game Design, Not Gamification, for Great Products.") This method shaped the entire vision for the service and allowed it to capture consumer attention in the crowded competitive space of workplace applications. The ultimate goal and reward around which Superhuman is built? Inbox zero. Anyone who deals with lots of email on a daily basis can appreciate, and enjoy, the process of achieving that.

Notes

a. Samir Agili, interview by author, January 24, 2022.

b. Jonna Koivisto and Juho Hamari, "The Rise of Motivational Information Systems: A Review of Gamification Research," *International Journal of Information Management* 45 (April 2019): 191–210, https://doi.org/10.1016/j.ijinfomgt.2018.10.013.

c. Yu-Kai Chou, *Actionable Gamification: Beyond Points, Badges, and Leaderboards* (published by the author, 2015).

d. Chou, *Actionable Gamification*.

is financially lucrative and that allows them to maintain a consistent touchpoint along the customer journey.

Making a Game: The Design Process

Regardless of whether your company wants to integrate with an existing game or create its own title, either with a partner or on its own, it is invaluable to understand the process of how video games are made. Doing so will set the right expectations and help avoid a rude awakening for your company and your potential partners along the way.

Why are the stakes high? Because making a video game is different from creating any other software or product. "You have to understand the differences between the development of traditional software and video games," says Jim Green, a product manager we met earlier who leads development of the team-building game-inspired workouts for Peloton's connected fitness devices.[23] After more than a decade of creating and managing video games across all genres and platforms, Green was intimately familiar with the intricacies of making great games. That knowledge allowed him to ensure that Peloton leadership's expectations regarding the process, outcomes, and timelines were aligned throughout the process of making the company's first game, Lanebreak, a reality.

Generally speaking, the video game development process is best described in the following six stages:

1. Ideation. The goal of this is exactly as the name indicates: to ideate. Teams explore a lot of different concepts for what a game could look and feel like, including the key features and mechanics that would make up the core experience, the visual appearance (namely the art style), and the theme. They

also explore who the target audience is, what their needs and preferences are, the market for the game, potential competitors, and examples of successful titles in the same space. These factors are key to ensuring that all ideas are anchored in who the team is actually making the game for.

Depending on your organization and target market, your ideal audience can be pretty clear. In the case of Peloton, fitness-oriented users were a far more nebulous crowd than the audience for a traditional game, and there were almost no best practices to rely on. "We were making a game-inspired workout for a stationary fitness bike. We were building a first-of-its-kind offering," remembered Green.[24] So even with all the possibilities for analysis, this stage typically brims with creativity. The more ideas, the better.

2. Concepting. Once ideas have been generated, the next step in the process is to reduce the set of options into a few viable concepts that the team believes have plenty of potential. A single concept will include ideas and hypotheses regarding components such as the theme, the art style, and the core features and mechanics. The goal is to arrive at three to five concepts that present clear ideas that can be tested and validated. This stage typically includes many user tests and iterations based on collected feedback and learnings. The goal should be to assess and understand the product-market fit for the target audience as precisely as possible along its most relevant attributes. (This topic is important enough that we're dedicating an entire section to it in chapter 4.)

The benefit of conducting user research early in the process? Not wasting budget on concepts that are bound to fail and doubling down on the ones that hold actual promise. There is really no set timeline, and it can be challenging to define when the team has struck gold. "The process of defining and finding the fun until you arrive at a video game concept that you want to invest in is unique," explained Green. "You can ideate and test for three months and not end up with something polished."[25] The muscle to discover the experiences you want to build and how to validate them is stronger in some organizations than in others. For companies that are used to building products in a straightforward manner, with clearly defined timelines and outcomes, it's easy to see how developing video games can feel unfamiliar—and maybe even uncomfortable.

3. Prototyping. When the concepting stage has yielded a clear winner that the team wants to prioritize, the prototyping starts. This is the stage where the actual building of the game's core gameplay begins. Frequent user testing is the cornerstone of measuring and tracking progress across important metrics regarding retention and engagement, and it is where you will encounter terms like session length, average number of daily sessions, and day seven and day thirty retention. These metrics let you gauge the "stickiness" of an experience, meaning whether it is ready to keep people playing over a sufficiently long period of time.

4. Soft launch. When the video game is largely complete and has enough content ready for players to enjoy, the real litmus test for the viability of the experience—and all the hard work in the months, if not years, leading up to this moment—is what is often referred to as a soft launch (or a beta launch, a closed alpha, or early access). Essentially, it is a live market rollout with a limited set of users or within selected territories, typically smaller markets first. This process allows the team to gauge real adoption from users, see whether the

performance metrics from the prototyping stage are holding up, and identify any issues that need to be addressed before a full rollout is possible.

The duration of the phase can vary greatly. As a rule of thumb, most mobile games stay in soft launch for about three to six months, whereas PC and console games often spend two to three years in this phase. The main drivers behind the length are the title's overall complexity, how strong the retention and engagement metrics are, and, frankly, how many things in the game are broken. Even companies like Supercell, which is considered to be one of the best mobile developers in the world, took a full eighteen months to tweak its video game Brawl Stars.[26] In Peloton's case, Green and his team released Lanebreak to a beta-testing audience of a few thousand. Paired with a post-ride survey after every level, the approach gave the team the confidence to move forward with the full launch.

5. Global launch. This is the moment of truth. Your new creation will be made available to the world. When Epic Games–owned developer Mediatonic launched the free-to-play version of its video game Fall Guys, an astonishing fifty million people downloaded it within the first two weeks.[27] Developer Scopely scaled from a few thousand players during the soft launch phase of its Scrabble Go, to two million daily players after the full release, making it the most successful word-game launch in the history of mobile games.[28] Supercell's Brawl Stars made over $60 million in revenue in the first month.[29] And Jim Green watched in awe as hundreds of thousands of Peloton riders played Lanebreak as their workout content of choice just in the first week. *Grab the champagne*, you might say after such results, *our work is done*. Not so fast.

6. Live operations. Video games in today's day and age are never really done. Due to the rise of games-as-a-service and free-to-plays, the global launch doesn't mark the end of the development process—because there is no true end (unless the game is shut down). The live operations phase focuses not only on the maintenance of the live experience but also on its enhancement and advancement through new ideas and content. Because updates can be made daily, companies have the opportunity to stay in sync in near-real time with their target audience's needs. "Games are a very powerful driver of daily engagement that create daily habits," emphasized Jonathan Knight, head of games at the *New York Times*.[30] It's hard to name something more powerful and potentially lucrative for a company or a brand than to become part of their consumers' everyday habits.

Despite the undeniable necessity of being data-informed through-out this entire process, there is no denying that developing a video game is inherently a creative endeavor. At its core are varying time-lines, a plethora of ideas, and any number of iterations before a product sees the light of day.

But it's not just the process that can be unfamiliar to companies—the talent required is also vastly different from what most organizations would traditionally count among their workforces. Yes, developers are important, but you will need developers who have experience with coding in environments that can support your project, such as game engines like Unity or Unreal. Video game development also requires artists who have a very different skill set from that of a company's user interface designers. The different capabilities required to be successful in gaming were actually the reason Unilever, after first bringing its Dove brand into the popular The

Sims franchise, waited almost a decade before it became serious about the opportunity that the industry presented as a whole. The organizational ramp-up required to execute successfully on a full-fledged video game strategy seemed too daunting at the time.

Partnering with a seasoned developer can be a sound strategy to alleviate the pressure your own organization is faced with. However, this approach is far from a silver bullet and comes with its own set of challenges and potential headaches.

Martin Reeves, senior partner at Boston Consulting Group and chair of the BCG Henderson Institute, remembers the steps he and his team went through with their development partner on the road toward pioneering a video game that let users experience, learn, and adopt distinct business strategies. "We needed to communicate between designers, coders, and business strategists. It was quite challenging, because everyone seemingly had their own language," he told me.[31]

Chris Rake, chief operating officer of the education organization *FIRST* Inspires, known for its global robotics competitions, shares a similar sentiment: "We're not game designers. We don't know the technicalities of designing video games. But we do know our community, our goals, and our vision."[32] The creation of games that effectively teach people about robotics required collaboration with experienced partners.

There is simply no getting around it. Making video games is hard—a lesson that some of the most successful companies in the world have had to learn.

Take Disney. Its thirty-year quest to create gaming experiences as magical as stepping into Disneyland or watching *Frozen* has been marked by ups and downs and complete pivots; in fact, the company has completely scrapped its in-house game development efforts a number of times. Only four years after its first attempt at an original creation, Walt Disney Computer Software, Inc. refocused on licensing Disney characters to other video games and their creators rather than actually creating these experiences itself.

Nearly a decade later, with Bob Iger's appointment as CEO, making games in-house was back on the menu. Iger established Disney Interactive Studios, which served as the home for all video game efforts and a number of studios and developers that Disney acquired at the time. While it saw some success, it faced more failures. In 2014, ten years after Disney Interactive Studios was established, seven hundred people were laid off. Two years later, Disney exited the in-house video gaming business (again) and refocused exclusively (again) on licensing its content and IP to third parties—a strategy that has its own challenges and isn't a guaranteed path to success.[33] Reflecting on the struggle to gain traction, Iger remarked, "We're obviously mindful of the size of that business, but over the years we've tried our hand at self-publishing . . . and we've found that we haven't been particularly good at [it]."[34]

Fast-forward to 2024 and Disney was once again rumored to be in the mix for acquiring a video game developer and publisher, including heavyweights like Electronic Arts, but the company announced a $1.5 billion investment in Epic Games to collaborate on a new entertainment universe tied to Fortnite.[35] "This marks Disney's biggest entry ever into the world of games, and offers significant opportunities for growth and expansion," Iger said in the public announcement.[36] Time will tell if the company's gaming journey will continue to feel like riding its Matterhorn Bobsleds roller coaster in Disneyland. But make no mistake, Disney is not alone in its struggles. The experiences of companies such as Hasbro and NBCUniversal, whose IP catalogs rival that of Disney, tell similar tales.[37]

If, after reading these examples, you're still interested in how video games can help your company grow and more effectively engage with customers, then read on. Now that we understand the power of play and the fundamental architecture of video games, it's time for the next level. We're ready to explore how games provide several ways for companies to establish a presence and connect with gamers on the modern customer journey. We'll start with simple but profound questions: Who is our audience? What are their needs? How can we authentically address them?

4

Consumer Engagement in the Twenty-First Century

Customer expectations are evolving. With people having more choices of goods and services than they can reasonably navigate, companies face a new reality when trying to reach their target audience: any marketing campaign, product, or experience must be personalized to resonate. In fact, 80 percent of consumers expect personalization.[1] This statistic makes intuitive sense, since what is appealing to you might not be to someone else. Personalization is good business as well—investing in deeply understanding customers can drive superior outcomes. And since how people find, evaluate, and buy products and services has fundamentally changed, video games provide a powerful way for your organization to be where new potential customers already are.

Different strategies are at your disposal to enter the gaming space. Which one is right for your company depends on your goals, risk appetite, resources, and time horizon. Do you want to be fast, test out video games as a playing field, and learn? Integrating with an existing game is a great starting point. Do you want to create a fully authentic brand experience and make games an integral part of your long-term strategy? Building your own title from scratch might be a better option. Both strategies—and others—can lead you to success.

But all strategies in this space share two foundational pillars:

- A clear understanding of who your customer is, along with their needs and desires.

- A clear sense of the company's identity, including its brand values and what it stands for—which must align with the needs of customers. Authenticity is crucial, because gamers have a sixth sense for when they're being "played."

Reimagining Consumer Engagement: Modern-Day Touchpoints

Traditionally, the customer journey is thought of as a funnel in which people consider a broad set of brands (and their offerings) and methodically narrow their choices until making a purchase. The stages of this funnel include awareness, familiarity, consideration, purchase, and loyalty. But with the proliferation of digital media, including video games, today's consumers evaluate brands before, during, and after making a purchase. So the customer journey needs to be rethought.

"How we have done user journeys or shopper journeys in the past—people don't want that traditional path to purchase anymore," Erika Wykes-Sneyd of Adidas, who we met earlier, told me. "As a company, you have to evoke emotions in your consumers. Traditionally, film and TV were the ways in which this was done. Now, video games are that medium—but on steroids."[2]

In research across twenty thousand customers in five industries on three continents, McKinsey & Company identified the modern customer journey as a circular one with four phases. Let's detail the phases, noting that video games can act as a highly effective performance enhancer:[3]

1. Initial consideration: A trigger event drives consumers to consider an initial set of products or brands based on brand perceptions and exposure to recent touchpoints. Remember that the average US consumer spends 16.5 hours per week playing video games, and that 13-to-17-year-olds spend 40 percent more time in video games than any other digital medium.[4] These numbers put games at the top of the list for companies looking to nudge consumers into the consideration phase, as well as to ensure that they are among the options people are evaluating. Offerings from brands that are part of this initial phase can be up to three times more likely to be purchased when the customer journey concludes.

2. Active evaluation: Consumers gather information and research potential purchase opportunities. Research has shown that, in contrast to the traditional funnel-based customer journey, consumers in this phase actually consider more, rather than fewer, products and brands.[5] In addition, companies that were under consideration in the first phase can be squeezed out by others that manage to leverage touchpoints in ways that allow them to arrive late to the party.

   Due to their consistent presence in daily life, video games can be those touchpoints and can present unique opportunities for companies to position themselves. The McKinsey researchers call out a second, very important change during this phase. About two-thirds of the touchpoints used by consumers during research involve customer-driven marketing activities, such as internet reviews or word-of-mouth recommendations, rather than company-driven marketing, which has been the traditional approach. Video games lend themselves naturally to a world beyond push-style marketing communication, as places where people socialize, chat, and hang out with friends.

3. Closure: The consumer ultimately selects a brand and commits to buying its product or service. Again, this is where video games can play a vital role, since consumers exhibit a high propensity to spend on both digital and physical items within the context of video games.[6] This highlights the opportunity for brands to be right there with the consumer in the moment of purchase, in their medium of choice, with a high likelihood of converting them into a transaction beyond the digital touchpoint—an opportunity that is, pun intended, game-changing.

4. Post-purchase: After buying a product or service, the customer's expectations and perception of the brand continue evolving through ongoing exposure to the product and service. This is a critical phase. For example, 60 percent of certain groups—such as buyers of facial skin care products—conduct further research online after they have made their initial purchase.

Consumer loyalty is not a given; companies have to work hard at staying relevant post-purchase to pave the way toward repeat business. This is a big reason coffee company Starbucks invested heavily in creating Odyssey—essentially a video game that lets customers collect "stamps" that tie back to real-life beverage purchases in any Starbucks store or online—and placed this initiative within its rewards program. Aside from the revenue generated from selling the next venti caffè mocha, Odyssey provides an additional revenue stream not previously accessible to Starbucks—monetizing the video game experience, especially through limited-edition stamps. While the rewards program was still in an invitation-only beta stage, the "Siren collection," featuring the brand's iconic logo, was released in March 2023 at a price of $100 per stamp. The entire collection of two thousand items sold out in eighteen minutes, and the resale market saw prices rise as high as $1,500. Not only did Starbucks generate $200,000, but it created a video-game-based touchpoint that allowed it to stay top of mind with consumers before their next purchase decision.[7]

As technology continues to advance, touchpoints will become even more connected since people expect to move seamlessly between them. Video games will continue to grow in importance as customers look for experiences that tie together shopping, socializing, and gaming in a highly personalized manner. This is why, as we've seen, companies should think about gaming as an entire ecosystem. If a customer sees an in-game placement for your product, then goes online to buy it, you want to be able to connect the dots between these two touchpoints and then persuade the customer to participate in future engagement efforts.

That is the key: rather than simply being active in all aspects of the customer journey, companies must tie these touchpoints together into a cohesive, personalized experience that feels authentic.

Your Video Gaming Strategy Option Space

Right now, you may be thinking: Where do we start, and how? What should *we* do? What corner of the video gaming world is the best entry point? Is it advertising in games? Selling virtual products? Creating our own games? Getting the answers to those questions will require clarity about your intended goals.

Kyle Price of Roblox works with thousands of brands on their journey toward leveraging the gaming platform and even designing their own immersive experiences. His view is that figuring out where to start comes down to three major goals and motivations:[8]

1. Activation: The company wants to generate awareness of its brand, which if done well enhances the path to purchase for customers, similar in essence to other top-of-funnel marketing activities but far more sophisticated.

2. Engagement: The company wants to engage its customers to enhance perceptions of and make its brand tangible for customers.

3. Monetization: The company wants to directly drive purchase transitions to generate revenue, whether online, offline, or both.

What makes video games so powerful for companies pursuing these three strategic goals is their ability to bring a brand and its values to life. "This is much harder to achieve in other channels where you can't design the entire experience and architect it in ways so that it optimally fits with your audience and with your brand," Price told me.

Athleisure company Alo Yoga is a great example of a values-driven company that capitalized on using immersive video game environments to allow customers to connect and interact with what its brand is all about. Conscientiousness and mindfulness are extremely important values for Alo Yoga, and it doesn't take much to understand why it would be challenging to make these values relatable for customers in a physical store or even on a website.

On Roblox, essentially a virtual universe that hosts a variety of games and immersive digital activities, the company was able to design and build an experience from the ground up and let its values come to life through three core areas. The "Yoga Tent" offers daily videos for practicing yoga, both in the video game as well as in real life. The "Sanctuary" is a meditation room with the goal of relaxing the body and mind. And the "Alo Store" showcases a five-piece digital fashion collection, which can be bought with points gained from participating in the yoga classes.[9] Alo Yoga's efforts clearly address the goals regarding activation and engagement. Through the digital collection, the company was also able to plant the seeds of further monetization through its clothing that people wear in real life.

As another example, luxury fashion house Burberry wanted to tap into a digital audience that it had been unable to reach. After doing extensive research on the target customer—no surprises here—Burberry learned that younger audiences play video games but also prefer to interact with brands. So the team explored using virtual characters to allow for exactly this kind of interactive experience, identifying Web3 games as the best avenue, particularly the game Blankos. Not only was Burberry able to address the early stages of the modern customer journey (initial consideration and active evaluation), but because of the monetary transactions for virtual clothes, as well as the ongoing gameplay post-transaction, it also catered to the latter stages of the journey—ensuring its brand would stay relevant throughout. What Burberry did worked well because its push into video games was based on a very clear understanding of the customer journey, the target audience, its brand value, and what it wanted to achieve.

That last part is critical, and I'm sure you've heard it before: you need clear goals and objectives. I know, it's like I'm telling you water is wet. Yet too many companies rush into creating strategies in order to enter new spaces, only to set themselves up for misaligned expectations and projects that fall short. The stakes are especially high when trying to break into video games, where the learning curve will inevitably be steep and failure can have severe implications for the future success of your business.

Adidas learned this the hard way. Its efforts to enter the gaming space originally centered on sponsoring esports teams and events (remember the distinction we drew between video games and esports earlier), which didn't generate the sustainable brand elevation and opportunities it was looking for. A lack of clarity around the goals Adidas was trying to achieve—combined with muddled perceptions around video games, esports, and the various pieces of the industry—resulted in a lot of one-off initiatives that didn't yield the results to justify the investment. These types of missteps can make companies rethink, and seriously doubt, their plans. "The premature takeaway was that the video gaming space wasn't for us," remembered Wykes-Sneyd.[10]

That conclusion shaped Adidas's gaming strategy going forward. After its first sponsorship initiatives for esports in 2016 and 2017, the company pretty much put a pause on video games. Only through the emerging space around Web3, nonfungible tokens (NFTs), and digital collectibles—a space tangential to video games—did it start thinking seriously again about games as a key strategy for consumer engagement.

Results like Adidas's early ones are why the investment in understanding your target audience is crucial. "Your goals should be ambitious," Jonathan Knight from the *New York Times* told me, "but you need to be very clear about what outcomes you want to drive."[11] A company might know *what* it wants to do, but if it is not clear *who* the efforts are for, plans about *how* it can cater to its audience and *what outcomes* it can drive with those plans will be vague at best. Erinrose Sullivan says,

> Companies are entering a different world when they go into
> video gaming. It pays to invest up front, to lay the foundation

first. If a company wants to be strategic about leveraging video games, this is the way to go. While one-off projects can be tempting with the idea of seeing quick, magical results, make no mistake: these one-off projects are just as much work and just as expensive as being strategic about it, but they carry the inherent risk of drawing the wrong conclusions and setting the company back overall.[12]

The basic premise you and your company have to address is the following: Are video games a short-term experiment for you as a channel and consumer touchpoint, or are you pursuing a more long-term strategy that establishes them as an integral part of your overall customer experience? Given the novelty and unfamiliarity that gaming might hold for your organization, as well as the inherent complexity, creativity, and talent required, your answer to the previous question will help you define how fast and how deep you want to go.

The goal of this book is not to explore every possible opportunity. The objective here is to equip you with a frame of reference that applies to most use cases and provides you with an immediate and actionable starting point to set your gaming strategy in motion.

The Four Strategic Options

There are four broad options for what a company might focus its gaming strategy on. Each of the following chapters is devoted to one of these options, and they're full of case studies of companies that have adopted them.

1. **Integrating with existing video games.** This is without a doubt the easiest jumping-off point. If your company is taking

more of a short-term view or wants to test the efficacy of video games, identifying existing titles that reach your desired audience is a sound strategy. It offers a fair amount of upside without the costs and potential risk associated with building new titles from scratch. From showing ads, to placing a product inside a game, to integrating an actual service, companies can leverage existing video games for a variety of use cases. Later we'll dig more deeply into how Unilever is using its Dove brand to address diversity in gaming, how WRTHY tackled child malnutrition with SpongeBob SquarePants, how Chipotle achieved record digital sales, and why it was worth it for Reckitt to scale its hygiene education efforts via Roblox.

2. **Creating new video games.** One of the greatest advantages that games offer over other touchpoints is the ability to fully control and shape the entire experience. While companies using social media channels are subject to the limitations of platforms like Instagram or TikTok, creating a video game from scratch allows for the design of an experience that perfectly aligns with a company's brand and goals.

   Going down this path is unquestionably harder, costlier, and riskier. But the potential upside is also greater. If video games are to play a central role in your long-term strategy, it's worth the effort. You also don't have to go it alone— there are a lot of partners experienced in building games that can do the heavy lifting for you. And because you have complete control over the touchpoint, your company can get close to your consumers, generate valuable first-party data that would be otherwise hard to obtain, and unlock business outcomes that are almost impossible to achieve through other channels. We'll learn more from organizations like NASCAR,

FIRST Inspires, and the *New York Times*, as well as fashion designer Tommy Hilfiger.

3. Leveraging Web3 games. This strategy encompasses the previous two, but we will explore it as a separate avenue due to a key underlying technical distinction: Web3 technology, namely blockchain. Web3 games provide an additional set of opportunities from both a marketing and a monetization perspective. While more complex to navigate, this space is a big part of the future of the gaming industry at large and holds many possibilities for meaningfully connecting digital and physical experiences. To be clear, whether you are integrating with an existing title or building a new one, the experience you bring to your customers is still the main attraction—enhanced by technology that opens up new pathways. Companies like Burberry, Starbucks, Puma, and Adidas will shine a light on what the future can look like.

4. Making the video game the product. Arguably the most advanced approach, this strategy sees games converge with products and services to the point where the video game itself ultimately becomes the product. Given how powerful games are at engaging consumers, this strategy holds a lot of promise and likely outsize returns. Not many companies have gone down this path to date, but we will learn from Peloton how a video game became the dominant workout form on its stationary bikes, from BMW how embracing games is helping it realize the vision of turning cars into our second living rooms, or from BCG how offering a video game complemented and enhanced traditional B2B consulting services.

You may have noticed that we're not explicitly focusing on pureplay advertising and marketing strategies. Here's the reason: treating video games as simply another advertising channel, and taking the traditional advertising approach to it, is not effective—it falls way short of the potential that games hold for your business. Too many organizations are stuck in that type of old-fashioned media thinking. "Many companies believe that because of their fame, consumers will just look at whatever they put in front of people," Marcus Holmström, who has worked with dozens of well-known brands and has helped them build their first gaming experiences, told me. "They try to replicate reality rather than use the possibilities of video games."[13] In addition to a sound strategy, a mindset shift is required—and with both in place, the sky's the limit.

Chris Brandt, chief brand officer and chief marketing officer at Chipotle, and a huge advocate of taking advantage of the unique opportunities video games provide, knows this better than anybody. To drive sign-ups for its loyalty program, Chipotle gave away $1 million in free burritos on Roblox. "It was one of the best digital promotions we ever had," Brandt said. "We know what the average lifetime value of a Chipotle Rewards member is. The return far exceeded our investment."[14] This is the power of video games in next-generation consumer engagement.

Given the significant potential that games have for your business, you're likely eager to dive in. The first step to set yourself up for success is to invest in a deep and robust understanding of your target audience.

Laying the Foundation: Deep Audience Understanding and Authentic Experiences

In today's experience-driven economy, the traditional method of thinking about consumers—solely in terms of demographic groups and behaviors—no longer provides the depth and insight needed to capture attention and foster meaningful engagement. For example, imagine that the following demographic profile described your target consumer, and you were tasked with coming up with strategies around building a video game that fits their customer journey:

Male

Born in 1948

Raised in the United Kingdom

Married twice

Lives in a castle

Is wealthy and famous

You might already have some ideas. Maybe you're thinking about collaborating with the existing video game Victoria: An Empire Under the Sun, which lets players strategize through the Victorian period. Or you might think about creating a game inspired by the TV show *Downton Abbey*, letting your audience dive into the aristocratic lifestyle and design the interior of a castle.

Now, what if I told you that both King Charles III of England and the musician John Michael Osbourne, better known as Ozzy Osbourne or the Prince of Darkness, share all the previously mentioned demographic details? So while they look similar at first glance, we can probably agree that the two are very different people and, when we take a closer look at their respective psychographic traits, we see that the experiences they enjoy might be very different (see table 4-1).

Cutting through the noise with personalized experiences that deeply resonate with customers requires companies to understand people much more holistically. Demographics, behaviors, and affinities all have their *raison d'être*. But your best insights will come

TABLE 4-1

Psychology-based personas

King Charles	Ozzy Osbourne
Top values are generosity, feeling heard, and reliability	Top values are creativity, transformation, and humor
Motivated by independence and working at his own pace	Motivated by difficult tasks and finding new ways to complete them
Motivated by compensatory effort and status orientation	Motivated by flow states and independence
Assertive, impulsive personality	Altruistic, fantasy personality
Competes to maintain self-esteem	Competes because it feels thrilling

from uncovering your audience's real needs and desires by grasping their unique motivations, personality traits, or values. Looking at your customers' behavior is like looking into the past; it's what they *already did*. Knowing their psychology, which is what compels their behavior, is like looking into the future; it reveals what they *will do*, and why. It forms a powerful baseline from which your company can connect with your customers, current and future, on a human level. The outcome? More meaningful engagement.

"The starting point has to be the consumer," Sullivan reiterated to me. In her career she has seen too many projects fail because they lacked a complete picture of the target audience. "Motivations, desires, needs, touchpoints—companies have to understand their audiences holistically and how they evolve over time."[15] This is true for any company that interacts with consumers, but it's especially true for those that want to embrace video games.

Wykes-Sneyd drove the message home: "You have to understand the human need and how gaming can fulfill it."[16] This is what Adidas did when it established its metaverse task force and ventured into the digital collectibles space as a segue into video games. Wykes-Sneyd described the foundational qualitative research into the target audience she and her team conducted with an external partner as "paramount."[17] Creating personas of your customers, along with outlines of their respective journeys, is a great place to start. Simply by putting yourselves in the shoes of consumers, the return on investment (ROI) of your efforts increases due to heightened levels of empathy. According to research firm Forrester, science-based personas provide returns of up to 400 percent.[18] It really does pay to make the up-front investment.

There are a number of frameworks, tools, methodologies, and partners available that companies can leverage to help them build this foundational knowledge of their audiences. On the lower end of the ROI scale, and specifically focused on why people play video games, are frameworks such as Steven Reiss's sixteen basic human motivators, Jon Radoff's ideas on how these motivators can be mapped to specific aspects of a video game, and Richard Bartle's classifications of the four main types of players.[19] These can be good starting points.

However, the limitations of many of these frameworks lie in their attempt to categorize all human beings and their needs into a boiled-down set of persona archetypes. Such thinking is useful for the simplicity that it can bring when forming an initial understanding of and establishing language around customer types. Yet this simplicity is also a downside, especially in combination with a lack of depth about and valid assessment of the true psychological drivers of the target audience. Organizations in gaming, retail, fitness, health care, fashion, and even the public sector have found the depth and breadth of audience insights from companies such as Solsten invaluable in their pursuit of deeper consumer engagement.

Grasping how audiences vary along different dimensions is crucial to building a winning strategy. Why? Customers crave authenticity, and gamers even more so. By getting into video games, you'll be encroaching on their territory, and they'll have their guard up. So you need to make sure your strategy is in sync with who your customers are, as well as your brand's identity.

"United Airlines is a good example of what 'good' can look like," said Jonathan Knight, referring to how the company integrated a game called Cleared to Land into its mobile app.[20] Mirroring the complex and busy operations of a real-world airport, players take on the role of an air traffic controller to try to coordinate the landing of several United planes with perfect timing—and no collisions. To complete the experience, United offers a second video game called Flight Simulator. Modeled after the actual simulators with which pilots are trained, players take a seat in the cockpit as they learn to successfully descend into San Francisco International Airport in varying conditions.

Both games are a great fit for United's brand. Sure, airplane-centric titles are an obvious match for an airline. But these two specifically promote safety and the complexity of working as an air traffic controller, helping customers to build empathy around the entire process—all of which fits perfectly with United's core values: fly right, fly friendly, fly together, and fly above and beyond.[21] "You need to be true to your brand values, because consumers can sniff out when things are not authentic," added Knight.[22] Or, in the words of Holmström, "Don't [make games] just for PR."[23]

Looking back at how Adidas laid the foundation for its gaming journey, Wykes-Sneyd offered a perfect synopsis:

> Foundational research into your target audience is critical. Then it is always important to start with who you are as a brand, because you live in the collective brain of people. So you have to understand who those people are, then tie it back into your own brand values and realize where you can stretch yourself. Because at the end of the day, we all offer far more

than just products to people. We sell experiences, access, and values. Aligning all of these aspects creates authentic, winning experiences.[24]

A winning experience is what Hasbro, a global player in toys and games, was able to create for its target audience. Together with video game developer MobilityWare, Hasbro leveraged its famous IP Monopoly for a new mobile game called Monopoly Solitaire, which more than doubled revenue expectations in its first year after launch.[25] But in the early stages, before the game was even built, success looked far from certain. If you roam the aisles of your favorite toy store, you'll notice many variations of the board game: a cheater's edition, a college edition, a women's edition. The list goes on. In its pursuit to "entertain and connect generations of fans through the wonder of storytelling and exhilaration of play," Hasbro opts for trying many variations and approaches with its famous board game.[26] The company applies the same strategy in the digital realm. But it was an odd combination to join an inherently social game like Monopoly with, as the name "Solitaire" might suggest, a predominantly one-player card game. There was a shared sentiment across the teams at Hasbro and MobilityWare that this was possibly the best idea they'd had in a while. Or, possibly, the worst.

"We needed to understand if this was chocolate and peanut butter, or chocolate and mustard," remembered Zach Pond, the vice president of marketing at MobilityWare. "We really invested in understanding the unique audiences of Monopoly and Solitaire, respectively, to then identify if there was a crossover . . . in terms of the underlying psychology of the consumers as well as their affinities and touchpoints."[27]

MobilityWare partnered with my company, Solsten, to establish its target audience personas. To meet future customers' needs, Pond and his team dove into our database from three angles: (1) Who are the fans of the Monopoly brand (as in, people who play the board game and have an affinity for the IP in general)? (2) Who are the traditional Solitaire players (to understand the overall market potential and the needs of the most valuable audience segments)? And (3) where do these two audiences overlap (to arrive at target personas that form the foundation for building Monopoly Solitaire)?

Some of the key findings of this audience-centered strategy were that the target customers highly valued entrepreneurship and mentorship, and that they were highly empathetic people. That knowledge paved the way for the Hasbro and MobilityWare teams to position the famous character Mr. Monopoly as an entrepreneurial father figure who mentored players by providing clues and feedback on how they could perform better, his facial expressions becoming more positive as they improved.

This is just one of the many examples of how the teams were able to create a chart-topping game and position the Monopoly brand with a distinct audience in the video games market. More than double-digit revenue performance later, both Hasbro and MobilityWare will tell you that it paid off to invest in audience insights rather than rushing into the project armed with stereotypes or too-high-level information.

At this point, you have a clear grasp of how video games connect to the modern customer journey, your strategies to enter the gaming space, and how to lay the foundation with deep insights into your audience. Now it's time to learn from some of the trailblazers in this space so that you can set your company on its video game path.

Part Two

THE
STRATEGIES

5

Integrate with Existing Games

Companies have been integrating with video games for more than four decades, but almost all these attempts were focused on advertising. For example, players in the racing game Crazy Taxi could drive to Pizza Hut and KFC, and more recently Forza Horizon 5 let people drive a Barbie-themed Corvette. Though these types of integrations are simple and can raise brand awareness, companies that look beyond advertising are finding better results.

Among the first to seriously team up with video games was Mastercard. In 2018 the company struck a partnership with Riot Games, maker of widely known titles like League of Legends (LoL) and Valorant. The initial deal focused on bringing LoL-themed credit cards to players. It complemented Mastercard's engagement strategy built around customer passion points; next to culinary and travel, gaming fit right in. The company's goal was clear as well: reach untapped and underserved audiences, specifically Gen Zers and millennials.

CASES

Chipotle: Fortune Favors the Bold

WRTHY: Breaking into People's Worlds

Unilever: Bringing Purpose to Life

Reckitt: Scaling a One-Hundred-Year Heritage

Execution was key. Contrary to the advertising playbooks most companies were running at the time, Mastercard knew that it couldn't simply slap a logo on something and expect gamers to embrace it. Instead, it integrated the credit cards with the game by allowing players to receive "Riot Cash," the currency used to buy in-game items, as rewards for purchases. Cardholders also received special discounts on Riot merchandise as well as access to special events, and Mastercard sent representatives to gaming events to engage with the community. The guiding strategy for the company is clear, said Raja Rajamannar, its chief marketing and communications officer and founding president of its health care business: "Gaming is a 365-day-a-year business for us, and to be successful in the space, you have to run it that way."[1]

The results speak for themselves. Of all the issued LoL "passion cards," as they're referred to internally, 80 percent have been renewed. Mastercard has launched seventeen credit cards focused on different video games since and has expanded its gaming strategy globally.[2] "That is a direct, straightforward increase in my business. If we didn't have League of Legends, those cards would not have been in existence, which means those revenues and those profits would not have happened," Rajamannar said in an interview with Digiday. "There is a direct correlation and causal relationship that we've established."[3]

Mastercard's efforts and success opened the door for more brands to explore gaming.

In 2019 French fashion house Louis Vuitton created a virtual trophy designed in the iconic style of its handbags and suitcases for the winning team of a League of Legends tournament. This collaboration also included the launch of a physical fashion line. Items ranged from $170 to $5,600, and despite the high price tags, the entire collection sold out in less than an hour.[4]

Balenciaga pushed the boundaries even further by launching its latest collection in the popular game Fortnite instead of on the runways in Milan, Paris, or New York. Consumers that bought a physical clothing item from a limited-edition collection also unlocked the digital version for their Fortnite character. Prices reached as high as $750 for a hooded sweatshirt, yet all items sold out in days.[5] Search volumes for Balenciaga on the web increased by 49 percent, and its YouTube channel saw more than six hundred thousand views during the virtual runway.[6]

Integrating with a video game might be enticing to your company for a few reasons. First and foremost, the title already has an established user base and provides instant access, at scale, to a target audience. Second, integrating with an existing game is far easier and faster than the complex process of developing a new one from scratch, meaning the approach is ideal for companies wanting to dip their toes into these waters without taking on too much risk. Third, an existing video game is a confined space that allows for faster experimentation and the quick measurement of results before committing bigger budgets and needing a full-on strategy. The key is to identify the game that provides the right access to your target audience and aligns authentically with your brand.

Chipotle: Fortune Favors the Bold

After a long day at the office, Chris Brandt returned home and ex-perienced a creative spark. Having spent more than twenty-five years in marketing leadership roles for companies such as Coca-Cola, Taco Bell, and Bloomin' Brands, Brandt, the chief brand officer of Chipotle Mexican Grill, knew all too well that ideas can come from anywhere and that sometimes you have to let them come to you. His source of inspiration on this day came from Fortnite—a favorite of his sons'. "When I saw the passion and time my sons invested into playing Fortnite, I immediately called a friend who is an executive at a video game company. I needed to learn more," Brandt told me.[7]

Before his team fully committed to working with the game, it decided to explore the gaming space to better understand the nu-ances and its audience's behaviors. This cautious, strategic approach allowed Chipotle to gain insights and avoid potential missteps in a new and unfamiliar market.

Its first foray into the gaming world was through a partnership with the Fortnite players of esports organization TSM and their "Fortnite house"—a real-life house where they lived together. These professional streamers had a social following of almost 2.3 million subscribers on YouTube alone. They regularly shared vid-eos of themselves playing Fortnite and participating in a variety of other activities and performances. Three of them were among the top fifteen Fortnite players globally. The gamers also regularly ate Chipotle. In the Fortnite house. On camera. Live streamed to their millions of followers.

Brandt and his team had found a place where Chipotle customers and video games collided. The company became a sponsor of the house, which included hosting a twelve-minute video of the players blind tasting beans, guacamole, burritos, and more from the Chipotle menu. This video was viewed more than 1.5 million times on YouTube.[8] But more importantly, Brandt walked away with some important realizations that would form the foundation of his company's massive future success in using video games: "To me, the community of video gaming is analogous to the community of freestyle skiing. Gamers are looking for community . . . It is literally the opposite of sponsoring a team. You can't take your traditional advertising approach to this new channel . . . Whatever you do, it has to fit into that world."

The five teams at Chipotle that report directly to Brandt—media, creative, brand, analytics, and social—collaborated on the proposal to expand its foray into gaming. The social team, for example, focused on the company's goal of becoming more culturally relevant. Through careful analysis and many conversations, Roblox quickly became the leading contender for Chipotle's second-ever video game integration, and its first in a metaverse-like environment. At the time the conversations inside Chipotle headquarters were taking place, Roblox had fifty million users engaging daily with the content on the platform (it has since grown to over eighty-eight million).[9] Demographically, the audience skewed a bit younger, in line with the age range Brandt had in mind. The platform is community-driven, with people meeting and playing together, plus Roblox supports brands with development resources so that integrations don't require a massive up-front investment. Chipotle's concept was to capitalize on Halloween and transform its popular offline event Boorito into a digital experience on Roblox.

For Brandt, the project ticked a lot of the boxes he was looking for. Yet because of the scale and public exposure, there was also a lot of risk involved should things not go as planned. In the end, his team decided to go for it. Brandt admits he has a personal affinity for charting new territory. "I like to be the first," he told me, adding that video games were a natural fit and Roblox was a great starting point. "How could I not do it?"

The team hired a third-party developer with a proven track record to build the gaming experience. The goal was to ensure that the environment on Roblox stayed authentic to Chipotle. Traditionally, fans dress up in costume for Boorito, visit a Chipotle restaurant, and receive a discounted entrée. The team offered similar features in Roblox: fans had the opportunity to dress up their avatars in new Chipotle-inspired costumes like Burrito Mummy or Guacenstein and visit the company's first virtual restaurant. The first thirty thousand Roblox players who visited Boorito during the four days leading up to Halloween received a code they could redeem online, on the Chipotle app, or in a restaurant for a free entrée.

The Roblox experience also featured the Chipotle Boorito Maze for players to navigate while collecting ingredients and avoiding monsters. Upon reaching the center of the maze, they unlocked exclusive virtual items for their Roblox avatars. The virtual restaurant and the costumes allowed Chipotle to be relevant on one of the most important holidays in the United States and to tie a new digital touchpoint to real transactions that would translate to the company's bottom line. The maze offered players a fun challenge—one they spent an average of 9.4 minutes exploring and to which they could come back after Halloween—that was instrumental in providing continued brand exposure.

On October 28, 2021, the Boorito Maze went live—and two hours later Roblox crashed. Headlines like "Chipotle Broke Roblox" quickly spread.[10] For a moment, it seemed like Brandt's worst nightmares had come true. Roblox was down for two days. But it turned out to be nothing more than a minor bump on the road to success, as the crash brought more attention to the project, ultimately driving more visitors once Roblox was back up. The campaign generated four billion impressions, and October 31, 2021, became one of Chipotle's most successful digital sales days.

In total, the company gave away $1 million in burritos—an investment Brandt says has paid off many times over. In the first week of the experience alone, Chipotle saw over 5.2 million gameplays and more than 2 million unique visitors. The integration with Roblox also boosted the company's rewards program, resulting in one of its top ten enrollment days of all time.

Buoyed by this success, the team doubled down on Roblox during National Burrito Day 2022 (April 7). Chipotle launched the Burrito Builder—a '90s-themed simulation reminiscent of the company's first location in Denver, Colorado, that challenged players to roll burritos. (If you have ever attempted to roll one yourself, it's not hard to see why this fairly complex tasks lends itself well to a video game.) Roblox players were able to earn and exchange virtual currency, Robux, for a real-world entrée from Chipotle. It might be hard to believe that rolling burritos inside a game would translate to offline impact for any company. But, once again, the results were remarkable: a top ten day for digital sales, one of the highest mobile transaction days to date, twenty-five million gameplays, and a staggering 83.1 percent week-over-week increase in Chipotle Rewards sign-ups.

While the company doesn't release specific figures about the average revenue generated per rewards member, it is hard to overstate the impact that these video game integrations on the Roblox platform have had. Twenty million active members have been added to Chipotle Rewards since its inception, and digital sales represent roughly a third of the company's total revenue of almost $11 billion.[11] Prior to its 2019 decision to make video games an integral part of its consumer engagement strategy, only 18 percent of its sales were digital.[12]

Chipotle has since intensified its gaming efforts. The company has invested deeply in experiences outside of Roblox, namely with the famous Street Fighter franchise. It also developed its own video game to further supercharge its rewards program, called Chipotle Race to Rewards Exchange. Fortune really does favor the bold.

Just how powerful video games can be for unlocking unprecedented consumer engagement becomes apparent when we look at our next example. It's a space that suffers from a chronic lack of consumer awareness: social impact initiatives.

WRTHY: Breaking into People's Worlds

Every eleven seconds a child dies from malnutrition, making it responsible for almost half of all children's deaths worldwide each year. Malnutrition is also the leading cause of death for kids under the age of five.[13] Did you know these troubling statistics? As a father of two young daughters, I was surprised that I hadn't come across them before, although the World Health Organization regularly publishes reports and statistics on the topic. This lack of familiarity highlights a challenge faced by many people who work to solve societal issues we face: how to improve awareness and increase social impact.

"Social impact initiatives typically focus on the weight of the issue. It's hard to break into people's worlds—but that is exactly what you need to do. You need a breakthrough around creativity," Jenifer Willig, CEO and founder of social impact agency WRTHY, told me.[14] Willig had spent her twenty-plus-year career in advertising, leading global brands including AT&T, Levi Strauss & Co., British Airways, the *Financial Times*, and more. Then her path led her to become the first chief marketing officer of (RED), the social impact organization founded by U2 frontman Bono and activist

Bobby Shriver in 2006. At the time, gaming principles had started to gain some traction, especially with younger people. (RED) introduced an American Express card that would donate a percentage of monthly spend to social causes. It also partnered with Apple to introduce a special-edition iPod for which the company would donate $10 for each purchase. Both are examples of leveraging clear objectives, offering a reward system, and signaling social status. To date, (RED) has raised $760 million.

Yet using video games to empower social impact initiatives never really took off. Today, though, that is changing. "Video gaming feels like such a natural storytelling platform," Willig said. "It is authentic, which gamers appreciate. It's a destination, not an advertising play. I worry that a lot of marketing is a knee-jerk reaction to solve things quickly. Gamers smell this right away." There's also an underlying demographic shift toward older people playing more that has allowed video games to become a more accepted medium in the context of social impact.

Willig took her observations to her next adventure when she cofounded social impact agency WRTHY. The team at WRTHY is putting video games at the core of its strategy. Together with the Eleanor Crook Foundation, a philanthropical organization, it created a games-focused initiative called LifePack. The goal: to combat child malnutrition. First, the team launched the website lifepack .org to educate people about this pressing issue. The site's focal point was a free-to-play game that the team built from the ground up, in which players use RUTFs (ready-to-use therapeutic food) to fight "malnutrition monsters." "Nobody knows that child malnutrition is the number one cause of child death," Willig explained. "So instead of asking people to donate, we asked them to play a video game. We met them where they were already at."

Because the game was highly accessible, anybody could support the cause right away. All players needed to do was tap the space bar on their keyboard to start the game; the space bar was also all that was needed to control the character—a child—as it jumped to avoid obstacles and monsters and ultimately collect RUTFs. To encourage play, the WRTHY team launched with a challenge: for every game played, a day's worth of RUTFs would be donated, which the Eleanor Crook Foundation ultimately paid for. The results were astonishing: in just twenty-six hours, the team achieved its initial goal of realizing ten thousand days of treatment for malnourished children. The significant impact of a fairly simple video game was all the proof Willig needed to start phase two of the initiative, with the goal of reaching even more people. Existing video games that already had a sizable audience were the perfect place for LifePack to go next.

From the get-go, WRTHY's team focused on learning about the gaming audience and the many different reasons they play video games. Rather than picking a list of prominent titles to pursue as partners, WRTHY identified key psychological attributes of players that the team felt would ensure they would connect with Life-Pack and its purpose. One of the attributes was people's levels of altruism. The hypothesis was the higher that player segments scored on altruism, the more they would care about and engage with a social impact initiative. Using audience insights tools like Solsten, WRTHY was able to identify highly altruistic gamers quickly, as well as uncover which titles they were already playing. That gave the team a blueprint for which partners to pursue.

In its first year the LifePack initiative partnered with games including PUBG: Battlegrounds, which is played by more than thirty million people daily, and SpongeBob: Krusty Cook-Off. Tilting Point, the company behind the latter, was the first developer and publisher to partner with WRTHY to implement LifePack. Because of the game's cooking theme and beloved cartoon character, the fit with raising awareness and funds for child malnutrition was perfect. In the video game, players control SpongeBob to manage a restaurant and fulfill orders coming in from the cartoon's familiar cast of characters. The first few levels focus on making pancakes—and the more delicious the pancakes, the happier SpongeBob's friends and customers are, and the more points and gems a player earns. As players earn points and gems, they can unlock additional levels and upgrade kitchen items, the decor of the restaurant, and ingredients for SpongeBob's ever-growing menu.

The teams at WRTHY and Tilting Point were evaluating the progression path that the video game provided. The goal was to make LifePack a seamless part of the player's journey through the SpongeBob universe. The solution the teams arrived at was fairly simple: some items would be labeled "LifePack," and any purchase of them would fund the distribution of RUTFs to at-risk children. To date more than ninety thousand packs have been delivered to children in need.

Given the overwhelmingly positive feedback from game developers, WRTHY continues to push the envelope of what is possible. The gaming space is a prime medium for engaging and mobilizing compassionate, committed people to help make positive change in the world. Most recently, the company has been exploring new areas, including partnering not only with developers but also with well-known gamers around the world to expand into other social issues, including gender and education. "To be clear," said Willig, "we're not making educational video games. We're making video games that educate." This mindset exemplifies the importance of connecting with players through the experience before introducing them to the issue at hand, rather than the other way around. Starting with the problem has been the go-to approach for social impact projects for ages, and it hasn't really been successful. The next big topic WRTHY will tackle? "Our climate crisis. We have no more time to waste," said Willig.

Finding the right entry point and having access to the right capabilities, either internally or through a partner, are essential to a successful integration with a video game. Otherwise companies risk prematurely concluding that games don't deliver the needed impact for their brand, or at the very least delaying their holistic gaming strategy from taking flight.

Unilever: Bringing Purpose to Life

When Electronic Arts teamed up with Unilever in 2012, the initial goal was to bring the latter's Dove shampoo brand into the former's uber-popular video game The Sims Social, a multiplayer spin-off of the Sims franchise that was designed specifically for Facebook. In addition, the two companies collaborated to launch the Dove Hair Spa, a virtual bathroom item that players could get by visiting the Dove Facebook page. This type of integration is essentially what this chapter has been all about: innovative partnerships between brands and video games.

After Unilever's video game strategy cooled off for a few years, the onset of the Covid-19 pandemic saw the company jump back in. To lay a solid foundation, Unilever hired Amanpreet Singh, a former professional gamer, to lead its efforts. As a part of the global media team, Singh established UPLAY, an internal gaming division. It has two major responsibilities: to define and support the development of the overall video game strategy, and to educate and support teams at Unilever across any gaming topic. Integrating with existing titles fits squarely into Unilever's holistic strategy, and its efforts allow us to explore just how impactful in the space shampoo—and even mayonnaise—can be.

Toward the end of 2022, Unilever's condiment brand Hellmann's teamed up with the Nintendo farming game Animal Crossing: New Horizons. The promise to players was that Hellmann's would donate food waste to a charity each time a player donated a virtual vegetable to charity within the game. The effort connected a purposeful, greater cause to a Unilever brand. But the UPLAY team didn't stop there.

Like many global companies, Unilever has a diversity and inclusion program, and its research uncovered some startling findings. An estimated 60 percent of girls start playing video games before the age of 10. And because female characters in video games oftentimes do not accurately represent the diverse gamer population, or are heavily sexualized while leaning on unrealistic beauty standards, 74 percent of girls wish those characters were more like women in real life.[15] (The fact that less than 10 percent of all video game developers are female very likely plays a role here.)

Unilever made it a goal to help represent people more objectively in virtual environments. Leveraging existing video games is a critical component of Dove's self-esteem project, which has a commitment to reach and support four million women. Enter Dove's partnership with Epic Games, whose Unreal Engine is the second most used game development engine globally.

The teams went to work by defining what stereotypes needed to be done away with to promote more-diverse beauty standards and overall body positivity. They collaborated with four women whose real-life personas served as the inspiration for the creation of digital avatars. These four avatars became the launchpad for what Dove calls the "Real Virtual Beauty Collection," character art that lives inside Unreal Engine to help developers using its tool kit to foster more accurate representation of female characters. Also included is a series of trainings that are geared toward avoiding unconscious bias in avatar development. Rather than trying to integrate with one game at a time, Dove partnered with Epic to have a chance to influence virtually every video game that is built using Unreal Engine. "Purpose is a big layer for us at Unilever," emphasized Singh—and gaming is a great vehicle to bring purpose to life.

The Dove team measured the impact of the integration through a brand power score, which evaluates the strength of a brand through three lenses: financial performance (e.g., revenue growth, profitability), equity (e.g., brand awareness, perception, loyalty), and market share (e.g., year-over-year change in the core market). "The score for Dove shampoo jumped significantly after the launch of the campaign," said Singh, so much so that the team doubled down by making its own video game on Roblox with a third-party developer. The team also extended the scope of the project to another shampoo brand in the Unilever portfolio, Sunsilk. Also on Roblox, it created Sunsilk Hair Care Lab Tycoon, where players in "Sunsilk City" can create their own hair salons or play other games with friends. Almost twelve years after Dove appeared in The Sims, Unilever's virtual hair spa for engaging with its consumers is a reality. "For Sunsilk specifically, not only has the share of voice gone up, but actual market share has as well," said Singh.

Considering the success, Unilever remains bullish on gaming as a cornerstone of how it interacts with customers. "Video games have become table stakes . . . Now for us, it's more about, What else can we do?" explained Singh. The numbers back him up. In 2022 alone Unilever executed on thirty gaming-related projects. In terms of importance as a media channel and consumer touchpoint, video games sit right next to social media or influencer marketing. The difference between now and Unilever's first attempt in 2012? It feels natural to the company instead of forced. "Gaming is in everything we do," said Luis di Como, who we met earlier.[16]

Reckitt: Scaling a One-Hundred-Year Heritage

UK household goods company Reckitt had everything going for it: growing revenues, a broad and successful portfolio of brands, and a legacy built on credibility. Yet there was a level of uneasiness among the senior executives due to a rapidly evolving technological landscape and swiftly changing consumer preferences. "Imagine the year 2030 or 2040. Nobody visits stores anymore," Raghunandan Srinivasan, director, emerging tech business models, told me. "Plus, Gen Z and Gen Alpha, which will be heads of households by then, question everything. This scenario poses a real risk to our brands staying relevant."[17] For example, Dettol, the company's hygiene brand, has a one-hundred-year heritage of doctors' recommendations. But this history was also built on customers' exposure to Dettol in their kitchens and bathrooms or from in-store visits—both of which are waning touchpoints.

Reckitt wanted a senior executive to make sense of the evolving world. With his twenty years of experience across sales and marketing and his insatiable curiosity about technologies, Srinivasan was the man for the job. In 2022 he began looking into what emerging technologies could offer; blockchain, AI, augmented reality, and video games were high on his agenda. While diving in headfirst, a couple of questions remained front and center for him: How do we build something that's relevant to people who will be future consumers and that's scalable? How can we be authentic while engaging with Gen Alpha in their world, their way? He was trying to find the bridge between new technologies and Reckitt's brand and product portfolio to identify paths forward.

Throughout the process, Srinivasan took a test-and-learn mindset, with a set of important guardrails steering his exploration. The consumer needed to be at the heart of the offering. Pilot projects and their entry points needed to hold low financial and reputational risk. The solution ultimately needed to be highly scalable. Alongside a couple of smaller experiments in blockchain and augmented reality, he landed on video games and especially Roblox, which ticked all of the boxes. Dettol's desired young customer base is omnipresent on Roblox. The platform's reach is global, and once a video gaming experience is built there, it can scale quickly and cost-efficiently to more than one hundred countries. Srinivasan's personal *aha* moment was when he noticed his eight-year-old nephew was hanging out with his friends on Roblox while they were physically in the same room. The platform seemed like a great pathway because "it is not just a video game; it's an immersive social platform where kids hang out, play, and engage with friends," he said.

Despite the evidence, internal concerns—mainly regarding some negative connotations video games still have and how they would fit with a brand like Dettol—needed to be overcome. Srinivasan looked for an internal stakeholder who would benefit from the company's foray into video games. He found the perfect fit: the social impact team.

Tasked with scaling hygiene education in schools across the globe, the team was doing a good job but was facing hurdles in expanding quickly. Physically going to schools was costly. Engaging kids on a boring topic like handwashing was challenging. A video game on Roblox would alleviate all of these pains. The social impact team was convinced and agreed to fund the project.

The focus would be on handwashing education, and the video game experience needed to keep Dettol's brand authentic while exploring ways in which digital goods and experiences can add value for the audience. Srinivasan used that framing to write a project brief and kick off the partner screening process. The closing sentences of the brief that was shared with agencies and partners painted a picture of his mindset and ambition: "Why can't a consumer goods company create value with goods or experiences that were never manufactured in a factory? We believe we can. We just need to figure out how."

The British Roblox development studio Dubit wholeheartedly agreed. For its team, the most important consideration in the beginning of the process was how to balance brand authenticity with the lift required to build a gaming experience. Headed by chief commercial officer Andrew Douthwaite, the team was looking for smart and effective solutions. While some companies' default approach to gaming is to create their own game, Douthwaite wondered if Dettol really needed one. There was a lot of opportunity to partner with existing games on Roblox, and Dubit had a network of one hundred of them that were open to integrations with brands. Douthwaite told me that working with existing titles offered multiple benefits for Dettol: It could choose games that provided access to the audience the brand cared about reaching the most. It would be a much smaller, and hence cheaper, effort. And the brand could learn quickly and then scale up what was working.[18]

The teams at Reckitt and Dettol were convinced. Rather than developing a brand-new game for six to twelve months, Dubit would need only two months to launch the project in existing titles on Roblox. The quest to bring awareness to critical issues around hygiene was underway.

The idea for Dettol Hygiene Quest was to place portals in a variety of games. These portals were infected by germs, and players were prompted with a call to action, asking them to help in fighting off the germs. The reward was an incentive, like an in-game item or a booster, for the actual video game they were playing. Once someone entered a portal, they were taken to Dettol Hygiene Quest, a roughly three-minute-long experience in which they killed germs with a sword. As they were taking care of the germ business, players had to repeatedly clean their swords before they could continue, learning about hygiene along the way.

Dubit monitored engagement metrics throughout to inform changes it would make to attract more players. For example, the positioning of the portals was adjusted. The number of germs on the portals was altered. The messaging to prompt a player to enter the portal was tweaked. And it worked—over a period of two months, 5.7 million kids played Dettol Hygiene Quest, which is far above the benchmark of 1 to 2 million players that these types of integrations normally engage. Douthwaite credited the selection of video games to integrate with as a key success driver: "We chose gameplay experiences where germs would naturally appear in the real world, like restaurants or train stations. This ensured that the narrative and the gameplay were authentic, and the Dettol Hygiene Quest even became additive to the video game players were already playing."[19]

Crucial to demonstrating success was the fact that measurement capabilities focused on the most essential metrics built into the game. The goal, according to Srinivasan, was to measure if users' hygiene and handwashing knowledge had improved because of it. The team conducted a short survey with a sample of twenty thousand players when they entered and left Dettol Hygiene Quest. The results exceeded their expectations. Players' knowledge around hygiene and handwashing increased by 19.7 percent from the three-minute experience—significantly more effective than traditional education methods. Better yet: time spent in the video game totaled 268,000 hours. That's more than thirty years of education.

The excitement across the company about solving real consumer problems through video games is high. The Dettol brand is now working with local brand teams to scale Dettol Hygiene Quest globally. And the impact continues to increase: fifteen million visits (and growing), more than a 20 percent improvement in hygiene knowledge, half a million hours played, and the status of number one game on Roblox for consumer goods/retail brands—all at a fraction of the on-the-ground cost to educate kids on handwashing.

Hygiene is just the starting point. Srinivasan is looking to expand his company's efforts into other social impact areas, like water conservation and sustainable clothing. As he summarized, "We believe video games and Roblox can become our scaled global education platform that allows us to associate our brands with the identity of consumers in really authentic and engaging ways."

What to Do

We've covered a lot of ground in this chapter. Here's what to remember.

- Be clear on your initial goals and the expectations you set. Keep it simple. In the beginning, less is more—but by zeroing in on a couple of metrics, you will be able to track and illustrate the tangible impact your entry into video games has on your business.

- Use existing video games to prove the value of a holistic gaming strategy for your company. These games offer access to an established audience, and the cost and risk of the technical integration is far lower than the potential upside.

- Be intentional about who you want to reach. Use audience insights tools to understand the needs of your target customers and which video games they play. Don't follow the most obvious path (read: the biggest games); choose the one that actually leads to your audience.

- Evaluate and identify the required skills, and which ones are currently missing in your organization. Close these skill gaps by partnering with experienced video game developers. If your goal is to lay the foundation for a long-term strategy, educate your organization and hire talent with a strong affinity for video games, potentially including people who have worked in the gaming industry.

- Don't copy playbooks from traditional advertising strategies and paste them into this new channel. Whatever your starting point is, it has to fit into the world of video games. Take advantage of the many ways in which games let you engage with your customers.

- Stay true to your brand and its values. Don't pretend to be something that your company isn't. Don't integrate with a video game just because it is popular. Identify the unique aspects of your brand and let those come to life in an experience that provides the proper setting for it.

6

Create New Video Game Experiences

uilding your own video game to engage with your target customers is a powerful strategy. But it is also a far more complex and hence riskier strategy than integrating into games that already exist. Why? It requires you to mold the experience from scratch. And if that wasn't enough of a commitment, there's the task of actually getting customers to play your new creation, plus maintenance after launching it. Integrating with existing titles doesn't pose these challenges, which is why most companies tend to start their journey there. However, building a new game has fundamental advantages that make the strategy so appealing—whether as a second step after a company has dipped its toes into the water through an integration or as a first step when jumping off the deep end.

Shell, the international energy company based in the United Kingdom, is a great example. The company first partnered with Fortnite to let players create customized racecourses, complete with Shell gas stations. The event was called Ultimate Road Trips and was the launchpad for Shell to make its own titles focused on car racing.[1]

CASES

HV Gaming and FashionVerse: Building the Future of Fashion Retail

FIRST **Inspires:** Turning Physical Robotics Competitions into Digital Ones

The *New York Times*: Achieving Digital Growth in an Industry in Decline

NASCAR: Turning Fans into Industry Professionals

Mars, owner of the M&M's brand, is another great example of this two-step approach. In 2016 the company had struck a deal to put its candy into the mobile game Two Dots. As players progressed, they could unlock an M&M's-inspired medallion. The integration allowed the brand to test the idea and engage an existing audience before settings its sights on a more ambitious endeavor: to reach a new audience beyond children and to provide experiences that its retail stores simply cannot achieve. To accomplish that mission, it created a game called M&M's Adventure, a fast-paced puzzle title that features anthropomorphized candy pieces as characters, as well as over one thousand levels in real-world locations around the globe. The data after launch proved that the strategy paid off. M&M's Adventure was enjoyed predominantly by adults ages 35 to 50 and resulted in elevated brand recognition and awareness within the target consumer group.[2]

Whatever kind of game a company opts for, the design process ultimately comes down to making trade-offs around speed, relevance, and potential impact for the business—which brings up an attribute that almost all companies that go down this path have in common. To them, video games are a long-term strategic priority. With that commitment, the benefits of shaping your virtual world from day one far outweigh the potential challenges along the way.

Here's some encouraging news: you don't have to go it alone. The vast majority of companies choose to partner with a game developer and rely on the partner's expertise in creating immersive experiences. Having people by your side who have been down this road more than once definitely makes the endeavor feel less daunting. The key is to find a partner that really understands your goals, vision, brand values, IP, and other relevant details, so the video game is authentic to your company. "Building gameplay mechanics is tough," Ed Kiang, the National Football League's vice president, video gaming, told the *Wall Street Journal*.[3] According to Kiang, the NFL went through an extensive vetting process to find the right partners for its two games on Roblox and its arcade-style mobile game NFL Rivals. The latter combines football gameplay with collecting and trading digital player cards, all running on the blockchain.

Once companies have found success in creating their own games, there is a case to be made that critical development expertise should be brought in-house (more on that in chapter 9). That's assuming, though, the goal is to expand the game portfolio and maintain these experiences as customer touchpoints. But the bottom line is that building new titles has a fundamental benefit: the first-party data they generate, which a company can use to understand its audience on an ongoing basis, including how their preferences may evolve over time. "The interaction data of players in these video games and how that shapes a brand's strategy is invaluable," Samir Agili of Tilting Point, who we met earlier in this book, told me. "It truly is the touchpoint of where your consumer is."[4] Armed with this kind of evidence, Agili had no problem convincing one of the most iconic fashion companies to let its brand and apparel come to virtual life—while shaping what the future of e-commerce might look like.

HV Gaming and FashionVerse: Building the Future of Fashion Retail

Fashion brands and retailers alike are attempting to revamp their strategies to keep up with changing consumer preferences and shopping behaviors. Foot Locker and Express exemplify this struggle, collectively closing over two hundred US stores in 2024 alone. Reports suggest that closures for all retail companies could reach forty-five thousand stores in the next five years.[5] The problem at hand: how to bring fashion to the next generation of digital-first consumers. Designer Tommy Hilfiger sees an opportunity in gaming.

Hilfiger's interest in video games was sparked by their high engagement levels and the diverse ways consumers use games as platforms for self-expression. "The fusion of fashion with digital pop culture through gaming provides an exciting opportunity to connect with a younger, tech-savvy audience," Hilfiger told me.[6] Together with his business partner Joseph Lamastra, he founded Hilfiger Ventures, a private investment vehicle focused on entertainment, media, digital content, and virtual experiences. The firm then formed HV Gaming to identify avenues to enter the video gaming space and develop a digital portfolio. Through connections with venture capital funds focused on similar investments, HV Gaming was introduced to Tilting Point and Agili.

Since 2015, Agili has been exploring avenues and seeking partners to leverage video games as a distribution channel to drive commerce. He envisions fully immersive virtual worlds that seamlessly connect online and physical shopping experiences. He also wants to tackle video gaming from different angles: outfitting digital avatars with the latest fashion lines, PC video games, and mobile video games.

The list to achieve the goal of bringing fashion to a younger, digital-first generation was long. But Agili had a great reference point that illustrated a less risky, but still ambitious, pathway: Covet Fashion, a 2013 mobile title that enables players to dress their avatars in virtual clothing from real-world brands. It's a video game that surpassed $435 million in lifetime revenue back in 2020 and today still makes around $200,000 in revenue.[7] Every week. Alongside mobile games' ease of use, vast accessibility, and relatively low development costs, these kinds of financial opportunities brought HV Gaming and Tilting Point together in their far-reaching vision of a fully immersive world.

The teams began to lay the groundwork for their project, called FashionVerse, by zeroing in on their target audience. The focus was consumers with disposable income who would be willing to make in-game purchases, so the brands could generate revenue from the game as well as from selling the corresponding physical items by introducing e-commerce capabilities into the game. This consideration led right into a second one: how to make the game so appealing that many different brands would feel proud to be a part of the experience. The teams leveraged HV Gaming's network to select the brands and focused a lot of attention on the art style of the experience as well as the right fashion trends. To support its research efforts, Tilting Point partnered with Solsten to dig into the motivations, needs, and preferences of different audiences: mobile gamers, players of existing titles like Covet Fashion, and the fans of each fashion brand. "This research was paramount in our ability to understand what would keep these different audiences engaged," explained Agili, "and how we could nurture them along an integral piece of our core game loop—an event-based system that would promote a single fashion brand at a time . . . to stay clear of creating direct competition between brands."[8]

With the foundation in place, the FashionVerse teams turned their vision into a reality. The mobile video game lets players act as a stylist and a photographer. They start out with a photorealistic avatar and are given challenges to dress it up for different types of events. The menu features clothing items from brands such as Michael Kors and movies including *Clueless,* and players can combine them into outfits while selecting a background they deem most fitting for the look and feel. The photorealistic style is key to the experience. "This gamer will want to see real fashion. It has to be elevated because they want to be inspired by it," said Hilfiger in an interview with *Vogue Business.*[9]

Players can submit their looks to the community, and users can vote for the best ones. Three days later, players find out if their look won and, if so, are rewarded with prizes as well as virtual cash that they can use to buy more items. In a way, the game mimics what every person has experienced when shopping in the physical world: going into a store and trying on clothes. The added element is feedback from other people—the perfect time to prompt players to purchase, in real life, the outfit they put together. That's the major advantage FashionVerse, and games in general, have over physical retail stores: It removes the barriers around time and space and offers instant, direct access to a continuously engaged consumer base.[10]

The results speak for themselves: increased user engagement and time spent on FashionVerse platforms, as well as effective market penetration of younger audiences, which addresses the overall goal of expanding brands' consumer bases. "Think about the amount of students in between class on public transportation and people just staying up late at night playing because they become so immersed in it," Hilfiger explained. "So many people are so immersed in

Instagram and TikTok and keep going and going and going. [FashionVerse] has those qualities of drawing people in."[11]

On the back of this success, the FashionVerse team has their eyes set on the next big thing: forever changing the nature of fashion retail. Traditionally, fashion games have integrated commerce by simply adding links that send players to a website to make their purchase. If it's up to the FashionVerse team, those days are over. The plan is to add true commerce natively to the game, so it becomes a part of the actual gaming experience, removing the friction for players having to leave the game in order to shop.[12] This approach offers the ability to mirror the modern-day customer journey and seamlessly blend gaming, social interaction, lifestyle, shopping—and making a purchase. Ultimately, it could take the traction that brands generate digitally and help turn it into physical purchases. As Foot Locker, Express, and many others revamp their consumer engagement strategies, they should take note of what HV Gaming and FashionVerse are up to.

FIRST Inspires: Turning Physical Robotics Competitions into Digital Ones

At the onset of the pandemic, Chris Rake—the executive vice president and chief operating officer of *FIRST* Inspires, the global robotics community known for its competitions that prepare young people for the future by advancing STEM education—had to scramble. With stay-at-home mandates and social distancing rules in place, he and his fellow executives were faced with an existential question: How could they keep delivering their mission as an organization? "We have been making robotics events for more than thirty years," Rake told me. "It's a proven recipe. When you deviate from that and you don't have the data on where to go exactly, it is hard for people to take the leap into something new and unknown."[13]

Given the lack of clarity around how long the pandemic would last, the *FIRST* team had no choice but to come up with new ways of bringing robotics to their community of more than one million people. The team eventually decided on building a video game.

Though the choice may seem obvious now, it was far from that. In 2018 the team had discussed trying out video games and virtual experiences. Over the ten years leading up to the pandemic, during which the community took it upon itself to build games like small robotics simulators, *FIRST* wasn't yet convinced that video games could lead to the same outcomes as in-person events; efforts were also fragmented. "We had no alignment nor the technical capability to actively pursue this," remembered Rake.

The pandemic forced the team to consider novel strategies that would enable it to deliver on *FIRST*'s mission while people were stuck at home. But it also required an entrepreneurial mindset from company founder Dean Kamen, who is known for inventing the Segway and iBOT. The team developed half a dozen ideas, one of which was to create a video game, realizing it had the opportunity to be a pioneer in the space. But what kind of game to build, and how, was far less clear. One conclusion the team reached quickly: it needed a partner to pull this off. "We're not game designers and we don't know the technicalities of designing video games. But we know our community, our goals, and our vision," Rake said.

So *FIRST* turned to Dan White and his company Filament Games. The two partners kicked off their journey in 2020, and throughout the year *FIRST* gave White's team the room to try different things. It also ensured that Filament would have dedicated and consistent counterparts within its organization. Rake, who was the vice president of programs at the time, overseeing the core verticals that provide events and services to the *FIRST* community, was the executive sponsor. Within each program vertical sat a group that typically focused on the in-person competitions. One game design lead gave input directly to Filament, meeting weekly to check on alignment and progress to provide visibility to *FIRST*'s leadership about the project's status. *FIRST* gave its partner a lot of trust and freedom to deliver the video game, which in turn made the lift for *FIRST* very manageable.

The area where Rake and his team spent the most time was the beginning of the process, providing Filament with the context to make the game as authentic to and as aligned with the mission of *FIRST* Inspires as possible. The two groups started by looking at robotics simulators and the previous grassroots efforts, to understand what worked with the community, what didn't, and which elements to carry over from the physical competitions so that the game would feel familiar. For example, *FIRST* is all about solving real-world problems, so the robots in the game would have to be helpful and constructive. In addition, the physical competitions often involve kits from which participants build robots from scratch—a concept that was adjusted but kept. While success is never guaranteed, *FIRST* got all the pieces in place: a clear strategy and vision, executive support, a safe space to experiment, and a partner that was in sync with its objectives. All these guidelines and findings served as important guardrails for discussions and for building rudimentary versions of the new game. A name emerged throughout that process as well: RoboCo.

In RoboCo players build robots to help humans in various daily-life situations. From delivering food at a restaurant or driving a tired person to their destination, to setting up a romantic date, doing yard work, or transporting large tree trunks, there's a robot to be built to solve almost any task. Players can choose from different robotic kits, customize the look and feel of their creations, and share their robots with the wider community. An important and unique feature of RoboCo is the ability to automate robots and teach them skills by writing a few lines of custom software—an integral aspect of the real-life competitions.[14]

From the day it launched, RoboCo was a resounding success. *FIRST* Global, a sister organization of *FIRST* Inspires, was the first team to test the game live and to replace a physical competition with a virtual one. Close to fifty teams competed against one another, building robots, learning about STEM topics, and voting for a winner—all within the game. The process pressure-tested RoboCo for the entire organization, making tangible the potential for video games to be part of *FIRST*'s programs even in a post-pandemic world. Rake and his colleagues now view gaming as supplemental to the core experiences they provide. "As the world largely returned to in-person education and resumption of activities that had to be suspended, we found that the physical gathering of young people to participate in STEM enrichment through robotics was extremely desirable from participant, mentor, parent, and educator perspectives," explained Rake, pointing to the rapid return to in-person events as well as the growth of participation since.

Yet the road ahead still needs to be explored, and *FIRST* doesn't fully know where its gaming efforts will go next. Similar to technologies like the drill press or the 3D printer, video games are and will remain part of the rich toolbox that the *FIRST* community makes use of to collaborate in solving the challenges thrown at them.

It took a global pandemic and the threat of its dominant customer touchpoints being wiped out for *FIRST* Inspires to take a leap of faith and dive into video games. In less than two years it managed to successfully transition from three decades of solely in-person competitions and open up a viable pathway for the future.

The *New York Times*: Achieving Digital Growth in an Industry in Decline

Games have been a part of the fabric of the *New York Times* for a long time—since 1942, to be exact. That was the year the Sunday crossword puzzle appeared. In a time where "people came for the news and stayed for the games," the crossword provided escapism from the dreadful events of World War II, but also a healthy challenge for the brain and a positive way for *NYT* to engage its audience.[15]

Yet games are now the driving force behind the company's tectonic shift toward digital subscriptions. When it began embracing digital, marked by the launch of its iOS app in 2009, *NYT* included the digital version of the crossword readers were so familiar with from the newspaper. Arguably, this was the publisher's first video game. It was the seed for what its digital subscriptions would eventually grow into: offerings with more than eleven million subscribers by 2024.[16]

"A lot of people are actually buying the subscription bundle through our Games product," said *NYT*'s chief product officer, Alex Hardiman. "That's a pretty big shift in terms of where we were a year and a half ago, two years ago. And that is what is so powerful about games as a funnel."[17]

In an industry that has been battered for decades by declining readerships, dramatically changing consumer preferences, and the rise of mighty digital-native competitors like Meta or Google, the *New York Times* is defying the odds. After the launch of its app, *NYT* pressed forward, meticulously and intentionally, with a shift toward a predominantly digital subscription–based business model. The focus was, and still is, high-quality journalism. But to provide enough value that readers keep paying their monthly fees, digital subscriptions needed a portfolio of content. And each content type needed the ability to attract a new audience and to serve as an entry point into the *NYT* ecosystem, while also showing users the other content pillars—and ideally the entire subscription bundle. So the company made acquisitions and investments in cooking, sports, e-commerce, audio, and video games.

Five years into its digital transition, in 2014, *NYT* expanded its games with the launch of the Mini Crossword. Four years later, it added Spelling Bee, which has roots in a puzzle that still runs in the newspaper. The slow but meticulous approach started to pay off: in 2017 the *Times* hit $1 billion in digital subscription revenue, accounting for 60 percent of its overall revenue. Digital subscriber growth rose to about 2.6 million. Crosswords, which is what the video game content was called at the time, was also growing healthily, to about 850,000 subscribers.[18] And subscriptions to just Spelling Bee were stacking up, too, helping to further diversify the audience *NYT* was able to reach. All signs were pointing in the same direction: a massive opportunity to build a video game portfolio to drive continued growth for the digital subscription business.

David Perpich, who was leading stand-alone products (including video games) and who is now the publisher of the paper's sports vertical, the Athletic, wasted no time. Crosswords was rebranded to NYT Games, and Perpich kicked off the search for a seasoned video game industry leader. Jonathan Knight, with his twenty-three years of experience at companies like Activision, Electronic Arts, Zynga, and Warner Bros. Games, fit the bill perfectly. "I came in at an inflection point and already had lots to work with," Knight said about the efforts leading up to his appointment as head of games.[19] "What makes games so engaging are their underlying loops. The systems have the ability to pull on people's motivations, aspirations, and deep human emotions. Games are not for gamers. They're for everyone."

What was missing at *NYT* was a clear strategy for future growth, which is where Knight and his team placed their initial focus. Their approach would be based on four critical pillars: an audience strategy to identify the right target customers, where to find them, and how to bring them into the NYT Games universe; a technical strategy to deliver the video games service; a big vision; and a content strategy to define the scope of what kinds of games they would create. Though it took a while to get all four of these in place, the audience and technical strategies required the most time and effort because of their foundational importance. "You have to create user value if you want to extract business model value. If you don't have a really good grasp on our audience, you won't be able to create value for them," Knight explained.

He and his team are guided by the principle of "time well spent" when thinking about their current games as well as which new ones to build. In essence, it's a philosophy similar to that of the games from the 1940s, and it still underpins the modern strategy. While the news cycle fluctuates, the puzzles are a consistent daily presence. And Knight's vision is for *NYT* to become the premier destination for digital puzzle games that reach larger and more diverse audiences.

That vision was paramount in anchoring the team on their road ahead. And therein laid another challenge: the initial team wasn't nearly big enough and lacked important skills in game production and design. Knight himself was experiencing his own learning curve from digging into *NYT*'s subscription business model and underlying drivers, which are different from those of the free-to-play world of mobile video games he had spent most of his career in. The key metrics now? How many users hit a paywall—in a news article, video, or any piece of *Times* content—and converted into paying subscribers. Number of conversions from landing pages. Starts and stops when people are reading an article. Net additions of digital subscribers. Knight had to figure out how to bring his video gaming past to bear on these kinds of measures.

He and his team went to work with the goal of building out a video game portfolio for the *Times*. Their first game, Digits, had good user engagement early on, but ultimately didn't quite meet the bar. But because they had invested in a technical strategy up front and made it a point to build a platform on which most, if not all, of their video games could be created, the team was able to experiment and pursue new projects quickly. Tiles and Vertex were its next projects; both have become staples in the NYT Games portfolio. Video game number four, a Hangman-inspired concept that was shaping up to become the team's own version of the widely popular Wordle, was already in the works. In just twelve months, *NYT* had made games a core part of its digital subscription offering and had a portfolio that by itself was attracting one million subscribers. Then the opportunity to accelerate everything presented itself.

"Wordle Is a Love Story."[20] When Daniel Victor wrote a *New York Times* article about the meteoric rise of Wordle, that headline was intended to reflect the fact that Josh Wardle, the game's creator, originally built it for his partner. Little did Victor know that the headline would carry far deeper meaning—for *NYT* itself. Two days later, Knight was on the phone with Wardle, asking if he wanted to sell his video game to the paper. Three weeks later, *NYT* had acquired it, helping catalyze an unparalleled growth story. "Wordle was a moment where the planets aligned," remembered Knight. "[It] brought in millions of players and people that had never been on nyt.com before." The game was a natural fit strategically, even though the team had to invest in software development, back-end infrastructure, and data storage to bring Wordle into its world and unify all of its platforms and systems. The result was that the digital subscription and video game audience grew tenfold within eighteen months.

With the integration well underway, the now roughly one-hundred-person-strong team turned its attention back to adding video games to its portfolio. While the group is predominantly focused on prototyping new titles, its internal resources are flexible, so it can easily shift from prototyping to carrying out the launch of a game. Ideas for video games can come from anyone on the team, as well as outside of it. If an idea gets the initial green light, it follows a process: build a prototype, test it internally, prepare for an external beta test with real players, conduct the beta test and gather results, do more research, and ultimately build the full game. Throughout, the concept committee—consisting of Knight, his executive producer of games, and his editorial director—vote on whether to move forward or abandon the project.

The team's latest, widely successful addition? Connections, which the company announced seventeen months after the acquisition of Wordle. It's a word association game that gives players a board of sixteen words organized in a grid. The goal is to find four groups of four associated words. Connections has been the next proof point that video games and *NYT* are a winning combination: only three months after launch, about ten million people were playing it in a given week, making it the company's most successful game after Wordle.[21] Overall growth for the subscription bundle saw another jump, to cross the ten million threshold. Shortly after followed another game, called Strands, which tasks players with uncovering themed words on a grid of randomly assembled letters. Filling the board with the required number of words, and hence uncovering its theme, unlocks the next board to solve.

In addition to bringing in new customers for the overall subscription bundle, video games have another attribute that is of critical business value to the *Times*: they create a far healthier long-term relationship with the customer. "If a subscriber engages with both news and games in a given week, we see by far the strongest long-term retention metrics of these customer segments," explained Knight. Given his team's success, it is no surprise that video games will play a key role for *NYT* on the way to achieving its goal of having fifteen million digital subscribers by 2027. At the time of this writing, the game portfolio has expanded to ten titles, and it is clear that more are coming. Knight wants his team to become the best in the world at digital puzzle games. For now, the focus remains on the word-game category, but the logic, visual, and trivia spaces are on the team's radar, as is international expansion.

Other publishers, like the *Washington Post*, have attempted to get their own video games off the ground as well—sometimes with lackluster and outright disappointing results.[22] Knight sees a big difference in the purpose those companies tend to ascribe to video games versus *NYT*'s approach. "For most publishers, games are a means to get eyeballs that you monetize via advertising," he said. "We are taking a different approach. We view games as creating a long-term relationship with customers that can be measured in a way only [they] let you achieve."

NASCAR: Turning Fans into Industry Professionals

The stock car racing company NASCAR and video games have a relationship that goes back all the way to 1984, when it licensed its IP for a game called Richard Petty's Talladega. In the twenty-five years that followed, more than forty video games were launched that leveraged the NASCAR brand and its IP.

Then, in 2009, the licensing agreement with Electronic Arts for its NASCAR racing games on consoles like Sony's PlayStation and Microsoft's Xbox expired. NASCAR's leadership had to reorient not only its video gaming strategy but its overall consumer engagement strategy, while facing multiple challenges. "At a time when our brand had peaked, in challenging markets on the back of the global financial crisis, we needed to engage with a younger, more digitally native audience that started interacting with sports far less via traditional broadcasting methods," Nick Rend, vice president, interactive and emerging platforms, told me.[23] What followed was a decade filled with ups and downs—but most importantly, one critical decision that would set the company on the right track to fully realize the promise video games held.

With the IP license up for grabs in 2010, NASCAR's executive team wanted to reevaluate the organization's presence in gaming. It signed a new licensing deal with a small development studio in the United Kingdom that would simply continue the video game franchise on consoles. A number of titles went live over the next five years with mixed results. "We made the mistake to prioritize revenue from selling console games over reach, relevance, and resonance with our actual target audience," said Rend.

Yet at about the same time, NASCAR partnered with development studio iRacing to build a brand-new game—a motorsports platform for competitive online racing on PCs. The goal was to create an experience that would be as close to racing a real car as possible and bridge the gap between NASCAR's established fan base and a new, younger audience that leaned toward online gaming. The teams developed a proof of concept for what they called the eNASCAR iRacing Series, which not only replicated the racing experience but also introduced innovative elements to enhance fan engagement and make NASCAR more accessible online. Creating a game that was as exhilarating as getting behind the wheel of a high-horsepower vehicle was the top priority. The two teams collaborated closely to fine-tune the physics engine, graphics, and user interface. Throughout the development, they brought in professional

NASCAR drivers to take the virtual cars for a spin. They liked what they saw—so much so that, within the same year, eNASCAR iRacing Series was ready to be launched alongside NASCAR's marquee event, the Daytona 500.

The game would see players compete on close approximations of real tracks, driving the virtual versions of the real cars. They would actually sit in a real racing seat, hands on a steering wheel, putting the pedal to the metal. The winner of the very first eNASCAR iRacing Series was none other than Dale Earnhardt Jr., NASCAR's most popular driver at the time, which significantly boosted the project's credibility and appeal. Since then, the competition series has featured the world's top forty simulation racers, who annually compete for over $500,000 and the Dale Earnhardt Jr. Cup—a trophy worth over $20,000. The project has expanded significantly to include a college series, with participation from over four hundred universities, and an international series that brings together NASCAR's global competitors—achieving the goal of reaching a younger, and global, audience. During the pandemic, when live sporting events were on hold, the virtual iRacing events took the place of the real races in the schedule and were even broadcast on TV. Not only did this ensure continuity of the sport, but 20 percent of the viewership was entirely new to NASCAR.

The remarkable power that video games have is arguably best illustrated by people like William Byron and Rajah Caruth. Both were avid players of the iRacing series—and eventually were able to take the leap and become professional NASCAR drivers offline after signing with youth racing teams and dominating the championships. Byron even won the Daytona 500 in 2024 and again in 2025, making him the first back-to-back winner since 2020 and only the fifth driver to accomplish that feat.[24] By making stock car racing globally accessible and less dependent on traditional audiences, who often passed their fandom down as a family heritage, NASCAR turned fans into industry professionals. "I can play football as a video game, but I couldn't step onto a football field and compete in the NFL," said Rend. "But with racing simulations, video games are so realistic that they allow players to train the very muscle memory that is needed for the sport in real life."

In 2021 NASCAR's IP was used by a development studio to build a video game for consoles for the last time. The game was called NASCAR 21: Ignition, and it faced significant backlash from players and the community after it launched. Bugs and subpar gameplay posed a serious threat to NASCAR's brand and reputation. At the same time, the IP licensing deal's expiration let iRacing pounce on the opportunity. It's now building a much-anticipated console game that will bring the fidelity and authenticity players expect to audiences beyond the competitive racing space.

With so much momentum, NASCAR has the confidence to significantly expand its commitment to video games. "What started as a simulation-style recreation of the world's premier motorsport has now become a hub of innovation and next-generation entertainment for us," explained Rend. The organization is looking to innovate across platforms like Roblox and Fortnite; its efforts include stand-alone video games aimed at casual fans, like NASCAR Arcade Rush, and a dedicated manager-style mobile game called NASCAR Manager.

The big difference now, compared with the challenging years in the 2010s? "Everything we do starts with our audience, who they are, and their needs," said Rend.

What to Do

The examples in this chapter offer plenty to think about. Here's what to remember.

- **Don't go it alone.** To realize your first video game, work with an experienced partner that has a track record of success.

- **But vet your partner.** The team needs to understand your vision, goals, brand, values, IP, and more. This robust understanding is the foundation of representing your company authentically in the digital world. If you are committed to making video games over the long term, consider hiring senior leadership and talent from the games industry and forming a dedicated internal team.

- **Be creative and bold.** Take advantage of the fact that you're creating a new video game. Shape the entire experience to optimally represent your brand and resonate with your target audience.

- **Be intentional about who your game is for.** Investing up front in deeply understanding your audience will reduce risk for the project and help ensure that consumers will love it.

- **Be strategic, both with the games you're building and with your overall strategy.** Understand and define how video games can complement your existing business model and allow you to expand on it.

- **Test, iterate, and learn along the way.** Involve real users in your development process to test and validate your hypotheses. Course-correct early when needed—this ensures critical aspects of your game will resonate with your ideal audience. Don't be afraid to kill projects if they don't meet the mark.

7

Unlock Revenue through Web3 Games

During the height of the global pandemic, a particular segment of the video gaming market experienced skyrocketing growth: Web3 games. These titles, which under the hood are powered by blockchain technology, saw a 2,000 percent increase between 2021 and 2022.[1] After the softening of cryptocurrency markets and related technologies in late 2022 and 2023, $600 million in fresh venture capital funding and a 12 percent increase in unique wallets owned by players to store virtual assets related to video games are clear signs: Web3 games are here to stay.[2]

To fully grasp the potential of these titles, we have to shine a light on their inner workings for a moment. Because of their technology, Web3 games allow companies to interact with consumers even more intimately than the traditional video games we have discussed do. (Web3 is an extension of cryptocurrency, using blockchain in new ways; this sentence's note has a wonderful primer in case you want to learn more.)[3] Essentially, these titles offer players the possibility to earn and outright own virtual items. Think of it this way:

CASES

Burberry: Reaching a New Audience in Twenty-Two Seconds

Starbucks: Taking Loyalty Programs to the Next Level

Puma: Making Exclusive Experiences Accessible to Everyone

Adidas: Selling Culture at a Premium

you play a game and progress toward a goal, at which point you are rewarded with a specific item that you now own—it's uniquely yours. There is a defined number of instances of this item available, and one instance belongs to you and no one else (the ownership aspect is verified via blockchain). Game developers have coined this approach *play-to-earn* or *play-to-own*—and it is only possible in Web3 games, because in traditional games an item's ownership cannot be verified. The ownership aspect creates a stronger emotional connection between the player and the game.

But there is more. The virtual items in Web3 titles do not only apply to the game itself. They also allow for a connection to real-world physical assets. Let's say you unlock and now own a pair of the latest Nike Air Force 1 sneakers in a game. A physical pair of that exact sneaker that is unique and linked to the digital sneaker version you own, verified via a token on the blockchain, is already on its way to your doorstep. Digitally owned items can often be transferred by the owner (the player) to other video games or sold to other players on secondary marketplaces. Because of the scarcity of certain items and the subjective value placed on them by consumers (just like in the real world), their worth will fluctuate. For companies and brands, this presents an incredible opportunity for long-tail engagement beyond the point of playing the game. Sustained, more frequent interaction with a brand and its products, even if it's driven by monitoring the value of digital assets, can create greater customer loyalty.

Take Kering's brand Gucci. It collaborated with Roblox, which has all the markings of a Web3 video game environment, to launch a virtual experience called Gucci Garden in 2012. As players entered, their avatars became blank, genderless, humanoid-like mannequins that absorbed elements of the various rooms they encountered—colors, designs, artifacts, and more, which paid homage to fifteen renowned Gucci campaigns and collections. Players could navigate freely and experience the rooms in different orders, which led to many unique creations at the end of each person's journey. Explore the Tokyo Tribe–themed maze first, and the colorful zigzag lights can become a patterned sleeve on your mannequin. As part of the exhibition, a digital version of a Gucci bag sold for $4,115 (or 350,000 Robux).[4]

Kering's archrival Louis Vuitton took its approach a step further. To celebrate the 200th birthday of its founder, in 2021 the company created Louis: The Game.[5] Players explored six different worlds through the eyes of the protagonist, Vivienne. Ultimately, the goal was to collect two hundred candles to commemorate Vuitton's birthday. Each candle revealed memorabilia related to the history of the company, and the protagonist's appearance could be customized with digital versions of its latest collections. The Web3 aspect came into play through thirty nonfungible tokens (NFTs)—unique cryptographic tokens that exist on the blockchain, can't be replicated, and represent digital or real-world items such as art or watches; they can be bought, sold, and traded—designed by the artist Beeple, who rose to global fame when his digital collage sold as an NFT at a Christie's auction for close to $69 million.[6] The NFTs could only be found by playing the game, and they could not be sold outside of it—creating a store of value that tied players to the Louis Vuitton experience.

Compared with more traditional games, the underlying tech for Web3 titles is different and the space is much newer (and quickly evolving). But the strategic options for companies to leverage these video games are identical to the pathways we highlighted in our previous two chapters. They can integrate with an existing game, or opt to create one from scratch.

Burberry: Reaching a New Audience in Twenty-Two Seconds

When we introduced Burberry's journey into gaming earlier in the book, you may have had a similar reaction to Mythical Games CEO John Linden when the British fashion house proposed a partnership. "I thought they were crazy," Linden told me, laughing.[7]

Typically, fashion houses launch their lines through traditional channels like runway shows or in-store promotions. Integrating high fashion with a digital environment, especially one based on blockchain, seemed out of character for Burberry. But as we learned, it had a plan in mind. The goal was to reach and build a meaningful connection with a younger audience—potential future aficionados of the company's iconic trench coat—and avoid becoming a brand of the past. It conducted extensive research on global shopping trends as well as consumer preferences and media consumption. The research was clear: Burberry's target audience follows and actively interacts with brands on social media, plays video games, prefers experiences over "things," and seeks personalization. Web3 games allowed Burberry to tick all of these boxes.

The company chose to work with Mythical's Blankos Block Party, which we introduced in chapter 1. The digital toys known as Blankos are customizable and come with a variety of designs and abilities. To start, Burberry decided to release limited-edition Blankos (750 of them, to be exact) at the steep price of $299.99 apiece. It also wanted to offer digital clothing items from its new collection that players could buy and sell on a virtual marketplace.

Linden wasn't sold. "At this price point, I thought this was going to fail," he recalled. "Three hundred dollars for a virtual character is a lot of money when you compare it to what players spend on average in a free-to-play game like Blankos." But once the offerings launched, just two months after Burberry and Mythical had announced their partnership, all 750 characters sold out—in twenty-two seconds. The price tag didn't deter players from purchasing them at all, but rather signaled exclusivity and a ticket to enter a special club—very similar to the signals sent by real-world Burberry fashion items.

"A big reason for the success of this launch, and you have to give a lot of credit to the team at Burberry for insisting on this, was the authenticity in how their brand was represented," said Linden. "The characters, the clothing items—everything felt authentically Burberry. This is important because gamers almost have a sixth sense for things that are trying too hard or attempt to take short-cuts. Burberry never compromised."

Building on this initial success, the British fashion house decided to expand its Web3 gaming efforts. Less than a year later, it launched a new limited-edition character in Blankos dressed in its latest summer wardrobe, along with a series of branded in-game accessories like boomboxes and slider sandals.

In the end, though on the surface it seemed odd for a luxury brand to create digital characters, Burberry found a strategic fit with Web3 gaming by being able to limit the number of available items as well as giving players the opportunity to make an item theirs. This collaboration wasn't just about blending physical and digital worlds.

The success of the Blankos project was the realization of where luxury and gaming intersect. As Rachel Waller, then Burberry's vice president, channel innovation, shared in a public company statement, "Luxury is an industry built on fantasy and expression, so in many ways, gaming is a canvas perfectly suited to bringing these dreams to life."[8]

Starbucks: Taking Loyalty Programs to the Next Level

The loyalty of consumers is not a given, and companies must work hard to stay relevant post-purchase to pave the way for repeat business. This understanding prompted senior management at Starbucks, a company that enjoys roughly 40 percent market share in the highly fragmented and fiercely competitive US coffee market, to develop the video game Odyssey.[9]

The company was starting in a strong position. Its loyalty program, known as Starbucks Rewards, has been tremendously successful in driving customer loyalty and increasing the frequency of visits and spending per visit. Per former chief financial officer Patrick Grismer, "We know from our experience that when customers join our rewards program, their total spend with Starbucks increases meaningfully."[10] In 2019 the company attributed its 7 percent increase in total revenues almost entirely to its rewards program. The same year, 40 percent of its entire revenue was attributed to the customer loyalty initiative.[11]

The program's integration with the Starbucks mobile app, which offers order-ahead and payment features, has significantly enhanced customer convenience and satisfaction. By using personalized offers and data-driven marketing, the company has effectively tailored its engagement strategies to individual preferences, boosting retention rates. Additionally, the program's tiered rewards system and exclusive member benefits have incentivized repeat purchases, making it one of the most praised loyalty programs in the retail sector. Now CEO Brian Niccol is looking to expand the company's focus beyond its rewards program members and attract more customers.[12]

Odyssey served as an extension of the rewards program. Customers would still earn points and redeem them for drinks, cookies, and other perks. What Starbucks wanted to build was an immersive experience to engage rewards members more frequently, more meaningfully, and to create an even stronger connection with the brand outside the transactional touchpoint of ordering coffee. Odyssey lets users go on choose-your-own-adventure interactive journeys to complete games, take quizzes, and collect Journey Stamps—NFTs that have a point value based on their rarity, making them sought-after items for collectors and traders. These stamps also unlock unique experiences online and offline. The rewards include virtual classes, early access to limited-edition merchandise, or, if a member has reached a high enough rewards tier, a trip to a Starbucks coffee farm.[13]

The results of Odyssey have been impressive. In chapter 4 we learned how the "Siren collection," whose two thousand stamps cost $100 each, sold out in just minutes upon its release in March 2023. Three months later, a second stamp collection was released. Called the "Starbucks First Store collection," it comprised five thousand stamps at a price of $99 apiece.[14] These stamps were initially available only to Odyssey members who had earned at least two unique Journey Stamps from playing the video game consistently. The more players engage, the greater and rarer the rewards become.

The impact on the company's financial performance has been strong. In the United States alone, the rewards program saw a

14 percent increase in its membership, taking its size beyond thirty-two million. Globally, the company's rewards program has ballooned to seventy-five million people.[15]

Odyssey's success can be attributed to the fact that it is an engaging game in its own right, but also to how it provides the opportunity to own, collect, and sell valuable digital items. Simply plugging in blockchain technology and calling Odyssey a Web3 game would have been destined to fail. Since 2018, 75 percent of all Web3 games have failed because they haven't justified their term-term value for audiences, leading to declining interest.[16] Starbucks got this one right.

The organizational setup was also instrumental in Odyssey's success. The project and the initial team were anchored in the overall loyalty organization of Starbucks. There were no playbooks to reference from similar experiences at other companies; the team was blazing a new path, which required space to experiment. Senior leadership was committed to building out Odyssey, though, and provided the necessary space and time. "It felt a bit like a playground," said Sydney Flynn, manager, loyalty partnerships and experiences, at the time.[17]

However, the playground had a few important guardrails. First, the team knew it had to make Odyssey accessible for two distinct audiences: Web3 enthusiasts and Starbucks rewards members. Second, Odyssey needed to be in line with the company's mission and values to ensure it was authentically Starbucks. The latter is a key reason that the game's content, especially player journeys, was designed in-house, whereas the team collaborated with partners for the technical components and overall building of the experience.

In the last quarter of 2023, Starbucks announced its "triple shot reinvention strategy" aimed at the long-term growth of the business. Among the core pillars are "strengthen and scale digital," with the explicit goal of doubling, by 2028, the rewards membership of seventy-five million people.[18] In light of the company's financial struggles throughout 2024, in which global sales slumped by 7 percent, Niccol called for a fundamental shift in strategy to reignite the coffee giant's growth. One aspect he wanted to focus on is a vision for community coffeehouses and the ability to bring people together.[19] Video games are sure to play a part.

Puma: Making Exclusive Experiences Accessible to Everyone

Puma has long been open to the possibilities that video games open up. "Our goal is to always be a part of culture, no matter where it happens," Ivan Dashkov, head of emerging marketing technology, told me. "Video games are a huge part of culture, across all generations."[20] To him, video games aren't just games anymore. They have become places where concerts take place, fashion shows are hosted, and more—they are places where culture happens. Thus including gaming integration in Puma's strategy to relaunch its basketball business for the 2018–2019 season was a no-brainer.

At that point, Puma already had experience in video games. The company's motorsport group had been integrated into the Need for Speed racing series for the past six installments. It had also launched collaborations in the physical world with series like Sonic the Hedgehog and Final Fantasy. The uplift for the Puma brand was definitely there. But the challenge was that all these initiatives were taking place in pockets across the company, without a cohesive strategy and dedicated team.

In 2022 Puma centralized all of its efforts into one team headed by Dashkov. At the same time, the cryptocurrency and NFT markets were cooling down. Despite the company's successful presence in the NFT space, Dashkov thinks this turned out to be a blessing in disguise. "We now have the space to focus on digital goods at large across multiple gaming genres and platforms, to really ensure we have a strong presence in all of the important touchpoints for our target customers," he explained.

One of these touchpoints is Roblox, which the Puma team groups into its Web3 strategy. The ability to create virtual worlds on Roblox gave the team the opportunity to design an experience that would represent Puma in a holistic, immersive way. It thought about all the ways in which consumers connect with the brand—on a basketball court, on a soccer pitch, in a race car, in the gym, in stores, and so on. This brainstorming formed the blueprint for what the team wanted to build, which was appropriately called Puma and the Land of Games. The virtual experience featured all the various sports as well as fields, courts, stadiums, and arenas Puma is a part of in the real world, plus a series of mini games people were able to compete in.

It was an ambitious project that saw seven million users and roughly three million item purchases. Yet it didn't quite have the impact that the size of the experience might suggest. "In hindsight, we tried to do a bit too much. Some of the mini games were actually getting lost inside of the world we built," Dashkov reflected.

Fueled by Puma's highly entrepreneurial culture, which encourages teams to experiment, test, and try new things, as well as an improving relationship with their partner Roblox, Dashkov and his colleagues collaborated closely with Puma's soccer business unit and built a second experience, Puma Futureland. It featured Neymar, the company's signature, world-renowned soccer player, and the launch was tied to the release of the new Future soccer cleat. Building on the learnings from Puma and the Land of Games, the new experience focused its gameplay to ensure users would immediately understand what to do and where to go.

While Dashkov acknowledges that it is still challenging to directly tie the impact of these virtual worlds to metrics like revenue increases, Puma experienced benefits. For the first two months after its launch, Futureland was the highest-ranking brand experience on Roblox, with a 94 percent rating given by users directly using a thumbs-up or thumbs-down button. Additionally, since Puma prioritized brand uplift over immediate revenue goals, its aim was to get players to wear its apparel as they were navigating the virtual world and Roblox more broadly. A digital red Puma hat was picked up by nearly three million players, and the jersey of beloved German soccer team Borussia Dortmund (full disclosure: big fan over here) was claimed 1.8 million times—mission accomplished for Dashkov and his team.

One advantage of Puma's virtual initiatives is they don't face a challenge encountered by its physical sneaker launches, which the company regularly hosts in the coolest locations around the world: namely, that only a limited number of people can attend. Video gaming and Web3 are the key enablers to break through this limitation and bring the brand to audiences around the world, at all times, on demand. In that respect, Puma's plans are working. Its Black Station and Black Station 2 projects are effectively a fully immersive shopping experience in the form of a Web3 video game. The shopping sessions of Black Station 2 users are three times longer than those of customers on puma.com. The company is on to something—and took home a Webby Award in April 2024 as a result.[21]

"For us, we are looking at the next five to seven years to build out more meaningful revenue streams from our video gaming efforts," Daskov said. "The low-hanging fruit is to let customers buy shoes and apparel in these virtual worlds . . . [but] I believe we have to think beyond shoes and apparel. The complexities and restrictions of the physical world disappear in video games and metaverse experiences."

Adidas: Selling Culture at a Premium

Erika Wykes-Sneyd joined Adidas as global vice president of marketing and brand for the company's Originals line of apparel. Just about a year and a half later, she was double-hatting as the global vice president and general manager of the business unit in charge of efforts around Web3, collectibles, blockchain, video games, and the metaverse. Her time at the company has seen her cannily weave together those two roles in innovative ways.

The Originals line is known for streetwear and an emphasis on fashion and lifestyle rather than performance sportswear. It includes a wide range of products such as shoes, clothing, and accessories, and is perhaps best known for its classic sneakers like the Superstar, the Stan Smith, and the Gazelle. The line has long by been embraced by athletes, artists, musicians, and other creatives, setting trends along the way. When Adidas sponsored the newly formed hip-hop group Run-DMC in the early 1980s, it was the first significant partnership between rap and fashion. However, over time, the company's collaborations shifted focus from prioritizing craftsmanship to capitalizing on the success of established artists and athletes. "We used to be the guardians of culture . . . Adidas had definitely lost its way," Wykes-Sneyd told me.[22]

With experience in leading the global launch of the Sony PlayStation 4 console and global marketing for companies like Google, Uber, and PayPal, Wykes-Sneyd set her sights on reestablishing Adidas's identity and appealing to a new audience in Gen Z. The brand principles she started to rework were aimed at taking the company back to its roots and the values that had made it so successful in the past.

Part of her thinking was about how to leverage Web3 and video games to execute on her plan. But Wykes-Sneyd knew she needed to "show, don't tell" to win over the decision-makers. One finding in particular stoked a fear that, by not embracing forward-looking digital initiatives, Adidas might be missing out on the next big opportunity: while its clothing items rarely sold at full price, a premium market for NFT collectors was emerging in which people spent money hand over fist on rare and exclusive digital collectibles. The ownership component of NFTs was key to Adidas, which is why the company leaned in to Web3 first before video gaming. "No one else was in our space. We realized we needed to sell culture at a premium," Wykes-Sneyd said. She wrote an internal brief for her plan in one night. Less than two months later, a metaverse task force was established with a clear objective: put Adidas back on the map and out in front of emerging digital culture.

The task force, essentially a steering committee for Adidas's venture into Web3, had the chief digital officer at the helm. The cross-functional team consisted of the senior vice president of Adidas Originals, the head of Adidas Confirmed (which distributes limited-edition items), and Wykes-Sneyd. Once the group had generated some initial traction and a framework for its strategy and goals, it expanded by including people from other business units and teams, at its peak growing to twenty-two employees who had passion and knowledge the organization at large didn't possess.

The starting point for the team was in-depth audience research. Wykes-Sneyd and her colleagues, taking an approach we've seen throughout this book, invested in getting a crystal-clear view of who their target customers were. They partnered with a highly experienced agency, onboarded the team to their brand strategy, and conducted qualitative research, including an ethnographic study of the audience at the edge of Web3. The team then explored what it would ultimately offer people. Sure, there would be a digital collectible of some sort. But there had to be more. "We sell way more than just products. We sell experiences, access, values," Wykes-Sneyd emphasized. Tapping into the cultural zeitgeist around NFTs, Adidas Originals partnered with Bored Ape Yacht Club, gmoney, and PUNKS Comic—all pioneers in the space—to launch an NFT called "Into the Metaverse," which gave owners access to a physical collection of a hoodie, a beanie, and a tracksuit. The project put Adidas on the Web3 map and set the stage for future NFT releases and continuous engagement of the target audience.

Nine months after Wykes-Sneyd wrote her brief, Adidas Originals put itself at the forefront of the major shifts in digital fashion with another project. In December 2021 it made thirty thousand tokens, which could be redeemed for exclusive Adidas hoodies, tracksuits, and orange beanies to be worn in the metaverse, available at a price of $800 each. They sold out in minutes. Adidas and its partners had generated roughly $24 million. But not only that, it was on the path to reclaiming what once made it successful—being deeply embedded in culture.

The hype among the target audience surprised even the most optimistic folks in Adidas HQ. The launch generated far more media mentions and a larger share of search volume, a key indicator for consumer purchase intent, than the original Louis Vuitton x Supreme collaboration that was hailed in 2017 as the ultimate partnership between two of the most sought-after fashion brands. Ten percent of all metaverse- and NFT-related Google searches in North America mentioned the project (extra impressive since Facebook changed its name to Meta around the same time). The impact of the launch showed Adidas where its future would lie, and the metaverse task force became a dedicated business unit for all activities related to virtual goods, including video gaming. Its goal: sustain and expand on the initial success. "This token drop really opened the door for Adidas's future in Web3 and video gaming," Wykes-Sneyd said. That future holds a lot of promise, and it definitely involves video games as a core piece, which people within Adidas are excited about. "We can no longer market in the way we have done it in the past," she added. "We have to evoke emotions along the way . . . Video games [can do] that—but on steroids."

In Wykes-Sneyd's view, the video gaming space has matured to a point where different platforms will converge. That would make it possible for players to transition between virtual worlds seamlessly, and best-in-the-world studios and developers are starting to build ownership elements into their games. "Our future lies in high-quality video gaming," Wykes-Sneyd said, "and we're bringing a community of three hundred million Adidas fans with us, through which we will unlock revenue streams that are simply not possible in the physical world." Adidas is well on its way. In July 2024 it launched the "Three Stripe Squad Bundle," a set of customizable items, in Fortnite.[23] The company is also actively evaluating integrations with a handful of other games.

What to Do

Web3 games are still not mainstream, and hence the people that play them are predominantly early adopters. Even though this is slowly changing, you need to conduct thorough research to understand whether the audience you are targeting is already present in the broader Web3 ecosystem, or if you would have to nurture customers not just into your game but into adopting Web3-related technologies and assets as well. One is exceedingly harder to do than the other. Here's what to remember.

- Design initiatives thoughtfully. Don't just plug in blockchain technology and call something a Web3 video game. At its very core, the experience you build needs to be and feel like an actual game in order to offer players the utility that results in sustained engagement. Blockchain and similar technologies should be an enabler under the hood, a means to an end.

- Authenticity is paramount. Representing your brand authentically is a continuous theme of this book, but it's arguably even more crucial in Web3 games. The digital assets you sell will live on for a long time, and they will reflect on your brand and company far beyond the initial purchase.

- Keep the long term in mind. You can use Web3 games to generate a quick revenue boost, but that should not be the goal. The goal should really be anchored in achieving sustained long-term customer engagement, and in the opportunities that earning, owning, and selling digital assets provide.

8

Make Video Games a
Part of a Product

The most advanced strategy for video games is to use them as extensions of a core service or as a core product themselves. Combining or enhancing an existing product with a game promises two major upsides for companies. One, the experience consumers will enjoy is more immersive, which results in greater engagement overall. And two, it unlocks the opportunity to increase revenue across the company's core product portfolio. Ultimately, a video game may even be(come) a product that completely reshapes how a service is delivered to consumers.

Look no further than Netflix. In 2021 the streaming company announced its plan to offer video games without ads or in-app purchases—the dominant ways in which games make money—a move that many people rolled their eyes at.[1] Fast-forward to the end of 2023, and Netflix had seen year-over-year growth in game downloads of more than 180 percent, with downloads of its app approaching one hundred million, user engagement tripling within one year, and roughly ten million subscribers playing games on Netflix on a

CASES

Boston Consulting Group: Letting Clients Experience Business
Strategies

Peloton: Making Video Games the Dominant Workout Format

BMW: Creating the Second Living Room

---

monthly basis.[2] Given its overall subscriber base of 260 million,
active gamers represent about 4 percent of the company's audience.[3]
That might not sound like a lot, but the growth is a clear sign of the
potential that still lies ahead. The addition of titles from the fan-
favorite Grand Theft Auto series illustrates this. It was the "most
successful launch to date in terms of installs and engagement, with
some consumers clearly signing up simply to play these games,"
according to the company.[4]

Netflix's core business being what it is, adding video games makes
a lot of sense strategically. Its massive IP catalog—including series
from *Stranger Things* to *Wednesday* to *Squid Game*—provides a rich
opportunity to further monetize its investments. Additionally,
games are able to keep people engaged in between seasons of their
favorite shows, which lowers the risk of canceled subscriptions.

While streaming and video games are adjacent verticals with intuitive fit, there are cases of games becoming core products that are
far less obvious. A company called Pymetrics, for example, has built
its own titles to assess soft skills in the recruiting and hiring process
for new talent.[5] Akili Interactive, a prescription digital medicine
company, made a game called EndeavorRx, which became the first
video game treatment for children with ADHD approved by the
US Food and Drug Administration.[6] But though the list of possible

applications for games as core products is long (and we'll explore some of those in the epilogue), there aren't too many companies that have gone down this path to date.

Fortunately for us, we have the opportunity to learn from three pioneers in completely different industries about how video games became a part of their core products. To start, we'll look at a game about a lemonade stand that was an effective way to teach senior executives about corporate strategy.

Boston Consulting Group: Letting Clients Experience Business Strategies

Martin Reeves, a senior managing partner at Boston Consulting Group and chair of the BCG Henderson Institute (essentially the firm's think tank), was looking out of his window in his office in midtown New York. He was thinking about how the latest work he and his team had done around using different strategy styles to help executives navigate changing market environments could be positioned more effectively to corporate leaders around the world. Reeves was writing a book on the subject as well. While that would certainly help in getting the word out, he was worried about waning attention spans, people not fully reading books (thank you for getting this far!), and whether the format would make the content and ideas tangible enough for executives to apply.

"We wanted these new concepts to be very useful for our clients. There is so much noise out there, and in today's world anyone can be a broadcaster," Reeves explained to me.[7] He wanted to break through the clutter while moving the new strategy concepts from theory to practice. The latter is of paramount importance for a professional services firm like BCG, and the team members needed a solution. That solution started to dawn on them when Reeves asked one crucial question: What media viewership is increasing? They only needed a few minutes to search for the statistics and find the answer: video games.

Gaming is hardly a traditional medium in the context of corporate strategy and professional services geared toward the most senior executives of the *Fortune* 1000. But Reeves wasn't deterred in his desire to explore this path. His intuition was telling him that it could be a fun, distinctive, and effective way to solve the challenge he was facing. The team started exploring the space, looking for inspiration and evidence to back up its intuition. After looking at games that were primarily designed for educational purposes, as well as searching for what he describes as the "million-dollar app" (a fun game that adds serious value), Reeves had seen enough. He couldn't find what he wanted—so the team pivoted. "Why shouldn't we be the first ones to pioneer this?" he wondered.

They began defining the specs of their game, which were grounded in the essential idea and purpose of his book's content: to help people understand five distinct strategy styles, evaluate changing market conditions, and choose and execute the most appropriate style to yield optimal business results given the environment. But Reeves didn't want this game to only serve marketing purposes. He was eager to build a tool BCG could use with its clients in workshops, one that had the ability to meaningfully engage people. By laying out the fundamental objectives this clearly, Reeves and his team identified a central piece of the puzzle that would be critical for the overall success of their project: "The learning environment . . . needed to be a serious simulation of real-world problems in order to facilitate true learning and future application."

The second big piece that required clarity was the story of the video game. It had to be understandable to all, but sophisticated enough to accurately illustrate fairly complex strategy problems. If you have taken even a basic economics course in your life, the story

Reeves's team landed on will not surprise you. They decided to pick a lemonade stand as the format to let players run a business and make strategic decisions amid changing conditions. The concept was sophisticated enough while also being highly accessible.

From there, the team members went a level deeper. They wrote out the actual narrative and created a table of contents to simulate all the different actions and behavioral patterns that could occur. There were some known challenges, such as tuning the level of difficulty for a variety of players. They also needed a way for people to progress within a given market environment while squaring off against an opponent that would be controlled by the game. BCG's founder, Bruce Henderson, would take on the role of the lemonade stand mogul that players would compete against.

There were also important insights along the way that led to iteration. For example, people needed a reason for why they won or lost a level so they could apply those learnings and continue playing. Making the simulation feel like real life took continual calibration of its logic and inner workings—which is tough to accomplish when changing one variable immediately affects another one. But Reeves knew that if their video game was going to take people from theory to practice effectively, they had to get it right. After three months of tweaking and obsessing over every detail, the software program that would run the game was built.

But Reeves and his team were far from done. Players needed a way to interact with the program, and to make that happen, BCG had to create the user interface. While they were able to rely on internal computer science skills to create the program, the team members didn't possess the skills to let their vision come to life visually. They needed a partner, and evaluated firms on three integral skills: the ability to create great graphics and gameplay, the ability to do advanced software programming to accurately simulate complex business strategies and environments, and the ability to effectively talk about and marry the previous two. Eventually the team found a video game developer in Germany that was able to take on the project.

Working with the partner brought forth a new set of challenges. Number one on the list was communication. Because of the different backgrounds of the various team members—designers, software developers, and business strategists—speaking the same language and being completely aligned in the vision and how to get there was, though critical, quite hard. For a while, the teams weren't clicking the way they needed to, and it was starting to jeopardize the project. The issues got to a point where the primary stakeholder on the vendor side was replaced. "We needed an actual translator between the different professional backgrounds," Reeves explained. It wasn't all smooth sailing from there, but the teams started to cruise along, and in two months the first user interface was built. BCG now had its first minimum viable product (MVP), which it gave the same name as the book whose content the game would let people experience viscerally: Your Strategy Needs a Strategy.[8]

The MVP allowed the team to put the game in front of people, rather than merely trying to explain its vision. In other words, show, don't tell—which is imperative in organizations that are more traditional or simply have not been exposed to video games before. At the next worldwide meeting of BCG senior executives, Reeves and his team showcased their game. They knew they had succeeded when the firm's CEO at the time, Rich Lesser, was standing by their booth and wouldn't stop playing it on his iPad. The MVP created the buy-in that would allow the team to turn it into a full-fledged product by adding features and capabilities that would make it effective with clients. Chief among these was a workshop mode with access to analytics and diagnostics tools to assess how players—workshop participants—were improving at applying the correct strategy over time. Programmed journeys to align the learnings across workshop participants was another key feature. A multiplayer feature and tournaments were also included.

While it is hard to precisely quantify the impact of Your Strategy Needs a Strategy on BCG, the game's success has been undeniable. First, it made Reeves's book stand out, bringing important awareness to the thought leadership he and BCG were putting forth. Second, it opened doors to top business schools, which is an important market for the company in terms of recruiting. But the team also saw a ton of success internally. The firm started using the video game as a tool for employees to test their strategic skills, with some senior executives becoming heavy users, which led to more requests for client-facing workshops than the team could handle. That was the signal that the game had unlocked commercial success for the organization at large. "People started coming to us, and we had to flip the script. We started to train the trainers to let this scale," said Reeves. He replicated the game approach for another book, *The Imagination Machine*, which comes with a stand-alone compendium of fifteen video and physical games to experience and apply to each step in the process of collective imagination.[9]

From theory to practice, Reeves and his team helped pioneer video games for learning in the business world.

Peloton: Making Video Games the Dominant Workout Format

It was near the end of 2020 when a team inside of Peloton conducted research about new types of workout content that people would enjoy. The team had a hunch that there was an audience that didn't gravitate toward the traditional instructor-led workouts. The research findings validated the hunch: scenic experiences, as well as virtual worlds and trainings, were what a subset of customers expected.

In true skunkworks fashion, Peloton product leaders got together with a couple of software developers and hashed out a plan. In their spare time, they would familiarize themselves with video game development and visualization tools like Unity, which we learned about earlier. The goal was to build a simple MVP they could use to pitch to the leadership team for additional resources. Given that Peloton had sold more than two million of its bikes, they were the natural starting point to host a new workout experience inspired by video games. Within just a few months, the team accomplished its goal. Funding secured, the real work began—and Peloton needed to find a development partner as soon as possible.

The ideal partner to make its game, Lanebreak, was a company called ustwo. What set ustwo apart was its collaborative working style and its user-centric design approach, which aligned well with Peloton's approach. "Many consultancies come at it from an angle of generic fun that is not connected to real user needs," Jim Green, group product manager, told me. "It can never just be a business objective, because if it is not connected to real user needs, you won't be able to deliver, and extract, value."[10] The alignment in approach, and a mutual understanding of both each other and video gaming concepts, was foundational to the success of the project.

The two teams followed a highly iterative development process that always tried to connect their efforts back to the needs of their audience. "Game-inspired workouts for fitness bikes . . . [don't really have] any best practices you can follow," Green explained. "And even if there were, simply following best practices often results in a generic experience for your audience." Lanebreak, a game-inspired workout that lets people compete, beat challenges, and collect points based on how they're riding their Peloton bike, quickly started to take shape.

The process of discovering what experiences to build and how to validate them, which industry veterans like Green refer to as "finding the fun," is innately different from the software-centric development process most companies nowadays are accustomed to—as are the skills involved. Creatives and artists are different from user interface designers, after all. This ideation process can in some cases take months before yielding tangible outcomes. Ultimately, Peloton's commitment was strong enough to see this new way of working through. In fact, the team focused on interactive workout experiences, which Green oversees, has now grown into a fully staffed, dedicated group.

After just a few months of development, Lanebreak went into an external beta launch with a few thousand Peloton members. The feedback was overwhelmingly positive. The team had launched a post-ride survey after every level that was designed to measure testers' satisfaction, and across all participants the satisfaction rating clocked in at 4.5 out of 5 stars. This feedback gave the team the confidence to roll out Lanebreak globally in February 2022, a mere twelve months after the initial skunkworks initiative, as well as to explore the viability of other game-inspired workouts as part of its strategy going forward. But there was a lot of work ahead of Green and his team prior to the big rollout. Changes and updates were necessary not just to the experience itself but to the overall organizational setup and to the relationship between Peloton and ustwo. That relationship evolved over time, and more responsibilities shifted over to Green as his team grew.

While Lanebreak's execution moved across milestones, Peloton and ustwo continuously worked on servicing the experience, which included testing and implementing new ideas. That is a crucial aspect of game development that organizations may not understand initially. A gamelike experience is rarely ever "done" and in many instances requires ongoing updates. "This also requires that you are not too constrained by project timelines and budgets," Green pointed out. Flexibility is key.

Yet the global rollout of Lanebreak would mark one of the most significant software updates in Peloton's history. Green told me that hundreds of thousands of members played it in the first week. As of this writing, two years later, Lanebreak continues to do well. Key performance indicators including number of sessions, time spent on bike, and workout days per month are all up for members who use Lanebreak; for a certain customer segment, Lanebreak is how they enjoy a full 50 percent of their workouts. Engagement with the game has also been shown to drive engagement with other non-instructor-led workouts the platform has.

Peloton's foray into gaming will have a lasting impact on the company's strategy. Green's team has been hard at work developing other workout experiences, but it's just the beginning. "Gaming-inspired fitness content will play a long-term role in . . . how we think about connected fitness experiences for a diverse, global audience," said Green. "Lanebreak opened the path for new ways to deliver workout experiences across platforms and devices." Ultimately, video games are now playing a key role in increasing engagement with riders by being part of the company's physical devices.

BMW: Creating the Second Living Room

In June 2019 Tesla announced that Cuphead, a well-known video game that had just released its latest version for the Nintendo Switch, would be playable on the built-in dashboard screen of different Tesla models.[11] By bringing video games into cars, Tesla was doing what it had done many times before: coming up with a pioneering idea and running away from its competitors.

In the BMW headquarters, the news couldn't have come at a better time. Senior leadership was wrestling with how to differentiate BMW from other automakers. Engine features or horsepower were no longer enough to stand out from the crowd. The team was thinking about the interior of the car and the freedom of design it offered. Their minds and conversations kept circling back to a central question: How do we make the interior an experience for our customers?

BMW had just finalized market research studies with consumers in China. Given that the country is the largest automotive market in the world, it holds critical importance. It is also the leading market for video gaming globally. The findings of the study painted a clear picture: Chinese consumers were enthusiastic about the promise of autonomous driving. Electric vehicles were set to take off and become the fastest-growing and largest segment in the market. And video games are an integral part of Chinese culture, especially for the consumers BMW was after.

Concurrently, the company was fostering the growth of its latest cohort of startups through its corporate incubation and venture program, known as Startup Garage. Among the cohort was a company called N-Dream, a video game developer that was working on a platform with potential to bring games into cars. To investigate the possibilities, the team around Stefan Butz, vice president of engineering information and communication platforms, and René Molle, senior line manager, entertainment and streaming features, evaluated whether games were a viable option. "We needed to understand if this truly fit with our target audience," Butz explained to me.[12] In their view, playing a game was an emotional experience not unlike driving a BMW on winding roads through the scenic countryside. *Freude am Fahren* ("sheer driving pleasure") has been the company's brand value proposition since 1972.

Butz and his team had been working on ideas to better represent BMW cars in the digital world. The company was already a part of established series such as Gran Turismo and Grand Theft Auto, but the efforts never went further than letting players drive its vehicles.

Now, cloud technology was starting to make the streaming of high-end gaming experiences possible. The conclusion was clear: video games would become the gateway for BMW to truly represent its cars in an increasingly digital world. "We asked ourselves many times: Is BMW playful? That's why these discussions took quite a while," Butz recalled. "But the harmony and fit with our brand made it clear to us that we needed to be a leader, and didn't want to, nor could afford to, be a follower."

A second enabling technology was at the heart of BMW's strategy: autonomous, or self-driving, cars. When our hands don't need to be on the steering wheel and our eyes don't need to be glued to the road, we can do other things while being driven to our destination. "The average person spends about two hours per day commuting. Autonomous driving will free up this time—and two hours is a lot of time," Molle pointed out. In the case of electric or hybrid vehicles, there's also the time you spend inside your car when it is charging. That all adds up—valuable hours that BMW can leverage to engage its customers and provide value. Combined with the fact that a car's interior offers the greatest degree of design freedom (experiences from the music industry have demonstrated it to be a perfect recording studio), BMW faced a crucial strategic consideration: how to provide the best possible customer experience when the car is the main touchpoint. "We regard the car, and specifically the interior of a car, as the second living for our customers," Butz said. By now it should be obvious how video games fit into that picture.

With the conclusion made, the team kicked off phase two. It needed to evaluate different solutions and the technical feasibility of bringing games into BMW cars. To begin, it studied Tesla's approach and in that process made two important discoveries. The graphics card Tesla was using required one hundred watts of power, which quickly drained the battery of an electric vehicle, and the approach required a high-end gaming controller. Overall, Tesla's method was too expensive, too big of a bet for BMW.

The team started to search for a cheaper solution that wouldn't compromise the experience. Enter AirConsole, the solution created by N-Dream. Requiring no additional hardware, AirConsole runs video games locally by leveraging the display inside of a car. The user's mobile phone becomes the controller, and multiple people can play together simply by entering a session code that connects them. Essentially, AirConsole can deliver high-quality gaming experiences at very low additional cost. It was exactly what Molle and his colleagues were searching for. "Bringing AirConsole into our cars didn't require additional people or budget on our end," he said.

The team ran its first tests with real BMW customers as soon as possible. The results added further fuel to the fire: when an electric vehicle was charging, kids and teenagers tended to simply stay inside the car and play video games delivered to them by AirConsole. Their parents often joined them as the fun went on. Usage during these waiting periods consistently increased as the team rolled out more field tests—a finding that surprised everyone. This evidence allowed Butz and his team to prioritize the project internally across the digital unit of the BMW Group. This gave them the visibility to create curiosity and demand with a critical group of stakeholders: the hardware teams who actually build BMW cars—and who would have to integrate the solution as a standardized feature.

Molle knew that to get his colleagues on board, his team would need a demo with a tangible product. They meticulously planned a demo day, for which AirConsole and a selection of games were ready to go in a BMW. The setup was meant to mirror the reality of customers as closely as possible so that the senior executives and key decision-makers could empathize easily with their future experience. "It was important that we . . . asked participants to use their own mobile phones. We wanted them to see how easy it was to do it themselves," Molle said. From Mario Kart to quiz games, it didn't take long for senior leadership to lose track of time and be fully immersed in playing video games. Inside of a BMW. "When you get your fellow VPs to play, you don't have any problems with creating buy-in and support for rolling out your solution," Butz said with a smile.

In fact, not having any problems is quite the understatement. The solution created so much excitement internally that senior leaders for each car model viewed it as an absolute must-have feature and wanted to talk about it during the global launches of their respective models. The first to feature the platform would be the BMW i5. The company launched the solution and showcased the new car at Gamescom 2023, the world's largest video gaming conference.[13] It even had a special announcement in its back pocket: a game of the renowned quiz show *Who Wants to Be a Millionaire* would be developed specifically for AirConsole in BMWs. Needless to say, the launch was a roaring success and BMW more than closed the gap on rival Tesla. Just a year later, the team added another staple to its offerings: the card game Uno.[14] If your living room feels anything like mine when an intense match of Uno is underway, you will surely see the potential in BMW's vision of the car as a second living room (if you're winning the match, that is).

However, the job is not done. When looking into the future, Butz says the freed-up time passengers will have due to autonomous driving capabilities is a massive opportunity that will inevitably attract fierce competition—from within the automotive industry as well as outside of it. "It will be an absolute battle over the control of the customer touchpoints," he explained. "Up until now, for us and other automakers, the touchpoints have mostly been physical. But these touchpoints are becoming more and more digital. Every company wants to enter that space . . . When the two hours per day are fully freed up, that's when the battle will really start."

For the senior executives at BMW, anticipating these kinds of shifts is critical to securing the company's future. Their vision of utilizing the interior of a car to create a level of immersion unrivaled by any other physical space is key to staying relevant and successful. Video games are an integral part of shifting that customer touchpoint from physical to digital. BMW's new focus will also help it maintain the premium prices consumers gladly pay to experience *Freude am Fahren*. Molle has zero hesitation about the company's commitment to video games over the next ten to fifteen years. "We will, without a doubt, integrate the best content and work with our partners to create an immersive experience," he said. If they succeed, *Freude* will likely still be a part of BMW's brand. But instead of *am Fahren*, it may be followed by *am Gefahren-werden* ("pleasure of being driven").

What to Do

The companies in this chapter offer rich examples to follow. Here's what to remember.

- Be intentional and strategic. Think carefully about how video games can become, complement, or elevate your existing product and service offering. Don't do it for the optics or because it sounds good on paper. It needs to make strategic sense and therefore unlock growth opportunities for your business.

- Be extremely clear on your customer needs. Conduct market and audience research before diving in to pinpoint the exact opportunity for your company. Leverage tools and data that you can get access to fairly quickly rather than falling into the trap of "analysis paralysis." Aim to start building and testing quickly.

- Start small. Skunkworks work. Don't let the lack of a dedicated budget hold you back. If you have to, begin with a small side project and a couple of like-minded people. Let the vision come to life by building a first prototype rather than relying on spreadsheets and slide decks.

- Use intermediate milestones and tangible progress. Doing so will help you win over internal stakeholders to broaden and deepen the support for your project. Show, don't tell. Remember, video games will likely be new terrain for your company and your key decision-makers. Let them experience the vision through the eyes of your customers.

- Evaluate partners for fit. They should align well with your company, your culture, and the skills required to do the job. There will be obstacles and iterations along the way. Having a partner that understands your goals and how you operate is just as important as possessing great game design and software development skills.

- Remain flexible. A video game is rarely ever a fully finished product. If your customers love what you have built for them, you will find yourself in a position where servicing and continually expanding it becomes necessary. Allow for flexible resource allocation internally and ensure that budgeting processes and timelines can accommodate shifting priorities.

Part Three

THE FUTURE

9

Priming Your Organization for Impact

Embarking on new journeys and exploring new avenues can feel daunting. Sometimes the current success of your business can create a false sense of security and lead you to conclude that change and exploration are not needed, or at least not right now. The innovator's dilemma, the disincentive that large, successful companies have to innovate, and companies like Kodak and Nokia, come to mind. For the majority of businesses, the world of video games presents uncharted territory whose landscape is unlike that of any other industry. But armed with the stories and insights in this book, you no longer have to start at zero.

While every organization is different, those featured in this book have all seen failure—and discovered where the pitfalls lie—on the road to success. Puma's first Web3 video game on Roblox was too complex for consumers to navigate effectively. Adidas prematurely concluded that games weren't right for it because the company's efforts in sponsoring esports didn't deliver sustainable results. Unilever waited a decade after its first gaming partnership before making a long-term commitment to the medium. Their stories provide valuable learnings and principles that can be applied to your organization and business.

In every interview I conducted, I asked the leaders and decision-makers what advice they would give a fellow executive, strategist, marketer, or product leader of a business that wants to get into the video gaming space. Their answers can help you learn, avoid failure, and succeed faster. This is what they shared.

Don't Copy and Paste Old Playbooks

Entering a vastly different space like video games but relying on tried-and-true methods from the past is a surefire recipe for failure. Consumer expectations have dramatically shifted over the past five years, across all demographic groups. If you default to strategies and channels that once worked successfully, expecting them to be just as effective in today's conditions, you're in for a rude awakening.

The proliferation of digital media, including video games, makes consumers today evaluate brands differently before, during, and after making a purchase. Adidas's Erika Wykes-Sneyd summarized it perfectly: "How we have done user journeys or shopper journeys in the past—people don't want that traditional path to purchase anymore."[1]

Serial entrepreneur Marcus Holmström, CEO of game developer The Gang, sees many brands and companies still falling into this trap. They think that due to their brand power and reputation, consumers will look at anything they put in front of them.[2] Chris Brandt of Chipotle echoed the folly of that sentiment: "Don't take the traditional advertising approach to this new channel called video games. Whatever initiatives you pursue, they have to fit into the world of video games."[3] This is where many companies struggle.

Deeply understanding games can be challenging at first, but it is necessary. "You need to throw your old playbook out to understand the video game experience and video game loops," asserted Nick Rend of NASCAR.[4] Taking inspiration from Reckitt's Raghunandan Srinivasan can set you up for success: his mindset of "unlearn to learn" ensured the company had the required openness to new ideas.[5]

The example of Unilever shows us what "good" looks like. For that organization, video games are a dedicated channel that sits right next to social media or influencer marketing, and all gaming-related projects answer a specific question up front: How can they address the specific challenge at hand? "You have to understand video gaming as a whole ecosystem," emphasized the company's Amanpreet Singh.[6] Then your playbooks will be unique and evolve naturally, rather than feeling forced or copied-and-pasted from times past.

Educate Your Organization

Educating stakeholders, especially senior executives, about games is a goal almost too obvious to state, but due to the vastly different nature of video games, and how they are built, this aspect is paramount for companies to succeed. Ivan Dashkov of Puma told me that having an insufficient knowledge base can further stoke fears and hesitations around building out a new business.[7] As a starting point, there needs to be clear alignment on what video games mean in the context of the organization and its strategy, because the applications, as this book has demonstrated, are manifold.

Additionally, executives must have a grasp of the process of how games are developed, since that is very different from how, for example, traditional software is made. "Understanding these differences was critical for our success at Peloton," recalled Jim Green. "Video game development depends on a huge amount of creativity.

It involves graphic artists, which are vastly different from traditional user interface designers. And the process to discover what experiences you want to build and how to validate that throughout your journey is highly iterative and rarely follows a straight line."[8]

This muscle for creative discovery exists in most organizations, but it's stronger in some than in others. Spending time to highlight the unique challenges of making video games builds a common understanding and allows all stakeholders to manage expectations to foster mutual alignment.

The UPLAY team, Unilever's video gaming consulting task force, went above and beyond in making sure the organization was strengthening both its knowledge base and its strategic muscle. The team went on an educational spree across the entire company, held monthly Q&A sessions, brought in experts from the gaming industry, held video game tournaments for employees, and even provided a tool kit for people to experiment and learn. Not only did this bring the whole organization up to speed, it also helped establish the UPLAY team as the internal focal point.

Manage Expectations and Set Clear Goals

Given the potential and the excitement surrounding video gaming, it would be easy for executives and leaders to regard it as their silver bullet to address all of their existing challenges around customer engagement, and to do so overnight. The reality is that this won't happen, and these expectations would put initiatives at risk from day one. "What are our objectives? What opportunities do we want to open up? The conversation around this needs to be very explicit," Green warned.

Given the creative discovery inherent to the game development process, it can be normal for teams tasked with making video games to ideate for months and not end up with a polished product. In fact, this aspect is so important that almost every person that was interviewed for this book said something along the same lines. "You have to set very clear goals. They can be ambitious, but they have to be clear. You have to create complete alignment regarding what outcomes you want to drive as an organization," emphasized Jonathan Knight of the *New York Times*.[9]

This is critical for two reasons: one, the clarity and alignment ensures that all stakeholders involved know where and why the ship is sailing and can support the plan accordingly, and two, the desired outcomes will shape the strategy of how your company enters the video gaming space. Is the objective to test games as a channel? You may want to start small, integrate with an existing title that already has your target audience, and get to initial results faster. Is the objective to establish a long-term presence in virtual worlds more broadly? You may want to explore making the investment in building a game from scratch, so you can define and shape the entire experience.

Leverage Partners That Have Done What You Need

Rather than immediately hiring expensive talent and building out an internal team, it can be highly beneficial for companies to work with partners for their early efforts. That is exactly how Jenifer Willig and her team at WRTHY started. "Bring in people who know how to do it and have done it before," she said.[10] WRTHY initially partnered with developers like Tilting Point and Krafton to implement its social impact initiatives into video games. Now with more experience under its belt, WRTHY's approach has evolved to a setup where the team still uses partners but also develops its own games.

This is similar to the path British fashion house Burberry followed. After partnering with developers, the company built out its internal digital teams, who have since built titles such as B Bounce and B Surf. In addition, Burberry still partners with developers like Mythical Games when it comes to Web3 projects.

In the case of Peloton, finding that first partner had far-reaching implications for its overall journey into video games. It was the foundational step that paved the way for an internal team that would focus full-time on interactive experiences. Green has reflected a lot on what made Peloton's first development partner such a great fit. "Obviously, the talent involved is important," he said. "But a mutual understanding of where each organization stands is just as important." In Peloton's case, the user-centric approach that developer ustwo brought to the table aligned very well with how the fitness company operated. "Many partners and consultancies don't tackle your challenges from this angle. Their approach often results in generic fun," he said. "For us at Peloton, what we do always has to connect to real member needs."[11]

Your partner's ability to listen and understand your objectives and your organization as a whole, including its culture and ways of working, rather than impose what they see as their ideal way of collaborating, is paramount to the success of the project. Chris Rake at *FIRST* Inspires ascribed all these attributes to partner Filament Games, which was the foundation for the successful launch of its video game RoboCo. "We would not have been able to build RoboCo without Filament," Rake asserted.[12]

The importance of finding the right partner can't be emphasized enough. As we saw earlier, NASCAR provides a cautionary tale of how the wrong partner can cause serious harm to your brand. A lack of understanding of your target audience, as well as your brand values, can result in video game experiences that receive backlash from customers.

Evolve Your Operating Model

As your company's video game strategy evolves, so should your organizational setup. There is no one-size-fits-all approach, and the setup that's right initially may not be right for the long term. Learning and remaining flexible are critical for any company in order to identify the right operating model.

When Adidas jumped on its opportunity in Web3, it created a task force that consisted of four senior decision-makers. Once the foundational strategy was in place, the team grew to be cross-functional and totaled as many as twenty-two people. With the success of its NFT launch in the books, the task force was elevated into a dedicated business unit. All within a span of just nine months.

The Lego Group is another great example of this. The company, which has been active in the gaming space since 1995, not only established a Lego Games business unit but also has dedicated teams with P&L responsibility for its gaming efforts that collectively form the holistic strategy. The latest focus? Hiring a vice president to oversee Lego's partnership with Fortnite and its maker, Epic Games.

Another piece of the organizational puzzle that is unique to building video games is how companies treat the engagement with their development partners, and how each one's responsibilities evolve from building the title to servicing it. One of the keys to Peloton's success was treating the separate teams as a collective that continuously worked on servicing Lanebreak while also experimenting with new ideas. This included a shift away from strict milestones to not be limited by project timelines and budgets in order to allow for a more fluid approach aimed at having the right team in place to continuously improve the experience for Peloton's customers.

Move Past Stereotypes

If you and your company are serious about establishing a video game strategy, you have to move beyond the stereotypes and misconceptions around gamers. Games are on the rise across all demographic groups, and even if consumers don't consider themselves gamers, chances are high that they have at least one title on their mobile phone. "My whole family, including my dad, plays video games," said Chris Rake of *FIRST* Inspires.[13]

If you're looking for inspiration on how to help your organization, or maybe even yourself, move past the stereotypes, look no further than Wykes-Sneyd: "Everyone has watched a movie or read a book. Video games allow a deeper connection to the extraordinary self. Put the stigmas to the side and approach the space with the understanding that people are playing video games to experience a better version of themselves. When you understand the behaviors, you understand the numbers. And then you understand the human need and how video games can fulfill that. Don't discount it."[14] When people play, their masks come off. They can live up to their true selves, away from the societal pressures of real life, with games providing a reality in which this can happen.

Understand Your Audience and Connect to User Needs

If you're still struggling to move past gamer stereotypes, then audience research and insights will help. Investing up front in deeply understanding who your ideal customer is, and what their underlying needs and desires are, is a nonnegotiable in a world where consumers are flooded with choice and companies battle over every ounce of attention they can get. In that type of environment, the tried-and-true methods of thinking about consumers in terms of demographic groups fails to provide the level of depth required to successfully engage with your audience.

To cut through the noise, we have to understand consumers much more holistically. Demographics, behaviors, affinities are important, but uncovering your audience's true needs and desires—by understanding their unique psychology, such as motivations, personality traits, values, communication styles, and cultures—is where the magic happens. "The starting point has to be the consumer," asserted Erinrose Sullivan, adding that a lack of a fundamental understanding of the target audience is the number one reason projects fail. "Motivations, desires, needs, touchpoints—companies have to understand their audiences holistically and how they evolve over time."[15]

This is true for any company that interacts with a consumer, but it's especially true for those exploring a space like gaming. Video games are so effective at engaging people because they have the ability to connect with deep emotions and motivations better than any other medium. If we don't understand the unique motivations and desires of our audiences, how can we expect to use video games to connect with them? The answer is, we can't. This is precisely the reason Knight made establishing an audience strategy the first step in the process of building the overall growth strategy for the *New York Times*, and why Wykes-Sneyd described Adidas's qualitative research as "paramount."[16] If we fail to understand who our audience is, all our efforts to reach them will fall flat.

Be Authentic and True to Who You Are

There's another integral piece we need to grasp: your company. Having a crystal-clear view of your brand values is necessary if you want to create experiences that feel authentic to the organization. And authenticity is critical because gamers have a sixth sense for when things are off. "Consumers can sniff out when things are not authentic," said Knight.[17] Chipotle's Brandt sees his company as "different"—a brand that should be in places that are different. (Remember the burrito tasting in the house where people played video games most of the day?) "You have to find the things that are unique to you and bring them to life," he said.[18]

Kyle Price of Roblox is constantly exposed to companies and brands looking to build virtual worlds. Because these experiences are interactive, "you have to be authentic because you're constantly engaging directly with your audience. It is very different from a 'push' sales motion," he explained.[19] The constant engagement with the audience, the communities inside of the games, requires attention and active management—whether the feedback is good, bad, or (I'm sure you have heard of internet trolls) ugly. You can't cherry-pick. You have to show up for the whole thing.

Follow the example of BMW, which deliberated for a long time about whether its brand was playful and whether video games fit it. "We needed to stay true to our values and our brand. It was important to take the time to evaluate that thoroughly," Stefan Butz said.[20]

Start Small, Learn, Grow, and Give Permission to Fail

There is a specific reason Chipotle started its journey into games by sponsoring a group of streamers: Brandt and his team found people who were eating Chipotle almost daily. "Find people who already use your brand" is a piece of advice he shared with me.[21] Doing so allows your company to get started more quickly without big upfront investments and the burden of lofty expectations. Pilot, trial, experiment with different things, and scale up what works. Chipotle lives by this mantra.

Puma's Dashkov offers a similar perspective: "I have seen companies with grandiose and robust plans but absolutely no learnings. You don't have to start with the biggest video games. It is better to find an easy entry point. For example, look for some of the smaller mobile video games. These video games can still attract five million players daily, and if there is overlap with your target audience, it is a terrific place to start and learn from."[22]

Not every project and game is going to be a big success right out of the gate. Your organization has to have a sufficient level of tolerance for experimentation and even failure. Remember that your company is likely entering uncharted waters. There's inherent risk to that, no doubt. But that is exactly why you will want your teams to know that failure is OK and a part of the process—it prevents them from playing things too safe and nudges them to be bold. The learnings this process facilitates will be invaluable.

Think back to Puma and the first Web3 game it built on Roblox. It was a grandiose, complex virtual world that ultimately failed to meet expectations. The senior leadership at Puma could have shut down the effort and concluded that video games weren't delivering the results they had hoped for. Instead, the team was encouraged to try again. By applying the learnings from the first launch, it was able to hit it out of the park with the second experience it built on Roblox. Video games are now an integral part of Puma's overall strategy—and are at the heart of future revenue streams that were previously out of reach for an apparel company that predominantly operated in the physical world. Imagine if Puma's team didn't have the permission to fail. Its future as a business would look pretty bleak.

. . .

A gaming strategy is no longer a nice-to-have. It's a must-have. To win over consumers and meet them where they are, the time to press play and set your organization on its journey into video games is now.

Which strategy is the right one for you depends on your starting point and your goals. The specifics and details will vary between the approaches different companies take as well. But all initiatives will benefit greatly from the learnings and insights of your fellow leaders. They will help you ensure that your company is entering this space full of confidence while giving yourself the best shot at being successful—and establishing video games as a foundational pillar in your overall customer engagement strategy, next to all the other channels and approaches we are so familiar with. Done right, it will feel like gaming should have been there a while ago.

Epilogue

Where Are We Going from Here?

Video games and virtual worlds are set to become even more pervasive and ubiquitous. As an increasing number of people regularly play games, and as these experiences continue to excel in immersing and engaging them, our baseline expectations will be elevated. To remain relevant, every company should take a hard look at video games and think about how to fit into this evolving world. As Jonathan Knight, the head of games at *NYT*, said, "Games are for everyone."[1] The sooner companies recognize the power of play, the better.

Advancements in technology will only make gaming more popular. For example, social opportunities and 3D will continue to converge, allowing even deeper levels of engagement. Roblox is a good example of this trend, and its growth is a clear sign of the potential of this convergence. In less than three years, Roblox more than doubled the amount of people who enjoy virtual experiences on the platform daily, from just under thirty million (Q1 2020) to over eighty-five million (Q4 2024).[2]

This kind of astonishing growth has given rise to many new projects and an inflow of venture capital. One ambitious project is Everywhere by a company called Build a Rocket Boy, founded by Leslie Benzies, a former producer at Rockstar Games who is known for his work on the Grand Theft Auto series. The project aims to blend multiple game genres into a single expansive platform, allowing players to engage in various activities within a shared world.[3] While details about Everywhere have been limited as of this writing, the vision for it includes experiences that mimic real-world interactions, which could encompass things like concerts, gyms, retail stores, social events, and user-generated content. The game is said to leverage cutting-edge technology and game design principles to create a platform that is both a game and a creative space, where the boundaries between playing and creating blur. Everywhere aims to offer an experience where the narrative evolves with the decisions and creations of its players, potentially reshaping the way stories are told in video games. "Nobody can say for certain what the next big thing is," PC Gamer's Harvey Randall wrote about the project, "and I'm not here to tell the future. But there's a raw spark of potential here that's really exciting."[4]

Technological progress regarding generative AI, no-code platforms and design tools, and user-generated content (UGC) are key enablers and accelerators for this movement. They significantly lower the barrier to entry for individual creators and companies alike. This gives businesses the ability to experiment faster, at much lower cost, and to get even closer to their target customers. If UGC is a part of a company's marketing campaign, engagement with the brand increases from 25 percent to 28 percent.[5] The ability to co-create bolsters a sense of ownership and identity on the side of the consumer, which, as we have learned in this book, is invaluable in the context of the modern customer journey.

Accompanying this, better methods are emerging to measure the impact and effectiveness of virtual initiatives on real-world business performance. For instance, Vans was able to link increases in store traffic directly to its virtual world on Roblox. But these examples are currently far and few between, and tracking and measurement capabilities are nascent. But Ivan Dashkov of Puma told me that they remind him of the early days of social media and anticipates similar advancements in measuring digital impact.[6] Kyle Price of Roblox agrees. "The more the virtual world becomes real, the more meaningful and accurate the signal companies will be able to draw from the virtual world to inform the real world," he said.[7]

Imagine you're an executive at a fashion company who created a video game to give out digital samples. There are some built-in guardrails on how to use the samples, but other than that, you let people create their own bags, purses, or belts. You could also let the community vote on their favorite items—and just like that you have a co-created, validated new collection with an early fan base that you can launch as a physical collection in the real world.

Any product company can leverage video games for this type of process and create tremendous efficiencies and improvements in R&D, testing, shipping, and needed shelf space. Games can de-risk the inherently laborious process around product development. This is exactly the reason Adidas looks at gaming and virtual worlds as its future.

Because video games and play are so powerful at connecting with the human brain, we will see a lot more usage of game mechanics, facets, and design principles in offerings for our daily lives. This process is generally referred to as gamification, but the superficial ways in which companies have tried to apply it in the past, by simply slapping video game features into their products, doesn't cut it. It needs to be done systematically, and ideally from the ground up.

We as consumers often might not notice that an app or a service we're using has all the inner workings of a video game under the hood, which can contribute to why we love the product so much. The financial services firm Robinhood is a great example. It has made stock trading accessible and highly engaging to a much wider audience by introducing gamelike mechanics in which users were celebrated for making their first stock investment. Language learning app Duolingo is an illustration as well. "The app is at a point where you are actually playing a game rather than primarily learning a language," said Knight.[8] Learning becomes the second-order effect that is enabled and facilitated by an effectively gamified experience.

Video games and gamification can make even the most mundane tasks fun. When Rahul Vohra, Superhuman's CEO who worked as a game designer in the past, built the email service, he used seven game design principles from day one and applied them to how he and his team imagined a modern email tool to work. The goal: let customers enjoy the process of getting to an inbox-zero state. If video games can make managing our finances, learning a language, and sending work emails enjoyable, then there's no limit to where they can elevate the customer experience.

Speaking of customer experience, Swedish furniture giant IKEA launched a game on Roblox called The Co-Worker, in which players can work alongside real employees. From serving meatballs to organizing showrooms to assembling furniture, people see what it would be like to be employed at an IKEA store. But here's the truly genius part. The company accepted applications for roles in the virtual store, offering paid shifts for ten new employees. Successful applicants, the company says, "will be able to flex their skills, help customers, and get promoted to move departments, just like in the real world."[9] All while playing a video game. The future of recruiting and talent management all of a sudden seems fun.

The implications for gaming technology go even further. Think about what games could do for the ongoing rise of mental health disorders, with the World Health Organization reporting a 25 percent increase in anxiety and depression among the global population post-pandemic.[10] Or how they could improve poor medication and behavioral adherence, which is responsible for around 50 percent of chronic illnesses and an estimated 125,000 deaths per year in the United States.[11] Joe Schaeppi, an adventure-based psychotherapist who uses adventure and nature experiences to improve mental health, CEO of audience insights company Solsten, and my business partner, knows why video games can usher in a completely new era of digital therapeutics and the patient experience: "The opposite of depression is to be in a physiological state of play. Companies and providers have to understand play beyond superficial gamification. If it's not fun to the patient, it's a task and not a video game. You have to start with the fun before you move to diagnosis and treatment. Video games can not only fix the treatment adherence issues, they can also improve our mental health."[12]

The power of video games is undeniable. For companies to be successful in this rapidly evolving world of virtual experiences, though, they have to understand the audience, who they are, and where they are going—and meet them there.

Video games allow companies to become an integral part of people's lives. The more that games evolve and proliferate, the higher the stakes for your organization will be. There's never been a better time to press play than now.

Notes

Chapter 1

1. B. Joseph Pine II and James H. Gilmore, *The Experience Economy* (Boston: Harvard Business Review Press, 2011).

2. "New Epsilon Research Indicates 80% of Consumers Are More Likely to Make a Purchase When Brands Offer Personalized Experiences," Epsilon, January 9, 2018, https://www.epsilon.com/us/about-us/pressroom/new-epsilon-research-indicates-80-of-consumers-are-more-likely-to-make-a-purchase-when-brands-offer-personalized-experiences; "The Future of Sales and Marketing Is Here," Boston Consulting Group, February 2022, https://media-publications.bcg.com/BCG-Executive-Perspectives-2022-Future-of-Marketing-and-Sales.pdf.

3. Ethan Cramer-Flood, "US Time Spent with Media 2022," Emarketer, June 15, 2022, https://www.emarketer.com/content/us-time-spent-with-media-2022; "The Future of Sales and Marketing Is Here," Boston Consulting Group; Arielle Feger, "Digital Media Makes Up Nearly Two-Thirds of Consumers' Total Time Spent with Media," Emarketer, August 13, 2024, https://www.emarketer.com/content/digital-media-makes-up-nearly-two-thirds-of-consumers-total-time-spent-with-media.

4. "Time Spent Playing Video Games Continues to Rise," Marketing Charts, October 26, 2021, https://www.marketingcharts.com/demographics-and-audiences-118663.

5. Sunil Gill, "How Many Gamers Are There in 2025? Latest Stats," Priori Data, January 26, 2025, https://prioridata.com/number-of-gamers; Tsion Tadesse, "There Will Be 3.8 Billion Gamers in the World by 2030," MIDiA Research, November 1, 2023, https://www.midiaresearch.com/blog/there-will-be-38-billion-gamers-in-the-world-by-2030.

6. Tommy Hilfiger, interview by author, July 10, 2024.

7. Tom Warren, "Microsoft to Acquire Activision Blizzard for $68.7 Billion," Verge, January 18, 2022, https://www.theverge.com/2022/1/18/22889258/microsoft-activision-blizzard-xbox-acquisition-call-of-duty-overwatch.

8. Dan Schulman, interview by author, November 3, 2024.

9. Ani Petrosyan, "Number of Internet and Social Media Users Worldwide as of October 2024," Statista, November 5, 2024, https://www.statista.com/statistics/617136/digital-population-worldwide/.

10. Sunil Gill, "Candy Crush Revenue and Usage Statistics 2024," Priori Data, March 26, 2024, https://prioridata.com/data/candy-crush-revenue.

Chapter 2

1. Thomas Reese, "Cable TV Statistics (2025)—Viewership and Subscribers," evoca.tv, January 4, 2025, https://evoca.tv/cable-tv-statistics/; "Data: Linear TV Consumption Continues to Decline Globally," Advanced Television, February 18, 2025, https://www.advanced-television.com/2025/02/18/data-linear-tv-consumption-continues-to-decline-globally/.

2. Jessica Clement, "Share of Internet Users Worldwide Who Play Video Games on Any Device as of 2nd Quarter 2024, by Region," Statista, November 5, 2024, https://www.statista.com/statistics/195768/global-gaming-reach-by-country/.

3. Entertainment Software Association, "U.S. Consumer Video Game Spending Totaled $60.4 Billion in 2021," PR Newswire, January 18, 2022, https://www.prnewswire.com/news-releases/us-consumer-video-game-spending-totaled-60-4-billion-in-2021--301462631.html.

4. Sean Murray, "Survey Finds the Average Gamer Spends $58,000 on Gaming in Their Life," TheGamer, April 25, 2022, https://www.thegamer.com/average-gamer-survey-spends-58000-lifetime/.

5. "The Future of Sales and Marketing Is Here," Boston Consulting Group, February 2022, https://media-publications.bcg.com/BCG-Executive-Perspectives-2022-Future-of-Marketing-and-Sales.pdf.

6. "The Future of Sales and Marketing Is Here," Boston Consulting Group.

7. "New Free Report: Meet the Gamers of 2023 and See How They Engage with Video Games," Newzoo, June 20, 2023, https://newzoo.com/resources/blog/how-consumers-engage-with-video-games-in-2023.

8. Daniel Hong et al., "Gaming Report 2024," Bain & Company, October 2024, https://www.bain.com/insights/topics/gaming-report.

9. "New Free Report," Newzoo.

10. Anders Christofferson et al., "Young Gamers and the Metaverse: How the Rules of Success Are Changing," Bain & Company, July 2022, https://www.bain.com/insights/young-gamers-and-the-metaverse-how-the-rules-of-success-are-changing/.

11. "Essential Facts about the U.S. Video Game Industry," Entertainment Software Association, 2024, https://www.theesa.com/wp-content/uploads/2024/05/Essential-Facts-2024-FINAL.pdf.

12. Lewis Rees, "48% of Gen Z-ers Have at Least Four Gaming Apps Downloaded," pocketgamer.biz, June 16, 2023, https://www.pocketgamer.biz/48-of-gen-z-ers-have-at-least-four-gaming-apps-downloaded/.

13. Christofferson et al., "Young Gamers and the Metaverse."

14. Raja Rajamannar, interview by author, October 17, 2024.

15. Ben Gilbert, "The Term 'Gamer' Is Quickly Becoming Meaningless," Business Insider, December 21, 2015, https://www.businessinsider.com/more-men-identify-as-gamers-than-women-2015-12.

16. Charlotte Rogers, "Highly Social, Gender Diverse and Age Agnostic: Why Brands Must Change Their View of Gamers," MarketingWeek, July 17, 2019, https://www.marketingweek.com/brands-change-view-gaming/.

17. "New Free Report," Newzoo.

18. Jessica Clement, "Distribution of Video Game Users in the United States as of June 2024, by Gender," Statista, August 15, 2024, https://www.statista.com/forecasts/494867/distribution-of-gamers-by-gender-usa.

19. Sisi Jiang, "This Mom Didn't Know She Was in a $250K Candy Crush Tournament, but She's Killing It," Kotaku, updated April 20, 2023, https://kotaku .com/candy-crush-competition-all-stars-2023-prizes-finals-1850353139.

20. Samir Agili, interview by author, January 24, 2022.

21. Jonathan Stringfield, *Get in the Game: How to Level Up Your Business with Gaming, Esports, and Emerging Technologies* (Hoboken, NJ: John Wiley & Sons, 2022).

22. Luis Di Como, interview by author, June 9, 2023.

23. Erika Wykes-Sneyd, interview by author, April 18, 2023.

24. Erinrose Sullivan, interview by author, June 29, 2023.

25. Dan White, interview by author, May 17, 2023.

26. Ashumi Sanghvi, interview by author, May 17, 2023.

27. Stefan Butz, interview by author, April 17, 2023.

28. Kyle Price, interview by author, May 31, 2023.

29. Sullivan, interview.

30. Kellen Browning, "Twitch Star xQc Signs $100 Million Deal with Kick, a Rival Platform," *New York Times*, updated June 21, 2023, https://www.nytimes.com /2023/06/16/business/twitch-kick-xqc.html.

31. Di Como, interview.

32. Amanpreet Singh, interview by author, June 9, 2023.

33. Tommy Hilfiger, interview by author, July 10, 2024.

Chapter 3

1. Raph Koster, interview by author, October 3, 2023.

2. Owen S. Good, "Henry Cavill Was Too Busy Playing Warcraft to Answer a Call to Play Superman," Polygon, April 2, 2016, https://www.polygon.com/2016/4 /2/11353442/henry-cavill-was-too-busy-playing-warcraft-to-answer-a-call-to-play.

3. "Spin Master Reports Q4 2024 and 2024 Financial Results 2024 Revenue Exceeds $2.2 Billion, Up 18.8%," Spin Master, February 24, 2025, https://www .spinmaster.com/en-US/corporate/media/press-releases/122980/; David Taylor, "Toys, Video Games, and Linear Entertainment Combined under a Single IP Are Creating Transmedia Bonfires of Excitement, Leading to Outsized Returns for Toy Companies Like Spin Master," LinkedIn, 2024, https://www.linkedin.com/posts /jdavetaylor_toys-video-games-and-linear-entertainment-activity-7212136548020 95105-1osH; "Spin Master Reports Fourth Quarter and Full Year 2023 Financial Results," Spin Master, February 28, 2024, https://www.spinmaster.com/en-GB /corporate/media/press-releases/122955/.

4. Samir Agili, interview by author, January 24, 2022.

5. "The Future of Sales and Marketing Is Here," Boston Consulting Group, February 2022, https://media-publications.bcg.com/BCG-Executive-Perspectives -2022-Future-of-Marketing-and-Sales.pdf.

6. Katie Salen and Eric Zimmerman, *Rules of Play: Game Design Fundamentals* (Boston: MIT Press, 2003).

7. Mihaly Csikszentmihalyi, *Flow: The Psychology of Optimal Experience* (New York: Harper Perennial, 2008).

8. Shubham Singh, "How Many People Use TikTok 2025 (Users Statistics)," Demandsage, January 1, 2025, https://www.demandsage.com/tiktok-user-statistics/.

9. Debra Aho Williamson, "Time Spent on TikTok," Emarketer, February 27, 2023, https://www.emarketer.com/content/time-spent-on-tiktok.

10. "Introducing the What's Next: Gaming Trend Report," TikTok Newsroom, July 12, 2023, https://newsroom.tiktok.com/en-us/whats-next-gaming-2023.

11. Erinrose Sullivan, interview by author, June 29, 2023.

12. Sarah Perez, "Netflix Thinks 'Fortnite' Is a Bigger Threat Than HBO," TechCrunch, January 18, 2019, https://techcrunch.com/2019/01/18/netflix-thinks -fortnite-is-a-bigger-threat-than-hbo/.

13. "Are Video Games Good for You and Your Brain?" Cleveland Clinic, December 2, 2024, https://health.clevelandclinic.org/are-video-games-good-for-you.

14. Ethan Gach, "Could Pricing *Grand Theft Auto* 6 at $100 Help Save the Game Industry?," Kokatu, January 15, 2025, https://kotaku.com/gta-6-price-video-game -industry-state-of-release-date-1851740553.

15. Scott Galloway, "Let's Get Ready to Rundle," *No Mercy/No Malice* (blog), July 10, 2020, https://www.profgalloway.com/lets-get-ready-to-rundle/.

16. Dan Avery, "Beyond Wordle: The New York Times Games Section, Explained," CNET, February 21, 2022, https://www.cnet.com/culture/internet /beyond-wordle-best-word-games-in-the-new-york-times/.

17. "The New York Times Company (NYT)," Yahoo Finance, https://finance .yahoo.com/quote/NYT/, accessed November 12, 2024; "The New York Times 2023 Annual Report," *New York Times*, 2024, https://nytco-assets.nytimes.com/2024/03 /2023-Annual-Report_WR_-Final.pdf.

18. Rida Khan, "$300 Billion of Video Gaming Revenue, by Segment (2017-2026F)," Visual Capitalist, August 15, 2023, https://www.visualcapitalist.com/sp/video -games-industry-revenue-growth-visual-capitalist/.

19. Jenifer Willig, interview by author, June 29, 2022.

20. Jonathan Stringfield, *Get in the Game: How to Level Up Your Business with Gaming, Esports, and Emerging Technologies* (Hoboken, NJ: John Wiley & Sons, 2022).

21. Ian Thomas, "How Free-to-Play and In-Game Purchases Took Over the Video Game Industry," CNBC, October 6, 2022, https://www.cnbc.com/2022/10/06/how -free-to-play-and-in-game-purchases-took-over-video-games.html.

22. "Electronic Arts Inc. (EA)," Yahoo Finance, https://finance.yahoo.com/quote /EA/, accessed November 12, 2024.

23. Jim Green, interview by author, September 6, 2022.

24. Green, interview.

25. Green, interview.

26. Craig Chapple, "Supercell Launches Brawl Stars Globally," pocketgamer.biz, December 12, 2018, https://www.pocketgamer.biz/supercell-launches-fifth-live -game-brawl-stars-globally/.

27. Amelia Zollner, "Fall Guys Has Reached 50 Million Players since Going Free-to-Play," IGN, July 6, 2022, https://www.ign.com/articles/fall-guys-has-reached -50-million-players-since-going-free-to-play.

28. Kayleigh Partleton, "Scrabble Go Experiences the Best Launch Ever for a Mobile Word Game," pocketgamer.biz, April 7, 2020, https://www.pocketgamer.biz /scrabble-go-best-launch-ever-mobile-word-game/.

29. Oliver Yeh, "Supercell's Brawl Stars Revenue Shoots Past $100 Million After Two Months," Sensor Tower, February 2019, https://sensortower.com/blog/brawl -stars-revenue-100-million.

30. Jonathan Knight, interview by author, August 8, 2023.

31. Martin Reeves, interview by author, June 29, 2023.

32. Chris Rake, interview by author, July 11, 2023.

33. Chris Morris, "Why Disney Unexpectedly Quit Video Game Publishing," CNBC, May 11, 2016, https://www.cnbc.com/2016/05/11/why-disney-unexpectedly-quite-the-video-game-business.html.

34. Patrick Shanley, "Bob Iger: Disney Isn't 'Particularly Good' at Self-Publishing Games," *Hollywood Reporter*, February 5, 2019, https://www.hollywood reporter.com/news/general-news/bob-iger-disney-isnt-particularly-good-at-publishing-games-1183088/.

35. Kat Bailey, "Disney's CEO Is Reportedly Being Urged to Consider Turning Company into a 'Gaming Giant,'" IGN, October 10, 2023, https://www.ign.com/articles/disneys-electronic-arts-acquisition.

36. "Disney and Epic Games to Create Expansive and Open Games and Entertainment Universe Connected to Fortnite," The Walt Disney Company, February 7, 2024, https://thewaltdisneycompany.com/disney-and-epic-games-fortnite/.

37. Dean Takahashi, "NBCUniversal Will Shut Down Its Game Publishing Business," VentureBeat, September 18, 2019, https://venturebeat.com/business/nbcuniversal-will-shut-down-its-game-publishing-business/.

Chapter 4

1. "New Epsilon Research Indicates 80% of Consumers Are More Likely to Make a Purchase when Brands Offer Personalized Experiences," Epsilon, January 9, 2018, https://www.epsilon.com/us/about-us/pressroom/new-epsilon-research-indicates-80-of-consumers-are-more-likely-to-make-a-purchase-when-brands-offer-personalized-experiences.

2. Erika Wykes-Sneyd, interview by author, April 18, 2023.

3. Court et al., "The Consumer Decision Journey," McKinsey & Company, June 1, 2009, https://www.mckinsey.com/capabilities/growth-marketing-and-sales/our-insights/the-consumer-decision-journey.

4. "Time Spent Playing Video Games Continues to Rise," Marketing Charts, October 26, 2021, https://www.marketingcharts.com/demographics-and-audiences-118663; Anders Christofferson et al., "Young Gamers and the Metaverse: How the Rules of Success Are Changing," Bain & Company, July 2022, https://www.bain.com/insights/young-gamers-and-the-metaverse-how-the-rules-of-success-are-changing/.

5. David Court et al., "The Consumer Decision Journey."

6. "The Future of Sales and Marketing Is Here," Boston Consulting Group, February 2022, https://media-publications.bcg.com/BCG-Executive-Perspectives-2022-Future-of-Marketing-and-Sales.pdf.

7. Jenn McMillen, "Starbucks Odyssey Gives Reward NFTs. Will Coffee Drinkers Care?" *Forbes*, October 3, 2023, https://www.forbes.com/sites/jennmcmillen/2023/10/03/starbucks-odyssey-gives-reward-nfts-will-coffee-drinkers-care/.

8. Kyle Price, interview by author, May 31, 2023.

9. Kellie Ell, "Exclusive: Alo Yoga Has Entered the Metaverse through Roblox," *Women's Wear Daily*, February 10, 2022, https://wwd.com/business-news/technology/alo-yoga-roblox-metaverse-1235066622/.

10. Wykes-Sneyd, interview.

11. Jonathan Knight, interview by author, August 8, 2023.

12. Erinrose Sullivan, interview by author, June 29, 2023.
13. Marcus Holmström, interview by author, July 12, 2023.
14. Chris Brandt, interview by author, June 7, 2023.
15. Sullivan, interview.
16. Wykes-Sneyd, interview.
17. Wykes-Sneyd, interview.
18. Vidya L. Drego et al., "The ROI of Personas," Forrester, August 3, 2010, https://www.forrester.com/report/the-roi-of-personas/RES55359.
19. Steven Reiss, *Who Am I?: The 16 Basic Desires That Motivate Our Actions and Define Our Personalities* (New York: Tarcher/Putnam, 2000); Jon Radoff, *Game On: Energize Your Business with Social Media Games* (Indianapolis: Wiley, 2011); Richard Bartle, "Hearts, Clubs, Diamonds, Spades: Players Who Suit MUDs," 1996, https://www.researchgate.net/publication/247190693_Hearts_clubs_diamonds_spades_Players_who_suit_MUDs.
20. Knight, interview.
21. Brianna Parker, "United Airlines Mission Statement, Vision, Core Values, Strategy (2024 Analysis)," Business Strategy Hub, March 22, 2024, https://bstrategyhub.com/united-airlines-mission-statement-vision-core-values-a-detailed-analysis/.
22. Knight, interview.
23. Holmström, interview.
24. Wykes-Sneyd, interview.
25. Zach Pond, interview by author, October 7, 2022.
26. "About Hasbro," Hasbro, https://corporate.hasbro.com/en-us, accessed November 14, 2024.
27. Pond, interview.

Chapter 5

1. Raja Rajamannar, interview by author, October 17, 2024.
2. Rajamannar, interview.
3. Alexander Lee, "Why Mastercard Is Advertising More with Riot Games Even as Other Brands Divest from Esports," Digiday, August 30, 2023, https://digiday.com/marketing/why-mastercard-is-advertising-more-with-riot-games-even-as-other-brands-divest-from-esports/.
4. Marta Juras, "Louis Vuitton Launches League of Legends Collection, Sells Out," win.gg, December 10, 2019, https://win.gg/news/louis-vuitton-launches-league-of-legends-collection-sells-out/.
5. Sam Cole, "'Fortnite' x Balenciaga Has Arrived & It's Selling Fast," Highsnobiety, 2021, https://www.highsnobiety.com/p/fortnite-balenciaga-collaboration-release-info/.
6. Yomi Sanghvi, "How Balenciaga Does Marketing in the Metaverse," Medium, October 3, 2022, https://yomivins.medium.com/how-balenciaga-does-marketing-in-the-metaverse-7ae069e1fd72.
7. Chris Brandt, interview by author, June 7, 2023. All materials in this case study stem from the interview unless otherwise indicated.
8. "Chipotle Sponsors TSM Fortnite! (Blind Taste Test Challenge)," May 31, 2018, posted by TSM, YouTube, https://www.youtube.com/watch?v=HErRdqK0-9Q.

9. "Roblox Reports Third Quarter 2024 Financial Results," Roblox, October 31, 2024, https://ir.roblox.com/news/news-details/2024/Roblox-Reports-Third-Quarter-2024-Financial-Results/default.aspx.

10. Paul Tassi, "'Roblox' Down: New Update Says It's Not Chipotle's Fault," *Forbes*, October 30, 2021, https://www.forbes.com/sites/paultassi/2021/10/30/roblox-down-new-update-says-its-not-chipotles-fault/.

11. "An Annual Report to Security Holders," Chipotle Mexican Grill, April 23, 2024, https://ir.chipotle.com/sec-filings?cat=1&year=2024; "Chipotle Announces Third Quarter 2024 Results," Chipotle Mexican Grill, October 29, 2024, https://ir.chipotle.com/2024-10-29-CHIPOTLE-ANNOUNCES-THIRD-QUARTER-2024-RESULTS.

12. "Annual Report and Proxy Statement," Chipotle Mexican Grill, February 5, 2020, https://ir.chipotle.com/sec-filings?cat=1&year=2020.

13. "Malnutrition," World Health Organization, https://www.who.int/health-topics/malnutrition, accessed June 17, 2022.

14. Jenifer Willig, interview by author, June 29, 2022. All materials in this case study stem from the interview unless otherwise indicated.

15. "We're Bringing Real Beauty to the Virtual World," Dove, n.d., https://www.dove.com/uk/stories/about-dove/dove-gaming.html, accessed March 4, 2025.

16. Luis Di Como, interview by author, June 9, 2023. All materials in this case study stem from the interview unless otherwise indicated.

17. Raghunandan Srinivasan, interview by author, April 15, 2024. All materials in this case study stem from the interview unless otherwise indicated.

18. Andrew Douthwaite, interview by author, May 1, 2024.

19. Douthwaite, interview.

Chapter 6

1. Paul Tassi, "Who Wouldn't Want to Visit the 'Fortnite' Shell Gasoline Island?," *Forbes*, October 6, 2023, https://www.forbes.com/sites/paultassi/2023/10/06/who-wouldnt-want-to-visit-the-fortnite-shell-gasoline-island/.

2. Samir Agili, interview by author, January 24, 2022.

3. Sarah E. Needleman, "Instead of Advertising in Videogames, These Companies Asked: 'Why Not Make Our Own?'" *Wall Street Journal*, June 16, 2023, https://www.wsj.com/articles/video-game-advertising-marketing-cbe9425f.

4. Agili, interview.

5. Dominick Reuter and Alex Bitter, "More Than 2,000 Stores Are Closing across the US in 2024. Here's the List," Yahoo News, October 24, 2024, https://www.yahoo.com/news/nearly-1-300-stores-closing-100701728.html.

6. Tommy Hilfiger, interview by author, July 10, 2024. All materials in this case study stem from the interview unless otherwise indicated.

7. Ivy Taylor, "Glu Mobile Avoids Second Year of Loss Thanks to Q4 Surge," GamesIndustry.biz, February 7, 2020, https://www.gamesindustry.biz/glu-mobile-income-exceeds-usd10m-last-year-thanks-to-q4-surge; Timothy, Your Friendly Neighborhood AI, "Top 5 Fashion Games on Android in Europe: Q2 2024 Performance," SensorTower, July 2024, https://sensortower.com/blog/2024-q2-android-top-5-fashion%20games-revenue-europe-6011f531241bc16eb85bc2b8.

8. Agili, interview.

9. Maghan McDowell, "Tommy Hilfiger on AI and His New Fashion Game," *Vogue Business*, December 19, 2023, https://www.voguebusiness.com/story/technology /tommy-hilfiger-on-ai-and-his-new-fashion-game.

10. Agili, interview.

11. McDowell, "Tommy Hilfiger on AI."

12. Agili, interview.

13. Chris Rake, interview by author, July 11, 2023. All materials in this case study stem from the interview unless otherwise indicated by additional sources.

14. Dan White, interview by author, May 17, 2023.

15. "Games," *New York Times*, https://www.nytco.com/products/games/, accessed November 28, 2024.

16. Katie Robertson, "The *New York Times* Passes 10 Million Subscribers," *New York Times*, November 8, 2023, https://www.nytimes.com/2023/11/08/business /media/new-york-times-q3-earnings.html.

17. Charlotte Klein, "Inside the *New York Times*' Big Bet on Games," *Vanity Fair*, December 19, 2023, https://www.vanityfair.com/news/inside-the-new-york-times -big-bet-on-games.

18. Sydney Ember, "New York Times Co. Subscription Revenue Surpassed $1 Billion in 2017," *New York Times*, February 8, 2018, https://www.nytimes.com/2018 /02/08/business/new-york-times-company-earnings.html.

19. Jonathan Knight, interview by author, August 8, 2023. All materials in case study stem from the interview unless otherwise indicated.

20. Daniel Victor, "Wordle Is a Love Story," *New York Times*, January 3, 2022, https://www.nytimes.com/2022/01/03/technology/wordle-word-game-creator.html.

21. Amanda Silberling, "Connections Is the *New York Times*' Most Played Game after Wordle," TechCrunch, August 28, 2023, https://techcrunch.com/2023/08/28 /connections-is-the-new-york-times-most-played-game-after-wordle/.

22. Brendan Sinclair, "*Washington Post* Reportedly Shutting Down Gaming Section," GamesIndustry.biz, January 24, 2023, https://www.gamesindustry.biz /washington-post-reportedly-shutting-down-gaming-section.

23. Nick Rend, interview by author, April 11, 2024. All materials in this case study stem from the interview unless otherwise indicated.

24. "Drivers Who Have Won Back-to-Back Daytona 500s," NASCAR, February 17, 2025, https://www.nascar.com/gallery/drivers-who-have-won-back-to-back -daytona-500s/.

Chapter 7

1. Dina Mattar, "Gaming Is Growing, and Web3 Is Coming with It," *Forbes*, January 9, 2024, https://www.forbes.com/councils/forbesbusinesscouncil/2024/01 /09/gaming-is-growing-and-web3-is-coming-with-it/.

2. Heather Somerville, "Andreessen Horowitz Debuts $600 Million Gaming Fund to Add to Web3 Bets," *Wall Street Journal*, May 18, 2022, https://www.wsj.com /articles/andreessen-horowitz-debuts-600-million-gaming-fund-to-add-to-web3 -bets-11652878800; Kelsey McGuire, "It's Time for Web3 Games to Embrace Play AND Earn," Nasdaq, November 1, 2023, https://www.nasdaq.com/articles/its-time -for-web3-games-to-embrace-play-and-earn.

3. Thomas Stackpole, "What Is Web3?," hbr.org, May 10, 2022, https://hbr.org /2022/05/what-is-web3.

4. Margaux MacColl, "After a Virtual Gucci Bag Sold for Over $4,000, More Than a Real One, VC Alexis Ohanian Predicts Virtual Fashion Will Be Huge. Gucci and Atari Agree," *Business Insider*, May 28, 2021, https://www.businessinsider.com/virtual-gucci-bag-sale-sign-digital-fashion-is-a-trend-2021-5.

5. Tora Northman, "Louis Vuitton's New Game Is Better Than 'Fortnite,'" Highsnobiety, 2022, https://www.highsnobiety.com/p/louis-vuitton-nft-game/.

6. Jacob Kastrenakes, "Beeple Sold an NFT for $69 Million," Verge, March 11, 2021, https://www.theverge.com/2021/3/11/22325054/beeple-christies-nft-sale-cost-everydays-69-million.

7. John Linden, interview by author, October 3, 2023. All materials in this case study stem from the interview unless otherwise indicated.

8. "Burberry X Blankos Block Party: New NFT Collection and Social Space," Burberry, June 22, 2022, https://www.burberryplc.com/news/brand/2022/burberry-x-blankos-block-party--new-nft-collection-and-social-sp.

9. Matt Lipson, Mike Philbin, and Lanie Beck, "Coffee Wars: Market Share Battles and Investment Opportunities from Starbucks to Startups," Northmarq, November 18, 2024, https://www.northmarq.com/insights/research/coffee-wars-market-share-battles-and-investment-opportunities-starbucks-startups.

10. Leah H., "Starbucks: Winning on Rewards, Loyalty, and Data," Harvard Business School, Digital Innovation and Transformation, February 9, 2020, https://d3.harvard.edu/platform-digit/submission/starbucks-winning-on-rewards-loyalty-and-data/.

11. Leah H., "Starbucks."

12. "Starbucks CEO: 'We Need to Fundamentally Change Our Strategy,'" NACS, October 24, 2024, https://www.convenience.org/Media/Daily/2024/October/24/3-Starbucks-CEO-Change-Strategy_CatMan.

13. Polygon Labs, "Starbucks Taps Polygon for Its 'Starbucks Odyssey' Web3 Experience," Polygon, September 12, 2022, https://polygon.technology/blog/starbucks-taps-polygon-for-its-starbucks-r-odyssey-web3-experience-nbsp.

14. Leah Alger, "Starbucks Drops 'the First Store Collection' NFTs Today!," NFT Lately, updated April 19, 2023, https://nftlately.com/starbucks-drops-the-first-store-collection-nfts-toda/.

15. "Starbucks Reports Q4 and Full Year Fiscal 2023 Results," Starbucks, November 2, 2023, https://investor.starbucks.com/news/financial-releases/news-details/2023/Starbucks-Reports-Q4-and-Full-Year-Fiscal-2023-Results/default.aspx.

16. "Over 75% of Web3 Games Fail Due to Declining User Interest, Study Finds," Binance Square, December 4, 2023, https://www.binance.com/en/square/post/2023-12-04-over-75-of-web3-games-fail-due-to-declining-user-interest-study-finds-909163218218.

17. Sydney Flynn, interview by author, March 17, 2023. All materials in case study stem from the interview unless otherwise indicated.

18. "Starbucks Announces Triple Shot Reinvention Strategy with Multiple Paths for Long-Term Growth," Starbucks, November 2, 2023, https://about.starbucks.com/press/2023/starbucks-announces-triple-shot-reinvention-strategy-with-multiple-paths-for-long-term-growth/.

19. "Starbucks CEO," NACS.

20. Ivan Dashkov, interview by author, January 30, 2024. All materials in this case study stem from the interview unless otherwise indicated.

21. "PUMA - Black Station 2," Webby Awards, 2024, https://winners
.webbyawards.com/2024/ai-metaverse-virtual/metaverse-immersive-features/best
-experiential-design/283429/puma--black-station-2.

22. Erika Wykes-Sneyd, interview by author, April 18, 2023. All materials in this
case study stem from the interview unless otherwise indicated by additional sources.

23. "Adidas Iconic Three-Stripes Land in Fortnite, Bringing Customizable
In-Game Cosmetics to Players Globally," Adidas, July 24, 2024, https://news.adidas
.com/partnerships/adidas-iconic-three-stripes-land-in-fortnite--bringing
-customizable-in-game-cosmetics-to-players-glo/s/153d0e1c-42b2-469c-acf0
-bdb43d911eab.

Chapter 8

1. Mike Verdu, "Let the Games Begin: A New Way to Experience Entertainment on Mobile" Netflix, November 2, 2021, https://about.netflix.com/en/news/let
-the-games-begin-a-new-way-to-experience-entertainment-on-mobile.

2. Sarah Perez, "Netflix Games Gains Traction with Installs Up 180% Year-
Over-Year in 2023, Thanks to GTA and Others," TechCrunch, January 10, 2024,
https://techcrunch.com/2024/01/10/netflix-games-gain-traction-with-installs-up
-180-year-over-year-in-2023-thanks-to-gta-and-others/.

3. Nicole Sperling, "Netflix Adds 5 Million Subscriptions in Quarter," *New
York Times*, October 17, 2024, https://www.nytimes.com/2024/10/17/business/media
/netflix-quarterly-report.html.

4. Rebekah Valentine, "Netflix Games Engagement Tripled in the Last Year, in
Part Thanks to GTA," IGN, January 23, 2024, https://www.ign.com/articles/netflix
-games-engagement-tripled-in-the-last-year-in-part-thanks-to-gta.

5. Shlomik Silbiger, "The Pymetrics Games—Overview and Practice Guidelines," Oxford University Careers Service, November 24, 2021, https://www.careers
.ox.ac.uk/article/the-pymetrics-games-overview-and-practice-guidelines.

6. "FDA Permits Marketing of First Game-Based Digital Therapeutic to Improve
Attention Function in Children with ADHD," US Food and Drug Administration,
June 15, 2020, https://www.fda.gov/news-events/press-announcements/fda-permits
-marketing-first-game-based-digital-therapeutic-improve-attention-function
-children-adhd.

7. Martin Reeves, interview by author, June 29, 2023. All materials in this case
study stem from the interview unless otherwise indicated.

8. Martin Reeves, Knut Haanaes, and Janmejaya Sinha, *Your Strategy Needs a
Strategy: How to Choose and Execute the Right Approach* (Boston: Harvard Business
Review Press, 2015).

9. Martin Reeves and Jack Fuller, *The Imagination Machine: How to Spark New
Ideas and Create Your Company's Future* (Boston: Harvard Business Review Press,
2021).

10. Jim Green, interview by author, September 6, 2022. All materials in this case
study stem from the interview unless otherwise indicated.

11. Joseph Knoop, "You Can Now Play Cuphead on Your Tesla Car," IGN,
September 28, 2019, https://www.ign.com/articles/2019/09/28/you-can-now-play
-cuphead-on-your-tesla-car.

12. Stefan Butz and René Molle, interview by author, April 17, 2023. All
materials in this case study stem from the interview unless otherwise indicated.

13. "BMW and AirConsole Celebrate In-Car Gaming Launch with Joint Appearance at Gamescom, Announcing New Game for 2024," BMW Group, August 22, 2023, https://www.press.bmwgroup.com/global/article/detail /T0429518EN/bmw-and-airconsole-celebrate-in-car-gaming-launch-with-joint -appearance-at-gamescom-announcing-new-game-for-2024.

14. "Mattel, AirConsole, and BMW Group Announce World Premiere of UNO Car Party! for In-Car Gaming," Yahoo Finance, August 15, 2024, https://finance .yahoo.com/news/mattel-airconsole-bmw-group-announce-110000365.html.

Chapter 9

1. Erika Wykes-Sneyd, interview by author, April 18, 2023.
2. Marcus Holmström, interview by author, July 12, 2023.
3. Chris Brandt, interview by author, June 7, 2023.
4. Nick Rend, interview by author, April 11, 2024.
5. Raghunandan Srinivasan, interview by author, April 15, 2024.
6. Amanpreet Singh, interview by author, June 9, 2023.
7. Ivan Dashkov, interview by author, January 30, 2024.
8. Jim Green, interview by author, September 6, 2022.
9. Jonathan Knight, interview by author, August 8, 2023.
10. Jenifer Willig, interview by author, June 29, 2022.
11. Jim Green, interview by author, September 6, 2022.
12. Chris Rake, interview by author, July 11, 2023.
13. Rake, interview.
14. Wykes-Sneyd, interview.
15. Erinrose Sullivan, interview by author, June 29, 2023.
16. Wykes-Sneyd, interview.
17. Knight, interview.
18. Brandt, interview.
19. Kyle Price, interview by author, May 31, 2023.
20. Stefan Butz, interview by author, April 17, 2023.
21. Brandt, interview.
22. Dashkov, interview.

Epilogue

1. Jonathan Knight, interview by author, August 8, 2023.

2. "Roblox Reports Third Quarter 2024 Financial Results," Roblox, October 31, 2024, https://ir.roblox.com/news/news-details/2024/Roblox-Reports-Third -Quarter-2024-Financial-Results/default.aspx.

3. Aaron Astle, "Leslie Benzies' Build a Rocket Boy Studio Raises $110M for 'Flagship' Trio of Projects," PocketGamer.biz, January 18, 2024, https://www .pocketgamer.biz/gta-v-lead-developer-leslie-benzies-raises-110m-for-build-a-rocket -boys-flagship-trio-of-projects/.

4. Harvey Randall, "Everywhere Wants to Build a Neverending Sandbox Where Players Can Become Game Designers—and I Think It Has a Real Chance of Pulling It Off," PC Gamer, November 30, 2023, https://www.pcgamer.com /everywhere-wants-to-build-a-neverending-sandbox-where-players-can-become -game-designersand-i-think-it-has-a-real-chance-of-pulling-it-off/.

5. Matthew Woodward, "These Are the User Generated Content Statistics You Need to Know," Search Logistics, updated July 17, 2024, https://www.searchlogistics.com/learn/statistics/user-generated-content-statistics/.

6. Ivan Dashkov, interview by author, January 30, 2024.

7. Kyle Price, interview by author, May 31, 2023.

8. Knight, interview.

9. Megan Farokhmanesh, "Ikea Will Pay You Real Money to Work in Its Virtual Roblox Store," *WIRED*, June 6, 2024, https://www.wired.com/story/ikea-is-hiring-its-next-generation-of-workers-on-roblox/.

10. "COVID-19 Pandemic Triggers 25% Increase in Prevalence of Anxiety and Depression Worldwide," World Health Organization, March 2, 2022, https://www.who.int/news/item/02-03-2022-covid-19-pandemic-triggers-25-increase-in-prevalence-of-anxiety-and-depression-worldwide.

11. Regina M. Benjamin, "Medication Adherence: Helping Patients Take Their Medicines as Directed," *Public Health Reports* 127, no. 1 (2012): 2–3, https://doi.org/10.1177/003335491212700102.

12. Joe Schaeppi, interview by author, January 31, 2024.

Index

Acknowledgments

It truly takes a village. It may be a cliché, but it couldn't be closer to the truth when it comes to the realization of this book. The list of people who influenced the course of this project and shaped its essence is longer than the space my publisher has granted me. At the risk of leaving out someone who deserves to be mentioned by name, I want to express my special gratitude to the following individuals, without whose contributions you would not be holding this book in your hands:

Melinda Merino, editorial director for Harvard Business Review Press, for believing in my idea based on only a few lines in an email and swinging open the doors for me; Kevin Evers, my editor at the Press, for encouraging me to play to my strengths as a writer and guiding my thought and writing processes with poise, patience, and a healthy dose of humor; Stephani Finks, the Press's design director, for embracing my vision for this book and letting it come to life visually, perfectly; my longtime mentor, Martin Reeves, for drawing me into the world of business-book writing and publishing more than a decade ago with the release of his seminal book *Your Strategy Needs a Strategy*; my business partner and close friend, Joe Schaeppi, for altering the course of my life, bringing me into the gaming industry, and affording me the space to write this book while continuing to grow our business; Sebastian Weyer, for being an early sounding board and solidifying many of the themes that form the foundation of this book; Regine Weiner, for reaffirming my belief that this book needed to be written and for opening doors to some key stories and protagonists; Jim Green, Kyle Price, Jonathan Knight, Chris Brandt, and all the executives and leaders who were so gracious with their time and knowledge—without them this book would never have been more than an idea; Johann Harnoss, Eliza Jäppinen, Christina Mayr, and everyone else who read early drafts of the manuscript and provided invaluable feedback; Michael Doetsch, for trusting me as a teenager to run the sports section of my hometown newspaper and pouring gasoline on the fire that was (and still is) my passion for writing; my parents, for picking up a local magazine that was looking for young writers and encouraging their twelve-year-old son to pursue his dream; and last, but certainly not least, my wife Lynn and my daughters Alexis and Tova for their unwavering support and understanding when I wrote at dawn, stayed up late at night, or missed another family dinner. I will forever be grateful, and I lack the words to express how much they mean to me.

About the Author

BASTIAN BERGMANN is the cofounder and chief operating officer of Solsten, a technology startup that empowers companies to deeply understand their audiences and create resonating experiences for them. Among its customers are globally recognized companies and brands such as Electronic Arts, Activision Blizzard, Sony, Supercell, Peloton, Dentsu, and many others. Before publishing this book, Bergmann frequently wrote articles on topics such as innovation strategy, data-driven creativity, and team management for publication in *Harvard Business Review*.

An economist and journalist by background, Bergmann has spent his entire career at the intersection of digital strategy, entertainment media, and AI. Prior to cofounding Solsten, he was the founder and CEO of WATTx, a company builder focused on machine learning and personalization of user experiences, and a strategy consultant at Boston Consulting Group, where he advised *Fortune* 1000 companies on their digital strategy across a number of industries. He is a frequently sought-after speaker for events and podcasts and advises startups, scale-ups, and public-sector organizations.